# The Office

# Equipment

# Adviser

# The Office Equipment Adviser

## Second Edition

John Derrick

What to Buy for Business

What to Buy for Business, Inc.
PO Box 22857
Santa Barbara, CA 93121–2857
Tel: 805 963 3539

**Publisher's Cataloging in Publication**
Derrick, John G.
       The office equipment adviser: the essential what-to-buy and how-to-buy resource for offices with one to 100 people / John Derrick — 2nd ed.
p. cm.
Includes index.
ISBN 1-88256-857-5


1. Office equipment and supplies — United States. I. Title.

HF5548.D47 1994                    381'.45'00029473
                                   94-61025

Printed in the United States of America

# Read This First

Welcome to *The Office Equipment Adviser* — a unique guide to all the main types of office equipment. The word "unique" is thrown about a great deal these days — but this time it's for real! There is, literally, no other book devoted to this subject matter. However, I won't let my monopoly lull me into complacency — this book sets itself high standards which, I hope, you will agree it meets.

This is the second edition of *The Office Equipment Adviser*. The first one — which was published in summer 1993 — received some excellent reviews. This edition has been fully updated and I have also added three new chapters — voice processing, color printers, color copiers, and multifunctional machines.

### How up to date is this book?

This edition was published in August 1994, and I finished working on it on July, 8 1994. In writing it, I have tried to take into account events in the pipeline — the book's useful shelf-life therefore easily extends for over a year.

### Ordering extra copies of this book

If you are reading this book at a library, or have borrowed someone else's copy, you might like to get hold of your own copy. You can order it through any good bookstore or you can call us at 800 247 2185 and order over the phone by credit card. We'd be happy to send you the book for $19.95 plus a $3 shipping charge. The book usually takes two to three business days to arrive if you order from us direct.

### Special "upgrade" offer for the next edition

There will be a further edition of the book published in August 1995. Owners of the current edition will be able to "upgrade" to the August '95 edition for just $15 plus shipping (a savings of about 25 percent on the cover price). All you need to do is clip the right hand corner of the front cover and mail it to:

OEA Upgrade Offer
What to Buy for Business, Inc.
PO Box 22857
Santa Barbara, CA 93101

Be sure to enclose a check for $18 (including the $3 shipping charge) payable to What to Buy for Business, Inc., or written authorization to charge the amount to your Visa/ MasterCard/American Express (remember to give your card number and expiration date). July '95 would be an excellent time to order the new edition — that way you'll get it as soon as it's published. This upgrade offer runs until December 31, 1995.

### What to expect from this book

Each chapter in *The Office Equipment Adviser* is a self-contained reference on a different subject. While I would be flattered if someone read this book cover to cover, I don't expect anyone to do so — it is a book to refer to when you want to brief yourself on a particular purchasing decision, when you want to learn about a particular type of equipment, brush up on technology, or check up on a vendor.

This is a serious book — to get the most out of it, you have to spend a bit of time with it. It is not one of the all-too-common genre of books written for people who do not want to read and, consequently, containing mostly lightweight information and trite advice.

The world is full of third-rate information these days. Late twentieth century America suffers from information overload, yet most of the information that comes our way is of dubious quality. All too often, information publishers — including those who publish information electronically — are obsessed with the medium, not with the content. Books are — literally — judged on their cover or on cute visual touches to the inside pages. Never mind the quality of the information inside — or the fact that a book is out-of-date even when published (let alone at the end of an excessively long two- or three-year shelf-life).

The aim of *The Office Equipment Adviser* is to provide high-caliber, timely information and experienced advice — that's what you're buying for your $19.95. But although it is a "serious" book, I have also tried to make it easy to use and — within the limitations of the subject matter — enjoyable to read.

The chapters are broken up into lots of sub-sections, each with their own further sub-headings — so it is quite easy to visually scan through the pages to look for parts that interest you. To further help you, there is an at-a-glance guide to the contents of each chapter at the start of every chapter. This is in addition to the Table of Contents for the whole book. The index at the back is another way of homing in on particular information.

Most of the chapters start with a discussion of technology options and features, then move on to "how to buy" advice, and end with vendor profiles which provide overviews of the companies vying for your business. Sometimes the how-to-buy advice precedes the features/technology discussion — especially in markets which are especially service-driven and where the question of who you buy from locally is as important as what you buy. The vendor profiles include addresses and phone numbers. (In the few chapters where there is not a full vendor profiles section, addresses and phone numbers may be shown on their own at the end of the chapter.)

### A few words about What to Buy for Business

This book is derived from *What to Buy for Business*, the almost-monthly, no-advertising guide to office equipment that I publish and edit. If you are looking for more "model-specific" information and advice than is included in this book, you may want to consider using *What to Buy for Business* as a further reference.

There is a full description of *What to Buy for Business* at the back of this book, in the appendix (page 591). Briefly, however, we publish 10 guides a year — each one devoted to a different subject or, in some cases, to two or three related subjects. We have guides available on all the subjects covered featured in this book (except typewriters) plus some others (at present, scanners and CD-ROM). You can either buy single issues or subscribe to the whole series.

The guides contain articles and vendor profiles — not unlike the material in this book — but what you get in addition is a lot more information and advice on specific models. For example, in most of the guides, there are extensive, double-page grid charts where you can look up all the main specifications and pricing on a particular model — as well as our "verdicts" on every machine. All the guides include our "Editor's Choice Shortlist" — a list of "Best Buy" recommendations. In some of the guides, there are also test results and user poll findings.

Purchased individually, these guides cost $23 each (plus $3 per order for shipping) or you can subscribe for $121 (10 issues). There are also some special offers — details in the appendix. Please call 800 247 2185 if you would like to be faxed an up-to-date list of reports or sent a free catalog.

*John Derrick*
*July 1994*

*What to Buy for Business, Inc.*
*PO Box 22857*
*Santa Barbara, CA 93121–2857*
*Tel: 805 963 3539*
*Fax: 805 963 3740*

# Table of Contents

# Chapter 1

# Computers

# Computers

This chapter covers personal computer hardware. It also covers operating systems — the software that allows you to run application-specific programs on your computers. However, I will not be talking about the applications programs themselves — software for tasks like accounting, word processing, spreadsheets, and so forth. That falls outside the scope of this book (not to mention my own expertise).

In this chapter, I'll be covering both desktop and notebook computers. Much of the discussion of desktops will also be relevant to so-called "towers," which are floor-standing PCs that are generally used as the central hubs of computer networks. The contents of this chapter are based on *The Business Computer Guide*, which is one of the *What to Buy for Business* series of office equipment guides. We've had a lot of great feedback on that guide — people seem to like the balance it strikes between going into the subject in reasonable detail, but not losing readers along the way. I hope that you'll feel the same way when reading what follows.

The second chapter in this book is on the subject of networks, and some other chapters cover computer-related things, such as printers.

## The PC Technology Jungle

Choosing computers is different from buying other types of office equipment: with notable exceptions, PC manufacturers are not so much developers of technology, but sources that make the technology available to users. The developers are, for the most part, the companies that make processors, that design computer bus architecture, and that develop operating systems.

For this reason, the secret in being a smart computer shopper is not to start by looking at brands and agonizing over whether to go with IBM, Dell, Compaq, Gateway — or whomever. Instead, you should be asking yourself what type of computer you want in terms of the technology and features. That's not to say that who you buy the computer from is unimportant — questions to do with service and support are of great concern, for example (and some obscure vendors should be viewed

---

**Inside This Chapter ...**

---

with caution on account of quality control shortcomings) — but it is in some senses secondary to getting the right ingredients. Keep in mind that all the major PC manufacturers source most of their technology and components from the same suppliers. Industry standards, more than individual vendors, define the PC market — though there are several industry standards to choose between.

Unfortunately, choosing the technology is not too easy. Most people who consider themselves computer-literate might know by now that 486 and Pentium systems are what's hot, and they may also have read a bit about the new PowerPC. But does this smattering of knowledge leave the buyer prepared to make rational purchasing decisions? Sadly not — things are a lot more complicated!

For example, do you know what a PC advertisement means if it says that a computer has a "PCI bus" or a "VESA bus" —

and do you know which is better? How do these differ from "ISA," "EISA," and "MCA" bus architecture? And if one type of bus makes sense for a 486, will it also be a smart choice for a Pentium? For that matter, what the heck is a "bus" in this context?

Talking of those two processors, how does a top-end, 486-series processor with a quoted "90MHz clock speed" compare with an entry-level Pentium with a "66MHz clock speed" — is the processor with the faster clock speed likely to perform better or worse than the one from the more upscale family, but with the slower clock speed? And when you hear about the new PowerPC standard, what is meant by "RISC" versus "CISC" architecture? Anyway, what is a PowerPC? (Clue: it is not a personal computer!)

You may have heard that Apple is a PowerPC exponent — what are the pros and cons of the latest Macs versus PCs running Windows and based on Intel processors? What major enhancements are in the pipeline for Windows? What is Windows NT? And what are the differences between the PowerPC products being introduced by IBM and those already available from Apple? If you are buying a Windows PC, does it matter whether it is driven by a processor made by Intel or one from AMD or Cyrix?

If you are buying a notebook PC, what should you know about 3.3-volt technology in order to identify the best models? What are PCMCIA slots — and what is the difference between Types I, II, and III? When it comes to networks, what is the difference between the peer-to-peer variety and the client/server species? How does Novell compare with LANtastic? And what do you need to know to understand Ethernet jargon?

### The aim of this chapter

I could continue with other examples of computer features — but the point is probably made by now: choosing computers without understanding today's PC technology would be an aimless, almost random, task. And that is why my mission in writing this chapter — and the one that follows on networks — has been to explain the technology options in language that is free of techno-babble, but without oversimplifying the subject matter or patronizing the reader.

### Picking "models"

Keep in mind that what defines a "model" in this industry is subject to change on a constant basis. PC vendors are forever rejigging the hardware ingredients and, in the process, introducing new models that have different numbers. Often, buyers can choose how their systems are configured so that the notion of a pre-defined model doesn't really apply. Some of the vendors sell literally dozens of models that do much the same thing, but that are slightly differentiated for the various distribution channels. And prices fluctuate on a constant basis, almost like a commodity market.

To try to keep track of each individual "model" of computer is, therefore, a hopeless task — as well as an unnecessary one. My advice to the buyer is to first define your own needs, and then identify two or three vendors that you think are the companies you want to buy from. Finally, you should identify a particular model from one of those vendors that best fits the bill. This chapter will take you fully through the first two parts of that decision process, and help you on your way in the third.

# Which Platform?

Before you choose your computer, pick your "platform." A computer "platform" is a combination of hardware standards and operating system standards. (An "operating system" is software that makes a computer work and that accommodates the applications programs — word processing, spreadsheets, graphics, etc. — that perform particular functions.)

Now is an interesting, though sometimes confusing, time to be looking at platforms: existing ones are on the move, and strange new alliances are forming in the PC industry to attempt to build new ones. I'll begin this chapter by examining the choices. Even if you know for a fact that you don't want to switch platforms — for example, if you know you want to run Windows and you have no interest whatsoever in the Apple Mac (or vice versa) — you should still read what follows, as I'll be telling you things you might not know concerning the future of your chosen platform.

### *Where the industry is at ...*
The most common "platform" in recent years has been the combination of a PC based on an Intel processor running operating software written by Microsoft. About 85 percent of all the personal computers in the US fall into this category. Right now, the Intel processors concerned are the 486 and Pentium series, and the Microsoft operating software is DOS working in conjunction with Windows. (The version of Windows current at press-time was not a complete operating system in its own right, but a sort

of overlay on top of DOS enhancing the latter's abilities and making it easier to use: more on this shortly.) Numerous vendors make Intel-based computers that run DOS/Windows.

There are a number of alternatives to the Intel-Microsoft platform, but by far the largest is the Apple Macintosh, which has about 14 percent of the US market. Apple's operating system — known as System 7 — is a more polished product than the Microsoft DOS/Windows combination: the latter shows too many signs of the early-generation operating software from which it is derived.

But because the Macintosh is proprietary, you have to buy Apple's own hardware — and only that hardware — in order to run the software. In recent years, that hardware, based on Motorola processors, developed a reputation for being more expensive than it was powerful. People bought Mac computers because of the software, and sometimes in spite of the hardware.

This helped the Intel-Microsoft combination become by far the dominant industry standard. Indeed, most buyers look no further — for them, the decision on what computer to buy simply becomes a decision on which brand of PC running DOS/Windows to buy.

There are a number of reasons why so many buyers have not felt it necessary to address the "which platform?" issue when buying new computers — the need to be compatible with other PCs and peripherals, preference for what is familiar, price/performance ratios, and so on. However, many of the assumptions that defined particular platforms in the past are in the process of changing, so now may be an excellent time to review your options.

### *Where the industry is going ...*

The computer market is in a major state of flux. Here are some highlights:

✔ Microsoft Windows is being upgraded to become more like the Apple Macintosh system software. This had not yet happened at press-time — but it will occur during the shelf-life of this book.

✔ Apple, in order to defend itself against the imminent onslaught, has stolen some of its rivals' clothes — for the first time ever, you can buy Mac hardware that matches, and sometimes beats, the DOS/Windows-compatible opposition in both performance and price terms. The Macs concerned use a new processor called the PowerPC, which was jointly developed by IBM, Motorola, and Apple itself. The first PowerPC-based Macs were launched in March 1994.

✔ The makers of DOS/Windows-compatible PCs are working hard to regain their hardware advantage: new and even more powerful versions of the Pentium and the PowerPC are in the pipeline, and each rival camp will be leap-frogging each other in 1995 with still-faster equipment.

✔ Apple is also trying to license its System 7 software to other makers of PC hardware, so you might soon be able to buy Mac-compatible computers from other well-known hardware manufacturers.

✔ Meanwhile, IBM will soon release its own PCs running on the PowerPC processor: while IBM's plans for the PowerPC seem sometimes confused, this could end up providing buyers with a further alternative to the traditional Intel-DOS/Windows platform. (IBM will continue to sell Intel-based PCs as well.)

✔ The industry is moving slowly towards a "multi-platform" ideal, where one hardware platform could run several different competing operating systems — so buyers need not be forced to decide between software standards when choosing their hardware. Don't, however, hold your breath — although there is movement in this direction, a combination of political and technical barriers ensure that buyers will have to wait a while before this ideal becomes reality.

### What follows ...

In short, all the platforms are moving. In the first part of this chapter, I will discuss all of the above and more. Most readers will probably end up sticking with the "moving platform" they are on already — the incumbent always has advantages. But what is perhaps most interesting is that the different platforms are all moving closer to each other: gone are the days when one could glibly assume that an Intel-based computer delivers more bang for the buck than a Mac, or that Mac software is necessarily vastly superior to Microsoft.

Later in this chapter, I'll look in more detail at the hardware features that affect your choice of model — desktop or notebook — once you have selected the platform. I'll also be advising on how to go about buying your computer. The chapter ends with the Vendor Profiles section, where I take a closer look at 11 of the largest makers of personal computers.

# A Brief Introduction to Windows

Many readers will already be familiar with Microsoft Windows, but here's a quick introduction for those who are new to it. Windows is a software program that comes preinstalled on most new PCs and included in the hardware price. It can work adequately with any PC with at least a 386SX processor and 2MB of RAM (I'll be discussing processors and RAM later), though be advised that these are the minimum — definitely not the optimum — requirements. It prefers you to have a color screen.

Windows provides a graphical operating environment — also known as a "graphical user interface" or "GUI" — which sits between the operating system (DOS) and your applications programs. (Remember that an applications program is a software package that handles a particular task — word processing, spreadsheet, database, etc.). Windows does not replace either DOS or the applications program, but instead creates an environment in which both are easier to use.

### Windows benefits in brief

These are the main benefits that Windows brings over DOS on its own:

✔ Windows allows you to keep more than one application program open at the same time (a capability known as "multitasking"). You can switch from one to another by clicking on different "windows" on the screen (a window is, effectively, like a screen within a screen — think of them as separate pieces of paper on your desk). You can have numerous windows open at once (layered on top of one another, if you like), each containing information drawn from different programs or from different parts of the same program. You are restricted in the number only by memory and, up to a point, by screen size.

✔ Windows allows you to copy data easily from one open program to another. It also goes some way to imposing a common set of commands on the way in which different programs work, so that when you have learned one you'll find it that much easier to master others.

✔ Windows makes learning and using software easier, as it employs graphical images to denote different commands. Using a mouse, you point to what you want to do, and click. Tedious, unintuitive keyboard commands are substantially reduced.

✔ The Windows environment allows you to create documents in a true "what-you-see-is-what-you-get" (WYSIWYG) manner. Type styles, type sizes, and graphical images show up on screen, in position, just as they will appear on paper. There's no more guesswork in designing attractive layouts.

### Moving over to Windows

To take advantage of Windows, you need to use the Windows versions of different software programs. If, for example, you currently use WordPerfect 5.1 for DOS, you'll need to get a hold of WordPerfect for Windows (or make the move to one of the other Windows word processing programs).

You can use your old DOS programs on a PC that is set up for Windows, but only by operating in DOS mode which is easy enough but slightly defeats the point of having Windows. Today, there are Windows versions of all leading business software programs. Most allow you to read files from their DOS equivalents, so you shouldn't need to worry about transferring all your old data.

### The case for Windows

I strongly encourage people using industry-standard DOS personal computers to make the move to Windows if they haven't done so already. True, there will be a learning curve. And there may be some extra expense in the short term. But software development has more or less halted for the pure DOS platform. If you stick with DOS, you'll effectively be sticking with 1980s vintage personal computing.

Like it or not, Windows is the industry standard for the 1990s. And, once you get the hang of it, it can be more productive than DOS — as well as more fun.

### The case against Windows

But while Windows wins hands-down over DOS, buyers should pause to consider other alternatives. Windows offers nothing that Apple Macintosh computers haven't been offering for quite some time. And the Mac operating environment is a lot more refined and that much more pleasurable to use.

Windows was designed to paper over the DOS operating system, which is still there underneath (with all its horrible CONFIG.SYS files and cumbersome "backslash culture" commands, like COPY C:\WORDPROC\DRAFT.DOC A:\WORK). By contrast, the Apple Mac was designed from the ground up to be what it is. In addition, unlike the Mac, DOS/Windows computers can be notoriously awkward when it comes to installing certain peripherals, such as sound cards, additional storage devices, and so on.

I have never come across anyone who, with personal knowledge of both systems and no vested interest, actually thinks that the combination of DOS and Windows 3.1 is better than the Apple Mac. More about the Mac alternative shortly.

### Why most people settle on Windows

If Windows isn't as good as the Mac, why do so many people choose it? There are several reasons. Perhaps the main one is that it is built on DOS, and DOS was established as the main standard in the business computer market long before Apple grew out of the low-end home/education market where it had its roots. For this reason, most businesses computerized around DOS when they first moved away from typewriters and ledger books — and once you've gone up this path, it's quite hard to change.

For example, businesses typically do not replace all the PC hardware and software they own at once — and so incremental purchases have to be compatible with what's already there. In addition, many businesses — even if they aren't encumbered by their own computer baggage — feel they have to be compatible with other businesses that they deal with.

And because there are so many more DOS/Windows users than Apple Mac owners, there is also more software around. That doesn't mean that Mac users are short of programs — most major programs are available for both platforms — but there is definitely more on the DOS/Windows side of the fence, and upgraded versions of the DOS/Windows packages are often introduced some time before the Mac versions are enhanced.

Also, because there are so many more DOS/Windows PCs being sold, hardware prices have traditionally been lower. And, to cap it all, the hardware has also been somewhat more powerful — top-end DOS/Windows equipment has significantly outperformed top-end Macs in recent years, while the mid-market and entry-level DOS/Windows models have delivered more computer power per dollar spent.

But, as I indicated, things are now changing, with the hardware and software designers on both sides attempting — with some success — to copy the strengths of their competing platform. I'll be talking about the changes to the Mac shortly, but first let's look at what Microsoft has up its sleeve....

### Coming soon: "Chicago" or "Windows 4.0"

Although it is widely agreed that the Mac's system software is classier than the combination of Windows 3.1 and DOS 6.0 — the latest releases from Microsoft at the time this chapter was written in summer '94 — a major enhancement for Windows is in the pipeline and should hit the market during the shelf-life of this book.

The new version of Windows — codenamed "Chicago" and likely to be called "Windows 4.0" — will be a complete operating system in its own right. In other words, it will not run as an overlay to DOS, but it will be a replacement for DOS — and it should be a lot more streamlined and less awkward as a result. It will also include built-in networking for smaller workgroups (something hitherto addressed by a separate Microsoft product called Windows for Workgroups).

In addition, Microsoft is working with hardware manufacturers to make it much easier for users to add peripherals and expansion boards without the tricky installation process that has been required in the past — Windows 4.0 should mark the start of a more Mac-like "plug-in-and-play" approach. Compaq and Microsoft have been working closely together to set new standards for tight integration between hardware and software, though the benefits should end up being industry-wide.

It remains to be seen to what extent Chicago might incorporate some of the less friendly aspects of DOS — having Windows take over from DOS will be less exciting if this means merging DOS-like things into Windows. Still, the consensus in the PC industry is that Chicago is a major step forward and that it will bring Windows significantly closer to the Mac.

Any DOS/Windows computer you buy today will be able to run Chicago. In other words, there is no need to delay your purchase to await the new version of Windows. You can simply get started with the current set-up, and then switch over when the time is right. Chicago is unlikely to cost more than $100 when it does become available and will in time be preinstalled on many new computers, just as DOS and Windows 3.1 are today. Keep in mind, though, that you may need new versions of your applications programs to get the best out of the new operating system.

# A Couple of Other DOS Offerings

The main version of DOS (which, incidentally, stands for "disk operating system") is MS-DOS (the "MS" standing for Microsoft). However, there are a couple of other products ending with the letters D-O-S. ...

### PC-DOS

PC-DOS is a slight variation of MS-DOS sold by IBM which, thanks to licensing agreements with Microsoft, sells its own version. PC-DOS is very similar to MS-DOS, but is enhanced in a few details. PC-DOS is used on IBM personal computers, but rarely on other brands.

### DR-DOS

You may come across something called DR-DOS. This is an early MS-DOS clone sold by a company called Digital Research (hence the "DR"), though DR-DOS has not been updated to keep up with MS-DOS.

Digital Research was the force behind an earlier standard of PC operating software called CP/M, which some readers may remember from the late 1970s and early 1980s: many people's first experience on office computers was running the WordStar word processing program on a CP/M "microcomputer" (as PCs tended to be called in those days). CP/M was more or less sunk when IBM introduced its first PC in 1981 and the world switched over to DOS.

Today, Digital Research is owned by Novell, which reigns supreme in the network operating software market. Despite this, I can't think of a good reason why anyone should want to opt for DR-DOS in place of MS-DOS — and sightings of this operating software have become increasingly rare.

# A Few Words About Some Other Operating Systems

The main alternative to DOS/Windows is the Apple Mac — I'll be talking about this shortly. Before I do, however, let's look briefly at some less popular and — in some cases — somewhat specialized alternatives. Frankly, most of these won't be of interest to most readers of this book, but I'm mentioning them here so that, if you hear about them elsewhere, you don't suffer "should-I-know-about-this-anxiety."

### IBM OS/2

OS/2 is an operating system that was originally developed jointly by Microsoft and IBM, until the former pulled out in 1990 leaving IBM to soldier on alone.

OS/2 presents the user with an operating environment that looks not unlike that of Windows. But unlike the current (as opposed to Chicago) version of Windows, OS/2 is a complete operating system — it does not rely on DOS. However, you can run DOS and Windows from within it.

Despite the superficial similarities with Windows, OS/2 is in some ways more sophisticated underneath. For example, it has superior multitasking abilities — you can load extra programs without slowing down other applications that are already open (Windows 3.1, by contrast, slows down its operation whenever another task begins).

OS/2 was a long time coming: for several years, people were told that it was almost ready, and that its heyday was just around the corner. But IBM only really got its act together in 1992 when it polished off the product and started promoting it with massive expenditures (having already sunk a fortune into its development). IBM claims that OS/2 is the industry standard of tomorrow. But OS/2's late arrival means that it is facing an uphill struggle — the market had already settled on Windows as the main industry standard by the time it got going.

And OS/2 isn't helped by the fact that not a great deal of software has been developed to work with it. You don't absolutely need to have special software, because — as noted above — you can run Windows from within it. However, getting OS/2 but then running mainly Windows applications largely defeats the object of choosing it in the first place (though IBM has worked in some enhancements to improve the Windows experience for OS/2 customers).

The main customers for OS/2 tend to be larger corporations running their own customized software. Unless you've got a particular reason for wanting OS/2, you can probably afford to overlook it. You can always get it later — it runs on the same hardware as Windows (though it requires more memory). The cost is pretty modest: you can buy OS/2 for about $125 (and it comes free with certain IBM PCs).

### Microsoft Windows NT

Microsoft Windows NT is a new and very upscale operating system with some ambitious features — including built-in networking capabilities and advanced multitasking — aimed at large corporate users. Windows NT has so far had little effect on the mainstream PC market and need not concern the vast majority of computer buyers. It is most definitely not a replacement for "regular" Windows.

One of the things that severely limits its mass-market appeal is its need for 16MB of RAM — plus whatever you need for your applications programs! However, a new "lite" version —

codenamed "Daytona" — was expected to reduce its hardware requirements later in 1994. Even when NT gets going, it will not be the main Microsoft operating system — it will continue to be focused on the very high end of the market.

In 1993, Microsoft and IBM got together and agreed that NT would be available on IBM's PowerPC computers. However, the latest word is that a combination of political and technical problems have got in the way of this plan: IBM PowerPC buyers should not count on being able to run NT in the near future.

### IBM Workplace OS

IBM is working to finalize a new operating system it refers to as "Workplace OS" (although this will apparently not be the official name when it's launched). Workplace OS will be promoted in conjunction with IBM's new computers using the PowerPC processor which are expected before the end of 1994.

It can best be described as a sort of "shell" operating system, which works in conjunction with the user's choice of "personalities," each of which is a separate operating system or an emulation of one. The idea is that you will be able to run more than one "personality" on the same machine at once.

The main personality will be OS/2, which itself can run DOS and Windows applications. However, versions of a number of upscale and specialized operating systems — Unix, Windows NT, etc. — are also planned. In addition, it's possible that Workplace OS will be able to host an Apple System 7 personality — effectively allowing you to run Macintosh software on your IBM PowerPC-based computer (though it is by no means certain that this will materialize in the near future). Readers who look forward to the dawn of the "multi-platform ideal" should keep an eye out for Workplace OS.

### Unix

Aside from the various Microsoft products and Apple, and aside from networking software, the main contender in the operating system market is Unix. This venerable, complex operating system is pitched at very high-end and usually pretty specialized markets — scientific and engineering applications, for example. It was first developed by AT&T many years ago, though it is now owned by Novell (of networking software fame).

Unix's main problem has been that there have been numerous different versions developed by vendors that use it. Although the differences have often seemed relatively small, they've been enough to make it harder for software developers to produce programs that work on different brands of Unix computer and this has generally acted as a brake on Unix's development.

However, Novell has handed over ownership of the Unix name, and responsibility for setting standards, to a 14-company organization called X/Open Co. (Novell retains ownership of the underlying program, however, and still derives royalties from its use). As a result, Unix could become more of a unitary force and pose a stronger challenge to Windows NT. The new unity in the Unix camp will not propel this operating system into the mass market, but it should assure it a continued role in its traditional territory.

### AIX

This is an IBM version of Unix, which is likely to be offered on IBM's forthcoming PowerPC-based models expected before the end of 1994.

### Taligent

This is a futuristic operating system being jointly developed by IBM, Apple, and Hewlett-Packard. Taligent is what is known as "object oriented software" — it is a very powerful tool whose main appeal is to program developers rather than end users. However, its benefits could eventually work their way into the upscale end-user market — it could help multiple users work on the same document simultaneously, for example.

Taligent will not ship until 1995 and is definitely not aimed at the mass market. I mention it here simply so that you know roughly what it is in case you hear mention of it elsewhere — I won't be discussing it further in this chapter.

### Microsoft "Cairo"

"Cairo" is the codename for another object-oriented operating system — this time being developed by Microsoft to rival Taligent (above). Like Taligent, Cairo is expected to ship in 1995 but is something of a specialized product that need not concern the vast majority of "ordinary" buyers. When it does arrive, it is likely to be marketed as an add-on to Windows NT.

# Introducing the Apple Mac

Apple is the only PC manufacturer that stayed apart from the original DOS industry standard and lived to tell the tale. In 1993, Apple sold its 10 millionth Macintosh, and the company now sells more computers than IBM.

For a long time, Apple's machines had a reputation for being best suited for "enthusiasts" and the company fought a battle to be accepted into the mainstream corporate market. Today, however, the Apple Mac is widely regarded as a very serious business tool.

Apple probably has its greatest penetration in the smaller business sector, but many pretty big businesses are sold on it for at least part of their PC needs. The Mac really shines in desktop publishing and upscale graphics applications — where it enjoys a distinct advantage over its DOS/Windows rivals — but there's also a good range of software catering to just about all mainstream applications.

Although people often talk about "the" Mac, there are, in fact, numerous Macintosh models ranging in price from under $1,000 to several thousand dollars. They include desktops and what are, arguably, still the coolest notebooks on the market.

The Mac has many plus points, but if there were just one I could stress, it would be this: if you compare computers in terms of megahertz or megabytes, Macs haven't always seemed anything special (though that has begun to change). Their real power has lain in the fact that because they're so easy and fun to use, people tend to use them more ambitiously.

People who have struggled for years with DOS machines — only to produce boring-looking documents and master basic applications — surprise themselves by the speed with which they achieve things they never managed before. People who use Windows still often envy the sheer simplicity with which things are done on the Mac. And Mac users tend to "love" their computers in a way that DOS/Windows users usually don't.

### What's so different about Apples?

The Mac provides an operating environment in which you can keep more than one program open at the same time, and easily switch data between them. You can have as many windows open at the same time as you like, either side by side or stacked on top of each other like a pile of paper on your desk. The number is limited only by available memory.

The Mac also provides an environment in which different application programs use a very similar set of commands, so once you've learned one, you're well on your way to mastering others. The system relies heavily on graphical images known as "icons" to represent programs, features, and commands available to the user — for example, outline drawings of folders represent files and a trash can represents a place to put work you want to delete. Using a mouse, you point and click to activate an icon.

"Wait a minute!" — you might say — "All this sounds pretty similar to Microsoft Windows." And, on paper, it is (Apple has tried unsuccessfully to sue Microsoft for patent infringements). But the Apple Mac operating environment is a lot more polished — "elegant" is a word often used to describe it. The current version of Windows is really an overlay on what is intrinsically an unfriendly operating system, as DOS undoubtedly is.

By contrast, the Apple Mac system software was designed from the ground up to be what it is. In addition, it has been around much longer than Windows, allowing for more revisions and enhancements. Microsoft is working hard to catch up — and could possibly get pretty close with the new "Chicago" version discussed above — but it isn't there yet.

### Why you might not want a Mac

There are two reasons why you might not want a Mac, and why you may decide to go with Windows instead — even if you accept the Mac's intrinsic advantages.

The first is if your whole organization is already geared to DOS-based personal computing — considering the size of your existing investment, it may make more sense to build on what you've got. But if you don't have baggage, my advice is to think seriously about the Mac. And even if you do have an investment in DOS/Windows equipment, Macs aren't totally incompatible as I'll show shortly.

The second reason why Macs may not be for you is that although there is now a very full set of software covering most general business applications, some more specialized programs are still only available in DOS/Windows versions. So if you are in the widget spray-painting business, and a niche software company in California has come up with a special program called "WidgeSpray for Windows" — which doesn't also come in a Mac version — you may decide to get a DOS/Windows computer for that reason alone. Keep in mind, though, that there are also some specialized applications that are geared more to the Mac world than to Windows — especially those involving complex graphics.

### Mac value

The third reason for not buying a Mac used to be that they cost more — but this is really no longer the case now that the PowerPC models have been introduced (more on these shortly). And Macs can be especially good values when you consider what's included in their standard specifications.

For example, all Macs have built-in networking capabilities — this is usually an extra in the DOS/Windows world. They can generally support a wide range of screens without the need for extra video boards. And they all have some built-in multimedia capabilities — they come standard with a microphone (enabling you to store voice input on your data files) and quite good sound output.

### More Mac differences

There are a number of other things about "Appledom" that are quite different from the DOS/Windows world. First, as I reminded you earlier, Apple makes both the computer hardware and the system software (the Mac system software, effectively its equivalent of DOS and Windows combined, is called System 7).

By contrast, Microsoft, which is the company behind DOS and Windows, only provides the operating software and does not make computer hardware. The tight integration between hardware and software is one of the contributing factors to the more polished and easy feel to the Mac operating environment (and it is also something that Microsoft is seeking to emulate).

Not only does Apple make the Mac hardware, it is currently the only company to do so — this is totally different from the DOS/Windows world, where numerous hardware manufacturers make PCs that are all fundamentally the same. So if you want an Apple Mac, you'll have to buy an Apple brand product.

This exclusiveness — protected by numerous patents — has had its pros and cons. On the one hand, it has allowed Apple to refine its product with nice touches that might have been sacrificed if it was constantly building Macs down to a price to compete with clones. For example, Apple's computers are unusually handsome in their appearance: the company tends to place more emphasis on design (of the non-technological kind) than its rivals in the Intel-based DOS/Windows camp.

But the drawback is that Apple has sometimes not treated its customers as well as other vendors facing more direct competition. For example, Apple support was until recently pretty poor and even now it is only average (more on this in the Apple entry in the Vendor Profiles section).

Likewise, Mac buyers have faced limited choices about where and how to buy their computers — for example, mail order sales have been non-existent or very limited (though this may be changing — see Vendor Profiles). And the exclusive approach also contributed to the high hardware prices that Apple managed to get away with until recently.

### The first Apple clones?

Either way, things are set to change. Following about a year of speculation, Apple formally went on the record early in 1994 to say that it did want to license its operating software to other computer makers — in other words, it is looking for companies to build Mac clones that run Apple system software.

It remains to be seen how many computer makers will come forward and how quickly — at press-time, Apple was talking to a number of leading makers of Intel-based PCs, but nothing definitive had emerged. It is also unclear whether Mac clones, when they do emerge, will be mass market products or whether they will be more specialized units aimed at niche markets.

The likelihood is that the first non-Apple computers to run Macintosh software will only be able to run Mac software and nothing else. However, as I explain later, the hope is that — eventually — the same computers will be able to run both Apple and Microsoft software.

### Mac add-ons

Although Apple itself currently makes all Mac computers, there's a thriving market in third-party peripherals, such as monitors, disk drives, and printers. Apple sells these add-ons itself, but it encourages other vendors to develop them as well. Most of the software is also third-party (although one of the biggest Mac software companies, Claris, is owned by Apple itself).

The choice of available screens is one of the big plus points in favor of the Mac. Apple users can choose between very high quality black-and-white, gray-scale, and color screens that come in half-page, full-page, and two-page sizes. The availability of excellent and very affordable full-page portrait screens makes Apple an excellent choice for word processing and desktop publishing applications, where it's a great help to be able to view a whole page at a time, in the size you're going to print it out — full-page screens are pretty rare in the DOS/Windows world.

### Mac compatibility with the rest of the world

Apples are not compatible with DOS/Windows machines, in the sense of allowing you to use the same software or swap disks just like that. On the other hand, they are not totally incompatible.

For a start, there are Mac versions of most of the main DOS/Windows programs — Microsoft Word and Excel, WordPerfect, and so on. These all have more than a passing resemblance to their DOS/Windows counterparts (though too strong a similarity is considered a bad thing, as it means that the program isn't taking full advantage of the Mac environment). There are also some excellent programs which were developed first and foremost for the Mac, which have now made their way over to DOS/Windows (the ClarisWorks multifunction integrated program and Claris's FileMaker Pro database, for example).

Second, it is a straightforward procedure to convert DOS/Windows files so that they can be read by your Mac. It's easiest to do this with text files and Macs come with a utility program designed with this in mind. Converting Mac text files back to DOS/Windows format is also possible.

In addition, a company called Insignia Solutions sells a series of programs called SoftPC that enable you to run DOS on a regular Mac, and Windows on a PowerPC-based Mac (SoftPC is "bundled" with some of the PowerPC Macs). Windows emulation on a PowerPC Mac delivers performance comparable to that of a 486SX Intel-based PC: as I'll be explaining soon, this is — by today's standards — an entry-level PC. You wouldn't want to run Windows on a Mac on a full-time basis — it would defeat the purpose of having one — but it can be useful if you're making the transition over to Macs or if you work in a mixed environment with people who have DOS/Windows equipment.

Finally, Apple sells one Macintosh that also includes an Intel 486SX processor and that allows you to run both Mac software and "actual" DOS/Windows at the same time. This is literally like having two computers in one, and it's the nearest thing there is right now to a genuine "multi-platform" computer. More on this in the Apple entry in the Vendor Profiles section.

# The Pentium Versus the PowerPC

The processor can be viewed as a computer's engine. Despite its tiny size, it is the most important factor determining how fast your computer will work. Until recently, "platform wars" tended to be defined more around the system software — you chose between DOS/Windows, OS/2, and Apple — and then you got whatever processor drove the computers that supported those software standards. Within each platform, there were different processors offering a choice of performance/price ratios, but you didn't typically spend much time comparing the types of processors on DOS/Windows computers against the ones used on Apples. That wasn't the angle from which buyers normally approached the buying decision.

### Processors get fashionable — and competitive

In 1994, however, the brand and design of processor has come to the fore. For the first time, users are being encouraged to make the processor design one of the key ingredients behind their choice of platform. The reason for this is the arrival of the PowerPC, a completely new super-powerful processor designed jointly by Motorola, IBM, and Apple — and manufactured both by Motorola and IBM. This has joined battle with Intel's Pentium processor — the latter is the high-end offering for computers that run DOS/Windows.

### Introducing the PowerPC

The name "PowerPC" can be confusing, because it makes it sound like the name of a complete computer. However, the PowerPC is a processor, not a whole computer. As an end-user, you can't go out and buy a PowerPC: you can only buy a computer that uses one.

The PowerPC is often associated with the Mac, because Apple was not only part of the troika that developed it, but was also the first computer manufacturer to release a computer that uses it and has been the loudest evangelist singing its praises. At present, Apple is in the process of moving its entire Macintosh product range onto a PowerPC-based platform — a process that should be complete by the end of 1995 (see the Apple entry in the Vendor Profiles for more on this and for details of compatibility with earlier Macintosh products).

However, Apple is not alone in using the PowerPC: IBM will release its own PowerPC-based products in 1995. However, whereas Apple plans to make its entire product range PowerPC-based as soon as it is able to, IBM is likely to target PowerPC systems at very high-end applications and specialized markets — IBM will continue to sell Intel-based products for the mainstream market. See the IBM entry in the Vendor Profiles section for more on the company's plans for the PowerPC.

Some other vendors will also get in on the PowerPC act — for example, Canon has announced that it will be building PowerPC computers that are compatible with the ones sold by IBM. However, the majority of big-name PC makers are remaining totally loyal to Intel.

### The multi-platform ideal?

Originally, there were high hopes that the PowerPC — supported as it was from opposite corners of the PC industry — would herald the start of a new multi-platform standard that would allow users to run Apple software on an IBM model and OS/2 (and hence DOS/Windows) on a Macintosh. In addition, IBM's PowerPC was meant to be an alternative platform for Microsoft's upscale Windows NT operating system.

For a combination of technical and political reasons, things aren't panning out that way — at least not yet. For the time being, Apple's PowerPC is best viewed as simply a much more powerful Macintosh with limited Windows emulation capabilities. And IBM's PowerPC is likely to first see the light of day as something of a niche product which won't run either Mac software or Windows NT. The ideal of having one very powerful computer which is equally comfortable running all the main industry-standard operating systems seems some way off.

### Introducing the Pentium

The PowerPC is the first processor to challenge Intel at the high end of the mainstream business computer market. It poses a strong challenge to the Intel Pentium — the Pentium was introduced in 1993 and, after a period of being something of a niche product for very upscale applications, it is now targeted at the high end of the DOS/Windows market.

The Pentium has not replaced Intel's 486 series of processors, which were first introduced in 1989, but the latter are now repositioned to cover the so-called "value" end of the market. The 486s have taken over from the old 386-series processors, which are now history (the latter were first introduced in 1985 and began to fizzle out around the end of 1992).

When the first PowerPC Macs appeared in spring 1994, they were more powerful than the current version of the Pentium. However, a speeded up Pentium was introduced soon afterwards. During the remainder of 1994 and throughout 1995, buyers can expect to see the highest-performing Pentiums and PowerPCs leapfrogging each other as new versions are released (more on this shortly).

### The RISC advantage

Despite all the leapfrogging, the PowerPC is in some ways the more intrinsically upscale of the two competing processors. This is because it uses something called "RISC" — standing for "reduced instruction set computing" — architecture. The Pentium, by contrast, uses "CISC" architecture — this standing for "complex instruction set computing."

In layman's language, a RISC processor is designed from the ground up to perform at super-high performance levels — it can do a lot more with much less circuitry. The Pentium, by contrast, is a stretched derivative of Intel's older and much less powerful processors — the CISC architecture causes it to be more expensive, larger, and more prone to get hot.

While the RISC-versus-CISC issue may not be enough to swing committed DOS/Windows users off their secure Intel platform, few independent people disagree that — in an ideal world — RISC is better than CISC. And the RISC architecture seems destined to ultimately win the race to drive the fastest personal computer: the most powerful planned version of the PowerPC charted to be introduced before 1997 will be faster than the most powerful Intel processor expected to be available during that time.

# What's in the Processor Pipeline?

Here's a quick look at the new versions of the super-fast PowerPC and Pentium processors that were on their way when this book was published, but not yet released. Note that processor speeds are rated in Megahertz (MHz) — I'll be talking more about that shortly.

### Future PowerPC processors

Here's what cooking in the PowerPC pot:

**PowerPC 601:** Launched March 1994 (already used by Apple and soon to be used by IBM), though faster versions of the 601 are still in the pipeline. First versions run at 66MHz; an 80MHz version is expected in the second half of '94; and a 100MHz one could appear by the end of the year. IBM may enter the PowerPC market with the 80MHz version, and skip the 66MHz level — but this was not certain at press-time.

**PowerPC 603:** Not yet out, though it could appear before the end of 1994: this version will be less powerful than the 601, but will be suitable for notebooks and low-end "affordable" desktop models. Likely to be the basis for Apple's future smaller office/home office/educational market products, and also for future Apple notebooks.

**PowerPC 604:** High-performance processor, which will be faster than the 601 — might see the light of day late in 1994, but probably won't ship in volume until 1995.

**PowerPC 620:** Top-of-the-line ultra-powerful unit likely to follow soon after the 604.

### Latest and future Intel processors

And here's what Intel has on the stove:

**Pentium 90/100MHz:** The launch of the super-fast 90MHz

and 100MHz versions of the Pentium was been brought forward
to respond to the PowerPC, and both should be shipping by the
time you read this. Both versions should outperform the 66MHz
version of the PowerPC 601 used on the models Apple introduced in March '94. Note that both versions run at their full
speed internally, but communicate with the rest of the computer at a slower speed — the 90MHz version communicates
internally at 60MHz and the 100MHz one does so at 66MHz.

*P6:* This is Intel's codename for the next-generation, post-
Pentium processor, expected to emerge in the second half of
1995, though unlikely to reach the end-user market in volume
until 1996. According to Intel, the P6 will be about three times
as fast as the first version of the Pentium (to further put things
in perspective, it will be 50 times faster than the first version of
Intel's 386 processor). When the P6 arrives, the Pentium is likely
to be repositioned as the mainstream processor for the masses,
and the 486 series will start to fade away.

*P7:* Intel has gone on the record to say that it has a team
working on the P7, the next generation after the P6. The
company's stated policy for the remainder of the decade is to
bring out a new generation of processors every two years, as
opposed to every four years as in the past.

### Future Pentium rivals from Intel's other competitors
As I discuss a little later in this chapter, Intel faces direct competition from two much smaller rivals that have been trying to
produce clones of its 486 and 386 processors. The two companies are American Micro Devices (AMD) and Cyrix Corporation.
Intel has done its best to block these rivals in the 386 and 486
markets, by pursuing never-ending lawsuits citing patent infringement. However, both AMD and Cyrix have Pentium rivals
in the pipeline which, they claim, will be safe from even the
most highly motivated Intel attorneys.

AMD's product is codenamed "K1," and Cyrix's is referred
to as "M1." Both should be available by the end of 1994, and are
intended to drive PCs running Windows applications.

It remains to be seen how many PC manufacturers will use
these chips — they lack the brand name appeal of the Pentium,
which is being heavily advertised to end users. Nonetheless,
Compaq's announcement early in 1994 that it will be using AMD
processors in some of its future products suggests that the PC
vendors don't want Intel to take their business for granted.

# 486-Generation Processors

Although the Pentium and the PowerPC are the hot topics in the PC industry, most computers being sold in 1994 still run on Intel's 486-series processors. The 486 series is far from obsolete — indeed, new versions were still being introduced in 1994 and this processor should remain strong throughout 1995.

If you are a confirmed Mac user, the following discussion of 486 and other Intel processors will be of little practical interest: the pre-PowerPC Macs run on Motorola 68000-series processors and I discuss these in the Apple entry in the Vendor Profiles towards the end of this chapter.

### The different types of 486 processor

The entry-level version of the 486 processor is called the 486SX. The mid-market version is the 486DX. At the time of this writing, there was a very new version called the SX2, which is positioned above the 486SX and just above the 486DX. Until recently, the top-end version was the 486DX2. The latest high-end version, which had recently begun to appear in PCs at around the time this book was published, is the DX4.

Note that in referring above to Intel's two latest processors, I said "SX2" and "DX4" — not "486SX2" or "486DX4." For trademark reasons that I confess to never having fully understood, Intel has been unable to prevent its rivals in the DOS/Windows-compatible processor market from replicating its mainly-numerical 386- and 486-series designations when naming their own equivalents. So, to better differentiate its products, Intel is moving away from the numbering system it has used in recent years to one that makes more use of letters and words.

Nonetheless, the SX2 and DX4 are members of the 486 processor family — they are not the start of a completely separate series. The DX4 may prove to be the last fundamental performance upgrade of the 486, which is now playing second fiddle to the Pentium.

The DX4 is the first new Intel processor to be introduced from day-one with 3.3-volt technology, the purpose of which is to boost the battery performance of portable PCs and lower the energy cost of desktop ones. Previously, Intel only offered 3.3-volt technology on special "SL" variants of its processors, which arrived on the scene some time after their original 5-volt counterparts. See the discussion in this chapter of notebook processors, and the section on energy-efficient PCs, for more on the SL variants and 3.3-volt technology.

Note that some of IBM's PCs use slightly different versions of the 486 series of processors. IBM has manufacturing rights to most of Intel's processors, but tweaks some of them in designing its own systems and varies the model numbers when doing so. IBM does not produce its own Pentiums.

### Co-processors

Today, almost all of the processors I am discussing come with an auxiliary processor that speeds up mathematical calculations — this is known as a math co-processor. The only one that does not is the entry-level 486SX, which has a socket for an optional co-processor called a 487SX which costs about $85. If you add this co-processor to your 486SX, you end up with what effectively amounts to a 486DX.

### Old processors to avoid

While there is still lots of life left in the 486, the 386 processor is now obsolete: it survived in the notebook PC market for a while after vendors started dropping it in desktops late in 1992 and during the first half of 1993, but it is now rapidly fading from the portable arena as well.

If you should come across a 386 product being remaindered in some place or other, do not be tempted by the price: the 386 is not an ideal platform for running Windows software and it is likely to be even less suitable for the new Windows 4.0 standard that I discussed earlier. Only die-hard DOS addicts are likely to be satisfied with a 386 purchased today.

As for the 286, this has joined Intel's original 8086 and 8088 behind a glass case in the processor museum.

### AMD and Cyrix: Intel's "unwelcome" competitors

For many years, Intel had a total monopoly in the market for processors driving computers that run DOS/Windows software. While it still has an overwhelming market share, it is now facing competition from two other much smaller vendors.

The one that has caused the most ripples is American Micro Devices (AMD), a $1.6 billion Californian corporation. It would be an understatement to say that AMD does not have a friendly relationship with Intel. Since 1992, the two companies have been locked in amazingly complex and seemingly endless litigation over AMD's alleged copyright infringements. This concerns something called the "microcode," which is internal software crucial to how the processor operates.

The litigation has been something of a roller-coaster for both parties, with each one enjoying pyrrhic victories, only to see them reversed on appeal or wasted by fresh legal action from another direction. At press-time, AMD seemed to have the upper hand and was managing to sell its range of 386 and 486 clones with the blessing of the courts. However, the battle was continuing — and it could last until the 486 design nears the end of its useful life. In fact, the ongoing dispute over AMD's alleged 386 infringements has already outlasted the 386 itself — in other words, the wrangle wears on despite the fact that 386 processors are basically obsolete.

Intel's other challenger is a company called Cyrix Corporation, which has also been engaged in legal battles with Intel. Cyrix is the smaller of the two players and has been less of a thorn in Intel's side.

At press-time, both AMD and Cyrix had a full range of 486 processors. As I indicated earlier, both companies have managed to give model numbers to these processors that are virtually identical to Intel's own. For example, AMD's equivalent of Intel's "i486DX2" is the "Am486DX2."

### *Are you better off with an Intel?*
Until recently, AMD and Cyrix processors tended to be found only in secondary brands of PCs. So although there might not have been anything wrong with getting an AMD or Cyrix processor as such, the overall package may not have appealed to conservative buyers who prefer to stick with the safest bets in the industry.

Today, AMD and Cyrix processors still tend to be used most often by smaller PC manufacturers, but this has recently begun to change to some extent. For example, IBM has announced that it will use Cyrix Pentium-class processors in some future products; moreover, IBM is actually making some Cyrix 486 clones under contract (although Cyrix designs its processors, it does not manufacture any of them). Likewise, Compaq announced early in 1994 that it would start to use AMD processors in some of its future computers (and the first AMD-equipped Compaqs were just hitting the market as this book neared completion).

To allay buyer concerns, and underline its acceptance within the computer industry establishment, AMD now ships all of its processors with a tiny "Microsoft Windows Compatible" logo etched on the side (it has to be tiny, because processors are themselves miniature). Of course, you'll probably never actually see the processor inside your computer, let alone look at it so closely that you'll spot this logo. However, AMD has begun advertising is processors to end-users — and it wants everyone to know about this implied Microsoft endorsement.

The AMD/Cyrix practice of referring to their processors using numbers that are near-identical to Intel's own makes instant comparisons easy — in general, any processor with the same set of numbers will deliver the same performance regardless of brand. That said, AMD and Cyrix may be obliged to come up with unique model numbers for their future processors, so it could become harder to instantly connect an AMD/Cyrix processor with a corresponding Intel.

Some buyers instinctively prefer Intel processors — in much the same way that people used to feel safer going with IBM in the early years of the PC market. Intel promotes brand loyalty by encouraging PC manufacturers that use its processors to display an "Intel Inside" logo on their packaging and advertising.

But although Intel likes to foster anxiety about whether an AMD or a Cyrix is as good as the "real thing," I know of no rational justification to support this fear. Still, these days there isn't usually much of a price savings associated with the lesser-known processors — and although AMD and Cyrix don't offer the end-user less performance or reliability than Intel, it is not clear that they offer any real advantages either (aside from making the processor market more competitive and thereby exerting downward pressure on prices).

Note that both AMD and Cyrix have Pentium rivals up their sleeves which, they claim, won't provide Intel's lawyers with work opportunities — see the earlier discussion of processors in the pipeline for details.

# How to Compare Intel Processors

Next, some guidance on how to compare the performance of different Intel processors.

### Clock speeds

Not all processors of the same family run at the same speed. Each processor has a rated "clock speed," which is measured in megahertz (MHz). If you're getting a 486SX machine, you'll find that speeds run from 20MHz to 33MHz. The new SX2 runs at 50MHz. Speeds in the 486DX and DX2 class go from 25MHz all the way to 66MHz. The DX4 runs at 75MHz and even 100MHz — and the Pentiums run at between 60MHz and 100MHz.

Clock speeds are often denoted with abbreviations such as "486DX2/66" meaning a "486DX2 processor running at 66MHz."

Note that the SX2, 486DX2, and DX4 processors work twice as fast internally as they do when communicating with the rest of the computer. This is what is meant by the jargon term "speed doubling." In these cases, the quoted MHz figure is usually the faster, internal speed. However, you may see a reference to, say, "SX2 25/50MHz" to denote an SX2 that works at 50MHz internally, but at 25MHz externally.

Sometimes you may have to choose between going for a faster clock speed or a faster family of processors. That used to be the case when both the 386 and the 486 family were current, and the top-end 386DX had a higher clock speed than an entry-level 486SX. Likewise, today, the fastest 486-series processor — the DX4 — has a higher clock speed than an entry-level Pentium. In a case like this, you can generally count on the higher level of processor family being faster regardless of clock speed — for example, a 66MHz Pentium is more powerful than a 100MHz DX4.

### Comparative processor performance
All of this raises a wider question as to exactly what the performance differentials are between all the different processor types. It's all very well saying that Processor A is faster than Processor B, but how are these differences quantified and what difference does it make in practice?

Intel has a rating system for its processors called "The iCOMP Index" — "iCOMP" stands for "Intel Comparative Microprocessor Performance." This is based on various technical categories, weighted by Intel's assumptions about how computers purchased today are likely to be used over a five-year period (the point being that powerful processors are only able to show what they're made of when they're given demanding work).

To some extent, Intel is biased in favor of showing its newest and most powerful processors in their most favorable light. Nonetheless, the figures — shown on the next page — make interesting reading.

### OverDrive processors: Intel's upgrade path
Intel introduced its OverDrive processors in 1992 as a means of enabling users of its 486-series processors to boost a computer's performance by effectively upgrading it to a higher level of processor. The upgrade involves adding an additional processor to the one your PC has to begin with — it does not involve replacing the first one. All 486-based systems being sold now have a socket for an OverDrive processor; OverDrives can also be added to most older 486-based systems which don't have the special socket.

## Intel's iCOMP index at-a-glance

Intel's "iCOMP Index" — discussed on the previous page — is based on relative performance: the 486SX/25MHz was arbitrarily given a rating of 100, and each of the other ratings is a figure relative to that one (although 386 processors are now obsolete as far as new computer purchases are concerned, I have included some 386 ratings for comparison purposes):

386SX/20MHz: 32
386DX/33MHz: 68
486SX/20MHz: 78
486SX/25MHz: 100*
486DX/25MHz: 122
486SX/33MHz: 136
486DX/33MHz: 166
SX2/50MHz: 180
486DX2/50MHz: 231
486DX/50MHz: 249
486DX2/66MHz: 297
DX4/75MHz: 319
DX4/100MHz: 435
Pentium Processor/60MHz: 510
Pentium Processor/66MHz: 567
Pentium Processor/90MHz: 735
Pentium Processor/100MHz: 815
(* All other figures are relative to this one)

At press-time, OverDrive upgrades were available for both the 486SX and 486DX. Users can expect a doubling of their processor's clock speed as a result. For example, adding an OverDrive processor to a 33MHz 486DX will double the speed to 66MHz: depending on the application, this can provide an over-all system performance boost of up to 70 percent. The 486SX upgrade includes a math coprocessor (which, you'll recall, is standard with the DX but not with the SX).

In addition, an OverDrive for DX2 users is expected soon which, says Intel, will offer Pentium performance. Keep in mind that you only upgrade one notch with an OverDrive: your 486SX can be brought up to DX levels, and your DX to DX2 levels — but you couldn't upgrade an SX to a DX2, or a DX to a Pentium.

Life is simpler if you choose the level of processor you need when you buy the machine, instead of aiming low to begin with and then upgrading 12 months later. But the OverDrive path is particularly useful when the type of processor you would ideally like isn't even available when you buy your computer — it's nice to know that you can upgrade to something totally new in a year or two's time without scrapping the PC you already have.

### Which processor to go for?

There's a school of thought that says you should always go for the most powerful computer you can afford. There's some truth in this, but it is a slightly glib piece of advice: many businesses are capable of writing a check that won't bounce for the most powerful Pentium desktop, but the real question is whether the money would be well spent.

It is a mistake to imagine that you have to be a pretty corporate sort of user to justify an upscale processor — the size of your business has nothing to do with it, only your ambition to do serious work on your computer. Arguably, a lot of small businesses need more powerful computers than many corporate departments: the reason is that a small business PC is often expected to handle a wide variety of functions — accounting, marketing/publicity, administration, planning, customer records, and so forth — whereas a corporate machine is often used only for one function, such as word processing.

In general, a 486SX is all you need for straightforward word processing using a Windows program, and for fairly unambitious use of other mainstream business programs. But remember that a 486SX is the entry-level processor these days — if you fancy a powerful computer, look for something faster.

How much faster is hard to advise — it is so application-specific. If in doubt, go up a few notches on that iCOMP Index. Examples of applications that benefit from faster processors include those that involve graphics, very long documents, large databases, and mega-spreadsheets. Also, a computer that is meant to be the hub of a network should have a powerful processor.

But don't overbuy: my sense is that many people end up with hardware that has much more latent power than they know what to do with. And think hard about whether a five-second delay while your computer completes a command constitutes a necessary reason to go out and buy a new and more expensive one.

Computers have become a bit like sports cars: people want a powerful one, even if they don't have the need, or roads, to drive it to its full potential. And some people see a powerful computer as the expression of their own potential and aspirations: to settle for an entry-level model is to admit to mediocre personal growth plans or to advertise to the world that your work is actually pretty straightforward. Powerful computers and large egos often go hand in hand.

Enough of amateur psychology. All the Intel processors I'm talking about are fully compatible. A 486SX can generally run the same programs as a DX4 or even a Pentium — the difference is the speed. Likewise, there is almost total compatibility between 486 and older 386 processors. And if you create a document on a PC using one type of processor, you can work with it on a machine using another.

In this sense, the Intel-DOS/Windows side of the industry offers an advantage over Apple: while the latter is moving over to the PowerPC, it is having to ask users to buy new software and convert their files in order to benefit from the new processor's speed; and for the next few years, incompatibilities between the old and the new Mac platforms will continue to bug users who operate a mix of machines.

# System Architecture: ISA, EISA, MCA, VESA, & PCI

Having grappled with the subject of platforms and processors, your next choice is the type of architecture. Keep in mind that this discussion of system architecture only applies to people buying Intel-based PCs (or ones using AMD/Cyrix clones) to run DOS/Windows — Mac buyers need not concern themselves with this.

### Bus lanes: ISA introduced
System architecture refers to the way in which information is sent along the "bus," which is a kind of highway in the computer for getting data and instructions from one part to another. Most PCs use what's known as "ISA" — this stands for "industry-standard architecture," and it's the latest evolution of the bus standard that IBM originally set when it launched the first PC back in 1982. ISA architecture today is "16-bit" — think of this as meaning that the data highway has 16 lanes (originally, it was only 8-bit).

### MCA & EISA
Back in 1987, IBM launched a new architecture called "MCA," standing for "Micro Channel Architecture." This is 32-bit architecture — meaning that twice as much traffic can go along the

highway at the same time. This enables better use to be made of the 32-bit processing power of Intel's current range of processors.

Other PC manufacturers weren't too keen on MCA and instead got together to launch a rival 32-bit architecture called "EISA" — standing for "Extended Industry Standard Architecture." Despite what may have been said at the time, their objections were not so much technical, but had more to do with not wanting to allow IBM to set industry standards.

Both MCA and EISA deliver some performance advantages over ISA. How much depends on what you're doing, but in general your needs have to be pretty heavy-duty for it to make much difference. In fact, with some applications you won't see much difference at all. Though technical wizards might argue late into the night about the relative merits of MCA and EISA, neither has any clear-cut performance advantage over the other.

The drawbacks to both are that they are expensive and that they require you to use a different type of expansion card in your computer from the regular ISA variety. I'll be talking more about expansion cards later, but these are boards you add to the inside of your computer to give it new features or to enhance performance. Examples include graphics cards, sound cards, network adapters, modem cards, and so forth.

MCA machines are totally incompatible with cards used on ISA computers. EISA machines do allow you to use ISA cards, but you have to have special EISA cards to get the benefit of the 32-bit architecture. MCA and EISA cards are not compatible with each other. Despite the incompatibilities between the three architectures when it comes to cards, they are compatible in other respects: they all use the same software, disks, peripherals, and so forth, and you can easily share data between them.

When the two rival 32-bit architectures were introduced in 1987–88, the official forecast was that all computer users would soon choose one or the other and that ISA would gradually fade into history. In fact, nothing of the kind happened. Today, manufacturers selling EISA machines only offer it on their high-end machines aimed at very power-hungry users. EISA never penetrated the 386-based market and, today, most 486- and even Pentium-based machines still use ISA.

The story with MCA is a little different, because IBM decided to make this its main architecture and gave up on ISA for about five years until making a monumental U-turn in 1992. The end may now be in sight for MCA: in 1994, IBM has been sending out signals that suggest it will be phasing out MCA entirely. For more on this, see the IBM entry in the Vendor Profiles section.

## Local bus architecture: PCI & VESA

If MCA is on the way out, and EISA is not widely used, does this mean that the PC industry has retreated into a complete reliance on the original ISA? No — one of the reasons ISA has survived for much longer than most pundits predicted is that PC manufacturers started tweaking it by creating special 32-bit buses for certain specific functions. For example, memory has for some time resided on a separate 32-bit bus of its own.

More recently, a new genre of auxiliary bus has appeared known as a "local bus" — so called because it performs a local function distinct from the overall data bus in the computer. The main practical benefit so far has been in handling complex graphics, and ensuring that images can be quickly redrawn on screen without getting slowed down by the congested 16-bit regular bus. Unlike ISA, EISA, and MCA, these local buses can directly access the computer's processor and keep up with its full clock speed.

When local buses started to appear in 1992, they were generally proprietary designs by particular PC manufacturers — some still are. The problem with this is that by going with a proprietary local bus, you're restricting your options later if you want to expand or modify your system. But by the end of 1992, a new industry standard had developed called VESA — short for The Video Electronics Standards Association (the body that was responsible for setting it). This is also known as the VL-Bus.

More recently, however, a new standard has come to the fore. This is PCI (Peripherals Component Interconnect), which is an Intel-developed product. PCI is widely acknowledged for delivering better performance with the Pentium processor in particular. In addition, it will more readily support simultaneous connections to different hard drives and networking devices. As a consequence, it has been adopted by most leading PC vendors as the local bus standard for their very high-end systems, though many still use VESA in their mid-market 486-based models.

Local bus architecture, such as PCI and VESA, can make a significant difference to the performance of your PC — it's a feature well worth insisting on if you're buying anything more than an entry-level model. Keep in mind that PCI and VESA can work with both an ISA or EISA main system bus. But a local bus is not a cure-all for congestion problems: there are other reasons why a computer may be slow to respond to your commands, such as a shortage of memory, the fact that your processor may be too weak to begin with, or that your network is overloaded.

# What the Heck is BIOS?

When you read technical blurb about computers, it doesn't generally take long until you come across the term "BIOS." Chances are that you don't quite know what this is — and you make a mental note to look into it one day, before letting your eyes skim down the page looking for something more understandable.

### *The answer:*

The good news is that buyers really don't have to understand BIOS. But for the record, BIOS — which stands for "Basic Input/Output System" — is the system-level software layer, built into the computer, that tightly integrates a hardware system with its operating system and applications.

IBM patented its own BIOS when it launched its first-ever personal computer and only made it available to other PC manufacturers (for a fee) late in 1992. But a company called Phoenix Technologies developed a fully compatible BIOS as early as 1984, and that's what helped put the clone makers in business. Today, several specialized vendors, such as Phoenix, sell the BIOS used in the vast majority of PCs; only a few PC vendors, such as IBM and Compaq, make their own.

If you hear about "flash BIOS," this means that it's possible to upgrade your BIOS from a floppy disk. Otherwise, this involves replacing the BIOS chip (but this isn't particularly important, as few people ever have a reason for wanting to replace their BIOS).

As a buyer, you don't choose your BIOS when you buy a computer — you take what the manufacturer has, in its best judgment, decided to build into the system. BIOS performs a critical function, but, unless you're keen to delve into the inner workings of your computer, you can safely carry on skimming over all references to it.

# Deciding on Memory

Although well over a decade has passed since the launch of the IBM PC, a surprising number of people still get memory mixed up with disk space. Memory is the part of your computer that handles the data and software you're working with at any given time, whereas disk space is the much larger archival area where you store data and programs permanently. When you switch off your computer, you lose what's in the memory — unless you have first saved it to disk.

## How much memory?

The amount of memory — or RAM (random access memory) — you have is very important. Without enough, your computer could run slowly and you may not be able to use some software programs. The absolute minimum that is acceptable these days is four megabytes (4MB), equivalent roughly to four million characters. This will allow you to run Microsoft Windows software in a fairly unambitious manner. Technically, you can run Windows with as little as 2MB, but this would be a frustrating experience and no new computers are sold with that amount any more.

Even 4MB is far from ideal, especially if you want to keep more than one program open at the same time (which is one of the main benefits of having Windows in the first place). It's much better, therefore, to buy your computer with 8MB — and you shouldn't consider 12MB to be a wild extravagance. In general, there's no need to have more than 12MB unless you have unusually upscale requirements. The above advice holds as much for Macs as for DOS/Windows machines, incidentally.

All PCs impose a ceiling on the amount of memory you can have, but in practice this isn't something to worry about as the ceiling always seems to be higher than the amount you could conceivably require on the given level of computer. Video RAM — or VRAM — is something different: I'll be talking about that shortly when I come to video adapters and monitors.

## Adding extra memory

Annoyingly, PC vendors often sell products with only 4MB as standard, despite the fact that this is only barely enough. The reason is that they want the advertised list prices to appear as low as possible. This is tedious, as it obliges you to think about upgrading the machine even before you use it.

This isn't such a big deal if you are buying from a direct sales/mail order manufacturer, as you can specify the amount of memory when ordering the computer and before taking delivery. It's also a relatively minor irritant if buying from a local PC dealer with its own in-house service technicians.

But it's a pain if you are buying from a retail store, as you're left on your own to obtain and install the additional memory. Adding extra memory isn't beyond the skills of most people, but it's a hassle — and it makes a mockery of the endless "ready-to-run" and "plug-in-and-play" boasts heard from PC vendors.

The price of extra memory varies depending on where and how you're buying it: 4MB could cost anything from $125 to

$200. For low cost memory upgrades that are easiest to install, check out machines that accept "SIMMs" (single in-line memory modules).

SIMMs have varying speed ratings, typically between 70 and 100 "nanoseconds" (one billionth of a second, believe it or not). The lower the figure, the faster the speed. In theory, faster chips mean better performance, but this doesn't always work out in practice — you should be guided by the recommendations of your PC manufacturer. Most PC software/peripherals catalogs sell SIMMs at low prices by mail.

### Cache memory

On a higher performance PC, look out for some cache memory in addition to your regular RAM. This beefs up performance by using high-speed memory chips — known as SRAM chips — to hold data that your cache controller predicts your CPU is going to require next. It makes the prediction based on what you're doing at the time, and then gets the data or program instructions from the hard disk, so that it's there for the CPU when needed. Think of it like an energetic assistant in your office, the keen type that always tries to think ahead about what you'll need next and makes sure it's there on your desk even before you've thought to ask for it.

Cache memory varies in quantity from 8K to 256K. Intel's 486DX and 486DX2 higher processors come with an 8K internal cache as standard, the DX4 comes with 16K, and the Pentium comes with two separate 8K caches. However, many PCs that use these processors also have additional — or "external" — cache. Keep in mind that 8K or 16K of internal cache is more effective than you might think: internal cache works faster than external cache on a per kilobyte basis.

# Disk Storage Discussed

All desktop PCs come equipped for two types of disk — floppy and hard.

### Floppy disks

Floppy disks are so common in the office that they hardly need explaining. But here goes, anyway. A floppy disk holds a relatively small amount of data — usually 1.44MB — and is used for loading software and copying files for back-up or transfer to another PC. There are two types of floppy disks. The main one used these days is the 3.5" variety (it's actually not "floppy," as it's enclosed in a rigid plastic case). These generally hold 1.44MB, though some IBM PCs use a version that holds twice that much (which, if you ask us, isn't much of an advantage, since it leads to compatibility problems with standard disks).

The older floppy disk size is the 5.25" variety, which is somewhat floppy or, at least, bendable. This type is becoming less common. The only reasons to go for a new PC that uses 5.25" disks are: (a) if you work with lots of other people who use them and you want to be compatible; or (b) if you've got a pile of old data that's stored on them. Even then, I'd recommend going for a PC that has both types of floppy drives — quite a few offer this as standard.

### Hard drives: how many megabytes?

You can get PCs without a hard drive — these days, you'd only do so if the PC was attached to a network and you only needed to access the central hard drive on the fileserver. Still, most network users prefer to have their own hard drive as well, and for single-user purposes it's essential to have one.

There are three main things to consider about a hard drive: capacity, speed, and controller type. The absolute minimum capacity you should consider is 120MB (in fact, it's now almost impossible to get less). A 120MB drive can be perfectly adequate for entry-level Windows applications. But you'll find those megabytes filling up depressingly quickly as you get into applications involving graphics — and these days, graphics are being incorporated into more and more mainstream office computing work. So, if you want to avoid disk space anxiety, there's a strong case to go for 170MB or, better still, 240MB (two fairly common larger sizes). In fact, an increasing number of PC manufacturers are offering drives holding over 200MB as standard even on their inexpensive lines.

Upgrading your hard drive later is possible, but it involves scrapping the old one (or, perhaps, keeping the old one but still adding a completely new one so that you end up with two). It's much more sensible, therefore, to get plenty of disk space to begin with — don't put disk storage in the same "I-can-always-add-more-later" category as memory.

Many buyers these days get 300MB–400MB drives, and that's usually about as high as you need to go for single-user storage unless you have truly exceptional requirements. Shared storage on a network is a different matter — and this clearly depends on the size of the network and the amount of shared data. The highest capacity disk drives take you to over one gigabyte (1GB) — that's a thousand megabytes, or a billion characters.

If you find that you underestimated your disk space requirements, you can buy software utilities that compress the size of files and hence free up more space. These programs sometimes claim to be able to double your disk space, but that's pretty optimistic. You find them in most decent software catalogs.

The problem about compressing your files is that you have to decompress them when you want to access them. This can be tedious and it can also make sharing data on a network awkward, though some compression software performs this task more speedily and automatically than others. By all means consider one of these programs if you find yourself stuck for disk space on a PC you already own, but I wouldn't advise planning on using one as a matter of course when you buy your computer. Microsoft offered disk compression as a standard feature on its latest version of DOS, but has had to withdraw this after losing a patent infringement suit.

### Hard drive speeds

Disk speeds — or "access times" — are measured in milliseconds (ms): the lower the figure, the better. The slowest drive you might still encounter is about 28ms, but this isn't very common and I wouldn't recommend accepting that. Most PC manufacturers now only use hard drives that work at under 20ms. Something around 17ms is reasonable, 15ms is considered pretty fast, and 11ms is about as speedy as you can get.

The differences in hard drive speeds and reliability are much less marked now than in the past — once you're talking about millisecond speeds in the mid-teens, the differences between a slightly faster and a marginally slower drive aren't all that noticeable. (If you're keen to improve the performance of your hard drive, look out for something called a "disk cache" software utility.)

Likewise, the shoddy hard drive manufacturers have been driven out of the business. If you're buying a leading brand of PC, you no longer need to worry about who makes the hard drive (all PC vendors buy in their hard drives from outside sources, such as Seagate, Conner, Quantum, etc.).

### Hard drive controller types

Finally, there are three different controller types. Most people go with IDE, which is generally the best bet for single-user applications and also okay for smaller networks. The largest IDE drives hold about 500MB. ESDI can be a good choice when very fast speeds are required, with large amounts of data being constantly accessed. SCSI is the most upmarket type, and is used in larger networked environments. Keep in mind that ESDI and SCSI drives are almost always pretty high capacity — below about 400MB, you'll probably find that all your choices are IDE.

# Monitors & Video Adapters

There are two aspects to getting fixed up with a monitor — you need to get the monitor itself, but you also need a video adapter that goes in the computer to act as a link between the central processing unit (CPU) and the screen.

Today, all PCs come with a video adapter of some sort as standard, often built into the main system board along with the processor and memory. If you want to upgrade your capabilities, you can add a different adapter using one of your computer's vacant expansion slots.

These days, all PCs sold are equipped to support VGA, which is the industry standard for graphics (remember that the term "graphics" encompasses not only displaying pictures, but also working with different styles and sizes of type and showing documents on-screen just as they'll be printed out). Graphics — black-and-white or color — have become an intrinsic part of mainstream computing. Forget about CGA, EGA, and Hercules — those old video/graphics standards are obsolete, and you'll only come across them if you're shopping for a secondhand computer.

### What to look for in video support

VGA comes in a number of levels, differing in the resolution of the image (which is made up of tiny dots called "pixels"). The higher the resolution density, the better (though you can go over the top, as I'll suggest below).

Regular VGA displays a resolution of 640 x 480, which is okay but not fantastic (text mode is slightly sharper at 720 x 400). So-called Super VGA usually goes up to 800 x 600. But these days, the resolution to shoot for is 1024 x 768. In fact, you can go higher than that: some monitors are capable of 1280 x 768 resolution, but this is a very expensive option which is usually only justified in fairly specialized circumstances.

Not all computers which support 1024 x 768 screens are equal: some can operate in that resolution with only 16 colors, others muster 256 colors or more. The key is the amount of video memory (also known as "video RAM" or "VRAM"). In order to show 16 colors at once with 1024 x 768 resolution, you need

512K of VRAM; without this, you can still have 16 colors on-screen at once, but the system will default to a lower resolution. To show 256 colors at the higher resolution, count on getting 1MB of video memory. A growing number of PC vendors throw this in as standard, but it's often an option. Either way, get it if you're keen on fancy color graphics.

Another must-have if you want no-compromises graphics is "local bus video" — refer back to the section of this chapter on system architecture for more on this and the two industry-standard versions (PCI and VESA).

### Buying monitors

These days, monitors are usually included in the standard packages offered by PC vendors. This is a relatively new development: until not so long ago, only the direct sales/mail order manufacturers routinely offered monitors in their standard pricing, but lately an increasing number of dealer-brand vendors have started doing the same on at least some of their products. Even when the manufacturer doesn't configure monitor-inclusive bundles, retailers often do so instead.

There are pros and cons about including monitors in the basic deal. Buying an all-inclusive system means you don't have to worry about compatibility and installation issues. On the other hand, buying your monitor separately from the PC gives you more choices — as I show below, some bundled monitors are less than ideal because the PC vendor is trying to keep the price down.

### Technical points for monitor buyers

Keep in mind that the most common effect of moving to a higher resolution monitor, without also moving to a larger size monitor, is that a greater number of same-size characters are squeezed onto the screen at the same size — instead of the ones that were there before looking crisper. For this reason, it generally makes sense to think larger monitor when you think higher resolution.

Ideally, all computer users with 1024 x 768 video support would choose monitors with 20" or 21" diagonal measurements (that's the viewable area). In practice, this isn't an option for most buyers because of the unwieldy size and steep cost — the largest monitors can easily set you back over $2,000.

Realistically, it generally makes sense to shoot for a monitor with a 15" or 17" diagonal measurement (there don't seem to be many 16" monitors around). A decent 15" monitor will probably cost you $500, while a good 17" one will be about $1,000.

Keep in mind that many monitors that are included as standard with PCs only have 14" screens, even though they have 1024 x 768 resolution. This is not the end of the world — just be advised that it is not ideal. (14" monitors, if purchased separately, generally cost around $250–$450.)

A vital thing to look out for when choosing a monitor is something called the "refresh rate" — this refers to the number of times the screen is redrawn each second, and it's measured in hertz (Hz). For flicker-free resolution, look for 70–72Hz. At 1024 x 768 resolution, a refresh rate of 60Hz will be too flickery for comfort. Many monitors have variable refresh rates, so that they can be optimized for the video board they're working with.

Another thing to check for is whether the monitor is non-interlaced. Interlaced screens scan every other horizontal line, and then come back and scan in the blank ones. Non-interlaced screens, by contrast, scan each horizontal line in sequence making for a clearer, steadier image. Non-interlaced monitors require a high refresh rate.

Another thing you'll come across when reading about a monitor's specifications is its "dot pitch." This refers to the spacing between the tiny dots that make up the image; it's generally measured in millimeters (mm). The lower the dot pitch, the better the image: a high dot pitch is about .40mm, and a low one is .25mm. The dot pitch is really another way of looking at the resolution: if two monitors have the same size screen, the one with the lower dot pitch will have the higher resolution.

You may hear the terms "multifrequency" and "multiscanning" used in a discussion of monitors: these are jargon terms referring to the abilities of monitors to handle frequencies produced by video adapters. The type of monitor I've recommended — non-interlaced, 70–72Hz — will always be one of these: there's no need to worry too much about which, though some techies argue that multiscanning (also called "multisync") is better in theory.

### Ergonomic & safety factors

One thing you may want to consider is whether the monitor has a reasonably flat screen. No monitor has a totally flat screen — despite suggestions to the contrary in some advertising — but the noticeably curved display of some models isn't to everyone's taste and it leads to some image distortion at the edges. Another ergonomic consideration is whether the monitor has a tilt/swivel base.

You may have heard about concerns relating to radiation emissions from monitors. The scientific evidence on this is mixed. However, almost all monitors now being sold are classified as low-emission, which means they meet the most stringent official standards that exist. As such, the question of emissions is unlikely to affect your choice of which monitor to buy. Sweden has some of the toughest regulations about monitor emissions, so vendors often refer in their publicity to the fact that they conform to all the Swedish rules.

### Portrait monitors

Most PC screens show only half a page at a time, despite the fact that most users create documents on their computers that will be printed on 8.5" x 11" paper. Even the larger screens are still landscape, rather than portrait, in orientation (i.e., the long side is the horizontal one). For example, a 19"-screen is neither able to show two side-by-side pages full size, nor one single page. A 21"-screen can show two full pages, but these are very expensive indeed — budget around $2,000 (more if you need a separate video card to support it).

The shape of modern screens is a throw-back to the time when computers were mainly used for data-entry purposes, and there was little concern for things like page layout. As a consequence, "portrait" screens that can display one full, same-size 8.5" x 11" page are rare in the world of Intel-based computers that run DOS/Windows.

The only one I know that works with DOS/Windows computers is an unusual color model called the Radius Pivot. What's unique about this screen is that it can be swiveled around in mid-use, so that it then works in landscape orientation. The Radius Pivot offers decent — though not unbeatable — image quality and usually retails for about $900. Be sure to check with Radius or your dealer to see whether the video adapter in your PC will support it, or whether you will require an extra board. You can call Radius at 800 227 2795 — or call 800 966 7360 if you would like to receive product information by fax. If you want to order this screen by mail, try calling The PC Zone at 800 258 2088.

In the Mac world, by contrast, portrait screens are pretty common. Every Macintosh computer is able to support them without the need for an additional video adapter, and there are many to choose from — some costing under $500.

The least expensive portrait screens for the Mac are black-and-white ones, but people whose work consists mainly of producing black-and-white pages using a word processing (WP) or desktop publishing (DTP) program often prefer these. A screen which shows jet-black images on a paper-white background may be better for WP/DTP than a full-color one, which tends to display black-and-white images with a certain lack of sharpness. If your work consists of producing documents destined for a black-and-white laser printer, there's a case for saying that a black-and-white screen is the closest there is to true "what you see is what you get."

You can also buy color portrait screens for the Mac, and these cost from around $700. A company to check out for very affordable full-page and two-page Mac screens is Mirror, which sells direct (rather than through dealers) — call 800 643 0631 (though avoid its color portrait screen, which isn't very good). In addition, the Radius Pivot screen mentioned above can also work with Macs. Apple, unfortunately, has recently discontinued its own excellent black-and-white portrait screen.

# Expansion Slots and Interfaces

The insides and back of a PC have all sorts of slots and plugs, which allow you to put extra boards in your computer and attach outside peripherals such as printers. Here's the low-down (the info on expansion slots need not concern Mac buyers: Apples also have these, but you don't have to worry about choosing between different types). ...

### Expansion slots

I've already made a number of passing references in this chapter to expansion slots. These allow you to add boards inside your computer that provide new features or enhance the performance of existing ones. Examples include video adapters, network cards, internal modems, sound cards, and so forth.

Keep in mind that the whole question of system architecture discussed earlier is linked in with expansion slots (I suggest you take a moment to read that section now if you haven't already done so). Computers have different types of slots, depending on whether they use ISA, EISA, or MCA architecture — and, as I explained earlier, these are not wholly compatible with each other. In addition, if the computer has a PCI or VESA local bus, you may have one or more additional expansion slots providing direct access to that high-speed bus lane.

Apart from the architecture type, there are two things to consider when assessing a computer's expansion board capabilities. One is the number of available slots, which can vary from as few as two or three to as many as seven or eight. Keep in mind that if a machine is advertised as having, say, seven expansion slots, this does not necessarily mean that all seven will be available for you to use — one or two may have been taken up by the system components installed when the machine was assembled. Some vendors exclude these when they quote the number of slots, but others don't. Always ask about the number of vacant slots.

The other thing to consider is that slots differ in size. Some are full-height, and others are half-height. This refers literally to the size of board you can install. A board's size isn't necessarily linked to its capabilities. However, if there's a particular board you have in mind, you'd better check that it will fit in a slot that's available.

Most users find that three or four vacant slots are sufficient, especially if the machine is fully configured to begin with. One reason not to go for more slots than you're likely to use is that they tend to make the machine quite bulky. A lot of people prefer to work with a machine that has low profile dimensions — in other words, a 4" system unit height, compared with the 6" height of some larger PCs.

### Interfaces

All DOS/Windows PCs come with at least one parallel interface and one serial interface. The parallel interface is the one you use for printers; the serial interface is for making other outside connections. With a Mac, you usually print either via a serial port or using an AppleTalk connection (that's the basic networking system that comes built into every Mac).

# The Energy-Efficient PC

Computers use more electricity than you might imagine — and the government, as part of its energy-efficiency drive, is eager that we should start buying ones that consume less. The Environmental Protection Agency (EPA) has come up with something called the Energy Star program that certifies computers that meet new guidelines for energy-efficiency. Since summer 1993, manufacturers whose PCs meet the EPA guidelines have been able to display a special Energy Star logo on their qualifying systems and in their promotional materials.

The EPA's strategy in promoting the program is to appeal to people's pockets, rather than to their consciences. It's trying to make buyers aware of the monetary savings they will enjoy from buying Energy Star computers, and it's trying to persuade manufacturers that the way to sell more machines is to cash in on the Energy Star advantage.

The Federal Government has already started buying only PCs that receive the certification. And the EPA is actively canvassing Fortune 1000 companies to encourage them to adopt similar purchasing policies. Energy Star programs covering monitors and laser printers are also in place.

Combined, the EPA hopes that these programs will save enough energy in the United States to eliminate the need for five coal-fired power plants (reducing carbon dioxide pollution each year equivalent to the exhaust from 2.5 million automobiles), and reduce the country's yearly electricity bill by over $1 billion. Bold hopes indeed — especially as the initial Energy Star requirements are quite modest.

### Where the waste occurs

PC-related energy waste occurs at two levels: (a) when computers are in use and, because of their design, they devour more electricity than they need to; and (b) when computers are left switched on even though they are not in use. The Energy Star program as it exists today is attempting to plug only the second of those two energy leaks.

The EPA estimates that 30–40 percent of computer users leave their systems switched on at night or over the weekend. Even during the work day, computers are used only a part of the time. An office worker is often engaged in other activities rather than working on the computer — answering the phone, going to meetings, having lunch, etc. Screen savers — that display things like flying toasters and fish tanks after a period of inactivity — are almost an encouragement to users to leave their machines switched on.

### How "sleep" cuts waste ...

Probably the main reason why people leave their computers switched on is the hassle of starting them up again after they have been shut down completely. What Energy Star-certified computers do is make the computers power down when not in use — but return quickly to an operational state at the touch of the keyboard or a button.

A system powers down by first recognizing that it has not been used for a certain amount of time, and then by putting itself in a "sleep mode" which turns off selected system components or places them in states where they consume less power. This concept will be familiar to people who use notebook portable computers — these have for some time done the same sort of thing to help conserve battery power.

### How much do you save?

Desktop PCs generally consume anywhere between 50–200 watts of power when in use (not including the monitor), and a typical system consumes around 120 watts. To receive Energy Star certification, a PC has to power down to 30 watts when it goes into sleep mode.

The EPA estimates that the resulting electricity savings per PC should average $120 a year. This is based on the assumption that a computer is in actual use for 15 hours per week; the EPA is also calculating the savings on the assumption that a computer was previously always left switched on (even at night and weekends).

This calculation shows a useful savings — though smaller benefits will clearly accrue to people who are less wasteful to begin with and who do make a point of switching off their PCs when they go home. Incidentally, the financial incentives to conserve energy are stronger in other countries than in the US (where electricity is priced relatively low) — in Europe, where energy costs are up to three times that of the US, the savings through using an Energy Star computer could reach $360 per year.

### Different types of sleep mode

Sleep modes vary in the number of components that are turned off or powered down, and in how "deep" a sleep a system is put into. For example, most notebooks have two sleep modes, a "standby" mode and a "suspend" mode.

Standby represents a "light sleep," where the power savings — though worthwhile — are reduced in order to ensure virtually no delay in returning the system to its full-on state. Suspend mode, by contrast, is a "deep sleep," which achieves maximum power savings at the expense of the time it takes to recover.

In order to receive Energy Star certification, PC vendors can get away with only implementing standby mode — and this is what most are likely to do on their desktop models.

### Further savings ahead

The Energy Star certification sets a relatively modest target for the PC industry — but technology already exists to go a great deal further. In particular, computers could be made to consume less power when they are being used, as opposed to only when they are switched on but not in use.

"Active power management" is the term that refers to techniques that reduce power while the system is in use, but with no impact on performance. This generally involves shutting off specific components that are not being exercised, or scaling down the power consumption of those that are not being fully utilized. Notebook PCs do this sort of thing already.

In addition, Intel has begun promoting "SL Enhanced" power-efficient versions of most of its 486-series processors to makers of desktop PCs: previously, these have only been used in notebooks. As I point out in the discussion of notebook processors later in this chapter, the SL versions provide energy-saving features at the hardware level that assist active power management.

Likewise, PCs could be made more energy-efficient if they made more use of 3.3-volt parts, which consume 50 percent less power than the traditional 5-volt variety. Intel's SL Enhanced 486-series processors come in both 3.3-volt and 5-volt versions. However, its new DX4 processor — the top of its 486 line — is the first to be made only as a 3.3-volt unit.

It remains to be seen how quickly PC manufacturers will move to bring out systems that significantly surpass the Energy Star standards, without the incentive of a further EPA certificate as a reward. The problem is that although the current Energy Star standards add very little to costs, some of the more advanced energy-saving designs, particularly those that are 3.3-volt oriented, could result in higher purchase prices — which is not what PC makers want to be messing with when they are in the middle of a price war.

### Who is getting Energy Stars?

Most major vendors have begun to introduce models that comply with Energy Star standards. Vendors are doing their best to squeeze maximum commercial advantage out of being seen to be green, though eventually just about all of them will comply with the standard — meaning that there will be no net advantage for any of them.

In the meantime, those who are quick off the mark with compliance can be expected to indulge in the heavy-handed "spend your money on our product to save the planet" style of advertising. Just remember when you come across this that what they are doing to reduce energy costs is the minimum required by the EPA — the real energy heroes will be those that go further of their own volition.

# Introducing Notebook Computers

Portable PCs are the fastest growing part of the computer market. Many of today's notebook machines can match the power of most desktops and, as a result, some people use them as their primary computer both on the road and while working in the office and at home.

This next part of this chapter tells you what you need to know about notebooks to choose the one that's right for you. Some notebook features overlap with those of desktops: in what follows, I'll be focusing on features and requirements that are notebook-specific.

### Early portable computers

Portable computers have come a long way since they became fashionable in the early eighties. The first portable to catch the imagination of the gadget-loving public was a bulky machine introduced in 1982 and named after its inventor, Mr. Adam Osborne. Compatible with IBM's original PC, the Osborne PC weighed about 25 lbs, and had neither battery power nor a hard disk. Owning an Osborne was a bit like carrying around a sewing machine. It was not so much portable, as luggable. Yet despite this, everyone wanted one. Having a portable computer meant taking more control over your life — many people saw the opportunity to do more of their work where they wanted, when they wanted. From then on, there was no looking back.

Osborne's machine was only on the market for a year or so before it was displaced in the public imagination by new and less bulky machines from a Texan upstart called Compaq. Its early machines offered superior performance and were a little less heavy, though they too only ran off AC power and weighed close to 20 lbs.

### The rise and fall of laptops

Compaq arguably did more than anyone else to set the portable bandwagon rolling, but it was a latecomer to the class of machine that redefined the concept. "Laptops" — the term coined to describe machines weighing 12–15 lbs — were pioneered mainly by Toshiba and Zenith and became popular around the mid-to-late eighties. During this time, they steadily became more powerful and less heavy. By the end of the decade, early models that made you choose between performance, screen quality, and battery power had been replaced by new ones that offered all three.

But laptop computers were never as portable as their proponents made out. People who bought them for mobile applications soon tired of carting around 14 lbs of hardware. The machines were a little bulky as well as heavy. True, they could fit on your lap, but they wouldn't fit into a normal briefcase. Cynics wondered whether the only people who actually did use them on airplanes were actors posing for laptop advertisements.

### The notebook revolution

So the R&D people worked overtime to come up with something better. And the result was a massive leap forward known as the "notebook" computer. These began to appear in late 1990, and really took off in 1991. Notebook computers are conceptually similar to laptops, but they are smaller and lighter. A typical notebook weighs 4–7 lbs and measures about 8.5" x 11" x 2" (sometimes the height is as low as 1.5"). In other words, notebooks are easy to carry around and they do fit in standard briefcases, leaving space for other items as well. All notebooks can run off rechargeable batteries.

If you define notebooks purely in terms of their size and weight, you could argue that they were around even in the late 1980s. Toshiba was selling briefcase-size machines for years, but its early models were bare-basics computers that were in no way comparable in performance terms with desktops.

Today's notebooks, by contrast, are as powerful as most desktops, and can have pretty large disk drives. A growing number have color screens, some of which are very good. In fact, today's notebooks are on the whole much better computers than yesterday's laptops which weighed more than twice as much.

As a result, laptops have more or less become obsolete (though many people have kept on using the word "laptops" to refer to notebooks). A few bulky laptops remain, pitched at the very high-end of the market in terms of performance capabilities, but even these are under threat from the latest upmarket notebooks. The very smallest and lightest notebooks are known as "sub-notebooks," incidentally — more on these soon.

### The limitations of notebooks

A notebook takes up considerably less space on a desk than a regular PC and is altogether a slicker piece of equipment. Once you have begun to use notebooks, you may begin to view desktop PCs as unwieldy and clumsy in a way that you never did before.

These days, a lot of people are wondering whether they can get by with using a notebook as their one and only computer, replacing rather than supplementing their desktop. And many have concluded that this is the way to go. But before you decide to put all your work onto notebooks and get rid of those big, boring desktops, consider the drawbacks and limitations.

First, notebooks are more expensive than desktops. A notebook will often cost you about 25–30 percent more than a comparable desktop. The differential will be larger if you want a notebook with a color screen. In fact, a color notebook can easily cost over twice as much as a desktop PC with a color monitor.

The next factor to consider before you abandon desktops is the durability of notebook computers. In their zeal to reduce dimensions, weight, and prices all at the same time, manufacturers sometimes cut corners on sturdiness and the quality of the finish. Don't count on getting five years use out of one of these machines. Arguably, though, the pace of technological change is such that you'll probably want to replace your notebook after two or three years anyway, because you'll consider it to be out of date.

A more fundamental limitation of notebooks concerns their suitability for certain types of work which are now becoming pretty mainstream in the desktop market. A notebook screen is fine for most plain-vanilla applications involving words and numbers. But notebooks are less than perfect for use as your primary computer if you want to run graphics. This makes them less than ideal for running Microsoft Windows.

There is nothing to stop you from running Windows on most notebook computers. In fact, most come with Windows preinstalled. But notebook screens are just a little too small for comfort — and have too low a resolution — given the amount of information and the number of images that are often displayed at once when Windows is in use. Also, Windows tends to assume you're working on a color screen, which most notebooks do not have.

A partial solution is to plug in an external monitor to your notebook when you're in the office or at home. This allows you to see everything in color even if the notebook itself only has a non-color screen. I'll be talking more about this later. But for now, keep in mind that most notebooks can only support a relatively humble quality of external monitor, not the type you'd probably get if you were buying a brand new desktop. In other words, it's another example of how using notebooks can involve making compromises.

If you are running Windows, you need more than a keyboard — you need either a mouse (the device you move around the top of your desk to control your position on the screen and to activate commands) or some mouse-substitute. It is perfectly possible to connect a regular mouse to any notebook through the serial port (there's one at the back of all machines) or through a dedicated mouse port. When you're using the notebook on a desk, it won't be any different from using a mouse with a regular PC. But operating a mouse is hard if you're using your notebook in a mobile environment where you don't have much desk space. In fact, it's impossible to use a mouse in a dignified manner if you literally are working off your lap.

For this reason, you really need some sort of a mouse substitute designed for use with notebooks. The problem is that by no means all notebooks come with these, and none are perfect. The best bet for Windows users is to get a notebook with an integrated mini-trackball (a little ball that you twiddle around to control your screen position). Surprisingly many notebooks do not have these, though they are becoming more common and some manufacturers have designed quite good trackball alternatives in their machines (more on these later).

I don't want to sound too negative about notebooks — I use them all the time myself — but there is a tendency among some people to be so gushing about notebooks as to overlook some quite significant practical drawbacks. Notebooks are one of the greatest inventions of the 1990s, and they can literally transform your life. Yes, you can run Windows on a notebook, especially if your notebook is a back-up machine to a desktop. But no, most of today's notebooks are not a perfect platform for this sort of work if they are your only computer. Don't let anyone convince you of the contrary.

# Notebook Features

Many of the same hardware considerations apply to notebook PCs as to desktop models. For example, you need the same amount of RAM to handle the same types of work. But there are differences in a number of features — the choice of processors, for example.

### Processors for notebook computers

Notebook buyers face a different range of processor options from their desktop counterparts. For a start, the Pentium is not currently an option for notebook buyers. The Pentium is not ideally suited for portable use, for reasons to do with its size and heat-generating tendencies — I expect that vendors will have gotten around the challenges before long, but the Pentium is not likely to make much impact in the notebook market until well into 1995.

On the Mac side of the fence, the PowerPC is also not yet an option as far as notebooks are concerned — though this was expected to change around the end of 1994 when a new version of the processor known as the PowerPC 603 becomes available (as I pointed out earlier, the 603 is specially designed for notebook and low-end desktop use). See the Apple entry in the Vendor Profiles for details of what the Mac notebook processor options are before then.

If you are looking for a DOS/Windows notebook, you will therefore almost certainly get a model using one of the 486-series processors — though, as I will show below, many notebooks use special versions developed for portable use.

The 386 family stuck around for a while in the notebook market after it became obsolete in the desktop arena — 386-based notebooks were still being sold for much of 1993 and you may still come across them today. This partly reflects the fact that notebooks are often purchased for less demanding workloads, and it also reflects the fact that notebook computers are more expensive than desktops and so people are less inclined to purchase performance they are not sure they really need. Nonetheless, my advice would be to turn down a 386 notebook should you be offered one now — you simply won't get the best out of the latest generation of software.

### 3.3.-volt and SL processors

Ideally, you should look for one of the Intel 486-series processors that uses 3.3-volt technology, rather than the 5-volt variety that is the norm. This is significantly more power-efficient — i.e., it allows you to enjoy high performance without sacrificing all-important battery power (which I'll be talking about shortly).

The original 3.3-volt processor was the 486SL, a special version of the 486SX and 486DX which was designed specially for the notebook market. First introduced late in 1992, this is still widely used by notebook vendors. You get SX-equivalent performance if the unit in your notebook does not have an on-board math co-processor, and DX performance if it does: either way, the processor is usually identified simply as a "486SL" (unless the vendor makes specific mention of a coprocessor, you can probably assume it's a 486SX equivalent). The advantage of the SL technology is that it consumes less battery power, because it slows down or goes to sleep during periods of inactivity while the computer is switched on.

Recently, Intel has introduced what it calls "SL Enhanced" 3.3-volt versions of its entire 486 series up to, and including, the 486DX2 (with the exception of the new SX2 processor, which is currently only available as a 5-volt unit). It now refers to these special versions by putting the designation "SL Enhanced" as a prefix to the regular model number of a processor. For example, it talks about the "SL Enhanced i486DX2." Note that the SL versions of the 486SX/DX, which used to be called the "486SL," are now being referred to by Intel in this new way — i.e., as the "SL Enhanced i486SX" and the "SL Enhanced i486DX." But to further confuse matters, many vendors are still just talking about the "486SL."

Assuming I haven't totally lost you at this point, there are a few other pieces of SL-related information to keep in mind.... Intel also supplies SL processors that use 5-volt technology and that don't, therefore, offer the full range of power savings (even though they do offer other SL benefits). Notebook buyers are better off with the 3.3-volt ones. Keep in mind that all the SL Enhanced processors deliver the same performance as their non-SL equivalents (they do not feature separately on Intel's iCOMP Index). Intel's SL technology is also being used to develop new highly energy-efficient desktop PCs (see the earlier discussion on this point).

Your other 3.3-volt option is Intel's new DX4, the top-end 486-series processor I discussed earlier in this chapter. This is the first Intel processor introduced simultaneously in the desktop and notebook markets to use 3.3-volt technology. In other words, you don't need to look out for an SL version of the DX4 — all DX4s are 3.3-volt. Note that the DX4 does incorporate the full SL technology, even though the letters "SL" do not appear in its model number. At the time of this writing, the first DX4-based notebooks were expected to reach the market soon, though none were yet available — these notebooks will be very desirable items for people wanting no-compromise mobile computers.

Although the ideal processors for portable use are those that use 3.3-volt technology, many notebooks still use the regular 5-volt 486SX, 486DX, and 486DX2 processors. These are not necessarily bad choices, just keep in mind that they are not optimized for the special needs of notebooks and that 3.3-volt/SL is better. AMD and Cyrix — the Intel rivals discussed earlier in this chapter — offer their own low-voltage processors to rival Intel's.

## Floppy drives & sub-notebooks

Today, all notebooks come with a hard drive and most also come with a built-in floppy drive. However, some very small notebooks — known as "sub-notebooks" — do not have a built-in floppy disk drive, but instead use an external one which you plug into the back. The advantage is that this reduces the weight and bulk of the main unit. Sub-notebooks weigh around 3–4.5 lbs and are usually pretty slim.

Opinions differ on whether not having a floppy drive built into your notebook makes sense. Some people feel exposed without one — for example, you can't make back-ups as you go about your travels. Others, who have previously used full-size notebooks, found that they rarely used the floppy drive while traveling — so keeping one in the office, or at home, to load software, copy files, and make back-ups seems sufficient. Also, there's nothing to stop you from packing your external floppy in your baggage if you do want to take it on trips (it shouldn't weigh more than a pound or so).

Sub-notebooks may have other drawbacks apart from their lack of a built-in floppy drive. In particular, they can have cramped keyboards and less than ideal screens.

## Notebook hard drives

When deciding what hard drive to get on a notebook, keep in mind that, unlike memory, disk drives on notebooks cannot as a rule be upgraded after you have bought the machine. (Exception: a handful of notebooks, including some of AST's and Compaq's, use removable hard drives.) Another point worth noting is that higher capacity drives do not result in heavier weights — for example, a machine with a 300MB drive weighs no more than the same unit equipped with 120MB.

Notebook computers tend to lag behind desktops when it comes to hard drives. It's still quite common to be offered 120MB hard drives on notebooks, even though that's quite low by desktop standards. Occasionally, you still come across 80MB notebook drives — these have now disappeared almost entirely from the desktop market. And the largest drives that are generally available on notebooks are about 200MB–350MB, somewhat smaller than the largest ones on desktops.

If you plan to use your notebook as a back-up PC, it's probably fine to settle for a smaller hard drive than you'd consider for your desktop. But if you're planning on using it as a primary computer for Windows applications, there's no logic in accepting lower specifications than you would on a desktop.

### Black-and-white notebook screens

These days, all notebook screens use LCD technology in one form or another. The vast majority of non-color LCD screens are the passive-matrix type. However, a small number have active-matrix, black-and-white screens — these boast sharper images, faster screen redraw times, and more legibility when you're viewing them outdoors or from an angle.

Sadly, black-and-white, active-matrix screens are not very common (and are quite expensive): most active-matrix screens are of the color variety (more on these in a moment). Apple sells notebooks that use them, but the only major vendor to do so on the DOS/Windows side of the fence is Compaq.

Screen size is important: ideally, you should look for a screen with a 10" diagonal measurement, though anything over 9" isn't too bad. The smallest screens are about 8.5" (but that size is quite rare on black-and-white models).

I mentioned earlier that the Windows operating environment tends to assume that you have a color screen, though it doesn't absolutely require this. If you only have a monochrome notebook, different colors will be represented by shades of gray. These days, most notebooks can show up to 32 or 64 gray scales which is plenty, though some only show 16.

In the early days of battery-powered portable computers, screens were not always fully lit from behind: this made them harder to read, but it saved a lot of juice. Today, virtually all notebooks do have screen backlighting so this has almost ceased to be an issue (exception: some sub-notebooks have edge-lit screens, which are not ideal).

### Color notebooks

Notebooks with full-color screens are now pretty mainstream — they are no longer the exotic items they seemed two years ago. Keep in mind that color notebooks tend to weigh more than their monochrome counterparts and have shorter battery lives. This, and their price, should make you think twice about buying one.

Color quality varies quite widely. The less expensive models use passive-matrix screens, which — in their regular versions — generally aren't terribly good. If you are buying a passive-matrix color notebook, try to get one with a so-called "dual-scan" screen: this produces significantly better results than the regular passive-matrix variety at a fairly affordable cost — though it is still by no means superb. Dual-scan is a sub-set of passive-matrix, not something entirely different.

By far the best type of full-color screen is the active-matrix variety — but this takes you into the premium end of the market price-wise. The colors are usually considerably brighter, and screen clarity should be much less sensitive to the viewing angle. If you can justify the cost, you should be very happy with an active-matrix color notebook.

### Screen resolutions

No matter whether you're getting a color or monochrome model, screen resolution will almost always be 640 x 480. This means that the image is constructed out of a matrix of 640 x 480 lines to the square inch. This resolution is equivalent to the basic VGA standard and is more than adequate given the size of notebook displays.

Today's desktop PCs usually support a 1024 x 768 screen resolution — but this is on monitors that are at least 4" larger (super-high resolutions on small screens tend not to work very well, for reasons discussed in the section on desktop monitors earlier in this chapter).

### Attaching an external monitor

I mentioned earlier that one way of compensating for the limitations of notebook screens is to attach an external desktop monitor when you're working in the office or at home. This allows you to work in color even if the notebook's own screen is monochrome. It also allows you to escape from the rigors of notebook screen size.

All notebooks allow you to attach an external screen, but their capabilities vary in a way that many buyers do not realize until it's too late. In particular, many notebooks will only support an external monitor with the same 640 x 480 resolution as the notebook's own screen. This is a pity, because today even relatively inexpensive desktop monitors are capable of doing a lot better than that. My advice to people who plan on working with external monitors is to look for a notebook that can support 800 x 600 or, better still, 1024 x 768 external video. You may have to probe to obtain this information — important though it is, external video support details do not often feature in published notebook specifications.

Another thing to check out is whether the notebook can simultaneously show your work on its own screen and on an external one. Most cannot. In fact, this is not necessarily a disadvantage. Some people find simultaneous displays mildly disconcerting and would prefer a blank notebook screen when working with the external one. Others, however, welcome the capability — especially when making a presentation to people gathered around a large screen plugged into the notebook.

### Notebook keyboard considerations

The number of keys on a notebook keyboard can be a clue as to how good the keyboard is. Some keyboards require certain functions to share a key with others; for example, in order to use the "page up/down" functions, you may have to press one of the cursor keys in conjunction with another key — the "Fn" key, for example. The more keys, the less doubling up. Around 82 is usually the sign of a good keyboard. Actually, the number of notebooks with poor keyboards is declining — as with most computer features, there's a general upward leveling out of standards. Keep in mind that virtually no notebooks include a numeric keypad on the right hand side of the keyboard, similar to the ones on desktops.

Keyboards are very subjective things and different people look for different qualities. Some machines have cursor keys that are smaller than the rest of the keys: that bothers some users, but leaves others indifferent. The exact position of certain keys can also be an important consideration for some people. Other users focus more on how "springy" the keys feel — a number of very compact notebooks have keys without much downward travel. There's no substitute for trying out a keyboard before you buy (though this can be difficult if you're ordering a machine through the mail).

In the same way that you can attach an external screen when you're working in the office or at home, you can also plug in an external keyboard. If you have both an external monitor and an external keyboard, you can generally keep the notebook shut even when it's switched on — you end up with what amounts to a desktop PC (albeit without the usual expansion slots). This can be a good compromise solution if you're torn between having a desktop and a portable computer, but prefer to keep all your work on one machine. (More on using notebooks as desktops later, when I talk about docking stations and port replicators.)

### Pointing devices

I mentioned earlier that if you're planning on running Windows applications on your notebook, you'll need some kind of pointing device, and I explained why a conventional mouse is not practical for truly mobile applications. Built-in trackballs on DOS/Windows machines are very small — generally about half the size of a marble. That said, they are easier to manipulate than you might imagine.

The main complaints tend to be that they are positioned awkwardly on the computer and that they are often separated from their accompanying "clicker" keys in a way that makes one-handed operation impossible. For example, some Compaq notebooks have built-in mini-trackballs situated on the vertical edge of the screen; on some other models, they are positioned next to the top row of keys on the right, but the clicker keys are all the way on the other side.

Much less satisfactory than even an awkwardly positioned built-in trackball is the type you clip onto the side of your notebook and plug into the back with wires. These are supplied by third parties, such as Microsoft and Logitech. While the actual ball itself is larger than on the built-in variety, it's a hassle to have to carry the external trackball around with you and fiddle with the wires. It may also be impossible to close the computer without disconnecting the trackball.

Microsoft sells a much better clip-on trackball called the BallPoint Mouse. This plugs directly into the side of the computer, eliminating the need for wires, but it only works with notebooks that have a special port at the side specifically for the purpose of supporting it. Several vendors — including Texas Instruments and Toshiba — have introduced models that have this port and are supplying the BallPoint Mouse as a standard accessory with their notebooks. Some other notebook vendors have developed their own plug-in wireless trackballs that plug into the front of the computer (the ideal position, in my opinion).

There are a number of other alternatives supported by different vendors. Some notebooks allow you to control the screen pointer from the keyboard: unlike cursor keys which move the cursor straight up, down and across, a "mouse key" allows you to move the pointer in any direction according to the way in which you press.

One of the most interesting trackball alternatives has been invented by IBM: its excellent ThinkPad notebooks sport a small rubber device in the middle of the keyboard — a little like a pencil eraser — which controls the screen pointer when you wiggle it. This might sound like an awkward method, but user feedback has been very enthusiastic. Toshiba has recently introduced a similar feature on one of its sub-notebooks.

Apple's latest PowerBook notebooks do away with the much-praised internal trackball on the earlier models, and instead come with something called a "Midas TouchPad" — a flat area in the place normally reserved for a PowerBook trackball, over which you move your finger to control the screen pointer. At the time this book was published, I had not had much of an opportunity to try this out for myself — but others report that it works nicely once you get used to it.

### PCMCIA slots

In the world of desktop PCs, there have long been industry standards that allow you to insert third-party expansion boards into vacant slots in the computer. The size of notebook computers precludes them from having this type of built-in slot, so all the add-ons available for notebooks have therefore been of proprietary design.

However, the computer industry has come up with a new standard which allows you to insert things the size of credit cards into the side of notebooks. There are a growing number of the new industry-standard cards available to serve different functions — extra memory, modems, enhanced external video support, network adapters, and so forth.

The new standard is known by the initials "PCMCIA" (standing for Personal Computer Memory Card International Association, the 475-member trade organization that created and maintains the standard). Recently, a large number of notebooks have begun to appear with PCMCIA slots — in fact, this is getting to be a "must-have" feature if you want a state-of-the-art machine. Some models have two slots — this makes a lot of sense, since once you start using these cards, you'll probably want more than one.

There are three types of PCMCIA cards, known as Types I, II, and III:

❑ **Type I:** This is the older variety, which has effectively been superseded by Type II.
❑ **Type II:** This is the main current standard, and it's typically used for things like extra memory, fax/data modems, and network connectors.
❑ **Type III:** This is not a replacement for Type II, but a standard that allows for thicker cards that may be needed for things like removable mass storage devices (i.e., hard disks on a card) and radio communication devices; the Type III standard is still pretty new.

All three card types measure the same length and width (roughly the size of a standard credit card) and use the same 68-pin edge connector for attachment to the computer. Where they differ is in the thickness: the thickness for Types I, II, and III are 3.3, 5.0, and 10.5 millimeters respectively (sorry, folks, but being an international standard, everything is metric). Just as the cards come in the three varieties, so do the slots that they go in — hence you will come across notebooks advertised as having Type II or Type III slots.

Because they differ only in thickness, a thinner card can be used in a thicker slot — but a thicker card cannot be used in a thinner slot. Therefore, if your notebook computer comes with Type III slots, you can be sure that you've got the widest range of options for future PCMCIA upgrades. Nonetheless, a lot of notebooks being sold at press-time only had Type II slots, and these can cater to most requirements.

As well as there being three different types of slots for the three types of cards, there are also different PCMCIA "releases" laying down technical standards to which the cards themselves conform. The current one is Release 2.1. A new release — probably to be called Release 3.0 and expected later in 1994 — will offer a number of performance advantages over Release 2.1. Some of these will take better advantage of the 3.3-volt design of the latest generation of Intel-based notebooks, and others could enable single cards to perform more than one function.

But do not confuse "Type" with "Release" — just as Release 2.1 works with all three Types (I/II/III), so Release 3.0 will do the same. The Type II and Type III standards will remain current for as far ahead as I can see, and the great thing about PCMCIA is that it's easy to replace your cards whenever you want to upgrade to get the benefits that Release 3.0 cards will offer. Keep in mind that there probably won't be many Release 3.0 cards available until some time in 1995. Note that the PCMCIA standard is also expected to make its way over to the desktop market during the next year or two.

### AC power considerations

Unlike some older laptops, all notebook PCs are able to run off both AC power and internally rechargeable batteries. When you're deskbound, it generally makes sense to run the machine on AC power. This saves your batteries for when you need them; often, you also get slightly better performance out of the machine when it's running on AC.

Almost all notebooks work with an external AC adapter. This is the small box-like unit that connects the power lead you plug into the wall with the cable that runs into the computer: its purpose is to reduce the AC voltage to a level that the internal battery can handle. However, one recently-introduced Compaq notebook has the AC adapter built-in — this saves having to carry around a separate item, though it adds to the weight of the computer itself.

An AC adapter comes standard with all machines. Some are larger than others. The best adapters are less than the size of a couple of decks of cards. Even the smallest adapters are a bit of a bore to carry around all the time, so you may want to consider getting a spare if you regularly transport the computer between the same two locations. For example, you could keep one in the office and the other at home. The cost is usually around $100.

All notebooks — at least, all the ones I know about — have automatic voltage sensing. This means that you can use them in countries with different AC power voltages without the need for a separate transformer. Keep in mind, though, that many countries have different power sockets (i.e., the pins that plug into the wall are a different shape). So although your machine is perfectly capable of being used on overseas voltages, you may need to get an inexpensive pin adapter (places like Radio Shack and some international airport drugstores sell these).

### Notebook batteries: the different types

The batteries used on notebooks are the internal rechargeable variety. There are two types: Nickel Cadmium (NiCad) batteries and Nickel Metal Hydride (NiMH). The latter are preferable for two reasons. First, they can often hold a charge for longer. Second, NiMHs do not suffer from an intrinsic drawback of NiCads relating to when the recharge takes place.

If you often recharge a NiCad battery which is not yet fully run down, it becomes addicted to recharges at the point that it is used to getting them. As a result, it starts to think it has run out of power even if it hasn't. Frequent premature recharges therefore end up reducing actual battery running times. This characteristic of NiCads is sometimes referred to as "memory effect" — presumably because of the way in which the battery "remembers" when it got its recent charges.

You can attempt to cure the battery of this addiction by running it down totally every now and then, but this ceases to be 100 percent effective after a point. Clearly, this aspect of NiCads is a major drawback. Often you'd like to recharge a half-spent battery before leaving your office so that you're running on "full tanks." With NiMH batteries, this isn't a problem — but with NiCads, doing so would contribute to possible memory effect. On a positive note, some recently introduced notebooks that work with NiCads are less prone to memory effect — but, on the whole, you're better off with the NiMHs.

An interesting development is the emergence of a new rechargeable NiMH battery from Duracell that could become an industry standard — in other words, the idea is that the same battery could be used in different brands of notebook. Previously, notebook rechargeable batteries have always been proprietary.

At the time of this writing, only one notebook used the new Duracell battery — a sub-notebook from Compaq called the Aero. If other vendors start to use it, spare batteries should be much easier to buy and also cheaper — industry-standard batteries would definitely be good news for the buyer.

Also at the time of this writing, only one vendor — AST — sold notebooks that can run off regular AA batteries in an emergency. This isn't a feature you'd want to use too often, since you'd spend a fortune on alkaline batteries: six AA batteries only keep you going for 90 minutes.

### Living with notebook batteries

Most notebooks claim battery lives of about two to four hours. In practice, three hours of actual usage is quite good and fairly common. Two hours is poor by today's standards. Four hours or more is excellent. However, you shouldn't take any quoted figure too literally, since a number of variables will affect the performance you get in reality.

In particular, applications which involve constantly accessing your hard drive will run the battery down much faster than those that don't. Likewise, the process of switching the machine on and loading a program uses quite a lot of battery. You'll get more time out of a charge if you use the machine continuously than if you have several short sessions with the machine turned off in between. Your taste in screen brightness is another major factor — the brighter you set it, the more power it consumes.

In addition, all current notebooks have — to a greater or lesser extent — various "intelligent" battery management functions. These enable them to conserve power by slowing down, or even shutting down, certain functions when they are not being used.

For example, most machines shut down the screen, and/ or slow down the hard drive, if you haven't touched the keyboard during the previous 10 minutes or so (users can generally alter the defaults). Many allow you to suspend operation at any moment of your choosing without actually switching it off, and then resume when you're ready (the machine will take you back to exactly the same place as you left off). While the machine is in suspend mode, it only uses a very low amount of power, so you save on battery usage compared with switching off and then booting up all over again.

Battery management features work best with the Intel SL processors, which, as I mentioned earlier, are specially designed for use with notebooks (unlike regular processors which are borrowed from the desktop PC market). The SLs have Intel's "instant on/off" feature which eliminates long, battery-draining boot-up and shutdown sequences when the machine is placed in what Intel terms "suspended animation."

You often hear quoted battery times of as much as six to eight hours on machines that use an SL processor. Do not take these too literally. They do not mean that you can run the computer continuously on full power for that long. The period quoted is the average time that you can use it without recharging, based on assumptions about how much, in normal usage, the system will be in suspended animation. The point is that in normal usage, an SL machine will constantly shut down and then instantly boot up; in practice, most of us use our computers on a stop/go basis, interrupting our keyboard pounding to refer to papers, speak to someone on the phone, grab some coffee, daydream, or whatever.

How do you know when you're getting low on battery power? Many older machines only warn you by means of a light that comes on when you've got about 10 or 15 minutes to go; usually, this is followed by a further signal when you're even closer to the limit and often the light is accompanied by an audible beep or on-screen message. But a growing number of machines go a step further and allow you to monitor available battery power continuously by means of a "fuel gauge." This is usually viewed on-screen by means of a software utility (occasionally, there's some sort of an LCD battery window built into the computer hardware).

When the battery does run down, you'll probably want to get it recharged as soon as possible. This is simply a matter of connecting the computer to an AC power supply and leaving it alone for a while. Until recently, this was often a painfully slow process — it could take as long as five or even eight hours.

The good news is that newer machines are mostly designed with much faster recharge times. Some allow you to perform a full recharge — with the machine switched off — in as little as one hour, though quite a few still take two or three hours. Recharges with the machine switched on generally take more than twice as long.

There is usually an option for an external recharger. There are two possible reasons for getting one of these: one is if it's quicker than doing an internal recharge; and the other is if you want to recharge more than one battery at the same time (most external rechargers can take two batteries at once and some manage three). If you're going to be on the road for longer periods, you may want to consider getting a spare battery. All machines allow you to take out a used battery and replace it with one that's fully recharged. The extra battery packs usually cost $80–$100.

Normally, you have to shut down the machine while you're switching batteries. However, some machines allow you to perform this task without doing so, as there's a built-in mini-battery that holds your data for about 10 minutes when the main one is removed. As well as being more convenient, this saves juice: if the first thing you do to a fresh battery is to make it boot up the computer, you'll immediately drain some of the charge.

### Docking stations

If you crave the mobility of a portable, but desire the expandability and convenience of a desktop, and if you don't like the idea of splitting your files between two computers (not to mention paying for two computers), then consider a notebook with a "docking station."

This is something that looks like a desktop PC with its guts ripped out. You insert your closed notebook computer into a mouth at the front and you end up with what amounts to a fully-configured desktop PC driven by the notebook's "engine" and using its hard drive; a full-size monitor sits on top and a normal desktop keyboard is also attached. The docking station contributes industry-standard desktop expansion slots (and, perhaps, space for one or two built-in peripherals) and these slots can be used for network cards and any other boards you care to add.

If you don't plan to network your computer, or use these expansion slots for other purposes, there will probably be limited practical benefits in having a docking station. After all, you can attach an external monitor and an external keyboard without one, thus giving your notebook the essential characteristics of a non-networked desktop PC.

However, a docking station can be a more streamlined and elegant way of making your notebook do double duty as a desktop. Not only does it make it look like a desktop, but it may deliver additional features. In particular, a few notebooks work with so-called "intelligent" docking stations, which streamline the process of switching from "notebook mode" to "dock mode" and back again.

Apple was the first vendor to bring out an intelligent dock, and the one it sells for use with its Duo sub-notebooks is still probably the best-designed you can get. Apple's slogan when marketing its sub-notebook/dock combination is "Best of Both Worlds" — which nicely sums up the case for the dock concept.

Recently, a few other vendors — including Texas Instruments and Compaq — have introduced intelligent docking stations for their DOS/Windows notebooks. Docking stations tend to cost between $500 and $750. Keep in mind that docking stations only work with the particular notebooks they are made for — there are no industry standards.

### Port replicators

If you don't get a full docking station, you may want to consider something called a port replicator. This is a sort of bar which plugs into all of the notebook's ports at the back; all of the ports are then replicated at the back of the bar itself.

What's the point of that? It's a way around the annoying problem that when you use your notebook on your desk and connect it to a screen, external keyboard, printer, and maybe one or two other peripherals, you're left with a bunch of loose wires and power cords orphaned on your desktop and falling on the floor every time you disconnect the computer.

With a port replicator, you just remove the bar, which remains on your desk to anchor all the wires. Port replicators, which aren't all that common, usually cost around $100. Like most add-ons in the notebook world, they are proprietary, so if your brand of notebook doesn't have one, you can't have one.

# PC Distribution, Service, & Support

Choosing where to buy your computer can be as important, and confusing, as figuring out what to buy. In fact, it's often quite difficult to separate the two decisions. The next part of this chapter examines how computers are sold and supported, and advises on how the smart buyer should approach the market. I'll be talking about buying strategies for both desktop and notebook PCs.

### Changing patterns of distribution

Not so very long ago, PC manufacturers fell neatly into two camps, which seemed to have relatively little in common. In one corner were the companies selling their machines direct, not through dealers — running factory-direct mail order operations and always providing support services to end-users. In the other corner were the manufacturers selling only through dealers — and leaving all service and support to the dealers. The big names tended to be found in the dealer channel, the upstarts in the mail order/direct channel. Most vendors fell squarely in one category or the other — few tried to operate in both channels.

During the past two years, the market has changed pretty fundamentally. As I'll show, manufacturers that sell through dealers have lately taken on a lot more responsibility for providing service and support to end-users. Moreover, some vendors that used to sell only through resellers have set up parallel mail order/direct sales operations of their own: you can now buy PCs direct from companies like IBM and Compaq, as an alternative to buying their products through dealers.

At the same time, the meaning of the word "dealer" has widened: today, a dealer is as likely to be a national chain of retail or warehouse stores as a smaller locally-operated business. In fact, the word "dealer" is giving way to "reseller," which, supposedly, has a more all-embracing meaning.

### Direct sales/mail order manufacturers

There are dozens of mail order, direct sales PC manufacturers — most of them pretty small. A few have made it to the big time, notably Dell and Gateway. Dell pioneered the concept, not only by undercutting the leading dealer-channel vendors when the latter were much less price-competitive than they are today, but also by offering lavish support policies at a time when companies like Compaq and IBM were pretty hopeless in this regard.

If you're wondering how come these mail order manufacturers are able to provide on-site service in just about every community across the 50 states, they do so by contracting third-party organizations to carry out the field maintenance on their behalf. GE Computer Service, a division of General Electric Company, is one of the three largest service providers in the country, with 1,000 authorized technicians in more than 250 locations. Other examples include Dow Jones, TRW, and NCR. In general, your initial point of contact if you have a problem is with the manufacturer, not with the third-party service provider.

The direct sales/mail order manufacturers market themselves with multi-page color ads in newsstand computer magazines; some of the larger ones also run ads in national media, such as the *Wall Street Journal*, and mail out glossy catalogs. All of them take orders over the phone and ship the goods using major carriers like UPS. In general, they serve the entire nation from a single location.

It's easier for a vendor to make a move from selling through resellers to selling direct than it is to go the other way around — there is limited shelf space in the stores and only a few of the direct sales/mail order manufacturers would have the clout to break into the retail channel. Dell is the only one to have done so in any significant way — it has been selling some of its products through certain warehouse club stores for a couple of years. Gateway, which has the muscle to move into the retail channel if it wanted to, has so far preferred to stay away.

Mail order manufacturers should not be confused with mail order dealers, which are something entirely different. Mail order dealers are firms which don't manufacture anything — they are simply resellers that deal with their customers by mail rather than in person. Examples include PCs Compleat.

### Manufacturers that sell mainly through resellers

The other type of PC manufacturer sells wholly or mainly through resellers. This category includes companies such as IBM, Compaq, Apple, AST, Acer, NEC, Leading Edge, and Packard Bell — to name but a few. Until a year or two ago, these companies generally wanted to have as little as possible to do with end-users. The idea was that dealers that sold the machines also provided repair services and general technical support.

Since the second half of 1992, all of these dealer-brand vendors have substantially upgraded their service and support arrangements, with the result that what they now provide to end-users often matches — and sometimes exceeds — what you get from the direct sales/mail order vendors.

The change came about for two reasons. One was that the dealer-brand vendors were losing sales to buyers who were choosing mail order largely because they were dissatisfied with the service they got from local computer dealers — not to mention the generally unhelpful attitudes of the manufacturers themselves.

The idea that local computer dealers are able to provide adequate after-sales service and support for all their customers harks back to the day when computers were more expensive items, sold in smaller quantities. It may have worked then, but it's less realistic in the cut-price, commodity business that PCs have now become. Today, computer dealers are forced to sell on price, and this means that they don't have the margins to provide support services locally that match those offered nationally by the mail order manufacturers — especially as the latter include a lot of support in the price of their machines.

The second reason why dealer-brand manufacturers were forced to take more responsibility for service is that they became keen on selling through consumer electronics and office warehouse stores, as well as through traditional computer dealers. These channels are vital for targeting the smaller office/ home office market — the so-called "SOHO" sector. However, the national retailers that provide the most effective coverage have little interest, or talent, in providing technical support and repair services — they're strictly in the cash-and-carry business. The PC manufacturers therefore had to provide their own service coverage in order to sell through these channels.

Once PC vendors had started offering service and support direct to their end-users, they were also able to start selling direct. As I indicated earlier, some vendors that have traditionally sold through resellers have lately opened up their own direct sales/mail order operations as well. In most cases, these only handle a limited product selection — typically, models targeted especially at smaller companies, though corporate buyers quite often find what they're looking for as well. By no means all the dealer/retail channel vendors have started to sell direct — those that have not include big names like AST, Toshiba, and Packard Bell.

### Mail order dealers

The past couple of years has also seen the emergence of a new type of dealer that attempts to bridge the gap between traditional dealer sales and manufacturer-direct channels. These are large mail order companies that handle a few top brands and provide support policies of their own in addition to those of the manufacturers. Dealers like this like to be referred to as the "super-channel."

The largest is a company called PCs Compleat which produces a catalog that includes top brands such as AST, Compaq, IBM, Leading Edge, Toshiba — and more. Dealing with PCs Compleat can be rather like dealing with a manufacturer's own direct sales/mail order operation, and it can be a particularly good choice for the brands — such as AST, Toshiba, etc. — that aren't also sold direct (in fact, PCs Compleat is authorized to use the words "Toshiba Direct" in marketing that company's products). The number to call is 800 669 4727. Another leading mail order company to consider is USA FLEX (800 876 5607).

One of the advantages of buying through a "super-channel" mail order dealer is that you generally get a 30-day money-back guarantee — which you don't, as a rule, if buying through other resellers.

### Specialized dealers

A "value added reseller" — or VAR — sells turnkey solutions addressed to vertical markets. It mixes hardware with niche software, often customized, and sells and supports it in a single package deal. A "systems integrator" is a dealer that takes various different types of hardware, software, and peripherals, and turns it all into a network that runs smoothly.

There is a large market for the services offered by VARs and systems integrators. By contrast, general purpose, small computer dealerships of the traditional mold are a declining breed. They are being squeezed between the superior skills of the VARS and systems integrators, and the low prices of the mail order and retail/warehouse-channel vendors.

### A closer look at warehouse stores

The smaller office/home office — SOHO — sector is the fastest-growing part of the computer industry, and the resellers that address it most effectively are the burgeoning warehouse stores. There are, in fact, several types, some more geared to business customers than others. The most business-oriented are the office warehouse stores, such as Staples, Office Depot, and OfficeMax.

These outlets devote most of their floorspace to office supplies and fixtures, but are getting increasingly into the lower end of the office equipment market. They like to sell equipment that comes in boxes, costs less than $2,500, and can be carried away: very low-volume copiers, fax machines, laser printers, small phone systems, and, of course, computers.

The next category are the specialized computer superstores, such as CompUSA and Computer City. These target SOHO buyers, and also people buying computers for educational or recreational purposes. Then there are the superstores, like Circuit City and The Wiz, that are mainly geared toward consumer electronics and household goods, but carry computers as well. Lastly there are the warehouse club stores like Sam's and Price Club which are expanding their electronics sections.

Distinct from the warehouse stores are the major department store retailers that have gotten into computers and other types of SOHO-oriented equipment. These include Sears — many of whose stores now include Sears Business Centers — and Montgomery Ward.

Some PC vendors have differentiated product ranges for these channels. But it would be a mistake to imagine that SOHO buyers are only interested in low-performance computers for somewhat undemanding applications. Manufacturers that made that mistake have been badly bruised — IBM, for example, with its original PS/1 line.

Today's SOHO buyer expects performance similar to what most corporate buyers are looking for. As a result, warehouse stores are already beginning to carry Pentium models. However, they don't carry the absolutely most powerful computers — EISA models, for example — or ones with the largest number of expansion slots. At the time of this writing, these stores had not begun selling the PowerPC-based Apple Macs — though it's only a matter of time before they do.

What distinguishes the retail/warehouse-channel computers from ones sold through other channels is often not so much the equipment itself, but the number of things that come included: warehouse channel PCs are often bundled with modems and applications software (often preinstalled). The trend is to sell computers that can be used for popular SOHO applications right out of the box — "plug-in-and-play," as some people call this.

Having bundled software can be attractive — especially when the hardware price is low to begin with — but it can also mean you end up using programs you might not have chosen had you picked them separately, which may not be ideal. Often, the bundled program is one of the growing number of multi-function packages whose name ends in "Works" — Microsoft Works, ClarisWorks, etc. These combine word processing with entry-level database, spreadsheet, graphics, and telecommunications modules. Often they are just about all the software a small business needs for everything other than accounting. Some are better, and more tightly integrated, than others (my favorite is ClarisWorks), but many people end up using the one they get with the machine simply because it's there.

Warehouse stores are fine if you have a pretty good idea what you want to buy when you go there. But the quality of pre-purchase support can leave something to be desired. Despite attempts by computer manufacturers to train store personnel, most of the sales assistants know little about computers and give advice lacking in caliber. Also, I never cease to be amazed at the number of demonstration computers in these stores that simply don't work — the mouse isn't connected properly, the software has jammed up, there's a permanently displayed error message, and so forth. To make matters worse, many of the display models are not only non-functioning, but they are also grubby.

In general, the after-sales service and support you get if you buy a computer through a warehouse store is okay — because the manufacturers now take care of this themselves, you don't ever again have to deal with the store after handing over your money at the register. But keep in mind that some manufacturers that are prominent in this channel are less good at support than others. For example, IBM's PS/1 line is not as well supported by IBM as its PS/ValuePoint products that are sold through other channels. Likewise, although Packard Bell — another prominent retail brand — offers decent support policies on paper, there is evidence that the company is not always as efficient at executing them as it might be.

# Pros & Cons of Direct & Reseller Channels

The big advantage of buying from a company that sells through the mail used to be that you got more support directly from the manufacturer. But, as I explained above, this plus has been neutralized somewhat by the much-improved support arrangements lately introduced by manufacturers that sell through resellers. So what are the pros and cons of the different channels in the new-look PC industry?

### Money-back guarantees

Buying direct is often a lot less hassle. It cuts out a whole tier of decision making. In the dealer market, you first have to figure out what to buy, and then you have to decide whom to buy it from. By contrast, the direct sales buyer makes one integrated decision. But one thing you don't get when buying direct is the chance to see what you're getting before you decide (though you'll probably see a picture in the sales literature).

Actually, this isn't as big a drawback as it sounds. First, you often don't get much of a chance to see the product when you buy it from a reseller, and there's a limit to what you can tell about a desktop PC from looking at it.

Second, just about all reputable mail order manufacturers have a 30-day unconditional money-back guarantee. If you don't like your computer for any reason, just send it back for a full refund — even if you've been using it. By contrast, few dealers will take a machine back once it has been sold, especially if there's nothing actually wrong with it. So in a sense, buying direct gives you more of a chance to get a close look at what you're getting before you say a final adieu to your hard-earned cash.

IBM is the only manufacturer to offer a 30-day money-back guarantee on PCs sold through its dealer channel, though this doesn't apply to all models. The dealers most likely to offer similar money-back guarantees of their own — in the absence of ones from the manufacturer — are the very large ones that sell by mail order (PCs Compleat, etc.).

### Pre-purchase information

One gripe about buying computers through dealers and retailers is that it's often almost impossible to get any detailed product sales literature. This means that you often only get verbal assurances about the exact specifications of what it is you're getting, or you have to rely on the sketchy details given in point-of-sale advertising material. I'm not saying that most computer salespeople try to mislead buyers — but it is a fact that a lot of them inadvertently give out wrong information.

In fact, the caliber of salespeople in many computer outlets is one reason why you're not really missing out by buying direct. In the average computer store, you will not be dealing with a computer expert. And well-intentioned, but ill-informed, advice is often worse than none at all.

On the whole, you get better pre-purchase information if you're buying direct from the manufacturer. By ordering direct, you can speak on the phone to technical specialists who can answer questions about specific features, and fax or mail you anything you want to see in writing. That said, you do sometimes encounter a pushy sort of salesperson when you call a manufacturer's mail order number — keep in mind the people on the phone are more likely to be operating on commission than the assistants in a store.

### The post-purchase convenience factor

Another benefit of buying from a mail order manufacturer is that it's often easier to get a hold of additional accessories you might want later on. This is especially true if you're buying a notebook computer, as these generally use proprietary parts for things like extra batteries, memory, and modems. With desktop PCs, this point is less critical as you can turn to third parties for this sort of thing.

Of course, if you buy your notebook from a dealer or retail store, you can still order extra accessories or enhancements later on — but this tends to be more bother, as the resellers don't usually carry them in stock and aren't always particularly helpful about telling you what your options are. (One manufacturer, AST, sells all of its notebooks through resellers, but sells accessories and expansion modules direct — a good way of addressing this problem.)

### Product differences

The quality of product you get is pretty well the same whether you buy from a mail order manufacturer, or through a dealer. There may be some dealer products around that use inferior components, and there may be some direct sales products of dubious quality. But this really isn't a factor relating to the type of distribution, providing you're talking about recognized vendors. Of course, all major vendors do have their occasional lemons, but the difference among them tends to be in the support arrangements to rectify problems, not in the frequency with which problems occur.

The only qualification I'd make to the above is that it's easier for a really obscure vendor to enter the market by selling direct than by going through dealers and retailers — and with obscure brands, there can sometimes be a higher risk of a quality problem. I'll be discussing the pros and cons of choosing really obscure brands shortly.

One product-related difference between direct and dealer vendors that I can detect is that the former are often nimbler in introducing new models with the latest features. Dealer/retail-channel sales vendors get there in the end, but often follow a few months behind. One of the reasons for this is that direct sales manufacturers often make each computer to order; dealer-brand manufacturers, by contrast, build up inventories, which then have to be cleared before new models can be introduced.

### The waiting factor

A consequence of the fact that mail order manufacturers make desktops and towers to order is that they generally aren't able to ship your machine right away. This drawback of the mail order channel often comes as an unwelcome surprise to buyers who assume that the goods will go out the door the same day.

Usually, a computer ships in about three days, and then you have to add another couple of days or so for delivery. In other words, you're talking about the best part of a week or more before you get it. On some models, moreover, the wait can be significantly longer (especially on top-selling notebooks, which tend not to be built to order and can get back-ordered).

These delays aren't necessarily the end of the world — a computer isn't usually an impulse buy that you think of the day before you really need it. Nonetheless, it can be an irritant. Sometimes, you're offered a machine that's ready to ship almost right away, but it's a slightly different configuration from the one you wanted and — chances are — it comes with some extras built into the price that you might not really need.

### Price comparisons

If you looked at list prices, direct sales products used to appear to be way less expensive than the stuff sold through dealers — but no one paid much attention to the dealer list prices, as these existed only as a marketing device to convince buyers that they were being given a great discount when, in fact, they were probably simply paying the going rate. With some brands, this still applies.

Lately, however, there has been a tendency for manufacturers to set suggested retail prices much closer to the prices that the machines actually get sold for. Some manufacturers have gone a step further and have abolished list prices altogether on some or all of their products.

Still, buying through dealer channels means that you are constantly prone to "am-I-getting-the-best-price?" anxiety. With direct sales products, by contrast, the advertised list price is the price everyone pays (unless, perhaps, you're placing a large order, in which case you may be eligible for volume discounts).

A further benefit of the direct sales/mail order channel is that the low prices are available nationwide: dealer prices, by contrast, tend to be lowest in, or close to, big cities where the resellers turn over high volumes — you don't get such good deals in smaller communities. Another plus about mail order is that you may be able to avoid paying sales tax, depending on where you and the vendor are located.

Of course, some of these benefits also apply if you buy computers through the large mail order dealers, not just if you buy direct from the manufacturers. And also remember that the manufacturers that sell direct and through dealers end up offering the best of both worlds.

### Be street-wise to dealer pricing

It's often quite difficult to make price comparisons when shopping in dealer channels. This is because dealers often customize the configuration of the computers they discount most heavily: for example, they might buy PCs from the manufacturer without any hard drives and with minimum memory, and then add the drives and additional memory from third-party sources. There's nothing intrinsically wrong with this. Sometimes, the dealer can offer you a better value — and equal quality — by reconfiguring the manufacturer's package. But it does make it a whole lot harder to compare prices when shopping around.

Dealer advertising is also confusing. Often, dealers advertise a product without making it exactly clear what the product is. I've seen numerous dealer ads citing vague model numbers that don't actually exist. Even when you call up, dealers are often pretty unspecific. Advertised dealer prices are often for systems without monitors, incidentally, whereas advertised direct sales prices almost always include them.

# Phone Support, Warranties, & On-Site Service

Next, I'll talk a little about what service and support actually entail. There are two aspects. One is getting help if you have a question when something doesn't seem to be working right, but you aren't quite sure whether it's you or the machine (or you know it's you, but you just can't figure out what to do about it!). The other is getting the computer fixed when there's a hardware fault.

### Phone support

The first is dealt with by phone support. All major mail order manufacturers have technical support lines, almost always using 800 numbers. During the past couple of years, almost all dealer-brand manufacturers have started offering them as well — with varying degrees of enthusiasm.

Phone support covers everything to do with the hardware (including questions relating to adding expansion boards and so forth). It usually also extends to questions to do with the system software (i.e., DOS and Windows) — at least those aspects of it that are hardware-linked, though this can be a bit of a gray area.

But don't expect your PC hardware vendor to help you out with questions relating to applications software (even any that comes bundled with the computer). Software difficulties are more likely to make you want to grab your phone than problems with the hardware, so it makes sense to check out the support policies that go with a program you're thinking of buying.

Some computer manufacturers' technical support lines are easier to get through to than others. Lately, there have been a growing number of complaints about unacceptable delays.

Also, some support lines are open for longer periods than others — these days, many vendors offer phone support 24 hours a day, seven days a week (though I sometimes wonder just who does call in at 4:45 a.m. on a Sunday morning). Others are only open during normal business hours — that's enough for some people, but less satisfactory if you use your machine in the evening or on weekends (details of different vendors' support arrangements appear in the Vendor Profiles section at the end of this chapter).

The best phone support is one that integrates smoothly with the service side. If the result of your call is a determination that your machine needs repairing, it's better if the people you're talking to stick with the problem and see it through to the next stage.

## Warranties & repair arrangements

Most computers are sold with one-year warranties. These days, most warranties on desktop and tower machines include on-site service — so if your machine needs fixing, you're entitled to a housecall. On-site warranties used to be associated with mail order manufacturers, but — as I explained earlier — they are now widely offered on computers sold through dealer/retail channels. These days, so many vendors offer on-site warranties on desktop PCs that I can't see any good reason to choose one that doesn't.

Keep in mind, though, that on-site service is not generally included in notebook PC warranties. If your notebook needs fixing, you usually have to send it back — if so, look for a promised turnaround of no more than 48 hours plus shipping times.

Some manufacturers offer standard warranties that run for longer than one year. Compaq offers three-year warranties on all its computers, though this only includes one year of on-site service. A number of other vendors offer three-year warranties on their premium models only. Warranty information is shown in the Vendor Profiles.

Most vendors offer optional extended on-site warranties — effectively all-inclusive service contracts covering parts and labor — and also allow you to purchase on-site service when required after your warranty has expired. Extended warranties on computers can make sense, especially if they include on-site service — they are worth pricing when you buy your computer, and they tend to be better values than the ones on consumer electronics items (which are usually a waste of money). For example, Dell's extended on-site warranties start at around $100 per year covering all parts and labor — a reasonable insurance against future disasters.

## Service response times

Most vendors that offer on-site service do not publish specific promises about how long it will take to arrive. However, when questioned, most say that service is generally next-day or, failing that, second-day.

Some vendors, generally the larger ones, do advertise response times and sometimes promise speedier service on their premium products. The larger vendors also usually allow you to purchase super-intensive service coverage, guaranteeing that a technician will visit within four business hours of your putting in a call.

### Other support services

There are a couple of other support services that are quite common among both dealer and direct sales vendors. On-line bulletin boards allow users with modems to communicate with both the manufacturers' technical support people and other users in order to retrieve technical information, share ideas, and ask questions. Bulletin boards are generally accessed via on-line services, such as CompuServe and America On-Line.

Fax-on-demand systems allow users to call a number, hear a menu of choices, and then use a touch-tone phone to request that specified technical information be sent automatically to a fax machine. In some cases, this type of system can also be used to obtain pre-purchase technical information.

# The Obscure Brand Option

If you shop the computer market, it probably won't be long before you come across a machine that appears to be an amazing bargain. It's loaded with features. It's priced well below what you'd normally expect to pay, even from a vendor with aggressive pricing. Usually, it's being sold by mail order. There's only one thing wrong. It's totally obscure.

I tend to advise caution in these circumstances. These products are generally assembled by very small businesses. The companies concerned have no recognized brand name to protect and, in order to tempt buyers with super-low prices, may be more prone to cut corners with component quality.

In addition, their size can make them less able to provide service and support should you need it. Even if they do offer support policies that sound good, you'll want to be sure that they are capable of living up to their promises: for example, there's no use having an on-site service warranty if the manufacturer falls behind on its payments to the third-party service provider it has contracted.

### "No names"

These companies are sometimes referred to as "no-names" — a throw-back to the time when some computers were literally sold without any name stuck on the side. Today, no-names, in the literal sense, are rare — but the designation is still sometimes used to refer to small vendors that use a brand name that hardly anyone has heard of.

### The perils of dealing with shoe-string vendors

It is a fact that many small computer manufacturers are finding it hard to survive following recent price wars. Some have gone out of business in the past year, and others are looking a bit perilous.

Fortunately, the communality of components between different brands of desktop PCs means that if your machine does develop a fault after its manufacturer has gone under, you can probably get it fixed somehow — but it will be a lot of hassle. Moreover, if this happens in the first year, you can forget about the warranty. Getting a notebook fixed after the manufacturer collapses may be more difficult: notebooks tend to use more non-standard parts.

If you look at some computer magazines, you'll see an awful lot of pretty obscure vendors reviewed editorially with the same prominence given to much larger manufacturers. Often, the computers recommended are made by vendors hardly anyone has ever heard of — but they frequently get the accolades because they narrowly outperform the more established competition in a benchmark test measuring speed by the split second.

That's fair enough, but it is worth keeping in mind that the magazines concerned have a vested interest in promoting a culture in which there is the largest possible number of smaller mail order manufacturers, rather than a reduced number of stronger ones. The mail order advertising from these companies is the livelihood of many of the magazines.

Don't get me wrong: I certainly don't want to suggest that all small-scale assemblers of PC products are untrustworthy (companies like Apple and Dell began in garages). But be advised that if you do go for a brand that few people have heard of, you are increasing your risk of ending up with a headache.

### Where to look

That said, when you see some of the prices, you may consider the risk worth taking. The best place to look for these bargains is in the computer magazines you'll find on newsstands. In particular, an oversized publication called *Computer Shopper* is the Mecca for direct sales buyers looking to stretch their dollars to the limit. Good luck, and be careful!

# Buying Software, Peripherals, & Accessories

Some mail order PC vendors also sell software programs. A few will install programs you purchase at the same time as the computer, so that everything is ready to run when you take it out of the box. (Don't confuse that with the much more widespread practice of preinstalling software that is thrown in "free" with the equipment itself.)

In general, though, you get the best prices on software if you buy it separately. And when deciding where to buy your software, price should be an overwhelming consideration. There is no benefit in paying more than you need to: the firms that sell software have no role in subsequent support arrangements. All you expect of the company that sells you software is that it handles your order efficiently and charges you as little as possible.

### Where to find the best deals

Fortunately, the suppliers that are cheapest are also usually very efficient. For the best deals, we recommend buying software by mail order. The worst prices — and the narrowest choices — tend to be offered by local computer dealers. There are a number of very respectable mail order suppliers which offer excellent service and produce first-class catalogs. These catalogs are also a great way of ordering extra memory, modems, accessories, and all sorts of other computer paraphernalia. (They sometimes sell their own brand of PC as well, though I wouldn't particularly recommend them for that.)

My favorite supplier is MicroWarehouse (tel: 800 367 7080). They are open 24 hours a day, seven days a week; what's more, you can order up to midnight (eastern time) for overnight delivery (there's a $7 shipping charge). I've found this company very efficient and its prices very competitive. It also runs a sister operation called MacWarehouse for Apple users (tel: 800 255 6227); for some reason, Mac users only have to pay $3 for overnight shipping. There is something very satisfying about deciding shortly before you go to bed that you'd like a software program, and then having it arrive the following morning — all for as little as three bucks over what's usually a rock-bottom price to begin with!

Also consider a company called The PC Zone (tel: 800 258 2088). It also offers overnight delivery ($6), though its catalog isn't as large. It too has a Mac equivalent, called The Mac Zone (tel: 800 248 0800); again, oddly, Mac users are just charged $3 for overnight shipping.

Dell Computer Corporation also has a catalog called *DellWare* for software and peripherals sales. This is a different catalog, and a separate operation, from Dell's mail order PC hardware business. The overnight delivery charge in this case is $5 (tel: 800 626 9530).

Likewise, the *IBM PC Direct Source Book* — put out by IBM's direct sales/mail order operation — offers quite a good selection of third-party software and other items, as well as IBM's own desktop and notebook PCs. However, IBM charges $6 for second-day air delivery.

# Computer Vendor Profiles

In the remainder of this chapter, I'll take a closer look at 11 of the leading vendors of both desktop and notebook PCs (all desktop vendors are also in the PC market, but two of the leading notebook vendors don't do desktops). In each profile, I provide an overview of the company, brief comments on its product range, and an examination of its policies on service and support. Also shown are addresses and phone numbers — including, when appropriate, the 800 numbers for direct sales.

The purpose of these profiles is to give you a general feel for the strengths, weaknesses, and overall focus of the vendors being examined. The companies profiled in this section are: Acer, AST, Apple, Compaq, Dell, Gateway, IBM, Leading Edge, Packard Bell, Texas Instruments, and Toshiba. In addition, there are much briefer comments on a selection of other vendors right at the end.

## *Acer*

*Acer American Corporation*
*401 Charcot Avenue*
*San Jose, CA 95131*
*Tel: 800 637 7000*
*Direct sales: 800 848 2237*

### Introduction

Founded in 1976 in Taiwan, where it still has its headquarters, Acer is now among the world's leading PC manufacturers, with operations in more than 70 countries. Worldwide, the company's annual revenues in 1993 were about $1.7 billion — this represents a gain of more than 40 percent over 1992. About one third of its revenues come from the US. Acer combines a solid product range with the financial stability that's lacking in parts of the computer industry.

The company is a darling of the Taiwanese government, as it's one of the few major Taiwanese corporations to trade worldwide under its own name, rather than selling components and products to others to sell under theirs. Acer is also one of the most vertically integrated PC manufacturers in the world — i.e., it makes more of its own components than most of its competitors. In addition, Acer claims to be the leading maker of computers that get sold under other vendors' brand names.

Acer is strong in desktop PCs, but it has had less success in the notebook market. It has lately been trying to move more upmarket in terms of the type of computers it supplies. In 1990, it paid $94 million for Altos Computer Systems, a loss-making Californian manufacturer of multi-user and networked Unix systems. This follows an earlier somewhat ill-judged acquisition of Counterpoint, another Californian multi-user computer manufacturer (Acer ended up shutting down almost all of Counterpoint's operations).

Until recently, Acer sold only through resellers, including some pretty big-name retail channel stores. However, in 1993 it also set up a direct sales/mail order operation which is promoted mainly through multi-page ads in newsstand computer magazines. At about the same time as it entered this channel, the company beefed up its support arrangements — more on this shortly. In a surprising move, Acer has recently entered the crowded fax market, with a line of low-end thermal paper models that it hopes to sell through the same retail channels that carry its PCs.

### Acer product overview

Acer's mainstream desktop PCs are its ACROS Series, which is the main focus of its marketing activity. The ACROS models are generally sold bundled with various extras such as fax modems and software: details of what's included vary according to the channel and reseller. These machines are generally good values, though they are not designed to appeal to performance buffs who look for refinements to tweak the maximum juice out of their 486-series processors.

More demanding users are offered the AcerPower Series — here the equipment is configured to deliver the highest levels of performance. There are both desktop and mini-tower versions of the AcerPower range, and both ISA and EISA models.

The high-performance tower servers are the AcerFrame

models, which are shipped network-ready with Novell NetWare. And the Altos brand name is still used to sell the company's Unix systems, which form the AcerAltos range. These products are sold through traditional computer dealers, systems integrators, and specialized VARs (value added resellers).

There is a separate range of multimedia systems aimed at techno-lusting home office buyers. This is known as the AcerPAC series: the letters "PAC" stand for "Personal Activity Center," and these machines combine a regular computer with a CD-ROM drive, fax modem, digital phone and answering device, and even an AM/FM stereo tuner, mixer, and CD player.

Acer's notebooks also go under the AcerNote name. Acer's notebooks are traditionally somewhat unexceptional and this isn't a vendor I would make a particular point of shortlisting for a portable computer — though that doesn't mean it can't be a reasonable choice, especially if you use Acer desktops and prefer single-vendor sourcing.

### Acer service & support

Acer's service and support arrangements are better than they used to be. Phone support is now available 7-days/24-hours; the number is toll-free for the first year, but you have to pay for the call thereafter.

All the machines are sold with a one-year warranty which — with the exception of the notebooks — includes on-site service. Acer guarantees that you will see a service representative within 48 hours; however, if you're located within 100 miles of one of the 633 service locations in the US, you can generally expect a next-day visit. Notebooks have to be sent back for fast-turnaround warranty repairs; coverage applies in more than 20 countries, in case your computer gets sick while you're traveling. If you buy from Acer direct, there's a 30-day money-back guarantee. There are also a number of extended and advanced service/warranty options.

### Summing up Acer

**For:** *Stable vendor; offers value and quality without too much hype; improved service and support; easy to find its products through leading retailers; new direct sales/mail order channel for those who prefer to buy that way.* **Against:** *Notebooks are nothing special.* **Verdict:** *Can be a very sensible choice for desktop PC buyers in particular.*

# Apple

*Apple Computer Inc.*
*20525 Mariani Avenue*
*Cupertino, CA 95014*
*Tel: 800 446 3000*
*Direct sales: 800 795 1000*

## Introduction

Most of this chapter is devoted to industry-standard PCs that run DOS/Windows operating software. But if you're thinking of buying some new PCs, you should take the opportunity to review whether a move over to the Apple Macintosh would be smart.

Apple is the only PC manufacturer that stayed apart from the industry standard and lived to tell the tale. The pros and cons of its Macintosh computers compared with DOS/Windows machines were discussed earlier in this chapter. That's also where I explained the new PowerPC — which is the most exciting thing happening in the Mac world this year. In this profile, I will describe Apple's hardware range, distribution methods, and service and support policies, and I suggest you refer to the earlier discussion for more on the pros-and-cons of being a Mac user.

## RIP Mac?

Apple has received quite a lot of negative press during the past year, and it has become fashionable in certain quarters to speculate about whether the company will survive in the long term. The negative view is that Apple's advantage has always been in the software arena and that Microsoft is catching up. It is only a matter of time, the doubters predict, before Apple finds itself being able to offer buyers little that they cannot get from the leading industry standard — in which case why would anyone bother with the smaller platform?

Perhaps one day Apple may find itself in the position of being unable to offer buyers a better alternative, but that doesn't seem likely to occur soon. In 1994, Apple for the first time offered hardware that should be the envy of many DOS/Windows users — and, looking at what's in the pipeline, this advantage should continue for several years. Moreover, the best that Microsoft is likely to offer most computer users in the next two years is operating software that is as polished as what Apple offers now. In addition, Apple benefits from huge brand loyalty — there is a very large user population that would be dismayed to see its demise.

Obituaries for the Macintosh seem in my view to be somewhat premature — but I can understand why some people might feel that the Mac legend will not last forever.

### Where's the Mac at?

Although people often talk about "the" Mac, there are, in fact, numerous Macintosh models ranging in price from under $1,000 to several thousand dollars. They include desktops, towers, and some of the most elegant notebooks on the market.

As I explained earlier in this chapter, Apple is in the middle of a major transformation as it begins the process of moving to a completely new hardware platform based on the PowerPC processor, which is a joint development of Apple, IBM, and Motorola. Initially, the PowerPC is being positioned at the top of the market — as a rival to Pentium-based products running DOS/Windows — but over the next year or two it will become the platform for the entire Mac range.

At the time of this writing, the first PowerPC models had recently been introduced, but the bulk of Macs being sold were still the traditional type. I will refer to these traditional Macs as the "680X0" models, because they are the ones based on the Motorola 68000-series processors (currently the 68030 and 68040 families).

Apple has got a tricky problem selling computers in 1994 and the first part of 1995: on the one hand, it has to talk up the PowerPC; on the other hand, it still has to sell its 680X0 models. It will take a while for a full range of PowerPC hardware to become available, and for software developers to get their act together to support it (more on this shortly). As I will show, Apple's answer to this problem is to make most of its last-generation 680X0 Macs upgradable to the PowerPC.

### A closer look at the 680X0 desktop Macs

Apple has already dropped the older versions of the 680X0 processor — namely the 68020 and the original 68000 itself. The 68030 processor is now only used in its older PowerBook notebooks and entry-level desktops. The desktop models targeted at business users, and the latest PowerBooks, now all use versions of the 68040 processor.

The 68040 comes in two shapes: the main one — the 68040 itself — runs at 33MHz and 40MHz and includes a built-in math coprocessor. The slower version (a kind of equivalent of an Intel SX processor) leaves out the math coprocessor and generally runs at 25MHz. This defeatured version is called the 68LC040 — the letters "LC" stand for "low cost."

Today, all 680X0-based Macs come with at least 4MB of

RAM. This is the minimum needed to get satisfactory use out of the System 7 software (System 7 is to Apple Macs what DOS/Windows is to Intel-based PCs). But — as with the DOS/Windows world — 4MB of RAM is insufficient for all but the most unambitious type of work. I recommend going for a minimum of 8MB and, ideally, 12MB.

Apple's desktop 680X0-based range consists of several separate, but overlapping lines:

❑ *LC series:* These days targeted mainly at educational markets.

❑ *Performa series:* Sold through retail channels and targeted at small business and home office users. Performa models are typically sold in "bundles" that include monitors and a selection of software.

❑ *Quadra series:* Originally positioned as a very high-end series, but now the mainstream business series. Quadra models are sold through traditional Apple dealers, and by Apple's own direct sales/mail order unit. Unlike the Performa models, the Quadras are not sold bundled — monitors, and even keyboards, are offered separately.

❑ *Workgroup Server series:* These, as their name suggests, are server products for small and medium size networks. There are both desktop and tower versions.

Keep in mind that in some cases, the same basic computer can feature in more than one of the above lines — although the overall package in terms of what's included may vary. The Centris series, which briefly filled the mid-market business slot during part of 1992 and 1993, is now history; the former Centris models have either been discontinued or renamed as Quadras.

Arguably, 1994 is not the ideal year to buy any desktop Mac — the non-PowerPC models are obviously on their last lap, while the PowerPC range is still limited, not to mention being more expensive and less powerful than it will be in '95. If you are going to buy a 680X0-series Mac in 1994, the smart choice is one with a PowerPC upgrade path. At press-time, Apple had announced PowerPC upgrades for the following current and discontinued desktop products (third-party upgrades may also be available for certain others):

✔ *Macintosh IIvx*
✔ *Macintosh Centris 610, 650, and 660AV*
✔ *Macintosh Quadra 610, 650, 660AV, 800, and 840AV*
✔ *Macintosh Performa 600*

Upgrades are priced from around $700. Still, there's a strong case at this stage to go straight for a PowerPC, rather than buy a fairly upscale Quadra and then upgrade it — even if this means waiting a while until the time is ripe to do so. The only people who I think should still be buying 680X0-based Macs at present are those choosing the most inexpensive models for entry-level applications (though keep in mind that these are the ones that will never be PowerPC-upgradable).

### Introducing the Power Macintosh
Apple unveiled its first PowerPC-based Macs on March 14, 1994, and named them the Power Macintosh series. The Power Macs run what, from the user's point of view, amounts to the same operating system as the 680X0-based models — in other words, the hardware platform may have changed, but the user interface that has always made Mac fans drool is basically the same.

The Power Macs can use the same monitors, keyboards, printers, and other peripherals as previous Macs. They can also run the same applications programs, but they won't do so any faster than a 68040-based Quadra — in order to benefit from the speed of the PowerPC processor, you have to run software that was developed specially for it. In fact, a Power Macintosh running software written for a 680X0-based Mac can actually be somewhat slower than a 68040-based model.

There is limited benefit in buying a Power Mac, therefore, unless you are prepared to get new software to go with it — keep this in mind when assessing costs. At press-time, special PowerPC versions of some popular upscale Mac programs were already available, and others will follow. In time, any software vendor wanting to sell to the Mac user base will need to adapt its programs for the PowerPC.

### Apple PowerBook notebook overview
Although Apple has launched its first PowerPC desktops, its notebook range is still all based on the 680X0 processor family and will be for a while longer. Apple was quite late launching its first notebooks — it waited until the end of 1991, after having previously offered only a very bulky (and pretty unsuccessful) larger-than-laptop Mac portable.

But the wait proved worth it: the Apple PowerBook notebooks became an instant cult. In fact, more PowerBooks were sold in their first year than any other computer product ever launched (including the original IBM PC). This partly reflected their excellent design, but it was also a consequence of pent-up demand — because these were the first Apple notebooks, Apple had to meet several years' worth of techno-lust rolled into a few months.

Much of what makes the PowerBooks so good is the same as what makes Apple desktops so good — namely the software and operating environment. But the PowerBooks have always had intrinsic hardware qualities of their own that have contributed to their success. Nonetheless, by the start of 1994, the main 100-series PowerBooks — the all-in-one models with built-in floppy disk drives and a full set of ports at the back — had begun to show their age. Although they had been enhanced since they were first launched late in 1991, their shape, size, and weight (almost 7 lbs) remained the same — as did a number of their other characteristics (such as indifferent NiCad battery performance). In addition, none of them worked with anything faster than a 68030/33MHz processor.

In May '94, however, Apple introduced a new series of updated and slicker 68LC040-based PowerBooks known as the 500-series; these will later be PowerPC-upgradable. Surprisingly, Apple has scrapped its much-praised internal trackball on these new models, which instead come with something called a "Midas TouchPad" — a flat area in the place normally reserved for a PowerBook trackball, over which you move your finger to control the screen pointer.

The other option for Apple notebook buyers is to get one of the PowerBook Duo models, which are sub-notebooks (without floppy drives or a full set of ports) that are designed to work with docking stations. These were first introduced at the end of 1992, and new models were introduced late in 1993 and early summer 1994. The Duos haven't proved as commercially successful as Apple had hoped, though the latest versions — which are 68LC040-based and will be PowerPC-upgradable at a later date — are superb machines in the finest tradition of PowerBooks.

The Duos are ideal products for people who want a very lightweight notebook when they are mobile, but who prefer the comfort and convenience of a desktop when they're in the office or at home — and that's exactly what you get if you use a Duo in conjunction with Apple's very elegant Duo Dock, a full-size "intelligent" docking station with its own floppy drive and expansion options.

Less ideal than the full docking station are the "mini docks" that Apple and a number of third-party vendors offer: these allow you to plug a full set of ports into the back of the Duo (which, on its own, only has serial and optional modem ports), but you still use the Duo in notebook, as opposed to desktop, mode.

### Apple distribution, service, & support

Apple Macs are sold mainly through dealers and — in the case of the Performa models — retail channels. Late in 1992, Apple set up a direct sales/mail order operation called *The Apple Catalog*. This originally only sold low-end products, but later took on most of the product line (except that the hottest Macs tended not to be available through this channel until demand began to ebb); it also sold some peripheral products from other vendors and a host of Mac paraphernalia, accessories, and gift items.

Early in 1994, Apple did away with *The Apple Catalog*, but replaced it with a non-catalog mail order/direct sales program selling only Apple products without the other sidelines. It was unclear at the time of this writing how high a profile this operation would have — in early summer '94, it was only carrying a small number of Mac products and it wasn't being promoted very heavily.

Until recently, Apple had a somewhat archaic rule requiring all of its dealers to see each customer in person: they were not allowed to take orders over the phone and ship the goods unless they had an established relationship with the customer. This precluded mail order, though there were "unauthorized" mail order Mac dealers. Recently, Apple has rescinded this rule and new mail order Mac operations were beginning to sprout as this book was being published.

In the last edition of this book, I wrote that Apple had the least satisfactory service and support policies of any major computer vendor. That was fair comment at the time, but the good news is that Apple has since upgraded its support policies. For a start, Apple now offers 800-number phone support covering all of its products. Previously, phone support was only available on PowerBooks and Performa desktops. However, Apple still keeps banker's hours compared with some of its rivals — phone support is only available Monday through Friday, 11 hours a day.

Another improvement is that the one-year warranty offered on desktop Macs now includes on-site service — previously, this only applied to Performa products and you had to take other models back to a dealer if you wanted free warranty service.

PowerBook service still requires taking the machine back to the dealer or returning it to Apple (at their expense), which is normal practice in the notebook market. Apple's PowerBook repair service is very good and you should get your computer back within about three business days of sending it away.

## Summing up Apple

**For:** *Better than Windows (in my opinion); elegant software and hardware design enhances personal productivity; outstanding range of monochrome and color video options; excellent platform for desktop publishing in particular; nice notebooks.* **Against:** *1994 is a difficult time to make the right purchasing decision, because the transition from the older Mac platform to the new PowerPC is just beginning; support policies, though improved, still fall short of the best; some niche software not available in Mac versions.* **Verdict:** *Not for everyone, but the best computers for many.*

# AST

*AST Research, Inc.*
*P.O. Box 57005*
*16215 Alton Parkway*
*Irvine, CA 92619–7005*
*Tel: 800 876 4278*

### Introduction

Founded in 1980, AST has become a very big player in the PC market. Its acquisition in 1993 of Tandy's computer manufacturing business was the latest boost to the growth of a company that ranks among the definite success stories of the PC industry. Revenues for the 1993 fiscal year topped $1.4 billion, up from $944 million in 1992. And in the first six months of its 1994 fiscal year, revenues shot up to $1.2 billion. Currently, AST is ranked number five in US PC sales, and is also in the top 10 worldwide. The company is still run by one of its original three founders.

AST has manufacturing operations in the US, the Far East, and Europe, and builds more of its own components than many of its competitors. AST sells only through dealers and retailers. Unlike just about all other vendors of its size, it has shown no signs of wanting to get involved in the direct sales/mail order channel. However, some national mail order resellers — notably PCs Compleat — carry its products in their catalogs.

AST is generally a conservative player in the PC market, preferring to cater to mainstream requirements rather than taking risks by being especially technologically innovative (some of its more exotic offerings, such as pen computers and multimedia systems, came with its Tandy acquisition). Partly as a result, it has developed a somewhat "neutral" brand image, but its machines are widely available and can be very good buys.

### AST product overview

AST is one of the prime exponents of the multi-brand school of PC marketing. There are several different product lines which often overlap, but are aimed at different distribution channels and market segments. In brief, these are currently as follows:

❑ *Advantage!:* This is AST's home office/small business series, consisting of desktops, mini-towers, and notebooks. Advantage! products are sold mainly through retail channels, and are typically bundled with software and other items such as modems; the emphasis is on turnkey, "plug-in-and-play" systems. The desktops include special multimedia systems. The notebooks are known as the Advantage! Explorer series.

❑ *Bravo:* This is AST's "value" line of desktop and notebook products for mainstream business use. These products are comparable to the Compaq ProLinea models or the IBM PS/ValuePoints. They aren't necessarily any more high-performance than ones sold in the Advantage! line. The Bravos are sold through business-oriented reseller channels.

❑ *PowerExec:* These are AST's more upmarket notebook computers (see below for more details).

*Premmia/Premium:* These lines take in AST's power-oriented desktops and servers for upscale corporate use.

❑ *Manhattan SMP:* At the top of AST's line are these large servers aimed at Fortune 1000 companies.

❑ *GRiD:* Specialized, mainly portable, products for vertical markets — this was a Tandy acquisition carry-over.

❑ *PenRight!:* Pen computers and data collection applications.

### AST service & support

All AST desktop and tower systems, with the exception of the Advantage! models, are now backed by a three-year warranty. This includes three years of on-site service in the case of the Premmia/Premium and Manhattan SMP products, and one year of on-site service for the others. You can expect to see a technician within 48 hours of putting in a call. Various additional programs offering quicker response times — as fast as four hours — are available as options, as are warranty extensions. The Advantage! desktops and towers are backed by one-year warranties, also with on-site service.

AST's notebooks have one-year warranties which — as is usually the case with portables — require you to send the machine back for repair. The standard warranty includes 48-hour repair on receipt of the product by AST. You can upgrade this to 24-hour turnaround at extra cost, and you can also pay to extend the warranty for a second year.

### Summing up AST

**For:** *Comprehensive desktop and tower range; excellent notebooks; wide availability; very good service policies; company appears to be stable.* **Against:** *No direct sales/mail order channel for people who prefer to buy that way.* **Verdict:** *A very strong supplier — one of the best if you're shopping in dealer/retail channels.*

# Compaq

*Compaq Computer Corporation*
*PO Box 692000*
*Houston, TX 77269–2000*
*Tel: 800 345 1518*
*Direct sales: 800 888 5858*

### Introduction

Founded in 1982, Compaq began life as a manufacturer of portable computers but soon became a major force in the desktop market. The company built its success in the eighties by out-maneuvering IBM in the value and performance race.

After a blip around 1990–91 when it showed signs of complacency and drift, Compaq virtually relaunched itself as a brand in 1992 and has since gone from strength to strength. Its 1993 sales reached $7.2 billion, representing a 75 percent increase over 1992. Worldwide, Compaq shipped 3.1 million computers in 1993.

All of Compaq's machines are designed and made by the company itself in its plants in the US, Far East, and Europe. Recently, it has brought more manufacturing back to America. Compaq does not use other offshore manufacturers, even for its least expensive product ranges. The company has traditionally been an all-Intel vendor, but has recently started using AMD processors in some of its models.

### Compaq desktop product overview

Compaq's most entry-level desktop systems are found in its Presario range, which was first introduced in 1993. The Presario models are targeted at home users and very small businesses, and are sold through retail channels.

The product line that has done the most to turn around Compaq's fortunes in the past couple of years has been the ProLinea series of desktop PCs. Originally targeted at the most price-conscious buyers, these have now become Compaq's main offering for business users. The ProLinea models are very comparable to IBM's PS/ValuePoint series, which was introduced later as a direct response. Depending on where you buy your ProLinea, it may be offered with various bundled extras such as a mouse, preinstalled software, a fax modem, and so forth.

In general, the ProLineas are not primarily intended to appeal to performance buffs wanting a computer that wins every benchmark test. Rather, what makes them tempting is the fact that you can be pretty sure you're getting high quality at a fair (though probably not unbeatable) price — backed up by very widespread distribution and excellent support (which I'll be talking about shortly). With some lesser and/or financially troubled rivals, there's always the anxiety that component quality might have been compromised in the struggle to keep corporate heads above water. Compaq, by contrast, has maintained its reputation for technical excellence while it's been making its product line more attractive to price-conscious buyers.

The ProLinea series has eclipsed, though certainly not replaced, the Deskpro series of computers that are now targeted at power users wanting more expandability, modularity, and, in some cases, EISA architecture. The latest Deskpro models at the time of this writing were the Deskpro/XL ones: introduced in spring '94, these represent Compaq's first PCI-based line of computers. The Deskpro/XL has a unique keyboard containing a small speaker in the upper-right hand corner and a built-in volume control knob; a small microphone is located in the upper-left corner.

Finally, Compaq offers a variety of server products — at the time of this writing, its current lines were the ProLiant, ProSignia, and Systempro/XL systems, all of which come in a number of sometimes overlapping shapes and sizes. The newest servers are the ProLiant models, which were introduced in fall '93.

### Compaq notebook overview

Compaq has always given portable computers a major role in its overall product strategy, and it's a leader in this field. Compaq's most affordable notebooks are its Contura models. The Conturas are effectively the notebook siblings of the ProLinea desktops: they were introduced at the same time, they are targeted at the same sort of buyers, and they are sold through the same channels.

These are relatively straightforward machines — most of the Contura models do not have any form of internal trackball or pointing device, for example (though the Conturas are often sold with an external clip-on trackball included in the price). Minus points on all the Contura models include limited external video support (only bare-basics 640 x 480 resolution).

Compaq was quite late coming to the sub-notebook market: its first model, announced early in 1994, is the Compaq Contura Aero, an excellent 486SX unit weighing just 3.5 lbs and coming with a choice of monochrome or color passive-matrix screens. There are a number of remarkable things about the Aero, which manages to include an integrated mini-trackball within its compact dimensions. One is that it can be powered by a new type of rechargeable industry-standard Duracell NiMH battery — Compaq is the first vendor to use this type of battery which will later be compatible with a variety of notebook computers from other vendors. Previously, notebook batteries were almost always proprietary.

Compaq's more upmarket, full-size notebooks are found in its LTE/Elite series, which was introduced in February '94 as a replacement for the earlier LTE/Lite series. The new machines weigh 6.8 lbs — that may not sound remarkable, but what's unusual is that the weight includes the AC adapter box which is built into the machine itself instead of being an external unit as is usually the case. Compaq argues that the LTE/Elite weighs less than other powerful notebooks when you include the latters' external adapters; it also argues that it's less cumbersome for the adapter to be internal.

The LTE/Elites are pretty powerful notebooks — for example, the series includes Intel's new DX4/75MHz processor. They come with a range of display options, including a rare active-matrix black-and-white screen (reminiscent of those used by Apple on some of its PowerBooks). There are a variety of expansion options, including an advanced "VCR-style" docking station, and there are also a number of user-upgradable features, such as a removable hard drive and even user-upgradable processors.

All the LTE/Elite models come with one or two PCMCIA slots and have built-in trackballs (though, in my opinion, these are rather awkwardly positioned on the vertical right-hand side of the screen, rather than level with the keyboard). If you're looking for a high-end notebook for DOS/Windows applications, these machines could well prove to be your best bets.

Compaq's most distinctive notebook product is its Concerto, which was announced in September '93. The Concerto has an unusual, flexible design: it has an adjustable built-in handle that doubles as a stand, and it also comes with a fully detachable, slimline keyboard. This allows the user to independently position both the keyboard and screen, as with a desktop model.

Also unusual is that the Concerto can work with an optional electronic pen that writes directly on the screen; you can either use the pen in conjunction with the keyboard, or put the keyboard away so that the unit resembles an "electronic tablet" (note that "pen" input in this context does not mean "handwriting recognition" — it's a specialized tool for data input in niche applications).

### Compaq distribution, service, & support

The ProLinea and Contura models are sold through a wide range of reseller channels. Traditional computer dealers carry them, but you can also buy selected models through retail channels, including both business- and consumer-oriented warehouse stores. The Presario models are sold only through retail channels. Other Compaq products — including the Deskpro models, the server products, and the LTE/Elite notebooks — are sold through traditional computer reseller channels and can't be found in retail stores.

In addition, most Compaq computers can be bought from Compaq's own direct sales/mail order operation, which is called Compaq DirectPlus. However, DirectPlus does not carry the server products. Compaq also sells through a number of leading third-party mail order and catalog resellers, such as PCs Compleat.

Compaq's excellent service and support policies go under the name of CompaqCare. Compaq is the only major vendor to offer a three-year warranty on all its computers — even the least expensive entry-level models. With the desktop and most portable models, you get on-site service during the first year: in subsequent years, you have to pay extra if you want a technician to carry out repairs in your office or home. However, the server products come with three years of on-site service included in the price.

Some of Compaq's latest notebooks — the Contura Aero and the Concerto — do not have warranties with on-site service: you have to send these models back for express repair even during the first year. It appears that Compaq will only be offering on-site warranties on its more upscale notebook products in the future. In fairness, few other vendors offer on-site service warranties on any of their notebooks.

The on-site service program has been enhanced to guarantee next business day response. If you buy from Compaq DirectPlus, you get the added benefit of a 30-day money back guarantee (this is not normally available if you buy from dealers, except in the case of some mail order resellers). A variety of extended and enhanced service options are also available. Various fee-based programs are available for advanced network support.

All Compaq owners have access to toll-free technical phone support. This is available 24 hours a day, seven days a week. Overall, I rate Compaq service and support policies as outstanding.

### Summing up Compaq

**For:** *Great product range, stressing quality, performance, and value; outstanding support policies (including three-year warranties on all computers); stable company.* **Against:** *Budget models can be outperformed by less blue chip rivals; on-site warranty service being withdrawn from less expensive notebook models.* **Verdict:** *Very safe bet.*

# Dell

*Dell Computer Corporation*
*9505 Arboretum Boulevard*
*Austin, TX 78759–7299*
*Tel: 512 338 4400*
*Direct sales: 800 289 3355*

### Introduction

Dell Computer Corporation was started in 1984 by Michael Dell who operated out of the proverbial garage when he was still in college; today, it is a Fortune 500 company and its fiscal 1993 revenues were in excess of $2 billion. The company pioneered the concept of mail order/direct sales — cutting out the dealer middleman — and, more than any other vendor, made this channel respectable in corporate America.

Recently, however, Dell has gone through a rough patch. In 1993, the company ran up its first losses since becoming a public company. It was also forced to admit publicly that some of its internal management procedures and controls had ceased to work effectively — things like inventory control had been allowed to slip.

In addition, it made a complete botch of the notebook market and for most of 1993 did not have any products of merit in this fast-growing sector (by way of illustration, Dell's notebook sales in the third quarter of fiscal 1994 were a mere $5 million, versus $62 million in the same period a year previously). To make matters worse, in October 1993 Dell had to recall 17,000 of its discontinued 320/325SLi sub-notebooks when it was discovered that the machines bore a risk of spontaneously combusting due to faulty wiring on the motherboard. And in May 1994, the company recalled 63,000 monitors made by an unnamed Taiwanese supplier because of an overheating/fire problem.

All of this took some of the shine off Dell's image, which had previously been one of great efficiency, savvy, and financial stability. Nonetheless, the worst is probably past — management changes should improve the way the company runs itself and Dell is slowly getting back into the notebook market, as I explain below.

The secret of Dell's rapid rise to fame lay partly in competitive pricing, but, above all, in delivering an excellent support package: Dell was offering its customers on-site service and toll-free phone support years before companies such as IBM and Compaq felt obliged to do the same. Lately, however, other companies have caught up: though Dell's service is still first class, it's no longer so different from what you get from some of its competitors in both the direct sales and reseller channels. In certain respects, indeed, Dell has fallen behind — for example, Compaq offers three-year warranties on all its computers, while Dell doesn't offer the same on any of its own.

Nonetheless, Dell has always had a very good reputation for the quality of its service and support — for example, there have been fewer complaints about over-stretched support services than you get with vendors such as Gateway. In addition, Dell offers a wider range of service options than most of its competitors, as I show below.

Though Dell pioneered direct selling, and though it remains very firmly committed to the concept, it has since widened its distribution system. For example, some of its "value" products are sold through CompUSA, Staples, Sam's, and Price Club. However, most Dell systems continue to be sold direct.

Dell's manufacturing operation is more assembly-oriented than those of certain rivals — Compaq, IBM, and AST, for example. Certain budget models are largely made by offshore suppliers working under contract to Dell. And, as I show below, Dell also relies on another PC manufacturer for its new notebook products.

## Dell product overview

In spring '94, the following product ranges made up Dell's desktop and server offerings:

❑ **Dimension series:** "Value" products.

❑ **Precision:** Broadly comparable to the Dimension models in terms of specifications, but sold only through retail channels (occasionally, certain Dimension models also turn up in retail locations).

❑ **Dimension XPS:** More powerful ISA-based, systems; emphasis on multimedia options.

❑ **OptiPlex series:** High-performance ISA-based 486/ Pentium systems, with emphasis on network-ready options and upgradability/modularity; replaced Dell's former Performance series.

❑ **Netplex:** Network-ready desktop PCs.

❑ **Power Edge & OmniPlex series:** Upscale servers.

## Dell notebook overview

In February '94, Dell re-entered the notebook market, from which it had effectively departed a year earlier as a result of difficulties in getting new products ready for the market. The new models are called the Latitude series. These are mid-market notebooks, which are decent but not terribly exciting — certainly, they are not a great monument to what Dell has achieved in its exile from the notebook market, not least because they are actually made for Dell by AST; they are somewhat similar to models in AST's own Bravo line.

Dell was likely to introduce new and more interesting notebooks later in 1994. There have been rumors that it will introduce a new sub-notebook which will be manufactured by Sony.

## Dell service & support

All Dell owners enjoy toll-free technical support for as long as they own the equipment; this is available seven days a week, 24 hours a day. The company calls this "Dell OpenLine." All of Dell's desktop and server products now come with next-day/on-site service included in the one-year warranty (with the usual exceptions about out-of-the way locations); the second-day service policy, which used to be offered on certain less expensive systems, has been discontinued. Like other vendors, Dell asks notebook users to return their products for express warranty repair. All products are sold with the 30-day money-back guarantee that's normal in the mail order market.

Dell is the only vendor to absolutely guarantee next-day

service visits to customers whose computers are under warranty or service contract. Should this fail to materialize, you are compensated with a one-month extension of your warranty or current service agreement. Furthermore, owners of OptiPlex, NetPlex, or server products calling for phone support are guaranteed either that they will talk to a technical specialist within five minutes or that one will call back within an hour; if neither of these happens, you get a check for $25 (certain conditions apply).

There are a wide range of enhanced and extended optional service plans catering to the needs of both smaller and larger businesses. For example, you can buy warranty extensions that run for up to five years. If you are a computer novice, you can pay $119 to have a technician visit to set up your computer when you first buy it and spend a bit of time explaining both it and the Windows operating environment. Larger offices can pay $299 to have someone visit and spend a day setting up a network and providing training.

If you want your new computer to be completely ready-to-run when you take it out of the box, you can buy software from Dell and have them install it for you before the equipment is shipped. Dell calls this service "ReadyWare," and offers it with over 100 popular software packages (do not confuse this with the bundled software that comes "free" and preloaded on many computers, but which you don't get to choose). There's a $15 installation charge covering any number of packages on a single machine — plus the cost of the software itself. In some cases, you'd save money buying the same programs from other vendors (particularly specialized software catalogs), but in other instances Dell offers very good prices — especially when it's a special promotion linked to a particular computer.

In addition to its main computer catalog selling PC hardware under the Dell brand name, there's also a completely separate catalog called *DellWare* which offers peripherals, software, and accessories under their own brand names. *DellWare* is run independently of Dell's main computer mail order business. It is, in effect, an alternative to computer catalogs such as *MicroWarehouse* and *The PC Zone* that I discussed earlier in this chapter in the section on how to go about buying computers.

### Summing up Dell

**For:** *The pioneer of the direct sales/mail order channel; very good reputation for service and support.* **Against:** *At press-time, only had a limited notebook range, following difficulties in keeping up to speed in this sector; no longer quite as blue-chip financially as* *it used to be.* **Verdict:** *Dell continues to be a good choice for desktop PC buyers wanting excellent support, but the company's recent troubles have tarnished its reputation for doing everything right.*

# Gateway

*Gateway 2000 Inc.*
*610 Gateway Drive*
*N. Sioux City, SD 57049*
*Tel: 605 232 2000*
*Direct sales: 800 846 2000*

### Introduction

Gateway is a direct sales/mail order PC manufacturer that made it from nowhere to Fortune 500 level in about nine years. It was founded in 1985 by Ted Waitt, a self-described maverick who strayed from his family's four-generation cattle business. Waitt set up offices on his family farm, a welcome contrast to the usual suburban garage origins of computer whiz-kids.

Today, Gateway still prides itself on being located in a low-cost, farm-belt part of the country, far away from the glitter of Silicon Valley. To reinforce the point, some of its advertisements show photographs of cows. Indicative of the company's "outsider" style is the fact that it never exhibits at any of the computer industry's trade shows. The company makes a point of trading on an "anti-establishment" (their words) image — some of its latest ads, when not featuring cows, show hippies using its equipment.

Still, a lot of pretty straight-laced business and government buyers choose Gateway, which has achieved a reputation for coupling very aggressive pricing with high-performance specifications. Gateway maintains that it achieves low prices by slashing overheads, not by compromising the quality of what it sells.

In December '93, the previously privately-held company went public. Lately, Gateway's revenues have been growing rapidly, and in 1993 they passed $1.7 billion, up from $1.1 billion the year before. However, there have been signs that Gateway may have increased its sales faster than it has expanded its service and support organization — more on this shortly.

### Gateway product overview

Unlike almost all other vendors of its size, Gateway offers a single product line: it does not have parallel and overlapping lines with their own brand identities — some offering higher specifications and more comprehensive support, the others lower prices and slightly reduced support. Instead, Gateway's approach is to sell a single line of computers, containing about three tiers, but all with very generous hardware specifications and all offered with a middle-of-the-road service package.

Gateway has lately started paying more attention to networking — in fact, it is the only major PC vendor to ship all of its products, even notebooks, with Windows for Workgroups preinstalled as standard. In addition, buyers can order products with Ethernet and other network cards preinstalled. In the past, Gateway computers were somewhat ungainly in appearance: today, however, they are quite nice-looking with an unusual, slightly curved front.

Gateway was late coming to the notebook market, but now has a fairly strong product range. Its most recent and alluring products are its Colorbook notebooks. The company's Handbook sub-notebooks are among the lightest around, and are undoubtedly good values, but you may be put off by the somewhat long, rectangular shape of the display which can distort images.

### Gateway service & support

Gateway has good service and support policies, though these aren't quite as comprehensive as those offered by Compaq, IBM, or Dell — and there is evidence that the company is not always as efficient at executing them as it should be.

All of its desktop computers come with a one-year warranty, including on-site service. However, there is no specific guarantee as to how long the service will take to arrive — the company's advertising makes no mention of "next-day" or "second-day" policies. Gateway tells me that service is "usually" within two business days.

With the notebook computers, on-site service is not included in the warranty, and users have to send machines back for repair. Again, there is no specific guarantee as to length of turnaround, though my impression is that it generally takes a few days plus shipping times (though you can get expedited service at extra cost).

Toll-free technical support is available for as long as you own the equipment; lines are open 18 hours a day, Monday through Friday, and for half the day on Saturdays. As with other mail order vendors, there's a 30-day money-back guarantee on all machines.

While Gateway's support policies seem reasonable on paper, user reports sometimes speak of unacceptable delays in getting through to the company's support lines, poor follow-up of problems, delays in shipping systems and parts, chronic backorders on certain products, and other organizational short-comings. Early in 1993, the company conceded that some of these problems existed and stated its commitment to addressing them; however, the signs were that they had not gone away entirely by spring of '94.

In fairness to Gateway, few people complain about the quality of its equipment. The complaints about support may prove to be temporary, though they are indicative of the problem faced by fast-growing PC vendors when it comes to keeping up with the rising expectations of users at a time when margins are at an all-time low.

### Summing-up Gateway

**For:** *Low prices; very generous hardware specifications; big-name vendor.* **Against:** *Support policies not as precise as those offered by Compaq, IBM, or Dell; user reports indicate difficulties in consistently delivering the level of support promised.* **Verdict:** *Gateway can generally be counted on to offer a heck of a lot of computer for the money; the equipment is first class, though the support is coach.*

# IBM

*IBM Corporation*
*Old Orchard Road*
*Armonk, NY 10504*
*Tel: 800 426 2468*
*Direct sales: 800 426 2968*

### Introduction

IBM — a.k.a. "Big Blue" — has been much in the news during the past two years, not always for the reasons it would like. Although it has revamped its presence in the PC market — in the process slaughtering some of its sacred cows — much of the company's publicity has concerned its staggering losses and massive layoffs.

In the mid-eighties, IBM was enjoying boom years. In 1984, it posted record profits, earning $6.6 billion on sales of $46 billion. Even as recently as 1990, its profits were not too far behind.

Since then, the company's fortunes have tumbled, as the PC price war wiped out margins, and sales of its expensive mainframes began to erode with the onslaught of ever-better PC-based local area networks. Early in 1993, IBM announced losses of $4.7 billion — the largest annual corporate loss ever (a record it only held for about two weeks, until General Motors released its 1992 results).

Even before the scale of these losses became apparent, IBM had begun to take an axe to its costs. IBM used to be the sort of company where, once you were hired, you had a job for life unless you were caught with your hands in the till. Today, whole layers of management are being dispensed with mercilessly. The company, which once insisted that all of its male employees wear white shirts, is now more concerned with getting rid of people than telling them how to dress.

There are signs that the worst may be over. The company's PC division has become nimbler and much more competitive. And early in spring '94, IBM as a whole began reporting its first profits for about three years. But with a large part of the company's fortunes still linked to the mainframe business, the payroll still larger than IBM's top management wants it to be, and the PC market become more and more of a commodity business, Big Blue's future size and market still seem uncertain.

### The rise and fall of the IBM PC
#### (or: Why the term "IBM-compatible" no longer means anything)
Most of the PC vendors discussed in this chapter began life in the 1980s. At the start of that decade, companies like Compaq and Dell didn't exist, nor did the personal computer (if you define the PC as a single-user computer conforming to industry standards).

IBM's history, by contrast, goes back to the early part of the century, when its founder, Thomas J. Watson, used questionable business practices to dominate the cash register market in many large cities. The company went on to use more mainstream business methods to develop computer technology, and it became the undisputed world leader of the business computer market — though its success sometimes owed more to marketing savvy than to technical superiority.

Either way, IBM's dominance of the computer market was so complete that when it launched its first personal computer — the original IBM PC — in 1981, that machine was bound to set the standard that other manufacturers would try to follow. And follow they did.

The critical parts of the IBM PC were not invented or manufactured by IBM itself. The hardware components — such as the Intel processors at the heart of the system — were readily available to other PC assemblers.

And the operating software was bought from a small start-up company called Microsoft, whose founder — a techie in his early twenties named Bill Gates — told IBM that he wanted to be able to sell his product to other PC manufacturers as well. IBM, in what must count as one of the most momentous decisions of its history, agreed (who would have thought then that, about 12 years later, Microsoft would overtake IBM in stock market value?).

Thus was born an open industry standard — simply because other computer companies could, legally, build machines that matched IBM's own in all vital respects.

In the years that followed, numerous companies introduced PCs that were dubbed "IBM-compatible," which meant they could use the same software and peripherals as IBM's own. Some manufacturers tried to score performance points over IBM's products, some tried to undercut IBM, and most attempted a combination of the two. IBM was able to handle this challenge, because none of the clone makers of the early- to mid-eighties managed to come close to Big Blue itself in terms of sheer corporate clout. In fact, the clone makers helped IBM, by enlarging the market for PCs and underlining the fact that IBM's standard was king — every time a clone maker claimed to be "IBM-compatible," it was paying an implicit compliment to the market leader.

After a while, however, the term "IBM-compatible" began to be a problem for Big Blue. It was one thing having small obscure companies paying you homage by legally cloning your machines. But it began to get worrisome when those clone makers gradually became very successful businesses in their own right, little by little edging their way into corporate America.

The first clone maker to become a serious force was Compaq. IBM could handle Compaq, but what it couldn't handle was a subtle change in the minds of buyers around the end of the eighties and the start of the nineties. That was when people increasingly began to think of products not as being "IBM-compatible," but instead began to regard IBM as just one of many manufacturers making computers that were DOS- or Windows-compatible.

The industry standard was being redefined around Microsoft. It was as though someone had thrown a party, to which so many people turned up uninvited, and which went on for so long, that people eventually began to think of it independently of the host, and then began to abuse the host for being a stuck-up hanger-on.

Today, buyers have moved on from talking about getting a

better deal than they can from IBM. They simply talk about getting the best deal they can on a machine that can run the software written for the industry standard. IBM became partly marginalized in the industry that it did so much to galvanize — though it has lately done its best to bounce back.

### MCA and PS/2

Although IBM originally set the industry standard for personal computing, it has since departed from it to some extent in an attempt to differentiate itself from the so-called "clones." After seeing its market share erode in the mid/late 1980s, IBM tried unsuccessfully to reassert its grip on the market in 1988 when it introduced its PS/2 range, the first fundamental relaunch of its personal computer series since the original PC was introduced in 1982. For several years, PS/2 was the company's only PC range targeted at business users, though it has since been repositioned as a premium line.

The main difference about PS/2, then and now, is that it uses a proprietary bus architecture that is only partly compatible with the original industry standard still used by the bulk of the industry (if you are puzzled by what I mean by "bus architecture," you should read the explanation in the features section earlier in this chapter). Called "Micro Channel Architecture" (MCA), this delivers enhanced performance, but the downside is that it is incompatible with the add-on expansion boards used by industry standard personal computers.

In introducing MCA, IBM was mindful of the lesson it had learned with the open architecture of the original IBM PC. By making MCA a proprietary standard, it ensured that other computer companies couldn't adopt it without paying a royalty. IBM hoped that the rest of the computer industry would follow the leader, just as they had in 1982, but that this time clone makers would pull out their checkbooks and make regular payments to Big Blue for the privilege. The idea was that even if users ended up choosing non-IBM brand computers, IBM would profit anyway. Unfortunately for IBM, things did not work out that way.

By the late 1980s, the clone makers were feeling pretty established and confident. So when IBM came up with MCA, they weren't too keen on falling into line and doing what they were told. Instead, they got together and — led by Compaq — set up their own rival enhanced standard called "Extended Industry Standard Architecture" (EISA). This is comparable to MCA in performance terms, but it is compatible with industry standard architecture expansion boards.

As it turned out, buyers were not overly impressed with either EISA or MCA. Contrary to what pundits predicted, most decided to stick with the original industry standard architecture (ISA), which is still used on a large majority of machines sold today (albeit increasingly in tandem with so-called local bus architecture which I spoke about earlier in the discussion of PC features). ISA machines are less expensive and — used in conjunction with a local bus — can be powerful enough to satisfy most requirements.

Despite this, IBM remained committed to MCA — so much so that until 1992, almost all of its machines relied on it. Even now, the PS/2 desktop and server series is virtually all-MCA, though the company has introduced less expensive product ranges that revert to ISA (more on this shortly) — and the latest indications are that it is preparing to ditch MCA entirely. Most of IBM's leading rivals sell EISA machines at the top of their ranges. For a while, a few did what IBM wanted and also paid royalties to produce MCA clones — but not many were sold and, subsequently, the cloned MCA computer vanished almost entirely.

### IBM and OS/2

IBM has been trying to differentiate itself from the market in other respects too. In particular, it has shown persistence — some say stubbornness — in sticking to OS/2, the Windows-like operating system it began to develop with Microsoft several years ago. While Microsoft has pulled out of supporting OS/2, putting all of its eggs in the DOS/Windows basket, IBM continues to insist that OS/2 is the wave of the future, citing the fact that it is more powerful than Windows (which it is).

Lately, IBM has sunk massive funds into promoting OS/2, and there are signs that the system is gaining more acceptance among large corporate users in particular. However, it seems unlikely that OS/2 will come close to Windows in terms of market share. Of course, all IBM PCs can also run DOS/Windows, just as OS/2 can run on non-IBM computers — so by choosing IBM, you are not committing yourself to OS/2 (or vice versa).

### Other IBM idiosyncrasies

Another respect in which IBM tries to separate itself from the crowd is in its floppy disk technology. Even in an age of large hard drives and computer networks, the floppy disk still has an important role in providing an easy medium for transporting data and software.

IBM — which several years ago was the first manufacturer

to abandon the 5.25" format in favor of 3.5" floppies — now supplies some PS/2 models with floppy drives that can take 2.8MB disks, instead of the usual 1.4MB ones. That sounds like an advantage, until you remember that in a mixed vendor computer environment, compatibility is everything. It really isn't helpful to have some PCs in your office using one type of floppy, and others taking different ones.

Another IBM difference is that the company uses its own versions of certain Intel processors in some of its computers, especially the more powerful ones. This is because it makes them under license from Intel itself. Again, the blessing can be mixed from the buyer's point of view — it makes it harder to make like-for-like comparisons with other brands of PCs.

### IBM desktop & server overview

Since reorganizing, IBM has revamped its PC product range, by dividing it into three separate brands:

❑ *PS/2*
The PS/2 line still continues as the upscale brand for large corporate users. All PS/2 desktops and towers currently use MCA architecture. Though PS/2 is not specifically tied to OS/2, IBM tends to market both in tandem.

For the most part, PS/2 computers remain expensive — they are not obvious choices for the typical office wanting computers for routine business applications on a standalone or smaller network basis. (This does not apply to IBM's ThinkPad notebook computers, some of which fall under the PS/2 umbrella — I'll be talking more about them shortly.) In fact, I have heard a figure — unconfirmed — that as few as 200 major corporations account for as much as 80 percent of PS/2 desktop and server sales.

At the time of this writing (June '94), there was widespread speculation in the PC industry about the future of PS/2. IBM seems to be coming around to the view that the MCA architecture has begun to near the end of its useful life: it seems likely that the company will slowly phase it out in favor of an industry-standard PCI bus. At presstime, the company had not formally acknowledged this — but it was about to start merging the PS/2 and ValuePoint (see below) lines into one from an organizational and marketing perspective. Technical problems had already led to delays in announcing PS/2 Premium, which is the first new PS/2 product line since September 1992.

### ❑ *PS/ValuePoint*

The centerpiece of IBM's product strategy is now its PS/ValuePoint series. First introduced in fall '92, this is targeted at the mainstream business PC market. It represents a huge climbdown by the company — one of the most blatant U-turns in recent business history. Using ISA architecture, ValuePoint is effectively an admission by IBM that it got it wrong by staking all on MCA. The ValuePoints substantially outsell the PS/2 models.

The PS/ValuePoint family is similar to the Compaq ProLinea line. There is little about the machines that's particularly special — these computers are, effectively, IBM's clones of the clones. But their very ordinariness is what's making them popular among mainstream PC buyers who previously felt that IBM had little to offer. With PS/ValuePoint, IBM computers are better values than they have been in recent memory. However, determined price chasers and performance buffs can still often find better deals elsewhere.

### ❑ *PS/1*

At about the same time that IBM introduced ValuePoint, it also relaunched its entry-level PS/1 line. This brand had been around for a while as IBM's offering to small office/home office ("SOHO") buyers. However, it had flunked because IBM made the mistake of imagining that SOHO buyers only wanted something simple and unpowerful to run somewhat trivial software. They didn't: today's home computer buyer typically expects a machine that matches or exceeds the capabilities of what he or she works with at the office.

The revamped and much improved PS/1 line mainly covers desktops, though there are also some notebooks sold under the PS/note brand name (not to be confused with the company's much better ThinkPad notebooks that I'll be talking about shortly). The PS/1 desktops are, for the most part, quite similar to the ValuePoint line in terms of the type of hardware they contain — the main differences are the distribution channels, the support arrangements, and the things they are bundled with.

The distribution is geared towards retail and consumer electronics channels, while the support is more limited than it is with the ValuePoint series (I'll be talking more about support shortly). In addition, the PS/1 products come bundled with more extras, such as applications software and modems. There are several different bundles available, but all tend to stress software and accessories likely to appeal to small business users.

IBM has introduced various "sub-brands" to distinguish those PS/1 models bundled with the most extras from the ones that come with fewer. The largest range of goodies comes with the so-called PS/1 Essential models; you get less on the PS/1 Expert models; fewer still with the PS/1 Consultant models; and least with the models that are sold as PS/1 pure and simple. All of this means that there are numerous variant models in the PS/1 series, though most retailers only carry a handful. Don't expect stylish looks if you choose a PS/1 computer, incidentally: they have a somewhat rudimentary, boxish appearance.

### IBM notebook overview

For a long time, IBM seemed incapable of producing decent portable computers. Throughout the whole of the laptop era, and the early days of the notebook market, it sold machines that lagged substantially behind the competition in just about every respect. Every time IBM introduced a new model, it seemed to be catching up with where other vendors had been a year or so earlier. The issue became symbolic of IBM's cumbersome product development process.

When IBM started to fight back in the PC industry in the second half of 1992, getting its act together in the fast-growing notebook market was a high priority. Today, few would dispute that it has succeeded: for the first time ever, IBM's portable range includes models that are numbered among the most desirable in their class. The notebooks that have revived IBM's reputation are the ones that it markets under the ThinkPad brand name.

Some people find this identity confusing, because the term "pad," when used in the context of portable computers, generally implies a pen-based product (pen computers are specialized devices used mainly for niche applications involving mobile data collection). To further complicate matters, the first product that IBM ever introduced under the ThinkPad name was, indeed, a pen computer. Today, however, the brand principally contains mainstream notebook PCs.

Aside from the pen-based model, there were several products in the ThinkPad line at the time of this writing. None include a built-in trackball, but all come with an interesting substitute that IBM calls "Trackpoint II." This is a small rubber button — it looks like an eraser at the end of a pencil — located in the middle of the keyboard within the circle formed by the

"G," "H," and "B" keys. The idea is that you use your index finger to wiggle it and control the position of your screen pointer. The clicker keys are located just below the spacebar, where they can be accessed easily with the thumb of the same hand that's manipulating the rubber key.

Like most new types of mouse substitute, Trackpoint II takes a little getting used to — but it's actually easy to use and quite effective. I consider it to be a clever idea and among the best solutions to the "what-to-use-instead-of-a-mouse-without-taking-up-too-much-space-on-a-notebook?" dilemma.

### IBM & the PowerPC

As I explained earlier in this chapter, IBM is a partner with Motorola and Apple in the development of the PowerPC, the new super-fast processor that is challenging Intel's Pentium. However, while Apple is making its position on the PowerPC very clear — i.e., that it plans to use it throughout its product range — IBM is planning on selling PowerPC systems alongside Intel-based equipment. Only one part of IBM — the division called Power Personal Systems — is wedded to the PowerPC, whereas all of Apple is organizationally loyal to the new processor.

At press-time, IBM had not announced its first PowerPC products. When it does (later in 1994), it seems that they will initially be targeted at niche workstation applications — in other words, at the technical and scientific market requiring super-high performance. It remains to be seen how actively IBM will push the new platform in conjunction with its OS/2 operating system towards the mainstream high-performance PC market.

It is possible that IBM's PowerPC products will be able to run Apple software — following Apple's decision to license its operating system — but the word is that this may be some way off because of certain technical incompatibilities between the two companies' PowerPC product lines. Instead, buyers should look for IBM PowerPC systems that run its new Workplace OS operating software, OS/2 (and, therefore, DOS/Windows), and AIX/Unix (see the discussion on operating software earlier in this chapter for brief descriptions of where all these fit into the big picture). It is not clear whether IBM will eventually sell PowerPC products that run DOS/Windows without OS/2.

The word is that IBM's direct sales/mail order operation (discussed below) will carry PowerPC products, indicating — perhaps — that the new platform may not be reserved for too narrow an audience. Nonetheless, the part of IBM that makes Intel-based equipment will effectively be competing against the part that uses the PowerPC, and it remains to be seen how comfortable this will work out in practice.

### Ambra — the other IBM

In 1993, IBM took a further step towards multi-level marketing by introducing a totally new brand called Ambra which is sold and operated completely independently of the IBM brand. Ambra is intended to be a direct challenge to the so-called clone makers. Products sold under this brand name are made for IBM by a third-party supplier in Asia and generally use processors made by Advanced Micro Devices (AMD), marking a break with IBM's traditionally close ties with Intel.

The Ambra experiment does not seem to have been a rip-roaring success, and some users have reported frustration at dealing with the new operation, citing delays in shipping and lost orders. Early in 1994, IBM shut down its Ambra business in Europe, where it was launched a year before it came to the US. It remains to be seen whether the American Ambra is here to stay.

### IBM starts selling direct

As part of its overall revamping, IBM has introduced a direct sales/mail order operation covering its PS/ValuePoint and ThinkPad (notebook) products. IBM PC Direct — as the division is known — is a parallel channel to the resellers which still account for the bulk of sales. You may sometimes be able to get better prices if you buy from a dealer, but don't count on big differences: the margins that dealers have on the ValuePoint products are low, making it hard for them to offer significantly better deals than you can get from IBM itself.

With IBM PC Direct's new "Net Select" option, customers can order entire built-to-order networks over the phone. IBM promises to get them up-and-running before shipping them, to ensure that they work.

### IBM service & support

Not so very long ago, IBM used to adopt a very standoffish approach to its end users. Unless you were a very large customer, they didn't really want to know you and all support was the responsibility of dealers. Now, as part of IBM's rebirth as a PC vendor, the company offers a service package — HelpWare — that ranks among the best in the industry. The level of support depends on the product range you're looking at. Here are the details:

❑ **PS/2 service:** The best deal of all is offered with the PS/2 series. Here, buyers get a three-year warranty on all machines. Unlike the three-year warranty offered by Compaq, this includes on-site service throughout the warranty period, not just in the first year. (Though, to be fair, Compaq's more limited three-year warranty is offered throughout its product line, not just on its premium models.) IBM quotes an average response time of just four hours on PS/2 service calls — so you can expect a technician to turn up on the day you make the request, or, at worst, on the next day.

There's also toll-free technical assistance for as long as you own the equipment. This is available 24 hours a day, seven days a week. I consider the PS/2 service package to be the best that comes standard with any product range, from any vendor. Just remember that the PS/2 machines are premium choices — most buyers tempted by IBM will want to focus on the less expensive ValuePoint line.

❑ *PS/ValuePoint service:* The service package offered on ValuePoint is not as generous, though it's still very good. You get a one-year warranty, which includes same-day or next-day on-site service. You also get the same toll-free, round-the-clock phone support for as long as you own the equipment. A unique benefit offered to both PS/ValuePoint and PS/2 buyers is a 30-day money-back-if-not-completely-satisfied guarantee: no other manufacturer offers this when selling through dealers (though it is routinely offered in direct sales/mail order channels).

❑ *PS/1 service:* The PS/1 product line comes with a more limited support package. The one-year warranty does not include on-site service — you have to send your machine back for repair. You can either send it back to the dealer or direct to IBM — if you choose the latter, you're promised 48-hour turnaround (plus shipping times) and they may either fix the old machine or send you a new one.

PS/1 owners do now get round-the-clock phone support on a toll-free number — this is relatively new, as there was no phone support offered on PS/1 products until not long ago. However, you don't get the 30-day money-back offer that applies to the other IBM PS product lines.

❑ *ThinkPad service:* Service on the ThinkPad notebooks corresponds to that of PS/ValuePoint or PS/2, depending on the model (except that the three-year warranty on the most expensive models only includes on-site service for the first year).

### Summing up IBM
**For:** *Very good service/support on PS/ValuePoint; excellent service/support policies on PS/2 models; competitive (though not unbeatable) pricing on PS/ValuePoint; notebook range includes interesting features; choice of buying direct from IBM or through a reseller.* **Against:** *PS/2 models are expensive and non-industry standard; PS/2 future looks uncertain; PS/1 models do not come with on-site service warranties; IBM still seems unstable.* **Verdict:** *IBM is a much better choice now than it has been for several years.*

# Leading Edge
Leading Edge Products Inc.
117 Flanders Road
Westborough, MA 01581–5020
Tel: 508 836 4800

### Introduction
Leading Edge focuses mainly on the lower and middle sectors of the business computer market, and on the home market, and it pursues an aggressive pricing policy. It describes its mission as "providing generous features at a low price." The company falls into the category of PC vendor that aims to be a source, not a developer, of advanced technology; it makes little effort to drive the technology forward itself.

The company was formed in the early 1980s by a US entrepreneur who had earlier made a lot of money in blue jeans. It had something of a roller-coaster existence until finding stability under the ownership of Daewoo, the $28-billion Korean conglomerate.

Leading Edge products are sold entirely through dealers, computer stores, and other resellers. There are no direct sales of any type. The brand is prominent in discount channels and you often find Leading Edge computers in consumer electronics stores, piled up high next to TVs and microwave ovens. Leading Edge claims to rank number-five in retail-channel market share.

### Leading Edge product overview
There are a large number of models at any given time — including desktops, mini-towers, and special multimedia systems — but all are variants of a smaller number of core machines and most retailers and dealers only carry a handful. The desktop models are known as the WinPro series, and the towers are called WinTowers. Leading Edge computers are usually sold with bundled software.

Unlike many of its competitors, Leading Edge has not developed parallel product lines for the budget-conscious and performance-seeking sectors of the market: it maintains a unitary brand image and, in practice, targets price chasers more than performance buffs.

Street prices for Leading Edge desktops can be hard to beat: while Leading Edge's computers can be outclassed in the detail, they are not often significantly undercut by any vendor of standing that has comparable distribution. Leading Edge also sells a number of notebooks: these tend to be less widely available than its desktops and not particularly exciting.

### Leading Edge service & support

Leading Edge has been obliged to upgrade its previously not very good service and support arrangements, to keep up with the general trend in the market for dealer-channel vendors to take more direct care of their end users. All desktop and mini-tower buyers are now offered a one-year warranty that includes next-day, on-site service.

Alternatively, buyers can select a two-year warranty that requires them to take their computer back to one of 800 authorized service centers for repair (usually that means taking it back to a dealer) — you have to pick which warranty you want at the time of purchase. Keep in mind that there are no published guarantees as to how long service center repairs will take. Notebook owners always have to return their machine to a service center. Warranty extensions are available for up to 12 months.

The company now has a toll-free technical support line. This is only open Monday through Friday, 11 hours a day. Since a large proportion of Leading Edge's customers buy their computers for home use, it would have been nicer to have had some phone support on weekends and longer into the weekday evenings.

### Summing up Leading Edge

**For:** *Low prices; widespread availability; improved service and support; very big company behind Leading Edge.* **Against:** *No direct sales/mail order option for buyers who prefer that channel; Leading Edge desktops and mini-towers tend to stress price, rather than the ultimate in performance refinement; notebook products tend to be fairly dull; phone support keeps banker's hours.* **Verdict:** *Can be a good choice for retail channel shoppers on tight budgets looking for a lot of computer from a stable vendor.*

# Packard Bell

*Packard Bell Inc.*
*9425 Canoga Avenue*
*Chatsworth, CA 91311*
*Tel: 800 773 5858*

## Introduction

Packard Bell is a major force in the lower end of the computer market — though in common with other vendors serving small business and home users, it's making its machines increasingly powerful realizing that so-called "small" users of equipment can still have demanding requirements.

Packard Bell's history goes all the way back to the 1950s, when it was a major TV manufacturer and a pioneer of color sets. It entered the computer market in the 1960s, but was not a major force in PCs until the late 1980s when it was acquired from Teledyne in a leveraged buy-out which brought in a new management team and a change of direction. Despite its name, the company has no connection with either Hewlett-Packard or the Bell telephone companies.

Packard Bell is an all dealer vendor (a brief experiment in direct sales/mail order was abandoned following disappointing results and complaints from dealers). Though it does chase some large accounts — in the government sector, for example — it is most prominent in the retail channel that caters to small businesses and home offices. Packard Bell claims to occupy more shelf space in the mass merchant channel than any other vendor. Its sales in 1993 exceeded $1.25 billion.

Packard Bell PCs tend to be very aggressively priced: in fact, the pricing is often almost as low as you can get from a vendor with an established brand name. While Packard Bell has never sought to lead the market in technology refinement, no one can doubt its track record as a leader in value.

## The Zenith Data connection

In mid-1993, Packard Bell formed a new alliance with Zenith Data Systems (ZDS): the two companies agreed to jointly manufacture desktop and notebook PCs, and ZDS's parent company took an almost 20 percent stake in Packard Bell. ZDS is no longer part of Zenith of TV and consumer appliance fame, but is now owned by Groupe Bull, a loss-making, French government-supported computer company.

ZDS has one of the most interesting and well-designed notebook ranges on the market. Its products often appeal most to larger corporate buyers: this is partly because some models come standard with built-in network adapters and networking software. The company is also present in the desktop PC market, but doesn't have a high profile there. Sales — other than to major accounts — used to be mainly through dealers, but the company has lately been spending heavily to promote a new direct sales/mail order operation called Z-Direct.

The new alliance looks promising: Packard Bell gains a strong notebook range to sell under its own colors (previously its notebooks were pretty nondescript), while ZDS obtains a source for more competitive desktop PCs as well as a share in a strong retail brand. In addition, the deal strengthens Packard Bell's finances which had begun to look shaky as a result of PC price wars.

### Packard Bell product overview

There are numerous different Packard Bell desktop models, even though a lot of them are very similar to each other — a while ago, I got a news release from the company headed: "Packard Bell launches 60 new 486 systems." The reason is that the company prefers to have differentiated models for specific distribution channels and major resellers. The company also offers entry-level tower servers.

Many of its products are sold bundled with extras such as software, modems, mice, etc.; details of what's in the bundle vary by distribution channel and individual retailer. Lately, Packard Bell has begun selling some desktops that come preconfigured for Windows for Workgroups — both the networking software and the network adapters are preinstalled.

Packard Bell's notebook range has gotten more interesting of late, as a consequence of the ZDS partnership discussed above.

### Packard Bell service & support

All of Packard Bell's desktops and towers come with a one-year warranty with on-site service. If your Packard Bell notebook needs fixing, you have to send it back; notebook repairs are turned around within 48 hours of the machine reaching the factory.

There is toll-free technical support available 24 hours a day/seven days a week, though I've heard some pretty negative feedback about how easy it is to get through. Furthermore, the toll-free support number is only intended for questions relating to the hardware itself. For "basic software installation and trouble-shooting questions," you have to call a toll-number. For more complex software questions (including those relating to DOS/Windows) — or to bypass the waits on the other numbers

— users are offered a 900 number which is charged at $3 for the first minute and $1.65 for each additional minute.

The use of 900 numbers for technical support is controversial and will not prove welcome with many users. In fairness to Packard Bell, it's always a gray area as to the extent to which a PC vendor is duty-bound to provide support on software that is bundled with its hardware. Many vendors are willing to provide basic assistance with the operating software, but refer you to the software publishers themselves for assistance with applications programs.

On the other hand, Packard Bell specifically offers the 900 number as a means of not only obtaining advanced software support, but also for receiving faster help on any matter. It could be argued that buyers are being charged a premium for prompt support to which they feel entitled anyway.

According to Packard Bell, the average cost of a call on the 900 number is $17; if a support person is not available instantly when you call, you get a busy signal, so you won't find yourself paying 900-number rates while on hold. Packard Bell is the first major PC vendor to use a 900 number for technical support. Keep in mind that many business phone systems are programmed to block 900-number calls.

### Summing up Packard Bell

**For:** *Widespread availability; low prices; lots of extras usually included in the price.* **Against:** *Support policies not as well executed as those from Compaq, Dell, etc.; confusing multiplicity of products.* **Verdict:** *Can be a decent choice for price chasers shopping in retail channels.*

## Texas Instruments

*Texas Instruments Inc.*
*PO Box 202230, ITG-009*
*Austin, TX 78720–2230*
*Tel: 800 527 3500*

### Introduction

Texas Instruments (TI) is a high-tech conglomerate with fingers in pies ranging from semi-conductors to defense systems. It was an early player in portable computing, and today has an excellent notebook product range backed by strong distribution. It does not sell desktop PCs. All sales are through dealers — there is no direct sales/mail order option.

### Texas Instruments product overview

TI calls its notebooks the TravelMate (TM) series. The range is biased towards the higher end of the market: the company started concentrating exclusively on 486 series products when some of its rivals were still immersed in 386 notebooks. TI can generally be counted on to sell nice-looking, powerful, and well-designed notebooks that offer good value to those willing to spend what it takes to get an upscale machine.

In most respects, these notebooks compare well with the best on the market (battery performance is generally pretty good, for example) — my only serious reservation is that none of the ones available at the time of this writing had any form of built-in trackball or any other integrated pointing device. Instead, every TravelMate comes with the rather bulky Microsoft BallPoint trackball which clips onto the side. This bothers some people more than others, but the omission may be rectified on new models released during the shelf-life of this book.

Another thing lacking in the TI range as it stood at press-time is a sub-notebook. On the plus side, TI offers an intelligent docking station — this is slightly reminiscent of Apple's class-leading Duo Dock, though not quite as elegant.

### Texas Instruments service & support

TI offers one-year warranties on its notebooks. These do not include on-site service — but, to be fair, that is still the exception rather than the rule in the notebook arena.

If you have a problem with your computer, your first point of contact is with TI's own technical support line; using an 800 number, this is available five days a week, 10 hours a day, for as long as you own the machine. If they determine that a repair is needed, you have to ship the machine back to one of over 20 NCR service depots (NCR has the contract to carry out maintenance on all of TI's notebooks).

While there are no published promises on turnaround, the repair should generally get done in a day or two — plus shipping times. On the whole, I rate TI's support policies to be adequate, but not as good as the machines themselves.

### Summing up Texas Instruments

**For:** *Excellent 486-based notebook range; offers value and high performance.* **Against:** *No integrated trackballs or other pointing devices; no sub-notebook; service and support only adequate.* **Verdict:** *Tempting choice for power notebook buyers, pity about the trackball.*

# Toshiba

*Toshiba America Information Systems, Inc.*
*Computer Systems Division*
*9740 Irvine Boulevard*
*Irvine, CA 92713–9724*
*Tel: 800 457 7777*

## Introduction

Toshiba does not sell desktop PCs, but its place in the history of portable computing is assured: it was a pioneer of laptop computers, a market which it dominated in the late 1980s. In those days, it made its name with superbly designed machines using the bronze-colored, gas-plasma screens that some people yearn for even now (plasma screens are, arguably, unbeatable for pure text work, but they add significantly to the weight and are less suitable for Windows and other graphically-oriented applications).

Toshiba has faced much stiffer competition in the notebook arena, where it has lost some of its reputation for innovation (though its reputation for quality remains intact). Nonetheless, it is still a big player, and it has one of the widest ranges. Where Toshiba tends to excel is at the premium end of the market: if you're looking for a really powerful machine with a great color screen, and aren't neurotic about the weight (or stingy about the price), Toshiba could be the vendor for you.

Toshiba only sells its notebooks through dealers: it has shown no interest in developing a direct sales/mail order channel. The company has lately made a big push to get its lower-end notebooks into more consumer electronics and office warehouse type outlets. The machines are also carried by some national mail order catalogs, such as PCs Compleat.

### Toshiba product overview

Toshiba's most affordable notebooks are those in its Satellite series. These are relatively plain-vanilla notebooks — not the sort that will draw many oohs-and-aahs from envious onlookers. For example, they lack any form of built-in pointing device, though they do come with the rather bulky Microsoft Ballpoint trackball which clips onto the side. But they are well made, and have traditional Toshiba qualities such as first class keyboards. You could do a lot worse.

One of Toshiba's latest models is a sub-notebook introduced late in 1993 called the Portégé (not a misprint). This very desirable model does have a built-in pointing device: called AccuPoint, this is reminiscent of the eraser-like one positioned in the middle of the keyboard of IBM's ThinkPads.

Toshiba also offers a range of more upscale full-size models, which make up its T4600 and T4700 series: some of these are quite expensive, but all are pretty impressive. For power and overall quality, they are hard to beat — unfortunately, however, they too lack integrated pointing devices and only come with the Microsoft clip-on BallPoint trackball. Doubtless, various new Toshiba notebooks will be introduced during the shelf-life of this book.

### Toshiba service & support

In the past, Toshiba was not noted for offering particularly good service and support policies, but the company is now looking somewhat better in this regard. Today, you get a three-year warranty on the more expensive notebooks — i.e., on all the ones mentioned above with the exception of the Satellites, which only come with one-year coverage.

For $49.95 per year, you can elect to have on-site service during your warranty period on any of the machines — that's a definite plus point, as on-site service for notebooks is generally not available at all. You have to select this option when you buy the machine.

If you don't receive on-site service, you generally have to take the machine back to a dealer — you can't send it back to Toshiba itself for express warranty repairs. However, for a modest $22.50, you can upgrade the warranty to cover you for no-cost overnight shipping to a so-called "Premier Authorized Service Provider" that will provide fast turnaround; the catch is that you have to take the machine to a "Mail Boxes Etc." location for shipping under this program.

There are a number of other service options, including no-fault coverage against screen damage costing $49.95 (monochrome) or $179.95 (color). It seems to me that Toshiba has a reasonable set of support policies, but too many options which people may not know about when they purchase the machine: it would be better if they simplified their program.

There is a toll-free technical support number that is open Monday through Friday, 10 hours a day. There is no technical support available on weekends. Phone support is available for as long as you own the equipment. Toshiba doesn't offer 30-day money-back guarantees — which is normal for an all-dealer vendor (though I know of at least one major national mail order reseller, PCs Compleat, that offers its own 30-day money-back guarantee on the Toshibas it sells).

**Summing up Toshiba**
*For:* *Strong pedigree in notebooks; excellent reputation for quality; on-site notebook service available for those who want it.*
*Against:* *No integrated trackballs or pointing devices on most models; service and support arrangements can be confusing.* **Verdict:** *Toshiba offers some fine notebooks, though some of its strength in this market is due to historical reasons.*

# Brief Comments on a Few Other PC Vendors

The preceding profiles covered 11 of the major vendors; I'll end this chapter with some much briefer comments on a selection of other players in this market....

**ALR** is not the force that it used to be. The company that had a string of "firsts" to its name in the 1980s (including bringing out the first 386-based PC) is hanging in there, now selling increasingly direct. The company is now under Singaporean ownership.

**Ambra** is a unit of IBM, selling low-cost products by mail; IBM has shut down the European Ambra operation which was set up about a year earlier than the US one (see the IBM entry in the Vendor Profiles section). Ambra PCs are actually manufactured in the Far East by the same company that owns ALR.

**Austin**, a Texas mail order/direct sales company, is still around, now under new Singaporean ownership, but it is less prominent than it once was.

**Canon** sells a limited range of fairly unexciting, but solid, products through retail channels — it mainly chases home office and very small business buyers.

**CompuAdd** is now out of Chapter 11, but it has closed down all of its computer stores and is refocusing itself as a smaller vendor concentrating only on the direct sales/mail order market.

**Compudyne** continues to offer buyers a lot of computer for the money: you can buy its aggressively-priced products either direct or through the CompUSA stores owned by its parent company.

**Digital Equipment Corporation (DEC)** continues to spend heavily to promote its mail order/direct sales PC business, generally targeting the corporate market. It has had some success building market share, though — at the time of this writing, DEC was one of the biggest loss-makers in the computer industry.

**Epson** has some nice notebooks and also sells desktops; sales are through dealer and retail channels only.

**Hewlett-Packard** has some interesting sub-notebooks, but it has still not managed to establish itself as a prominent supplier in the mainstream desktop PC market; it sells only through dealers.

**NEC** has been putting most of its marketing energies into the notebook market, where it has some interesting products; it continues to push desktops, however, and it has beefed up support. When you hear NEC numbered among the top few PC manufacturers, you should keep in mind that this is due largely to its strength in the Japanese market, where it sells proprietary, non-industry standard PCs.

**Northgate**, a direct sales/mail order vendor is still in business, defying rumors that it would be a victim of PC price wars.

**PC Brand** is now out of business, and warranties have proved useless.

**Sharp's** presence in the computer market is limited to notebooks (and hand-held organizers, etc.). It sells some nice machines, but support has always been its weak spot.

**Tandy** is now out of the PC manufacturing business, having sold to AST; however, its Radio Shack stores now sell relabeled equipment made by the latter.

**Zenith Data Systems** has gone into partnership with Packard Bell (see that company's entry in the Vendor Profiles).

**Zeos** may have put the worst of its financial problems behind it, though there are still occasional rumors that it will have to merge with someone else. Note that, unlike most direct sales/mail order vendors, Zeos makes on-site service an extra-cost item not included in its advertised prices. Note too that it calls one of its product lines "Ambra," despite the fact that this is the name used by a unit of IBM (see above). Make what you will of that. ✍

# Chapter 2
# Computer Networks

# Computer Networks

The whole subject of computer networks is surrounded by an aura of confusion, not helped by the plethora of arcane jargon (often promoted by consultants who see the democratization of networking as a threat to their livelihoods). There are many businesses that would quite like a network, but have held back simply because they don't understand the subject, don't know what their options are, and don't know how to take the first few steps.

In this chapter, I aim to answer many of the most commonly asked questions, and leave you feeling well-briefed about the basics of networking and ready to enter the market.

## Introduction

Computer networks allow you to transfer files between PCs, to share central databases of information, and to share peripherals such as printers. They also allow you to run an electronic mail system, allowing users to exchange messages and even coordinate group calendars in order to set up meetings.

Once mainly a tool for larger businesses, networks are now available to the masses. Even if you have as few as two computers, there's often a strong case to set up a network of some sort, and businesses with up to 20 computers will find it much easier to network now than they would have a few years ago. Costs have also become more reasonable. You can set up a pretty decent network for five computers for a total cost of around $1,200 (maybe less). If you only need to network two computers, your costs could be lower than $100.

### What makes a network?
There are several ingredients that can make up a network: the "fileserver" (jargon for the computer at the hub of many networks), the adapters that connect the individual computers and other devices to the system, the cable that links them, the network software that allows you to share your data and programs, and the industry standards that allow all the different parts of the system to work together.

At the lower end of the market, some vendors have at-

---

**Inside This Chapter ...**

---

tempted to provide one-stop solutions to networking, by sup-plying all the different elements (apart from the computers them-selves) under a single brand name package. In some cases, you can literally buy a network in a box — more on this later. But with medium and larger networks, the different ingredients are generally provided by different vendors (though you may still be able to get them all from the same dealer).

You've probably heard of many of the industry standards and top vendors in the network game — names like Ethernet, Token Ring, Novell, LANtastic, Windows for Workgroups, for example. What you may be less clear about is how they all link in and what they do. For example, some newcomers to network-ing assume that Ethernet and Novell are alternatives, when the reality is that they are complementary. What I aim to do in this chapter is to explain clearly what the ingredients of a network are and how they all relate. In the process, I'll introduce you to some of the big names in the network industry — including those that specialize in smaller networks — and I'll advise on how to go about buying and installing a network.

Be warned that the subject is quite complex: to make it easier to understand, I'll leave out a lot of non-essential infor-mation and gloss over some of the technical detail, but I won't oversimplify matters so that you're left only a little wiser than you were at the start. I'll be assuming that you are already fa-miliar with computer terminology that isn't network-specific (if not, I suggest you first refer to the previous chapter where I explained this). I'll start by introducing you to a few basic terms and concepts, and then I'll move on to talk about the different types of networks.

## LANs and WANs

You'll often hear the term "local area network" — or LAN — used to describe networks in offices. This term was devised to differentiate networks within offices (LANs) with so-called "wide area networks" (WANs) that link computers in different offices over digital phone lines. In this book, I am only discussing LANs and I'll use the terms "local area network" and "network" interchangeably.

## What you can network

Computers that are attached to a LAN are often referred to as "workstations" or, simply, "stations." This gets a bit confusing, because in another context the term "workstation" describes specialized and immensely powerful PCs used for engineering and computer-aided design applications. While those types of workstations can be attached to LANs, most computers on a network are regular PCs — just like the ones used on a standalone basis. Every PC you buy today is capable of being networked, though, as I'll explain later, you usually have to upgrade them with an appropriate adapter.

The word "device" is often used to refer generically to anything connected to a network — thus a network device may be a printer or CD-ROM drive, for example, as well as a computer. There is no such thing as a dedicated network "terminal" — in fact, the word "terminal" doesn't really belong in a discussion of LANs (it's a word that's at home in the world of mainframe and old-fashioned minicomputers, where terminals are "dumb" devices without any processing power of their own).

Having said that, some network users get stripped-down PCs without their own disk drives, or with only a floppy drive and no hard drive. In these cases, the PC is only able to access data and programs on the network's central shared hard drive. However, the majority of networked PCs do have their own floppy and hard drives, enabling users to perform some functions on a standalone basis and others on the network. In practice, diskless workstations don't offer huge savings, mainly because they are made in much smaller quantities than PCs with disks. Another reason not to get diskless workstations is that networked PCs with their own hard drives make it possible to carry on working if the network itself goes down.

## What's a "node"?

You'll often hear this word used in a discussion of networks: all it refers to is a connection between the network and a device on the system.

### Applications programs & networks

When people talk about network software, they are generally referring to the software that provides networking services to everyone on the system — I'll be talking about this soon. But there are also special network versions of some applications programs (remember that an applications program is something like a database, accounting, or word processing package). In most cases, however, you use the regular single-user version of a software package, because there isn't a separate network version.

Depending on the program and the network you're installing, you may keep the software loaded on each individual workstation, or you may have the network users access centrally-loaded software as well as centrally-held data. In either case, you'll need to pay for each user on the system to use the software. Pirating software across a network should not be viewed as acceptable. Most software vendors have special pricing plans for multiple use on a single site. Don't assume that any applications program will work on any network without problems: compatibility problems do occur, though it can be hard to find out about them other than via the hard way.

# Entry-Level Solutions: Printer Sharing & Zero-Slot LANs

In small offices, the most cost-effective way of transferring data from one computer to another may simply be to copy it onto a floppy disk, walk over to the other user, and hand the disk over — "SneakerNet," as computer wits never tire of calling it.

The main reason to set up a fully-fledged local area network is if you regularly need to share the same central database, as opposed to occasionally exchanging files. However, many smaller users with only two or three PCs don't have major data sharing applications, but still find it inefficient to keep their computers totally unconnected.

For example, it makes a lot of sense to share printers between more than one computer. Likewise, you may sometimes want to share files that are too big to fit onto a single floppy disk. The good news is that there are some options that sit between mere SneakerNet and setting up a full-fledged network.

### Printer sharing devices

If all you want to do is share a printer between more than one

PC, your best bet may not be to set up a small network, but instead to buy a printer sharing device. You can connect several computers to one of these using normal printer cables, and then plug the device into the back of the printer itself. This enables several users to print their files, without having to manually juggle the cables.

Prices are fairly inexpensive: you'll probably spend about $100–$200. Printer sharing devices can be found in many computer accessories catalogs; alternatively, local computer dealers sometimes carry them or can order them for you from their wholesalers.

### Zero-slot LANs

If your office is small, but you want to do more than just share printers, consider getting a "zero-slot LAN." This is an entry-level network that allows you to connect two or three computers without the need for the special network adapters that are required with other LANs.

All you need to do is plug the cables into the serial or parallel ports that come standard with just about every PC. If possible, use the parallel port, because this will result in faster file transfer times. The problem is that many PCs only come with one parallel port and this is often used for a printer — you may, therefore, have to settle for the serial port, which is likely to work at about half the speed.

The advantages of zero-slot networks are that they are inexpensive to buy and easy to set up. The drawback, apart from their limited size, is that they are quite slow compared with larger networks — but this need not matter too much if your data sharing needs are modest.

Do not confuse zero-slot LANs with programs, such as Traveling Software's LapLink, that are only file transfer utilities. These utilities have their niche (such as copying data from a notebook PC to a desktop), but a true zero-slot LAN should do more than just allow you to pass a file over a wire — look for basic network features such as printer control, built-in electronic mail, password security, and so forth.

In my opinion, the best zero-slot LAN is LANtastic Z from Artisoft (not to be confused with Artisoft's more upmarket networking products, which also use the LANtastic brand name). A two-station LANtastic Z kit, including the special software and both parallel and serial cables, usually sells for around $95. Setting it all up is a breeze.

Keep in mind that LANtastic Z can only support up to two PCs per network (plus your printer). Clearly, it has its limitations, but it's a good starting point for very small offices, and it will set you up well to transition to the other versions of LANtastic if your business grows.

Other less polished zero-slot LANs may be able to support three or more users, but speeds with more than two users can get pretty slow. My view is that zero-slot LANs are great investments for two-computer offices, but that people with three or more computers are probably better off with one of the other network types I'll be talking about next.

# The Difference Between Peer-to-Peer and Client/Server LANs

Once you get beyond the world of zero-slot LANs, networks come in two flavors: "peer-to-peer" LANs are the less expensive and lower performance variety, and are often the best bets for groups of between three and 10–20 users; and "client/server" LANs are most suitable for medium- and larger-size users and also for smaller networks that happen to have fairly upscale database sharing requirements.

### Peer-to-peer LANs introduced

A peer-to-peer LAN is one where all the computers in the network are equal: no one computer is designated as the hub. Any two stations on the network can share information and use the same peripherals, such as printers.

You need to have special software to run a peer-to-peer network, but this can work under DOS or Windows — it does not work independently of them. Examples of peer-to-peer networks include Artisoft's LANtastic, Microsoft's Windows for Workgroups, and Apple Computer's AppleTalk (which comes standard with every Macintosh).

### Client/server LANs introduced

By contrast, a client/server LAN designates one computer to be the hub of the system. This computer, which is usually a very powerful PC with a very large hard drive, is known as the "fileserver" or, simply, as the "server." The fileserver stores centrally shared data and also the programs that are used across the network.

The individual computers that are connected to the network — the "clients" — route everything through the server. In other words, even if you want to transfer a file to the person sitting next to you, it will journey through the server to get there.

A client/server LAN uses special networking operating system (NOS) software, which runs on the fileserver. The NOS is independent of DOS/Windows, but does not replace them — in other words, you still run applications that are DOS/Windows-based, but the NOS controls the sharing of information and the network functions. The bestselling NOS software is Novell NetWare, which can work with networked PCs running DOS/Windows applications and also with Apple Mac and UNIX computers.

### Pros and cons

Peer-to-peer networks are all that most smaller offices need. They are cheaper to buy, easier to install, and simpler to manage once they are up and running. Their main drawback is that some can become quite slow if you want to connect more than 20 users — in fact, some people recommend using them for no more than a dozen users.

Client/server LANs can grow much larger. But they are much more complex to run even when set up: you are more or less obliged to designate someone to be the "network administrator." On the plus side, client/server LANs generally use industry-standard adapters and cables (more on this later, when I talk about Ethernet and Token Ring).

It is hard to come up with a precise cut-off point, above which it generally makes more sense to go with a client/server network, and below which it makes more sense to take the peer-to-peer route. Much depends on your workload.

For example, a 12-person office doing mainly word processing would probably be best off with a peer-to-peer network. But an eight-person office taking orders over the phone and constantly accessing the same large database may be better off with a Novell system. As I point out later, the leading peer-to-peer vendor is trying to position its product as suitable for very large networks — but the vast majority of installations to date have been for less than 20 users.

There can be quite a lot of overlap between peer-to-peer and client/server networking. For example, although peer-to-peer networks do not require you to have one hub computer acting as a server, there is nothing to stop you from designating one computer to be the hub holding the most commonly accessed shared data if this suits you.

Likewise, if you have a client/server network serving the whole of a large organization, you can still have peer-to-peer networks for workgroups such as individual departments. In this case, users would operate on the peer-to-peer level when communicating with their immediate workgroup, and would connect into the client/server network when accessing or sending data elsewhere in the organization.

### More about fileservers

Fileservers are simply very powerful PCs. Although some PC manufacturers designate certain upscale models as servers in their marketing, it's possible for any moderately powerful PC to act as a server. For example, you could use a PC based on an Intel 486SX processor as the server in a small network containing only a handful of PCs.

But with the price of powerful PCs at an all-time low, it makes more sense to choose one of the more powerful 486-series processors when you're buying a server: the price difference isn't all that much, and the extra speed is worth it. Upscale network users should consider Intel's new Pentium processor discussed in the previous chapter.

Remember that having a very powerful server does not require you to use the same processor in all your workstations: in most networks, the majority of workstations use less powerful ones than the server at the hub. Many networks are made up largely of 386-based PCs, and some still include vintage 286-based ones. A server's hard disk capacity is likely to be more than you'd ever think of getting for a standalone PC.

Often, PCs that are mainly marketed for use as fileservers are floor-standing, as opposed to desktop. These are often known as "tower" machines. This sometimes amounts to little more than packaging, as when you find machines with more or less identical performance capabilities offered in both desktop and tower versions (some vendors apparently believe that tower machines "look" more powerful and therefore stress that design). The term "mini-towers" is sometimes used to refer to the smaller floor-standing models.

It is sometimes possible for a server to double up as a client workstation — in other words, as well as acting as the shared hub, it can also be the computer on which one person on the network does his or her own work. Often, though, this is not possible and, for a host of operational reasons, it may not be a good idea even when it is possible.

For this reason, it usually makes sense to specify an inexpensive monitor, since no one is likely to be sitting in front of it all day. Instead, server buyers are better off putting their money into getting the fastest processor and the biggest and fastest hard drive they can afford. All major PC vendors have models that are suitable for use as fileservers.

Although people often use the words "fileserver" and "server" interchangeably, not all servers are, in fact, fileservers. For example, "printservers" are computers that control access to printers across a larger network (not all networks require these and, in many cases, the same computer performs the roles of fileserver and printserver).

# A Closer Look at Peer-to-Peer Networks: LANtastic, Windows for Workgroups, & AppleTalk

Having introduced you to peer-to-peer networks, let's look a little closer at the leading exponents of the genre.

### Artisoft LANtastic

The bestselling peer-to-peer LAN to date has been Artisoft's LANtastic. Artisoft, headquartered in Tucson, AZ, was started in the mid-eighties, but took off in a big way around the end of the decade. The company has made peer-to-peer LANs the core of its business. At the end of 1993, there were believed to be over 300,000 LANtastic networks installed worldwide.

Though conventional wisdom has it that peer-to-peer networks are suitable for linking up to around 20 PCs, Artisoft is keen to promote the idea that LANtastic can be used in much larger environments of up to 300 stations. This may be true, but, in practice, the typical LANtastic installation is much smaller.

In fact, using the company's own figures for the number of networks in use and the total number of PCs connected, the average size turns out to be less than six. In fairness, this average is pulled down by the fact that these numbers include the LANtastic Z zero-slot LAN (discussed earlier), which can only handle two PCs.

The latest release at the time of this writing was LANtastic 6.0, which was introduced early in 1994. This major upgrade includes advanced electronic mail, network scheduling/group calendar, faxing, and paging features. Other improvements over the earlier LANtastic 5.0 include better network printing support. In addition, version 6.0 provides excellent connectivity for workgroups who want to link into their organization's Novell client/server network.

In the past, buyers were offered a choice between Artisoft's proprietary adapters and LANtastic Ethernet adapters, but to-day LANtastic is all-Ethernet (I'll be talking more about Ethernet later, but the bottom line is that Ethernet, an industry standard more commonly associated with client/server networking, is a whole lot faster). You can use Artisoft's own Ethernet adapters — attractive to people who want a single-source network — or you can use other types.

Artisoft sells LANtastic Starter Kits, where you get everything you need for linking your first two computers in a single box. A two-PC kit used always to include network software that was licensed for up to several hundred computers — in other words, once you got your Starter Kit, you could expand your system only by getting more adapters and cable and you didn't have to pay anything more for the networking software.

However, with the introduction of LANtastic 6.0, the kits only include the software for the first two PCs and you are expected to upgrade your software license on a "per node" basis (remember that a "node" is a connection between the network and a device on the system).

A LANtastic 6.0 Starter Kit including two adapters, software for two PCs, and cabling has a list price of $519; add-on kits list at $239 per PC. In addition, you can buy software-only kits in a number of sizes ranging from one to 100 users: for example, a 5-user software kit is $499, a 25-user kit is $1,799; and a 50-user kit is $2,999.

### Simply LANtastic — new entry-level alternative

LANtastic 6.0 is quite sophisticated, and the danger is that Artisoft could be abandoning its "keep it simple and straightforward" roots. To prevent this from happening, Artisoft launched a new product a few months before releasing LANtastic 6.0 that's called Simply LANtastic.

This is an entry-level system designed to meet the basic networking requirements of small businesses and home offices — it will typically be used in offices with between two and 10 people. The Simply LANtastic network provides basic file-, printer- and CD-ROM-sharing features and is specially designed for easy installation and and simplicity of use. This peer-to-peer product sits between the LANtastic Z zero-slot product and the main LANtastic 6.0 offering.

A hardware bundle comprising the Simply LANtastic software, two of the new low-cost LANtastic Ethernet adapters, and cabling lists for just $299, with additional nodes priced from $149. There is a choice of internal or external adapters — the latter plug into a PC's parallel port and appeal to people who want the easiest possible installation process and who don't want to open up their computer to get at the expansion slots. People who begin with Simply LANtastic can later upgrade to LANtastic 6.0. There are also software-only kits for people who want to provide their own adapters and cabling.

### Microsoft Windows for Workgroups

The main alternative to LANtastic comes from Microsoft, which introduced a product called Windows for Workgroups at the end of 1992. Windows for Workgroups — which is essentially a version of Windows 3.1 with integrated peer-to-peer networking — includes some powerful features, such as built-in electronic mail and an excellent scheduling system.

Once installed, this is an impressive system — and operation should be reasonably intuitive to anyone who has already mastered the Windows operating environment. Unfortunately, some users have found the installation process itself to be less than intuitive — though the latest version — Windows for Workgroups 3.11 — addresses some of these concerns. A few PC vendors — including Gateway — ship their computers with Windows for Workgroups preinstalled, and that clearly takes away the set-up headaches.

If you already have your computers, there are everything-you-need-in-a-box Starter Kits that are priced according to whether you already have the Windows operating environment installed, and whether you are using Microsoft's own adapters or compatible ones sold by third parties (although the adapters used are a proprietary type, Microsoft encourages other vendors to develop third-party versions). As an example, $299 typically buys you a starter kit including two adapters, two copies of the Windows for Workgroups add-on software (this assumes you already have Windows itself), and some cable.

Keep in mind that Windows 4.0 — discussed in the previous chapter and expected to be introduced during the shelf-life of this book — is likely to have workgroup networking capabilities built in.

### AppleTalk — standard with every Mac

Apple Mac users are lucky, as every Macintosh includes a peer-to-peer networking system called AppleTalk that is simplicity itself. Most smaller offices buy inexpensive external adapters costing less than $30 that allow you to link up all your computers and printers using regular phone wire — that's the only extra expense over what comes standard with the Macintosh itself.

The best known supplier of these adapters is a company called Farallon, whose PhoneNET adapters are featured in just about all Mac catalogs and are carried by most Mac dealers. Alternatively, you can buy Apple's own LocalTalk cable from a dealer — this doesn't require adapters, but it's usually more expensive and less convenient.

PhoneNET and LocalTalk provide the ultimate in low-cost, easy networking, but the drawback is that they are quite slow. However, Mac users can also use Ethernet to run AppleTalk and thereby enjoy much faster file transfer rates. In fact, the new PowerPC Macs all include built-in Ethernet adapters (I'll be talking more about Ethernet soon). Apple Macs can also be included in mixed-platform client/server networks in which they share resources with computers running DOS/Windows.

# A Closer Look at Server Operating Systems: Novell, Microsoft, IBM, & Banyan

Next, more on the software systems that control server-based networks. Remember that these networks are mostly suitable for medium to larger networks with over 20 workstations, or for smaller ones with upscale shared database requirements.

### *Novell NetWare*

Novell Data Systems, headquartered in Orem, UT, was one of the stars of the software revolution of the 1980s and early 1990s. After a shaky start as a general purpose vendor in the early days of personal computers, it dedicated itself to PC networking. For a while, it sold computers designed specifically to be used as servers. Subsequently, it abandoned the network hardware market and now concentrates exclusively on software.

More companies use Novell than all other network operating systems put together. If you take the PC software market as a whole, Novell ranks second only to Microsoft. And despite challenges from mighty names such as Microsoft and IBM, Novell NetWare is the effective industry standard in the client/server system software market.

Recently, Novell has been making some pretty fancy acquisitions. Late in 1992, Novell bought Unix Systems Laboratories from AT&T, thereby gaining control of the Unix operating system (discussed briefly in the previous chapter). And early in 1994, it was announced that Novell was acquiring WordPerfect — its Utah neighbor. Novell also owns a Microsoft DOS-compatible operating system called DR-DOS, which was originally developed by Digital Research (this was also discussed briefly in the previous chapter).

There are good reasons why so many people who want to set up client/server LANs choose Novell NetWare. In a nutshell, the system works very well: it is fast and it offers excellent expansion capabilities and gateways to other types of networks. It has an excellent set of features, including first-class administration and security functions.

And because Novell is so widely used, it is very well supported: there are a huge number of products designed to work with it, and numerous companies that support and install it. In short, Novell is a safe-bet choice: the only reason why you might regret choosing it is if you don't really need it, and could have managed with a peer-to-peer network that is simpler and cheaper.

Though Novell is very powerful and has extensive capabilities, the flip side of the coin is that it can be difficult to get to grips with. It also uses a lot more memory on workstations than peer-to-peer networking software. Do not underestimate the complexities involved in becoming a Novell user, or the importance of getting first-class support. It is a fine system to master, but not an easy one.

As with other network operating systems, Novell has a price structure that's governed by the number of users on the network. Though prices vary by reseller, a five-user license of version 3.12 typically costs around $650, a 10-user version is about $1,450, and a 25-user license sells for $2,150. Larger versions are also available, of course. Prices for version 4.01 — which is more sophisticated — are higher.

If you're shopping for PCs, you'll see quite a lot of products advertised as being "Novell certified," and this may give you anxieties about buying another brand that doesn't boast the same. My advice is not to worry too much about "Novell certification" — the fact is that just about any mainstream PC can work on a Novell network. The "Novell certification" business is a kind of mutual backscratching marketing exercise involving Novell and certain PC vendors.

### Network operating systems from Microsoft & IBM

In recent years, the main direct challenger to Novell NetWare has been a product that was jointly developed principally by Microsoft and IBM (in the days when those two companies enjoyed better relations than they do now), though they were joined by various other names in the network industry such as 3-Com.

The software is probably best known as Microsoft LAN Manager, but all the parties to its development sell slightly modified versions under their own names, often to work with their own computer hardware. For example, IBM calls its version IBM LAN Server.

When it first came out, LAN Manager got a somewhat unenthusiastic reception, but subsequent versions have generated better responses from corporate networking aficionados. IBM markets its version very much in tandem with OS/2, its upscale operating system discussed in the last chapter.

Today, Microsoft tends not to actively promote LAN Manager, and is instead putting its energies into Windows NT Advanced Server, the network version of its new NT operating system (also discussed in the last chapter). Existing LAN Manager users can use NT in conjunction with LAN Manager, but new users looking for the latest and greatest that Microsoft has to offer in this department are more likely to be offered Advanced Server.

### Banyan VINES
The other main contender in the client/server network operating system software market is VINES, which comes from a company called Banyan Systems. It is actually based on the UNIX operating system. Though it has its disciples in some large corporations, VINES is much less well established — and widely supported — than Novell NetWare.

# Ethernet, Token Ring, & ARCnet

If you get a client/server network, you'll need to turn to one vendor, such as Novell, for your server software, and to a PC manufacturer, such as IBM, Compaq, Dell, etc., for your server; the other key hardware ingredient — the adapters — are sold by third-party vendors that make them according to established industry standards (the main one of which is also used in some peer-to-peer networks). Joining everything together is the cable itself, which comes in several varieties. In this section of the chapter, I'll tell you what you need to know about adapter standards and cabling.

### IEEE standards
The most established of the industry standards for network adapters are Ethernet and Token Ring. These are controlled internationally by an august body called the Institute of Electri-

cal & Electronic Engineers (IEEE). The benefit of IEEE standards is that they ensure compatibility between network components supplied by different vendors.

There's also a third standard called ARCnet, which isn't IEEE-regulated, but which is something of an unofficial industry standard nonetheless. I'll be talking a little about all three shortly, but first an introduction to cabling — the reason being that one of the things that distinguishes different standards is the type of cabling they use.

### Cable types

There are several types of cable. Perhaps the most common is "coaxial" cable, which comes in two varieties — thick and thin, or "ThickNet" and "ThinNet" in network-speak.

ThickNet may be required in some larger networks, but its bulk (0.4 inches in diameter) and cost — typically around $1 a foot — means that it is not the medium of choice unless you have a very good reason for needing it. The most compelling reason to get ThickNet is if you want individual segments in your network to be longer than 500 meters (sorry, but network industry standards are usually expressed in metric: one meter is equal to 3.28 feet).

ThinNet — also known as "CheaperNet" — can generally be bought for 20–30 cents a foot, and is much more manageable and widely used. ThinNet can handle segments up to 185 meters, but if you want to connect more than 30 devices you'll probably need to pay extra for "repeaters" to boost the signal.

Alternatively, you can opt for "twisted-pair" cable, which also comes in two guises. "Unshielded" twisted pair (UTP) looks like telephone wire and has lately become increasingly popular in small and medium-size networks due to its low cost — often 10 cents per foot or less — and easy handling. UTP wiring has become a lot more reliable than it used to be and can also handle high-speed data transfers — which wasn't the case in the past.

However, in certain installations it can attract interference from major electrical or motorized items — such as elevators — and in this case "shielded" twisted pair (STP) may be the answer; this looks like the wires that carry electricity in your office or home, and usually costs about 40 cents a foot.

Finally on cable types, some upscale networks have begun to use fiber optic cables. However, you've got to be a pretty large user to even want to consider this option, which is very expensive and complex to install and maintain.

### Wireless networks

It's worth noting briefly that some networks don't require cables at all: some vendors, such as Motorola, have developed "wireless networks" that use sound waves to carry data. That market is still pretty young, and right now the technology is mainly being implemented in niche markets. Still, there's a lot of momentum behind anything with the word "wireless" in it these days, so this could be the wave of the future.

### Network topologies

Sometimes, a single piece of cable runs from station to station, taking in all the servers, computers, and peripherals on the way. This type of network topology is usually referred to as a "bus" (some people prefer to call it a "daisychain").

In other cases, a separate cable runs from the fileserver to each workstation and peripheral on the system. This type of arrangement is known as a "star." A "tree" is a variation on a star, where you have several mini-hubs with branches going out to individual stations, rather than just one central cable hub.

Buses use less cable than stars, but problems with the wiring have more far-reaching consequences and can be harder to isolate. With a star, by contrast, if one piece of cable fails or is removed, the rest of the system should be intact. When low-cost UTP wire is used, it is usually in a star network.

### Baseband & broadband

You quite often hear these terms in a discussion of networks: they refer to how signals are sent down the cables. In practice, you don't really need to know about them, as broadband signals — essentially the type used by cable TV — are for mega-huge networks. The network you install will almost certainly be baseband and you can safely ignore this as a factor.

### Introducing Ethernet

Having introduced you to the cable types and topologies, let's return to the IEEE networking standards I mentioned earlier. The most common standard in corporate America is Ethernet. This was developed by Xerox well over a decade ago; it remains the most successful monument to that company's largely frustrated attempt to become a force in the computer systems and software markets. Today, Xerox is not involved in marketing Ethernet. Numerous vendors sell products that are Ethernet-compatible, but there is no actual company or brand called Ethernet.

The overall Ethernet standard is known in IEEE circles as "802.3," but this actually comes in several versions for different cable types. So-called "Standard Ethernet" — known to the IEEE as "10BASE5" — uses ThickNet cables. If you want to use ThinNet, you should look for network adapters that use the "10BASE2" Ethernet standard. Less expensive than CheaperNet is a standard called "1BASE5," or "StarLAN," which uses UTP wire. The most basic version of this standard is pretty slow, but an enhanced version called "10BASE-T" is a popular choice for people wanting a good mix of speed and economy.

### How Ethernet works

An Ethernet network is silent, except when one workstation decides to talk to another device on the system — in other words, there is no traffic of any type between data transfers. But because only two computers can communicate through one piece of cable at any time, a characteristic of Ethernet is that frequent "collisions" occur when more than one user tries to do something simultaneously.

The adapters that connect devices to an Ethernet LAN are able to detect collisions and sort them out. In moderate traffic environments, users should be unaware of what's going on. This is thanks to something called "Carrier Sense Multiple Access with Collision Detection" (CSMA/CD), which is the core of the Ethernet standard. Don't worry about how it works: just think of it as a bit like a super-high tech version of a four-way stop sign, with various protocols determining who goes first.

The problem with Ethernet is that in very busy networks, sorting out the collisions can lead to a degradation in response times. In plain English, the network slows down: it'll take you longer to access or transfer a file, or print something out, than it would when fewer people are trying to use the system at once.

### Token Ring — a faster alternative

The main alternative to Ethernet is a standard called Token Ring. IBM was its main sponsor, and remains its main protagonist. Token Ring — or "802.5" in IEEE parlance — uses twisted-pair cable and is designed to work faster in very heavy data traffic environments. It differs from Ethernet in how it manages the flow of data from one bit of the network to another.

A Token Ring network constantly sends around an electronic message box — known as a "token" — to each station on the system at very high speeds. As soon as the token reaches a station that has something to send, it collects the data and takes it where it needs to go — then it resumes its journey around the network.

Described in this sort of layman's language, Token Ring might sound somewhat ponderous but, in reality, the opposite is the case. It takes hardly any time at all for a token to zap around a network of 100 or 200 stations and the result is that there are fewer delays in busy environments than with Ethernet. To further enhance productivity, you can design a network so that certain critical stations are visited more frequently by the token than others.

Don't infer from this that Token Ring is usually the smart choice: it is generally chosen only by pretty large network users and will be overkill for most readers of this book.

### ARCnet

ARCnet falls outside the IEEE's control. It was originally developed by Datapoint Corporation (the letters "ARC" stand for "Attached Resource Computing," incidentally), but it has become something of an unofficial industry standard — quite a few vendors sell products that are ARCnet-compatible.

The way it works is something like the Token Ring method described above, but it isn't as fast (though an enhanced version was introduced in 1992). ARCnet is less widely used than Ethernet and Token Ring, and it isn't a particularly obvious choice unless you have some special reason for wanting it (e.g., because your organization already has some special expertise or investment in it, or because you have a close relationship with a vendor that specializes in supporting it).

### Network speeds

Network speeds are measured in megabits per second (mbps). Ethernet runs at 10mbps; Token Ring generally runs at 4 or 16mbps, though there's also a super-fast 100mbps version; and ARCnet in its most common form works at 2.5mbps. A new, faster Ethernet standard is under development, incidentally.

You should treat these speed figures with some caution: they provide a good general indication of comparative performance, but actual speeds will be affected by a variety of factors, such as the network operating software and the network adapters used. Remember that a network is generally only as fast as the slowest thing on the system.

As an idea of what mbps figures mean in practice, a network that works at 4mbps takes about two or three seconds to transfer the equivalent of a fully-loaded floppy disk. The actual distance over which the data has to travel has no noticeable impact on the speed.

### Network adapters

Assuming that you want to hook up to something more than a zero-slot LAN, few personal computers leave the factory "network-ready" (that's the term referring to when you can take a PC out of the box and plug it straight into a network).

There are exceptions, however. As already noted, Apple Macintosh computers leave the factory ready to work with Apple's own peer-to-peer network — and a few PC vendors on the other side of the fence preinstall Windows for Workgroups on their PCs. Also, some DOS/Windows PC manufacturers are beginning to make some of their models Ethernet-ready — as is Apple in the case of its PowerPC models. Notwithstanding these exceptions, the general rule is that you have to install a third-party adapter in your computer before you can hook it up to a network.

A network adapter is a computer board that goes into one of your PC's vacant expansion slots. Installation can sometimes be a bit tricky, because of the array of set-up options relating to how the rest of your system is configured.

There are dozens of network adapters to choose from, especially if you've decided on Ethernet. Most are made by companies you probably haven't heard of, but you should be okay if you buy from a reputable dealer or catalog. In particular, there are different adapters for all three PC architecture types (ISA, EISA, and MCA — as discussed earlier in the previous chapter), for the different cable types, and for 8- and 16-bit data transfer (16-bit is faster and generally the better choice).

Prices for Ethernet adapters typically range from under $100 to over $250. Token Ring adapters tend to cost more than their Ethernet counterparts: expect to pay from $250 to over $500. ARCnet adapters, by contrast, typically sell for around $100–$150. Some Ethernet cards come with extra on-board memory, but this doesn't generally make a vast difference to performance. When funds are limited, it makes sense to put the most upscale adapter in your network fileserver, the computer at the hub of your system — this is the unit that will be under the most pressure.

### External adapters

If you don't like opening up your computer and fiddling with boards, if you don't have any vacant expansion slots, or if you want to network a notebook PC, consider buying an external Ethernet adapter that you plug into the back of your computer via the parallel port.

A good bet are the Pocket LAN Adapters sold by a company

called Xircom; these are widely available through computer catalogs and dealers, and cost from around $290. Catalog browsers will also find lesser-known external adapters costing as little as $140. Most of the latest generation of notebook computers have PCMCIA slots, which accept network adapters that look like slightly overweight credit cards and that slide easily into a slot at the side of the computer (PCMCIA cards and slots were discussed in the previous chapter, in the section dealing with notebook PC features).

# Buying, Installing, & Managing a Network

How you go about buying and installing a network depends very much on the type of network you're getting. It also depends partly on how computer-proficient you are — and your skills with a drill may be a further factor.

### Buying and installing a small network

If you're setting up a small zero-slot network for a couple of computers and a printer, you should be prepared to do everything yourself. Since the network itself — something like LANtastic Z — costs only about $100, you're not going to get any hands-on help other than at a disproportionate cost. Nor do you need it. The network vendor should offer phone support if you get stuck, however.

Setting up a small peer-to-peer network for under 10 users is a little more complex, largely because you have to install adapter boards, but it should not be beyond the abilities of most people who are prepared to read the manuals and show a little patience. Peer-to-peer buyers should consider getting one of the everything-you-need-in-a-box starter kits I've referred to earlier. (Remember that these generally include all the software, hardware, and cables you need to network your first two PCs.)

See how you get on with that before deciding whether you need help. Apart from anything else, setting up a small network yourself is a good way of bonding with it and learning all about it — and that will help you when you come to use it. Still, if time is in short supply, and if you know a good local firm, you may decide to opt for the simple life and pay someone to do the work for you.

Obtaining outside help may be especially sensible if putting down the cable to link all the computers is difficult. If your office is spread over several finely decorated rooms, or over two floors, and if getting out drills and hammers presents a problem, you may want to call in someone with the necessary aptitude.

### Where to buy a small network

The best way of getting a zero-slot network kit, or a starter kit for a peer-to-peer LAN, is by mail order or from a computer store in your area. You do not need to go to a company with carpeted offices and a sofa in the reception area that offers network consulting services. I find that mail order is often the most painless way to buy this type of product (see "Network Contacts" section at the end of this chapter).

### Buying medium-size LANs

If you're buying a medium-size peer-to-peer network — say one with 10–20 computers — there's a stronger case to buy from a local dealer that offers more support. For a start, the installation of the cable is likely to be that much more complex. In addition, you may want to have more formal staff training.

And, at this level where the peer-to-peer market begins to overlap with the client/server market, you may want to have someone analyze your requirements in case you're making a mistake in your initial choice. That said, beware of people who sell networks that are more complex and expensive than necessary.

If you are buying a client/server network — one based on Novell NetWare, for example — you definitely should deal with a local vendor able to offer expert assistance before, during, and after the installation. As I mentioned earlier, this type of network can be very sophisticated: if you don't know what you're doing, you'll be in for a bumpy ride.

By no means all local computer dealers have the necessary skills to give you good advice and support in setting up a client/server network. Beware of those whose apparent wisdom is a reflection of your innocence. References from recent customers are one of the best sources of comfort — always check these yourself. *The Yellow Pages* can be as good a place as any to start looking if you have no idea who to turn to in your area.

### Network consultants

As well as dealers that offer advice and training as part of their overall sales package, there are LAN consultants who work for a flat retainer (though some also take a cut from dealers who supply equipment they recommend — a potential conflict of interest). The word "consultant" covers a multitude of sinners and saints: a good consultant can be worth every penny, but some are the type who try to make everything more complicated than it need be. Perhaps they want you to get so confused that you end up thinking that their outrageous bills must be worth paying — just to get everything sorted out.

Choose a consultant with care — and always insist on names and phone numbers of recent clients. Beware of the ones who are gratuitously rude about peer-to-peer LANs for, say, 10–20 computer offices that aren't running particularly complex databases: that's a tell-tale sign of someone trying to steer you into something much more upscale than you might really need.

### Network administrators

Once your network is installed, it's essential to make sure that everyone is trained to make good use of it. And unless your network is very small, it's also essential to place one person in your office in charge of a network. Offices with over 40 workstations often make the job of "network administrator" a full-time position. Smaller offices may make the function double up with other office administration tasks — looking after copier matters, for example. Either way, this is an important job, requiring excellent computer skills.

Duties include making sure that daily backups occur (absolutely vital), making sure that weekly backups are kept in a different location (in case your office burns down one night), deleting old files that aren't needed and clutter up disk space, determining priority in printer usage, managing data security and access questions, updating user name and password tables, keeping shared laser printers replenished with supplies, choosing and installing adapter cards (and deciding who gets which ones) — plus training for new employees and general troubleshooting. The buck has to stop in one place for this type of thing: otherwise, your network could end up a mess.

# Network Contacts

If you want to buy starter kits for small networks, or additional adapters for a larger one, one of the easiest and least expensive methods is mail order. There are a number of very respectable mail-order suppliers which offer excellent service and produce first-class catalogs which they'll gladly send you. One of the best is called Data Comm Warehouse — this has widest range of network items I've seen in a single source (tel: 800 328 2261). There is a listing on the next page showing the addresses and phone numbers of the network vendors listed in this chapter. ✍

### Network vendors

Here's how to contact the main network vendors discussed in this chapter:

**Artisoft Inc. (LANtastic)**
2202 North Forbes Boulevard
Tucson, AZ 85745
Tel: 800 233 5564

**Banyan Systems, Inc.**
115 Flanders Road
Westborough, MA 01581
Tel: 508 898 1000

**Microsoft Corporation**
One Microsoft Way
Redmond, WA 98052–6399
Tel: 800 642 7676

**Novell, Inc.**
122 East 1700 South
Provo, UT 84606
Tel: 800 638 9273

# Chapter 3

# Laser, LED, & Ink Jet Printers

# Laser, LED, & Ink Jet Printers

The printer market suffers from a large measure of information clutter. But in order to make a rational purchasing decision, it's important to have a grasp of the main technical issues. This chapter uses plain language to explain what you need to know, and why you need to know it.

What are the differences between the PCL 4 and PCL 5 printer languages? What is PostScript and when do you need it? Can you use PostScript fonts if you don't have a PostScript printer? What is TrueType? How can you make sure that the fonts built into your printer show up on your computer screen? Should you get Adobe Type Manager?

How much better is so-called "600dpi" resolution than "300dpi" — and when might a supposedly 600dpi printer only be capable of printing at 300dpi? What is meant by "resolution enhancement technology?"

Why is the quoted "pages per minute" speed an incomplete indicator of a printer's actual speed — and what other features impact performance in reality? What is a RISC processor? How much memory should you have in your printer? What devices are available to help you print onto envelopes? Can laser printers handle 11" x 17" paper?

How suitable are ink jet printers for business use? Can their higher running costs wipe out the savings afforded by their lower purchase prices? Do the newer entrants to the ink jet market offer advantages over the vendors that have traditionally dominated it? Read on for answers to these and similar questions....

## Introduction

This chapter covers both laser and ink jet printers. The laser coverage also takes in LED printers, which are conceptually very similar — I'll be talking more about LEDs later but, for now, consider them as one and the same. I am only talking about black-and-white printers in this chapter — if you are looking for a color printer, turn instead to Chapter 7.

The lasers I'm discussing cost from under $500 to $5,000 in the discount market. They have engine speeds ranging from 4 pages per minute (ppm) to 20ppm. A few of the machines can print onto paper sizes up to 11" x 17", but most only go up to letter/legal.

The ink jet machines I'm talking about mostly sell for less than $300. They offer print quality and speeds that are not quite as good as those of entry-level lasers, but that can get reasonably close. These machines can be ideal for home offices and other small offices.

I am not covering dot matrix printers in any detail in this book. The only reason to consider these nowadays is if you want to print onto multi-part (i.e., carbonized) forms. The three leading vendors to consider are Epson, Oki, and Panasonic.

### Multifunctional printers

Keep in mind that there's a new genre of combined printer-copier-scanner-fax beginning to appear. For the most part, these are suitable for people with either very entry-level or pretty upmarket requirements — mid-market buyers are less likely to find these machines of interest. I won't be discussing them in this chapter — but they are covered in Chapter 9 which is devoted to multifunctional equipment.

# What's Doing in Laser Printers?

I'll start with a brief review of the main developments in the laser market: this will also serve as an opportunity to introduce one or two technical issues. The laser printer market went through a major transition during 1993 and the first half of 1994, as second generation models started to give way to new ones that print at much higher resolutions.

Laser printers form their images out of tiny dots — the more dots, the higher the resolution and the better the print quality. For years, industry standard printers worked with a matrix of 300 vertical by 300 horizontal lines to the square inch: where each of the lines meets, a dot forms part of the image — in other words, a black solid area measuring one square inch would be made up of 90,000 dots. This resolution is commonly referred to as "300dpi" ("dpi" stands for "dots per inch"), though a more accurate shorthand is "300 x 300."

The 300dpi standard delivers quality that's good enough for most business purposes. If the technology had stood still for the time being, there would not have been riots in corporate America. But it can be improved, and the printer industry is keen to make it better — how else do you give all those satisfied owners of reliable laser printers a reason to buy new equipment?

Some improvements over the basic 300dpi standard have been around for a while. Since 1990, many 300dpi printers have offered so-called "resolution enhancement technology" — I'll be talking about this later, but the bottom line is that the printer varies the size of dots in places where it helps to even out jagged edges that can be evident with 300dpi (especially on large size type).

Also, some vendors began offering printers that worked at resolutions higher than 300dpi several years ago. In most cases, however, these were software-enhanced versions of 300dpi printers, rather than from-the-ground-up higher resolution machines, and they tended to be very expensive devices aimed at specialized applications.

### The October revolution

But, towards the end of 1992, high resolution was brought to the masses. On October 26, 1992, Hewlett-Packard (HP) launched two new mid-level printers that began to transform the market. The HP LaserJet 4 and 4M were the first laser printers built from the ground up on 600dpi engines to produce high resolution output for all types of software at affordable prices.

These machines were not launched as upmarket luxury items: they replaced the mid-market 300dpi workhorse in HP's range. They were followed in 1993 by 600dpi siblings aimed at low-volume users and at people needing fast network printers. Today, Hewlett-Packard — which leads the laser market in every sense — sells only one 300dpi printer, a budget model costing under $650.

Though the arrival of HP's 600dpi printers was not completely unexpected, it stunned much of the rest of the industry: other vendors were left with product lines clearly not as good in terms of quality and/or value. During 1993, prices tumbled as a consequence and rival vendors rushed to bring out 600dpi models of their own.

However, by mid-way through 1994, few had yet caught up. The reason is that almost all non-HP printers capable of 600dpi output are only able to print at that resolution when working with PostScript, a print language which I'll be talking about later but that tends to be associated with either the Apple Macintosh or with graphics and desktop publishing work on DOS/Windows PCs. In other print modes, these machines default down to 300dpi.

If you're a little confused at this point, hang in there — I'll be explaining things further as this chapter continues. For the time being, just remember that HP's 600dpi output is somewhat more all-embracing than what you get from other vendors' 600dpi machines.

### Is 300dpi obsolete?

It would be quite wrong to regard 300dpi printing as a thing of the past. At the bottom end of the market, 300dpi continues to be the norm. If you want to spend much less than $900 on your printer, you will be getting a 300dpi model, period. The lowest price I saw in early summer '94 on HP's least expensive 600dpi printer was $959. By contrast, the least expensive 300dpi laser/LED printer from any vendor was selling for around $475 at press-time. While further price falls will occur during the shelf-life of this book, the threshold for true 600dpi printing is unlikely to drop much below $900 for a while.

Also, the difference in print quality between 300dpi and 600dpi should not be exaggerated. With plain vanilla word processing — the staple diet of most budget laser printers — the differences will not necessarily be very apparent. You'll find them more noticeable if you work with large type sizes, or if you print large black solid areas and graphics.

### What's next in this chapter?

What you've just read should have given you some idea of where the main activity in the laser/LED market is right now. It will also have introduced you to the concept of resolution, which will be cropping up throughout this chapter.

Before I delve deeper into laser issues, I'd like to introduce you to the ink jet budget alternative. If you know already that you don't want an ink jet, skip to the section after that where I resume the discussion on lasers by looking at the confusing, but important, topic of "printer languages" (PCL 4, PCL 5, PostScript, and so on).

# Ink Jets Introduced

With laser prices starting at a little under $500 in the discount market, you don't have to be a plutocrat to buy one. But if you print very small amounts of material, if you need a portable printer, or if you want one for occasional use at home, you might want to consider an ink jet. They can also be suitable for small branch offices of larger organizations.

### Ink jet quality

Ink jet printers are just as versatile as lasers for text and graphics: any image that can be printed on a laser can also be handled by an ink jet. However, print quality is somewhat coarser. An ink jet literally squirts ink directly on the paper and, as a consequence, print quality is often quite paper-sensitive. Paper that absorbs ink usually leads to an image that is less crisp; conversely, non-absorbent paper can cause smudging if you run your fingers over it immediately after printing.

Ink jets have improved dramatically in recent years, and now get fairly close to laser quality — I'd say that a decent ink jet is about 70 percent as good as an average laser in terms of print quality. That's good enough for many types of business correspondence, but the difference is noticeable: people who tell you that ink jets are "every bit as good as lasers" are overstating the case.

High resolution, 600dpi output is not available in the ink jet market, incidentally: all machines currently work at either 300dpi or 360dpi.

### Ink jet speeds

On the plus side, the price of a typical ink jet is about half that of a low-end laser. Most desktop models sell for between $250 and $300 in the discount market. However, speeds are somewhat slower: a typical ink jet will probably be only half as fast (or twice as slow) as an entry-level laser.

Direct speed comparisons from published specifications can be difficult, because whereas laser speeds are routinely quoted in "pages per minute," ink jet speeds are usually quoted in "characters per second" (cps) — the same calibration used on matrix and old-fashioned daisywheel printers. To help you make comparisons, you should consider a quoted speed of 125–150cps as broadly equating to 1.5ppm, and likewise 250–300cps is about 3ppm.

To further confuse matters, ink jet printers can normally be set to work at different modes, allowing you to trade off speed for print quality — something that isn't available with lasers and LEDs. The fastest speeds will be in so-called "draft quality," whereas the slowest ones will be in "letter quality" (LQ) or "near letter quality" (NLQ).

### Ink jet running costs

While the typical ink jet might cost around $200–$300 less than an entry-level laser or LED printer to buy, that saving can be eroded by higher running costs. The cost of consumables on an ink jet can work out to over 8 cents per page, though a figure of around 4 cents is average. By contrast, laser and LED running costs usually work out to around 2.5–3 cents per page, and can be as low as 2 cents.

If you assume that an ink jet costs 1.5 cents per page more than a laser, someone printing 500 pages a month will end up spending $180 more in consumables over a two-year period than they would have with a laser or LED. That can almost wipe out the initial savings by going for the cheaper machine. Ink jet running costs are falling, however, and newer models tend to offer running costs closer to 3 cents per page.

### Who's who in ink jets?

Two vendors have historically dominated the ink jet market: Canon (with its Bubble Jet series), and Hewlett-Packard (with its DeskJet and DeskWriter models). Other vendors include Lexmark, Epson, and Texas Instruments.

### Ink jets and color

While this chapter is not focusing on color printing — that's covered separately in Chapter 7 — it is worth noting here that color is what really makes ink jet technology shine. Whereas with monochrome (i.e., black-and-white) printing, ink jets are something of the poor relation and laser tends to be the technology of choice, that certainly isn't the case in the color market.

There, laser technology is barely an option at all (unless you're willing to part with over $10,000) and ink jet is the leading print method for mainstream business applications. As black-and-white laser costs fall, the attraction of ink jet printing for purely monochrome applications may diminish, but there should be a bright future for those machines that combine competent black-and-white with attractive color output.

### What to read next

One of the nice things about monochrome ink jet printers is that they are pretty straightforward — there aren't a vast number of features to get to grips with. For this reason, much of what follows in the rest of this chapter will not be particularly relevant if you've already decided that an ink jet is all you need.

There's no need to agonize over PostScript, for example, because it isn't an option. You don't need to worry about how much memory is needed, because you hardly get any — and you can't specify more. You don't need to worry about the processor inside the printer, because ink jets are essentially passive devices that let the host computer they're connected to do all the work.

You therefore do not need to read all of the rest of this chapter if black-and-white ink jets are all that concern you. You might still want to skim through it — and pick up on certain parts, such as the discussion of fonts — but a lot of the material will not be relevant. That said, I will be referring to ink jet features in parts of the chapter where it seems relevant to do so.

# Printer Languages Introduced

Back to lasers and LEDs. A printer language has to do with the way your printer receives instructions from your computer software and then formulates the image. Although the subject can get quite technical, it has some very real practical implications relating to what you can and can't do with your equipment — so it pays to get to grips with the topic.

### Language perspectives

Historically, the printer industry has always adopted one or two manufacturers' own printer languages for each different printer technology and these have become the industry standards. For example, Epson has traditionally been the bestselling brand of dot matrix printer and any matrix vendor wanting to be taken seriously has had to offer Epson emulation.

The reason is simple: the best way of selling printers is to make them compatible with the software used on computers; and the safest way of ensuring compatibility is to fall into line with the bestselling models you're competing against. If you develop your own language, you run the risk that software companies won't consider it worthwhile "driving" your printers; so even the vendors that do develop their own usually also "emulate" industry standards as a back-up.

Sometimes, a standard developed for one technology is carried over into another, if not as the primary standard then as a supporting one. For example, some laser printers still boast "Diablo 630 emulation," despite the fact that the Diablo 630 was an old-fashioned daisywheel printer and that Diablo — a Xerox subsidiary — vanished from the printer scene several years ago.

Why? It's a kind of lowest common denominator to ensure compatibility if all else fails — though I can't see who really does use Diablo 630 emulation on a laser printer, since the laser market has developed its own standards which make infinitely better use of the technology.

### The three main laser languages

In practice, there are three main industry standards that should concern the laser and LED printer buyer (though one or two others are knocking on the door, as I'll show later). Two of them — PCL 4 and PCL 5 — were developed by Hewlett-Packard; the other, called PostScript, comes from a company called Adobe Systems.

If you're an Apple Macintosh user, you might as well skip the discussion of the PCL languages, as these are not an option in the Mac environment. (However, Mac users have a further option called QuickDraw: see the Apple entry in the Vendor Profiles section at the end of this chapter for more on this.)

If you work with DOS/Windows PCs, you do have a choice of all the main industry standard printer languages. Which is best for you will depend on the type of work you want to do — in particular, whether you want to create documents that only incorporate straightforward typewriter-style text, or whether you want to create ones that incorporate different type sizes, special effects, and graphics.

Your decision may also be influenced by ambitions you have to print at very high resolutions, and by whether you're working on things like brochures, annual reports, catalogs, and so on, that will later get sent to a firm of commercial printers (here I'm using the word "printers" in the other sense, to refer to firms with offset or web printing presses).

### Ink jet print languages

The choice of languages in the ink jet market is different. As I remarked earlier, PostScript is not an option (except in the color ink jet market). There is Hewlett-Packard emulation, but a different type — look for HP PCL 3. Various forms of matrix printer emulation are common, because ink jets and matrix printers tend to overlap in the market they address. Canon, one of the two market leaders in ink jets, has a proprietary print language in this market.

# Introducing PCL 4 & PCL 5

Hewlett-Packard sells more laser printers than anyone else and has set the leading industry standards. The entry-level language used by most brands of laser printer is HP PCL 4; the more advanced version is HP PCL 5. You don't have to get a Hewlett-Packard printer to use either of these languages, as other brands are able to emulate HP.

The main difference between the two PCLs is that PCL 4 uses built-in fonts (i.e., typefaces) that are fixed in size: these are known as "bitmapped" fonts. By contrast, PCL 5 uses built-in "scalable" fonts as well as bitmapped ones — in other words, a PCL 5 machine has built-in (or "resident") fonts that can be printed in any size you're likely to want. With PCL 4, you can print in different sizes using your resident fonts, but in order to do so you have to install a separate font for each size; this is much less versatile and it can become quite expensive (though you shouldn't get too hung up about resident fonts, for reasons I'll be coming to).

PCL 5 also offers a number of other built-in enhancements over PCL 4. For example, there are much better line drawing capabilities, you can rotate text and images to any angle, and introduce various special effects such as shades of gray within boxes and reversed-out images (white out of black). It also incorporates a special graphics language called HP GL; this is available separately on some PCL 4 machines — often as an option — but with PCL 5 it's enhanced and fully integrated.

Machines that use PCL 5 also have other advantages which, while not intrinsically part of PCL 5, are nonetheless closely related to it. In particular, almost all offer resolution enhancement technology, which helps improve print quality — more on this later.

### Printing screen fonts with PCL 4

Does all of the above mean that if you get a PCL 4 printer, you can't use software on your computer that allows you to select the type size? No. What I've been talking about so far is what you can do with your resident fonts — the ones that are built into the printer. But you can also use scalable screen fonts on your computer and then download these into the printer each time you output a job.

This way, a PCL 4 machine can produce a document combining lots of different type sizes and styles. In the same way, it can also produce special effects such as reversed out images. The drawback is that downloading the fonts results in longer print times and — depending on how many sizes and styles you want to use — it may require you to add more memory to the printer (I'll be talking more about memory later).

Keep in mind that even if you get PCL 5, you may still end up downloading some fonts if the ones you use on your computer do not match the ones that are resident in the printer. More on that later when I talk about fonts in greater detail.

### PCL 4/5: the bottom line

The bottom line is that if you already have a PCL 4 printer (an old LaserJet II, for example) and are now making the move over to Windows and want to use scalable fonts, you are not obliged to go out and buy a new printer — the one you have can do the job using the downloading method.

But if you are buying a new printer, it probably makes more sense to go with PCL 5 unless all you want to do is produce typewriter-style, plain-vanilla documents. Not only will you get better performance out of the printer, but you'll also get a little better quality as a result of the resolution enhancement that accompanies PCL 5.

A PCL 5 machine typically costs $100–$200 more than an equivalent PCL 4 model: that premium seems quite fair when you consider the benefits. The likelihood is that PCL 4 is eventually going to fade away, though — slightly to my surprise — new models are still being introduced that use it.

### Extended PCL 5

Until not so very long ago, both PCL languages could only work with 300dpi resolution, which has been the dominant standard in the laser market for some years. (Remember, I talked about "resolution" at the start of this chapter and I'll be returning to the subject shortly.)

What this means is that if you bought one of the lasers that boasts, say, 600dpi output, you didn't get the benefit of the higher print quality when in PCL mode — instead, the swanky 600dpi machine would default down to boring old 300dpi. With most brands, this is still the case and you only get high resolution output if you use the PostScript language which I'm about to discuss.

However, most of the Hewlett-Packard LaserJet 4 models are able to produce 600dpi output without PostScript, as they use what HP calls "Extended PCL 5" (PCL 5e). At press-time, only three other vendors — Brother, Canon, and Lexmark — were selling laser printers that emulated PCL 5e.

### Microsoft's Windows Printing System

Microsoft — the software mega-giant responsible for DOS, Windows, and countless other things — has introduced a product called Windows Printing System (WPS). This is an upgrade for Hewlett-Packard (and compatible) printer owners. It consists of an add-in cartridge for the printer, and software for both the printer and the host PC.

WPS enables you to effectively bypass PCL and PostScript when printing out Windows documents. This improves the printing performance of Windows, which has never been totally satisfactory. WPS was launched in mid-1993, and it appears to be more of an alternative to PCL 5 than to PostScript (Microsoft has a separate product called TrueImage, which is a PostScript clone: more on that later). WPS will not work with the HP LaserJet 4 models.

There has been quite a lot of cooperation lately between Microsoft and Hewlett-Packard, and it is still early to judge how much significance should be attached to WPS in a discussion of printer languages. However, the early signs are that WPS has failed to make much impact, and it may end up fizzling out before it ever catches on.

# Introducing PostScript

Having introduced you to the two PCL languages, let's now take a look at the alternative. This comes from a company called Adobe Systems and it's called PostScript. Unlike Hewlett-Packard, Adobe does not make or market printer hardware. It's a software company that licenses its product to printer manufacturers which build it into their machines.

PostScript has more in common with PCL 5 than with PCL 4. So if you've decided that PCL 4 is suitable for your needs, you can forget about PostScript. If, on the other hand, you were tempted by what I said about PCL 5, you should also consider PostScript as an alternative. (Adobe would probably put it the other way around — PostScript has been on the scene a lot longer than PCL 5.)

Like PCL 5, PostScript works with scalable fonts. The main differences between the two concerns not so much the images they can create (although there is a bit of that), but the way in which they work and their compatibility with different types of output device. As I will show, PostScript is especially suitable for applications involving desktop publishing and graphics. It is also the dominant printer language for the Apple Macintosh environment (PCL 4/5 only work with DOS/Windows computers, and are not an option for Mac users).

### PCL 5 & PostScript: the technical differences

OK, brace yourself for a bit of technical stuff. With PCL 5, your computer software sends commands to the printer one at a time — print this, print that, print this, and so forth. Most of the interpretative work is done by the computer — the printer just does what it's told. With PostScript, by contrast, your computer software sends the "big picture" to the printer all in one go; the software in the printer then interprets the data and prints the image accordingly. In jargon terms, PCL 5 is known as a "command language," while PostScript is known as a "page description language."

One consequence of this is that the actual speed you get from a PostScript printer will be determined significantly not just by the mechanical speed of its engine, but by the power of its built-in processor — simply because with PostScript, a lot more of the computing work goes on inside the printer, rather than inside the PC.

That doesn't mean that the processing power of the printer is of no importance with PCL: it's a matter of degree. I'll be talking more about this later in the chapter when I focus on the matter of print speeds and processors, but it's worth trying to keep this technical difference in mind because it does help make various other things a whole lot clearer.

### Device independence

PostScript's most clear-cut advantage over PCL 5 is its ability to drive printers that work at any resolution. No matter whether your printer works at 300dpi, 600dpi, 800dpi, or even 1,200dpi, PostScript can drive it. The technical term that describes PostScript's ability to work with any laser at its highest achievable resolution is "device independence."

By contrast, PCL 5 has until recently tied you to 300dpi. Even now, 600dpi is the limit and that is only achievable with PCL5e which is still almost exclusively the preserve of Hewlett-Packard's own LaserJet 4 models.

Many businesses occasionally need very high resolution output, but can't justify buying an in-house printer capable of delivering it. For example, if you need absolutely top-notch artwork for your brochures, annual reports, and so forth, you probably won't want your final output to be done on a 300dpi machine — on the other hand, your volume of work may not warrant buying your own 1,000dpi PostScript model.

In this case, the solution is to do your proofing on your own lower resolution PostScript laser printer, and then give the disks to a bureau that has specialist ultra-high resolution laser printers aimed mainly at the commercial printing, publishing, and graphic arts markets.

These are not machines that are used in normal office environments — they fall into a light industrial category of their own — but they also use the PostScript language, just like humble office lasers. The best known equipment in this category is the Linotronic 300, which uses laser beams to draw images directly onto light-sensitive paper, which is then developed photographically. This equipment can actually work at resolutions far higher than 1,000dpi. There are thousands of service bureaus across the country which offer Linotronic output from your disks — you can look them up in your local *Yellow Pages*. It is PostScript's compatibility with so many output devices — and the fact that it is the only language to span both the DOS/Windows and Apple Mac platforms — that gives it its biggest advantage.

Of course, you could still do your proofing on a PCL 5 printer, and then give the disk to the Linotronic bureau for final output. But you may find that the proof copies would differ from the final ones in details other than the resolution. PostScript printers tend to offer more typographical finesse in matters such as the precise spacing between characters. They also have better line drawing abilities, and they can print in more shades of gray. In addition, the PostScript printer in your office is able to have the identical resident fonts as the bureau's Linotronic (remember what I said earlier about built-in fonts resulting in faster printing than ones that are downloaded from a computer).

For all of these reasons and more, the desktop publishing (DTP) and graphics software markets are geared around PostScript. If you plan to use advanced DTP and drawing programs — such as Aldus PageMaker, Quark Xpress, Aldus Freehand, or Adobe Illustrator — then you should definitely get a PostScript printer. That doesn't mean that PCL 5 machines can't print documents produced on these programs — they can, but they simply aren't quite as suitable and there may be certain graphical images that they will have a problem printing at all.

### PostScript and word processing

Keep in mind, though, that the distinctions between upmarket word processing (WP) and desktop publishing are diminishing. Windows WP programs — such as Microsoft Word, Lotus Ami, and WordPerfect for Windows — can produce layouts and special effects that come close to straightforward DTP.

Most people who use these advanced WP programs choose PCL rather than PostScript: this is the type of upscale office work where PCL 5 can hold its own very well. The same applies to the growing breed of entry-level, sub-$100 DTP programs (such as Microsoft Publisher). It's only when you get into fairly serious DTP work that PostScript begins to be *de rigeur*.

### PostScript and PCL 5 prices

Two or three years ago, PostScript was a premium technology — it was head and shoulders more advanced than PCL 4. But PostScript prices have since fallen considerably in response to the growth of PCL 5. The least expensive PostScript machine can now be bought for a street price of around $700. Street prices for an entry-level PCL 5 laser start at just under $600 (these prices were accurate as of spring 1994).

### Having your cake and eating it

The good news is that if you're torn between PCL 4, PCL 5, and PostScript, you can have your cake and eat it. All PCL 5 models are downwardly compatible with PCL 4 (useful if you come across an older piece of software that only has a PCL 4 driver). A few PCL 4 models have PCL 5 upgrades; likewise, many PCL 4 and some PCL 5 models have PostScript upgrades. Finally, most PostScript models also come standard with PCL 4 or 5.

So you needn't worry too much about making an irreversible mistake. It's not like the VHS versus BETA debate in the early days of VCRs, when a wrong decision at the outset meant you couldn't rent *Star Wars* three years later.

Upgrades are often accomplished simply by inserting a plug-in cartridge. Be warned, though, that PostScript upgrades often result in slower speeds than you get from a factory-ready PostScript model. If PostScript is your prime requirement, I suggest getting it on a machine that has it as standard.

In much the same way, you may find bugs with the PCL emulations on machines that are mainly marketed as PostScript printers. In short, although it's nice to know that you can switch emulation without switching printer, it's safer to choose a printer that is specifically and primarily intended for the language that you will work with most.

### Automatic emulation switching

If you use different software — some PCL oriented, and some better suited to PostScript, and especially if more than one computer is sharing the same printer — you may want to look for a model with automatic emulation switching. This way, the printer recognizes the language that the computer is using and resets itself automatically for each job. The alternatives involve either flicking a switch on the printer each time you need to change language, or resetting it using software on the computer.

Auto emulation switching was pioneered by QMS — a printer vendor mainly addressing PostScript users — which first introduced it a few years ago. It is now offered by numerous vendors. It's a handy feature, but be advised that it does not always work in practice quite as well as it's meant to. It's a good idea, which has yet to be perfected.

### Variations on PostScript

Although I have been talking about PostScript in general terms, it actually comes in two different versions — and there are also clone languages from other software companies. The original one is Adobe Level I. In 1991, Adobe introduced a new version called Level 2. This has not replaced Level I, which Adobe continues to license to numerous printer vendors, but it is gradually taking over.

Level 2 offers certain detailed speed-related improvements; it also offers additional functionality in some types of work, such as printing new data onto form layouts already created; and there are additional features for supporting color (outside the orbit of this chapter). All other things being equal, Level 2 is more desirable than Level 1, but the differences aren't huge and there's no need for most people to fret unduly about which version to go with. Level 2 is downwardly compatible with Level 1.

### Microsoft TrueImage

Microsoft has for some time been trying to get into the page description language business, as part of its strategy of dominating as many major areas of business software as possible. It now has a device-independent PostScript clone of its own called TrueImage, which it is trying to license to printer manufacturers as an alternative to Adobe.

Microsoft markets TrueImage as a natural companion to its Windows operating environment and to its TrueType fonts (I'll be talking more about fonts later). However, there is no requirement for Windows users to get TrueImage and it's by no means clear that it offers major benefits to the type of users who are drawn to PostScript. (Do not confuse TrueImage with Microsoft's Windows Printing System that I discussed earlier.)

At the time of this writing, few vendors had embraced TrueImage. It may well end up fading away.

### Other PostScript clones

Apart from this, there are quite a few PostScript clones developed by smaller software specialists and, occasionally, by printer manufacturers themselves. Most of these are copies of Adobe Level 1, but a few emulate Level 2. Sometimes, the buyer may not be aware that a printer uses PostScript clone software rather than the real Adobe product — it only becomes clear when you peruse the small print and notice tell-tale phrases like "PostScript-compatible quality."

In theory, a PostScript clone is no different from the real thing. And, in practice, this is indeed usually the case. But sometimes, you do run into compatibility problems with the programs in your computer. While this may be less common now than in the past, it is also the case that you no longer have to pay much of a premium to get the genuine Adobe article. Buyers who wish to play it safe should keep this in mind, but not make too big a deal of it.

# Laser Engines Explained

So far, I've been talking about the software aspects of laser printers. Next, I'll turn to the hardware.

### How lasers print

A lot of people don't realize that the printing technology used by laser printers is based on that developed for xerographic copiers. Like a copier, a laser printer includes a drum; however, the printer's drum is exposed to light from a laser beam, rather than to an optical reflection of the image.

The electronic signals sent from the computer have the effect of switching the laser on and off, so that the drum is charged positively or negatively. The positive areas attract particles of electrostatically charged toner to create an image, which is offset from the drum onto the page and fused to the paper using a heat process. Excess toner is then cleaned from the drum, readying it for the next image. Get it?

### Who makes the engines?

The part of a laser printer that performs the operation described above is known as the "engine." Most vendors of laser printers don't make their own engines, but source them from other manufacturers. Often, the same engines are used on several different brands of machine. For example, Canon engines are used by Canon itself, Hewlett-Packard, QMS, and Apple — among others. Likewise, Sharp engines are used by Sharp itself, Texas Instruments, and Dataproducts. Other engines which are used by several different printer vendors include ones made by TEC, Samsung, Minolta, and Fuji Xerox.

Often, different brands of printers using the same print engine also share other common hardware features. For example, many Canon- and Sharp-based lasers with the same engines look alike and have the same paper handling features; there may be important differences "inside," however, such as the type of processor (more on that soon) and software enhancements to increase the resolution.

A few printer manufacturers use their own proprietary engines and don't supply them to other vendors. These include Panasonic, Lexmark/IBM, and Kyocera. There are persistent rumors in the industry that Hewlett-Packard is developing its own engines and that its next generation of LaserJets will not, therefore, be Canon-based.

### Engine pros and cons

The question of who makes a printer's engine is quite important. Some engines with comparable resolution produce better print quality than others, though these days the differences tend to be picked up only by perfectionists.

Some engines are a lot easier to maintain in terms of keeping them supplied with consumables. The simplest are the ones where the drum, toner, developer, and fuser all come in a single sealed cartridge — in other words, you've only got one thing to replace. Canon engines use all-in-one cartridges, which are generally good for about 3,500–6,000 pages depending on the model. Minolta engines also have them; its cartridges are generally good for 6,000 pages.

Among the less satisfactory engines in this respect are Panasonic's: some of its machines require you to change the toner every 5,000 pages, the drum every 13,000 pages, and the developer every 20,000 pages. To make matters worse, Panasonic's method of adding toner is somewhat messy. TEC engines are also far from ideal: they require you to add new toner after only 1,500–2,000 pages.

On the whole, it makes sense to buy a laser printer based on a widely-used engine. This is because it'll be easier to shop for supplies. In general, different brands of laser using the same engine can use the same consumables, so if you're going with something like a Canon, Sharp, or Minolta engine you should be able to get better discounts and you needn't have anxiety about whether supplies will still be readily available in a few years' time.

### Running costs
The cost of all the consumables typically works out to around 3 cents per page on a laser printer, or a bit less. However, there are signs that running costs on some newer engines are falling closer to 2 cents a page.

Most quoted running costs assume that five percent of a page will be covered by part of a black image — this may sound little, but it is, in fact, a reasonable average (especially when you account for white areas such as the holes in a letter "e" or "o," etc.).

### Recycling toner cartridges
Environment- and value-conscious people are often uneasy about throwing out used toner cartridges and buying brand new ones. Why not reuse them, they ask? Adding new toner to an empty cartridge yourself is not a practical option, but there are third-party companies that take back old cartridges and sell you ones that they have recycled themselves. In addition, some of the printer vendors have started their own recycling programs.

The feedback I get from users suggests that, in general, recycled cartridges work, but that some have a higher failure rate than new ones. I have not heard of a recycled toner cartridge failing and causing damage to the machine, and a reputable vendor will replace faulty ones.

One vendor gets around the "what to do with old cartridges?" dilemma by doing away with cartridges and disposable drums entirely: Kyocera's laser printers, which use proprietary technology, simply require you to add toner from a bottle — the drum does not need replacing. See "The Green Printer" section later in this chapter for more on how environmental issues impact the printer world.

### The LED alternative

Not all the machines which fall loosely under the "laser" heading do use laser engines. All of Oki's and Kyocera's printers use LED technology instead, as do some of the latest models introduced by Panasonic, Texas Instruments, and Lexmark.

LED is very similar to laser technology and the differences need not concern the end user unduly. LED proponents argue that it's more reliable, since fewer moving parts are employed — but the excellent dependability of laser printers speaks for itself. Either way, LED printers are certainly not "poor people's lasers" as some make out — I'm not convinced that the technology is intrinsically superior, but it's certainly not inferior and it often offers better value. My advice is to treat lasers and LEDs as one and the same when it comes to choosing what to buy.

However, it is worth noting that, so far, LED engines have only been developed for the lower and middle levels of the printer market. Currently, all are 300dpi units in the 4–8 pages per minute sector.

You'll sometimes hear the term "page printers" used to embrace both technologies. However, when I use the term "laser printers," I generally use it in a loose sense to cover LED models as well — though every now and then I refer to "lasers/LEDs" to remind you that the distinction does exist!

# More on Print Resolution

At the start of this chapter (in the "What's Doing in Laser Printers?" section), I introduced you to print resolutions and described how the standard is shifting upward from the 300dpi level where it has been for the past few years. And in the part where I discussed the PostScript and PCL printer languages, I explained how higher-than-300dpi has hitherto been the province of PostScript — until the new 600dpi Hewlett-Packard LaserJet 4 series came on the scene. Next, a few other points to round out my explanation of resolutions.

### Higher-than-300dpi output

Anything better than 300dpi can claim to be "high resolution," but some resolutions are a great deal higher than others. A 400dpi printer will scarcely be better than a 300dpi one — you'll have to look pretty hard to spot the difference. The most popular level for high resolution output is 600dpi. With 600dpi printing, a solid black area measuring one square inch is formed out of 360,000 dots, compared with 90,000 on a 300dpi model.

Anything higher than 600dpi is only for upscale PostScript desktop publishing applications. The very highest resolution office lasers go all the way up to 1,200dpi and are worthy alternatives to the Linotronic laser typesetters that I talked about earlier — more about these shortly.

### *"True" high resolution*

Within the printer industry, there are some fierce squabbles raging about what can really be considered "true" high resolution output. Many of the laser printers that boast resolutions higher than 300dpi are actually based on what were originally designed to be 300dpi engines, but they use software that causes the laser beam to create a higher resolution image by placing tens of thousands of additional tiny dots. This process is sometimes known as "software interpolation" or "modulation."

Only a few engines — such as those made by Lexmark, some of Sharp's, and various Canon units used by Hewlett-Packard — are designed from the ground up to be high resolution. The technical arguments get pretty complex, but purists argue that "from-the-ground-up" means "better." The phrase "native resolution" is sometimes used to refer to the base resolution of an engine before any software modulation kicks in. No engine currently in production has a native resolution higher than 600dpi, incidentally — so whenever you come across something like 800dpi, 1,000dpi or more, you can be sure it's software interpolated.

### *Resolution enhancement*

As I indicated earlier, 300dpi PCL 5 printers generally include a form of resolution enhancement technology. This results in smoother curves and sharper edges than you normally get — conventional 300dpi printing can leave slightly jagged edges. The feature is often referred to as "image enhancement" or "smoothing," and several vendors give it their own trademarked names — but it's basically the same in all cases.

The way resolution enhancement works is by changing the actual size and position of dots in relation to the ones around them; this helps fill in and smooth out potentially jagged parts of an image. The difference it makes should not be overstated, but it definitely helps make 300dpi as good as can be hoped for. It is also available on 600dpi engines.

Note that a 300dpi engine with resolution enhancement is still termed "300dpi" — it takes more than this to count as a software-interpolated high resolution engine. The generally accepted view is that in order for an engine to be referred to with a higher dpi figure than its native resolution, the software modulation must increase the number of dots, not just their size and position. And that involves something more than what's normally implied by resolution enhancement.

However, there are gray areas in these definitions, and a certain lack of unanimity and consistency in how all the terms are applied. For example, some vendors use terms such as "600dpi effective resolution" when all they are really referring to is 300dpi with image enhancement. When checking a vendor's claims, always be on the look-out for tell-tale phrases such as "equivalent to" which imply that the resolution may not be quite what is being hinted at!

### Gray scales treatment

Some vendors have developed another form of image enhancement that gives special treatment to photos by increasing the number of gray scales that can be printed. This used to be quite a rare feature, but it's becoming more common — about one in five machines now seem to have it.

# Super-High Resolution Lasers

If you are an advanced user of desktop publishing software, and produce your own layouts for brochures, catalogs, annual reports, and so forth, you probably send your PostScript files on disk, or by modem, to an outside bureau for typesetting at the very highest resolutions.

However, a growing number of in-house DTP users are considering buying their own super-high resolution PostScript lasers to enable them to produce final copy output in-house. Several vendors sell machines that, using software interpolation, extend the resolution of office lasers to as much as 1,200dpi.

The technology used by these in-house machines differs from that used by a bureau's Linotronic which, as I explained earlier, uses a process that involves exposing light-sensitive paper to a laser beam and then developing it with photographic chemicals.

### Pros and cons

While the results of in-house 1,200dpi machines are not quite as good as those from a bureau's Linotronic, they can get very close on text work. The difference is more noticeable with photographic and other shaded images, including color separations, where resolutions of over 2,500dpi can give professional typesetting equipment — or "imagesetting" equipment, as it's sometimes known — a distinct advantage.

The price of 1,200dpi laser printers has fallen during the past year, though it is still not cheap. Most of these machines are able to print onto 11" x 17" paper, and list prices are generally in the $7,000–$10,000 range.

One factor that will influence the price within the above range is whether you want to have "bleed" on 11" x 17" paper — in other words, images that go right up to the edge of the page. This requires you to print onto oversized paper that is, in fact, larger than 11" x 17"; a further benefit of doing so is that you can then also display printer's crop marks, etc.

If you seem to be writing a lot of checks to a service bureau, it may make sense to figure out how much of your work could be done in-house with one of these machines, and then do some calculations to determine which would be the more cost-effective approach. Keep in mind that if all you want is 11" x 17" printing — for proofing purposes, perhaps — and you don't really want 1,200dpi output for final copy, you can get away with a regular laser printer that has ledger-paper capability costing a lot less (check out machines from Dataproducts if you're looking for low-cost 11" x 17" capability). Also keep in mind that the bureau business has gotten a lot more competitive lately, and if you haven't checked prices recently, now might be a good time to shop around a little.

### Vendors to consider

The three main vendors to consider if you are thinking of buying 1,200dpi laser equipment are LaserMaster (tel: 800 950 6868), NewGen (tel: 800 756 0556), and Xante (tel: 800 926 8839). LaserMaster and Xante both sell equipment based on Toshiba 8ppm engines, and Xante uses an 8ppm Canon engine.

# Engine Speeds and Processors

Three main factors influence the speed you'll get out of your laser printer: the speed of the print engine, the type of processor, and the amount of memory.

### Engine speeds

All print engines have manufacturers' rated print speeds. The slowest engines print at 4 pages per minute (ppm), the fastest in what currently constitutes the mainstream office market cruise at 20ppm (there are also super-high-volume models that go faster still, but these tend to be somewhat specialized).

In general, 15–20ppm engines are mostly aimed at network environments where the machine will be shared by more than 10 users. By contrast, 8–12ppm engines tend to be for smaller workgroups sharing a printer. And 4–5ppm engines are suitable for use by one or two computers only. In spring '94, the industry standard defining a "mid-range" laser was effectively upgraded when Hewlett-Packard replaced its 8ppm LaserJet 4 with the new LaserJet 4 Plus models. Today, 10–12ppm has become the main mid-market level, and 8ppm is beginning to look a little slow.

Keep in mind, though, that all rated ppm speeds should be taken with a grain of salt. They represent the fastest speed an engine is capable of working at; the actual speed is dependent on other factors, among them the type of processor.

### Processors

A laser printer contains a microprocessor, similar to a computer's, for processing and interpreting the data it receives from a PC. The more work the printer has to do to process information, the more powerful the processor will have to be in order for the machine to perform close to its rated engine speed.

Let's flash back to an earlier section of this chapter. You'll recall that a characteristic of PostScript printers is that they receive all the information concerning a page in one go, and then set about interpreting the data inside the printer; by contrast, PCL printers adopt a more passive role vis-à-vis the computer, carrying out single instructions and then receiving new ones. The result is that if a PostScript printer is to work as fast as a non-PostScript printer using the same engine, it needs to have a more powerful processor.

### Choosing the right processor

A common processor in the lower end of the laser printer market is the Motorola 68000. This isn't especially powerful, but it's good enough for most straightforward work under PCL emulation. Its slightly more powerful sibling is the Motorola 68020. Both these Motorola processors can be used in PostScript printers, and often are at the lower end of the price spectrum. But they do result in quite sluggish performance, especially the straightforward 68000.

Increasingly, therefore, PostScript vendors are using a more powerful type of processor that uses something known as "RISC" ("reduced instruction set computing") architecture. Several chip makers have RISC processors, including Intel, AMD, and Weitek. RISC processors are also found on some PCL 5 models.

A year or two ago, RISC processors were considered pretty exotic items, reserved for the premium end of the market. Today, while they are not exactly chips for the masses, they have become much less exclusive. In fact, one Oki printer selling for under $500 uses one, though that isn't typical.

### Watch those MegaHertz

Keep in mind that the same processor may run faster on some machines than on others. The measure of a processor's speed to look for is the "MegaHertz" (MHz) rating; the higher it is, the better.

For example, the Motorola 68000 processor usually runs at 10–12MHz, but on some models it cruises along at 16MHz. That said, you can only make instant, at-a-glance MHz comparisons if two printers use the identical processor: a RISC processor with a low MHz figure will probably be faster than a non-RISC one with high MHz.

# Printer Memory

The third ingredient in the speed equation is memory, though this also has other implications about what you can do with your laser printer. All laser printers come with at least 512K — or half a megabyte (MB) — of random access memory (RAM); quite a few come with 1–2MB as standard; and a number have 4MB or more as standard. Having more memory can help a printer do its job faster; it can also determine the sort of graphics printing you can do.

### Memory for PCL 4

The amount of memory you need is dependent on the type of work you do. For fairly straightforward text work under PCL 4, 512K is sufficient; this can also allow you to print straightforward half-page graphics. If you want to print full-page graphics, you should get 1.5MB. These suggested amounts of memory assume that you aren't using part of your memory for additional downloaded fonts (more on that later) — if you are, you'll need more on top.

### Memory for PCL 5

PCL 5 machines generally come with 1MB of memory as standard. This is sufficient for producing half-page graphics at 300dpi. If you want to print full-page graphics, look for at least 2MB of installed memory — plus extra for any downloaded fonts.

### Memory for PostScript

For PostScript applications, 1.5MB is the absolute minimum; 2–3MB is preferable, and around 4–6MB is generally ideal. More memory may be required for certain types of upscale graphics work.

### Adding memory

Whatever amount of memory is standard, you can almost always add more at any time as an option. Be warned, though, that adding memory later often works out to be more expensive than getting a similar machine equipped with the higher amount in the first place — and you've also got the hassle of the installation.

Memory upgrade prices vary: as an example, a 1MB upgrade for the HP LaserJet 4 lists for $109; 2MB is $199; and 4MB is $299. However, memory upgrades are often as heavily discounted as the printers themselves. Some niche mail order dealers specialize in cut-price memory — look for ads in the computer magazines sold on newsstands.

### Data compression

Some vendors have developed techniques that compress data sent from the computer to the printer. This effectively allows them to squeeze more out of the memory that's built into the printer — for example, 512K with data compression may be equivalent to 1MB without it.

# Summing up Speed

Because of all the variables in the speed equation, it can be quite difficult to get a firm handle on how two printers will compare in practice — especially as the machine that's faster on one job may be slower on another. It can be hard to determine, for example, whether you're better off with a slightly slower engine and a faster processor, or a faster engine and a slower processor. However, the following points should be kept in mind:

✔ For straightforward non-PostScript applications, especially those mainly involving text, it isn't necessary to have a super-powerful RISC processor. A Motorola 68000 or 68020 is adequate.

✔ Because the processor matters less on non-PostScript work, the rated speed of the print engine is probably more important.

✔ With PostScript work, the relative importance of engine-versus-processor is different. There's little point in getting a fast engine if the processor can't keep up with it. For example, you could find that a 4ppm machine with a fast processor will match or even beat the performance of an 8ppm model with a slower one. But all sorts of variables affect this (such as the nature of what you're printing).

✔ If speed is paramount, and you can afford it, look for both a faster engine and a RISC processor!

# Paper Handling

No one likes running out of paper all the time, so the larger your paper supply, the more convenient it is. Most machines use removable paper cassettes — similar to the ones on copiers — that hold 200–250 sheets. However, some budget lasers and LEDs only take 50–100 sheets (as do most ink jets).

### Dual cassettes

Most laser printers come with a single on-line paper cassette; you might own an extra cassette for a different paper size, but you can only have one in the machine at a time. However, some machines come with two on-line cassettes, or allow you to add a second one as an option. This means that you can keep two different types of paper in the machine at once — letterheads in one tray, for example, and continuation sheets in the other. Be sure, though, that your PC software will support this feature.

If you don't get a dual-cassette machine, most paper cassettes have a by-pass feature, which allows you to place one or more sheets of a different paper stock on top of the regular cassette without having to remove and unload it. This is usually the way you print multi-page correspondence — the letterhead goes in the by-pass and is printed first, and the subsequent pages are printed onto blank sheets drawn from the cassette. (The concept is identical to the by-pass feature found on most copiers.)

### Feeding envelopes

Addressing envelopes is one of the general pains of office automation — software and hardware manufacturers have been slow in coming up with brilliant methods of integrating this smoothly into the rest of the word processing operation, though things are better than they were.

Just about all laser printers can take standard-size envelopes — you either feed them through using one of the normal paper cassettes or you insert a special envelope cassette in place of the regular one. Even then, you have to make sure that the software will cause the image to print in the right place. Some of NEC's laser printers have a handy pull-out envelope tray that's built into the machine in addition to the regular paper cassette; this comes standard and holds 15 envelopes.

If you plan to do a lot of envelope printing, you may want to choose a machine that has an optional power envelope feeder. As an example, the power feeder on the HP LaserJet 4 Plus holds 75 envelopes, does not require you to take out the normal paper cassette, and lists for $349. Not very many mid-market lasers do offer power envelope feeders, however.

### Printing on 11" x 17" paper

The vast majority of laser printers can only print on paper sizes up to letter (8.5" x 11") and legal (8.5" x 14"). Machines that can handle 11" x 17" paper have traditionally been regarded as niche products, and have been expensive.

This is still the case up to a point, but there are signs that it's changing. For example, Compaq made 11" x 17" printing a standard feature of its network printers introduced in 1992, and you don't really appear to be paying a premium for the capability — the problem is that these machines won't be available for much longer, as Compaq is pulling out of the printer market. Likewise Dataproducts introduced some pretty competitive 11" x 17" models around the same time. None of Hewlett-Packard's current models have this capability, incidentally — though this is a gap that the company might fill before long.

### Duplex printing

Vast areas of forest are wasted each year because of people's reluctance to print onto both sides of the paper, but the laser industry doesn't make it very easy — automatic double-sided printing is not widely available, and manual double-sided printing (i.e., turning the paper over and running it through a second time) is a pain and can lead to jams.

The jargon term for automatic double-sided printing is "duplex." This feature is generally only found in the 15–20ppm network printer market, and is often an option. The good news is that duplex will be an option on HP's new mid-market LaserJet 4 Plus models — at the time of this writing, the company was saying this will be available in the last quarter of 1994.

# Interfaces & Network Connectivity

Next, a few words about linking your laser printer to the rest of your computer system.

## Interfaces

Most laser printers come with both parallel and serial interfaces as standard; this ensures that they are compatible with all DOS PCs. Unless there's a special reason to the contrary, you'll almost always use the parallel interface, as this works significantly faster. As a result, some cheaper models do not have serial interfaces as standard. If you're using a PostScript printer with an Apple Mac, you'll need an AppleTalk interface: this is standard with most PostScript printers.

Many machines with two or more interfaces keep them all "live," and switch from one to the other automatically depending on the job that's coming in.

## Direct network connectivity

A growing number of printers, usually faster ones, can be fitted with network interface cards that allow you to connect them directly to Ethernet and Token Ring networks without the need to go through a special PC performing the role of print server. Occasionally, network interfaces come standard.

All printers with an AppleTalk interface can be connected directly to an AppleShare network without the need for additional upgrades — this networking capability is also built into every Macintosh computer as standard. No ink jet printers can be connected directly to a network, except that some models designed for Macs can work with AppleShare.

# A Font Primer

The subject of fonts (i.e., typefaces) is surprisingly complicated. One of the reasons is that the printer industry the font industry, and the PC software industry, have not yet settled on a single set of standards. Here's a plain English guide that should answer most of the font issues that buyers find confusing.

As I mentioned earlier, your laser or LED printer will include a number of built-in — or "resident" — fonts when you take it out of the box. (Few ink jet printers include resident fonts.) However, the actual range of typestyles you get with the machine may turn out to be smaller in reality than it appears from the quoted number of resident fonts — this applies especially to PCL 4 machines, as I show below.

In addition, be advised that the fonts built into your printer may not match the ones that you work with on your computer screen. Finally, keep in mind that the more you get into fonts, the less important the ones that are resident will become. All of the above assertions are explained below. ...

### PCL 4 resident fonts

Typically, a PCL 4 printer comes with something like 14 resident fonts. All of these are "bitmapped" (i.e., fixed in size). This doesn't mean that you get 14 totally separate typefaces — you may find that almost all of the 14 are different versions of the same basic typeface, usually Courier (the leading typewriter-lookalike font).

For example, a typical PCL 4 machine with 14 resident fonts would really give you: Courier Medium/12 point; Courier Bold/12 point; Courier Italic/12 point; Courier Medium/10 point; Courier Bold/10 point; Courier Italic/10 point; Line Printer Medium/8.5 point. That makes seven fonts in all — but each comes in both portrait and landscape orientation, which is how you get to the quoted total of 14.

So although you get this high-sounding number of 14 fonts, what you really get is Courier in all the styles you're likely to want (and some you probably don't want) and Line Printer (a small-size face suitable for printing out piles of computer data) — not quite as much as you might have hoped for. (Remember, incidentally, that the word "point" refers to the typesize; the smallest type is usually 6 point and a good size headline is unlikely to be more than 48 point; what you're reading now is 10 point.)

### PCL 5 resident fonts

If you're getting a PCL 5 machine, your built-in fonts will include some that are bitmapped and a selection that are scalable. Typically, you might get two or three typeface families in four separate styles (normal, bold, italic, bold italic, etc.), each of which can be printed out in any size you're likely to want. In addition, you'll get the same range of bitmapped fonts that you would on a PCL 4 machine (i.e., endless fixed-size/style versions of something like Courier).

### PostScript resident fonts

Most Adobe PostScript machines come with 35 resident fonts, all scalable. These consist of several type families in various styles, including one set of special symbols (or "dingbats"). The resident font set you get standard with a PostScript machine is significantly wider than what usually comes built into a PCL 5 printer.

### Bold and italic styles

Sometimes you get separate bold and italic styles of a scalable font (either PCL 5 or PostScript), but in other cases you just get one generic style and the bold/italic effects are created from within the application program on your computer. Typographical purists argue that having dedicated bold and italic styles is better; this is more true with some typefaces than with others, but it need not concern mainstream business users unduly.

### Showing fonts on screen

A problem that arises from having fonts that are resident in a printer is this: how do you get them to show up on your computer screen, so that you can see what you're working with? The chances are this won't happen of its own accord — you'll have to do something to make it happen. In practice, a lot of people don't bother.

This didn't used to be an issue in the days of plain-vanilla DOS, when people didn't expect "what you see is what you get" (WYSIWYG) screen displays and when, accordingly, people's use of fonts was generally extremely unambitious. But it is a factor with Windows, when WYSIWYG — or something very close to it — is the norm.

The scalable fonts that are built into most PCL printers come from a company called Intellifont, which is a division of Agfa. Although Windows 3.1 comes with its own very good collection of screen fonts, including ones that resemble the fonts built into PCL 5 printers, they are not the same. Instead of coming from Intellifont, they're what's known as TrueType fonts — TrueType is a format that was developed jointly by Microsoft and Apple.

This does not mean that you can't print your Windows screen fonts — far from it. As a Windows user, you can have your TrueType fonts downloaded to your printer every time you output a file (drawback: slows down print speed, wastes all your built-in Intellifont typefaces, and may force you to get more printer memory).

Alternatively, you can have the printer use the resident fonts that most closely resemble the TrueType ones that you are working with on screen (drawback: means that what you see on screen may not exactly match what you'll get on paper).

If neither of these arrangements seems ideal, one option is to get a hold of a utility program called Intellifont-for-Windows 3.1, which displays your printer's resident fonts on screen alongside your TrueType fonts and lets you add other Intellifont typefaces for the screen or printer. (This program is available free from Hewlett-Packard, though it is not shipped with any of its printers; to order it, call 303 353 7650.)

Life would be a lot simpler if the printers would themselves come with resident TrueType fonts that exactly match the ones built into Windows. Then you'd get the speed/memory benefits of resident fonts, without the hassle/anxiety of matching them to screen fonts.

The good news is that this is exactly what is slowly beginning to happen. The 600dpi Hewlett-Packard LaserJet 4 models do come with the standard TrueType faces contained in Windows 3.1, alongside a full set of 35 Intellifont typefaces. At the time of this writing, few other vendors had started doing the same, but this should become increasingly common.

Moreover, the Windows Printing System upgrade for LaserJet II and III (and compatible) printers that I discussed earlier contains the full set of Windows TrueType fonts and thereby ensures that the fonts built into your printer match those you are working with on screen.

### Adding extra fonts

Many people make do with the fonts they get with their computer and with their printer. Because the ones that come with the computer are, literally, a lot more visible, these are the ones that users focus on and work with. In other words, most people don't really think in terms of the fonts that are resident in their printer and instead choose to work with the ones that they have on their computer — which may or may not be the same.

There are a number of ways of adding extra fonts to your overall computer/printer system. The first method is to get a font cartridge and insert it into a special slot built into the side of the printer: the extra typefaces then become additional resident fonts. Most lasers come with one or two font slots. These are especially convenient for PCL users if your printer accepts Hewlett-Packard cartridges, which most do; if yours doesn't, the range of fonts available on cartridges may be narrower and it'll be harder to shop for discounts.

The other way of adding fonts is to buy them on floppy disks which you install on your computer hard drive. If you are using Windows or Apple Mac software, they'll show up on screen in your range of font options and be automatically downloaded into your printer's memory each time you output a document that uses them.

This method may require you to add more memory to the printer, but it does allow you to take advantage of some bargain priced font offerings. Many computer catalogs offer package deals where you get a pretty fine collection of fonts for around $40. There's a big price war taking place in the font industry. Not long ago, Adobe introduced a "ValuePack" containing a great selection of typefaces for $39 — only a few months earlier, the same fonts would have cost over $1,000 if purchased separately!

If you are shopping for font deals, think quality as well as price: stick to fonts from the best sources such as Adobe, Microsoft, Monotype, and Apple. All of the above usually offer excellent deals and fine typography. Some of the lesser vendors tend to offer more quantity than quality in their low-priced font bundles.

Because disk fonts have now become so inexpensive, there's usually not much of a case to add extra resident fonts — the latter haven't fallen much in price and those HP-compatible font cartridges are not very good buys. In fact, they aren't even offered in many computer catalogs. What's more, you've got the problem referred to earlier about fonts that are resident in your printer not showing up of their own accord on your computer screen.

The result is that once you have added lots of downloadable fonts, the whole subject of resident fonts will probably fade from your consciousness — you'll probably stop thinking in those terms. Many font addicts keep over 50 fonts in their computers, and the majority of the ones that they use most often are not resident in their printers. In fact, a lot of people who are pretty computer-proficient don't even know what fonts are built into their printer.

For all of these reasons, I don't think that the number of resident fonts in a printer should be a particularly important factor in your selection criteria — despite the fact that vendors often make quite a big deal of it.

### Hard disks on printers

I've given you the impression above that the only way of making your new fonts resident is to get them on cartridges and that, because font cartridges aren't nearly as good values as fonts on disks, you should forget about adding new resident fonts and instead think downloading. And, in the vast majority of cases, that advice seems to me to make sense.

However, a few laser printers offer ways of buying fonts on disk, and then making them permanently resident in your printer. One is to get a laser printer with its own hard disk, which can accept and then permanently store downloaded fonts. As you might guess, this option is not only expensive, it is also only available on a few pretty upscale printers.

Another option — also not very common — is to get a printer that can accept fonts downloaded from your computer into a special permanent "read only memory" (ROM), the contents of which survive even when the printer is switched off.

Both of these options are worth considering if you consider yourself a pretty serious font user. For the vast majority of users, however, the way to go is to buy fonts on disk, load them in your computer, and then download them to the printer on a daily basis as you print your documents. Choose the screen fonts you like — and don't worry about whether they match ones that live in your printer.

### Type 1 fonts, PostScript, & Adobe Type Manager

Both TrueType and Intellifont typefaces are good for all mainstream business applications. However, the finest library of fonts, and the best-crafted, typographical detail, comes from a third category known as Type 1 fonts. This is the format that's used with PostScript — you'll sometimes hear Type 1 fonts loosely referred to as "PostScript fonts."

The leading supplier of Type 1 fonts is Adobe Systems itself; others include Bitstream, Monotype, Linotype-Hell, and Agfa. All of these are very reputable. If you are a committed PostScript user, you'll probably want to standardize on Type 1 fonts. This is more or less essential if you plan to use a Linotronic bureau for your high resolution, final copy output — almost all bureaus work only with Type 1 fonts.

However, you do not have to buy a PostScript printer in order to use Type 1 fonts. If you buy yourself a piece of software for your computer called Adobe Type Manager (ATM), you can display any Type 1 fonts in your Windows or Apple Mac screen environment and download them to virtually any printer (ink jets, as well as lasers and LEDs).

With ATM, you can also be sure that the appearance of your Type 1 screen fonts will exactly match the Type 1 fonts built into your PostScript printer. ATM usually sells for about $60 — I regard it as an essential part of any well-equipped computer. (Note that it often comes free with Adobe font bundles.)

Keep in mind that some popular typefaces are available in TrueType, Intellifont, and Type 1 formats; in other cases, you get fonts that look very similar indeed, but that have different names depending on the format. But many fonts are only available in one format and, as I indicated above, Type 1 gives you the richest choice.

### Font substitution — and SuperATM

One of the problems of working with lots of different fonts is that you may create a file using fonts on your computer, then transfer that file to someone else to work with — only to find they don't have the same fonts loaded in their system.

When that happens, all your fancy fonts default to some generic typeface like Courier: the fine-looking document that you created will look pretty awful and a lot of the line-breaks, spacing, and layout will change because of the different typographical qualities of the default font.

A version of Adobe Type Manager, called SuperATM, gets around this problem with a clever feature called "font substitution." SuperATM automatically creates a simulated version of the original fonts used on a document when you don't have the same ones on your system. The simulated fonts will be close enough to the originals to preserve the look and feel of the document.

SuperATM also includes another clever Adobe feature that organizes excessively-long, drop-down font menus on your screen into shorter ones, by bunching all the members of the same font family into their own sub-menus.

# The Green Printer

Printer buyers are seeing an increasing number of machines sporting a new "Energy Star" logo, developed by the Environmental Protection Agency (EPA). The right to display this logo is conferred if a vendor's machine complies with new EPA guidelines designed to reduce wasteful use of electricity.

To qualify, a printer has to shut itself off after 15 minutes of inactivity, so that it only consumes a tiny trickle of power until being woken again by an incoming print job. In other words, you save power without having to remember to switch the thing off.

According to the EPA, an amazing 30–40 percent of office workers leave their computers and printers running at night and at weekends. Even people who are good at switching off their computer often don't get around to turning off the printer. Screen-saver software — the type that makes your computer display flying toasters and goldfish when it's left unattended — are almost an encouragement to leave the thing on.

The EPA further estimates that the typical saving by turning off a PC and printer during non-work hours would be $73–$126 per year — enough, they point out, to drive 1,825 to 3,150 miles.

And, while I'm quoting EPA statistics, they also say that if everyone switched off their computers and printers when going home, the electricity saved would be enough to power Vermont, Maine, and New Hampshire — and that carbon dioxide emissions would be reduced by the equivalent of cutting out five million automobiles.

Most laser printers being introduced in 1994 and 1995 are Energy Star compliant. Vendors are doing their best to squeeze maximum commercial advantage out of being seen to be green. Eventually, however, just about all printers will comply with this standard, so that there will be no net advantage for any of them. In the meantime, vendors who were quick off the mark with compliance can be expected to indulge in the heavy-handed "spend-your-money-on-our-product-to-save-the-planet" style of advertising.

### Cutting down on ozone

Buyers might also like to note that the most environmentally friendly lasers do away with ozone-generating corona wires for charging the drum and transferring images. Instead, they use charge rollers.

# Buying a Printer

Next, some advice on how to go about buying your printer.

### Discounts

There are two things that you should keep in mind about printer prices. The first is that they are falling, and probably will continue to do so during the shelf-life of this book. The second is that most brands are widely available at discount prices well below the official list prices.

However, this second statement is less universally true than it used to be, as some vendors have begun to set list prices quite a lot closer to what they expect actual street prices to be, instead of setting list prices that more or less invite discounts of 30 percent or more in order for a machine to be competitive.

Other vendors have taken the view that list prices are so meaningless that they won't even quote them. The most you can get out of them is an "estimated selling price," which usually equates to something toward the high end of the actual street price range.

Some models, and a few entire brands, are rarely openly advertised in discount channels. This does not mean that discounts cannot be obtained, just that they may be harder to find, subject to negotiation, and often smaller in percentage terms.

### Where to buy

You can buy discount printers from a variety of sources, but the lowest prices often come from mail order dealers that advertise in the newsstand computer magazines and in some newspapers. Also look out for mail order printers in computer supplies/peripherals catalogs. Remember that buying by mail may save you local sales tax (depending on where you, and the seller, are located): this could more than offset shipping charges.

Local computer dealers also offer discounts, though their asking prices tend to be higher. Computer warehouse stores can be another good place to look. In addition, discounted low-end printers can be bought at many office supplies warehouse stores, at consumer electronics stores, and in some major department stores, including Sears.

If you're buying a computer, you can choose to go to a manufacturer that sells direct to end users, cutting out the middleman. These direct sales vendors — such as Dell and Gateway — offer low prices combined with excellent service and support arrangements, including warranties with on-site service. Unfortunately, this option is rarely available if you're buying a printer.

Some PC direct sales vendors do sell printers as a sideline, but only acting as resellers for other manufacturers. In these cases, the printers are sold under their original brand names — and they don't come with the same on-site service warranties and support arrangements that you get with the vendor's own-brand computers.

### Laser warranties, reliability, and service

Obtaining a hefty discount should not affect your warranty rights, despite suggestions to the contrary often put around by dealers who charge higher prices. However, you should confirm this in each case with the dealer selling the machine: if you buy from an unauthorized dealer, the manufacturer may try to argue that you lose your warranty protection.

In the overwhelming majority of cases, printer warranties only cover you for repairs if you send the machine back to the dealer or the manufacturer's service depot — "carry-in" service, in industry jargon. That whole process can easily take two weeks or more, including shipping times; usually, moreover, you, the buyer, have to pay for the outbound shipping.

Some dealers carry out repairs themselves, though they generally still have to order parts; others will simply ship the machine on your behalf to the manufacturer or another service organization. Only a few models, mainly upscale ones aimed at larger corporate network users, come with warranties that include manufacturer-arranged on-site service. This type of service — which can also be purchased as an option on other models or after a warranty has expired — may be contracted out to a national third-party service organization.

Having said that, some local dealers may promise to carry out on-site warranty repairs at no charge if you buy from them. Also, sometimes you will be given a new machine if yours breaks down very soon after you bought it, rather than having to send yours away for repair.

The good news is that laser printers are, in general, very reliable: only a very small proportion of buyers need repairs during the first year, and you probably won't need any over a period of three or four years. So you could be paying an excessive insurance premium if you cough up a high price for a machine largely because you were impressed with the warranty arrangements.

That said, a longer warranty is obviously a plus point to take into consideration if you're finding it hard to decide between two models which seem pretty equal in hardware terms. Two-year warranties are becoming quite common in the printer world, especially in the ink jet market where they are now the norm. Most suppliers of LED machines offer five-year warranties on the LED printhead — a way of reassuring people affected by "what's-LED-anxiety?" — and one year on the rest of the machine.

By now, I hope you're feeling reasonably proficient on the technicalities of laser, LED, and ink jet printers — and sufficiently street-wise about how to go about buying one. Next, I'll introduce you to the vendors. ...

# Vendor Profiles

Here, in alphabetical order of brand names, are overviews on the leading vendors in the laser, LED, and ink jet markets — this information should help you to narrow down your choice of suppliers. Also shown are addresses and phone numbers.

## *Apple*

*Apple Computer, Inc.*
*20525 Mariani Avenue*
*Cupertino, CA 95014*
*Tel: 800 776 2333*

Apple is the only mass market PC manufacturer to have stayed away from the DOS/Windows set of industry standards and lived to tell the tale. But when it comes to printers, Apple is more in the mainstream. The main printer language used in the Apple Mac environment is PostScript, which is also widely used in the DOS/Windows market. However, Apple Macintosh computers do not work with either of the PCL printer languages.

Although Apple Mac computers don't work with PCL, a number of Apple's PostScript laser printers do. This is because Apple is keen to market its printers to users of DOS/Windows PCs, as well as to Mac owners. It also wants to sell to companies that have a mixture of Macs and PCs in the same office. In practice, though, Apple has had limited success in marketing its printers outside the Mac world. Apple Mac computers can also work with most other brands of PostScript laser, providing that the latter have an AppleTalk interface (most do).

There was a time when Apple's printers tended to sell at a premium and buyers could usually find much better values by looking at other brands. Today, Apple is much more competitive, though Mac owners can still sometimes do better by shopping elsewhere. Apple has traditionally been one of the vendors most concerned with the styling of its laser printers, although the differences are less pronounced now that other vendors have begun to be more design-conscious themselves.

Although PostScript is dominant in the Mac world, Apple's ink jets and its entry-level lasers use the company's own printer driver called QuickDraw. A QuickDraw printer is a completely passive device without its own built-in processor — in other words, a lot of the work which is normally done inside the printer is left to the host computer which does the driving.

This helps to keep printer costs down, but it also means

that how close actual speeds come to the theoretical speed of the print engine will depend on the power of the host Macintosh computer and on whether the computer is being used for other things at the same time. Since the type of users who buy QuickDraw printers tend to have only moderately powerful Macs, QuickDraw printers often turn out to be quite slow — especially when handling graphics.

Apple has recently introduced something called "GrayShare," which is effectively an enhanced version of the QuickDraw printer driver. GrayShare serves two purposes: the "Gray" part of the name refers to the ability to handle sophisticated gray scales printing, and the "Share" part refers to the fact that you can share the printer between more than one computer using a serial port connection.

Printer sharing via GrayShare is not the method of choice for making a printer available to more than one Macintosh in an office. A better way — when available — is to use the AppleShare networking feature that's built into every Macintosh computer as standard. However, a printer needs to have an AppleTalk interface in order to network on AppleShare, and Apple's entry-level QuickDraw models do not have these.

One odd — and somewhat irritating — fact about Apple's approach to the laser market is that whereas the company's printers are mostly PostScript models, Apple Macintosh computers themselves come with TrueType fonts, which do not correspond to the resident fonts inside the PostScript printers. Even the extra font packs that Apple sells are TrueType, rather than PostScript. Apple's commitment to TrueType dates back a few years, and — although it may have seemed a good idea at the time — it seems to me to be a bit of an anomaly today.

Of course, Mac owners can add third-party Type 1 (i.e., PostScript) fonts to their computers to match and expand the range that are resident in their printers — but it's strange that Apple itself remains wedded to TrueType on Macs when not a single Apple printer has TrueType resident fonts.

In the case of Apple's QuickDraw printers, this isn't so much of an issue, as these machines don't have resident fonts anyway and QuickDraw users by definition don't have any particular ties to PostScript. If you do buy a QuickDraw printer, you'll find that it comes with a set of fonts on disk to load into your computer — somewhat similar to one of those inexpensive font collections you see in computer catalogs — but this is done for marketing purposes only and really has nothing to do with the features and capabilities of the printer itself. Any QuickDraw printer can print any fonts loaded into your Mac — including

PostScript ones (providing you have Adobe Type Manager installed). By the way, if all this discussion of fonts seems confusing, you ought to read the section on fonts earlier in this chapter!

Apple used to be an all-Canon vendor, in terms of the engines it used in its laser printers. However, although some of its models still use Canon engines, a number now use ones supplied by Fuji Xerox. At press-time, Apple's top-of-the-line model — one of its Fuji Xerox-based units — was a relabeled version of a Dataproducts printer. Apple's ink jet printers are manufactured by Canon.

Apple sells its printer line through the same authorized dealers and retailers that handle its Macintosh computers, though also through some other channels such as third-party Mac software/peripherals catalogs. For a while, Apple was selling printers direct by mail order — at press-time, it had recently stopped doing so following the termination of *The Apple Catalog* and it was unclear whether and/or how it would do so in the future (see the Apple entry in the Vendor Profiles in Chapter 1 for more on this).

Late in 1993, Apple abolished conventional list prices and instead now quotes "estimated selling prices," which it also refers to as "ApplePrices." These prices correspond to the upper end of the street price level — you can sometimes beat them by shopping around, but not by a great deal. All Apple printers come with one-year warranties.

## *Brother*

*Brother International Corporation*
*200 Cottontail Lane*
*Somerset, NJ 08875*
*Tel: 800 227 6843*

Brother International — the US subsidiary of Brother Industries Ltd., of Nagoya, Japan — markets a number of laser printers, including some PostScript-compatible models. It also sells one Canon-based ink jet, which — at the time of this writing — was the only black-and-white ink jet that comes equipped to work on both DOS/Windows PCs and Apple Macs.

Brother used to sell lasers based on Canon engines, as well as some models that used its own. Today, however, all its models use Brother engines. The latest Brother engines have been cleverly designed to work with the same cartridges as Canon engines.

Brother is better known as a PCL vendor, and is not noted

as a PostScript specialist — though it does sell models that use its own PostScript-emulating language called BR-Script.

Brother was one of the first vendors, apart from Hewlett-Packard itself, to sell a laser that uses the extended version of HP's PCL 5 print language (PCL 5e). The significance is that this enables its 600dpi engine to deliver high resolution working with PCL as well as with PostScript emulation — other vendors which have 600dpi engines working under regular PCL 5 default to 300dpi when in PCL mode and can only deliver the higher resolution with PostScript.

Brother addresses the lower middle sectors of the laser market — its current range includes models that work at 6ppm and 10ppm. Availability is reasonably good, though Brother isn't as prominent as some other printer vendors discussed in this chapter. Brother now offers two-year warranties on most of its models. It has made arrangements for on-site service to be provided by Dow Jones at extra cost.

## *Canon*

*Canon Computer Systems Inc.*
*123 East Paularino Avenue*
*Costa Mesa, CA 92628–5048*
*Tel: 800 848 4123*

The Canon brand name is mostly seen in the printer market on the company's hugely successful ink jet printers, known as "Bubble Jets." These machines deliver excellent print quality, though they can be a little slow.

Canon has traditionally occupied a slightly strange position in the laser printer market. Canon makes the engines used by Hewlett-Packard and a number of other laser printer vendors (actually, Canon does more than this: it actually manufactures entire HP printers in its Virginia factory). But despite this, Canon's own-brand laser printers until recently did not use HP PCL emulation but, instead, ran on Canon's own proprietary page description language called CaPSL III. I believe this was the result of some obscure agreement made between Canon and HP a number of years ago, though no one at either company seems able to remember the reasons. Either way, the result was that Canon became a somewhat marginal brand.

However, a new division of Canon was formed in 1992 called Canon Computer Systems Inc. (CCSI). Its mission was to focus on the small business/home office market with new lines of computer and printer products. It also took over the existing Bubble Jet line. Among CCSI's latest products are a new generation of HP-emulating Canon brand lasers. These machines are fine, but the range tends to trail Hewlett-Packard's and is also focused on the lower end of the market — for example, Canon only introduced its first equivalent of the 600dpi/8ppm HP LaserJet 4 in spring '94 and, a few weeks later, HP replaced its version with the faster LaserJet 4 Plus.

Canon's ink jets and lasers are being targeted through retail outlets such as computer stores, office supplies warehouse stores, and consumer electronics stores. Availability is excellent. Two-year warranties are offered on carry-in terms.

## *Dataproducts*

*Dataproducts Corporation*
*6200 Canoga Avenue*
*Woodland Hills, CA 91367*
*Tel: 818 887 8000*

Dataproducts is a relative old-timer in the printer market, having been founded in 1962. Originally an American manufacturer, it is now a wholly-owned subsidiary of Hitachi and Nissei Sangyo (no, that isn't a misprint for Sanyo). Its laser printers are based on Sharp and Fuji Xerox engines. It also sells fairly upscale color printers and various types of niche printers outside the scope of this chapter.

Realizing that a smaller player has to be different in order to survive, Dataproducts has a tradition of being innovative and has quite a long list of "firsts" and "only's" to its name — though some of its advantages have proved to be relatively short-lived. Its latest innovation is a highly sophisticated software function built into its faster models to help users who have computer networks comprising a mixture of different hardware platforms and software. It calls this "Virtual Printer Technology" (VPT).

Dataproducts can be an interesting vendor to consider if you are a large network user, or if you have niche requirements (11" x 17" printing, for example). However, it is not a particularly obvious choice if you consider your needs to fall in the pretty mainstream, mid-volume general office category. Dataproducts's 20ppm model is also relabeled by Apple.

Dataproducts is not highly visible in the mass discount market, but its products can be found there if you look around a little. Warranties are either one or two years, depending on the model, and on-site service is included with the faster ones.

# Epson

*Epson America Inc.*
*23530 Hawthorne Boulevard*
*Torrance, CA 90505*
*Tel: 800 922 8911*

Epson America is part of Seiko Epson, the giant Japanese manufacturer of computers, computer peripherals, and other high-tech products (not to mention watches). Epson is best known in printers for its very strong position in the struggling dot matrix industry, but has also built a good name in the lower and middle sectors of the laser market where it has good distribution. At press-time, all of its lasers were based on Minolta 300dpi engines.

Late in 1993, the company re-launched itself back into ink jets, a market which it had previously had difficulty in entering. Its Stylus-series ink jets are competitively priced and have some unusual design features. However, it remains to be seen how easy it will be for Epson to ease the hold that Canon and Hewlett-Packard have on this immensely competitive market.

Epson is not a pacesetter in lasers: its machines — which are chiefly aimed at PCL users — tend to have specifications aimed at less demanding users. It backs its laser and ink jet printers with two-year warranties on carry-in terms.

# Hewlett-Packard

*Hewlett-Packard Company*
*PO Box 58059, MS511L-SJ*
*Santa Clara, CA 95051–8059*
*Tel: 800 752 0900*

Hewlett-Packard (HP) has lately been one of the big success stories of the American computer industry — a case study in how versatility can pay off. Originally a manufacturer specializing in large minicomputer systems — the type of equipment that took a major knock with the advance of PCs — it could have gone the way of companies such as Data General and faded away from the mainstream computer market (worse, it could have followed minicomputer manufacturers, such as Wang, into terminal decline). Instead, it successfully diversified into a major supplier of peripherals (its attempts to become a force in PCs have had more mixed results).

In particular, HP established itself as the undisputed market leader in laser printers and as one of two dominant forces in ink jets. Not only does HP sell more lasers than anyone else, but its own PCL printer languages have become the main industry standards, rivaled only by PostScript. This means that all PC-oriented software vendors ensure that their programs communicate with HP printers, and just about all other laser printer manufacturers also ensure that their machines are fully compatible with them.

Setting the industry standard can be a mixed blessing, however, as IBM found out in the PC market. Once other vendors are able to follow it — often adding their own enhancements — what advantage is there to the buyer in sticking with the original?

One tactic HP has used to stay ahead is to update its standard faster than its competitors can follow. When HP introduced PCL 5, it took some rivals the best part of a year to update their own PCL 4 emulations. And a year after HP introduced the first 600dpi lasers to run under the extended version of PCL 5, most of its competitors had still not caught up. Just as some started doing so in 1994, HP increased the speed of its own machines.

With the exception of the 300dpi entry-level LaserJet 4L models, all HP's lasers now use 600dpi engines which — unlike most other vendors' higher-than-300dpi models — are able to work at full resolution under PCL as opposed to only under PostScript.

All of HP's printers have PostScript options and variants — you can either add PostScript or buy a model that is factory-equipped. The PostScript variants are recognizable by the letter "M" in their model numbers — "M" apparently standing for "Macintosh," as Apple users are viewed as the main customers for these models.

HP sometimes gives the impression of having a slightly ambivalent attitude towards PostScript, which up to a point is a competitor to its own PCL language. It can't afford not to support it, but it prefers to compartmentalize it in its own niche.

All of HP's lasers are well made and superbly documented. There is a feeling of quality and commitment surrounding the whole company, which you don't get with all its rivals. HP's lasers are very widely available at competitive discount prices. All come with Canon engines and most actually come out of a Canon factory in Virginia. However, there are rumors that HP and Canon will part ways with the next round of machines: according to some published reports in trade newspapers, HP is developing its own print engine.

HP is also a leader in the ink jet market. However, although HP's black-and-white desktop ink jets have superb reputations for quality and sturdiness, they have in some senses begun to show their age: in particular, they could be faster and they have an appearance which is utilitarian to the point of being ugly. This may change during the shelf-life of this book, however. By contrast, HP's portable ink jets are very sleek units. Incidentally, HP's DeskJet models are the ink jets for DOS/Windows PCs, while the DeskWriter versions are for Macintosh users.

HP's printers come with one-year warranties mostly on carry-in terms, though the 4Si-series network models have on-site service included. On-site service is available on all the machines, if you're willing to pay.

There's a helpful telephone support line — the wait can be quite long (and the number is not toll-free), but the attitude and knowledge of the people you talk to is usually first class when you do get through.

## Kyocera

*Kyocera Electronics, Inc.*
*100 Randolph Road*
*Somerset, NJ 08875*
*Tel: 800 323 0470*

Kyocera is a Japanese manufacturer with interests in fields ranging from ceramics to printers. Its page printers use LED, rather than laser, technology. The company has been in the printer market for quite a long time. After a period of selling fairly boring machines, it began selling some rather distinctive models in 1992.

What sets Kyocera's printers apart from the crowd is that they do away with environmentally-unfriendly, non-biodegradable disposable print cartridges. Instead, patented technology allows you to add toner from a bottle to work with a permanently installed drum.

This — and the company's claims that its machines are ozone-friendly — are the basis for its distinctly "green" style of marketing: Kyocera would like you to choose its machines not just for their print quality, but also because they are better for the planet. But the company also appeals to your pocket: it claims that running costs work out under a penny a page (compared with around 2–3 cents on most "normal" laser printers).

At the time of this writing, Kyocera had two models, one running at 10ppm, and the other at 18ppm. Both have some interesting options, including copier-style sorter bins. Though some of the company's literature talks about "300 x 1,200" printing, these machines are really 300dpi models with image enhancement.

Sales are through dealers, but you can also order direct

from Kyocera. This brand is rarely advertised in discount channels, so you'll have to satisfy yourself that any deal offered is competitive.

# Lexmark

*Lexmark International Inc.*
*740 New Circle Road*
*Lexington, KY 40511*
*Tel: 800 426 2468*

IBM itself pulled out of the printer and typewriter markets about two years ago, selling its business in March '91 to a new venture capital-backed company called Lexmark. I always understood that the name was chosen after the Lexington, KY location of the main plant — but then I came across some PR blurb that said: "The name was created by combining LEX — an abbreviation of Lexicon, pertaining to word — and MARK, which refers to marks on paper." Take your pick.

Lexmark purchased not only the assets, but also the right to use the IBM brand name on these products. Its management is largely ex-IBM, so the whole operation still looks and smells like Big Blue (IBM retains a 10 percent stake). However, there is a gradual shift towards downplaying the IBM connection, and giving more emphasis to the Lexmark brand.

All of Lexmark's laser and LED printers use the company's own engines. In 1991, Lexmark became the first engine manufacturer to offer 600dpi lasers to the general business market — beating Hewlett-Packard by a year. Like most other non-HP models, Lexmark's older 600dpi units only offered high resolution in PostScript mode. However, the company did introduce its first PCL 5e models in summer '94 (enabling it to offer high-resolution printing in PCL mode as well).

Lexmark has sold ink jet printers for some time, but until recently its machines were all Canon-based. Late in 1993 it introduced the first machine using its own ink jet engine — this seems a very good machine, though it will face new competition when Hewlett-Packard and Canon update their own ink jet ranges in 1994.

Lexmark printers can be bought in the mass discount market, though they are also sold through more corporate channels. All are backed by one-year warranties (except that its LED model has a five-year warranty on the printhead). On-site service is included with the higher-end models and is optional on the others; this is carried out either by dealers or by IBM which still has the contract to provide maintenance. Some of Lexmark's printers are now being sold relabeled by Gestetner.

Lexmark still manufactures heavy-duty office typewriters, as well as keyboards and supplies. In addition, it recently started making notebook computers (this has placed it in indirect competition with IBM itself). According to the PR blurb referred to above, Lexmark would rank among the top 200 corporations on the Fortune 500 list were it a public company.

# NEC

*NEC Technologies Inc.*
*1414 Massachusetts Avenue*
*Boxborough, MA 01719–2298*
*Tel: 800 632 4636*

NEC sells some fine machines. Most are based on Minolta engines, though its entry-level model uses NEC's own. That machine — the Silentwriter SuperScript 610 — is unusual, as it is a "slave" to the computer it works with: in other words, it allows the computer to do a lot of the print processing work that would normally take place inside the printer itself.

At the time of this writing, NEC was only selling 6ppm and 10ppm printers; one of its 10ppm models had a 600dpi engine. NEC printers have some nice design features, and they're quite easy to find in the discount market: they are solid mid-market buys. They're backed by one- or two-year warranties, depending on the model, on carry-in terms.

# Oki

*Oki America Inc.*
*532 Fellowship Road*
*Mount Laurel, NJ 08054*
*Tel: 800 800 7333*

Oki is a major player in the printer market, focusing on the low and middle sectors, and addressing both PCL and PostScript users. Its machines are not lasers, but LED printers; all use Oki's own engines. Oki's printers can be very good values. The brand is easily found in the mass discount market.

Currently, Oki only sells 4ppm and 8ppm models; all its machines have 300dpi engines. It remains to be seen whether Oki is content to focus on this sector of the market, or whether faster and/or higher resolution engines are in the works.

Possibly to counter a misapprehension in some quarters that LED is less of a known quantity than laser technology, Oki backs all of its machines with a five-year warranty on the LED printhead, as well as a one-year warranty on the rest of the machine. This policy has recently been emulated by other vendors selling LED models. The company makes arrangements for on-site service to be available, though the standard warranties are on carry-in terms.

## Panasonic

*Panasonic Communications & Systems Company*
*Two Panasonic Way*
*Secaucus, NJ 07094*
*Tel: 800 742 8086*
Panasonic — part of the giant Matsushita empire — has a fairly high profile in the low and middle levels of the laser printer market and has recently introduced its first LED models (easily recognized by their unusual, space-saving upright design). Its machines, which use Matsushita engines, are mainly aimed at PCL users and tend to sell on price more than on stunning performance.

The brand is widely available in discount channels. Panasonic printers come with a one-year warranty on carry-in terms (the printheads on the LED machines are guaranteed for five years); on-site service arrangements are left to individual dealers.

## QMS

*QMS Inc.*
*One Magnum Pass*
*Mobile, AL 36618*
*Tel: 205 639 4400*
QMS specializes in pretty upmarket printers, all of which are supplied with PostScript as well as PCL as standard. The product range includes high resolution, 11" x 17", and fast network models. The ones that fall within the scope of this chapter are all based on Canon engines. QMS also sells faster network printers that fall outside the scope of this chapter and is, in addition, a prominent player in the color printer market.

QMS's strength in the printer market is its Crown architecture, sophisticated software that is built into its printers to enhance their performance in network environments. QMS Crown significantly enhances actual speed and overall productivity in busy workgroup and network environments.

QMS's Crown-based products have the most advanced internal controllers in the industry. Keep this in mind, as these printers can perform better in demanding, heavy-use situations than rival machines which, on the surface, appear to have similar hardware specifications.

It seems fair to say that the more demanding your requirements, the more interesting QMS is likely to be as a supplier. Though the company does sell 4ppm and 8ppm machines, these are unlikely to be your best values in that level of the market — unless, perhaps, you are also getting the company's faster printers and you want to source all your machines from the same vendor. QMS printers are backed by one- or two-year warranties, depending on the model. On-site service, provided either by QMS or dealers, is available at extra cost.


## Sharp

*Sharp Electronics Corporation*
*Sharp Plaza*
*Mahwah, NJ 07430*
*Tel: 201 529 9600*

Sharp seems to make everything from vacuum cleaners to banking systems and is a major force in several of the areas of office equipment covered by this book. It has quite a large slice of the laser pie, but most of its business is supplying engines to other vendors: several, including Texas Instruments and Dataproducts, use Sharp engines for part of their product lines.

The company's own-brand machines, including both 300dpi and 600dpi models, are less common in discount channels, but can be good values when you do come across them. They come with one-year warranties on carry-in terms; on-site service is left to individual dealers.


## Texas Instruments

*Texas Instruments Inc.*
*Information Technology Group*
*PO Box 202230, ITG-9136*
*Austin, TX 78720*
*Tel: 800 527 3500*

Texas Instruments (TI) is a high-tech company with fingers in pies ranging from semiconductors to defense electronics systems. It has quite a strong presence in the laser printer market, with a product range comprising Sharp engine-based machines — PostScript and non-PostScript — aimed at mid-market and network users. In addition, the company now sells some very competitive, low-end LED models based on Samsung engines.

In 1993, Texas Instruments entered the ink jet market for the first time. It currently has one machine which uses a print engine made by Tokyo Electric (TEC) in conjunction with Xerox. This machine is quite similar to a new ink jet sold under the Xerox brand name.

The brand is easily found in discount channels. One-year warranties are offered on carry-in terms (the LED models also have a five-year warranty on their printheads); on-site service is available at extra cost.

## *Xerox*

*Xerox Corporation*
*PO Box 1600*
*Stamford, CT 06904–1600*
*Tel: 800 832 6979*

Xerox's main presence in the printer market has traditionally been at the very high end of the document production arena. Until recently, its least expensive laser was a newly-introduced 20ppm network printer, using a Fuji Xerox engine, with a list price starting at $8,750. In spring '94, however, the company introduced a new range of 600dpi 5ppm and 10ppm models, as well as a much more affordable 20ppm one. All of these are also based on Fuji Xerox engines. It remains to be seen how much impact Xerox will have on this market as a latecomer.

Xerox has also recently entered the ink jet market. Actually, the company has been involved in ink jet technology for a considerable time, but it has hitherto not sold a product under its own name. Xerox's new ink jet printer uses an engine that it was partially responsible for designing, but that is manufactured by Tokyo Electric (TEC), a Toshiba subsidiary. This is the same engine that is used in the Texas Instruments ink jet. A separate ink jet product — a multifunctional fax/printer — was expected to be launched later in 1994.

Like all Xerox office products, its printers come with the company's excellent "Total Satisfaction Guarantee," promising a replacement machine during the first three years if the customer is not satisfied with performance. ✍

# Chapter 4

# Low-Volume Copiers

# Low-Volume Copiers

This chapter covers copiers which cruise at below 25 copies per minute (cpm) and are mainly suitable for monthly workloads of up to 10,000 copies. Some of these models do have options like document feeders, sorters, and automatic double-sided copying, but many do not. If you're on higher volumes, you should read Chapter 5 on mid/high-volume copiers.

## What's "Low-Volume?"

There is no hard and fast definition of what constitutes "low volume." Some people making fewer than 10,000 copies prefer a faster machine, which I would classify as "mid-volume." They may just like their copies in a hurry, their copying workload may be concentrated in particular parts of the month, or they may have a need for particular features that are harder to find on slower machines.

Many sub-25cpm machines are officially rated by their manufacturers as suitable for 20,000 copies a month or more. In my opinion, these figures are pretty worthless and somewhat arbitrary. In fact, the official volume figures are largely ignored by the manufacturers themselves and by their dealers — you tend to find that copier salespeople go to the other extreme, and push people towards faster machines than they really need.

Still on the subject of copy volumes, I quite often hear from people who have made, say, 250,000 copies in total on a three- to four-year-old, low-volume copier, and are being told by their supplier that the machine is due for early retirement because it's been worked too hard. But when one looks at the manufacturer's own copy volume figures, it turns out that the machine is well within what the manufacturer originally said it was good for.

In other words, there seems to be a double standard. When the copier industry sells us copiers, they give out these high copy volume figures and tell us that we can get five years' use out of a machine. But when we get to within 30 or 40 percent of those figures, they tell us we're using the machines too heavily and should trade up to something newer and better.

---

**Inside This Chapter ...**

---

### How laser printers are reducing low volume copier usage

One quick thought before I get started. The rapid growth of laser printers in the past two years — prompted by major price drops — has reduced some smaller offices' copier requirements. Rather than making additional sets of computer-generated documents on a copier, some people choose simply to print out additional originals on their laser. The quality ought to be better, and sometimes it's a lot less bother.

The laser option is only practical, and economical, up to a point. You won't have productivity features, such as automatic sorting of completed sets. Double-sided printing is not normally available. Speeds will be quite slow. And the running cost of lasers is quite a lot higher than that of most copiers.

But laser running costs aren't necessarily higher than those of copiers used for less than 3,000–4,000 copies per month. And they should be quite a lot lower than those of copiers designed for under 1,000 copies a month — and those machines don't have much of a speed or productivity edge over laser printers anyway. Keep this in mind if you are a very low-volume user trying to figure out your copier requirements.

### The multifunctional factor

Recognizing the fact that copying and printing requirements can overlap, the copier vendors are working on new "multifunctional" machines that combine both functions in one — along with scanning and faxing functions. These are discussed in Chapter 9.

But don't hold your breath: the multifunctional market is taking a long time to get going, and first-generation multifunctional machines are likely to deliver performance that doesn't compare all that favorably with the dedicated, single-function machines they are hoping to replace.

# The Two Types of Low-Volume Copier

For many years, the low-volume arena has been the sleepy part of the copier industry, with not much going on. Currently, however, some fairly fundamental changes are underway: these have important implications for buyers, as they affect where you can buy your copier, the cost of ownership, and the amount of service you'll need. Here's what's cooking. ...

### Introducing "mini-copiers"

Traditionally, the low-volume copier market has been divided into two sectors. People on very low volumes (less than 1,000 copies per month) have been served by what I call "mini-copiers" — these are very small and compact machines that are generally sold through retail channels. You find them at office supply warehouse stores — such as Office Depot, OfficeMax, and Staples — and also in some warehouse clubs, consumer electronics stores, and office supply catalogs.

Mini-copiers run at 10cpm or less and are pretty basic — they don't have document feeder or sorter accessories, for example. Prices are appropriately low, starting at under $300 and usually topping out at below $1,000. Despite this, copy quality is as good as what you get from much larger and more expensive machines.

Mini-copiers require no maintenance, because they use sealed cartridges in place of parts which, on a regular copier, need servicing by a dealer. When one cartridge runs out, you just take it out and replace it with another. This is something that a user does, and it's pretty easy — no different, in fact, from changing a cartridge on a laser printer. It's almost like getting a whole new copier.

### Introducing "traditional" low-volume copiers

The other part of the low-volume market has comprised machines that run at speeds greater than 10 copies per minute, and that have been sold through the same office equipment dealers that also handle much larger copiers. Traditionally, these machines have not been cartridge-based (or, when they have been cartridge-based, this fact has been played down).

These low-volume copiers, running at speeds of more than 10cpm, have required regular dealer service in order to keep on producing decent copies. As a consequence, people buying them have been obliged to enter into a fairly service-intensive relationship with their dealer, much as they would in the mid-volume market. If they don't, or if the dealer turns out to be no good, the copies will suffer.

### How things have begun to change ...

That's how things have been up until now — and how, up to a point, they still are today. But two new trends are apparent, which have very important implications for the buyer:

> **(1) Retail-channel copiers get bigger:** Some manufacturers are beginning to place larger cartridge-based copiers through the retail channel. You can now buy low-volume copiers at office supply superstores that run at speeds as high as 18 copies per minute and that are good for several thousand copies per month. It is no longer true to say that the only retail-channel copiers are "minis" suitable for the very lowest volumes.

> **(2) Dealer-channel copiers get simpler:** Conversely, cartridge-based copiers — using the same technology as retail-channel ones — are now becoming more common in the traditional dealer channel. So if you buy a low-volume copier from a dealer, you may not need much in the way of routine service after you take delivery. Whether or not the dealer will tell you that is another matter, however.

### The benefits of cartridge-based copiers

Cartridge-based copiers are clearly gaining ground, though they have their pros and cons. The advantage of owning one is that the need for routine service is minimized or even eliminated — these machines are a whole lot simpler and more straightforward. They have a lot in common with laser printers. On the smallest models — the ones I call "mini-copiers" — there should be no need for routine service at all.

On slightly larger cartridge-based models in the 12–18cpm level, some service may be required. For example, the replacement of "fuser rollers" may be a service item — but that isn't a frequent occurrence (depending on the model, this only crops up every 80,000–200,000 copies, which is a heck of a lot of copies for a low-volume user).

Likewise, cartridge-based models with automatic document feeder and sorter options are likely to need periodic service. Those accessories can be fickle on the best of copiers, and may need adjusting from time to time. But what you shouldn't need on any cartridge-based copier are regular visits from a service technician to perform routine cleaning, etc. — something which is required on the non-cartridge variety. And you certainly don't need a technician to put in a new drum. A full service contract on such a machine may, therefore, be unnecessary.

A further advantage of the cartridge design is that, because it reduces or eliminates the need for routine service, it opens up new possibilities for distribution — and this puts downward pressure on prices. Historically, low-volume copier prices have been quite high, because buyers have had to rely on local vendors, with relatively high overheads, for machines running at speeds of over 10cpm. Once you take away the need for intensive service, you open up the possibility of selling these machines through mass market channels that work on much lower margins — and this is exactly what's beginning to happen in the sector of the low-volume market serving people making under 5,000 copies a month.

### The drawback of cartridge-based copiers

The drawback of cartridge-based copiers is that the consumables costs are high. There are three items that figure into calculations about a copier's running costs: toner, developer, and drum (some machines do not need separate developer). On a conventional copier, if you take the list price of these items, and divide them by the estimated yield, you typically get a combined consumables cost of somewhere around 1¢ per copy, give or take a little.

With a cartridge-based machine, by contrast, the copy cost is likely to be anywhere from a bit under 2.5¢ to a bit over 5¢. The highest cartridge copy costs tend to be found on the smallest machines running at speeds of 10cpm or less. The lower cartridge prices in the region of 2.2¢–2.9¢ tend to be found on the faster models running at speeds of between 13cpm and 20cpm plus.

### Cartridge and non-cartridge running costs compared

Does this mean that cartridge-based copiers are always going to be more expensive to own than conventional ones? Not necessarily — it depends on your volume. Below 4,000–5,000 copies per month, the cartridge method can hold its own cost-wise. For a start, cartridge-based copiers may be less expensive to buy, because some are sold by low-overhead retailers that move large quantities of boxes on pretty low margins.

Secondly, although you pay a premium for your consumables, you save money by not needing much in the way of service. It is very hard to generalize about what service does cost on a traditional, non-cartridge low-volume copier. In the mid- and high-volume copier markets, dealers manage to combine consumables and full parts-and-labor service into a single cost per copy charge which they often manage to keep below 1.5¢ (a meter inside the machine keeps track of copies made, and you are billed for each one; alternatively, the price you pay for supplies may include full service for as long as you go on using them).

In the low-volume market, dealers often charge for service in a similar manner, but the cost per copy will be higher because users are not making enough copies to amortize the fixed costs of service into a low per copy charge. For example, if you pay $360 a year for service plus the cost of consumables, and if you make 3,000 copies a month, the service works out at about 1¢ per copy; if you add this to the supplies cost, you can easily get a total cost per copy of about 2¢ or more. If someone is only making 2,000 copies per month, but paying for the same service contract, the total cost per copy could then reach 3¢. In other words, the greater your copy volume, the lower your total cost per copy on a conventional, non-cartridge machine.

There are so many different ways of charging for service, and so many different service values offered, that it's very hard to generalize about the volume point at which cartridge-based copiers become significantly more expensive to own than conventional ones. This is especially true if your calculations take account of purchase prices, and if you make the necessary (but difficult) assumptions about discounts that can be negotiated from dealers versus the low prices offered in retail channels (not that all cartridge copiers are sold through retail stores).

This is one of those areas where two different people could come up with plausible examples that support exactly contrary opinions! I therefore encourage readers to make their own copy cost calculations based on the specific options they have available.

That said, my gut feeling is that mini-copiers that run at up to 10cpm can be reasonably economical for up to about 750 copies a month; that 12–18cpm cartridge-based copiers, with somewhat less expensive supplies, can be appealing for up to about 4,000–5,000 copies per month; but that conventional copiers usually have the advantage between 5,000 and 10,000 copies per month (and can be competitive for as little as 2,000–3,000 copies a month). The non-cartridge low-volume copiers that look least interesting these days are those in the 12–14cpm sector.

I have mentioned that cartridge copiers are now being sold not only by retail stores, but also by dealers that carry full copier lines. Things start getting very expensive if you buy a cartridge model from such a dealer, but then get roped into paying a bundle for service on top — this service may not be required, but that doesn't mean it won't be offered! More on this soon.

Feature requirements, as well as copy volumes, may determine whether you end up with a cartridge-based copier or a traditional one. Cartridge models are usually quite low on frills. For example, Xerox is the only manufacturer to sell cartridge copiers with both document feeder and sorter options (though Minolta has models with document feeders only, and Sharp will also have such a model soon).

### Who makes cartridge copiers?

Of the nine companies to manufacture low-volume copiers worldwide, six currently produce at least one model that uses cartridges and one (Xerox) uses this technology in all its models covered by this chapter. Interestingly, not one of the six sells cartridge-based models exclusively through the retail channel — in fact, three of them aren't in the retail channel at all.

Canon pioneered the concept back in the early 1980s, when it launched its "Personal Copiers" — usually abbreviated to PCs, despite the obvious "personal computer" confusion this causes. Until very recently, the Canon PC line only went up to 10cpm. However, in summer 1994 the company introduced a 16cpm model called the PC-850, which is its first copier suitable for several thousand copies a month to be sold through retail channels. One of Canon's NP series of non-retail, low-volume copiers also uses cartridges, though the rest do not.

The second largest manufacturer of cartridge-based machines is Sharp, which launched its Z-series retail-channel line in the wake of the Canon PCs. Right now, all the Z-series models run at 10cpm or under and are, therefore, what I define as "minis." However, a 14cpm model is expected towards the end of 1994, and this will be targeted at people making up to a few thousand copies per month; moreover, this model will have a low-cost document feeder option (something that's still novel in the retail channel).

One of Sharp's 10cpm Z-series models is also repackaged for the company's non-retail SF-series line handled by traditional dealers. Those dealers will also get the new 14cpm model referred to above, so Sharp clearly no longer sees cartridge-based technology as suitable only for the retail channel.

As well as selling mini-copiers under its own brand name, Sharp makes them for Xerox which has, over the past three years, risen to become the number-two copier vendor in the retail channel. These days, Xerox sells more Sharp-made retail copiers than Sharp does itself.

However, all the low-volume copiers that Xerox manufactures are also cartridge-based — Xerox takes the cartridge design further up the copier market than anyone else, even into what I classify as the mid-volume sector (i.e., over 25cpm). These Xerox-made cartridge models are sold both through the retail channel and through its direct sales/agents channel.

At press-time, the fastest Xerox model to be sold nationally through the retail channel was an 18cpm model called the 5016, and a mid-volume model was being test-marketed in selected locations. If you buy these Xerox-made models through an office supply superstore, Xerox itself installs the machine and the regular Xerox field organization covers you for service. The store, which doesn't hold inventory of these machines, really acts as little more than a showroom and an order-taker, and you have no continuing relationship with it once you have signed the paperwork and handed over your money.

Minolta also makes cartridge copiers, but does not sell them through retail stores (though it has tried, with limited success, to do so in the past) — instead, these machines go through the same dealers that carry its larger machines. The Minolta copiers concerned run at 13cpm and 15cpm, and typically get used for monthly copy volumes up to 5,000.

Mita makes a 10cpm cartridge-based machine which is sold through its Copystar dealer operation. A slightly faster 12cpm variant is also being introduced into Mita's main dealer channel. Mita is not present in the retail channel. The rest of Mita's product range is not cartridge-based. Finally, Panasonic has one 8cpm cartridge-based mini-copier which has all the characteristics of a retail-channel copier, except that it isn't carried by any major retailers.

The other three low-volume copier manufacturers — Konica, Ricoh, and Toshiba — don't have any cartridge products.

### The service needs of cartridge copiers

The smallest mini-copiers do not need any service whatsoever in the normal course of events, any more than a $200 camera does. Keeping the machine up to scratch is just a matter of switching cartridges.

Does this mean that a mini-copier can never go wrong, that no one has ever had to worry about getting one fixed? No, not quite. Some things that might fail can't just be replaced with another cartridge. You could have an electrical problem, for example — the control panel, perhaps. And, if that happened, you'd have to send the machine back — it's like having a consumer appliance fail. The store that sold you the machine will be able to arrange service, even though it probably won't carry it out itself.

But you'd be unlucky if you had that sort of glitch, even if you owned one of these machines for a few years. What I'm saying isn't that mini-copiers are intrinsically fault-free, but that they do away with the need for the *routine* maintenance, and labor-intensive replacement of wearing parts, that on a regular copier are vital.

If you're buying a cartridge copier that's larger than a mini, you should make sure that on-site service is available, should you need it. However, that does not necessarily mean you should pay for a service contract — with the amount of service that's required on copy volumes of below 4,000 copies per month, it's probably cheaper simply to pay for service on the rare occasions when you need it.

The key thing is to make sure that the service is available when you want it. If you buy a cartridge-based copier through a dealer, availability is not the problem: the challenge you face as a buyer isn't being able to obtain service, it's declining, in the face of slick sales pressure, to purchase coverage that's overkill!

With faster-than-12cpm copiers sold through retail outlets, you may want to be a bit more careful. In fact, there were only two brands in that sector of the retail market at the time of this writing: Xerox and Canon. Xerox — which is currently the only retail-channel vendor to offer optional document feeders and sorters — offers three-year warranties on all its low-volume copiers, and the service is on-site on the models that run at 12cpm and faster. In other words, for the first three years, there are no service costs whatsoever over the price of the consumables (which are priced a little above average by cartridge standards).

With Canon, on-site service arrangements are not yet in place for its 16cpm PC-850 referred to above, though this may change during the shelf-life of this book (that machine was not yet in the stores at press-time). A future version of the PC-850 is likely to have document feeder and sorter options, and these will definitely require on-site service coverage. Canon might end up arranging this through a third-party national service provider — for a variety of reasons, its regular NP-series copier dealers may be unwilling and/or unsuitable to take on this task.

### Service overkill on cartridge copiers

Companies like Minolta, Canon, Sharp, and Mita, which sell some 12–16cpm cartridge copiers through their traditional full-line copier dealers, face an awkward dilemma when it comes to advising users about service requirements. While it is important that these 12–16cpm models should have on-site service available, it's by no means clear that smart users should pay for a full service contract (as they would on a regular copier).

But if the copier manufacturers tell users how maintenance-free these machines really are, they risk alienating their dealers who are accustomed to earning revenues from lucrative service contracts. If, by contrast, they encourage end-users to pay for service contracts on top of the not-inexpensive cartridges, they risk pushing the cost of ownership up to uncompetitive levels. In practice, the manufacturers usually duck the issue and give very little steer to end-users — their instinct is to let the dealers sort it out with the customers.

Not surprisingly, some dealers end up treating cartridge copiers as though they were regular copiers — and offer service deals that make no allowance for the cartridge-based design that should make most routine service unnecessary. The customers, unaware of how simple these copiers really are, end up paying the dealer to send someone around to change cartridges and "clean" the machine (it's unclear exactly what a technician is cleaning under these circumstances, as the parts that normally need attention are sealed inside the cartridges).

In the case of Minolta, the cartridges actually contain copy-count meters, so that dealers are able to charge users a fixed cost per copy as they would on a regular, service-intensive machine. That's fine if the fixed copy cost adds up to something close to the price for the consumables, but it's not so great if it pushes the copy cost over 3¢.

### The different types of copier cartridge

Most cartridge-based copiers actually use two separate cartridges — one mainly comprising the drum and the other the toner. Canon, however, uses all-in-one cartridges, so there's only one thing to worry about. But Canon's cartridges are usually the priciest around, and the big drawback is that you don't get any cartridge included in the price of a PC-series copier to begin with.

With two-cartridge copiers, by contrast, the first drum cartridge — usually good for 12,000–20,000 copies — invariably comes standard with the machine, so you only have to pay for toner for your first x-thousand copies. Since the drum element in the copy cost is higher than the toner element, this gives you a worthwhile break on your initial running costs. On a very low-volume mini-copier, it takes a long, long time to get through the initial drum. Canon PC buyers don't get this break.

# How to Buy Non-Cartridge-Based Low-Volume Copiers

Much of the previous discussion has concerned buying cartridge-based low-volume copiers, as these represent a growing part of the market. However, most machines that run at speeds of above 10cpm, but below 25cpm, still use traditional, non-cartridge-based technology. Moreover, aside from Xerox models, all low-volume copiers with both automatic document feeder and sorter options are not cartridge-based and, therefore, do require full service. I expect this to change in the future, but that's how things stand right now.

### Hail to the dealer

Copiers of this type are, for the most part, sold through dealers. Therefore, despite the views I expressed above in the context of cartridge-based models, it is a fact that traditional, service-intensive dealers still have a pivotal role in keeping the nation's low-volume copiers up-and-running.

The typical copier dealer handles just one brand; few handle more than a couple. Most are independent owner-run businesses, though a growing number belong to one of two large conglomerates (Alco and Danka) that have grown mainly through acquisitions. Even those that are part of Alco or Danka operate to a large extent as local businesses, with their own separate identities.

### The direct sales alternative

A few brands are sold direct. Xerox is still the main direct-seller of office copiers, though its low-volume emphasis is increasingly in the retail channel. Some of the Japanese brands, notably Konica and Minolta, have direct sales operations in major cities, even though they are mainly dealer-oriented. And there are also the companies that relabel copiers, and sell them through their direct sales organizations (and sometimes through their own dealers as well); examples include Gestetner, Lanier, and Pitney Bowes.

In general, direct sales organizations concentrate on juicier business. They do sell low-volume copiers, but mainly to companies that need these in addition to somewhat larger machines. You shouldn't be made to feel unwelcome if you approach a direct sales office about purchasing just one low-volume copier, but you probably won't be made to feel particularly important either — and you may not get the best price.

### Dealers matter

These days, most copiers are born equal. When they leave the factory, there aren't usually significant differences in reliability. The days of really bad copiers are largely over. Manufacturers that made terrible machines, such as Olympus, have been driven from the market.

That doesn't mean that lemons are never made — but the point is that all manufacturers have some lemons and, when one particular copier performs badly, it generally isn't symptomatic of a problem affecting that whole product line. Yet, lemons aside, we all know that some copiers seem to work a lot better than others. How come? The answer is that it depends in large part on how well a copier is treated and, in particular, on how well it is serviced.

Despite electronic control panels, the insides of non-cartridge copiers are far more service-intensive than other types of office equipment, such as faxes or personal computers. And that makes the buying process different — you need to establish a continuing relationship with a local supplier you can rely on.

In practice, you generally have to use the dealer that sells you a copier for the service. Do-it-yourself service is not a realistic option on a copier that is not cartridge-based. In some cases, you may find that another dealer in your area can also service your brand of copier — particularly when the same machine is sold under more than one brand name — but you can't count on this. What this means is that choosing the right dealer can be as important as choosing the right copier.

### Judging dealers

Unfortunately, assessing a dealer's service capabilities is difficult. The task isn't made easier by the fact that lesson-one in how to become a copier salesperson is to stress service — all copier reps are programmed to spout boasts about superb service as a matter of course, regardless of the reality of what their employers are geared up to provide. I'm not saying that all copier salespeople who promise good service are bluffing; but I am reminding you that many simply say what they think is necessary to close the deal.

The best recommendations in choosing a dealer are personal experience and word of mouth. If you already know a good dealer who has never let you down, there's a strong case to stick with them (even if their machine is a shade slower, or a mite more expensive, than something else). Otherwise, ask business acquaintances in your area who they use and how satisfied they are.

It shouldn't be too much to expect on-site service within, say, six normal business hours of putting in a request (i.e., same-day if you have a problem in the morning, or next-day if the fault occurs in the afternoon); however, response times in rural areas may be longer, because of the distances.

You should also expect routine service visits to be made at intervals that reflect your copy volume. If you're on an all-inclusive service contract, you should make sure that you actually get all the preventative service calls you're entitled to — sometimes you pay for a contract that supposedly includes them, but somehow not all the visits actually take place (and your copies suffer as a consequence).

Technical competence is paramount. There's not much point in the technician turning up promptly if the fault persists after he or she has left. The most frustrating type of fault can be one involving degraded copy quality or periodic jams/misfeeds — the technician may claim that the machine is "working" (simply because it is producing copies), but you know that it isn't working as well as it should be!

Ideally, the repair people should have been trained by the copier manufacturer on the specific product line you have. In practice, this isn't something you can count on — nor can you always count on a straight answer if you ask the question. A copier dealership that retains its service technicians is likely to have more experienced people on the job than one that is always losing people and hiring replacements — but, again, it can be difficult for the buyer to get a handle on this.

### Low-volume copier warranties

Many people take out a service agreement from day-one of having the machine. This can make sense, but the terms ought theoretically to reflect the fact that the machine comes with a manufacturer's warranty. Copier warranties tend to be amazingly short, however, often lasting no more than a mere 90 days. (As mentioned earlier, Xerox offers three-year, on-site warranties on all of its low-volume copiers, but these are all cartridge models and none are sold through dealers: in these cases, the savings in service costs are effectively negated by the price of the cartridges required to keep the machines running.)

Your dealer may argue that the warranty only covers you for sending the machine back to be repaired, and that on-site service has to be paid for in full from day-one. This is something you'll have to argue out in each case. Also, if you are on a fixed cost per copy agreement, the price you pay for your first x-thousand copies should take into account that you paid for the drum

— a major element in the total copy cost — with the machine. Don't be afraid to haggle about service terms — these things are definitely negotiable!

### Satisfaction guarantees

A few copiers come with extra-special warranties. Xerox is noted for its famous "Total Satisfaction Guarantee." If you aren't satisfied with your Xerox's performance for any reason during the first three years (sometimes longer if Xerox provides the financing), you can insist on a replacement model. Unlike some other guarantees, you — the customer — are the arbiter on whether a replacement is called for. The only catch is that you have to purchase your supplies (other than paper) and service from Xerox — but that's reasonable under the circumstances. The offer applies to all Xerox copiers, from its minis to its very largest office machines.

Lanier's guarantee goes two steps further by promising you financial compensation if your machine has more than two percent downtime and a free loaner if the machine is out of service for more than eight hours. No other vendors have policies that match this, though a few offer diluted guarantees.

Canon, for example, offers a three-year performance guarantee on some of its NP-series copiers, but the problem is that it doesn't explicitly make the customer the arbiter of whether he or she is entitled to a new machine — it simply states that the customer is entitled to a new machine if the existing one can't be repaired.

This could prove unsatisfactory, since it is often far from clear whether a machine has been "repaired." A copier may be "working," for example, but simply not producing very good copies. Or it may be jamming more than the customer finds acceptable, but less than the dealer defines as constituting a breakdown. Also, the Canon contract is between dealer and customer, while Xerox's is between manufacturer and customer.

### Discounts

The "d-word" is guaranteed to make certain copier dealers froth at the mouth. They accuse people like me of undermining their ability to do business, by encouraging buyers to believe that it is possible to obtain both a decent discount and good service to follow.

I stick by my view, however, because the fact is that discounting is rife in the copier market and always has been. To write about the copier market without mentioning discounts would be like writing about the car market and giving the impression that the sticker price is the price you pay.

In general, most low-volume copiers sold through dealers can be bought at discounts of 25 percent below the manufacturer's recommended price, sometimes more. Often, you'll have to negotiate — low-volume copier prices tend not to be advertised openly as much as fax or computer discounts. The problem is sometimes knowing exactly what the list price is — and that's one of many good reasons why you should subscribe to the *What to Buy for Business* series of office equipment guides which provide this information and a whole lot more detailed stuff on individual machines (details in the Appendix)!

Certainly, there would be little point in obtaining a rock-bottom price on a copier if it meant having to rely on a dealer that wasn't geared up to supporting you afterwards. But the argument that discounting is necessarily incompatible with good service ignores the fact that service is a profitable business in itself. Indeed, I suspect that many dealers currently make most of their profits on service. Moreover, it is only discounting that makes dealer pricing remotely competitive with warehouse-store pricing in the low-volume market sectors where the two channels overlap.

# Low-Volume Copier Features

The level of features on low-volume office copiers is, in general, mercifully low. Compared with their feature-laden, mid-volume cousins, low-volume copiers are mostly equipped only with the features necessary to get the job done and offer little in the way of gimmicks and frills.

These days, most people are pretty familiar with the features on low-volume copiers, so I won't explain them all in laborious detail. But here's a brisk review of what they are, just to remind you of what to look out for.

### Copy speeds

As with all copiers, quoted speeds are based on continuous copying onto 8.5" x 11" paper from an original placed on the platen. Remember that copying onto legal or 11" x 17" paper will lead to a speed reduction. The same applies to automatic double-sided copying — not that this is very common in the low-volume market — and often to the use of a document feeder.

Low-volume copier buyers should also pay close attention to the first-copy time. That's the only speed figure that counts when you're making single copies of one-page originals. Some copiers are quite leisurely in producing that all-important first copy, taking around 12 seconds (easily enough time for a yawn or two). Others take only around six seconds or less — that may not sound like a big deal, but my experience is that the difference between six and 12 seconds seems bigger than you'd think.

Almost all the machines in the 10–25cpm sector allow you to preselect up to 99 copies of an original; a few manage 999.

### Copy sizes

All low-volume copiers can copy onto both 8.5" x 11" (i.e., letter-size) paper and most can handle 8.5" x 14" (i.e., legal-size) as well (the exceptions being some minis). Most machines that copy at speeds of 15cpm or more can also copy onto 11" x 17" (i.e., ledger-size) paper.

Even if a machine can't copy onto 11" x 17" paper, it may be able to reduce from 11" x 17" originals or, if not, perhaps from originals up to 10" x 14" in size. Reduction/enlargement is common in the low-volume copier market; most machines with this feature have "zoom," which allows you to select ratios in one percent increments, though some models restrict you to a handful of fixed ratios. The widest zoom range is around 50–200 percent, though some machines can only manage something like 60–140 percent.

### Paper supply features

All office copiers in the 10–25cpm sector come with at least one on-line paper cassette holding at least 250 sheets. Some come with a second one, standard or optional; in a number of cases, the second cassette holds 500 sheets giving a total of 750 sheets on-line. A few machines have 1,000-sheet paper tray options, though these aren't nearly as common in the low-volume market as they are among mid-market machines (nor are they nearly as useful). Some low-volume machines with more than one on-line tray have a feature that makes the machine automatically switch over to the next tray if the first one runs out of paper mid-job.

If possible, look for a copier that has a frontloading paper supply — this means that the paper cassettes take the form of slide-in trays at the front of the machine, instead of sticking out at the side. Frontloading trays take up less space and generally look neater.

A bypass is a handy feature on a copier. This allows you to feed in alternative paper stock without having to unload your regular paper cassette and fill it up with non-standard paper. This can be useful if, for example, you occasionally need to copy onto a letterhead or onto colored paper — but not so often that you want to pay to have a special paper cassette devoted to it. Also, most copiers are more tolerant of very heavy or very flimsy paper when it's fed through a bypass, rather than from a cassette — the chances of jamming will be reduced.

Virtually all low-volume copiers have a bypass of some sort, but they differ in capacity. Some machines only allow you to place a single sheet in a bypass; others allow you to stack a pile of up to 50 sheets, which can be a lot more convenient when you need to make multiple copies onto non-standard paper stock.

### Double-sided copying

Printing on both sides of the paper helps save trees, but it probably won't save many low-volume users any money — that's because duplex (i.e., automatic double-sided copying) is quite a pricey option, costing an average of around $1,000.

That can be worth paying on a copier handling higher volumes, but it's less tempting at the end of the market we're looking at here. Not all vendors even offer it — Canon, for example, does not on any of its sub-25cpm machines. Keep in mind, moreover, that duplex generally slows down a copier's performance, and the effect on low-volume machines tends to be particularly pronounced. Tests carried out by What to Buy for Business show that, at the time of this writing, Sharp and Minolta made the low-volume copiers that work best on double-sided copying.

If you are thinking of getting this feature, check out the capacity of the internal duplex tray — this represents the maximum number of sheets that can be copied onto in one double-sided operation. And, if you think you might want to make double-sided copes of 11" x 17" paper, check out whether a machine you're thinking of buying can manage this.

### Document feeders and sorters

Toward the bottom of the 10–25cpm copier sector, most machines do not have automatic document feeder (ADF) or sorter options. In other words, you always have to raise the lid, position the originals on the platen, make sure they're straight, lower the lid, and press start — the old-fashioned way.

That's not such a big deal when you're copying single-page documents, and you don't make all that many copies anyway. But it begins to be pretty tedious when you often need to copy longer multi-page originals, and also if you do large quantities of single-page copying.

A document feeder and sorter take the effort out of that type of work — at a price. You place the originals in the feeder, dial the required number of copies, press start — and then, paper jams allowing, you just sit back and enjoy, while the machine gets on with producing the correct number of fully-collated sets all on its own.

As you go up the low-volume ladder, document feeder and sorter options become more common, but they are expensive compared with the cost of the basic copier. Some low-volume copier document feeders list for around $600, but most are around $1,200–$1,400; the sorters generally run around $900–$1,200 at list price. On some machines, the document feeders and sorters can be as much as around $1,700 apiece — especially when the accessories are the same ones that are used on the manufacturer's mid-volume machines, as opposed to being specially built for the low-volume sector.

When you consider that the machines which these options work with tend to cost around $3,000–$5,000 in their basic form, it's clear that selecting them can add well over 50 percent to the overall cost. On the whole, there's little point in selecting a document feeder without a sorter or vice versa — my advice is generally to go for both, or neither.

It's worth mentioning, though, that Minolta has developed a very inexpensive type of low-volume document handler able to make collated sets of a multi-page original, one at a time, without the need for a sorter. This unit, which Minolta calls its "set document handler," adds about $600 to the price of two of its low-volume models. It's a very good value — and it's one of the reasons why Minolta has lately become a very tempting choice in this part of the copier market.

### Further feeder & sorter tips

Here are some points to look out for when assessing the abilities of feeders and sorters. First, consider their capacity. Most document feeders in this sector of the copier market can hold up to 30 or 50 originals. Most sorters have 10 bins, and some have 20; each of the bins can hold 20–50 sheets (though 50-sheet capacities are not very common in the low-volume market).

Remember that the document feeder and sorter bin capacities each determine the length of document you can copy automatically, while the number of sorter bins limits the number of sets you can make at a time. For example, let's assume you have a 50-page document feeder working with a sorter that has 15 bins, each with a 30-page capacity. In that example, you could make up to 15 copies of a document no longer than 30 pages — the larger 50-page capacity of the document feeder is effectively wasted, as the smaller capacity of the sorter bins determines the length of multi-page document you can copy.

Most low-volume copier document feeders can only copy from single-sided originals. However, a "recirculating automatic document feeder" (RADF), optional on some machines (sometimes as an alternative to a regular ADF), can also make copies from double-sided originals. If you have a duplex copier, an RADF will be able to make single- or double-sided copies from single- or double-sided originals; if you have a non-duplex (or "simplex") copier, an RADF will still be able to make copies from double-sided originals, but the copies will only be single-sided.

An RADF is generally overkill on a non-duplex, low-volume copier. When it is the only feeder offered, it's usually because the manufacturer hasn't come up with a document feeder specially for its low-volume models and has had to borrow something from higher up its product range.

Incidentally, you may come across the term "semi-automatic document feeder" (SADF): this type doesn't allow you to place a pile of documents in the feeder, and you have to manually feed them in one by one (the feeder grabs each one from you, copies it, and then grabs the next one). If you're copying just one page, this may be a little faster than using a full ADF; with several pages, an SADF is slower than an ADF, but still works out faster than placing the originals on the platen. SADFs are not all that common in the low-volume market; when available, they are incorporated into fully-automatic feeders.

### New in low-volume copiers: stapler-sorters

During the past couple of years, stapler-sorters have made their debut in the low-volume copier market — these are sorters that automatically staple multi-page sets. Previously, they were only available on somewhat larger copiers.

A few of these cost less than you might imagine. For example, the 10-bin stapler-sorter option on Canon's 21cpm NP 2120 copier costs $1,282 (list price) and can produce up to 10 stapled sets, each up to 20 pages long (you can make unstapled sorted sets up to 30 pages).

### Other common features

Finally, a quick review of the "special features" behind those mystery buttons on the control panel that many users never get around to pressing (except when they do so accidentally, and then can't figure out what they've done wrong). Some can be quite useful if you do make the effort to master them, others verge on gimmickry. Here's what they are. ...

**Serial copying**, also known as **book copying**, allows you to place an open book or magazine on the platen, and then obtain same-size copies of each page on separate sheets in a single operation — you don't have to reposition the original for the second page. If you have a duplex copier, both pages can be copied onto different sides of the same sheet.

**Image shift**, also known as **margin shift**, allows you to shunt the image area a little bit to create a margin.

A **photo mode** helps you obtain slightly better quality when you make copies of photographs and other half-tones (though the difference isn't usually all that great).

**Edge erase** removes the shadow around the edge of an original that you sometimes get when it's placed on the platen. Some people refer to this as **border erase**.

**Image overlay** allows you to superimpose two images onto a single copy.

**Copy editing** is a feature that allows you to perform basic "mask and trim" operations — in other words, you can define which parts of an original you want copied. On a few machines, you can also perform more advanced editing functions that involve altering the lay-out of an original before it is copied. (This capability, beloved of copier reps in the 1980s, never met with a very enthusiastic response from buyers and has faded into the background somewhat.)

**Pushbutton color change** is a feature found on a few machines that allows you to keep two toner colors in the machine at once and switch at the press of a button. A handful of models go a step further, with a feature that allows you to make copies in more than one color in a single pass through the machine (you can't make color reproductions of color originals, but you can define which parts of an original you want copied in a second toner color).

All those features are fairly dandy, and some can actually be quite useful. In general, though, low-volume buyers are more concerned with good old-fashioned things like price, copy quality, and getting the best speed that their money can buy.

# Vendor Profiles

Next, a brief look at the vendors that sell low-volume copiers. You can find somewhat fuller profiles of many of these companies, with more background information, in the next chapter on mid/high-volume copiers.

## AB Dick

*AB Dick Company*
*5700 West Touhy Avenue*
*Niles, IL 60718*
*Tel: 312 763 1900*
AB Dick is an old American reprographics manufacturer, now British-owned, with its roots in smaller and medium-size offset printing equipment. In the late 1980s, AB Dick earned its place in copier history books by being the only company to sell relabeled Xerox equipment. Today, AB Dick's copiers are relabeled Konica machines.

These days, AB Dick concentrates on selling copiers mainly to large accounts. It does not actively court smaller businesses. AB Dick is far from being a huge force in copiers. Sales are both direct and through dealers.

## Canon

*Canon USA, Inc.*
*One Canon Plaza*
*Lake Success, NY 11042*
*Tel: 516 488 6700*
Canon entered the copier market in 1968. Today, it is one of the five Japanese companies to manufacture an entire copier range stretching from the low end to the 80cpm level. For the past 12 years, it has been number-one in US market share if you measure by the number of units sold (Xerox is ahead in terms of revenues).

Canon is one of only two Japanese copier companies to manufacture copiers in the US (the other is Ricoh). At presstime, two copiers were being made in the company's US plant, which is located in Newport News, Virginia; these are both low-volume units.

At the very bottom end of the market, Canon is the market leader in cartridge-based "mini-copiers." Remember that these are the machines suitable for volumes below 1,000 copies a month that are sold through retail channels mainly to smaller office and home office buyers. At that level, Canon's only serious opposition is from Sharp and Xerox.

Canon designates its mini-copiers as the "PC" line — those letters standing for "personal copiers." The PC line is being extended upwards in 1994, beyond the mini-copier level, and now includes one 16cpm machine that should be good for something close to 2,000–3,000 copies per month.

Canon's regular office copiers have model numbers that are prefixed with the letters "NP." The NP-series low-volume models are generally priced very competitively. One of them, a 15cpm unit, is cartridge-based.

Canon sells under its own name entirely through dealers. But while it doesn't have direct sales branches as such, it owns subsidiaries in the New York, Chicago, Philadelphia, and Los Angeles metropolitan areas which operate as dealers.

## Copystar

*Mita Copystar America, Inc.*
*225 Sand Road*
*PO Box 40008*
*Fairfield, NJ 07004*
*Tel: 201 808 8444*

Copystar is Mita's secondary brand, created for its smaller dealers. The Copystar models are, for the most part, identical to the equivalent Mita ones and sell at the same prices. However, there is one Mita-manufactured, cartridge-based mini-copier sold through the Copystar channel that does not correspond exactly to anything sold under the Mita name — though a slightly faster Mita-brand variant was just being introduced at press-time.

## Gestetner

*Gestetner Corporation*
*599 West Putnam Avenue*
*Greenwich, CT 06836*
*Tel: 203 863 5551*

Gestetner is a long-established British reprographics company that has undergone changes in ownership in recent years. The Gestetner family sold out to Australian investors several years ago and, subsequently, Ricoh acquired a 25 percent stake.

Gestetner — which trades worldwide — is not a copier manufacturer. Its low-volume copiers are all relabeled Mita models. Gestetner sells through dealers and 35 direct sales branches. Traditionally, the brand has been strongest in the schools/churches/government markets, which have been drawn to Gestetner on account of its background in stencil and electronic duplicators.

# Konica

*Konica Business Machines USA Inc.*
*500 Day Hill Road*
*Windsor, CT 06095*
*Tel: 203 683 2222*

Konica is one of the five Japanese vendors to make all of its own machines, from the bottom to the top of the market. It has been very successful in selling to major accounts under its own name. Indeed, Konica sells a higher proportion of its machines to major national accounts than any other Japanese manufacturer.

Konica's ability to target national accounts has been helped by the fact that the company has far more direct sales branches than any other copier manufacturer apart from Xerox and Kodak — currently, the total is 48. This enables it to bid for multi-location contracts where the buyer wants to deal with only one vendor, preferably the manufacturer.

However, Konica also has a strong dealer network, and should by no means only be considered a major account vendor. Indeed, it has one of the best balanced distribution networks of all the Japanese companies. Konica's copiers are also relabeled by AB Dick.

Konica has never gone out of its way to develop conventional copier products likely to excite smaller businesses. For example, it has only very recently offered a sub-20cpm copier with a document feeder — and even that is a feeder borrowed from its mid-volume range. That said, Konica's initial multi-functional offerings will be targeted at the low end of the market.

Konica is one of only three copier manufacturers not to make any products that are cartridge-based. Its slowest model is a 12cpm unit, and it does not have any presence in the retail channel.

# Lanier

*Lanier Worldwide Inc.*
*2300 Parklake Drive NE*
*Atlanta, GA 30345–2979*
*Tel: 800 708 7088*

Lanier is a major national, and international, office equipment vendor which sells relabeled products direct to end users, as well as through a limited dealer network. The company has excellent distribution: it claims to serve every parish and county in the United States. Its appeal is chiefly to larger buyers, especially those with multiple locations: you can negotiate one deal and get one bill. However, Lanier also sells to medium- and smaller-size offices.

Lanier's low-volume copiers are made by Sharp, Panasonic, and Toshiba. Lanier has an excellent reputation for service, and offers one of the most comprehensive total satisfaction guarantees in the industry. Nonetheless, Lanier's focus in this market makes it less of an obvious choice in the low-volume market than it is in the mid- and high-volume sectors.

# Minolta

*Minolta Corporation*
*Business Equipment Division*
*101 Williams Drive*
*Ramsey, NJ 07446*
*Tel: 201 825 4000*

Minolta tries harder than most of its copier-manufacturing rivals to offer something special to smaller businesses. The company has an excellent low-volume range, consisting of cartridge-based models in the 13–15cpm level, and non-cartridge models beyond that. Minolta does not have anything below 13cpm, and it is not in the retail channel.

Minolta's cartridge-based copiers have an innovative and inexpensive type of document handler suitable for making single copies of multi-page documents one at a time (most other manufacturers do not offer document feeder or sorter options on machines for people only making a few thousand copies a month, or charge significantly higher prices when they do).

Although Minolta sells mainly through dealers, it also has about 20 direct sales offices in major markets. One of Minolta's low-volume copiers is sold through distributors which sell to small dealers that are not authorized to carry the full product line. Minolta low-volume copiers are also sold relabeled by Olympia.

# Mita

*Mita Copystar America, Inc.*
*225 Sand Road*
*PO Box 40008*
*Fairfield, NJ 07004*
*Tel: 201 808 8444*

Mita is the only Japanese company to be a copier specialist: apart from minor sidelines in fax and laser printers, copiers are all it makes. Mita's low-volume range contains a decent mix of new and older models. A new 12cpm model, introduced at about the same time this book was published, will be cartridge-based.

Mita manufactures all of its copiers and, except for one direct sales office in New York City, sells them only through dealers. Mita's machines are also relabeled by three other vendors: Gestetner, Monroe, and Pitney Bowes. In addition, some are sold under the Copystar brand name, which is now owned by Mita itself (see separate entry in these Vendor Profiles). Mita has a factory in South Carolina which produces some parts for its copiers, as well as toner.

# Monroe

*Monroe Systems for Business*
*The American Road*
*Morris Plains, NJ 07950*
*Tel: 201 993 2000*

Monroe is an old name in the American office equipment market. Its copiers are relabeled Mita machines. These days, Monroe only actively chases large accounts. All sales are direct — there are no Monroe copier dealers. Monroe's copiers are relabeled Mitas.

# Olympia

*Olympia USA. Inc.*
*1330 River Bend*
*Dallas, TX 75247–4953*
*Tel: 800 926 6456*

Olympia is an old German office equipment company that never fully recovered from the demise of its former mainstay, the good-old, heavy-duty office typewriter

The copiers that Olympia sells are relabeled Minoltas. Olympia tends to focus on selling low- and mid-volume machines to smaller- and medium-size businesses. Olympia's dealer network is far from the best developed, though the company is making efforts to enlarge it.

## Panasonic

*Panasonic Communications & Systems Company*
*Two Panasonic Way*
*Secaucus, NJ 07094*
*Tel: 201 348 7000*

Panasonic is one of the smaller players in the copier market (it has the lowest market share of all the Japanese manufacturers). It — or, rather, its Matsushita parent — produces a line of low- and mid-volume machines, but its high-volume copiers are relabeled Minoltas. Until recently, Panasonic also sold relabeled Minolta equipment in the bottom half of the low-volume market, but it has recently stopped doing so.

Panasonic only has about 200 active dealers. There are no direct sales. However, some models are relabeled by Lanier and Pitney Bowes. Most of Panasonic's dealers also carry other brands of copiers.

## Pitney Bowes

*Pitney Bowes Inc.*
*Walter H. Wheeler Jr. Drive*
*Stamford, CT 06926*
*Tel: 203 356 5000*

Pitney Bowes — best known as a mailroom giant — sells copiers that are relabeled Mita and Panasonic models. Lately, its selection of low-volume models has been looking a bit uninspiring. Pitney Bowes doesn't have any dealers: all sales are direct. Although the copier sales reps are separate from their mailing equipment counterparts, the two sometimes work together on a local basis.

## Ricoh

*Ricoh Corporation*
*5 Dedrick Place*
*West Caldwell, NJ 07006*
*Tel: 201 882 2000*

Ricoh is one of the five Japanese copier manufacturers to make all of its own machines, from low- to very high-volume models. It has a solid range of products and a good dealer network. Ricoh copiers are also relabeled by Savin.

Ricoh is one of the three low-volume copier manufacturers not to make any cartridge-based models whatsoever; its smallest low-volume models run at 13cpm (though students of copier history will recall that this wasn't always the case: there was a time back in the 1980s when Ricoh did make some cartridge-based mini-copiers, which were never very successful). Ricoh's low-volume copier range is solid, but perhaps unexceptional in terms of what it offers to smaller businesses.

Ricoh only sells through dealers in most parts of the country, though it has direct sales operations in the New York tri-state area and in Washington, DC. The typical Ricoh dealer tends to focus on selling to medium size and larger accounts in its area. In general, Ricoh does not go out of its way to target smaller businesses — though that doesn't mean that low-volume copier users aren't welcome.

## Savin

*Savin Corporation*
*9 West Broad Street*
*Stamford, CT 06904–2270*
*Tel: 203 967 5000*

Savin is a distributor of relabeled Ricohs, which has recently emerged from Chapter 11. Savin's copier list prices tend to be consistently higher than those set by Ricoh for the identical machines. Sales are through dealers.

## Sharp

*Sharp Electronics Corporation*
*Sharp Plaza*
*Mahwah, NJ 07430–2135*
*Tel: 201 529 8200*

Sharp is a strong vendor, both in terms of its market share and the quality of its equipment and dealer network. It is one of the five Japanese vendors to manufacture a full line of copiers from the low-volume sector to the high end of the market.

And it is the second-largest manufacturer of mini-copiers designed for people making under 1,000 copies a month. Its Z-series, retail-channel mini-copiers challenge Canon's Personal Copier models at the very bottom end of the market. Sharp also manufactures most of the mini-copiers sold by Xerox, though the majority of these don't correspond exactly to ones that Sharp sells under its own brand name. During the past year, Xerox has been selling more Sharp-made minis than Sharp has under its own name — such is the strength of the Xerox brand.

Sharp's main line of copiers, sold through its dealer network, is its SF-series — this stretches from the 10cpm level all the way into the high-volume market. Recently, there have been signs of a coming together of the top end of Sharp's Z-series and the low end of its SF-series. The entry-level, 10cpm SF-series model is a cartridge-based unit that is basically the same as the top-end Z-series model. And a new 14cpm cartridge-based machine with a low-cost document feeder option will be marketed both through the Z-series retail channel and the SF-series dealer channel after its introduction late in 1994.

Sharp has a strong dealer network. There are no direct sales: Sharp is the only one of the big players in the copier market without a direct sales branch or subsidiary in any US city.

## Toshiba

*Toshiba America Information Systems Inc.*
*Electronic Imaging Division*
*9740 Irvine Boulevard*
*PO Box 19724*
*Irvine, CA 92713–9724*
*Tel: 714 583 3000*

Toshiba has one of the lowest profiles of all the Japanese manufacturers, and ranks second from last in US market share. The company is stronger as a low- and mid-volume vendor — its high-volume range is quite limited and some of its dealers lack experience supporting high-volume users.

Most of the machines it makes itself are also relabeled by Lanier. All of Toshiba's own-brand sales are through dealers. The company has no presence in the retail channel and is one of the three low-volume copier manufacturers not to produce any cartridge-based models; its smallest model is a 13cpm unit. Despite the company's low profile, it makes decent copiers.

## Xerox

*Xerox Corporation*
*Xerox Square — 05B*
*Rochester, NY 14644*
*Tel: 800 832 6979*

Xerox pioneered the office photocopier and is still the market leader. It has lately become a lot more interesting in the low-volume sector — largely as a result of its bold venture into the retail channel (more on this shortly). Alone of all copier vendors,

Xerox sells a low-volume range that is entirely cartridge-based.

Aside from the retail channel, Xerox does not sell through dealers in the normal sense: it relies instead mainly on its own direct sales force, which covers most of the country with a network of branches. However, it supports this with what it calls "agents." A Xerox agent is a self-employed person, or a small business, that sells copiers but does not stock, resell, or service them — the agent simply wins the orders and is paid on commission only.

In the past, Xerox agents only operated in rural areas. Since then, however, Xerox has extended the program to major cities. In general, the urban agents are most active pushing the low- and mid-volume machines to smaller accounts, leaving the direct sales office to concentrate on the juicier business. In rural areas, which the branches do not cover, the agents peddle the entire range.

The low-volume copiers that Xerox sells through its direct/agents channels tend to be pretty unexciting machines, and are not always very temptingly priced. I can see users of Xerox's larger copiers buying these models through the direct/agents channel, in order to maintain one-stop shopping — but the local Xerox branch is not a particularly obvious choice for smaller offices needing only a low-volume copier.

Part of the problem is that Xerox's direct sales organization does not, as a rule, discount as readily and by as much as its dealer competitors. So even if you find the list prices comparable, street prices are likely to be higher. When you are buying its larger copiers, or if you are buying low-volume ones as part of a bigger order, Xerox can get pretty creative with the terms and offer tempting deals. But if someone is only buying a low-volume copier, the scope for creativity is somewhat reduced.

The story with Xerox in the retail channel is quite different. Xerox can be a very appealing brand if you prefer to buy through retail stores, not least because it is currently the only vendor to offer copiers through this channel that are good for volumes up to 5,000 copies a month and that also have document feeder and sorter options. Xerox is very prominent in the office supply warehouse channel — all three major chains carry its products — and in some more consumer-oriented stores, such as warehouse clubs.

Xerox's mini-copiers (10cpm and below) are actually manufactured by Sharp. The machines do not always correspond exactly to the ones sold under the Sharp brand name, though they are sometimes identical and generally come pretty close. Xerox is making a big push in this market, and now sells more of these copiers than Sharp itself.

This success is pretty remarkable — Xerox has come from virtually nowhere in the personal copier market to about 30 percent in only three years. The company's Personal Documents Division, which handles the retail channel, operates autonomously from the part of Xerox that sells copiers through the branch network, and seems to have a different culture.

As I indicated above, Xerox's presence in the retail channel now extends further up the ladder — following a low-key start in 1993, the company's retail-channel line now takes in copiers in the 18–26cpm range with document feeder and sorter options. The machines at this level are older low-volume models lifted out of Xerox's direct-sales channel; they are "genuine" Xerox copiers, not rebadged Sharps (though one Sharp-made 14cpm model with a document feeder option is expected to join the Xerox retail range toward the end of 1994). The model numbers of these older Xeroxes are changed for the retail channel, but the machines are the same. As copiers, these machines are pretty unremarkable: what makes them special is how they are sold, not what they do.

The Xerox-made 18–26cpm retail copiers are sold only through the big-three office warehouse stores (Office Depot, OfficeMax, and Staples). The stores do not carry them in stock, but simply display them and take orders: if you buy one, Xerox itself will undertake the delivery and installation (low-volume copiers of this size are too big for customers to take away themselves). If all goes according to plan, the Xerox retail-channel range should rise into the 30–40cpm mid-volume sector in 1995, and it will also take in duplex models.

Other vendors will find it harder to develop retail-channel distribution to the same extent, because of the problem of who is going to install and service the machines. While basic low-volume copiers can be designed to be largely user-maintained, the slightly larger models with document feeder and sorter options are going to require support.

Xerox — as a direct sales company — is able to offer its regular service network to support its retail-channel copiers. All Xerox low-volume copiers come with a three-year warranty; service on the Xerox-made models is generally on-site — though the cartridge-based design minimizes the amount of service that is required in practice.

By contrast, few of the Japanese vendors have their own directly-employed field-service organizations (none have any that are totally national), and their traditional dealers could prove reluctant to support a retail channel that threatens to undermine their own low/mid-volume copier sales (moreover, national retailers prefer to have national service organizations supporting the products they sell).

The solution may be to retain third-party national service organizations — just as computer manufacturers do. Nonetheless, having people service copiers between repair jobs on fridges may not provide sufficient assurance to buyers used to dealing with local, service-intensive dealers. For these reasons, it is unlikely that any Japanese vendor will offer a retail-channel copier faster than 20cpm in the near future. Xerox has, therefore, got something of a clear run in that market — if it fails, it won't be because of direct competition.

One thing that you should be aware of is that Xerox-manufactured retail-channel copiers may be remanufactured units, rather than brand new ones. In fact, people buying Xerox-made retail models during the shelf-life of this book are almost certain to get a machine that has been remanufactured. If a machine is remanufactured, it makes no difference to the price or the warranty — and, in my opinion, the quality is also the same.

Xerox informs me that, prior to April 1994, none of its retail-channel copiers were remanufactured, aside from some being test-marketed in limited locations. They also assure me that the information will be disclosed adequately to buyers, both in the point-of-sale literature and in the paperwork that buyers sign when placing their order.

It is a fact, however, that the remanufactured factor is perceived as a "negative": while Xerox will doubtless fulfill its legal obligations to disclose this information, it is likely to play down this aspect as much as possible (its direct sales organization sometimes uses obscure language to describe the build status of copiers that are not brand new).

I have observed that in at least some test marketing in northern California, remanufactured Xerox copiers have been sold by Office Depot without any disclosures being made — this, apparently, was an oversight. It remains to be seen whether the retailers themselves will disclose the information in their own catalogs.

The retail-channel copiers are by no means the only Xerox models to be sold remanufactured. The company has a policy of factory remanufacturing its trade-ins and then repositioning them in the direct-sales front-line with the same prominence given to equipment that is brand new. Therefore, the low-volume copiers sold through the company's direct sales/agents channel are also often remanufactured. The price is always the same, but Xerox states that it may "at its sole discretion" supply you with a remanufactured unit instead of a new one. The older models tend only to be available remanufactured.

While I believe that buyers should be made aware of the build status, I do not feel that people should avoid buying Xerox copiers because they may be remanufactured. When a Xerox copier is remanufactured, numerous parts are replaced with new ones. In addition, a machine is enhanced to incorporate any improvements that have been developed since it was first manufactured. The quality control process is identical, whether a machine is new or remanufactured. Sometimes, the same production line is used.

Xerox offers an exceptionally good guarantee of satisfaction on all of its copiers — from the smallest mini to the largest giant. The bottom line is that they'll replace a machine at any time during the first three years if you're dissatisfied for any reason (the term may be longer if you're leasing the equipment through Xerox's finance subsidiary). What's more, you — the user — are the arbiter of whether a replacement is called for. This guarantee applies to all Xerox copiers, regardless of their build status (new, remanufactured, etc.) and distribution channel. ✍

# Chapter 5

# Mid/High-Volume Copiers

# Mid/High-Volume Copiers

This chapter is relevant to people planning to make from 10,000 to over 100,000 copies a month on a single machine. If you make fewer than 10,000 copies a month, you should be reading the previous chapter on low-volume copiers.

When I refer to "mid-volume" copiers, I'll be talking about machines that cruise at between 25 and 49 copies per minute (cpm) and that are generally good for about 10,000–40,000 copies per month. "Low" and "high" volume are either side of that ("very high volume" means over 100cpm). This chapter includes a discussion of how to match your copy volume to the speed of a machine.

## A Very Brief History of the Photocopier

Chester Carlson, born in 1906, was a barber's son from Jackson Heights, NY, whose career began on an unpromising note. A physics graduate, he applied to 82 companies for employment, received only two replies, and worked briefly for Bell Labs before being laid off. (Sounds like the 1990s?) Having finally found a new job in an electrical company, Chet — as he was known to friends — noticed that there were rarely enough carbon copies of documents he had to work with. In his spare time, he began to dream up a technology for making copies of documents using the science of photoconductivity. In 1937, he filed a patent for what later became known as "xerography."

### Early Xerox copiers

Unlike earlier methods of copying documents which were essentially photographic in nature and therefore slow, messy, and expensive to operate, xerography was intended to make document copying easy and reasonably affordable. The technology — which, in essence, is unchanged to this day — focuses an image onto a cylindrical device, called a "drum," in the form of electrically charged static. Toner, a powdered ink-type substance, is then attracted to the charge and the image is printed onto plain paper that passes through the machine. The name "Xerox" is based on the Greek word "xeros," meaning "dry" — a contrast to the photographic method of document copying which relied on liquid chemicals.

Nothing came easily to Chet Carlson and no fewer than 20 companies, including Eastman Kodak, turned down his invention in the seven years that followed the filing of his patent. Undeterred, Carlson pressed on and, in 1944, managed to get support from a non-profit research organization called the Battelle Memorial Institute. Three years later, Haloid, a manufacturer of paper for photographic document copiers, eventually agreed to lend commercial support.

The process that Carlson had stubbornly promoted was still far from perfect, and Haloid was not a huge company. It took a further 12 years, and the involvement of a British company called the Rank Organization, before the first Xerox copier — the 914 — was born in 1959. Early production models of the 914 were supplied to users complete with a fire extinguisher, a necessary precaution given certain combustive tendencies. In 1961, Haloid turned itself into Xerox Corporation.

### Early Japanese copiers

Xerox's patents ran until the mid-1970s and the company used this period to establish a dominant position in document copying in the US and, with its Rank Xerox joint venture, worldwide. But the Japanese competition began early. By the late 1960s, Canon and Ricoh had developed a process that circumvented the Xerox patents by using liquid toner. Though inferior to the Xerox products, the early liquid toner copiers were cheaper.

By the mid-1970s, the Xerox patents had run out and rival dry toner machines began to emerge both from the Japanese and from several European manufacturers (almost all of which were later driven out of the market). A few other American companies tried to get into copier manufacturing, though only one, Eastman Kodak, has stayed in that business; Kodak only focuses on the top end of the market.

By the early 1980s, most of the Japanese companies had abandoned liquid toner entirely and were becoming increasingly aggressive in building market share. In contrast to Xerox which has always sold its copiers direct to end users, the Japanese moved into the US market using dealers which had lower overheads, but which were less geared up to chase large corporate accounts.

### Copier wars

In the decade that followed, Xerox saw its grip on the copier market slide, due partly to the increased competition, but also to its own complacency during the 1980s which resulted in high prices and a lack of new models. When Xerox did begin to fight back towards the end of the 1980s, it did so by relying increasingly on low- and mid-market models sourced from its Fuji Xerox joint venture in Japan.

Only the very high end of the market has withstood the Japanese onslaught, and even that has taken some hits. Whereas six years ago, no Japanese copier worked faster than 65 copies per minute (cpm), leaving Xerox and Kodak more or less unchallenged in the 70–125cpm sector, today the fastest Japanese machines reach around 100cpm. Nonetheless, as I'll show later in this chapter, the fastest Japanese machines tend, in practice, to be used for substantially lower copy volumes than Xerox and Kodak machines with the same quoted copies per minute speed. Indeed, Canon relabels a Kodak 85cpm super-high-volume machine, because its own 83cpm models are, frankly, in a different league.

Throughout the 1980s, the copier industry boomed. Successful manufacturers and dealers made a lot of money. But the footnotes of history are also littered with companies that tried to manufacture copiers, but were forced to pull out during the first great copier shakeout during the mid-1980s: AB Dick, Agfa, Apéco, Eskofot, IBM, Lumoprint, Olivetti, Olympia, Olympus, Rex Rotary, Savin, Saxon, 3M, and Yorktown. Some of these companies live on as copier relabelers; others have pulled out of copiers altogether, but have other core businesses; and several have vanished entirely. Only one of them, Olympus, was Japanese: all the others were American and European.

Today, the industry is leaner. For example, apart from Rank

Xerox, there is only one remaining European copier manufacturer, Océ (a high-volume specialist). The 1990s have seen the market reach what is euphemistically termed a "mature" stage. Sales are flat, smaller dealers are hurting. This prompts speculation about a further shakeout, this one involving Japanese manufacturers.

The Japanese copier manufacturing industry is gradually dividing into two camps: the companies that are able to make all their machines themselves and those that are not. The practice of relabeling other vendors' equipment is far from new. What is noticeable is the increasing tendency for some vendors that used to make all of their own machines to buy in some of their ranges from elsewhere because they don't have the in-house strength to keep up with the competition. The two main examples are Panasonic and Toshiba. Previously, relabelers tended to be vendors that didn't make any of their own machines.

The Japanese copier companies that are totally self-sufficient in their product ranges now number just five: Canon, Konica, Mita, Ricoh, and Sharp. (That's not including the unique Canon/Kodak super-high-volume deal I referred to above. Minolta looks as though it may become self-sufficient, though at the time of this writing it was still selling one relabeled Ricoh model.) These companies, together with Xerox, are the ones that will dominate the market in the years ahead. Others may not drop out of copiers altogether, but they could become further marginalized.

# Trends in the Copier Market

The copier market lacks the hectic pace of the computer or fax markets, but it's not entirely dormant. In the last year, one vendor has departed the market — Sanyo, a real basket case in this industry, has finally fizzled out.

But while there has been little earth-shattering headline news in the copier industry lately, a number of trends have been particularly noticeable during the past year — and copier circles are full of speculation on whether there's a technology revolution around the corner. Here's a look at what's cooking. ...

### Trend #1: Upwardly creeping prices
First, the bad news. After a decade of falling steadily, copier prices have been slinking slowly back up. This trend had recently begun when the last edition of this book was published in 1993, and has continued since. Typical year-on-year increases have been as much as 10 percent.

Copier price increases come as a bit of a shock to office equipment buyers who have come to associate price "changes" with price "cuts." In fact, office copiers are one of the few areas of office equipment where there is much upward price movement. In part, the increases reflect the weak dollar and sharp declines in earnings of the Japanese companies that make copiers. However, these factors have not prevented prices from falling in other areas of equipment, such as fax machines.

I expect prices to rise further during 1995. List prices, however, can mean little in the copier market. It is easy to obtain discounts of 25 percent or more — often around 35 percent when a machine is laden with options. Copier dealers are not going through boom years, and are hungry for your business.

## Trend #2: Downwardly migrating features

Next, the good news. You may be able to beat the increases and actually pay less for a copier now than you would have done three years ago. How come? The answer has to do with the downward migration of upscale features. Advanced features that only used to be available on pretty fast and expensive machines are now becoming common on somewhat slower and more affordable ones.

Possibly, therefore, you may be able to settle for, say, a 35 copies per minute (cpm) machine when in the past you would have felt obliged to fork out the cash for, say, a 45cpm model because that was the only way to get X, Y, and Z features. (This is especially so as today's 35cpm copiers may in practice operate faster than yesterday's 35cpm models, for reasons I'll come to shortly.)

This trend is not completely new — it began a while ago when duplex (i.e., automatic double-sided copying) started to make its way down first to the mid-volume market and then to the low-volume sector. But the trend has accelerated recently. Take a feature such as automatic covers insertion (this enables a copier to automatically print the covers of a multi-page document on a different paper stock). Not so long ago, this was only available on "giant" copiers aimed at people making over 100,000 copies a month. Then it moved down into the mainstream high-volume sector. But today, it is becoming more common in the 25–49cpm mid-volume market and it even crops up on a handful of low-volume models.

Mid-volume copiers also have much larger standard on-line paper supplies than they used to. The dual 250-sheet trays that we all used to put up with now look pretty dated, and few machines offer them outside the low-volume sector. In their place, you'll often find dual trays offering a combined capacity of 1,500 sheets; moreover, quite a few class-of-'94 mid-volume machines have triple trays included in their basic list price. Similarly, automatic tray switching has become more common (this is the feature that makes the machine switch to the next tray without stopping when the first runs out of paper).

### Trend #3: A new emphasis on productivity features

The third trend links into the last one quite neatly. Manufacturers have lately begun de-emphasizing the gimmicky features that obsessed many of them during the eighties and that spilled over into this decade. Instead, most are working on making their copiers perform closer in practice to their theoretical copies per minute cruising speeds.

The best example is the way in which the latest generation of automatic document feeders operate at the same speed as the copier engines they work with. Traditionally, document feeders have worked significantly slower resulting in a degradation of actual copying speeds. Today, however, you don't have to suffer this deterioration. More on this later, but, for now, consider this as another reason why you may be able to justify buying a theoretically "slower" copier than you would have in the past.

I don't want to overstate this point. I don't think that someone who rationally purchased a 60 copies per minute machine a few years ago could today sensibly buy a 35 copies per minute model to cope with the same needs. But I do think that someone who previously bought, say, a 45cpm unit, should at least consider one of today's much-improved 35cpm machines.

What are the gimmicky features that you hear less of now that attention is being turned to genuine productivity? One example is "copy editing" (the ability to alter the layout of images that you are copying or to block out selected parts). Another is "spot-color copying" (mixing black with another toner color, or making all of your copies in a color other than black).

These features still exist, but manufacturers have belatedly realized that few people use them in practice. For a while, they made sales demos interesting, but they never caught on in the real world of office life. Today, the novelty has gone — in the copier world, as in other walks of life, the nineties are proving a less flamboyant and more down-to-earth decade than their predecessor.

Again, I don't want to overstate this point. Gimmicky features are still out there, and some manufacturers tout them with more enthusiasm than others (also, in some specialized environments, they may even prove useful). But they are less common, and dealers and end-users alike are less easily impressed.

### Trend #4: How laser printers are reducing copier usage

While I'm on the subject of trends, the rapid growth of laser printers in the past three years — prompted by major price drops — has reduced some offices' copier requirements. Rather than making additional sets of computer-generated documents on a copier, some people choose simply to print out additional originals on their laser. The quality ought to be a shade better, and sometimes it's a lot less bother: you can press all the buttons without getting up from your chair.

The laser option is only practical up to a point, however. You won't have productivity features, such as automatic sorting of completed sets, and speeds will be quite slow. But what makes the laser option bad policy if adopted on any significant scale is the fact that printer running costs are a lot higher than those of all but pretty low-volume copiers. Typically, lasers are two to three times as expensive to run as office copiers.

Be that as it may, a lot of people in big offices are using their PC keyboards to make laser copies — or, perhaps one should say, "laz-ee" copies! Some companies have taken steps to discourage this by modifying their networks to limit the number of prints that can be made of the same document in a single go.

### Trend #5: Emerging multifunctional technology

One response to the tendency of people to make expensive "copies" on laser printers is to develop combo machines which include copier and laser printer functions in one unit — and which have running costs akin to those of conventional copiers. Some of these emerging multifunctional machines can also act as scanners and fax machines.

These machines use digital technology, rather than the conventional analog "light-lens" method of traditional xerographic machines. What digital technology means in this context is that originals are scanned electronically and the stored images — consisting of millions of computer instructions — are then processed in much the same way as data sent to a PC printer.

The good news is that such multifunctional machines exist — several of the copier manufacturers either have models available or waiting in the wings (most of the momentum is coming from the copier side of the fence, not the printer vendors — this is despite the fact that multifunctional machines seem likely to be used more as printers than copiers).

The bad news is that the early ones tend to be pricey and

usually offer performance that doesn't compare favorably with that of the dedicated, single-function machines they seek to replace. Moreover, most early multifunctional machines are pitched either at the very low or very high ends of the market — you typically need to have very modest requirements or exceptionally upscale ones and there is little available in the middle.

Integration, as such, is not necessarily a huge benefit — while it does offer savings in space, it also invites possible user conflict. In my opinion, the multifunctional market will only take off when buyers are given a price incentive and when they are not forced to make performance compromises. There is a full discussion of the developing multifunctional market in Chapter 9. The rest of this chapter focuses on traditional, single-function copiers.

# Copy Volumes & Copier Prices

All manufacturers quote recommended monthly copy volumes, but these figures tend to be very optimistic. Often, they are also pretty arbitrary. For example, in 1991 Xerox literally doubled the recommended volumes of most of its copiers overnight (without making any physical adjustments to the machines themselves). In practice, few people run their copiers to the manufacturers' quoted maximums. In fact, if you get within 30 percent of the official limits, you often get told by the dealer that you've outgrown the machine and that you should be thinking of trading up to a new one.

I've prepared some guidelines to give you an idea of how fast a machine you probably need for your monthly workload; at the same time I thought it would make sense to give you ballpark figures warning what each level of copier is likely to cost you in list price terms.

My advice on copy volumes is necessarily generalized — it may not apply to your own particular circumstances. For example, if you make 20,000 copies a month, but 15,000 of them are made in the last week of each month, you'll need a faster copier than someone who makes the same total number of copies spread evenly. To an extent, the speed of machine you need also depends on how patient you are. Some people like their copies in a hurry when producing long multi-page sets and are prepared to pay a premium not to be kept waiting. Others would rather pay less even if it means hanging around by the copier for a while longer. You should also take account of your future plans to grow or — dare I say it? — contract: in general, it makes sense to plan on keeping a copier for about four years (good luck to you if you do better than that but, in reality, it usually doesn't work out that way for one reason or another).

Keep in mind that while faster machines are generally constructed for higher workloads than slower ones, this isn't always the case when the speed differences are comparatively small. A 30 copies per minute (cpm) machine may not necessarily be more heavy duty than, say, a 25cpm one — the difference may be in the speed and nothing else. Finally, remember that not all machines with the same quoted cpm speed actually deliver the same number of copies per minute in practice — more on this later when I talk about productivity.

In coming up with the price guidelines below, I've made what I hope are sensible assumptions about the type of options people are likely to want at each level of the market, and you should treat these prices as broad indications only. Keep in mind also that no one should pay list price for a copier. I'll be talking more about discounts later, but if you mentally discount most of the figures below by around 25 percent you won't be too far off the mark.

So, with all these caveats and health warnings, here are my copy volume and copier price guidelines (remember that if you are making much fewer than 10,000 copies per month, you're reading the wrong chapter — you should turn instead to the earlier discussion in Chapter 4):

### Mid-volume copiers: 10,000–40,000 copies per month

❑ *10,000–20,000 copies per month:* At this level, a 25–30cpm machine is likely to be your best bet. Depending on the machine and the options you select, the list price will probably be in the region of $8,000–$10,000.

❑ *20,000–30,000 copies per month:* I'd be inclined to go with a 35–40cpm copier. Expect to pay anywhere from $9,500–$15,000 in list price terms depending on the machine and required options.

❑ *30,000–40,000 copies per month:* Now you're getting into upper mid-volume territory. I'd probably be looking at 45cpm machines, possibly breaking into the high-volume market by considering 50–55cpm models if I was doing closer to 40,000 and wanted a bit more speed. Around the 45cpm mark segment, list prices are likely to be in the $10,500–$16,000 range depending on the machine and options.

### High-volume copiers: more than 40,000 copies per month

The phrase "high-volume copier market" actually embraces quite a wide range of equipment. Just consider the price range: the least expensive machines in the 50–135cpm market list for under $12,000 with no options, and the most expensive sell for over $150,000 (most are in the $17,000–$38,000 sector). I think it's helpful to segment the market into three distinct categories (though there are some overlaps, and a few machines don't fall neatly into any one of them):

❏ *50–70cpm machines:* The high-volume market begins with copiers that cruise at 50–70 copies per minute (cpm). These are conceptually pretty similar to the equipment you get in the mid-volume market, but they are simply faster. The maximum recommended monthly copy volumes quoted by the manufacturers are typically around 60,000–125,000. In practice, most of these machines get used for about half that amount or less. They have list prices of between about $12,000 and $25,000, depending on speed and the options you select.

❏ *75–100cpm fast copiers from Japanese manufacturers:* The second category is made up of the Japanese machines that cruise at 75–100cpm. This class of copier is still fairly new: not so long ago, the Japanese product ranges topped out at around 70cpm, and the first models to cruise at 80–85cpm only appeared on the Pacific horizon in 1991. During 1994, however, several are being introduced — the fastest is the Ricoh FT9101 which runs at 101cpm. (I stress that I am using the word "fast" in a loose sense — as I'll be pointing out later, the "copies per minute" figure is a somewhat notional speed which doesn't provide a complete picture of a machine's actual productivity. On double-sided work involving the use of document feeders, you might find that Machine A, which runs at, say, 75cpm, completes a job quicker than Machine B, which notionally runs at 85cpm.)

Japanese manufacturers' recommended maximum volumes in the 75–90cpm level are typically up to 150,000–175,000 a month. Again, however, most machines only get used for half that or less. What this means is that many people who buy them could get by with one of the less expensive 50–70cpm models if they were willing to accept something slower in return for a lower price. List prices in the 75–85cpm Japanese-built sector are typically around the $28,000–$38,000 level.

Some Japanese manufacturers, notably Canon, have

been more successful than others at selling to users who make more than 100,000 copies a month on a single machine. However, those volumes are the exceptions rather than the rule. It's debatable whether this is because the machines are not totally suitable for more demanding copy environments, or because buyers on those volumes have yet to accept them. My view is that it's a little bit of both — but I also sense that copy volumes on these Japanese machines are creeping up as the equipment becomes more of a known quantity. However, as I remarked earlier, the fact that Canon sells a relabeled Kodak 85cpm copier, even though it makes its own much less expensive 83cpm models, is an indication that the Japanese manufacturers tacitly admit that their high-speed machines have limitations next to US-made equipment with the same notional cpm speeds.

❏ *85–135cpm "giant copiers" from US and European manufacturers:* Two American companies, Xerox and Kodak, make "giant copiers" for the very highest volume users. A Dutch manufacturer, Océ, is also in this market (most of its machines aren't terribly fast, but are nonetheless engineered to cope with very high volumes). On paper, these machines don't always appear a great deal faster than the Japanese machines discussed above — the "notional" speeds of recently introduced giant copiers are mostly around 85–110cpm. In practice, however, they have superior document and paper handling capabilities resulting in greater productivity advantages than the difference in quoted cpm speeds would suggest. Giant copiers — often referred to as "copier-duplicators" — are also much more heavy duty: they usually last over a decade and are often remanufactured every few years before being supplied to new owners.

Machines in this category are widely used for over 100,000 copies a month. Some are suitable for up to 250,000 a month, and the highest are rated for up to one million. By no means all people who buy Xerox, Kodak, and Océ giant copiers do use them for over 100,000 copies a month: some could comfortably get by with less expensive Japanese 75–90cpm equipment. But there is a sizable base of users who work these machines very hard indeed: their high-volume credentials are not in doubt. Giant copiers are not cheap. Don't expect a lot of change from $75,000 in list price terms (unless you're looking at one of the oldest remanufactured units). The most expensive machine lists for over $150,000. Even though these machines are definitely more productive than the fastest Japanese copiers, some high-volume buyers are beginning to wonder whether the premium is worth paying.

# How to Buy a Mid/High-Volume Copier

America is littered with the corpses of copiers discarded prematurely because copy quality deteriorated or because jamming and other problems became intolerable. Sometimes, the machines concerned were just plain bad copiers. But that's much less common now than it used to be — differences in reliability between the major brands are becoming harder to detect every year. Often, therefore, a copier's premature demise is not the fault of machinery. It's the fault of people.

No other piece of office equipment needs such tender loving care and attention as the photocopier. Unlike computers or fax machines, copiers quite often go wrong. And even the most reliable models require regular preventative maintenance in order to give their best. That's hardly surprising: compared with other types of office equipment, copiers rely on a large number of moving parts, not to mention messy toners and chemicals. Though manufacturing processes have improved substantially over the past decade, the fundamental technology has remained remarkably constant. What this means is that who you buy from can be as important as what you buy. In a nutshell, the service and support arrangements are critical.

I am not one of those who slavishly argues that service and support are paramount in all fields of equipment. Quite often, arguments about service are used as an excuse to squeeze more money out of buyers by playing on anxieties. You can overdo service anxiety, like when you pay for an extended warranty on something like a fax machine. Likewise, some low-volume copiers actually require very little in the way of service (a point I discussed in the previous chapter). But mid- and high-volume copiers are different, and I'm stressing this point because although this chapter will help you form an opinion on the machines themselves, these opinions should be considered in conjunction with the local support arrangements for each brand. And the key word here is "local" — the best buy in one town may not be the best buy in another.

### Direct sales & service
Vendors which sell and support their copiers direct, rather than

through dealers, tend to be more predictable, no matter what the location. For example, Kodak service is widely regarded as being superb across the whole nation. Likewise, Xerox has support policies and pricing which apply nationwide; if you're unhappy with your service, it's easier to complain and get satisfaction because your service comes from the manufacturer rather than from a dealer over which a manufacturer has limited control.

### Dealer sales & service

However, the majority of high-volume copiers are sold through dealers. And dealer type and caliber varies both within brands and between them. Most of the major Japanese manufacturers are represented by some dealers whose high-volume service is every bit as good as the service from Xerox and Kodak — but not all of their dealers reach those standards. You can find an excellent dealer for a given brand in one state, but find that in the next door state that very same brand has acquired a less good reputation due to the quality of local support.

Also, some dealers may provide good service on, say, mid-volume copiers, but be out of their depth on high-volume machines. In general, the vendors with the strongest high-volume copier model lines are likely to be the ones with dealers who have the most experience in servicing high-volume users. This means, for example, that a high-volume user is more likely to get good service from, say, a Canon or Sharp dealer than from a Panasonic or Toshiba dealer. But that is clearly a generalized comment, to which there will be exceptions.

To an extent, of course, a dealer can only be as efficient as the manufacturer it represents. An inefficient parts operation run by a manufacturer may not be the fault of a dealer, but will still result in the dealer delivering poor service.

### Dealer conglomerates

Some of the dealer brands are represented by very large dealer conglomerates. There has lately been a steady process of consolidation involving larger copier dealers swallowing up smaller ones. The largest of the conglomerates is Alco Office Products, whose dealer operations grossed almost $1.8 billion in their financial year ended September 1993. By the start of 1994, Alco had approximately 500 copier locations in the US, most of which were the result of acquisitions.

Two facts illustrate how important Alco has become in the copier market: first, its total number of placements (i.e., the number of machines it sells a year) represents a seven percent market share, or about half that of Xerox; second, an amazing 38 percent of Canon's copier sales now go through dealerships which are part of Alco (though Alco dealers also carry other brands, especially Sharp). Despite these impressive numbers, few people have actually heard of Alco unless they work within the copier industry — the reason is that all the dealerships trade independently under their original names. The only other dealer conglomerate which even approaches Alco is Danka Business Systems, which currently has about 160 dealers under its belt. Danka dealers mostly handle Konica, Minolta, Canon, and Sharp copiers.

### Dealer vendors that also sell direct

A few dealer sales manufacturers also have direct sales and service operations in major cities, which is good for users who prefer to deal direct with the manufacturer. Konica and Minolta are prominent examples in this category. Other vendors tend only to have direct sales operations — or wholly-owned subsidiaries that operate as dealers — in a few major centers, especially the New York/New Jersey area. Details of each vendor's distribution channels appear in the Vendor Profiles section later in this chapter.

### Relabelers

There are several major distributors which relabel other vendors' equipment and then sell and support it through their national sales and service organizations. Examples include Lanier (a relabeler of Panasonic, Toshiba, Canon, and Kodak equipment), Pitney Bowes (a Mita and Panasonic relabeler), Gestetner (a Mita and Ricoh relabeler), Savin (a Ricoh relabeler), Olympia (a Minolta relabeler), and AB Dick (a Konica relabeler). Some of these relabelers sell copiers through dealers of their own as well as through their direct sales branches. Details of who relabels what, and how they sell it, are included in the Vendor Profiles section of this chapter.

For some archaic reason I have never comprehended, companies that relabel equipment are known in the industry as "OEMs," standing for "original equipment manufacturers" — despite the fact that they don't manufacture anything! Thus, for example, you might hear people talking about Savin as an OEM for Ricoh — I've always considered this to be a misnomer, which is why I don't use it myself. However, other people use the term "OEM" to refer to the company that does manufacture the stuff, not to the relabeler — this would seem to make more sense, but I'm not sure it's the correct usage.

In almost all cases, the relabeled models are the same as the manufacturer's own-brand equipment — despite some not very convincing attempts in certain quarters to conjure up perceived differences. Usually, the list prices are also the same — but certain relabelers, especially Savin and Pitney Bowes, routinely quote higher list prices than the manufacturers themselves.

### Multilocation sales

Vendors that sell direct are usually best able to bid for major accounts spread across locations in different parts of the country. It takes a lot to convince national account buyers that life isn't simpler if dealing with one vendor, one set of pricing, one lot of bills, and one type of machine.

However, the other vendors have special sales teams that work with their dealers to coordinate national account bids. Those with dealers that form part of a national or regional grouping are in the best position to do this effectively.

### When to think about service

In theory, you may be able to buy a copier from one dealer and — if you're not happy with the support — subsequently have it serviced by another. After all, that's common if you're buying something like a car. In practice, that's not always an option. For a start, you may find that there's only one dealer for a particular machine in your area.

Secondly, a dealership that thinks it's being taken advantage of may be reluctant to take on your service business, or may only do so on unfavorable terms. After all, no dealer wants to keep a cut-price rival in business by offering a safety net to its disgruntled customers. Also, you don't want to go through a period of bad support that forces you to want to change service providers.

For these reasons, you should be assessing a dealer's service capability (or that of a direct sales/support organization) at the same time as you're assessing the equipment itself.

### Common sense checks

Unfortunately, it can be quite difficult to judge the quality of service before you buy. There's no hard and fast distinction between dealers that are service-oriented and those that are not — it's not like the fax market where some vendors quote low prices and make no pretense of offering service. All copier dealers are required to service the machines they sell as a condition of their dealership and all copier dealers make sales pitches based on the claim that their service is the best.

Often, therefore, you have to take quite a lot on trust and gut feeling. But there are a few common sense checks that you can carry out. You should definitely visit the dealer's premises before placing your order — in fact, you'll probably have to anyway in order to get a hands-on demonstration of the equipment. When you go to the dealer, don't just be shepherded into the showroom, try to walk through the service department and talk to the technicians: get a feeling for the culture of the dealership.

Years in business can be a good indicator of how established a dealer is; the owner of a new business may be more motivated to please you, but it's less certain that he or she will be around in a year or two's time (that said, not many new copier dealerships are being set up these days). The location of the dealer is also important: a dealer in your town is likely to be more efficient in servicing your needs than one 30 or 40 miles away. Also, a local dealership is more conscious of protecting its reputation in the business community it's part of.

If at all possible, speak to existing customers before placing your order. A dealer should be able to give you the names of several in your area who you can call. Make sure that the people you contact have copying workloads comparable to your own: words of recommendation from someone making only 3,000 copies a month are of limited help if your volume is 10 times that amount. An inability or unwillingness on the dealer's part to provide you with names should set alarm bells ringing: either it suggests that there's something to hide, or it simply suggests a generally unhelpful attitude that may manifest itself later in other ways.

### Technical competence

Good copier service is a little like good fun — you can't pin it down to just one ingredient, but you know when you're having it. The first aspect is straightforward technical competence. This is absolutely vital: there is nothing more annoying to a copier owner than a fault which keeps on recurring. And there is nothing more frustrating than watching a copier gradually deteriorate because there's some idiot who comes around to do the maintenance (or, worse still, a different idiot every month).

Technical competence is more likely to be achieved if a dealer is experienced in selling and supporting the particular copier you're buying. If you're the only local user of a particular machine — or if you make a lot more copies than most of its other customers — you won't be able to draw on a reservoir of experience appropriate to your requirements. Beyond that, technical competence depends on how well a dealer trains its technicians and on how much turnover there is in its support staff. Are the technicians trained by the copier manufacturer, for example, or do they simply learn on the job? How many years of experience do they have servicing copiers?

But these are very difficult issues for you, the buyer, to judge. Ask a salesperson the questions, and you'll get predictably reassuring answers — but little in the way of hard evidence. Realistically, you'll have to rely on your instinct and experience — backed up by any feedback you are able to get from other customers.

### Service coverage — how long you have to wait

Apart from technical competence, the other considerations in assessing service are: coverage, back-up, "total satisfaction," and cost. By "coverage," I mainly mean how quickly a dealer responds to service calls — in other words, the level of service cover that's provided. Users should expect a written guarantee that service will be forthcoming within a stated number of business hours. Unless you're located in an out-of-the-way area, you should expect same-day visits if you put in a service call earlier in the day, or next-morning if you call later.

Very high-volume users should demand even faster response — guaranteed four-hour response, for example. Some very high-volume users operate around the clock and may need service outside normal business hours. Xerox and Kodak offer support plans in major locations that include service availability 24 hours a day, seven days a week.

These days, most manufacturers offer some form of remote diagnostics on mid- and high-volume copiers, which enables service centers to access certain information via modem and even perform some bug-fixes over the phone. This feature is typically used mainly for collecting usage information to assist with billing — it's especially useful where information needs to be pulled from multiple locations in order to be put on one bill.

However, certain very high-volume models from Xerox and Kodak are able to automatically send out data about copier performance and usage over a phone line to a service center computer that predicts maintenance requirements and dispatches a technician without the user even putting in a request. For example, the computer can monitor the number of jams and automatically place a service call if the frequency rises above a preset threshold.

### Back-up — loaners when yours is down

By "back-up," I mean whether a dealer or direct sales vendor is prepared to guarantee that you will not be down for more than a day. This means that you're entitled to a loaner at no extra charge if your machine can't be fixed right away. The loaner may not be exactly the same as your own machine, but it should be a reasonable substitute.

### Copier performance guarantees

By "total satisfaction," I mean whether you are entitled to have your machine replaced permanently if you aren't satisfied with it — even if you have purchased it outright (as opposed to leasing or renting it). This type of guarantee is not common, though watered-down versions are becoming less rare.

Xerox and Lanier lead the field in this regard: if you, the buyer, aren't totally satisfied with your copier during the first three years (longer if they provide the financing), they will replace it with a similar machine that is acceptable to you. What's especially good about both guarantees is that they explicitly make you, rather than the supplier, the arbiter. Lanier's guarantee goes two steps further by promising you financial compensation if your machine has more than two percent downtime and a free loaner if the machine is out of service for more than eight hours. No other vendors have policies that match this, though a few offer diluted guarantees.

Canon, for example, offers a three-year performance guarantee on some of its NP-series copiers, but the problem is that it doesn't explicitly make the customer the arbiter of whether he or she is entitled to a new machine — it simply states that the customer is entitled to a new machine if the existing one can't be repaired. This could prove unsatisfactory, since it is often far from clear whether a machine has been "repaired." A copier may be "working," for example, but simply not producing very good copies. Or it may be jamming more than the customer finds acceptable, but less than the dealer defines as constituting a breakdown. Also, the Canon contract is between dealer and customer, while Xerox's is between manufacturer and customer.

Minolta's guarantee is better, though still not perfectly watertight. This promises you a replacement machine during a three-year period, and also makes you, the customer, the decision-maker. If the replacement is required within the first year, it will be a new unit; after that, it may be a used one. Also, Minolta's guarantee promises you a loaner if your machine has to go into the shop. The flaw is some slightly loose wording that defines your coverage as applying if the machine, or its accessories, "do not operate within Minolta's specifications." Since there are no published specifications concerning things like copy quality, and what constitutes an acceptable number of jams, this guarantee seems somewhat vague if taken literally (and wise buyers should take any guarantee literally — the vendors don't pay lawyers to spend hours working on the wording for nothing). Also, Minolta's guarantee only applies if a dealer chooses to participate — and it does not apply to all models. Still, this is currently the best you can get from a Japanese manufacturer selling through dealers — most other vendors don't offer anything.

Keep in mind that the regular warranties you get on copiers are almost unbelievably abysmal — the typical copier warranty runs for just 90 days! Even then, you're often asked to pay for a service contract from day one — more on this shortly.

### Service costs

Cheap service can turn out to be a false economy, but value matters. It clearly makes sense to get a firm handle on what good service is going to cost you. There are several different elements that make up the overall cost: toner, developer (a separate chemical substance required on most copiers), the cost of a replacement drum, the cost of replacement fuser rollers, the labor cost of routine preventive maintenance, the labor cost of fixing the machine when it breaks down, and the cost of replacement parts.

You can pay for all of these items separately, as and when you need them. But it's preferable to have a service contract: at the risk of stating the obvious, this is the only way of ensuring that you're contractually entitled to a given level of support. The simplest way of budgeting is to have a fixed price contract that covers everything. This will be linked in some manner to the number of copies you make.

For example, you may pay a monthly service cost which includes all supplies (other than paper), parts, and labor up to a specified number of copies a month, and then there will be an additional charge for each copy over that amount (copier usage is recorded by a meter inside the machine). Alternatively, some dealers quote terms where the cost of the toner includes the full-service package — providing you go on buying the toner from them, you're fully covered for your maintenance and repairs at no additional cost.

A further variation is when you rent a machine and pay "nothing" for the equipment itself, but only for the copies you make. The cost per copy includes the cost of the equipment. Beware that rental contracts are not always as flexible as you might hope for, especially in the case of a brand new machine when you're likely to be locked in as much as if you were financing it through a lease. Always read the small print! Sometimes, this type of rental deal involves being given used equipment and in these cases you should expect more flexibility.

### *Your service check-list*

No one method of charging is necessarily better than others. Paying for service and then getting "free" toner is not intrinsically better or worse than paying for toner and then getting "free" service. You're going to pay for what you need one way or another — "there's no such thing as a free drum." But there are some important considerations whichever way you structure it:

✔ Don't commit to a service contract based on higher copy minimums than you are likely to make.

✔ Make sure you know what each copy is going to end up costing you taking into account all the cost ingredients other than paper (it should be around a penny, less if you're on very high volumes).

✔ Do ensure that you have adequate assurances about the quality of service you're going to receive in return.

✔ Check out price escalation clauses and whether you're entitled to go on receiving service at a reasonable price. You don't want to be in a position where a dealer can effectively disown you at renewal time, if it turns out it's sold you a lemon, by pricing the service at a level where it simply becomes uneconomical.

✔ Never — under any circumstances — enter into an agreement where you prepay service for an excessive period! One-year prepayment is the most I would ever contemplate and even that seems high — quarterly or monthly billing makes more sense. Dealers with cash flow difficulties sometimes try to offer deals where the price of the copier includes several years' worth of service and supplies — the mere mention of such an offer should set alarm bells ringing that you are dealing with someone who may not stick around!

Keep in mind that it is common practice for copier users to pay for the full service package from day one of getting the machine. This, in effect, means that you don't get any price break to reflect the warranty. This seems pretty unfair, and you can always try negotiating the matter — but, like it or not, this is the way of the copier world.

## Discounts when buying your copier

With the exception of very low-volume machines, copiers are rarely openly advertised at a discount — in fact, prices are not generally mentioned at all in the advertising — but most buyers should pay significantly below list price. You should not be talked out of a discount by a salesperson who argues that discounting is incompatible with good service. The fact is that list prices exist as a starting point for negotiations, not as the minimum price a dealer can live with.

Also, remember that a copier vendor makes a lot of money out of keeping your machine up-and-running — the profit on the sale of the machine is only the start of your business relationship. In fact, dealer margins on service are often a good deal higher than those on equipment sales. The most successful copier dealers operate their service business on gross margins in excess of 40 percent.

The feedback I get suggests that discounts of 25–30 percent are widespread. Quite often, they are larger: discounts of 35 percent are by no means unheard of. This applies as much to direct sales vendors as to dealer brands. Anyone who pays list price for a copier is getting a terrible deal, period. Keep in mind that discounts should be applied to option prices too, not just to the price of a basic machine. Document feeders and sorters, which are often necessities, rarely come standard and can easily add $3,000 to the list price of a mid-volume copier.

Throughout the business equipment industry, the end of the year is often a good time to get better-than-average discounts. In addition, *High-Speed Copy News* — an excellent newsletter produced mainly for the quick-print industry (Larry Hunt Publications/813 886 9107) — reports that the best time to get deep discounts from Xerox is at the start of each quarter (except January), when districts have special funds for deals which are used on a first-come, first-served basis.

I think it is fair to say that a dealer who operates on the slimmest margins is unlikely to maintain the overhead required to support a decent service organization — unless it makes up for this by charging excessively for the service, in which case you're no better off. On the other hand, there is a case for trying to drive a hard bargain from a dealer who charges high prices to most of its other customers — in other words, if you sense that other people's money is paying for the dealer's overhead, you can feel more comfortable about pressing hard for a maximum discount than you might if you were buying from a dealer who seems to offer rock bottom prices to just about everyone!

So by all means try to get yourself a good deal, but don't let price be your only consideration — keep in mind that if you go too far chasing the lowest price in the wrong quarters, you may end up doing business with a second-rate dealer. That would be a false economy — use your good judgment.

### Leasing copiers

Many users choose to lease their high-volume copiers. Remember that leasing is effectively just a form of borrowing dressed up to look like a trading transaction. The day you sign a lease contract, a finance company sends a check to your copier supplier (sometimes, the finance company is a subsidiary of the copier manufacturer, but the principle still applies). Leasing is not the same as renting from the copier company.

Leasing may make sense for tax reasons, or to conserve cash and lines of bank credit. However, any lease is based on a capital value — the higher the value, the higher your monthly payments. It is important, therefore, that if you do lease a copier, you establish the value on which the lease is being based. That value should represent a discount on the list price similar to what you'd get if you were buying outright. This can be quite hard to figure out, because sometimes lease payments include a service element built in.

However, building service into your lease payments is not something I generally recommend, because if you grow unhappy with the quality of service, the lease company, which is really just the finance provider, won't want to know — if it has paid a check to the dealer, all it wants is monthly checks from you that arrive on time and it couldn't care less if your copier is jamming all the time. In fact, third-party lease companies generally aren't even willing to enter into agreements that include service. The problem is that some dealers tell the customer that part of the payment covers service, but tell the lease company that it is all for the equipment. This amounts to the same thing as asking a cash buyer to prepay several years' worth of service at the time of purchase — something I definitely advise against. Different advice may apply if you are financing the copier through a lease company owned by the copier vendor.

If you are leasing, check out what happens to the copier at the end of the lease period. Although a smaller copier might not have much of a residual value at the end of three to five years, that is not the case with many high-volume machines. Under most leases, ownership at the end of the lease reverts to the lessor, but you may have a right to purchase the equipment using a predetermined formula.

# Copier Scams

Beware of unscrupulous salespeople who pretend that they are giving you a big discount by inflating the list price. A variation of this is the trade-in scam: the dealer offers what looks like a good trade-in on your old machine, but bloats the price of the new one to accommodate this (or reduces the discount that would have been offered). The practice of bloating list prices is especially common with copier leases. By expressing the price in terms of monthly payments, a salesperson can hide the capital value on which the lease finance is based.

While on the subject of scams, beware of used copiers posing as new. Likewise, a machine that is described as a "demonstrator" may be a lot more used than you're told. I certainly don't want to cast doubt on the scruples of most who work in the copier industry. But anyone who is familiar with this market knows that dirty tricks do occur — so be vigilant!

### *Beware of toner phoners!*

Beware of the scam outfits that sell toner over the phone. These scuzzballs — who are not copier machine dealers — employ devious tricks to confuse buyers into thinking that they are ordering from their regular suppliers. The toner supplied is always outrageously expensive and often of questionable quality.

This is how they typically operate. They first call to obtain the name of an administrative manager in a medium-size office ("person A"). Soon afterwards, they call someone else in that office ("person B"), and refer to a fictitious "order" that had been placed by person A. They ask person B whether it would be okay to deliver a bunch of toner the following day. Person B, assuming from the mention of A's name that everything is okay, says "fine." To give more credibility to their call to person B, the scam supplier will often have already found out the exact copier that the office uses (this in a separate phone call, under some false pretense): person B is even more likely to assume it's legitimate if the caller refers to the equipment, as well as to another person in the office, by name.

The next day, the delivery arrives, for the attention of B. That person signs for it, or someone else signs on B's behalf. Soon afterwards, an invoice arrives for an excessive sum. Often the invoice is paid. If challenged, the scam supplier refers to its conversation with B and says that this constituted an order in response to a sales call. There are several variations of this scam and they don't only involve copier toner — some scam-artists operate similar schemes involving typewriter ribbons and laser printer cartridges.

My advice to anyone who does get tricked is not to give these creeps a dime. When the invoice arrives, send it back with a note saying that the goods were delivered as a result of deception and that you will destroy them unless they are collected within 30 days. Do not waste your energy or money to send them back yourself. If the goods ended up being used accidentally, I still wouldn't pay for them. You are not being dishonest by refusing — the fact is that you are the victim. And these scam artists won't take you to court: crooks don't go there unless they are taken.

# Speeds, Feeders, Sorters, & Finishers

By now, I hope you're feeling reasonably street-wise about the copier market. Now it's time for copier features. Try to pay attention to these, as there's more to them than the lists that appear on the glossy brochures. Let's start by looking at how to assess those copy speeds. ...

### Copy speeds — not always what they appear

The manufacturer's figures for a copier's speed are more a theoretical maximum than a realistic average. The secret in making a sound decision is knowing which types of machines are most likely to operate reasonably close to their "notional" speeds — and which will fall significantly short.

The most commonly quoted indicator of a copier's speed is its copies per minute (cpm) figure: I've been blithely using that all through this chapter. It is effectively a measure of how fast the machine cruises if it's making same-size copies of an 8.5" x 11" single-sided original placed on the glass. In practice, though, a lot of office copying jobs involve more than that — typically, you'll be using a document feeder, sometimes you'll be doing double-sided work, frequently you'll be producing sorted sets (perhaps ones that are automatically stapled), and occasionally you'll be copying onto other sizes of paper, such as 11" x 17". Any of these variations can lead to a degradation in actual copying speeds.

The first-copy time is another factor that will impact speed, especially on short-run convenience copying. Some machines take about four seconds or less to make their first copy, but others take almost seven. The first-copy time is most significant when much of your work consists of short-run convenience copying — and when you're making just one copy of one original, it's the only speed figure that matters.

It is pretty well impossible to come up with any precise figure as to the actual speed you'll get out of a given copier in practice, since it all depends on the job you're doing. Not surprisingly, copier manufacturers tend to play down all the ways in which their machines may work slower in practice than their cpm figures lead buyers to hope for. Most copier brochures make no mention of speed apart from the cpm cruising figure and they don't even hint at slower operation when boasting about a machine's document feeder, duplex, and 11" x 17" functions.

However, *What to Buy for Business* conducts independent tests on copiers, by timing their actual speeds on a series of different benchmark jobs — the results of these tests tell you much more about actual copier productivity than any information you'll ever get out of salespeople. The test results are published in *The Mid-Volume Copier Guide* and *The High-Volume Copier Guide*, both of which also include full specifications, pricing, and ratings on all machines (each of these guides cost $21 at press-time, plus $3 per order for shipping; to order by credit card, call 800 247 2185). If you're spending thousands of dollars on a copier, it makes sense to study this information before you choose a machine — the differences in actual speeds are far greater in many cases than you might imagine.

### Introducing ADFs, RADFs, and sorters

Document feeders are virtual necessities on mid- and high-volume copiers, unless your work consists of making long runs of single-page originals. There's little point in paying good money for a moderately fast copier if you spend ages feeding in piles of multi-page originals.

There are several types of feeders, plus a few variations and several types of auxiliary feeders. The most straightforward is known simply as an ADF (automatic document feeder). An ADF-equipped machine takes a pile of single-sided originals and makes all the required copies of each page before moving onto the next page; one copy of each page is deposited in a sorter bin, so that at the end of the operation each bin will contain a complete copied set of the whole document. A straightforward ADF typically adds around $1,000–$1,300 to the list price of a copier.

This type of plain-vanilla feeder is the norm in the low-volume market, fairly common in the mid-volume market, but increasingly rare in the high-volume market. In sectors of the market where the basic ADF has been edged out, it has generally been replaced by something called an RADF (recirculating automatic document feeder). This works in much the same way, except that it's also able to take double-sided originals and then make single- or double-sided copies; it can also make double-sided copies from single-sided originals.

In the mid-volume market, RADFs tend to be optional items (sometimes you can choose between an RADF or a less expensive ADF). In the high-volume market, however, they tend to be standard items bundled into the basic list price of the equipment. When priced separately from the copiers they work with, RADFs typically cost $1,300–$1,600.

Like straightforward ADFs, RADFs work with sorter bins — the latter acting as repositories for the completed sets. Sorters generally have either 10 or 20 bins and cost anywhere from $900 to $2,000 (more if you want automatic stapling, which I'll be coming to soon). With some mid- and high-volume copiers, you can connect two or three 20-bin sorters together to create a 40- or 60-bin system. Remember that the number of bins determines the number of copied sets of a multi-page document that you can conveniently make in one uninterrupted run.

### Introducing RDHs and OCTs

The other main type of document feeder is known as an RDH (recirculating document handler). The difference is that this type makes one complete copy of a whole document before proceeding to the next one; in other words, each original page is copied just once before the machine makes a copy of the next page; when one whole set has been produced, the machine goes back to the first page and starts producing another set. All RDHs are able to handle single- or double-sided originals, and make single- or double-sided copies. If you didn't quite get all of that, the bottom line is that an RDH makes one set at a time — the other feeders I talked about above make all the copies of each page at a time.

An RDH is generally able to work without sorter bins, because the completed sets are deposited in something known as an "offset catch tray" (OCT), a stacking device in which the sets are offset from one another for separation purposes. However, a few machines with RDHs do use sorter bins as the repositories for their completed sets. Sometimes, RDHs work with a wider range of finishing options, such as automatic folders (more on this shortly).

RDHs are not very common among mid-volume machines, but they become more common the further you go up the high-volume market. Sometimes, a vendor offers a high-volume copier that can be configured with either an RADF or an RDH, but in most cases you can only get one type or the other. When available, high-volume copier RDHs are generally included in the basic list price of the equipment, rather than being priced separately as options. When comparing the cost of RDH-equipped machines with that of RADF equipment, keep in mind that you will probably be saving the cost of sorter bins.

### RADFs & RDHs: pros and cons

The advantage of an RDH is that it allows you to get your hands on one complete copied set at an earlier stage. With an RADF, by contrast, you can't grab one finished set until just about all the sets have been copied.

A further advantage of RDHs is that they can make it easier to produce a large number of copies of a multi-page original. Most RADF machines are only equipped with 20 sorter bins (40-bin options, when available, tend to be very expensive and take up a lot of space). The problem is that if you only have 20 bins, you're generally restricted to making just 20 copies of a multi-page document at a time: if you need 100 sets, for example, you have to do the job five times over.

With an RDH/OCT, by contrast, you can specify any number of sets up to the maximum preselection limit on the machine (generally 999). You may have to empty the catch tray from time to time during a very long run, but you can generally do this without stopping.

Having said all of the above, some RADF/sorter machines do now have a "continuous sort" function, which means that you can select any number of sets up to 999 providing you keep on emptying the bins. However, this is a bit awkward in practice compared with the RDH/OCT method, because you have less flexibility about when you can clear out the copied sets: if you think about it, you can only do so at exactly the point when the machine has finished copying the last page of each batch of 20 sets and, if you aren't quick about it, the machine will pause. One vendor, Mita, has come up with an innovative method of allowing one of its 20-bin RADF/sorter machines to go on producing multiple sets without interruption: a unique robotic arm empties the sets as they are completed, and transports them to a special catch tray.

A drawback of RDHs is that they result in your originals being shuffled around much more than with an RADF. The constant movement can result in more wear and tear to the originals and more document feeder jams. The problem shows up most if the originals are in poor condition to begin with or are on flimsy paper. Sometimes, users get around this by making duplicate master copies of the originals and then copying the masters. The drawback, apart from the time this takes, is that you end up with second-generation copies which may result in less sharp image quality.

It's hard to generalize about which type of feeder is faster: it all depends on which feeders you're comparing and on the jobs they are performing. RDHs sometimes move the originals faster than RADFs — whereas some older RADFs work at only 80 percent of a copier's cruising speed, RDHs generally move originals at the same speed as the copier can duplicate them. Having said that, most recently-introduced RADFs also work at full machine speed.

The RDH method of making just one copy of each original, and then making one copy of the next one, can be intrinsically slower than the ADF process of making all the copies of each page in one go: that's because even though the RDH may move the originals at a faster rate, it has a lot more moving to do. And you may not get the benefit of the full cruising speed when you make what amounts to hundreds of single copies one after the other. If, however, you're only producing one copy of a multi-page set, then the RDH may have an advantage.

Keep in mind that the RDHs found on machines manufactured by Xerox, Kodak, and Océ are in a class of their own when it comes to productivity. These document feeders use proprietary technology — for example, they feed the sheets using a vacuum rather than friction method — and are able to offer outstanding performance in terms of the actual time it takes to complete a long job as a proportion of the theoretical time based on cpm cruising speed.

By contrast, some of the Japanese RDHs are really quite poor: even though the actual recirculating mechanism is able to work at full machine speed, the machines concerned move paper around the copier in such a way that double-sided productivity falls well short of what you should expect. For example, Ricoh's 80cpm FT8880 is terrible on double-sided work — in the *What to Buy for Business* tests that involve making double-sided copies of 10-page, single-sided documents, this machine ran at only 33 percent of its "notional" 80cpm speed! There is nothing in the specifications of this machine that would give you a clue to this ("on paper," the FT8880 looks great) — it's something you would only find out about the hard way or by studying independent test figures (or by carrying out your own tests before buying).

On the same jobs, certain models from Xerox, Kodak, and Océ run at between 95 and 100 percent of full speed. The best Japanese RDHs available at press-time were found on high-volume copiers produced by Sharp (I understand that Sharp has licensed some Kodak patents, though I haven't been able to obtain confirmation).

In summary, there is no clear-cut winner in the RADF versus RDH debate. To some extent, it's a cultural matter: high-volume users who have been brought up on a diet of Xerox and Kodak may start with a built-in presumption in favor of RDHs, because that's what they are used to; by contrast, other people may be more comfortable with the RADF/sorter configuration if their previous exposure to copiers has largely been to Japanese mid-volume machines.

### Other types of document feeders

Let's move on from RDHs and RADFs, but stay on the subject of document feeders — because there are three other types you might encounter. SADFs (semi-automatic document feeders) are a type used in conjunction with some RADFs/RDHs — and occasionally on their own — which allow you to hand-feed single sheets into the machine.

This is much quicker than manually positioning an original on the platen, and it can be quicker than copying a single sheet using a fully automatic document feeder. Another advantage of SADFs is that they sometimes allow you to feed larger-size originals than a regular document feeder will accept.

Computer forms feeders (CFFs) allow you to feed and copy unburst computer forms. Quite a few vendors offer these in the high-volume market, in contrast to the mid-volume market where CFFs are something of a rare species. Sometimes they are standard, but in other cases they are options — expect to pay around $1,400 or so.

Less common are "sub-feeders" or "dual-job feeders." The way in which these work varies, but the idea is that you can place a second job in a feeder and key in the appropriate instructions while the machine is busily processing the first; when the first job is complete, the second one is copied automatically without further user intervention.

### Document feeder and sorter capacities

Check how many sheets of paper can be held by a document feeder and each of your sorter bins. In the mid- and high-volume market, the answer for both is usually 50 — but a handful of models can handle more and a few can only take less.

Occasionally, you'll find that the document feeder capacity is higher than the sorter bin capacity on the same machine, or vice versa. But in these cases, the lower figure is the one that matters: there's limited benefit in having a document feeder that can take, say, 100 sheets if your bins can only hold 70 (the only advantage in that case would be that you could take 100 single-sided originals and make double-sided copies onto 50 sheets of paper; but you wouldn't be able to use all 70 sorter bins unless you were making single-sided copies, in which case you wouldn't be utilizing the full capacity of the feeder).

### Automatic stapling

An increasingly popular feature on both mid- and high-volume copiers is automatic stapling of completed sets, a process often referred to as "finishing." This is available on both sorter- and OCT-configured models. Sometimes it's standard, but usually it's an option — few high-volume machines don't offer it at all.

Stapler-sorters are generally expensive — a 20-bin stapler-sorter generally lists for over $3,000. "Finishing" on an RDH/OCT machine is similarly pricey, though it is often bundled into the cost of the offset catch tray that it works with — few people these days purchase RDH machines without finishing. (For some reason, the word "finishing" is generally used to describe the stapling process on RDH/OCT machines, while plain-and-simple "stapling" is the norm when referring to it on RADF/sorter machines. Don't ask me why!)

Make sure that a machine you're considering is able to staple a sufficient number of pages for your needs: quite a few high-volume machines can manage 50 pages, but some can only handle 25. Another important thing to check are the number and location of available staple positions: some machines can only put one staple in the top left-hand corner, but others give you a choice of, say, one or two staples in up to three positions (for example, you could have two down the left-hand margin for booklet-style finishing). Also worth checking out, though less important, is the size of the staple reservoir.

Keep in mind that RDH-equipped machines have an advantage over RADF models when it comes to stapling, as the process is done more or less simultaneously with the delivery of each completed set — it does not add to the total job time. With an RADF/sorter machine, by contrast, stapling usually only begins when the last page of all the sets has been copied and delivered to the sorter bins. However, a few RADF/sorter models save time by stapling each set as soon as its last page is delivered to the sorter bin (even though the final page hasn't reached all the other bins).

### Folding & other finishing options

Certain upscale models from Kodak and Xerox can take 11" x

17" copied sets, fold them to 8.5" x 11", and then staple them down the middle like a magazine ("saddle-stitching," to use the jargon term). Canon also makes some copiers that take 11" x 17" sheets and fold them into a z-fold for inclusion in an 8.5" x 11" document.

Another form of finishing is automatic on-line thermal binding: Kodak offers this in the high-volume market, and Mita offers it on some mid-volume machines. Mita also offers automatic on-line hole punching as an option on certain models.

# More Document & Paper Handling Features

Next, a look at other features that concern the handling of originals and paper. ...

### Duplex (automatic double-sided) copying

Almost all mid- and high-volume copiers can handle automatic double-sided — or "duplex" — copying, though this is sometimes an option. If you're doing double-sided copying, look for the size of the machine's internal duplex tray. This determines how many double-sided copies a machine can make of each original in a single run; the figure is generally 50 sheets (i.e., 100 double-sided images). Keep in mind that not all machines can make double-sided 11" x 17" copies, even if they can handle that size on single-sided work. Also, remember what I said earlier about duplex copying often slowing down overall speed: duplex, more than anything else, is what slows down copiers, but whereas the effect is very marked on some models it is barely noticeable on others.

A few high-end machines use a different type of duplex technology, known as "one-pass" double-sided copying. In this case, the machine copies onto both sides of the paper in a single run, in contrast to the conventional duplex tray method where the paper is copied on one side, inverted automatically, and then run through a second time. Proponents of the one-pass method claim that it results in fewer paper jams. Kodak and Océ both use this method on certain models.

### Paper and original sizes

Most mid- and high-volume copiers can copy onto all standard paper sizes up to 11" x 17" and can also copy from originals up to that size. A handful of machines can take larger size originals and make reduced-size copies.

However, some older high-volume copiers — mostly from

Xerox and Kodak — are only able to copy onto letter- and legal-size paper, and can't do 11" x 17" copies. These machines are document duplicators in the traditional mold, aimed at people on very high monthly volumes (well into six figures). Sometimes, these older machines can copy from 11" x 17" originals. Even then, you may not be able to use the main document feeder, but instead have to position the original directly on the platen, or use the SADF.

### Reduction/enlargement

Just about all mid- and high-volume machines offer both reduction and enlargement as standard, though a handful of models have this as an option or only allow you to reduce but not enlarge. Reduction and enlargement is almost always in the form of a continuous zoom range, supported by various preset ratios; many models offer a 50–200 percent range, though some only have something like 64–141 or 64–155 percent.

### On-line paper supplies

There's a marked trend for copier manufacturers to introduce new models that have significantly larger on-line paper supplies than their predecessors. For example, mid-volume buyers can now usually expect at least two trays holding 1,000 sheets between them. Dual 250-sheet trays are now only acceptable in the low-volume sector, and even there you often get something like one 250-sheet tray plus one 500-sheet tray.

In the mid-volume sector, it's also becoming increasingly common for the standard paper supply to include one tray handling 1,000 sheets or more — previously, large capacity trays tended to be options. For example, you might get one 500-sheet tray and one 1,000-sheet tray. Some mid-volume machines offer three or even four on-line trays as standard: in these cases, none may hold as many as 1,000 sheets, but their combined capacity may be an impressive 1,500–2,000 sheets.

Not surprisingly, the largest standard paper supplies are to be found in the high-volume sector, where you get machines able to hold 2,000–5,000 sheets. However, an irony in the high-volume copier market is that some of the machines with the very highest copy volume capabilities also have the smallest on-line paper supplies. This is because these machines, sold by Kodak and Xerox, are derivatives of machines that were first developed in the mid-1980s when a 2,000-sheet capacity was considered pretty hefty.

Some copier buyers prefer the emphasis to be on having as many trays as possible, while others are more concerned with the total on-line capacity. If virtually all of your copying is onto the same size and type of paper, you won't be too bothered about the number of trays and will focus on the total capacity — arguably having fewer trays that hold more paper is an advantage. If, however, you want to be able to press buttons to switch between different paper sizes and types (regular copying paper, colored paper, letterheads, 11" x 17", etc.), the number of trays will be important. In practice, most people look for a combination. (Incidentally, I use the terms "tray" and "cassette" interchangeably when referring to paper supplies, though some purists reserve "tray" for the units with higher capacities. Paper "drawers" are a sub-set of trays: more on these shortly.)

### Auto tray switching

If you use more than one tray to hold the same size and type of paper, you may want to look for a feature called "automatic tray switching." This means that when the machine runs out of paper from one tray, it will switch to the next one without stopping.

Some machines with auto tray switching also allow you to refill an empty tray while the machine is copying and drawing paper from another. Some also allow you to refill the toner while the machine is running. Combined, these features can enable you to complete very long jobs without stopping at all — paper jams allowing!

### Bypasses

A bypass allows you to feed non-standard paper without having to put it in one of the trays. Almost all copiers have a bypass of some sort: with some you can only feed one sheet at a time, while others allow you to stack up to 50 sheets.

A bypass is also useful when you want to feed paper that's especially difficult to copy onto — for example, very light or heavy paper — as the paper path is straighter and the chances of jamming are reduced.

### Front-loading paper supplies

If the last time you bought a copier was a few years ago, you'll probably think of paper trays as cassettes that stick out at the side. Today, however, the rage is paper "drawers" that slide out at the front. Paper drawers are usually considered a plus point: they make the copier neater to look at, they can be easier to get at, and the copier takes up less room.

On the other hand, the upward paper path from a front-loading drawer can be more complicated than the more horizontal path from a side-loading cassette, so the chance of jamming may be increased. On the whole, though, the copier manufacturers have gotten their paper paths working pretty well — I'd be inclined to go for front-loading machines, rather than avoiding them on account of paper jam angst.

A few machines have both front-loading trays and side-loading cassettes. This really gives you the worst of both worlds: having just one side-loading cassette sticking out means that the machine ends up using more floor space, yet you still have the possible jam anxiety associated with front-loading supplies.

### Automatic selection

If you've got more than one size or type of paper on-line in different trays, you can press a button to select which you want the machine to copy onto. But these days, all machines with zoom reduction/enlargement also have an automatic selection feature — this means that the machine recognizes the size of the original and automatically selects the right paper tray to match it, taking account of the magnification ratio you've chosen. I stress the word "all" because copier salespeople have a habit of raving about this feature as though it were a characteristic of their brand in particular, rather than of copiers in general.

The feature operates the other way too: if you insert a particular original, and select the paper size you want it copied onto, the machine automatically selects the right magnification ratio to do the job. (Keep in mind that this feature usually only operates when you're copying documents placed in the feeder, not on the platen.)

# Other Mid/High-Volume Copier Features

Next, a brief tour through the other main features of office copiers. ...

### Preselection

This refers to the number of copies you can tell your copier to make in one run. Mid-volume machines usually go up to either 99 or 999; high-volume models almost always go up to 999.

### TV-style displays

Copier control panels have gotten a lot more user-friendly in recent years, though most still have a way to go. One feature that a lot of users like on larger machines is a small TV-style display to prompt users through their options. Some manufacturers have gone a step further and introduced touch-screen displays on their high-volume machines.

### Photo mode

Many copiers have a special mode for enhancing the reproduction quality of photos. This usually doesn't make a great deal of difference, as you can often achieve comparable results by adjusting the contrast control. However, a few models at the top end of the market do have more sophisticated functions, especially certain models from Kodak and Xerox.

### Serial/book copying

Also known as "dual-page copying," this very common feature enables you to place an open book or magazine on the platen, and obtain separate copies of both the left and right hand pages in a single operation. On duplex machines, you can use this feature to obtain copies of each facing page on both sides of a single sheet.

Occasionally, salespeople get confused if you ask about "book copying" and think all you want to know is whether you can copy from open books or magazines by placing them on the platen: this is a throw-back to the olden days when some machines couldn't handle that.

### Border/edge erase

This feature allows you to erase the border around the edge of your copy. It's useful if there are marks around the edge or if you're copying something, such as a book or newspaper, that creates a shadow.

### Margin/image shift

This allows you to shift the image of your original a little way across the page to leave a decent margin for binding. With duplex copiers, the margin position can be altered automatically from left to right according to whether the pages are odd- or even-numbered.

### Image overlay

This somewhat less common feature allows you to superimpose two originals onto one copy automatically. You place the two originals onto the platen side-by-side and press a special button.

### Covers insertion

This enables you to load one of your paper trays with document covers; these might be a different colored paper or, perhaps, a light card. The covers can automatically be added to the front and, usually, back of each multi-page set. Usually, the covers can also be copied onto.

This feature can be especially effective when used with automatic finishing (i.e., stapling), as it enables you to produce well-presented documents with minimum operator involvement. Originally just a high-volume copier feature, it has also become more common in the mid-volume sector.

### Chapterization

Chapterization enables you to separate each section of a document by instructing the machine to insert divider pages held in one of the alternate paper trays. This feature is usually only found in the high-volume market, but can be found on some mid-volume models. On some machines, you can also request the machine to begin each new chapter on a right hand page when you're copying onto both sides of the paper. Keep in mind that some models offer a limited version of this feature, which enables them to insert the divider pages, but doesn't allow you to copy onto them.

### OHP interleaving

All copiers can copy onto overhead transparencies ("OHPs," in copier jargon). However, the problem with being handed a pile of transparencies is that, unless they come with a sheet of blank backing paper, it's very hard to see what each one is.

The solution is to have the copier automatically insert a blank "slip sheet" between each transparency when it's copying multiple images onto OHPs. This feature is generally only found in the high-volume market. You can usually also have the machine copy the image onto the slip sheets.

### Copy editing

This allows you not only to copy an original but to alter it in the process. This feature comes in two guises: built-in copy editing and add-on copy editing. The editing facilities built into some copiers are usually restricted to "mask and trim" — this enables you to block out certain parts of an original that you don't want to appear in the copies. Basic built-in copy editing is not exactly a rarity, but most machines do not have it — and most people who get the feature seldom end up using it.

More advanced copy editing typically requires something

called an "edit board," which is offered as an option on some machines. This is an external device connected to a copier. You place your original on the board and mark out the areas you want to copy or block off using an "electronic pen."

Edit boards are generally a little easier to use than built-in copy editing features and offer more features, including the ability to alter the layout of an original (i.e., move the position of certain parts) and create special effects (such as reversals, where black areas turn to white and vice versa).

But edit boards are also expensive items which have not caught on. I regard them as, for the most part, gimmicks. If you have a real need or burning desire to alter an original before copying it, you'd probably be much better off doing so in the pre-copying stage by manipulating the image on a computer.

### Job programming

This feature allows you to program a sequence of instructions needed to execute a complicated copying job, so that you can set it all in motion whenever you want at the press of just one or two buttons. It's potentially useful for complicated jobs that come up over and over again, but in reality it's the sort of feature that many people never get around to using.

### Color features

This chapter isn't covering full color copiers, which make same-color copies of full color originals — but these are covered in Chapter 8. However, some regular office copiers do have color capabilities of a much more limited nature — they allow you to substitute the regular black toner color with another color on all or part of your copies.

This often requires you to open up the side of the machine, take out the black toner, and replace it with toner of another color — an awkward process which few users care to get involved in. However, a few machines allow you to keep more than one toner color in the machine at once and switch between them at the press of a button.

A handful of models go a step further and allow you to make copies in more than one toner color in a single pass through the machine — a headline might be in red, for example, and the rest of the text in black. This is accomplished in tandem with a copy editing feature.

### Copy auditing

Finally, a growing number of mid- and high-volume machines have "copy auditor" features which restrict access to authorized persons and/or record details of copier usage. This can be useful when copies have to be costed to different departments or billed to different clients.

How the feature works varies, but it usually operates by means of users entering PIN-style codes on a copier's control panel. Check out the number of accounts the auditor can handle — this varies from fewer than 50 to several thousand.

# Vendor Profiles

Here are overviews introducing you to the vendors which make or relabel mid- and high-volume copiers. Also shown are their addresses and phone numbers; contact them for details of dealers and/or direct sales offices in your area.

## *AB Dick*

*AB Dick Company*
*5700 West Touhy Avenue*
*Niles, IL 60718*
*Tel: 312 763 1900*

### *Introduction*
AB Dick is an old American reprographics manufacturer, now British-owned, with its roots in smaller and medium-size offset printing equipment. In the late 1980s, AB Dick earned its place in copier history books by being the only company to sell relabeled Xerox equipment. Unfortunately, this arrangement didn't seem to work as it only lasted a short while. Today, AB Dick's copiers are relabeled Konica machines.

### *AB Dick's focus*
These days, AB Dick concentrates on selling copiers mainly to large accounts. It has made its copier business more autonomous than it was previously — it's eager to stress that it isn't only in the business of selling to companies that already use its printing equipment. AB Dick is not a huge force in copiers, but it stresses its commitment to this market and can be considered as an alternative to other major account specialists such as Lanier, Pitney Bowes, and, indeed, Xerox. Sales are both direct and through dealers.

# Canon

*Canon USA, Inc.*
*One Canon Plaza*
*Lake Success, NY 11042*
*Tel: 516 488 6700*

## Introduction

Canon's roots go back to the 1930s, when it began life in Japan as a camera manufacturer known as Precision Optical Research Laboratory. The name "Canon" is derived from "Kwanon," the Buddhist goddess of mercy after whom the company's first camera was named.

Canon entered the copier market in 1968. Today, it is one of the five Japanese companies to manufacture an entire copier range stretching from the low end to the 80cpm level. For the past 12 years, it has been number-one in US market share if you measure by the number of units sold (Xerox is ahead in terms of revenues). Canon USA Inc.'s revenues in 1993 amounted to $5.3 billion, of which 87 percent came from office equipment. The US operation accounts for about one third of Canon's worldwide business.

As I show in Chapter 9, Canon has taken a lead in the copier-based multifunctional market, with a mid-market unit called the GP55. And as I show in Chapter 8, it is also the leader in color copiers. Also, as I discussed in Chapter 4, Canon is the leader in retail-channel copiers for very low-volume users.

## Made in the USA — up to a point

Canon is one of only two Japanese copier companies to manufacture copiers in the US (the other is Ricoh). At press-time, two Canon copiers — both low-end models — were being made in the company's US plant, which is located in Newport News, Virginia. However, this facility also makes laser printers — including Hewlett-Packard's LaserJet 4 series — as well as printer cartridges and toner. As with other manufacturing operations of this type, by no means all components are US-sourced — however, the local content is high enough to enable Canon to placard the factory's output as "Made in the USA."

## "NP" copier product line

Canon's regular office copiers (as opposed to its retail-channel, low-volume copiers) have model numbers that are prefixed with the letters "NP" (originally standing for "new process," though the company — keen as all copier vendors are to be "seen to be green" — has taken to pointing out that these letters are also short for "non-polluting"). Lately, the NP series has looked best in the low- and higher-volume ends of the market, and the mid-volume range has seemed in need of a facelift — by the time you read this, Canon may have rectified this situation.

Canon is one of the most impressive Japanese companies in the high-volume copier market. It makes some of the best machines (especially at the 50–60cpm level), has some of the largest dealers, and boasts a track record second to none: no other Japanese vendor has so many machines installed which actually get used for very high volumes.

### The Canon-Kodak deal

Canon's position in high-volume copiers has recently gotten stronger still: since 1993, it has been relabeling Kodak super-giant copiers, suitable for workloads of 100,000–250,000 copies a month (no Japanese company makes copiers at that level, which historically has been a three-horse race between Xerox, Kodak, and Océ). At the time of this writing, Canon only had one Kodak model in its stable, though a second and faster one should have been announced by the end of 1994.

Canon is only selling the Kodak equipment through its largest dealers — about 40–50 in total. This is the first time that a Japanese vendor has challenged Xerox at the very top end of the market, albeit not with its own equipment. As a result of this deal, Canon has also become the only vendor, apart from Xerox itself, to offer a product line that stretches all the way from mini copiers, for several hundred copies a month, to giant copiers for several hundred thousand.

This isn't the first time that the two companies have worked together. Kodak has been relabeling certain Canon 50–60cpm machines for a while, selling them to users of its larger equipment who want one-stop shopping. During the shelf-life of this book, Kodak will take on additional Canon products, relabeling mid-volume models all the way down to 30cpm. In addition, Kodak relabels Canon color copiers. Further details and comment on the Kodak-Canon alliance appear in the Kodak entry in these Vendor Profiles. Note that the 83cpm models that Canon manufactures are also relabeled by Lanier — which, to complete the triangle, itself relabels a Kodak 100cpm unit.

### Canon's copier distribution

Canon sells its NP-series copiers entirely through dealers. But while it doesn't have direct sales branches as such, it owns subsidiaries in the New York, Chicago, Philadelphia, and Los Angeles metropolitan areas which operate as dealers.

In all, Canon has approximately 500 dealers. Approximately 40 percent of Canon's US office copier sales are now through Alco dealerships: as I explained earlier in this chapter, Alco is a conglomerate that, through an aggressive acquisitions policy, now owns hundreds of copier dealerships across the nation. All of these operate under individual names, rather than under the Alco name. The Alco coverage provides Canon with powerful distribution: while this is envied by other vendors, some people wonder whether Canon has exposed itself by putting so many eggs in one distribution basket.

Some Canon sales to government and a few other major accounts go under the Selex brand name. The Selex models are made by Copyer, a Canon subsidiary, and are similar, though not identical, to Canon's own.


# Gestetner

*Gestetner Corporation*
*599 West Putnam Avenue*
*Greenwich, CT 06836*
*Tel: 203 863 5551*

### Introduction

Gestetner is a long-established British reprographics company that has undergone changes in ownership in recent years. The Gestetner family sold out to Australian investors several years ago and, subsequently, Ricoh acquired a 25 percent stake.

Gestetner — which trades worldwide — is not a copier manufacturer. It has traditionally sold relabeled Mita copiers, and still does. However, it has recently begun selling some relabeled Ricoh models as well. In Europe — where the company also trades under the Nashuatec and Rex Rotary brands — Gestetner has become more heavily slanted to Ricoh products, but in the US the plan seems to be to remain more Mita-oriented. The dealer network appears to prefer the Mita products, which tend to have more of an edge on price.

### Gestetner's focus

Gestetner sells through a network of approximately 450 dealers and 35 direct sales branches. Traditionally, the brand has been strongest in the schools/churches/government markets, which have been drawn to Gestetner on account of its background in stencil and electronic duplicators.

There has recently been a shake-up in Gestetner's North American management. While Gestetner will remain one of the smaller vendors in this market, there does seem to be more drive in growing its US business and making it more visible outside its traditional core markets.

# Kodak

*Eastman Kodak Company*
*343 State Street*
*Rochester, NY 14650*
*Tel: 800 344 0006*

### Introduction

Kodak specializes in the top end of the copier market: the slowest machine it manufactures is a 70cpm unit and the fastest is a 110cpm model. In this respect, Kodak has just two major competitors: Xerox and Océ. However, Kodak also competes indirectly against several Japanese vendors selling 70–100cpm machines that are significantly less heavy-duty and productive.

Kodak does sell 50–60cpm models, but these are relabeled Canons; they are not marketed aggressively and are generally only sold to companies that are buying faster Kodaks and want single-vendor sourcing for all of their high-volume requirements. However, Kodak is likely to expand its presence in the mid-volume market during the shelf-life of this book, when it introduces relabeled versions of other Canon models going all the way down to 30cpm.

While these machines will likewise only be offered to buyers of Kodak's larger copiers, the company is making noises to indicate that it wishes to place more emphasis on its ability to satisfy its customers' mid-volume needs. This relabeling of Canon equipment is part of a broader alliance in the copier business between the two companies, which I will discuss later in this profile.

### Kodak's commitment to the copier market

Eastman Kodak has been much in the news in the past year for reasons not always of its choosing: it has reported disappointing results, and gone through a major internal rumpus over the speed and extent of restructuring and refocusing — culminating in the replacement of its CEO. In the midst of this, rumors flew about the condition and future of a number of divisions, including its copier business. There was speculation that Kodak might get out of copiers, by selling the division to Canon.

While it's unclear how serious an option that ever was, it now seems certain that Kodak does plan to stay in this business — the new CEO went on the record in January 1994 to categorically rule out a sale. And Kodak's copier business seemed in good shape financially at the start of 1994, after a disappointing period in 1991 and 1992. This isn't immediately apparent to outsiders, because copiers have formed part of a segment of Kodak whose results have not lately been reported separately from certain loss-making operations.

Kodak's Copy Products business forms the larger part of the Office Imaging organization, which also includes Business Imaging Systems (which handles microfilm, scanning, and related products and supplies). Office Imaging, in turn, is — for the purpose of financial reporting — part of the Information Segment (Eastman Kodak currently reports its results in three "segments," Information, Imaging, and Health).

In 1993, revenues from Office Imaging amounted to $2.5 billion — of which $1.8 billion came from Copy Products — and earnings were in the region of $200 million. Approximately 60 percent of Office Imaging's business is in the US. If the Office Imaging organization were to be spun off from the rest of Kodak (which it won't be), it would be a Fortune 300 company in its own right. It seems right to stress these figures, to balance the uncertainty that has surrounded Kodak's copier business as a result of the clouds hanging over the company as a whole.

Kodak's copier division has earned a superb reputation for the quality of its service and support. The service organization has been enhanced with a remote service and diagnostics function, enabling Kodak technicians to monitor performance and predict problems on certain models from data sent over a phone line from the copier to a central Kodak computer.

### The "build status" of Kodak copiers

As with Xerox, many of the copiers supplied by Kodak are remanufactured, not brand new. The reason is simple: copiers that are built for the highest volumes are incredibly sturdy units that have a natural life of over 10 years. If a customer wants to change a machine after two or three years, it makes no sense to scrap the old one and it's also a waste to sell it merely as a used machine.

Instead, the policy is to bring it back to the factory, put it back on a production line, and make it as good as new. Typically, a Kodak copier will begin to be supplied remanufactured a year or two after it was first supplied new; there will usually be an overlap period when both new and remanufactured units are shipped concurrently and sold for the same price.

Like Xerox, Kodak has not always been as forthcoming on

the build status of its machines as it might be. It prefers to play down the fact that many of its copiers are not new: this information is omitted from most of the marketing literature, for example.

Kodak argues that the information is not particularly important, since all the machines — new and old — meet the same quality standards. While I agree that this is so, I also feel that the build status of any office machine ought to be made clear to buyers — it is a slippery slope if vendors only provide this information selectively.

However, toward the end of 1993, Kodak for the first time began defining the build status of all of its models — a welcome step towards openness. It did so by placing them in three categories — one for machines that are essentially brand new (even though they may contain some remanufactured parts), another for machines that are remanufactured, and a third for "derivative" machines that are upgraded from one model to another during the course of a remanufacturing process.

Readers will note that these three categories correspond exactly to the three that had been defined by Xerox for its own product range almost a year earlier. What's more, Kodak's exact description of these categories is copied — in large parts verbatim — from Xerox's carefully (and sometimes obscurely) worded explanations. Here, then, is how Kodak defines the build status of its copiers in its own words (or, rather, in words inspired by its main competitor):

❑ ***"Factory Produced New Model Equipment*** — Equipment that has been converted to new model status which maintains features and/or functions not available on the previous model. The new model has been disassembled to a predetermined standard established by Kodak and manufactured to a new model status. It has a new serial number. The new model contains new, reprocessed and/or recovered parts that fully meet new product productivity and reliability specifications."

❑ ***"Remanufactured Equipment*** — Remanufactured equipment is restored to be functionally equivalent to new equipment through the following processes: (i) Disassembly to levels established by Kodak; (ii) Thorough cleaning and lubrication; (iii) Replacement of components with either new, remanufactured, or used components as determined by Kodak; (iv) Installation of all mandatory modifications and any deemed desirable by Kodak effective the date of remanufacture; (v) Inspection and testing to assure that remanufactured equipment functions within new equipment performance requirements."

❑ ***"Newly Manufactured Equipment*** — Newly Manufactured Equipment is newly assembled equipment which may contain used components that have been subject to rigorous inspection and functional testing to assure machine compliance with product performance and reliability specifications."

Keep in mind that most models can be supplied in more than one of the above categories. Kodak's price list, should you get to see this, indicates which build categories apply to each model. Like Xerox, Kodak reserves the right at its sole discretion to supply you with a machine that falls in any of the applicable categories — and the company's pricing policy does not in any way distinguish between the categories. For example, if you buy a Kodak 2085, you may get one that is brand new (though possibly containing some remanufactured parts) or you may get one that is a completely remanufactured Ektaprint 235 — but you'll probably never know which you're getting (even when you've got it). The price is the same either way. I have been unable to discover how many remanufactured parts can go into a brand new copier before the copier as a whole is termed "remanufactured" rather than "newly manufactured."

You should take a look at the points I make in the Xerox entry about build status, as many of these are applicable to Kodak as well. In particular, I do want to stress that, in my opinion, build status is not a quality issue. I am providing you with all this information about build status, because I think that buyers have a right to know — I am not giving it to deter you in any way from buying a Kodak copier on the grounds that what you are getting may not be brand new.

Readers should also know that the build status of a Kodak copier makes no difference whatsoever to what you pay for service, or to the quality of support that you get. Kodak is noted for giving the same excellent support to users of its older copiers that it does to buyers of its latest models.

That does not mean that its older models are necessarily as good or productive as its latest ones — machines introduced for the first time in the past three years may be superior in a number of ways to ones that were brought to the market eight years ago. However, the idea is that Kodak maintains an older machine to the same standard that was enjoyed when that particular machine was new — indeed, field upgrades sometimes result in an eight-year-old machine becoming better than when it was new.

In some cases, remanufacturing may take place on the same production line responsible for brand new models. This is especially likely to occur with models introduced for the first time within the past few years that are not derivatives of older ones. Older machines are likely to be remanufactured in other locations. Indeed, much of Kodak's remanufacturing for the North American market takes place in Mexico.

A few very old machines that are from time to time offered may not be remanufactured as such, but may simply be sold as used equipment. These are veteran models, such as the Ektaprint 100 and 150, which are effectively discontinued but which are occasionally offered to customers — especially in the public sector — who are looking for the absolute cheapest equipment capable of high-volume duplicating.

### Kodak support & distribution policies

Kodak does not have a formal customer satisfaction guarantee similar to that offered by Xerox (which promises to replace a machine at any time during the first three years if a dissatisfied customer requests this). However, in practice Kodak's policy is to do what it takes to keep on the right side of its customers — and that generally includes replacing problematic machines rather than expecting buyers to live with them. Kodak lays great (and genuine) emphasis on building "life-long relationships" with its customers: it does not want to squander goodwill on occasions when a machine fails to live up to expectations.

Nonetheless, Kodak is currently looking at the possibility of some sort of formal satisfaction guarantee — more for appearance's sake than because it perceives an actual need to change its attitude towards problem machines. (The only Kodak copier whose reliability has been anything other than excellent in recent years has been the 2110: while I have received some negative feedback about that model, I have only heard positive things about how Kodak has responded to problems.)

Until 1993, Kodak only sold its copiers direct — there were no dealers and no distribution agreements with other vendors. However, since 1993, two different Kodak giant copiers have also been sold relabeled by Canon and Lanier. Kodak is continuing to sell its full line through its own sales force: there is no evidence that the Canon and Lanier deals are the start of a winding down of its own sales operation (in fact, the sales force has lately been growing by over 100 people a year).

### More on the Kodak-Canon/Lanier relationships

Canon is likely to take on a second Kodak copier towards the end of 1994 — probably a planned enhancement of the 2110. I imagine that Lanier also plans to take on an additional Kodak product at a later date; Kodak appears to prefer that Canon and Lanier don't end up relabeling the same models as each other, though that rule isn't necessarily written in stone.

Canon and Lanier are both doing their own servicing on the Kodak machines they relabel. Kodak refuses to service machines sold by the other two, and supplies have been tweaked to make them incompatible. It is possible that Kodak will take back used models sold by Canon and Lanier for remanufacturing, but it seems more likely that the relabelers will set up operations to carry out this work themselves (though it remains to be seen whether their remanufacturing could be done as thoroughly as Kodak's own).

The risk facing Kodak with these deals is that there are now three companies selling its copiers to the same users, possibly confusing customers and resulting in the direct sales operation losing business to the relabelers. If I were thinking of buying a Kodak copier, I'd certainly get competing proposals from Canon and/or Lanier in the hope of being offered a better deal. Kodak's policy is not to allow itself to be undercut, so — even if your gut preference is to buy from Kodak itself on account of the company's experience in supporting high-volume users — you can use Canon and/or Lanier as leverage in your price negotiation.

However, Kodak believes that the main effect of its Canon/ Lanier deals will be to widen its distribution base and cause Kodak-manufactured copiers to challenge Xerox in significantly more installations than at present. Kodak expects that only about 10–15 percent of its copier sales will route through Canon/Lanier in the next year or two. Of the two relabelers, Canon is selling more equipment.

Canon's decision to start relabeling Kodak's 2085 duplicator marked a new stage in the already significant alliance between the two companies. This alliance had already resulted in technology exchanges, as well as in Kodak relabeling certain Canon 50–60cpm copiers and color laser copiers. Lately, the two companies have discussed other ways of extending their relationship. One consequence is that they may start working together on joint bids for major contracts (though this is by no means certain). In addition, the two companies are jointly developing a totally new copier product slated for introduction in the mid-nineties which — according to senior Kodak sources — will "knock my socks off."

### Kodak's strategy for product development

A very important aspect of Kodak's developing strategy is to market high-volume digital copiers that are multifunctional units capable of doubling up as high-speed network printers. Its 1575 digital copier, introduced in 1991, can now be upgraded with a printer option or can be purchased as a 1580 with this option preinstalled: this machine is by no means perfect, but it is the only machine of its type at this level of the market and it has some very interesting features.

Kodak is also promising to place increasing emphasis on making high-volume copiers easier to use. People at the company talk about making future Kodak copiers "as easy to use as Macs." Beyond this, Kodak's strategy in this market is to exploit what it terms its "media independence" — a reference to the fact that it is able to offer large organizations the choice of copying documents, printing them across a network, storing them on CD, or outputting them to microfilm/fiche.

# Konica

*Konica Business Machines USA Inc.*
*500 Day Hill Road*
*Windsor, CT 06095*
*Tel: 203 683 2222*

### Introduction

Konica is one of the five Japanese vendors to make all of its own machines, from the bottom to the top of the market. It has been very successful in selling to major accounts under its own name. Indeed, Konica sells a higher proportion of its machines to major national accounts than any other Japanese manufacturer.

### Konica's distribution strategy

Konica's ability to target national accounts has been helped by the fact that the company has far more direct sales branches than any other copier manufacturer apart from Xerox and Kodak — currently, the total is 48. This enables it to bid for multi-location contracts where the buyer wants to deal with only one vendor, preferably the manufacturer. I get good feedback from major account customers about their dealings with the company.

However, Konica also has a strong dealer network, and should by no means only be considered a major account vendor. Indeed, it has one of the best balanced distribution networks of all the Japanese companies. There are about 360 Konica dealers, of which about 20 are rated as "super-strong." There don't appear to be any Alco dealers in the Konica fraternity, though there are a number of Danka ones. In general, Konica dealers located in areas also covered by direct sales offices tend to focus on smaller accounts. Konica's copiers are also relabeled by AB Dick.

### Konica's focus
Konica has never gone out of its way to develop conventional copier products likely to excite smaller businesses. For example, it has only very recently offered a low-volume copier with a document feeder — and even that is an expensive one borrowed from its mid-volume range. That said, Konica's initial multifunctional offerings are targeted at the low end of the market.

The main event in Konica's 1994 calendar is the launch of two new 90cpm machines, which were first shown as prototypes in 1992. Previously, Konica's high-volume range stopped with a fairly mediocre 80cpm product.

# Lanier

*Lanier Worldwide Inc.*
*2300 Parklake Drive NE*
*Atlanta, GA 30345–2979*
*Tel: 800 708 7088*

### Introduction
Lanier is a major national, and international, office equipment vendor which sells relabeled products direct to end users, as well as through a limited dealer network. The company has excellent distribution: it claims to serve every parish and county in the United States. Its appeal is chiefly to larger buyers, especially those with multiple locations: you can negotiate one deal and get one bill. However, Lanier also sells to medium- and smaller-size offices.

### Lanier's multi-manufacturer portfolio
Lanier's copiers have lately been relabeled Toshibas, Panasonics, and Sharps in the low-volume sector, relabeled Toshibas in the mid-volume market and at the lower end of the high-volume sector, and relabeled Canons further up the high-volume ladder. In addition, Lanier started selling a relabeled version of a Kodak 100cpm giant copier in 1993 — see the Kodak entry for more on this.

### Lanier support

Lanier has a very good reputation for service, and backs its products and service contracts with the most comprehensive total satisfaction guarantee in the industry. What's more, the feedback I get from people who have bought from Lanier lately is that the company has become a lot more competitive in discount prices — so don't be afraid to negotiate yourself a deal.

# Minolta

*Minolta Corporation*
*Business Equipment Division*
*101 Williams Drive*
*Ramsey, NJ 07446*
*Tel: 201 825 4000*

### Introduction

Minolta has improved its product range immeasurably in the past couple of years, and it is a strong candidate for users who expect to make between 1,000 and about 50,000 copies on a single machine.

Historically, Minolta has a tradition of innovation when it comes to copier features. For example, it was the first vendor to introduce zoom reduction/enlargement back in the 1980s, and it was the first to introduce auto paper/magnification ratio select. There were times a few years ago when Minolta could be accused of being too features-driven, at the expense of real-world productivity, but that is no longer the case: even though Minolta still likes to come up with unusual features, productivity on core copying jobs now ranks very high.

Minolta is still absent from the very high end of the market — at the time of this writing, its fastest high-volume machine was a 76cpm RADF-equipped unit with no more than 20 sorter bins. Minolta will doubtless launch some faster equipment in the next year or so — but whether or not this will be Minolta-manufactured remains to be seen (recently, one Minolta 71cpm copier has been a rebadged Ricoh).

Nonetheless, Minolta's product range is excellent as far as it goes, and the brand has been gaining significant market share in the mid-volume market and the lower part of the high-volume sector where it was previously weaker.

### Minolta distribution

Although Minolta sells mainly through a network of over 350 dealers, it also has about 20 direct sales offices in major markets. Most Minolta dealers are independents, though about 25 are part of the Danka consortium and there is also a sprinkling of Alco representation. Several Minolta copiers are also sold relabeled by Olympia and Panasonic. In Minolta's favor is the fact that it offers the best performance guarantee of any of the Japanese vendors selling through dealers (see the discussion on that topic earlier in this chapter) — though this does not apply to all models.

# Mita

*Mita Copystar America, Inc.*
*225 Sand Road*
*Fairfield, NJ 07004*
*Tel: 201 808 8444*

### Introduction

Mita is the only Japanese company to be a copier specialist: apart from minor sidelines in fax and laser printers, copiers are all it makes. The Osaka-based company — which is still privately held — has roots in the lower and middle sectors of the copier market. But in recent years, it has been moving steadily upmarket: throughout 1992 and 1993, its 85cpm model was the fastest Japanese machine being sold in the US in terms of its notional cruising speed (that speed record was lost in 1994, however).

### Mita product comments

Parts of Mita's product range have been looking somewhat uninspiring lately, with price, rather than stunning performance, often standing out as the main thing in its favor. However, the range received a boost in mid-1994 from the launch of the new 60cpm DC-6090: this model is an innovative unit which should emerge as one of the most exciting machines in its class.

Further up the market, Mita's 85cpm DC-8585 has achieved an excellent reputation as a workhorse copier. This machine, which cynics once suggested was too big for Mita to handle, has proved itself to be a solid trooper — a dependable duplicator which can cope comfortably with six-figure workloads. It has its limitations, however (duplex productivity could be better, for example), and an enhanced 92cpm derivative will emerge during the shelf-life of this book.

### Mita distribution

Mita manufactures all of its copiers and, except for one direct sales office in New York City, sells them only through dealers. It has more dealers than its rivals — the number is currently around 550 (about 200 more than average). However, many of these are in smaller markets and Mita is not generally counted among the strongest players in the major account market.

Most of Mita's machines are also relabeled by three other vendors in the US: Gestetner, Monroe, and Pitney Bowes. In addition, some are sold under the Royal Copystar brand name, which is now owned by Mita itself (see separate entry in these Vendor Profiles). Mita has a factory in South Carolina which produces some parts for its copiers, as well as toner.

# Monroe

*Monroe Systems for Business*
*The American Road*
*Morris Plains, NJ 07950*
*Tel: 201 993 2000*

### Introduction
Monroe is an old name in the American office equipment market. Its copiers are relabeled Mita machines. All sales are direct — there are no Monroe copier dealers. At present, there are about 55 main district sales offices, and about 150 smaller satellite branches. Lately, the company has closed down some of its smaller offices.

### Monroe's focus
These days, Monroe only actively chases large accounts. Monroe falls in the same category of supplier as Lanier and Pitney Bowes (though it's a smaller version): in other words, it appeals to larger buyers who want to deal with a national vendor, rather than local dealers, and who want an alternative to Xerox.

# Océ

*Océ Systems for Business*
*5450 North Cumberland Avenue*
*Chicago, IL 60656*
*Tel: 312 714 8500*

### Introduction
Océ-USA is a subsidiary of Océ-van der Grinten, a $1.3-billion Dutch company, which is the only surviving all-European manufacturer of copiers (a separate division of Océ makes specialized

engineering/large-format copiers). Océ is a high-volume specialist: although the company has three 45cpm office copiers, most of its machines are in the 60–100cpm sector.

All have a well-deserved reputation for sturdiness, and most are engineered for significantly higher volumes than their cpm speeds might lead you to expect. There is not a single Océ copier that is rated by the manufacturer for less than 150,000 copies per month, though the company targets users with monthly volumes as low as 15,000 with its slower models.

Some of the newer models display outstanding productivity, in terms of how close they run to their "notional" cpm speeds on complex jobs involving duplexing multi-page sets. However, Océ is a strong prominent exponent of the "total productivity" view of copiers, usually stressing ease of use and reliability over features.

Océ copiers are actually pretty low on features: fans welcome this, praising the company for concentrating on the fundamentals of copying instead of developing party tricks which look great in sales demonstrations but rarely get used in practice. However, other users feel that Océ sometimes takes the "spartan" image just a little too far.

One thing most people agree on is that Océ service is generally very good. Buyers who are used to dealing with Xerox or Kodak, but who want to consider an alternative, can do well to contact Océ.

### What's different about Océ copiers?

Océ's implementation of analog copier technology is different from that of its rivals: time spent being shown the inside of Océ copiers is time spent being shown how they depart from the xerographic norm.

Océ copiers have much shorter and straighter paper paths. They go about bonding the image onto the paper in a different way (instead of melting toner onto the paper, they press it onto the surface in a manner somewhat reminiscent of offset printing). As a consequence, only one electrical charge is required to make a copy (other copiers need 4–8). This, points out Océ, reduces static, which can be one of the main causes of jams. The duplexing method on the newer models is the one-pass variety, which means that the paper is copied on both sides in a single run through the machine eliminating the need for a duplex tray to act as a transit area for paper waiting to be run through a second time and further reducing the chance of jams (Kodak is the only other vendor that uses one-pass duplexing). The monocomponent toner system eliminates the need for separate developer, which complicates the copying process and can lead to inconsistent copy quality. In place of a conventional drum, Océ copiers use a photoreceptor "belt" which doesn't come into contact with the paper and is also much less expensive to replace.

Those are the main technical differences, expressed in layman's language: there are a few others as well. For example, Océ makes a big deal out of environmental issues in its copier marketing, claiming various "green" advantages in terms of how its machines are built and how they operate.

Océ copiers are undoubtedly reliable — on certain machines, ordinary users can't even get into the copier to clear a jam, because paper path jams are almost unheard of. (Keeping users out of the inside of the machines is an Océ hallmark: on most models, adding toner is something only done by a technician on a routine service call.)

But although Océ's copy quality on text work compares with the best of the rest, you don't get the very black solid areas that you do from Xerox. Océ responds that the ultra-black solids of its competitors are less solid than they first appear: the sales reps are trained to show how competitors' images can be cracked and how they may peel off on other surfaces (a plastic folder, for example).

### Océ's changing distribution

For years, Océ was steadfastly a direct-sales vendor and did not come close to rubbing shoulders with the dealer brethren, nor did it allow its products to be relabeled by other vendors. The price that Océ has paid for this exclusiveness has been relatively poor penetration in the US market. With about 25 branch offices, covering about 60 cities, Océ is not represented in many medium-size markets which — between them — amount to a large part of the American copier pie.

All of this is in the process of changing, however. Océ has decided — some would argue after a somewhat lengthy period of reflection — that it has to become more sociable in order to grow. At the time of this writing, Océ had recently begun selling through some Alco copier dealers: this arrangement was meant to be linked to so-called "facilities management" (FM) contracts, where the dealer not only supplies a copier, but provides a full inplant copying service. In practice, however, Alco dealers have been selling Océ equipment on non-FM terms.

In addition, Océ is likely to start selling through another copier vendor which will relabel its equipment. Several reliable sources have told me that Océ was having discussions with Sharp in 1993 and early 1994 about a deal involving Océ's fastest copier — a 100cpm model — though Océ's spokesperson flatly denied that any such talks had taken place. Pitney Bowes is another possible partner that comes up in conversations.

# Olympia

*Olympia USA, Inc.*
*1330 River Bend*
*Dallas, TX 75247–4953*
*Tel: 800 926 6456*

### Introduction
Olympia is an old German office equipment company that never fully recovered from the demise of its former mainstay, the good-old, heavy-duty office typewriter. Olympia went through a rough period in the past few years — at one point teetering on the edge of bankruptcy — and the US operation seemed to drift with its German parent.

Today, there is a new team of people at Olympia in the US and, although the company remains a small player in copiers, the American subsidiary seems to have developed more drive and direction. Olympia remains involved in some other areas of office equipment, including shredders and typewriters.

### Olympia's focus
The copiers that Olympia sells are relabeled Minoltas. The company focuses on low- and mid-volume users, and is a very small force in the high-volume market. Sales are through dealers. Olympia's dealer network is far from the best developed, though the company is making efforts to enlarge it.

# Panasonic

*Panasonic Communications & Systems Company*
*Two Panasonic Way*
*Secaucus, NJ 07094*
*Tel: 201 348 7000*

### Introduction
Panasonic is one of the smaller players in the copier market — in fact, it has the lowest market share of all the Japanese manufacturers. It — or, rather, its Matsushita parent — produces a full line of mid-volume machines, and is also resuming making all of its low-volume ones, but its high-volume copiers are rela-

beled Minoltas. In fact, the fastest copier Matsushita was manufacturing at the time of this writing was a 50cpm model which was introduced back in 1989.

All the copiers that Panasonic was manufacturing at presstime have the same shell and, to a large extent, they share the same accessories. This means that Panasonic's low-volume, 16cpm model looks somewhat on the large side — it would be easy to mistake it visually for a mid-volume machine — though, conversely, its 40cpm model is relatively compact for its level of the market.

### Panasonic's commitment to copiers

Panasonic's lack of a full product line of its own prompts occasional speculation in copier circles on whether the company has its heart in this market. The folks at Panasonic in the US argue vigorously that their company is fully committed to copiers, and also point to innovative technology in the models that Matsushita does produce and to the investment that the Japanese company has recently made in copier manufacturing.

And, to be fair, speculation on whether Panasonic is in the market to stay has been going on for a few years, yet the company is still around and bringing out new models. While no one can confidently forecast where the copier industry will be 10 years from now, there seems no good reason to suppose that any of the current manufacturers, including Panasonic, is going to leave the market in the foreseeable future.

In addition, the mid-volume copiers that Matsushita does produce are pretty good — copy quality, for example, is generally excellent (even if productivity is only average). The company places great emphasis in its marketing on the internal circuitry of its copiers, citing advanced electronics — termed "Fuzzy Logic" — which are intended, among other things, to enhance the consistency of copy quality.

### Panasonic's distribution

One of the reasons why Panasonic is not rushing to bring out new high-volume models of its own is that it has quite weak distribution. In the US, it only has about 200 active dealers. There are no direct sales. However, some models are relabeled by Pitney Bowes and Lanier. Put bluntly, Panasonic's problem is that it would find it difficult to sell enough copiers to justify the cost of developing and manufacturing a new high-volume product range of its own.

But this is a bit of a vicious circle, as the small dealer network is itself a consequence of the narrow product range:

Panasonic has traditionally lost dealers almost as quickly as it has recruited new ones — though there has lately been some net increase — and one of the reasons is that the dealers prefer vendors with fuller lines. The company hopes that having a 76cpm model in its range (a relabeled Minolta) will help to cement dealer loyalties more effectively.

Most of Panasonic's dealers also carry other brands of copiers. To encourage them to carry its line, Panasonic offers larger margins than other vendors. This can result in list prices that appear on the steep side (not that any right-thinking person pays list price). Dealers who only carry Panasonic copiers tend not to be very experienced in supporting higher-volume users, but a Panasonic dealer that also carries other brands might be well versed in the needs of heavier users.

# Pitney Bowes

*Pitney Bowes Inc.*
*Walter H. Wheeler Jr. Drive*
*Stamford, CT 06926*
*Tel: 203 356 5000*

## Introduction

Pitney Bowes — best known as a mailroom giant — went through a period in recent years when it tried to get into copier remanufacturing by rebuilding old machines from companies such as Ricoh and then placing them on long-term rental contracts. It has now abandoned that strategy in favor of selling and renting new machines.

### Pitney's range, focus, & distribution

Pitney Bowes's current copiers are relabeled Mita and Panasonic models. Recently, its range has been looking somewhat in need of revamping and expanding: there have been gaps (especially at the high end) and much of what has been there has not been especially inspiring. However, some major introductions — possibly involving a new supplier — are expected during the shelf-life of this book.

The company reorganized its copier division about three years ago and turned it into an autonomous unit. Since then, the division appears to have shed the complacency that sometimes goes with the near-monopoly culture of Pitney's mailroom business. In particular, it has become much more willing to discount in order to compete with dealer brands. Keep in mind, though, that Pitney's list prices tend to be higher than Mita's own.

Pitney Bowes doesn't have any dealers itself: all sales are direct. Although the copier sales reps are separate from their mailing equipment counterparts, the two sometimes work together on a local basis. Pitney's national direct sales structure gives it a good platform to address the major account market, but it will need to do something about its product range before it can make significant progress.

From time to time, Pitney specifies detailed enhancements, which supposedly give its equipment productivity advantages over the versions sold under their original brand names. For example, both the Pitney high-volume machines have quoted speeds which are 1cpm faster than the original Mita brand equivalents. However, the changes are more symbolic than substantive.

# Ricoh

*Ricoh Corporation*
*5 Dedrick Place*
*West Caldwell, NJ 07006*
*Tel: 201 882 2000*

## Introduction

Ricoh is one of the five Japanese copier manufacturers to make all of its own machines, from low- to very high-volume models. It has a solid range of products and a good dealer network.

Ricoh was one of the last of the Japanese copier vendors to enter the US market under its own brand name, though it was one of the first to challenge Xerox in the worldwide market — outside of Japan, it initially operated mostly through OEMs (i.e., other companies relabeling its machines). Partly as a consequence, its US dealer profile differs a bit from most of its competitors' — it contains fewer of the ex-typewriter sort, for example, and more ex-Xerox folk.

## Ricoh distribution

Ricoh sells only through dealers in most parts of the country, though it has direct sales operations in the New York tri-state area and in Washington, DC. It has about 300 dealers, with about 600 locations between them. A large majority are independent, owner-managed businesses, as opposed to being part of dealer conglomerates. However, there are some Alco dealers among them — especially in the larger markets.

The typical Ricoh dealer tends to focus on selling to medium size and larger accounts in its area. In general, Ricoh does not go out of its way to target smaller businesses — though that doesn't mean that low-volume copier users aren't welcome.

### Ricoh's US manufacturing

Another thing that distinguishes Ricoh from the opposition is that it has a copier manufacturing operation in the US. Located in Orange County, California, this produces a number of mid- and highish-volume models with a significant local component content. Ricoh gives surprisingly little prominence to this in its marketing.

### Ricoh high-volume product notes

The main event in Ricoh's 1994 calendar is the launch of a new machine called the FT9101 — this 101cpm copier is the fastest ever to come out of Japan. A version has been sold in Japan for about three years and in Europe for about one year.

High-volume buyers considering Ricoh should note that the company's 80cpm RDH-equipped model — the FT8880 — delivers terrible productivity on double-sided work — by far the worst in the industry for its class, according to tests carried out by *What to Buy for Business*. It remains to be seen whether that model will remain in the range for the shelf-life of this book.

### Relabeler relationships

Ricoh now owns a major stake in Gestetner, and the latter has started to relabel certain Ricoh models alongside its branded Mita machines; at present, however, only one high-volume Ricoh is sold under Gestetner's colors in the US. A long-standing relabeler of Ricoh copiers is Savin, which is now out of Chapter 11. Two high-volume models are also relabeled by Toshiba.


# Royal Copystar

*Mita Copystar America, Inc.*
*225 Sand Road*
*PO Box 40008*
*Fairfield, NJ 07004*
*Tel: 201 808 8444*


### Introduction

Copystar was launched about four years ago as Mita's second-tier brand, created originally for its smaller dealers which aren't geared to selling and servicing the larger machines. Unlike the other Mita relabeling operations, Copystar was set up as a wholly-owned Mita subsidiary.

### The Royal connection

In 1992, the Royal copier business — previously owned by troubled Italian office equipment giant Olivetti — was merged into the Copystar operation. Out of this emerged the new Royal Copystar brand. Royal had previously been an independent relabeler of Mita machines. Following the Royal deal, the brand's mandate was extended upwards and it now takes in Mita copiers up to 70cpm. The Royal Copystar models are identical to the equivalent Mita ones and sell at the same prices.

Note that, for some reason, the low-volume models still tend to be referred to only under the "Copystar" brand name, without the "Royal" prefix — however, "Royal Copystar" and plain "Copystar" are effectively one unified brand and the dealers are all the same.

# Savin

*Savin Corporation*
*9 West Broad Street*
*Stamford, CT 06904–2270*
*Tel: 203 967 5000*

### Introduction

Founded in 1959, Savin is a distributor of relabeled Ricohs, selling entirely through dealers. It went into Chapter 11 in summer 1992, following a difficult period that stretches back to its ill-conceived attempt in the mid-eighties to become a copier manufacturer rather than a mere distributor. This had been followed by an equally misguided attempt several years later to become a major force in full-color copiers.

However, Savin emerged from bankruptcy protection in December 1993 following a settlement in which creditors received stock in lieu of cash — I was unable to obtain verification as to what this stock was valued at, but the company had previously forecast that it could be worth as little as 25 cents on the dollar owed.

At a press conference to announce this, the company's present management touted the outcome as "a great American success story" — which is one way of describing it. Either way, the strategy is now to focus entirely on the company's core business of selling relabeled black-and-white copiers as well as fax machines.

### Savin distribution and pricing

Savin's dealers have, for the most part, stayed loyal — the company has a strong dealer network which is its major asset. At press-time, Savin's copier list prices were consistently higher than those set by Ricoh for the identical machines — in one case, the difference was over $2,400 (this was with a high-volume model).

It is possible that the worst excesses of Savin's pricing may be ironed out in the discount process. But it is unclear why Savin is making itself appear uncompetitive at the very time when it needs to restore credibility to its brand name. Perhaps giving its dealers larger margins was one way of keeping them sweet during the dark days of Chapter 11.

### Savin and liquid toner

Although all Savin copiers are manufactured by Ricoh, not all correspond to machines sold under the Ricoh brand name. Some are Savin exclusives that use the company's proprietary liquid toner technology. Liquid toner used to have a somewhat second-rate reputation in the copier industry — copies tended to smudge and you needed to use very smooth paper in order to get acceptable results. For this reason, it was long ago dropped by all other copier vendors.

To Savin's credit, the version of liquid toner that it has developed for its Ricoh-manufactured machines is free from all the drawbacks of the old-fashioned variety. However, I am not convinced that it offers real advantages, and I am puzzled why Savin continues to go out on a limb promoting it — especially as the machines concerned are not particularly exciting in other respects.

# Sharp

*Sharp Electronics Corporation*
*Sharp Plaza*
*Mahwah, NJ 07430–2135*
*Tel: 201 529 8200*

### Introduction

Sharp is a strong vendor, both in terms of its market share and the quality of its equipment and dealer network. It is one of the five Japanese vendors to manufacture a full line of copiers from the low-volume sector to the high end of the market.

Sharp is generally a conservative choice — and Sharp users seem, on the whole, to be a pretty satisfied bunch. The company has solid products in the low-, mid-, and high-volume sectors.

### Sharp's high-volume copiers

At the time of this writing, Sharp's high-volume product range stopped short of most of its competitors' if you measure it just in terms of the quoted copies per minute speed — the fastest Sharp machine currently on the market cruises at 75cpm.

However, as I point out elsewhere in this chapter, cpm figures provide an incomplete picture of actual productivity. And Sharp has been more successful than most at bringing very high-volume design features down into the mainstream of the high-volume market — the result is that Sharp's 75cpm machines can be compared with rivals that cruise at 80–85cpm. For example, Sharp makes by far the best RDHs of any Japanese manufacturer and its machines incorporate things like vacuum-fed paper feeds (as opposed to the friction-fed variety which is the norm at this level).

Nonetheless, Sharp is anxious to have a product that is faster still and, at the time of this writing, there were rumors that Sharp would start relabeling the Océ 2600, a super-high-volume 100cpm model that is capable of copy volumes that the Japanese have yet to master. This deal — if it goes through — would be comparable to Canon's relabeling of Kodak giant copiers.

### Sharp distribution

Sharp has a strong dealer network, numbering around 550. There are no direct sales: Sharp is the only one of the big players in the copier market not to have opened a direct sales branch or subsidiary in any US city. About 200 of Sharp's dealers are designated as part of the "Master Series," which means that they are sufficiently large and well qualified to carry the full product line; those that are not part of this series can sell everything other than the high-end RDH models.

Although Sharp doesn't give out an exact figure, it appears that about 10 percent of its dealers — give or take — belong to either the Alco or Danka conglomerates. Certain low-volume Sharp copiers are sold relabeled by Lanier, and its retail channel low-volume copiers are also relabeled by Xerox — however, none of Sharp's mid/high-volume copiers are relabeled by anyone else.

# Toshiba

*Toshiba America Information Systems Inc.*
*Electronic Imaging Division*
*9740 Irvine Boulevard*
*PO Box 19724*
*Irvine, CA 92713–9724*
*Tel: 714 583 3000*

### Introduction

Toshiba copiers are good and deserve more prominence than they enjoy (Toshiba has one of the lowest profiles of all the Japanese manufacturers). However, the company is stronger as a low- and mid-volume vendor — its high-volume range is quite limited and some of its dealers lack experience supporting high-volume users. The fastest copier that Toshiba manufactures is a 65cpm unit; the faster models in its range are relabeled Ricohs.

### Toshiba distribution

All of Toshiba's own-brand sales are through dealers. Toshiba-manufactured copiers are also relabeled by Lanier.

# Xerox

*Xerox Corporation*
*Xerox Square — 05B*
*Rochester, NY 14644*
*Tel: 800 832 6979*

### Introduction

Xerox pioneered the office photocopier and is still the market leader. Its main strength lies in the high-volume sector: several of its fastest machines are still able to outperform anything the Japanese have come up with, both in terms of overall speed and copy volumes.

At the very top of the high-volume market, Xerox has only two serious manufacturing rivals: Kodak and, to a lesser extent, Océ. However, it is facing new challenges now that Canon and Lanier have started to use their strong distribution platforms to sell certain Kodak machines under their own labels, with Sharp threatening to do the same with Océ equipment.

Xerox is less interesting as a mid-volume supplier: its machines in that sector tend to be expensive without always offering performance advantages over the Japanese competition. However, Xerox has lately become a lot more interesting in the low-volume sector — largely as a result of its bold venture into the retail channel (see discussion in Chapter 4).

### Xerox pros and cons

Xerox still enjoys considerable loyalty among large corporations that want one-stop shopping for all their copiers across multiple locations. And its prices can be highly competitive when it's bidding for major account business. Where Xerox tends to be least competitive is in selling to companies wanting a fairly small number of machines in the 25–50cpm sector: not only can its front-end prices be high, but its service and supplies costs can mean that you'll go on paying a premium month after month.

Part of the problem is that Xerox does not, as a rule, discount as readily and by as much as its dealer competitors. So even if you find the list prices comparable, street prices are likely to be higher. In general, you can get 15 percent off the price of a Xerox copier if you walk in off the street wanting to buy one of its mid-volume machines, and possibly 20 percent. Dealers, by contrast, routinely offer 25 percent discounts and often more. However, you may be offered alternative packages by Xerox — such as sweet deals on the service and, if you're financing the machine, on the interest. The larger the deal, the more creative the solutions — and the bigger the break on the price.

But while Xerox can be an expensive choice, it also offers buyers qualities that not all of its rivals can match. Its machines are built to last. Copy quality is generally excellent — a well-maintained Xerox often produces solids that are hard to beat. As a buyer, you generally deal with the manufacturer, not with a middleman. And the guarantees are excellent (more on these later).

### Where Xerox copiers are made

Much of Xerox's copier manufacturing takes place in the US, though certain models are made overseas by its worldwide joint ventures: Fuji Xerox, which makes some low- and high-volume models in Japan; and Rank Xerox, which makes mid-volume copiers in Holland. The policy, however, is to bring production of many Fuji and Rank models to the US, even if the design and some initial manufacturing takes place offshore.

### How Xerox sells mid/high-volume copiers

Xerox does not have any copier dealers — in the normal sense of the term — for its main line of copiers (i.e., all its machines other than the mostly low-volume models sold through retail channels): it relies principally on its own direct sales force, which covers most of the country with a network of branches.

However, it supports this with what it calls "agents." A Xerox agent is a self-employed person, or a small business, that sells copiers but does not stock, resell, or service them — the agent simply wins the orders and is paid on commission only.

In the past, Xerox agents only operated in rural areas. Since then, however, Xerox has extended the program to major cities. In general, the urban agents are most active pushing the low- and mid-volume machines to smaller accounts, leaving the direct sales office to concentrate on the juicier business. In rural areas, which the branches do not cover, the agents peddle the entire range.

### Xerox takes mid-volume copiers into the retail channel
I pointed out in the previous chapter that Xerox is increasingly strong selling low-volume copiers through the retail channel. In 1994, Xerox is extending its retail channel line upwards to include one 26cpm model that falls just inside my definition of mid-volume: this model is being sold through office supply warehouse stores. If this goes well, the likelihood is that the Xerox retail-channel range will rise into the 30-40cpm mid-volume sector in 1995, and that it will also take in duplex models.

Xerox is the only vendor to sell mid-volume copiers through this channel. The equipment offered is so far pretty unexceptional stuff, but the mere fact that it is being sold through office supply warehouse stores is what is remarkable. See Chapter 4 for more on how Xerox handles the retail channel, and on the pros and cons to the buyer.

One thing that you should be aware of is that all of Xerox's mid-volume retail channel models are likely to be remanufactured units, rather than brand new ones. This is not something that only affects Xerox customers in the retail channel: as I explain below, much of Xerox's entire copier business involves remanufacturing machines it takes back, rather than only producing totally new ones. There is nothing "second rate" about Xerox's remanufactured copiers: in my opinion, they literally are as good as new (more on this shortly).

Xerox assures me that the build status of its remanufactured retail channel copiers will be clearly disclosed to buyers, both in the point-of-sale literature and in the paperwork that buyers sign when placing their order. I have observed, however, that in at least some test marketing in northern California, remanufactured Xerox copiers have been sold by Office Depot without any disclosures being made — this, apparently, was an oversight.

### What you always wanted to know about Xerox
### build status, but never dared to ask

Xerox's retail channel copiers are by no means the only ones to be sold as remanufactured. The company has a policy of factory remanufacturing its trade-ins and then repositioning them in the direct-sales front line with the same prominence given to equipment that is brand new. The price is the same either way, but Xerox states that it may "at its sole discretion" supply you with a remanufactured unit instead of a new one. The older models tend only to be available remanufactured.

At any given time, most Xerox mid/high-volume copiers are in the stage in their product cycles when at least some of the units being shipped are remanufactured. It is possible that some models may be remanufactured from the very day they are first launched: Xerox's product development strategy at present is to increase the rate at which it introduces new models, but to make most of them direct derivatives of ones that currently exist. Already, some machines that go through Xerox's remanufacturing process emerge at the other end sporting a different model number from the one they had when they went in.

On two occasions in the past couple of years, I have visited Xerox's remanufacturing operation at Webster, NY (close to the Rochester location where xerography first began). Actually, it might be more accurate to say that I visited a Xerox manufacturing plant, since what I was being shown was a new set-up where older machines are remanufactured on the same production line that handles brand new ones (previously, the two operations were separate and, with some models, they still are).

When a Xerox copier is remanufactured, numerous parts are replaced with new ones. In addition, a machine is enhanced to incorporate any improvements that have been developed since it was first manufactured. The transformation is even more complete in cases where the machine is being remanufactured into a newer derivative model. The quality control process is identical, whether a machine is new or remanufactured. And all remanufactured machines are sold with the same excellent warranties and satisfaction guarantees that Xerox offers with its new ones.

I was impressed with what I saw at Webster, and see no reason to doubt Xerox's claim that its remanufactured copiers really are as good as new. That doesn't mean that a six-year-old Xerox is necessarily as good as a new model introduced for the first time last year: it only means that it's as good as it was six years ago when it was first made. The older Xerox models with roots in the 1980s are in some ways quite dated, but there are newer models, newly-built and remanufactured, which cost more and are better.

I also agree that it makes good sense to remanufacture copiers, especially high-volume ones. Some of these machines are built to endure for well over a decade, and there's no reason to scrap them after the first owner moves on to something else. When you look at what some of the parts actually are, it's hard to think of a good reason not to use them again. These days, Xerox cites environmental grounds to support its remanufacturing policy — that's fair enough, but the main motivation is strictly commercial.

Until recently, Xerox seemed reluctant to bring its remanufacturing policy to the limelight; mention of the whole process tended to be confined to necessary small print. It's hardly surprising — this whole issue can be awkward for a salesperson to handle and it is liable to be exploited, and sometimes distorted, by competitors.

Lately, however, Xerox has been more open in its treatment of the issue in its direct sales channel, partly as a result of pressure from *What to Buy for Business* and certain state consumer protection agencies. Still, some of the language it uses to describe its remanufacturing policy is obfuscated — and it is still quite possible for a reasonably diligent buyer to purchase a Xerox copier without realizing its build status.

Xerox now places the build status of each of its copiers into one of the following three categories: "Newly Manufactured," "Factory Produced New Model," and "Remanufactured." And, for the first time, it has come up with official definitions. These are as follows:

> ❏ *Category (1): "Newly Manufactured"* — This is defined as: "Equipment that has been assembled for the first time from new parts; it may also contain some used components that have been reprocessed to new part standards."
>
> Xerox's lawyers appear to take the position that up to 20 percent of a copier (measured in value) can be made of reprocessed parts, without the whole machine being called "remanufactured." I have not seen this 20 percent figure in writing, but it has been given to me verbally by different sources at Xerox on two occasions. Measuring the 20 percent can be a slightly inexact science, however, as there are a number of gray areas when it comes to actually determining the proportion and value of the parts that are not brand new.

❏ *Category (2): "Factory Produced New Model"* — This second category is something of a misnomer, in my opinion, as the machines in this category are not brand new. They are trade-ins that are remanufactured, and substantially enhanced in the process. They are likely to contain reprocessed parts that take them over the magic 20 percent level referred to above.

The official definition of this category is as follows: "Xerox equipment that has been converted to New Model status, and maintains features and/or functions of the previous model and adds new features and/or functions not available on the previous model. The New Model has been disassembled to a predetermined standard established by Xerox and manufactured to New Model status. It has a new serial number. The New Model contains reprocessed and/or recovered parts that fully meet new product specifications."

Translation: What Xerox is saying is that these are remanufactured machines which, during the remanufacturing process, are converted into different models from their previous incarnation (i.e., they have different model numbers), such that the new models are clear descendants of the old ones but have additional features and/or functions (a "function" seems to be defined as a fairly fundamental feature).

The use of the word "New" is confusing. Xerox argues that it applies to the features and functions, which give rise to a new model number, rather than to the core hardware around which the machine is built. Fair enough, but this meaning is hardly intuitive — most reasonable people would naturally assume that the phrase "Factory Produced New Model" means "brand new."

Also odd is the phrase "Factory Produced" — where else are copiers produced? The answer here is that the use of the word "factory" is meant to underline the fact that the remanufacturing takes place on the same production line as new copiers. The category-two process is, perhaps, the equivalent of the way Boeing zero-times its 1970s vintage 747 jumbo jets, by reequipping and refurbishing them to the extent that some airlines flying them claim to have the "newest" fleets in the air.

❏ *Category (3): "Remanufactured"* — The third Xerox build classification is defined by the company as follows: "Equipment that has been disassembled to a predetermined standard, then reassembled by adding new parts and some used components which have been reprocessed to new-part standards. With remanufactured equipment, the features, functions and model number remain the same." That's a reasonable definition, and Xerox could add to this the fact that some enhancements take place during the remanufacturing process, reflecting design changes that have been made to the model since the original unit was first produced.

Astute readers may already have deduced that a category-three "remanufactured" Xerox may, in fact, be a newer copier in one sense than a category-two "Factory Built New Model." For example, a model that is traded in two years after it was first built is more likely to go through a category-three remanufacturing process and retain its original model number. However, a six-year-old trade-in is more likely to be transformed into an enhanced new model and, hence, be given a new identity — thus it would be a category-two "New Model." However, the older machine (i.e., the New Model, if you see what I mean) will probably have more new parts.

A point to keep in mind is that not one of the build status categories — which between them cover all Xerox copiers — guarantees that a machine is brand new, containing no remanufactured parts. You will recall that the "newest" category of all — "Newly Manufactured Equipment" (category-one) — does allow for up to 20 percent of parts to be reprocessed. But the key thing to remember is that Xerox claims to build all the machines to the same quality standards — and I believe them.

### Disclosing the build status

Historically, Xerox has been less than forthcoming about the build status of its machines. While it has never misled people, it has presented the information in a way that could make it quite easy for people to miss what's going on, or misunderstand it. However, as I indicated earlier, there are signs that the company has begun taking a positive line, rather than a defensive one, about its remanufacturing policy. For example, when it launched the Xerox 5365 in April 1993, it produced a brochure that said the following in the same size type as the general sales blurb: "The Xerox 5365 copier is either newly manufactured or remanufactured at Xerox's option."

That's plain English, and it's clear for all to see. But there is still some inconsistency in the presentation of other models. For example, on the same day that Xerox introduced the 5365, it introduced another new model called the 5388 which is a remanufactured version of the old Xerox 1090 (a high-volume machine first launched in 1985). In this case, the only public indication of the machine's build status is some small print at the bottom of the brochure saying: "The Xerox 5388 is factory-produced new equipment." While that statement is consistent with the official Xerox definitions — except for the use of the word "equipment" — the intended meaning of those words is unlikely to be apparent to most people.

And I have not yet seen any Xerox literature made available to customers which defines its three build-classifications (the definitions I was quoting earlier are from material Xerox gave to industry analysts in 1993). Another of the phrases Xerox still uses to refer indirectly to the fact that machines are not brand new is its old standby: "Build status subject to change without notice."

The bottom line, therefore, is that Xerox is still using some language to describe the build status of its equipment that is vague and obscure — but it is moving towards greater clarity and openness and, in my opinion, it has a good story to tell (because its remanufactured machines really are as good as new).

Keep in mind that even if you are aware of Xerox's remanufacturing policy, you will not generally be told in advance whether the specific machine that will be delivered to your office will be new or remanufactured (though in the case of some older models, the status will be fairly obvious to anyone familiar with Xerox's product line).

However, I have heard of some buyers of more recent Xerox models insisting on a newly-manufactured machine; although Xerox does not encourage this type of request, it will, where possible, honor it. When you get your machine, the only way to tell that it's remanufactured is to check for the letters "RMFD" engraved in the plaque next to the serial number on the inside — but remember that this does not apply to the so-called "Factory Built New Models," as these are given new serial numbers when they go through their reincarnation process.

### *Xerox's customer satisfaction guarantee*

Xerox offers an exceptionally good guarantee of satisfaction on all of its copiers — from the smallest mini to the largest giant. The bottom line is that they'll replace a machine at any time during the first three years if you're dissatisfied for any reason (the term may be longer if you're leasing the equipment through Xerox's finance subsidiary). What's more, you — the user — are the arbiter of whether a replacement is called for.

The only catch is that you have to pay for a maintenance agreement and/or purchase Xerox supplies — and Xerox running costs are often higher than those of other copiers. Still, Xerox's guarantee is the ultimate lemon protection — you can't get much fairer. The guarantee applies to all Xerox copiers, regardless of their build status (new, remanufactured, etc.).

Certain Xerox copiers also have three-year warranties, covering all replacement parts and all service. However, this is not quite as good as it sounds, as the cost is effectively built into the price you have to pay for the supplies. What's more, this pricing method can leave you with exceptionally high running costs after the initial three-year period, when you have to pay for parts and service and still pay the same high price for the supplies.

### Final thoughts about Xerox

In general, Xerox looks like a much stronger and more attractive supplier now than it did a few years ago. It has shed the smugness and sleepiness of the 1980s. It is proving more flexible and more responsive, it is experimenting with new distribution channels, and it is introducing better copiers faster — in 1993, it brought more new models to the market than in any previous year of its history (counting those that are derivatives of earlier ones). It still has its weaker areas — the value it offers in the mid-volume market, for example — but the movement is in the right direction.

Finally, Xerox has taken a lead with multifunction copiers/laser printers at the very high end of the market. Its DocuTech system, introduced in 1990, is a highly advanced document production system that lists for $220,000 and falls outside of the scope of this book. ✍

# Chapter 6

# Fax Machines

# Fax Machines

Contrary to what is sometimes thought, fax is not a particularly new technology. It was invented in the last century by a Scotsman named Alexander Bayne, who dreamed up a pendulum device to scan an image and send electrical pulses over a phone line representing lighter and darker areas. The first international use took place in 1901, when a picture of the Pope was transmitted from London to Paris, a touching merger of new technology and traditional beliefs, one might say.

That makes fax one of the oldest types of office technology — much older, in fact, than xerography or electronic computing. What is fairly recent is its widespread use. For decades, fax was used mainly in specialized fields such as publishing and the military. The only place it developed faster was Japan, where the complexity of the alphabet gave it an edge over telex.

But in the seventies, fax machines began to be more common sights in large corporations in the US and Europe and, in the eighties, the market began to snowball. The more people had fax, the more useful it became, so the more people got it. Fax became a symbol of 1980's yuppiedom: a sort of office equipment equivalent of Perrier. Meanwhile, prices tumbled: the sort of machine which cost several thousands of dollars 10 years ago today costs only several hundred.

Now, fax machines in homes are becoming increasingly common; in offices, more people are getting a fax of their own instead of sharing one. The technology is developing too, as the emphasis shifts over to plain paper printing and a new modem standard emerges to allow different brands of machine to communicate at very high speeds.

### Big growth area: plain paper fax

The biggest growth sector in fax is plain paper. Most medium-size offices that are replacing older machines — those that print onto that all-too-familiar crinkly fax paper that comes in rolls — are opting for new ones that print onto regular sheets of paper — like a copier or laser printer. The starting price for plain paper fax has fallen significantly, as I'll be showing later — you can now buy one of these machines for not much more than $600 (though most cost quite a lot more than that) — and the entry-level price point could fall to as low as $500 during the shelf-life of this book. Nonetheless, "thermal" — i.e, non-plain paper — machines are still selling heavily at the bottom of the market, to people who only want to spend around $200–$400.

### What's in this chapter?

I'll start the discussion of fax features by looking at paper handling features that relate to these thermal machines; after that, I'll introduce you to plain paper fax; and then I'll talk about other fax features that apply to both types of machines. After reviewing features, I'll give you some advice on how to buy a fax — this is definitely a market where it pays to be street-wise. Then I'll introduce you to the vendors.

This chapter will also talk a little about fax modems that work with PCs. You should refer to Chapter 9 for a discussion of "combo" machines that incorporate fax in a multifunctional unit that also does duty as a scanner, printer, and/or copier.

# Thermal Paper Faxes Introduced

Non-plain paper fax machines use heat to draw an image directly onto special heat-sensitive, or "thermal," paper. There are no chemicals inside, no toner, no ribbons. The main drawback of thermal paper is that it's harder to handle — it tends to curl up and it can be awkward to write on.

Moreover, the image fades after a year or so — as some

people have discovered to their horror when trying to dig up important faxes that were filed away. Print quality is adequate, though rarely outstanding. However, the image quality is only partly determined by the printing method used — the main shortcomings are due to how a document is scanned at the sending end (more on that later).

If all fax machines cost the same, no one would buy ones that used thermal paper — their only advantage over plain paper fax is price. Non-plain paper faxes start at just below $250 in the discount market, and I don't generally recommend spending more than $400 on any thermal model. By contrast, plain paper faxes generally start at around $600 for entry-level models, and the majority cost between $1,250 and $2,500. Running costs for thermal paper fax are often also lower, as I'll explain shortly.

### Auto paper cutters

Thermal fax paper always comes on special rolls, but most machines have automatic cutters which chop up incoming multi-page faxes into neat cut pages as they exit the machine. Without a paper cutter, an incoming multi-page fax prints out in a long continuous strip, which you manually tear off your machine's paper roll using a cutting edge.

Some people argue that auto paper cutters are indispensable on a thermal machine, and that you shouldn't consider buying a machine without one. I don't fully share that view. The benefit of a cutter depends in part on how many long faxes you receive — they're not such a big deal if most of your incoming faxes consist of only a page or two. Also, be warned that the paper cutter is the most mechanical feature on a fax machine and is, therefore, the most likely to go wrong. And, arguably, it's better to receive a long fax in one continuous scroll, rather than endless individual curled-up pages.

Having said that, the market research people employed by fax manufacturers invariably report that a paper cutter is the one feature that budget buyers want most. As a result, cutters are becoming increasingly common even at the bottom end. You can now get models with paper cutters from around $299 — that's within about $60 of the absolute rock bottom of the fax market. (Remember that when I refer to prices in this article, I'm talking about easily-obtainable discount prices: there'll be advice on how to obtain good prices later.)

### Thermal paper roll size

Thermal paper fax machines take rolls that are 98', 164', or

328' long. The length of the paper roll is a function of the machine design — you can't buy a machine that comes with a 98' roll and then, when that roll runs out, replace it with a 328' one. You'll have to put in another 98' roll, because that's what the machine takes. Less expensive machines generally have shorter rolls.

The advantage of having a longer paper roll is simply that you don't have to replace the paper so often; longer rolls should also work out to be a bit cheaper on a per page basis. Paper width is almost always 8.5". A few specialized machines do allow you to print onto 10.1"-wide paper — useful if you're receiving wider documents and don't want the size to be reduced automatically to fit onto the 8.5" width — but these are few and far between and tend to be somewhat expensive. Different brands of machine can generally use the same paper rolls, even though some vendors encourage you to use their own.

### Making thermal paper better

A small number of machines have a feature designed to counter the irritating tendency of fax paper to curl up after a transmission is received. This feature — usually known as "anti-curl" — is moderately effective (especially on machines with the shorter 98' paper rolls where the curl tends to be more accentuated).

In addition, some vendors are bringing out thermal fax paper that looks and feels a bit more like regular paper. Sometimes, this paper is intended specifically for use with a particular brand — it may not work well in other machines. Check out Brother and Sharp if you're looking for vendors that are making an effort in this direction. Beware that this paper can cost about twice as much as regular fax paper. However, if you buy a machine that is able to take this paper, you aren't obliged to use it — you can stick with the regular stuff if you prefer.

### Honey, I faxed the kids!

If you plan to keep your fax on your desk (maybe in order to double up as your regular phone), or if it's a home machine that has to battle for space on your kitchen counter, size is all-important — and this is one area in which some thermal paper machines still have an advantage over their more glamorous plain paper siblings.

A number of vendors are bringing out very compact thermal paper machines designed specifically for the home market. These can weigh as little as 5–6 lbs and have a footprint of around 8" x 12", yet still incorporate the essential bottom-end features (the typical weight of thermal faxes these days is around 10–14 lbs). One Sharp model can be wall-mounted. By contrast, the smallest plain paper fax weighs around 12 lbs, and most weigh quite a bit more and also take up as much space as a laser printer.

### The end in sight?

Several vendors that used to sell thermal faxes have now stopped doing so in order to concentrate on the plain paper market. These include Xerox, NEC, Pitney Bowes, and Minolta. Other vendors, which technically have a few thermal models in their range, do little to promote them. Some people speculate that in a few years' time, the thermal paper fax market will be finished, and that all models sold will use plain paper. That's what happened to the copier market which, as recently as 12 years ago, still had a low-end, non-plain paper sector.

My view is that the thermal paper fax market will continue to be active for quite a while, catering to the most price-sensitive, low-volume users — home users, very small businesses, and small branch offices of larger companies. Also, people whose workload consists overwhelmingly of sending, rather than receiving, faxes almost by definition have little to gain from having plain paper machines.

And while some vendors are deserting the thermal market, others are entering at this late stage: for example, Smith Corona (of typewriter fame) has introduced a line of thermal faxes (which is actually made by Samsung); another new and unexpected arrival is Acer, the Taiwanese computer manufacturer.

Entry-level prices may fall to $199 or less within a year or two, and the trend for these machines to be sold mainly through retail channels will continue. However, I also believe that most businesses with only moderate incoming fax traffic — say, 10–20 pages a day — are going to move over to plain paper. In fact, that process is already underway.

# Plain Paper Fax Introduced

Plain paper fax may seem more of a luxury than a necessity, but as people's fax traffic increases — and as the cost of the machines falls — it's one that's becoming easier to justify. The benefits of plain paper fax are:

✔ Incoming faxes are easier to handle (especially longer multi-page documents).
✔ The paper doesn't curl up.

✔ Faxes received on plain paper don't fade over time, as regular faxes do.

✔ Image quality is generally better (though not by as much as you might expect, since the shortcomings of regular fax output have more to do with the way in which documents are sent than with the paper and printing technology).

✔ It's much easier to write on plain paper than on thermal fax paper.

✔ It's also a lot easier to re-fax a document you've received if it came in on plain paper (thermal paper is a bit too flimsy to be easily fed into a fax machine as an original).

✔ You can use recycled plain paper.

✔ You could reduce your copier running costs, if you presently photocopy incoming faxes as a means of transferring them onto plain paper.

✔ With most plain paper machines, it's easier to keep track of how much paper is left in the machine — so you can say good-bye to "Am-I-going-to-run-out-of-paper-unexpectedly?" anxiety.

Another reason to consider a plain paper fax is that because they are at the cutting edge of fax technology, they are more likely to benefit from other enhancements which — while not relating to the paper used or to the printing method — can result in much higher productivity.

For example, one of the most interesting developments in fax right now is the increasing popularity of the 14,400 bits per second (bps) modem standard. I'll be talking about this later in this chapter, but its significance is that it allows six-second per page transmission between different brands of machine. (Previously, fax "fast" modes were not only slower, but also proprietary so they could only work between compatible machines made by the same manufacturer.) These 14,400 bps modems are not a function of plain paper technology, but you're more likely to find one on a plain paper machine than on a regular thermal paper fax.

### The cost of plain paper fax

The only case against buying a plain paper fax that I can think of is that they cost more. Discount prices for plain paper faxes range from a little over $600 to $3,000 (you'd need to have exceptionally upscale needs to justify spending more). The price depends largely on the type of plain paper technology selected — there are some significant differences in quality and functionality as I show below. Most businesses that buy plain paper faxes these days spend between $800 and $2,500 per machine.

But many buyers are going to find that they don't have much choice about whether or not to go with plain paper. That's because the market is drying up for non-plain paper machines that are also heavy duty. The only part of the thermal paper market that is flourishing is right at the bottom of the ladder — I'm talking about machines that sell for a few hundred dollars and that are suitable only for light to moderate usage (hard to define, but probably up to 15 pages a day, incoming or outgoing). I'm not saying that heavy-duty thermal paper machines have already ceased to exist. There are still some out there, selling for close to $1,000 or more. But not many are being introduced and, in my opinion, they are pretty poor buys in their twilight.

So, the only people who need to agonize a little about whether or not to go with plain paper are those on the verge of spending $350–$500 on a fairly low-volume, but not rock-bottom, thermal paper model. People in that position have a rich choice of thermal paper models, but can also switch to plain paper for a relatively modest premium. You can make a rational case for both options: my gut feeling is that plain paper is worth paying for, but I recognize that some people would rather pocket the savings. Keep in mind, though, that aside from the printing/paper aspect, the features offered by a $650 plain paper machine may be fewer than those offered by a $450 thermal paper model.

Also keep in mind that no plain paper fax costing less than $1,000 is going to be all that heavy-duty. The day when $999 can buy you the sort of machine you'd put in a busy six-person attorney's office, for example, is not yet here — though it's drawing closer. Corporate fax prices have remained artificially high for quite a while (a fact privately acknowledged by many in the fax industry), and it's only a matter of time before price wars result in better values for the buyer. Right now, however, there are compromises when you buy a sub-$1,000 plain paper fax — which leads me onto the next subject....

# The Four Types of Plain Paper Fax

Your first decision in choosing a plain paper fax is to decide what type of printing technology to go with. You have four to choose from:

### Thermal transfer plain paper

This is the oldest-established type of plain paper fax technology. It is also one of the least expensive and, arguably, the least desirable. Like conventional fax, it uses a heat process to etch the image onto the paper. However, whereas conventional fax draws the image directly onto special heat-sensitive paper, this type of machine etches it onto a heat-sensitive thermal ribbon, which then deposits a carbon image onto regular paper.

Print quality can be very good, though it's not always superb on the less expensive models. You'll generally get better results with paper that has an unusually smooth grain — using the paper in your copier can lead to disappointing results.

One thing that's good about most thermal transfer machines is their price. Most cost below $1,500 and Brother has introduced some very aggressively-priced models selling from around $600. Only one vendor — Xerox — sells thermal transfer models that compete in the higher echelons of the plain paper fax market.

Although purchase prices are generally quite low, thermal transfer running costs are fairly high. Depending on the machine, consumables generally run 5–7 cents for each page you receive (other types of plain paper fax usually work out to around 2–4 cents a page). Moreover, these running costs are fixed regardless of image density — so a page with hardly anything on it will cost you the same as one that's full of type.

With a couple of older, but still current, Canon models, you are obliged to use special rolls of plain paper. That's better than using thermal paper rolls, but it's not exactly ideal. Having to buy "plain" paper in special rolls defeats a lot of the purpose of getting a plain paper fax — most people rightly assume that plain paper fax ought to mean using regular cut sheets.

Some vendors believe that the term "thermal transfer" conjures up negative implications for plain paper fax buyers — the word "thermal" is generally associated with non-plain paper technology. For example, Muratec has taken to calling its thermal transfer models "film imaging" faxes — this sounds a bit more high-tech, but the difference is only semantic.

### Ink jet fax

Ink jet technology is well established in the computer printer market, where it provides an economical alternative to lasers; although ink jet PC printers are not quite as good as lasers, some get pretty close. Ink jet fax is a more recent development, but it serves a similar function as a budget alternative to laser and LED fax (the latter, as I explain below, are the premium plain paper technologies, though they are just beginning to break into the sub-$1,000 market).

Print quality is not quite as good as a laser's, but it is, by any standards, very acceptable. You can print onto just about any plain paper; you do not have to use special plain paper rolls. But keep in mind that print quality can be affected by the exact stock of plain paper used: if you print onto paper with a more absorbent surface, you may get a less crisp image.

Not surprisingly, ink jet faxes are sold by some of the same vendors that sell ink jet PC printers. Hewlett-Packard (HP), an ink jet printer leader, sells two models. These are actually manufactured by Matsushita, the parent company of Panasonic, though they use HP's own print engines. They are very similar to machines sold by Panasonic itself. Recently, Sharp has also begun selling ink jets using the same HP print engine.

The other big name in ink jet PC printing is Canon, which sells faxes based on its highly successful Bubble Jet printers. Late in 1993, Ricoh launched its first ink jet fax, which is based on a Canon engine. At the time of this writing, newly-introduced ink jet faxes based on the Hewlett-Packard engine were generally better than those based on the older Canon engine: HP's latest engine is faster, and less expensive to run.

However, Canon was, at press-time, on the verge of introducing new models based on a different ink jet engine that use a new ink jet cartridge called the BX-2. This engine features a newly-designed printhead for faster printing. The earlier models using the older engine, which are easily identifiable by their unusual upright design, were still widely available at press-time but are probably best avoided at this stage unless you are trying to get the absolute lowest-priced ink jet model regardless of features and performance.

An ink jet fax generally costs from around $650–$1,100 (remember that I'm talking about discount prices). However, at the time of this writing, rebate deals on the older entry-level Canons sometimes take the price down to as little as $479 — and keep in mind that today's rebate deal is usually tomorrow's street price. I expect, therefore, that the very cheapest ink jet faxes will be readily available for around $500 by spring 1995.

Ink jet running costs are a little steep at about 4–6 cents per page, and may be somewhat higher when the image density is very high. However, this may not matter too much as ink jet machines are only suitable for light to moderate workloads.

One of the reasons why ink jet faxes aren't optimum for heavier fax users is that their print speeds are quite slow. Models using older engines, and this includes the older Canon models that were still current at press-time, can only print at about one page per minute (ppm). Since all fax machines can transmit and receive at a minimum rate of approximately 3ppm, the result is that you may be kept waiting for your printed pages to appear after the actual transmission has finished. This is something that ink jet vendors never mention in their sales pitch. However, the good news is that ink jet faxes based on the new Hewlett-Packard engine, and the new Canon engine, manage to print at about 2ppm — a lot better, though still not ideal.

By contrast, low-cost laser and LED faxes generally print at the rate of 4ppm (some more expensive models go up to 10ppm). This limitation of ink jets will obviously be most noticeable if you receive a lot of long faxes or if you want to print from your fax machine's memory (more on that later). Thermal transfer plain paper faxes generally print at about 2ppm, incidentally — in other words, at roughly the same speed as the latest ink jets.

A quick thought. ... Thermal paper faxes (i.e., non-plain paper models) print their images as they are received — it's simultaneous, so the image comes out of your machine at more or less the same time it goes through the sending machine. If you are on a very tight budget, but regard instant print-outs with no irritating delays as paramount, you may want to reconsider your interest in plain paper fax and stick with the thermal variety. Remember that while a pricey plain paper fax is infinitely better than a cheap thermal fax, a decent thermal fax may have some benefits over a cheap plain paper model!

To underline the low-volume design of ink jet faxes, some have modest document and paper handling capabilities. For example, Canon's older — but still current — ink jets (the upright-looking models with the slower engine) only allow you to feed documents up to five pages long automatically, and can only hold up to 50 sheets of plain paper for printing.

### Laser fax

Laser fax (along with LED fax, explained below) offers the best print quality, the lowest running costs, and the fastest print speeds. It also requires you to pay the most for your machine at the outset: at the time of this writing, discount prices started at a little under $1,500 — though the first $999 model was on the horizon — but most people end up spending somewhere between $1,750 and $2,500. The printing technology is the same as that of a computer laser printer. You can use pretty well any type of plain paper.

Don't expect the image you receive to be as good as what

you get from a laser printer connected to a PC — the reason is that the output of any fax is, largely, only as good as the image it can receive; and existing fax technology imposes limits on the resolution (i.e., the crispness and sharpness) of transmissions. However, some machines do have the ability to enhance received images (more on this shortly).

Laser fax is the easiest and cleanest type of plain paper fax to use and maintain. Replenishing supplies can involve nothing more than taking out an old cartridge and putting in a new one. (Some brands are better in this respect than others: Canon is probably the most streamlined.)

Running costs are generally around 2–3 cents per page (plus the cost of the plain paper; expect higher per-page running costs if receiving originals with very heavy densities of type or solid areas). This means that lasers — unlike thermal transfers and ink jets — can be no more expensive to run than non-plain paper thermal machines.

### LED fax

The fourth category of plain paper fax is basically a variation of laser technology — and is well worth your attention. LED technology tends to be found at the lower end of the laser price spectrum, and just below — there are some great machines which kick in at a little under $1,300, and you can get something very fancy in the way of features without going much over $2,000. In other words, LEDs often cost about 10–20 percent less than comparable lasers. Running costs are similar to a laser's.

Some people argue that LED technology is more reliable, as it contains fewer moving parts. I'm not impressed by that point of view, since lasers have proved extremely reliable in all their applications in the office. Others maintain that LEDs don't produce output quality quite as good as a laser's. Again, I don't go along with that, as I find the differences to be indiscernible. My advice, therefore, is that buyers should regard lasers and LEDs as effectively one and the same. The reason I like LEDs isn't that they are better machines than lasers, just that they are frequently better values.

Often, LEDs are sold by the "lesser" brand names — by that I definitely do not mean the brands that offer lesser quality, but the ones that have a little less name recognition. For example, you don't find vendors like Canon, Ricoh, or Sharp selling LEDs. You do find vendors like Oki, Muratec, and Dex selling them. If I were the sort of person who went in for bumper stickers (which I'm not), I might display one saying: "Smart Faxers Use LEDs."

# Fax Image Features

Any type of fax — and plain paper machines in particular — would be capable of giving better quality print-outs, if only the signals sent down the phone line added up to a higher-definition picture. The image quality you get doesn't generally do justice to the printing capabilities of the receiving machine.

However, there are three features that are designed to spruce up the look of the faxes you send or receive: superfine, gray scales, and image enhancement. Here's what you need to know about them.

### Superfine

A brief reminder at this point about how fax machines work. A fax machine at the sending end scans an image and turns it into a grid comprising thousands of tiny dots; it then transmits electrical signals representing the pattern down the phone line to the receiving machine, which reconstructs the image out of the information provided.

Normally, the sending fax scans an image using a grid with 203 x 98 vertical/horizontal lines. In fine mode — selectable on virtually all machines — this rises to 203 x 196; this ensures that greater detail is picked up, but it is still a relatively low resolution (computer printers, for example, print at resolutions of at least 300 x 300). The result is that certain images remain less than perfect — large-size type has a noticcably jagged edge, for example, and curves are less than perfectly smooth.

Superfine mode, selectable on most faxes, but by no means all, goes a step further with a resolution of 203 x 392 — better, but still not great. Superfine would be a more useful feature, were it not for the fact that it only works between compatible machines from the same manufacturer (something that will be changing, however, thanks to a new industry standard that should be implemented by most vendors during the next couple of years or so). Also, a document takes longer to send if you've selected superfine. Moreover, superfine doesn't do anything to improve the image of documents you receive — it's purely a way of sending them more clearly.

### Gray scales

This is another feature that improves the look of the faxes you send, not the ones you receive. The number of gray scales quoted in a machine's specifications refers to the number of shades of gray a machine can transmit representing different colors or halftones.

All plain paper faxes — and many thermal paper ones — have gray scales of some sort, though less expensive models generally only operate in up to 16 shades. That's sufficient for most purposes, but if top-notch reproduction of photos is important, look for a machine with 32 or even 64 gray scales. The highest number you can get is 128, but this is pretty rare (and an optometrist once told me that the human eye is incapable of distinguishing anything like that number of shades of gray).

There can be two drawbacks to selecting gray scales mode. First, it slows down transmission time (but, of course, you can still transmit in the regular way without the gray scales feature selected). Second, it may degrade the image quality of the parts of a document that aren't halftones, though some machines apply the feature "intelligently" only to the halftone portions.

### Image smoothing

The features I've just talked about — superfine and gray scales — are ones that improve the look of your outgoing faxes. "Image smoothing" sounds like some public relations exercise for a beleaguered politician, but it is, in fact, a feature found on a growing number of faxes — mostly lasers — which enables a receiving machine to enhance the defects of incoming transmissions by smoothing lines and edges and removing some of the fuzziness.

It works by making intelligent assumptions about where to fill in the gaps — effectively, it prints the image at a higher resolution than the one it received. The results are less noticeable on regular-size type than on larger images. This feature works no matter what machine is doing the sending — it isn't one of those advanced fax features that only works between compatible machines from the same manufacturer. Details vary between different manufacturers (some of whom give it their own trademarked names to make it sound as though it was somehow special to them).

Do not expect more from this feature than it is able to deliver — it helps improve images at the margin, so to speak, but having it or not having it is not exactly like the difference between night and day.

### Greater than 300dpi printing

Image smoothing is a software feature, which interpolates an image into something better than it really is. Some plain paper print engines also have enhanced print capabilities built into their hardware. In the sub-$1,000 sector market, this only applies to certain ink jets — the Canon models print at resolutions of 360 x 360 dots per inch (360dpi), compared with the 300dpi resolution found on most plain paper faxes. Further up the market, some laser faxes have 400dpi resolutions. But this doesn't make a lot of difference in practice, especially since the fax images themselves are sent at lower resolutions.

# Paper Handling on Plain Paper Faxes

If you're getting a plain paper machine that prints onto cut sheets, check out the number of on-line paper cassettes, their capacity, and the size of paper they can hold.

### Single cassette models

Most models only have a single paper cassette on-line, usually with a 200- or 250-sheet capacity. What this means is that you can only be set up to receive onto one size of paper at any given time. That's fine if just about all your incoming faxes are pages that were transmitted on letter-size paper (which is usually the case). However, it's less satisfactory if you receive a lot of documents that were sent on legal-size paper.

If you only have letter-size paper in your fax and you receive a document consisting of legal-size pages, one of two things can happen depending on the machine and how it is set up: either the incoming pages are automatically reduced to fit onto the smaller paper; or the bottom part may print onto a second letter-size sheet, with no reduction taking place. Neither outcome is ideal.

That's the one drawback of a cut-sheet plain paper fax over a thermal roll machine — with the latter, you're automatically set up to receive onto both sizes of paper, because both are 8.5" wide and the machine simply cuts off whatever length is appropriate.

### Dual-cassette models

If you want to receive onto different paper sizes, the solution is to get a machine with dual on-line cassettes. Like dual cassettes on a copier, this enables you to keep different sizes on-line at the same time. Your machine will automatically select from the paper source appropriate to the page size of the incoming fax. If one cassette is empty, the machine switches to the other regardless of the page size of incoming faxes.

There's usually not much point in getting dual cassettes unless you're going to use the second one for a different paper size. Simply using it to enlarge your on-line supply of one size is an expensive luxury, as a dual-cassette feature typically adds several hundred dollars to the price. The only exception would be if your incoming fax traffic was so heavy that keeping a 250-sheet drawer topped off would be a real nuisance. Some machines have single cassettes that hold as many as 500 sheets, incidentally.

Ideally, look for a paper supply that takes the form of a frontloading drawer at the bottom of the machine. These are more streamlined than the older design with paper cassettes sticking out at the side.

If you only have a single-cassette machine, you can almost always choose whether to have letter or legal paper on-line, even though you can't have both simultaneously. Sometimes, the single cassette is adjustable for both paper sizes, but in other cases you have to pay about $80 extra for a legal cassette to substitute for your letter one. At the time of this writing, only one plain paper fax — made by NEC — could print onto 11" x 17" paper.

# Document Feeders

Almost all faxes — even pretty inexpensive thermal paper ones — have document feeders of some sort, except for a handful of really small ones that require you to feed in each original manually. Document feeders on faxes are similar to the ones you get on copiers — you simply place all the pages in a pile, start the transmission, and then wander off, confident that the machine will take one page after another out of the feeder until it's done transmitting. At least that's the idea.

The reality is that on low-cost machines, document feeders don't always work too well. More often than manufacturers care to admit, a machine fails to pick up the next page and then cuts out, or accidentally picks up two pages at once. Once you find you cannot trust your feeder implicitly, you'll probably loiter around the machine while it's transmitting — you'll want to check that everything is going through properly. Document feeders on more heavy-duty machines — notably laser and LED models — tend to perform more reliably.

### Document feeder capacities

At the risk of stating the obvious, the size of feeder you require relates to the length of documents you fax. A 30-page feeder is a waste of money if none of your fax transmissions are more than 15 pages long. Conversely, you'll soon rue the day you bought a machine with only a 15-page feeder if you regularly need to send 30-page documents.

### Document widths

Some faxes can handle originals up to 11" wide, though most less expensive models can only transmit ones that are 8.5" or 10" wide. If much of your work consists of transmitting wide originals, be sure also to check the maximum scanning width — some machines that can take 11" wide documents are only able to scan a significantly narrower width.

If you are sending a wide document to a machine that only has 8.5" wide paper (as almost all do), the larger image will be automatically reduced to fit at the receiving end. If you only occasionally need to fax wide documents, you can always reduce them on a copier and then fax them — rather than paying extra to get a machine with a wide feeder.

# Sharing a Phone Line

An increasing number of fax machines are designed to share a phone line with regular voice traffic, instead of having a line of their own. These machines have something called a "fax/tel switch," a device whose function is to distinguish automatically between incoming voice and fax calls.

### Fax/tel switches explained

Fax/tel switches are less common in the plain paper fax market than in the thermal paper sector (where they are now found on most machines). The reason is that manufacturers assume that if you are willing to spend the money required to buy a plain paper fax, it must mean that you receive a good number of faxes; and if you do receive that many, it would be much more practical for the machine to have a line of its own.

There's some logic in that reasoning. I don't count myself among the most ardent supporters of fax/tel switches outside home office environments (and, even there, I have my doubts) — but there's nevertheless also some demand for plain paper faxes with auto switching, and a number of machines do have it.

Fax/tel switches can be useful, though your enthusiasm for the concept shouldn't blind you to the fact that they are usually a bit of a compromise on having a dedicated fax line. They can cause confusion and irritation when people are trying to fax you; in practice, they don't always work out quite as smoothly as the vendors would have you believe. If you can jus-tify the cost of a separate phone line for your fax, it's generally money well spent.

That said, it's easier to justify line sharing if most of your traffic consists of sending, rather than receiving: when you're sending a fax over a regular phone line, the only downsides are that callers won't be able to get through and that a call-waiting signal — if you have this feature — could interfere with your fax transmission.

The exact way in which fax/tel switches operate varies from brand to brand, but here's a generic description of how they function. Let's imagine that you've got a fax/tel-equipped ma-chine and someone is trying to send you a fax. Your machine will answer the call, usually on the first ring, and as soon as it hears the fax signal from the other machine it'll send a fax sig-nal back in the normal way (the so-called "handshake") so that transmission can begin.

It's when someone makes a voice call that things are dif-ferent. In this case, when the machine picks up on the first ring it recognizes that the incoming call is a person, and not another fax, by the absence of a fax signal. It then immediately resumes ringing at the receiving end — thereby signaling to you that a human call is on the line. Sometimes, the machine gives a short voice announcement to callers to let them know what's going on.

### Faxes and answering machines

Some machines with fax/tel switches have interfaces to con-nect to an answering machine. These allow you to set the fax so that when it determines that an incoming call is a human and not a fax, the call is automatically picked up by the answering machine. If, on the other hand, the machine recognizes that the call is coming from a fax, it will issue a fax signal and the an-swering machine will not be disturbed.

Alternatively, consider a fax with a built-in telephone an-swering machine. There are more of these now than there were a year or two ago. Panasonic used to have this market largely to itself, but it is now joined by Canon, Sharp, and Samsung (among others). You can also get plain paper combo machines (until not long ago, all were thermal faxes).

Personally, I question the wisdom of integrating both func-tions into one combo machine. While fax machines are gener-ally pretty reliable, answering machines can be fickle. I'd think twice about risking the integrity of a fax by building in a rela-tively inexpensive and potentially troublesome answering device. It can be smarter to connect an external answering machine, especially if you have one already. On the other hand, when you look at the price of some of the combo machines, you may be tempted to go buy one anyway — Panasonic's models start at around $350.

If you come across the acronym "TAD" in your perusal of the fax market, this stands for "telephone answering device." Likewise, a "TAD interface" is jargon for the feature you need to link a fax to an answering machine.

### Extension transfer

If you do share a phone line between a regular phone and a fax, you may decide to put the latter on "manual receive" — this means that it only gives out a fax signal when you press a button. You might do this if you don't have a fax/tel switch, or if you do have one but don't get a lot of faxes. Extension transfer means that if you pick up another phone sharing the line, and hear an incoming fax, you can remotely activate your fax machine's signal using a touch-tone command.

Keep in mind that, as with other aspects of line sharing, this can cause problems — I've heard a few gripes lately from people who had found that the feature is not all it's cracked up to be. This backs up my advice that it's preferable to give your fax its own line if at all possible. Technologically speaking, it's really the best way to go!

### Other phone features

If you do plan to use the same machine for both your voice and fax traffic, look for a machine that incorporates the features you'd look for on a regular phone. Some have things like hands-free speakerphones and music on hold.

If a speakerphone is important, make sure that the machine's advertised speaker isn't the type that just allows you to pick up when the party you're calling answers, and that doesn't let you conduct two-way, hands-free conversations: sales people often give inadvertently misleading information on this point, not grasping the distinction between the two types of speakers. Full, two-way speakerphones are actually a little rare on fax machines (though they do exist).

Keep in mind also that this type of phone-feature is more likely to be found on a relatively low-cost thermal machine than on a more expensive plain paper model. The reason is simply that thermal faxes tend to be bought for personal use (which makes it more likely that you will use the same machine as a fax and a phone) while plain paper faxes tend — by virtue of their price — to be shared devices.

# Dialing Features

Almost all fax machines have automatic dialing capabilities, but the extent varies quite considerably. Here's a briefing on the main features to look for.

### Speed dialing

This feature is just like the one you get on regular phones. It enables you to store frequently faxed numbers in a memory, so that they can be dialed automatically at the press of one or two (or possibly more) keys. The best type is the one-touch variety, which gives each number its own dedicated key. You can often label each key with the name of the party whose fax number it controls.

Most machines offer a combination of one- and two-touch speed dialing, but the thing I always focus on is the number of one-touch keys — generally, you can get anything from a low of about five to a high of about 50.

Some machines offer as many as 100 two-touch numbers. This sounds great, but the difficulty — apart from thinking of 100 people to whom you regularly send faxes (in addition to those on your one-touch keys) — is remembering who has what two-digit number.

A solution is a feature called "LCD scroll auto-dial." This allows you to set up an alphanumeric directory in the machine's memory and then visually scroll through it using the machine's LCD display; when you get to the name/number you want, simply press "start" and the number is dialed for you. This feature is also known as "directory dialing."

### Delayed send & auto-retry

Both of these features are found on all plain paper fax machines and on most thermal models. Delayed send allows you to program your machine to transmit a document at a specific time; this allows you to take advantage of cheap phone rates in the middle of the night. It's one of those features that often gets disregarded in practice — in general, fax messages have a sense of urgency that makes you want to send them right away rather than saving a few cents on the cost of the call.

Auto-retry means what it says: if the number you're calling is busy, the machine will automatically try again a few times at intervals of two or three minutes. A less common variation is "auto alternate-number retry" — in this case, the machine will try alternate numbers which you have programmed in as backups to the ones stored in memory for speed dialing.

### Programmable keys

Programmable command keys enable your fax to "memorize" certain complex instructions, so that they can be executed by pressing just one button. It's quite handy if you regularly send documents to the same number and with the same instructions on how they should be transmitted. For example, a single programmed command could tell the machine to transmit to a confidential mailbox (explained later) at a given fax number using superfine mode.

Most mid- and upmarket faxes have some programmable keys, though, again, I suspect that most people never get around to using them.

### Transmission reservation

This feature can save you the bother of hanging around waiting for an incoming fax to finish before you prepare your next transmission. It allows you to enter dialing instructions for your next outgoing fax while the machine is still receiving; you then leave the outgoing document in the feeder and walk away — as soon as the line is clear, your document will be sent out.

### Talk reservation/voice request

Don't confuse transmission reservation with what many people call "talk reservation," but which others call "voice request." Talk reservation is a feature which lets you tell the fax machine that when it's through faxing, you'd like to talk to someone at the other end — so the machine shouldn't hang up automatically.

### Polling

This is a feature that allows you to leave a document in your machine, so that it will be sent to another machine when that one calls yours. Why not just send the fax to the other machine in the normal way? Well, you might want the other party to carry the cost of the phone call. Fair enough, but a bit stingy and hardly worth the bother.

Potentially more useful is an upgrade of this feature called "sequential polling." Say you're in the headquarters of a company with 20 branch offices. Let's also suppose that you require a daily report from each branch. This feature means that you can tell each branch office to leave its report in its machine at the close of business; you can program your machine to call each branch automatically in the middle of the night, one after the other, to receive all the reports. When you turn up bleary-eyed in the morning, there'll be a pile of reports for your perusal.

That can make more sense than asking all 20 branches to fax you, as they'd have a problem getting through if they all tried at the same time. What's more, with programmable command keys you can activate this entire routine, every day, with the touch of a single key. There are usually various security features to prevent unauthorized persons from "collecting" the documents before you do. A lot of machines can also poll documents stored in other machines' memories — more on document memory soon.

### Departmental codes

If you need to charge outgoing faxes to clients, or to different cost centers in your organization, you may want to look for a machine with this feature. It requires users to enter a PIN-code before they can send a fax. Reports are then generated summarizing usage by account number.

# Transmission Features

I've been talking above about fax features relating to dialing and setting everything up for a transmission. Next, I'll brief you on the main ones to do with the actual sending.

### Fast mode

Pick up some fax brochures, and the chances are that they'll boast of fast mode transmission times — 10 or 12 seconds per page, for example, which is roughly half the time it normally takes to send a page of text. What the brochures rarely make clear is that these fast speeds are almost always proprietary — in other words, they only work between compatible machines from the same manufacturer. If you're faxing another brand of machine, there will be no speed advantage whatsoever — even if that machine also has its own fast mode.

This means that most fast modes are not as exciting as they first appear, though they can be very useful if you know that a significant amount of your fax traffic is between machines from the same manufacturer. Keep in mind that not all machines in a given manufacturer's range will necessarily be fast mode compatible.

### 14,400bps modems

The one exception to what I've just said about fast modes being proprietary is if two machines have a super-fast 14,400 bits per second (bps) modem, instead of the regular 9,600bps modems used on most faxes. These 14,400bps modems — also known as 14.4 modems — can transmit a standard page in just six seconds and are now part of the industry standard, which means that different brands can communicate at high speed providing that both the sending and receiving machines are equipped. If only one party has a 14,400bps modem, transmission will take place at the slower speed.

Sometimes, there is a small proprietary element to 14,400bps transmission. A few vendors, including Canon and Pitney Bowes, have developed ways of shortening transmission times further when their own 14.4-equipped machines are communicating with each other. They achieve this with proprietary protocols that reduce the "handshakes" that take place at the start of transmissions.

Conversely, although two machines of different brands should always work at high speed if both are 14,400bps-equipped, the full six-second speed may not always be achieved. Some vendors quote 14,400bps speeds of seven or eight seconds, presumably to take account of this; others don't, but this point may still apply to them in practice. But the differences are pretty small, so you shouldn't worry about this unduly.

Anyway, it would be a pointless exercise to stand over any machine with a stopwatch and fret if you don't get exactly six seconds every time: the six-second speed assumes you are sending the fax industry's definition of a "standard" page; originals with a dense image area will take longer to transmit than ones with less on the page. Also, keep in mind that even if each page does take exactly six seconds, you won't be able to send exactly 10 pages in a minute — you have to allow a short gap between each page.

The number of 14,400bps machines installed is still fairly small as a proportion of the entire fax population. However, they are catching on — especially in the plain paper market. I wouldn't be surprised if, in a couple of years, most plain paper fax machines sold have 14,400bps modems.

Getting a 14,400bps modem may not bring great benefits overnight, but you should enjoy significant benefits in the future. Moreover, you'll be doing your bit to enlarge the 14,400bps population — and the faster it grows, the quicker fax gridlock will be eased for all of us. That said, 14.4 may itself come to be regarded as slow some day — the fax industry is already working on a new 28,800bps standard which could be introduced by the end of 1995 (though don't count on it).

### Data compression methods

This refers to the method by which the machine encodes an image into a series of digital signals when transmitting. Most machines sending to other brands of fax are capable of two industry-standard compression methods — "Modified Huffman" and "Modified Read" (don't ask me who thought up those names, though I guess it was two people called Huffman and Read!).

Modified Read (MR) is a little faster than Modified Huffman (MH), and these days almost all plain paper faxes have both. Those that don't are at the low end of the market — in these cases, the workload is likely to be fairly modest, so the fairly marginal difference in transmission time won't amount to a big deal anyway. My advice, therefore, is not to worry too much about this.

You'll also come across "Modified Modified Read" (MMR). This isn't a misprint for Modified Read, but the data compression method that operates when you're in fast mode (discussed above).

### Error correction

If you're transmitting over a poor phone line, the image you're sending may become distorted. However, machines with error correction mode (ECM) automatically retransmit signals that are affected by line quality problems.

These days, error correction always works to an industry standard — in other words, you no longer need to have the same brand of machine at either end of the phone line for the feature to work. However, you still do need to have an ECM machine, of whatever brand, at both ends — ECM will not work unless both the sending and receiving machines have it. ECM is widely found on mid- and upmarket machines and is becoming increasingly common in the budget sector too.

### "Overseas modes"

A few vendors sell a feature that allows you to make your fax machine operate at a slower transmission speed, supposedly to reduce the chance of being cut off due to line interference when working with dodgy overseas phone connections.

This might possibly be worth thinking about if you fax some pretty out of the way countries — but it's completely unnecessary for faxing "mainstream" destinations in Europe and Pacific Asia, for example. Using this feature may do more to raise your phone bills than it does to improve your fax transmission success rate.

### Automatic cover sheets

A few machines have the ability to produce automatically generated cover sheets, drawing information about the recipient (the person's name, etc.) from information stored in the auto-dialer. Potentially a time-saver — though I've never seen the necessity to always use dedicated cover sheets anyway.

### Closed user groups

This feature enables you to restrict who you receive faxes from. The way it works varies from brand to brand, but the general aim is to bar your fax from accepting incoming transmissions from machines that are not designated members of the "group." The idea is to keep your fax lines clear for important transmissions.

To some extent, the feature is a reaction against so-called "junk fax" (i.e., unwanted sales transmissions which tie up your machine and use up your paper). But unless you're installing a fax in the Oval Office, this feature may be something of a sledgehammer to crack a walnut. Also, junk fax seems to be drying up anyway (some states have passed laws that outlaw it).

### Verification stamps

With this feature, each original page in a multi-page transmission can be discreetly stamped by the machine to show that it was transmitted successfully. You can deactivate this feature if you don't want it. Just about all machines produce a variety of printed reports summarizing your fax traffic and confirming that transmissions were successful.

# Document Memory Features

Almost all fax machines offer a basic memory feature in the form of speed dialing (see above), but document memory is something different. This allows you to scan an outgoing document into memory before transmission and/or to receive an incoming transmission into memory before printing it out. There are several applications.

### Broadcasting

The first is broadcasting. If you want to send the same document to a number of different locations, you'll save time if you enter it into memory and then tell the machine all the locations you want it to go to. This is a lot faster than having to load it into the document feeder, set up the transmission for the first recipient, watch all the sheets go through, and then repeat that process separately for each other recipient.

### Batch transmission

This feature is potentially useful in offices where several people frequently need to send non-urgent faxes to the same long-distance destination. It allows different documents, entered into memory for transmission at a later time, to be batched together automatically and sent all in one single phone call. This saves on costs, as one continuous call usually works out cheaper than several short ones.

I've yet to meet anyone who actually uses batch transmission, though it might be particularly useful if you need to send faxes to third-world countries where getting a phone connection is a chancy business requiring endless tries and lengthy delays.

### Relay broadcasting

Some higher-end machines are able to receive documents sent from other faxes, and then broadcast them on to further fax locations. These are known as relay broadcast hub machines, and the idea behind the feature is to save on phone costs.

Imagine, for example, that you've got a head office on the west coast that wants to send information to 10 branch offices in the east. Instead of sending 10 transcontinental faxes, relay hub broadcasting allows you to send just one fax to a hub unit in the east, which then retransmits it nine times within its own region taking advantage of cheaper (on account of the shorter distances) phone costs.

Many machines which don't have the capability to act as a relay hub unit are able to transmit to relay hub units for onward retransmission — look out for the feature known as "relay broadcast request." Keep in mind that this feature is one of those that only operates between compatible machines from the same manufacturer.

### Confidential transmission & reception

Another memory application is sending and receiving confidential material. If you don't want prying eyes to see your incoming faxes, look for a machine with confidential reception. This means that an incoming fax will only print out if you enter a special PIN-code; until then, it'll be held in memory. This only works if the sender selects a feature called confidential transmission.

Quite a few machines that don't have confidential reception nonetheless can send confidentially. Remember, though, that this feature — like relay broadcasting — only works between compatible machines from the same manufacturer (though it may be brought into the industry standard before long).

Many machines allow you to set up multiple "mailboxes," each with their own PIN-code, for different people in your office who share a machine; however, you'll need to specify quite a large amount of memory for this to be worthwhile.

### Out of paper reception

This means that if your machine runs out of paper and no one in your office notices, an incoming fax will go into memory rather than into thin air. This can be especially handy if there's a run of incoming faxes during the night when there's no one around to check on how the paper's doing.

This is the most common document memory feature. Every machine with memory has out-of-paper receive and, therefore, if a machine has only one memory feature, you can count on it being this one. (In other words, don't be impressed if the salesperson boasts about it in glowing terms.)

### Memory size

Virtually all plain paper machines offer some document memory. But the usefulness of some of the memory features is determined by the memory size. This is usually measured in the number of pages (the fax industry has come up with an agreed definition of how much is on a page to ensure that apples are compared with apples). However, some vendors talk in terms of kilobytes (256K of memory is equal to approximately 15–20 typical pages).

Memory sizes in the fax market may seem very small to people used to storing vast amounts of data on computers. The typical quantity that comes standard is between seven and 70 pages, though you can often upgrade the memory to a total of between 100–200 pages and, occasionally, to as much 1,000 pages.

If you only have a little memory, it's not the end of the world — you can get a lot of value out of a plain paper fax without ever using the memory features. However, if you are hoping to use the memory, you should aim to get a reasonable amount — say 30 pages or more — because otherwise you'll find that there isn't, in practice, a great deal you can do with it. Likewise, check out whether the memory is "multi-file" — in other words, whether you can store only one long document up to the overall memory capacity, or several shorter ones.

### Dual access

This feature allows you to do two things on your fax at once, providing you've got a machine with document memory. For example, you can be scanning a document into memory while the machine is transmitting or receiving something else; the document will be sent as soon as the line becomes free. Likewise, you could be printing out a document received into memory while you are sending or receiving. Dual access is becoming increasingly common in the plain paper fax market, and a growing number of moderately priced units now offer it.

A few low-end machines that don't have dual access nonetheless manage something called "semi-dual access." This means that while the machine is printing out, you can be sending another document, but you can't be scanning one into memory.

### Fast scan

Some plain paper machines with document memory enable you to scan a document into memory in just a few seconds. The fastest quoted scan time is about two seconds, though about five or six seconds is also fast compared with regular speeds. This feature can be a welcome time-saver if you're entering a large number of pages into memory using the dual access feature or for broadcasting.

# Using Your Fax as a Copier?

Be warned that some highly misleading sales claims are circulated about the ability of regular fax machines to double up as copiers.

It is true that all fax machines are capable of making reproductions of originals, as well as transmitting them. If you have a thermal fax machine, the copies will be made on your regular fax paper and will look no better than the faxes you receive. Copies made on a plain paper fax might "feel" more like regular copies — but reproduction quality is significantly worse than that of regular copiers and the process is also pretty slow (added to which you miss out on all the productivity features of dedicated copiers).

Despite this, some fax vendors have a habit of shamelessly making out that their machines are able to double up as copiers — they do so in order to make them appear to offer additional value. The only machines that can plausibly claim to be fax-copier combos are the specially designed — and pretty expensive — multifunctional units discussed in Chapter 9 ... and even there, performance and productivity may not compare all that favorably with that of dedicated copiers.

# Fax "Groups"

In the olden days, fax machines from different manufacturers couldn't talk to each other. Then a Swiss-based organization called the Consultative Committee for International Telephone & Telegraphy (CCITT) laid down industry standards, which all manufacturers adopted.

Today, by far the dominant industry standard is CCITT Group 3. Originally established in 1980, this ended up replacing the older and much slower Group 1 and 2 standards which are obsolete. Occasionally you still come across machines in use that were built only for the older standards; Group 3 models are mostly downwardly compatible if you do need to transmit to an older machine.

### Group 4

There is also a Group 4 standard. This isn't particularly new, and it certainly is not a replacement for Group 3. It offers super-fast transmission — speeds can be less than two seconds a page — but it requires all-digital phone lines and is currently only a practical option for major corporations with privately leased phone networks. The new six-second Group 3 14,400bps modem standard (described earlier in this chapter), which works over regular phone lines, threatens to slow down the development of Group 4, as it significantly narrows the latter's performance advantage.

Most fax vendors do not sell Group 4 machines. If you are interested in getting one, your best shortlist of suppliers would be Canon, NEC and Ricoh. Available models are very expensive, and are rarely found in normal discount channels. Occasionally, Group 3 models have Group 4 upgrade options.

### Color fax

So far, there is no industry standard for color fax — in fact, color fax is still in its infancy. Several manufacturers are working on it, but only one — Sharp — had brought a machine to the market by spring 1993. Color fax is likely to be a very expensive, proprietary, and specialized tool for several years. The Sharp model costs over $20,000, and remember that you need one at both ends of a phone line. Transmission times are also very slow — a page can take up to two minutes.

# Portable Fax

Quite a few budget machines are described by their makers as portable, but often it turns out that all this means is that they're compact desktop units, weighing 5–6 lbs, that are offered with optional canvas carrying cases on which the dealer makes a disproportionately high profit. However, there are a handful of smaller machines that are designed specifically for portable applications. These machines can be used with any phone, including — in theory — cellular phones, and the most useful are the ones that run on rechargeable batteries.

These tend to be expensive items: the portable fax market has never really taken off, partly because people tend to find it more convenient and less expensive to get a fax modem for their notebook computers (I'll be talking about these next). However, portable fax should get a new lease on life when cellular fax comes of age — right now, this is an immature market, not least because the analog cellular network gives iffy line quality for data communications. Digital cellular is on the way, however — and this should improve things.

Right now, I tend to advise people with mobile fax applications to settle for a fax modem for their notebook for the time being and await further developments (in time, wireless faxing direct from your computer will become commonplace).

# Fax Modems and PC Hooks-Ups

A fax modem is a relatively inexpensive device that allows you to send any document you create on your computer to someone else's fax machine without first making a print-out — with one of these faxes, you can transmit directly from your PC and you may, therefore, be able to do away with having a dedicated fax altogether. You can also receive faxes on your computer, and view them on screen or print them out.

If you already have a computer and a laser or ink jet printer, this is the cheapest way of getting yourself set up for plain paper faxing. In fact, it's even cheaper than buying a non-plain paper budget fax. Fax modems — which always come with the special software you need — usually cost between $100 and $200. Since this is a lot less than the price of a dedicated plain paper fax, why doesn't everyone get one?

### The downside of fax modems

The answer is that fax modems have their limitations. First, they only allow you to fax documents that you create, or import, as computer files. You can't fax a handwritten note, or a newspaper clipping, or a photo. Actually, there is a way around this, and that's to get a scanner and import those types of originals into your computer as graphical images — but this is a slow and awkward solution.

The other problem is that fax modems can interfere with the rest of the work you do on your computer. These days, most are advertised as being capable of sending and receiving faxes in background — in other words, they can operate while you are using the computer for other things. And up to a point, they can do just that.

In practice, however, you may find that you put a strain on your computer, especially when you send or receive long faxes at the same time as you perform other complex tasks. For example, you may find that everything on the computer slows down. Worse still, you may run out of memory. I don't want to overstate this problem, and it does depend in part on how powerful a computer you have and on the fax software you're using. But take it from me: the fact that a fax modem can operate in background mode does not necessarily mean that it won't get in the way at all.

Another problem is that some fax software is a little slow. Although you save the time of having to first print out your document and then fax it on a regular machine, you still have to convert your document into fax format before transmission can take place — this can take up just as much time as outputting it on a printer. In fact, sometimes it takes rather longer (this depends on the computer, the document, and your fax software).

Also, by their nature, fax modems are more suitable for use by one person, than for general use by a whole department or office. They are not suitable for walk-up use by a bunch of different people. Conversely, they can be handy devices for people who have a computer at home.

Still on the drawbacks of fax modems, the whole business can be a bit fiddly — while there are real productivity gains to be had, there are also bugs and irritations to be encountered (details vary, but if it isn't one thing, it'll probably be another).

Many people agree that fax modems are particularly "moody" when it comes to receiving faxes — in my opinion, they are better tools for sending them. In my office, I am set up to send most of my outbound faxes on a fax modem, but I use an LED plain paper machine for receiving faxes; the fax modem and the regular fax share the same phone line, but I turn off the auto-answer feature on the modem.

### The advantages of fax modems

Fax modems compare well with dedicated faxes in terms of features. For example, you can get fax modems with auto fax/tel switching if you want to share a phone line with your regular voice traffic. And in some respects, fax modems are friendlier to use than regular faxes, especially if you're operating in the Microsoft Windows or — better still — Apple Mac environments.

I find that features like delayed send, automatic dialing, and broadcasting, can be a lot easier to use with good PC fax software than they are on dedicated fax machines which often have user interfaces about as friendly as those of VCRs. Also, anyone who has been frustrated by the small amounts of document memory you get on a dedicated fax should be happy with a fax modem — your entire hard disk can be used for fax document storage.

### Choosing a fax modem

If you are considering a fax modem, be sure to get one that can receive faxes as well as send them. A few are send-only, though these are no longer very common.

Also, check out its speed. To be as fast as a regular fax, a fax modem should operate at 9,600bps, but some older and/or less expensive ones only operate at 4,800bps (sometimes, a machine may be able to send faxes at 9,600bps, but only receive them at 4,800bps). There are also 14,400bps fax modems, which have the same speed advantages as 14,400bps dedicated fax machines (discussed earlier). Incidentally, a fax modem is always able to double up as a regular modem for sending data to other computers and accessing databases and electronic mail services.

Fax modems are sold by most computer dealers and computer software/peripherals catalogs. A growing number of retail-channel PCs come with them as part of the standard package. Fax dealers that handle dedicated machines do not, in general, sell them (and tend, therefore, to have a vested interest in belittling them).

Fax modems are either external devices, the size of a regular modem, or they can be fitted internally in one of your computer's expansion slots. They are especially useful on notebook computers, as they give you the benefit of a fully portable fax while you're traveling (though the hassle of connecting them to hotel phone jacks, and then figuring out how to fax out on the hotel phone system while room service is tripping over you, can be a disincentive to using them).

Most notebook vendors sell internal fax modems designed specially for their machines; this is often the only one that will work with the machine in question, though there is a move toward standardized slots for notebooks — see the discussion of PCMCIA slots in Chapter 1.

### Hooking up a fax machine to a PC

Some fax machines have optional interfaces that allow you to hook up to a PC. There are several possible benefits from doing so. One is that you may be able to send faxes straight from your PC, rather than making paper print-outs and then feeding them into the machine. Fax salespeople tend to demonstrate this feature as though it was a staggering technology breakthrough — but it actually amounts to little more than making the fax machine act as a regular PC fax modem.

The second possible reason for interfacing your fax to a PC is that you may be able to use the fax as a scanner for inputting graphical images into the computer — that's fair enough, but the scanning capabilities are unlikely to compare very favorably with those of dedicated scanners.

The third benefit from a fax-PC hook-up is that you may be able to use the fax as a computer printer — but, again, the speed and print quality won't impress anyone used to the latest and greatest from the dedicated laser printer arena. There is further discussion of fax-PC integration in Chapter 9 which focuses on multifunctional machines.

# Smart Buying Tactics

Choosing what to buy is only part of the story. You've also got to decide where to buy. The next part of this chapter explains the pros and cons of different types of dealers and suppliers.

Your "how/where-to-buy" options depend in part on the type of fax machine you are buying. If you are looking for a sub-$1,000 machine (plain paper or thermal), you are best off going into the so-called retail channel — budget fax has taken on the characteristics of the consumer electronics market, in which low-overhead distributors vie with one another to move as many brown cardboard boxes as possible in as short a time as possible — and in as impersonal a way as possible.

However, if you are looking for a more expensive fax, you'll probably have to deal with a more traditional office equipment

dealer which works on higher margins. At the time of this writing, faxes costing more than $1,000 were rare sights in the re-
tail channel — in part because businesses seem to have anxieties (unjustified, in my opinion) about buying more expensive
equipment that way.

### Office warehouse stores

These days, the best and easiest places to buy sub-$1,000 fax
machines are often office supply warehouse stores, especially
the big-three national chains — OfficeMax, Office Depot, and
Staples. All three sell a good selection of leading brands at prices
that are hard to beat.

Typically these stores carry about five or six budget plain
paper faxes at any time, usually from about three of four different brands. They also give you about the same number of thermal paper models to choose from starting from under $250. In
my experience, the range of options they offer between them is
usually plenty.

If getting to a warehouse store isn't convenient, keep in
mind that they take orders over the phone and deliver anywhere.
Some numbers to call:

*Office Depot: 800 685 8800*
*Staples: 800 333 3330*
*Office Max: 800 688 6278*

Keep in mind that these stores do deliver (often at no charge)
and that they also sell discounted fax supplies.

### Other retail stores

Next are the consumer electronics retailers that sell faxes in
their shops alongside things like video cameras, cellular phones,
and notebook computers. Consumer electronics retailers tend
only to offer pretty low-end faxes, though they often sell the
very-entry-level plain paper models such as the Brothers and
the older upright-looking Canons. They generally carry a smaller
selection of brands than the office warehouse stores and often
charge slightly higher prices.

Another possibility are certain well-known chains of computer stores that sell low-end fax equipment as a sideline. For
example, CompUSA sells some pretty aggressively-priced equipment.

Still on the subject of retailers, warehouse stores like Sam's
and Price Club can be good places to turn for budget faxes,
including ink jet models — you sometimes find these stores sell-

ing a slightly different range of models from the office warehouse stores.

### Small mail order dealers

Small mail order dealers — often New York-based — which used to be good sources for budget fax machines, no longer usually have any significant price advantage at this end of the market. They can offer tempting prices on more expensive laser faxes, but some of them have a way of doing business that leaves something to be desired.

Never, ever send a check to one of these companies — you should always pay by credit card, as you'll have more redress that way if the transaction turns sour. Be alert for small mail order dealers who advertise exceptionally low prices on models that they then seem to have difficulty in supplying — this is the so-called "bait and switch" trap, where buyers are lured into the net in order to be sold something else. Watch out for machines that turn out not to be brand new. And expect stiff delivery charges, a technique that these dealers use to claw back some of their margins.

If these warnings have not put you off (and buying this way can result in the lowest possible prices on good machines), check out advertisements in the Science Section of the *New York Times* (this is published every Tuesday in both the national and regional editions).

If you buy from one of these mail order dealers, you can still turn to a local dealer in your area for service should you need it — but warranty work can be a problem. Surprisingly, there are no blue chip, national mail order catalogs that sell anything other than budget, sub-$1,000 faxes.

### Traditional office equipment dealers

The various types of discount retailers have made life difficult for conventional office equipment dealers trying to operate in the budget fax arena. These traditional dealerships, which are generally built on product areas such as copiers and typewriters, are mainly smaller businesses that only sell in their own local areas, though some are part of larger dealer conglomerates.

Requiring higher margins to show a profit, they often find it hard to compete on price with the retail-channel competition discussed above. However, they still have their strength selling more expensive fax machines — as I indicated above, retail-channel vendors have not managed to make much headway peddling faxes for more than $1,000.

Traditional office equipment dealers mostly only handle a single brand, or perhaps a couple. Often the one they sell is the same as the copier brand that their business relies on.

In fact, if you are looking for a fairly heavy-duty, and somewhat feature-rich, laser fax, you may well find that one of these dealers is your only option short of calling one of the mail order dealers discussed above (and aside from buying from the manufacturers with their own direct sales offices — more on this shortly).

Don't be afraid to negotiate — these dealers tend to charge what they think they can get away with. Laser fax prices have been kept artificially high, in my opinion, partly because they have only been sold through this sort of dealer — rather than through national retailers working on lower margins and creating more competition.

It is in the area where the retail-channel faxes overlap with those sold by traditional office equipment dealers that the latter seem most uncompetitive. For example, traditional dealers often sell ink jet faxes, but can charge 30 percent more than office warehouse stores on identical or near-identical equipment.

Some manufacturers sell virtually the same machines through both channels, but make very minor feature adjustments and allocate different model numbers in order to create some semblance of product differentiation. For example, Sharp does this — the faxes that are prefixed with the letters "UX" go through the retail channel, while the ones prefixed with "FO" go through the dealer channel and generally sell at higher prices.

### The direct sales option

A few fax manufacturers have direct sales offices in some major cities, even though they mainly sell through dealers. In general, these offices concentrate on larger accounts — they'll gladly sell you just one or two machines, but you probably won't get a great deal.

Also, there are a number of fax distributors that relabel equipment which they then sell under their own brand names through direct sales offices and/or dealers. Examples include Pitney Bowes (which only sells direct) and Lanier (which sells direct and through dealers). These vendors tend to sell at fairly high prices, making much of any "added value" they provide in terms of service and, occasionally, slightly tweaked features.

### The service factor

Traditional office equipment dealers, and direct sales vendors, do have one advantage over the discount crowd: service. In many cases, they employ their own technicians who can fix machines in need of repair. They'll also be more likely to answer questions about how to use the equipment. And they'll install the equipment for you (not that this is anything requiring a modicum of skill).

Discount, retail-channel dealers, by contrast, usually offer little, if anything, in the way of after-sales service and support. If you have a problem with your machine, the most they may be able to do is refer you to a service center, to which you'll have to ship or take the machine.

You may infer from this that it's a false economy to buy from a discount dealer. But that isn't necessarily so. For a start, budget fax machines are, in general, very reliable. If you buy smartly in the first place, you'd be unfortunate if your machine needed repairing over a period of three to four years. Most don't. And unlike most copiers, fax machines do not require routine preventive maintenance.

What this means is that paying a hefty premium for your fax in return for the expectation of good service in the future may equate to paying an excessive insurance premium to protect yourself against a relatively low risk. Also, how can you be sure that a higher price dealer really will provide good service — especially in a year or two's time? The fact is that many more office equipment dealers talk about good service than actually deliver it.

Another point to keep in mind is that if you are unfortunate enough to need repair work, there's no reason why you have to rely on the firm that sold you the machine. Just as you can take your car to a different dealer from the one that sold it, you can likewise call up another fax dealer if the one you bought from isn't geared up to provide support. If you have a problem locating a service outlet, the manufacturer could provide a referral.

Having made these points, I should remind you again that the choice of whether to buy through retail channels or traditional dealers is not an option in most cases — that's because retail channels rarely sell anything other than thermal faxes, ink jet models, thermal transfer plain paper faxes, and very entry-level laser/LED ones. More upscale laser faxes simply aren't available through these channels and so the chances are that you'll be obliged to buy from a local dealer which charges quite high prices but does at least offer decent service back-up.

Keep in mind that some manufacturers take direct responsibility for service, meaning that you may not have to rely on a dealer at all. Some do so with more enthusiasm than others. In

— but the drawback is that its warranty, like most in the fax industry, only lasts for 90 days.

## Canon

*Canon USA Inc.*
*One Canon Plaza*
*Lake Success, NY 11042*
*Tel: 516 488 6700*

Canon has traditionally had one of the strongest overall product ranges in the fax market and some of the best distribution. The company sells a range of inexpensive thermal machines, which are widely available through retail channels. In addition, it has a very comprehensive range of plain paper models, comprising both ink jets and lasers.

The older ink jets — characterized by their somewhat upright design and compact footprints — have slow print speeds and are probably best avoided: it's unclear how much longer these models will stick around. The newer ink jets, introduced in spring 1994, have a more "normal" appearance, are faster, and are better in other respects.

The venerable L700-series laser faxes (which in some senses are showing their age) now occupy the premium position in Canon's range, while the newer Laser Class 5000-series models, also introduced in spring 1994, occupy the mid-market slot. Soon after this book was published, Canon was expected to introduce the Laser Class 7000 series, which will replace the L700-series models. Note that none of Canon's laser faxes can print at more than four pages per minute — a drawback when you get to the high end of the market, where 14,400bps modems and large amounts of memory are becoming the norm.

Canon's laser faxes are based on the same engines that dominate the laser PC printer market (Canon-manufactured laser engines are used by numerous printer vendors, including Hewlett-Packard). And its ink jet faxes use the same printing technology as the company's excellent BubbleJet PC printers.

Canon sells ink jets through retail stores and dealers, while the laser faxes go only through dealers. While Canon doesn't have direct sales branches as such, it owns subsidiaries in the New York, Chicago, Philadelphia, and Los Angeles metropolitan areas which operate as dealers. The warranty is the usual 90 days.

# *Dex*

*Dex Business Systems, Inc.*
*36 Apple Ridge Road*
*Danbury, CT 06810–7300*
*Tel: 203 796 5400*

Dex used to be the brand name used by Fujitsu to market its fax machines (students of fax history will recall that the same name had previously been used by Burroughs, which sold its fax business to Fujitsu in 1986). When Fujitsu announced early in 1992 that it was pulling out of the fax market, Danka Industries - a large office equipment distributor headquartered in St. Petersburg, FL — bought up Fujitsu's fax inventory and the remnants of its US fax distribution business.

Danka formed a new subsidiary called Dex Business Systems. This initially sold off the remaining Fujitsu machines under the Dex brand name, but went on to relabel other manufacturers' fax equipment.

Dex now has two separate plain paper fax lines. The older, and less interesting, machines are a couple of relabeled Toshibas. The newer ones, which offer great value for money, are LEDs manufactured by Samsung. It looks as though Dex will have an exclusive on most of these — Samsung is only selling the entry-level model under its own brand name (that model is also relabeled by AT&T). Dex sales are mainly through traditional office equipment dealers. The warranty is only 90 days.

In fall 1993, Danka acquired Telautograph, the fax distributor that owned the Omnifax brand name (see separate entry in these Vendor Profiles). Omnifax is a relabeler concentrating on selling to medium and large corporations via direct sales offices.


# *Gestetner*

*Gestetner Corporation*
*599 West Putnam Avenue*
*Greenwich, CT 06836*
*Tel: 203 863 5551*

Gestetner is a long-established British reprographics company that has undergone changes in ownership in recent years. The Gestetner family sold out to Australian investors several years ago and, subsequently, Ricoh acquired a major stake.

Gestetner used to sell relabeled Mita faxes but, following the Ricoh deal, it is now selling branded Ricoh plain paper models. Gestetner is not prominent in the fax market; the most obvious reason to consider it would be if you already had a relationship with a Gestetner dealer for your copier requirements.

# Hewlett-Packard

*Hewlett-Packard Company*
*19310 Pruneridge Avenue*
*Cupertino, CA 95014*
*Tel: 800 752 0900*

HP — the California computer and peripherals giant — entered the fax arena for the first time in 1991, and has done very well by concentrating on the low end of the plain paper market. Hewlett-Packard's faxes are ink jets. They are very similar — though not identical — to the ones sold under the Panafax brand name: they are made by Matsushita, Panasonic's parent company, though HP supplies the print engines (which were originally developed for its very successful ink jet printers).

HP is unusual in offering a return-to-manufacturer express repair service for its faxes. If your machine needs fixing, you can call HP and, providing you give them a credit card number, they'll overnight you a new model. If your machine is under warranty, your card will not be charged if you ship the old machine back within a few days (you pay for the shipping); if the machine is not under warranty, you can still use this service, but there will be a charge for repairs. The other unusual thing about HP's warranties is that they run for a full year — most vendors in this industry only offer a miserly 90 days.

Perhaps surprisingly, in view of its dominance in the laser printer market, HP does not sell any laser faxes. It used to sell a device that turned your existing HP laser printer into a plain paper fax, though this has now been discontinued. HP fax sales are through dealers and retail stores (office supply warehouse stores in particular), and the brand is well represented in discount channels.

# JetFax

*JetFax, Inc.*
*978 Hamilton Court*
*Menlo Park, CA 94025*
*Tel: 415 324 0600*

JetFax — formerly known as Hybrid Fax, Inc. — was formed in 1988 and initially concentrated on selling add-on products that allow users to upgrade their laser PC printers into plain paper fax machines. It went on to sell a relabeled Minolta receive-only fax.

In 1992, it introduced its first full-function standalone fax. This is assembled by JetFax in California, using a Samsung laser engine and parts sourced from China. The machine has some interesting characteristics, most notably the fact that it can be upgraded to work with two phone lines sending and/or receiving simultaneously.

JetFax seems a decent company, with some brainy people working on product development. Part of its strategy is to team up with larger vendors — I believe that JetFax is working on a multifunctional ink jet product for Xerox that will be introduced during the shelf-life of this book. It will also be selling a version of this machine under its own name.

# Konica

*Konica Business Machines USA, Inc.*
*500 Day Hill Road*
*Windsor, CT 06095*
*Tel: 800 456 6422*

Konica has a stronger presence in copiers than it does in fax. It seems to be gradually pulling out of thermal fax, and now concentrates mainly on the plain paper sector. Its plain paper faxes are based on engines bought in from other manufacturers, though all of its current models are built to its specifications and are not straight relabelings. The least expensive of its three models uses a Matsushita laser engine, and the other two models are built around Casio LED engines.

Sales are mainly through dealers, though Konica also sells and supports its equipment direct in over 40 major cities. This direct sales presence is one of the reasons why the company has been quite successful supplying major accounts.

# Lanier

*Lanier Worldwide Inc.*
*1700 Chantilly Drive NE*
*Atlanta, GA 30324*
*Tel: 404 496 9500*

Lanier is a major office equipment distributor. These days, it is more or less out of thermal fax, and it's concentrating on the plain paper sector where its range currently consists of relabeled Toshiba, Sanyo, and Ricoh models. Until recently, it was also selling some rebadged Oki equipment, but this has now been discontinued. Keep in mind that Lanier sometimes offers reconditioned equipment.

Lanier mainly sells direct, and concentrates on larger buyers through its direct sales force; however, it also has some dealers. Lanier is a service-intensive supplier; its prices include delivery, installation, training, and initial supplies.

Although the company only offers a 90-day formal warranty, it backs this up with a three-year "satisfaction guarantee" entitling you to a new machine if you aren't happy with the performance of the one you bought (certain conditions apply).

## Minolta

*Minolta Corporation*
*Business Equipment Division*
*101 Williams Drive*
*Ramsey, NJ 07446*
*Tel: 201 825 4000*

Minolta is not a strong player in the fax market, though in 1993 it introduced two new laser models which are the first all-Minolta fax send-and-receive products it has built. Sources tell me that the company will soon introduce a sub-$1,000 laser fax — this will be one of the first lasers to hit the market at that price point. I believe that the model concerned will be made by Sharp.

Minolta has direct sales offices in some major cities, but mostly sells through dealers. While Minolta is not one of the first companies that usually comes to mind when thinking of fax vendors, its background in making laser products is strong — in fact, the company claims to be the world's second biggest producer of laser engines after Canon (these are used in a number of brands of laser printer, though no one else is currently using them in the fax market).

## Mita

*Mita Copystar America, Inc.*
*225 Sand Road*
*PO Box 40008*
*Fairfield, NJ 07004*
*Tel: 201 808 8444*

Mita is a copier specialist that has branched out into fax. It no longer sells thermal fax machines, but it does have some decent laser plain paper models. Some of these are sold relabeled, and with certain enhancements, by Pitney Bowes. One is also rebadged by Swintec.

Mita is not a leader in the fax market. Most of its dealers are ones that also handle its copiers. The list prices are competitive, and Mita faxes can be good values in parts of the country where the lowest office equipment prices may be hard to obtain. However, Mita is not very prominent in discount fax channels in the big metropolitan areas. The warranty is the usual 90 days.

# Monroe

*Monroe Systems for Business*
*1000 American Road*
*Morris Plains, NJ 07950*
*Tel: 201 993 2000*
An old name in the American office equipment marketplace, Monroe today concentrates mainly on selling relabeled office products to major accounts through its network of local branches. However, it has recently gone back into the dealer market for some of its fax sales. Monroe's fax machines were until recently relabeled Mitas, but the company has now started selling rebadged Toshibas instead. The warranty is the standard 90 days.

# Muratec

*Muratec Inc.*
*5560 Tennyson Parkway*
*Plano, TX 75024*
*Tel: 214 403 3300*
Muratec — until recently known as Murata — is a Japanese fax specialist. It is a subsidiary of Murata Machinery, Ltd., a privately-held Japanese company with interests in various diversified manufacturing businesses. Long known only for fax machines, Muratec now also sells cellular phones.

It competes in the middle ground of the plain paper fax market, concentrating on people with budgets between $1,000 and $2,000, and it also sells some inexpensive thermal models through retail channels. Its first ink jet fax was likely to be introduced not long after this book was published, though it was not clear whose engine this would use.

Aside from the forthcoming ink jet, Muratec's less expensive plain paper models use thermal transfer technology — or "film imaging" as Muratec has taken to calling it — and its other ones use LED engines. In the past, Muratec used to buy in Casio LED engines, but the company tells me that its current ones are its own. One of its low-end thermal faxes is made by Samsung.

Muratec fax machines are generally pretty good values,

sometimes very good ones. It sells both through dealers and retail channels, though it is not represented in any of the big-three office supply warehouse chains.

Recently, Muratec has been test marketing mail order direct sales, though it isn't clear whether this is going to be rolled out into a continuing program. Muratec has also beefed up its customer support policies, and now offers 800-number phone support and remote diagnostics. Its machines only come with 90-day warranties, however.

## NEC

*NEC America Inc.*
*Facsimile Division*
*383 Omni Drive*
*Richardson, TX 75080*
*Tel: 800 782 7329*
NEC was a fax leader during the mid-1980s when the market first began to take off, but it later became much less prominent. For a while, it began selling relabeled Mita plain paper models. Today, NEC seems to be gaining back a bit of its past strength: it no longer sells thermal paper models, but it has quite a strong, if small, plain paper range which it manufactures itself. This includes one very upscale niche machine which is the only plain paper fax able to print onto 11" x 17" paper. NEC also makes Group 4 faxes.

NEC sells both direct and through dealers. It usually offers six month warranties on its fax machines.

## Oki

*Okidata Inc.*
*532 Fellowship Road*
*Mount Laurel, NJ 08054*
*Tel: 800 654 3282*
Oki makes plain paper faxes based on the LED technology used in its highly successful computer printers. The company focuses most of its efforts on the mid-level — there are some great Oki buys for people going shopping with $1,300–$2,000, particularly at the lower end of that price range.

Sales are through dealers. Oki faxes are also sold relabeled by AT&T and Omnifax. Oki still has a couple of quite expensive thermal paper models in its range.

To show its confidence in LED technology, Oki backs the printhead on its plain paper fax machines with a five-year guar-

antee. The rest of the machines are covered by one-year warranties, and you get free on-site service for the first 90 days —
these warranty terms are a lot better than those offered on most
other plain paper faxes. Oki faxes are sold only through dealers.

## Omnifax

*Omnifax, Inc.*
*8700 Bellanca Avenue*
*Los Angeles, CA 90045*
*Tel: 310 641 3690*

Omnifax is a fairly prominent brand in the fax market, especially at the more corporate end. A variety of relabeled equipment is marketed under the Omnifax brand name, which, until
recently, was owned by a privately-held company called
Telautograph. The Omnifax range consists mostly of relabeled
Ricoh faxes, though there is also some Oki and Toshiba equipment.

In the second half of 1993, Telautograph was acquired by
Danka Industries, which also owns Dex, a distributor of relabeled Samsung and Toshiba fax machines (see separate entry
in these Vendor Profiles). It is unclear what plans, if any, Danka
has to exploit the synergy between Omnifax and Dex.

Omnifax operates mainly through direct sales offices, and
targets medium and larger users; there are, however, some
Omnifax dealers, generally covering less populated markets.

Omnifax has a good reputation for service. It is a vendor
worth checking out if you are a serious fax user needing a fair
number of machines, and it is also geared up to compete for
complex multi-location bids. It is less of an obvious choice if
you just need one or two machines and are shopping for the
best price.

## Panasonic/Panafax/Quasar

*Panasonic Communications & Systems Company*
*Two Panasonic Way*
*Secaucus, NJ 07094*
*Tel: 201 348 7000*

Panasonic is big in fax — and good at it. It has two separate
product lines, which are marketed by different divisions of the
company.

The Panasonic KX-F series is sold through consumer electronics, office warehouse, and mail order channels, and consists of thermal models and low-end LEDs; all of the thermal

models, and one of the LEDs, incorporate built-in telephone answering machines (Panasonic has by far the largest share of the fax/answering machine combo market).

The LEDs have a very strange upright design, which is supposedly meant to save deskspace. These machines give the impression of being built down to a price: at press-time, Panasonic was the only vendor to offer an LED/laser class machine for less than $1,000 in the retail channel (though other machines can be expected to emerge at the $999 price point during the shelf-life of this book).

The KX-F models are now backed by an express replacement or return service, allowing you to ship a broken machine directly back to Panasonic, bypassing the dealer. What's more, the warranty on the KX-F models lasts for one year — a lot better than the 90 days that you usually get in this industry. Some of the KX-F thermal models are also relabeled under the Quasar name, which is a parallel brand developed by Panasonic for parts of the retail market.

The Panafax series is the more upscale line; this includes some thermal models, but it is more geared to plain paper fax. The budget plain paper models are ink jets, which are very similar to the ones sold by Hewlett-Packard: both lots of machines are manufactured by Matsushita — Panasonic's parent company — but use HP print engines. The Panafax versions have a few more features, though the warranty arrangements are not as good.

The mid- and upmarket plain paper Panafaxes are lasers using Matsushita engines. Some of these are very competitively priced. Panafax sales are mainly through dealers; the manufacturer service arrangements mentioned above do not apply — if a Panafax unit breaks down, you have to rely on a dealer.

The part of Panasonic that sells the Panafax machines is quite separate from the part that sells the Panasonic KX-F series — the two divisions seem to have little to do with each other even though they operate out of opposite ends of Panasonic's giant office complex in Secaucus, New Jersey. The Panafax name ends up replacing the Panasonic brand name, except when the Panafax division sells ink jets through retail channels — on these occasions, they revert to the Panasonic name instead. It's a bit confusing, but that's the way it is!

Most of Pitney Bowes'ss plain paper faxes are made by Matsushita, though none correspond to products sold under the Panafax or Panasonic brand names.

# *Pitney Bowes*

*Pitney Bowes Inc.*
*Facsimile Systems Division*
*3191 Broadbridge Avenue*
*Stratford, CT 06497–2559*
*Tel: 203 381 7000*

Pitney Bowes, the mailing equipment giant, has made a major effort in the plain paper fax market, and it has had significant success (it does not supply thermal paper models). Pitney Bowes targets quite large users of fax equipment: it does not go out of its way to chase single machine sales. All of its sales are direct — there are no Pitney Bowes dealers.

Pitney Bowes does not manufacture any of its fax machines — they are all made by Matsushita and Mita. The Matsushita models, which are the older ones, are built entirely to Pitney Bowes'ss specifications — they do not correspond to models sold under Matsushita's Panasonic or Panafax brand names. The Mita-made models do bear more than a passing resemblance to equivalent models sold under the Mita brand name, but there are differences.

The enhancements Pitney Bowes makes when it buys in faxes to sell under its own name fall into three broad categories. First, there may be a different "user interface" — in other words, there may be modifications to the control panel and to the way in which you interact with the machine. Second, there may be a few additional features added (for example, one Pitney Bowes model has a quick-scan feature, which the equivalent Mita does not).

Third, there may be proprietary protocols to increase the speed of the handshake when two Pitney Bowes machines communicate and, hence, cut down on overall transmission time. Much of Pitney Bowes's sales pitch relates to the substantial phone bill savings that can be made by establishing corporate fax networks designed to shorten transmission times as much as possible. (That's fair enough, but it also raises the question of how much internal company traffic between different locations should go by fax, rather than e-mail.)

There is no doubt, therefore, that Pitney Bowes does add value to the machines it sells. It also offers exemplary support, which includes the most ambitious remote diagnostics program in the fax industry.

But, you may be wondering, what does all this cost? If you look at Pitney Bowes's list prices for fax machines, you'll find that they are way out of sight. The difference can be well over

$1,000 on a single machine. Even allowing for the usual Pitney Bowes enhancements, the gap is huge — added to which, in this case, the Pitney Bowes version comes with a lot less standard memory than you get on the Mita, so not all the differences do count as enhancements.

Pitney Bowes's response is that its list prices for outright purchase are not a fair indication of the terms on which it does business. In practice, the company tries to place as many of its machines as possible on rental contracts. Pitney Bowes does not make rental price lists available, arguing that each deal is priced individually — I imagine, however, that there must be some set basis on which it prepares quotes for smaller orders.

Rentals form the cornerstone of Pitney Bowes's highly profitable mailroom business — the idea is to get people to sign up for cash-generating rental agreements, covering equipment, supplies, and service, that are renewed from one period to another with minimum fuss.

In the mailing world, Pitney Bowes has been helped by the fact that one key piece of equipment — the postage meter itself — can, according to archaic postal regulations, only be rented and may not be sold outright. No such imperative exists in the fax market to get a rental culture going, but Pitney Bowes seems nonetheless to have been very successful in persuading its customers to rent rather than buy.

The benefit of renting is that it is, theoretically, more flexible. How much more is debatable: Pitney Bowes would not show me a rental contract, again saying that all contracts were individually negotiable, but it assured me that customers could change machines during the course of a rental agreement with no penalties and without being forced to extend their commitment. When pressed, they told me that this includes downgrading or reducing the number of machines. Buyers would be well advised to carefully read the small print of any rental agreement, and satisfy themselves that the terms are, in reality, as flexible as is verbally represented. The other benefit of rentals is that one payment covers you not only for the machine itself, but also for supplies and service.

Against this is the argument that renting from Pitney Bowes is likely, over time, to work out to be more expensive than purchasing discounted equipment from dealer brands and then paying for service only when you need it. This is especially so as fax machines usually require minimal service — they are not like copiers which require frequent preventive maintenance in order to give their best (evidenced by the fact that even Pitney Bowes's rental contracts do not include preventive service visits).

Pitney Bowes disagrees with this view, arguing that fax machines are so critical in corporate life that absolutely nothing should be done to compromise service standards. The company points out that its diagnostics center receives 40,000 calls a month from people with potential problems on their machines, evidence that corporate users really do require a high level of support.

In conclusion, the case against Pitney Bowes as a fax supplier is that while it enhances the machines it sells in order to make them as good and productive as possible, it then markets them at a premium which exaggerates the value it adds to the equipment. And by placing too much emphasis on the importance of intensive service, it manages to charge high prices for support which, while excellent, is not always necessary. Evidence that Pitney Bowes is a premium supplier is its noticeable weakness in the government sector — where buyers tend to go for the lowest bid, rather than agreeing to pay higher prices because of additional perceived value.

The case for Pitney Bowes, however, is that it offers one-stop shopping and excellent support for large companies with multiple locations that want to negotiate a single contract for their fax machines nationwide. While Pitney Bowes is not the only company to offer this, it is an obvious vendor to consider if this is what you need. And while smaller and medium size companies might be deterred by the cost of doing business with Pitney Bowes, major accounts may have the muscle to command pretty favorable terms and benefit from what the company has to offer.

## *Ricoh*

*Ricoh Corporation*
*5 Dedrick Place*
*West Caldwell, NJ 07006*
*Tel: 201 882 2000*

Ricoh is a strong player in plain paper fax; it also has some slightly pricey thermal models in its range. The company is strongest at the higher end of the laser market — the greater your fax traffic, the more likely you are to be impressed with what Ricoh has to offer. For example, all of Ricoh's laser faxes print from memory at 10 pages per minute (most plain paper faxes print at four pages per minute or less). Ricoh also sells Group 4 models.

Late in 1993, Ricoh did introduce its first sub-$1,000 plain paper fax — an ink jet — though this isn't the most tempting machine in its class (it's based on a Canon engine — not the same one that Canon uses on its own latest equipment, but the older and slower one that Canon is moving way from). Ricoh tried to get that machine into retail channels, but not with much success. There is a bit of a gap between the ink jet and where the company's laser range starts — Ricoh could use a mid-market laser product (and it's possible, indeed, that one will emerge during the shelf-life of this book).

Most Ricoh fax sales are through dealers, though the company does have some direct sales offices in some major markets — mainly going after major account business. The warranty is the usual 90 days that's all too common in this market. Some Ricoh models are also relabeled by Gestetner (in which Ricoh has a major stake), Omnifax, Savin, and Lanier.

## Samsung

*Samsung Electronics America, Inc.*
*105 Challenger Road*
*Ridgefield Park, NJ 07660*
*Tel: 201 229 4000*

Samsung, the South Korean electronics giant, is a relative newcomer to the US fax market, and is very new to the plain paper sector — which helps explain its very low profile. It makes a full line of very affordable LED machines, but it's only selling one of these under its own brand name — and its dealer network is spread pretty thin. It also makes a range of thermal models which are sold through retail channels.

Most of Samsung's plain paper fax business is going through relabelers. Dex, the fax distributor listed separately in these Vendor Profiles, sells the full range under its own colors, and the entry-level LED is also relabeled by AT&T. One entry-level Muratec thermal machine is made by Samsung, and I believe that Smith Corona's new line of thermal faxes is also Samsung-manufactured.

## Sanyo

*Sanyo Business Systems Corporation*
*51 Joseph Street*
*Moonachie, NJ 07074*
*Tel: 201 440 9300*

Sanyo is not a particularly strong player in the fax market (nor, for that matter, in any area of business equipment). However, it seems to be making some progress. It is currently selling one model under its own brand name through its sparse dealer network, but — more significantly — it has also started selling this and two other units to Lanier for relabeling. The likelihood is that most Sanyo plain paper fax sales in the US in 1994 will be through Lanier. In addition, Sanyo sells some budget thermal models.

## Savin

*Savin Corporation*
*9 West Broad Street*
*Stamford, CT 06904–2270*
*Tel: 203 967 5000*

Founded in 1959, Savin is a major distributor of relabeled office equipment, selling entirely through dealers and concentrating on Ricoh-manufactured equipment. It went into Chapter 11 in summer 1992, following a difficult period that stretches back to its ill-conceived attempt in the mid-eighties to become a copier manufacturer rather than a mere distributor. This had been followed by an equally misguided attempt several years later to become a major force in full-color copiers. Savin emerged from bankruptcy protection late in 1993 following a settlement in which creditors said by goodbye to most of their money and hardly anyone got any cash.

The strategy is now to focus entirely on the company's core business of selling relabeled black-and-white copiers as well as fax machines. Savin's dealers have, for the most part, stayed loyal — the company has a strong dealer network, which is its major asset, though this focuses a lot more on the copier side of the business than on faxes.

Savin faxes are identical to the equivalent machines sold under the Ricoh brand name. In general, Savin fax dealers are the same ones that sell its copiers.

## Sharp

*Sharp Electronics Corporation*
*Sharp Plaza*
*Mahwah, NJ 07430–2135*
*Tel: 201 529 8200*

Sharp is a leading manufacturer of faxes. It has a full range of low-cost thermal models, it sells some excellent ink jets (based on Hewlett-Packard print engines), and it has a competitively priced laser range. The laser line-up was enhanced in 1993 by the introduction of a new print engine that's faster than the old one, easier to keep replenished with supplies, and less expensive to run (consumables work out at a very low two cents per page). This engine is now used on all the Sharp laser models.

Sharp faxes whose model numbers begin with the letters "FO" are generally sold through traditional office equipment dealers, while models beginning with "UX" go through retail channels. Sharp's thermal paper and ink jet faxes come in both FO and UX versions — the UX ones are usually the better values. At press-time, Sharp's laser models only came in FO versions — however, a new entry-level model likely to sell for around $999 was expected soon after this book was published and this is likely to come in both FO and UX versions.

Sharp follows the usual pattern in this industry of only giving a 90-day warranty on its fax machines.

## Smith Corona

*Smith Corona Corporation*
*320 W. Commercial Avenue*
*Moonachie, NJ 07074*
*Tel: 800 225 0867*

Smith Corona — often known as SCM (the "M" stands for "Machines") — is best known for its low-cost typewriter line, but has recently made a late debut in the fax market. It is only selling thermal machines, which I believe are actually manufactured by Samsung.

## Swintec

*Swintec Corporation*
*320 W. Commercial Avenue*
*Moonachie, NJ 07074*
*Tel: 800 225 0867*

Swintec is an office equipment distributor, mainly operating through traditional office machines dealers. It's best known in the typewriter market, where it has a leading position selling fairly heavy-duty equipment (helped, in part, by the withdrawal of some of its competitors).

In the fax market, it sells some thermal paper models, and it has recently started selling a relabeled Mita plain paper model. I'm not sure who actually makes the thermal models — Swintec refuses to talk about these things — but they don't correspond to anything sold under other brand names.

# Toshiba

*Toshiba America Information Systems, Inc.*
*Electronic Imaging Division*
*9740 Irvine Boulevard*
*PO Box 19724*
*Irvine, CA 92713–9724*
*Tel: 714 583 3000*

Toshiba sells thermal fax machines and also plain paper models covering three of the four printing technologies: thermal transfer, LED, and laser. Toshiba's thermal transfer print engines are bought in from an unidentified source, though its laser and LED engines are its own.

Toshiba — which is something of a secondary force in fax — sells through dealers. Some models are also relabeled by Dex, Lanier, and Monroe.

# Xerox

*Xerox Corporation*
*Xerox Square — 05B*
*Rochester, NY 14644*
*Tel: 800 832 6979*

Xerox is now an all-plain paper fax vendor: it no longer sells thermal paper fax machines. It is also the only vendor that continues to use thermal transfer plain paper technology in the middle and upper levels of the fax market. At press-time, it had one laser model, a modified version of a unit made by TEC (Tokyo Electric Corporation, a Toshiba subsidiary). The least expensive Xerox plain paper fax — one of its thermal transfer models — is a relabeled Muratec.

Xerox — which likes to call faxes "telecopiers" — mostly sells fax machines through its direct sales force and its independent agents (self-employed people and small businesses that solicit orders on behalf of Xerox, but do not buy and resell the machines). However, it also has some fax dealers — late in 1992, the company reversed an earlier decision to pull out of the fax dealer market.

An ink jet fax product was likely to be launched soon after this book was published — this will be a combined printer/fax product that will be pitched at the entry-level multifunctional market and will be sold mainly through the retail channel. ✍

# Chapter 7

# Color Printers

# Color Printers

This chapter discusses computer printers that deliver full-color output and that cost below $10,000 (the cheapest models discussed can be bought for around $500–$600).

I'm focusing on the three technology types that make the most sense for offices wanting to introduce color into mainstream business documents: ink jet, thermal wax transfer, and laser (don't worry if you don't understand the differences, as all will be explained shortly). I'll also offer pointers on some of the other more specialized color technologies, such as dye sublimation.

Keep in mind that some color copiers can also be interfaced with PCs so that they double up as color printers. Most of these are very expensive devices, costing tens of thousands of dollars, but Canon has one color copier that costs a little over $8,000 including the PC interface. I won't be talking about the combo copier/printer option in this chapter, but you can read all about it in the chapter on color copiers that follows.

## Introducing Color Printers

Color printers have been around for a while, but have not so far become mainstream business tools. This could be about to change, however, since a number of factors are making more people more interested in color than ever before. Trends working in color's favor include:

✔ Improvements in monochrome printing technology have already opened users' eyes to endless font and style options. Once you have put plain vanilla, typewriter-style printing behind you, color is a logical progression.

✔ The Windows software environment is heavily geared around working with color screens, even if users aren't actually producing color documents. This has meant that computer users have become more color-conscious, and some have become frustrated at the gap between the colorful images they are able to create on-screen and the dull ones they are able to print out on paper.

✔ Computer software is becoming easier to use, and PC users are becoming more experienced — both these factors lead to a more ambitious use of graphics in business documents.

### What's been holding it back?

These trends have been evident for some time, yet many people are still holding back from buying their first color printer. According to most industry estimates, less than five percent of offices have them.

Buyers have been put off by the traditionally high prices on the machines that deliver good results, and by iffy output and slow speeds on those that seem most affordable. In addition, color printers have not generally been very suitable for doubling up as regular printers for monochrome work. For example, some require special paper, most are slow, and not all are particularly good at printing black-and-white text. In other words, to justify one of these machines, you often need to have quite a large amount of niche color work.

To some extent, these popular perceptions do not take full account of changes in the market during the past 18 months, particularly at the low end — more on this shortly. Still, the perceptions linger on.

### Confusion reigns

In addition, there is widespread confusion among users about the technology. There are six different mainstream color printing methods, most of them unfamiliar to the novice buyer, as well as other more specialized ones. What's more, laser color printers — which intuitively seem the most obvious bet to the person who is happily using black-and-white lasers — are not usually an option because they all have price tags of over $7,500. The fact that most buyers feel they don't really have a grip on what their color options are is a constant disincentive to buying a machine — especially when the need is not exactly hypercritical.

### Signs of life

The good news is that the past 18 months have seen a lot of activity, especially at the lower end of the market. New, affordable machines are hitting the streets which are able to produce very good color print quality; some can also produce near-laser quality in black-and-white, making them serious contenders to be your one-and-only printer. Running costs, which have been another color gripe, have also shown signs of falling.

The high end is also becoming less forbidding: color laser prices, though still very high, are a little less astronomical than they were at the start of 1994 — and should continue to fall during the shelf-life of this book. While it would be premature to say that the color printer market is really taking off, it is certainly moving.

# Color Basics

Before I introduce you to the different color printing technologies and discuss their pros and cons, let's focus briefly on some of the main issues that crop up in any discussion of color printers. Keep in mind, incidentally, that I will not be spending much time in this chapter explaining printer terms and concepts that are not color-specific, but that apply equally to regular black-and-white models.

So if you have very little technical grasp of printers — for example, if you have little understanding about what's meant by the word "PostScript" — you may want to read Chapter 3 which, as well as focusing on black-and-white printers, serves as a general printer primer. That said, I will be reminding you about a few printer basics in this chapter, so what follows should be reasonably easy to follow if you consider yourself moderately printer-proficient.

### The colors themselves
All the print technologies I'll be talking about involve mixing three or four basic colors to create millions of color combinations. You'll often hear a three-color palette abbreviated to "CYM," standing for cyan, yellow, and magenta. To form a composite black, CYM printers combine the three primary colors.

However, most printers now have a separate, true black (designated as "K" in printer lingo). This four-color palette is referred to as "CYMK." The colors themselves come in the form of different substances — such as ink, ribbons, and toner — depending on the print technology.

Keep in mind that computer monitors use a different red/green/blue (RGB) palette to mix their colors. To reconcile the two color sets, some printers include color-matching software that lets users specify which monitor they have, enabling the printer to adjust the output to match the monitor.

In addition, there is a whole sub-industry devoted to third-party software and hardware tools designed to match and calibrate color to satisfy the pickiest people. However, all of this is only a factor if you are dealing in very precise shades. It might be a concern if you are in the graphics arts, publishing, or design business, for example, but it's not something that mainstream business users need generally lose sleep about.

### Output quality

For most of the color technologies, print quality is partly a function of resolution — just as it is in the black-and-white market. Resolution is measured by the numbers of columns and rows of dots per square inch (dpi) that make up an image.

Today, most color printers still offer 300 x 300 dpi resolution measured on vertical and horizontal axes (usually referred to simply as "300dpi"). A few offer 360dpi, but this makes little difference in practice.

However, a growing number now offer at least partial 600dpi output. In theory, 600dpi should make quite a big difference, but in the color market you tend only to get a restricted version with 600 rows of dots on one axis, but still only 300 on the other. This is better than nothing — but it's not the real thing! Xerox's color laser printer offers 1,200 x 300 dpi.

Watch out for printers that are only able to print in resolutions higher than 300dpi in black-and-white and not in color. Keep in mind also that on less expensive models, high resolution printing tends to slow down color output significantly.

Output quality is also determined by how vividly colors are printed, and how crisp black appears (particularly in small type sizes). Printers with separate black (i.e., the CYMK models) typically generate richer-looking black text than printers that combine the CYM colors to create composite black. Beyond this, color quality is a function of the printing technologies and their implementation by different vendors — I'll be comparing the different types shortly.

### Performance — mind your p's and m's

Generally, a printer's speed is measured by the number of pages a device can output per minute — "ppm" stands for "pages per minute." However, in the case of color printers, the figure quoted is often "minutes per page" (or "mpp") — that's because some color printers can take several minutes to print just one page. Be careful about this — it's very easy to mistake "mpp" for "ppm" when skimming printer specifications, but those m's and p's make a big difference!

With some color printing technologies, vendors talk in terms of characters per second (cps). This tends to be a slightly meaningless measure when you're talking about printing graphics or large-size text (it is usually based on the assumption of a type size that allows 10 characters to the inch in a "typewriter-style" typeface).

Speeds quoted by printer vendors are generally for color prints, except where noted to the contrary. Black-and-white prints generally come out of the machine quite a bit faster. Keep in mind that actual speeds are likely to depend on the image being printed, the computer being used, and/or the print mode selected (some printers give you the option of producing slightly less good output at faster speeds).

At the time of this writing, the fastest sub-$10,000 color printer churned out full-color pages at the rate of about three a minute, and black-and-white ones at 12 per minute. Many machines are a great deal slower than that, however.

### Media

Some color printers require special paper which neither looks nor feels like normal copier or laser printer paper — plain paper isn't even an option. Other machines can technically print on regular plain paper, but the manufacturers encourage you to use a special, very smooth variety in order to get best results. A minority of machines can produce excellent results on just about any type of paper you put through them.

Special color paper adds to the printer's running costs and can be less convenient. Most color printers are also able to print onto transparent film for overhead projector presentations.

# Color Printing Technologies Introduced

Having introduced you to some basic issues that crop up in any review of color printers, let's now look at the six main types of printing technology. Each has its pros and cons — before you even begin to think about which specific model or brand to consider, it's essential to decide which technology is most appropriate for the type of work you do. I'll start with the most basic technology, and then work my way up the ladder of sophistication....

### (1) Dot matrix

This is the oldest office color printing technology, the least expensive, and by far the least desirable. Dot matrix printers — often referred to simply as "matrix printers" — fall in a category known as "impact printers," which means that they create an image by having a printhead strike a ribbon.

The printhead is a matrix of needles: depending on which character is being printed, a different combination of needles is deployed. The more needles — i.e., dots — in the matrix, the better the print quality. Most people choose 9-pin or 24-pin matrix printers. Color matrix printers include a multicolor ribbon and special software drivers to decode the color commands from the software being used on the PC.

Color-capable matrix printers are inexpensive, mostly costing a few hundred dollars, but there's evidence that most people who buy them only use them for black-and-white print jobs in practice. The color quality isn't particularly good, and the color print speeds are very slow — you'll often have to wait four minutes, or more, per page. On the other hand, you can print onto regular paper.

Dot matrix printers in general are a declining breed. The market has been shot to bits by the new generation of inexpensive ink jet printers. The only plus point of matrix machines is their ability to print onto multi-part (i.e., carbon) sets.

I do not recommend that anyone looking for a color printer consider the matrix option, unless they have a very specific reason for needing one, and I won't be giving it much attention in this chapter. If you do want to pursue the option on your own, the three most obvious brands to consider are Epson, Oki, and Panasonic.

### (2) Thermal ink jets (a.k.a. liquid ink jets)

This is the fastest-growing part of the color printer market. If you are looking for a color printer to produce business documents that mix black-and-white text with colored headlines and graphics, the chances are that an ink jet is going to be your best bet. In fact, if you want high-quality output and want to keep your total expenditure below $2,500, there isn't a great deal else to consider.

Ink jets are, above all, flexible. No other type of affordable printer is as suitable for meeting both your monochrome and color needs. In fact, a lot of people who buy color-capable ink jets use them more for black-and-white printing than for color. If you want the absolute finest color quality money can buy, and if you have the volume of work to justify getting a printer more or less only for your color output, then thermal ink jet may not be your best bet. But if you're looking for a more general-purpose sort of printer that can handle color, then ink jet has a heck of a lot going for it.

Thermal ink jet technology works through a heat vaporization process. Ink is supplied in self-contained, replaceable cartridges: the ink is heated to a vaporization temperature, causing a vapor bubble to expand, and it is then forced out through nozzles.

Thermal ink jets offer quiet operation and moderately fast — by color standards — print speeds. Some older models required special paper, but most newer machines work reasonably well with regular plain paper. However, even the newest machines generally work best with paper that has a particularly smooth finish. On paper with a more absorbent surface, there can still be a slight tendency for the ink to run as it hits the paper (a bit like when you use a fountain pen on certain types of writing paper) and the output is generally less crisp.

Color ink jet prices generally begin at around $550 (unless you're looking at a discontinued model that's priced to sell) and the best amount for business users to go shopping with is something between $1,500 and $2,250 — that can buy you a really nice color printer, as I'll be showing later. Running costs are reasonable by color standards, unless you're printing pages with a very dense color image area in which case they usually become quite expensive (I'll be focusing on running costs later in this chapter).

The big two in this market are Hewlett-Packard and Canon. Other names include Apple (which sells relabeled Canons) and Epson (a promising newcomer to this market). There is another form of ink jet printing — discussed below — but because thermal ink jets are much more common, the term "ink jet" used on its own usually refers to this type unless there is any indication to the contrary.

### (3) Solid ink jets

Don't confuse the thermal ink jets discussed above with "solid" ink jet models. These are more fancy machines; they are also quite a lot more expensive and, largely for that reason, they are not really suitable for doubling up as regular computer printers.

This technology relies on a solid block, or "crayon," of ink that is melted in a slot and dropped onto the paper. The ink resolidifies immediately in a process designed to maintain its clarity.

Because very little ink soaks into the paper, solid ink jets can deliver more brilliant colors than regular liquid ink jets. Overall, I would rate typical print quality as excellent.

In addition, solid ink jets aren't fussy about what type of plain paper they print onto — they generally work fine with regular copier and laser printer paper. Note that the solid ink tends to create a slightly embossed feel, which you may or may not consider an advantage. One benefit of the technology is that the output doesn't smudge if it gets wet.

On the other hand, this technology is not generally recommended for transparencies — the solid ink diffuses the passage of light through the transparency, giving the projections a generally inferior appearance. Some models attempt to get around this problem, but anyone who does a lot of color printing on transparencies is probably better off with one of the other technologies.

Solid ink jet printers list for between $5,000 and $10,000. Running costs are usually higher than those of regular ink jets, but not out of sight. There aren't that many models available. Tektronix and Dataproducts are the two most obvious vendors to consider if you're interested. Brother also has a model, but does little to promote it.

You may sometimes hear solid ink jets referred to as "phase change" printers, a term that refers to the melting/resolidifying process — there's no special significance to this, and the term is synonymous with "solid ink jet."

### (4) Thermal wax transfer

This is the main rival to ink jets in the battle to popularize color printing. With thermal wax transfer printing — often referred to as "thermal wax" or "thermal transfer" printing for short — heat fuses colored wax from film onto paper. The printing is a one-color-at-a-time process, meaning that with the standard CYM or CYMK color mix, the paper goes through the printer three or four times. Thermal transfer printers create images at 200dpi to 300dpi. Finished documents look fairly glossy, and the colors are vivid.

Though an increasing number of new thermal wax transfer printers have plain paper capabilities, this technology has traditionally required special paper and transparency media. The special paper tends to have a slightly flimsy feel to it, making it less than ideal if you want to combine pages with regular monochrome lasered pages in a bound document. Even the machines which are able to print onto plain paper tend to need premium quality plain paper — something better than what you probably use in your copier or monochrome laser printer.

Thermal transfer technology is particularly well suited for business-presentation graphics. For example, you can get truly excellent results on transparencies. If this is your main application, this is probably the best technology for you. Keep in mind, though, that creases or scratches in the media may cause the wax to flake or peel off the page.

An unusual characteristic of thermal wax transfer printing is that the per page consumables costs are fixed regardless of the size of the image you're printing — that is not the case with most other color printing technologies. I'll be talking more about running costs later, but for now keep in mind that a thermal wax transfer page can be a lot more expensive to produce than an ink jet page if the color image area is quite small, but it can be cheaper if you need to print out full-page color pictures.

List prices are usually in the $3,000–$8,000 bracket. However, one vendor — Fargo — has caused a stir in printer circles by introducing a model for under $1,000. The two most prominent mainstream vendors in this market are Tektronix and QMS, both of whom sell excellent machines.

### (5) Dye sublimation (a.k.a. dye thermal)

If you want a color printer that produces near-photographic quality, this is the type for you. Dye sublimation printing (erroneously referred to in one newsstand computer magazine as "dye subliminal" printing!) uses heating elements to change solid dyes on ribbons into a gas. The gaseous, transparent dye diffuses into the chemical coating of a special type of paper, where it reverts to solid form.

Note that some people call these machines "dye thermal" or "dye diffusion" printers, and others refer to them as "dye sub" printers for short. The thing to keep in mind is that any printer with the word "dye" in it is one of these.

Because colors can be very closely matched to the original image, this technology is particularly useful in the advertising and commercial printing markets. And the glossiness of the prints can make them look suitably snazzy for presentation purposes. You can also get superb results on transparencies.

But these machines are definitely not aimed at offices wanting a printer to introduce some color into general-purpose business documents. For example, running costs are out of sight, as I'll show later. And the same qualities that create these dazzling photo-like prints also result in slight fuzziness when you're printing text, especially in small sizes. Detailed line work also lacks a certain sharpness.

Some dye sublimation printers can take up to five minutes

to create a color page. Machine prices mostly range from about $3,000 to $20,000, with the highest concentration between $6,000 and $10,000.

Because of their niche nature, I won't be focusing much on these machines in this chapter. However, the vendors to consider if you're interested include Kodak, Mitsubishi, RasterOps, Sharp, SuperMac, and Tektronix. In addition, Fargo offers a very cheap dye thermal option on its low-cost thermal transfer printer referred to above.

### (6) Laser color printers

If all color printers cost the same, most of us would probably choose a laser. Print quality can be very good and print speeds can be quite fast. Unfortunately, these machines are very expensive — so much so that they will simply not be an option for most readers of this book. When QMS announced a $12,500 color laser printer in June 1993, it was considered a breakthrough price — color lasers have traditionally cost $20,000–$50,000. More recently, color lasers (including those sold by QMS) have begun to fall in price — though don't expect to pay very much less than $8,000.

As with monochrome machines, color laser printers work by having a light source etch an image on a photosensitive drum which then attracts toner; the toner is transferred to paper, heated, and fused, and an image is created. The difference is that with monochrome lasers, the process is completed with one pass through the machine, but with color models the imaging takes place a total of four times — one for each of the CYMK colors.

The problem facing color laser vendors is that in their efforts to make color lasers more affordable, they are having to restrict capabilities. At press-time, the fastest machine costing under $10,000 could make color prints at the rate of three pages a minute — not bad, but hardly a landmark speed.

It is sometimes hard to see what benefits color laser printers have to justify the size of the premium over the latest ink jets costing around a quarter of the price or less. The notion that "lasers-are-best" has been ingrained deep in American corporate consciousness in recent years — because of the excellence of the HP-led monochrome LaserJet tradition — but it could be that this is not going to be the technology of choice for color.

Still, the range of color lasers is increasing. Just before this book was published, Xerox introduced a model setting a new record low list price of about $8,500. QMS also cut its prices, and increased its range. And the first models from Hewlett-Packard, Apple, and others were expected before long. Color lasers will remain premium items, but will become more common during the next couple of years.

# Running Costs

Running cost comparisons can be quite tricky to make in the color printer market. In the monochrome market, there's a consensus among vendors that quoted running cost figures are based on an assumption of the image area covering five percent of a page (which is more than it sounds, when you think about the white space in the middle of a letter like an "e" or an "o"). Although that five percent figure may or may not be an accurate representation of what occurs in practice, it does provide a constant standard against which you can make like-for-like comparisons between different monochrome machines.

### Color variables
In the color market, however, numerous variables enter into a cost per page analysis. For example, with an ink jet printer, the cost of a printed page depends not only on the size of the image area, but on the color mix and the type of image being printed.

With thermal wax machines, the running cost is the same regardless of image size — the way in which the machine uses wax color ribbons means that it costs the same to print a full-page color image as it does to print a page with only five percent coverage. That makes for easy running cost forecasts, but it makes it hard to come up with cost comparisons with ink jets. In addition, the special paper required, or preferred, by some machines is another thing you have to factor in.

### Some generalized comparisons
Having said all of the above, it is possible to make some generalized comparisons. Typically, a thermal wax printer is likely to cost you in the region of 55–65 cents per page, regardless of what you're printing. Traditionally, ink jet printers have been cheaper to run in applications requiring less than 35 percent coverage.

So if you are producing documents containing black-and-white text, with color only added to highlight headlines and some graphics, an ink jet printer is going to be cheaper to run. However, if much more than a third of the page is actually covered by color, you'll probably find that you're paying as much as you would with a thermal wax transfer machine (or more).

At least, that applies to most ink jets. But some newer models have reduced running costs. For example, the Hewlett-Packard 1200C has managed to reduce ink jet running costs substantially, without making any compromise on quality. With this machine, running costs are likely to be cheaper than on a thermal wax transfer machine regardless of what you're printing. For example, at 30 percent coverage, running costs on the HP are less than a third of those of a typical wax transfer machine; at 100 percent coverage, the HP works out to about about 10 cents less per page. This comparison does not take into account the special paper required on many thermal wax machines, which typically adds around 7–8 cents to the per page cost.

### What about the other technologies?

I've focused above on ink jet versus thermal wax transfer running costs, because those are the two technologies that most readers are likely to choose between. Here's a steer on what to expect with the other technologies.

Matrix running costs are cheapest of all — but so they should be, considering the poor results. Solid ink jets are a little more expensive to run than regular liquid ink jets. Dye thermal printers are hyper-expensive to run — expect to pay several dollars for every print you make. The photographic results can justify the cost if you have the right application, but this type of printer clearly isn't an economical contender if you're looking for a general-purpose color machine.

Color laser running costs are highly variable, depending on what you're printing, but they tend to be roughly in the same ballpark as those of color ink jets, or a bit higher — depending on which models and print jobs you're comparing. What rules out color lasers for most offices is not the cost of running them, but the cost of buying them in the first place.

# More About Features

Next a few words on features to look for — but because none of these are color-specific, I won't go into a lot of detail.

### PostScript tips

PostScript is what's known as a "page description language" — it is software that resides within the printer that governs the way in which the machine handles instructions from the computer. If you want to read more about it, there's a detailed discussion in Chapter 3. For now, I'll just remind you about when you do and don't need it.

If you use serious desktop publishing programs (PageMaker, Quark, etc.), you should definitely get a PostScript printer. The same applies if you use upscale graphics programs, such as Illustrator and Freehand.

If, however, you only use word processing programs — such as Microsoft Word or WordPerfect — you probably don't need a PostScript printer (a PostScript printer will be able to work with these programs, but it isn't necessary or even particularly advantageous). The same applies if you use spreadsheet programs, or if you use one of the multifunction programs such as Microsoft Works or ClarisWorks.

If you are in the market for a PostScript printer, you should ideally get one with Adobe PostScript Level 2 — this has a number of detailed enhancements over Level 1, some of which concern color in particular. A few printers do not use the original Adobe PostScript, but instead use a PostScript-compatible print language developed by third parties. The chances are that these will work fine with major software packages, but you may be increasing the risk of incompatibility bugs.

Once you get beyond the $3,000 price level, you'll generally find that just about any color printer is a PostScript machine anyway. For example, all solid ink jet models and most thermal wax transfer ones are PostScript devices. It's only in the low end of the color market — and especially in the thermal ink jet arena — that you find yourself with a choice.

### Memory and processors

The least expensive color printers have virtually no memory to speak of — they are passive devices that let the sending computer do most of the work. However, the more desirable color printers have both memory of their own and powerful processors that enable the printer to handle large and complex print jobs with more alacrity. If a printer's memory is quoted in kilobytes, abbreviated to "K," as opposed to megabytes, abbreviated to "MB," it means that it hardly has any memory.

The relationship and role of memory and processors is discussed in Chapter 3 and I am not going to dwell much on it here, save to say that more memory and powerful processors enhance a printer's speed and are essential for more ambitious types of work. For example, if you're getting a PostScript color printer, you need quite a lot of memory in your printer — 4MB–6MB or more — and you should ideally have a processor using something known as "RISC" technology.

### Paper handling

Some color printers are able to output onto 11" x 17" paper, though others can only manage sizes up to letter and legal. If 11" x 17" paper is important to you, check out whether your machine can print on that size with "bleed" — this means that the color goes right up to the edge on all four sides.

The size of the paper supply is also worth looking at — some machines have trays that can hold around 200 sheets, but others take quite a lot less — this may not matter if you plan to use the machine only for specialized color output (because your volumes will probably be lower), but it's less than ideal if you want to use it as a more general-purpose office printer.

### Fonts

Most color printers come with a number of built-in (or "resident") fonts (i.e., typefaces). Keep in mind that fonts that are supplied with the printer on floppy disks, as opposed to being built into the machine, are not particularly significant — they have no benefit over any disk-based fonts you buy in one of those inexpensive font collections to load into your computer. Hence the range of disk fonts that are supplied with a printer is really not a big deal — fonts on disk are not a feature of the printer itself (even though printer vendors tend to describe them as though they were), but are an added value that the vendors throw in as an extra.

Beware that some vendors do not make it very clear in their literature and advertising whether the fonts they say come with a printer are resident or supplied on disks. Either way, any color printer can print any font you keep in your computer — the ability to handle certain typefaces is not, therefore, something that distinguishes one model from another.

The advantage of printer-resident fonts is that they may help increase actual print speeds, compared with fonts that come on disks and that reside in the computer. The problem, however, can be matching the fonts you work with on-screen to those that live in the printer. There is a full discussion of this somewhat tricky subject in Chapter 3 — I won't get drawn into it further here, except to say that, in my opinion, the number of resident fonts is not something that should be a major factor in choosing a color printer.

### Interfaces and network connectivity

Almost all color printers come with both parallel and serial interfaces as standard; this ensures that they are compatible with all DOS/Windows PCs. In addition, all PostScript color printers

— and a few others — can work with Apple printers using an AppleTalk interface.

A growing number of color printers can be fitted with network interface cards that allow you to connect them directly to Ethernet and Token Ring networks without the need to go through a special PC performing the role of print server. Mac users can usually connect their printer to an AppleTalk network without the need for additional upgrades.

# Buying a Color Printer

Because color printers have not yet taken off in a big way, they can be harder to buy than their monochrome siblings. A lot of places you can turn to for black-and-white printers simply do not sell color models or only carry one or two low-end ones costing less than $600. Be prepared, therefore, to do a bit of calling around to locate a computer dealer that sells a fuller range of products.

Another thing to keep in mind is that you won't have many options when it comes to where to buy supplies. You can't walk into an office supply warehouse and buy the consumables required for most color printers, and you'll probably end up buying them from the dealer that sells you the machine.

In time, color printers will become easier to buy and you'll have more choice about where to shop. Then, there should also be more downward pressure on prices. Right now, however, this market is where the monochrome laser market was about eight years ago — it is, as us office equipment scribes like to say, not yet "mature."

# Color Printer Vendor Profiles

Next, brief comments on some of the companies that are most prominent in the section of the color market that this chapter is focusing on.

## Apple

*Apple Computer Inc.*
*20525 Mariani Avenue*
*Cupertino, CA 95014*
*Tel: 800 446 3000*
Apple was late coming to the color printer market, entering for the first time in 1993. At press-time, it was only selling a low-end ink jet that is a relabeled and only slightly modified Canon. However, I expect Apple to introduce a color laser printer during the shelf-life of this book.

## Canon

*Canon Computer Systems Inc.*
*123 East Paularino Avenue*
*Costa Mesa, CA 92628–5048*
*Tel: 800 848 4123*
Canon is big in ink jets and, together with HP, dominates the sub-$1,000 color printer market. Canon has beefed up its printer support lately, and now offers toll-free phone assistance 11 hours a day, five days a week.

## Dataproducts

*Dataproducts Corporation*
*6200 Canoga Avenue*
*Woodland Hills, CA 91367*
*Tel: 818 887 8000*
Dataproducts is one of the three established vendors of solid ink jet color printers. As you may have gleaned from reading the earlier explanation, this technology is more expensive than the thermal ink jet variety used by vendors such as Hewlett-Packard and Canon, but it works well with just about any type of plain paper and it also produces more vivid colors.

# Epson

*Epson America Inc.*
*23530 Hawthorne Boulevard*
*Torrance, CA 90505*
*Tel: 800 922 8911*

Epson America is part of Seiko Epson, the giant Japanese manufacturer of computers, computer peripherals, and other high-tech products (not to mention watches).

Epson entered the color ink jet market in 1994, with an interesting entry-level product called the Stylus Color. This machine offers the highest resolution of any machine in its class, as well as some of the lowest running costs. Of the companies attempting to challenge the HP/Canon ink jet stranglehold, Epson seems to me to be the most interesting.

# Fargo

*Fargo Electronics Inc.*
*7901 Flying Cloud Drive*
*Eden Prairie, MN 55344*
*Tel: 612 941 9470*

Fargo is a bit of an odd-ball in the color printer market. The company's background is in bar code printers and, until not long ago, it had no presence in any part of the mainstream office printer market. In 1992, however, it decided to get into the color printer business and it introduced a thermal transfer model called the Fargo Primera. A few months later, Fargo sold its bar code printer business, which means it is now a one-product company selling only this somewhat atypical color printer.

What is remarkable about this printer is its price — just $995, which is far less than anything else that uses this technology (the street price is about $675). As you might imagine, the low price was not achieved without sacrificing something in terms of quality or speed.

To broaden the appeal, Fargo has introduced a low-cost option that allows the Primera to double up as a dye thermal printer — remember that this is the printing technology that produces near-photographic results (albeit at very high running costs). This option costs $250 — while the results may not be on a level with the best dedicated dye thermal machines, this does seem a remarkable value.

# Hewlett-Packard

*Hewlett-Packard Company*
*PO Box 58059, MS511L-SJ*
*Santa Clara, CA 95051–8059*
*Tel: 800 752 0900*

Hewlett-Packard (HP) needs little introduction in any discussion of the printer market. The company leads the monochrome laser market (in fact, it defines the industry standard), and it is one of two manufacturers to dominate the monochrome and color ink jet markets. One thing that was still absent from HP's printer range at press-time was a color laser — however, it is probable that such a machine will be announced within a few months of this book being published.

HP's color ink jet market comprises three tiers: the entry-level DeskJet/DeskWriter models; the highly-impressive, mid-market 1200C-series models; and the PaintJet models, which actually don't do much that the 1200C models can't do with the exception of 11" x 17" printing.

# Lexmark

*Lexmark International Inc.*
*740 New Circle Road*
*Lexington, KY 40511*
*Tel: 800 426 2468*

IBM itself pulled out of the printer and typewriter markets over three years ago, selling its business in 1991 to a new venture capital-backed company called Lexmark. The new enterprise purchased not only the assets but also the right to use the IBM brand name on these products; its management is largely ex-IBM, so the whole operation still looks and smells like Big Blue (IBM retains a 10 percent stake).

At press-time, Lexmark was only selling one color printer, an enhanced version of an older Canon ink jet. A more mass-market thermal ink jet, using Lexmark's own engine, was expected to be introduced by late summer 1994.

# QMS

*QMS, Inc.*
*One Magnum Pass*
*PO Box 81250*
*Mobile, AL 36689–1250*
*Tel: 205 633 4300*

QMS is a highly respected name in the printer industry. It tends to focus on upscale and niche products, rather than competing in mass markets. In the color arena, it sells models using laser and thermal transfer technology.

QMS was the first company to introduce color laser printers into the section of the market covered by this book. Its laser printers are based on Hitachi engines, and its thermal transfer models are based on Mitsubishi engines.

All QMS printers use proprietary operating software known as QMS Crown, which significantly enhances actual speed and overall productivity in busy workgroup and network environments. QMS Crown-based products have the most sophisticated internal controllers in the industry — keep this in mind, as these printers can perform better in demanding, heavy-use situations than rival machines which, on the surface, appear to have similar hardware specifications.

## Tektronix

*Tektronix Inc.*
*Wilsonville Industrial Park*
*PO Box 1000*
*Wilsonville, OR 97070–1000*
*Tel: 800 835 6100*

Tektronix is a color printer specialist with a first-class reputation. It sells machines in three of the technology categories: solid ink jet, thermal wax transfer, and dye sublimation.

The thermal transfer models — the Phaser 200/220 series — are arguably the best in their class. The range — which is based on Sharp-manufactured hardware — was enhanced early in 1994. You should definitely take a look at what Tektronix has to offer if, having weighed up your technology options, you have decided in favor of thermal transfer.

Tektronix makes its own solid ink jet printers. It currently has one model, which, while not inexpensive, has a loyal following in the graphics arts and publishing sectors.

## Texas Instruments

*Texas Instruments Inc.*
*Information Technology Group*
*PO Box 202230, ITG-9136*
*Austin, TX 78720*
*Tel: 800 527 3500*

Texas Instruments (TI) is a high-tech company with fingers in pies ranging from semiconductors to defense electronics systems. It has quite a strong presence in the laser printer market. It was in the course of introducing its first color printer — an entry-level thermal ink jet — at about the time this book was being published. TI's machine is a relabeled model that is manufactured by Olivetti (the troubled Italian office equipment giant).

## *Xerox*

*Xerox Corporation*
*PO Box 1600*
*Stamford, CT 06904–1600*
*Tel: 800 979 7355*

Until recently, Xerox's presence in the color printer market was limited to very upscale lasers costing tens of thousands of dollars. However, shortly before this book was published, the company entered the sub-$10,000 color laser market with a new and very aggressively priced high-resolution machine with a street price below $8,000. Xerox was the second vendor to offer a sub-$10,000 laser (QMS was the first). Like QMS, Xerox bases its color laser on an Hitachi engine.

Like all Xerox office products, its color laser comes with the company's excellent "Total Satisfaction Guarantee," promising a replacement machine during the first three years if the customer is not satisfied with performance. ✍

# Chapter 8

# Color
# Copiers

# Color Copiers

Before we get going, let's get straight what I mean by the term "color copier." I'm talking about machines that let you take a full-color original and obtain a full-color copy. This may sound obvious, but some people get confused because there are also copiers with much more limited color capabilities.

The latter only allow you to add "spot color" to black-and-white originals — for example, you could make a copy of a black-and-white document so that a headline comes out highlighted in red. Full-color copiers often share this ability, but the crucial difference is that they can also make same-color copies of colored originals.

It may be that a regular copier with spot-color capabilities is all you need. You won't find them covered in this chapter, and you should turn instead to Chapters 4 and 5 covering regular low-, mid-, and high-volume copiers.

Keep in mind that some full-color copiers can also be used as color printers connected to a PC. Many also allow you to edit and manipulate images, as well as copying them. More on this later.

A number of full-color copiers are also suitable for doing plain-vanilla, black-and-white work, so they could, in theory, be your one-and-only copier (though there are a number of reasons why this doesn't usually work out in practice). Again, I'll be talking about this later in the chapter.

### Who sells these machines?

Full-color copiers are made by the same companies that provide us with regular black-and-white ones. All major copier manufacturers, with the exception of Mita, Sharp, Panasonic, and Océ, were selling some sort of full-color copier in the USA at press-time.

Few of the major copier relabelers have yet entered the color business — you can't buy these machines from companies such as Lanier and Pitney Bowes, for example.

### What I'm assuming

In this chapter, I'm assuming a reasonable working knowledge of general copier features and I won't spend much time explaining or discussing terms that are not color copier-specific. If you consider yourself something of a copier neophyte, and a color machine is your first purchase (unlikely, but possible), you may find it worthwhile looking at Chapters 4/5 for a general tutorial.

# A Reality Check

This chapter may end up disappointing you. Not, I hope, on account of the quality of the writing or research, but because it may contain information that will force you to reconsider your interest in color copiers (depending, of course, on how much you already know about this subject).

Here's the bottom line: these machines are seriously expensive (and this isn't a market where prices are in a free-fall). The models that cost less than $20,000 in list price terms are the ones that are described as "low cost." Most under that price point have significant limitations. For example, nothing under $10,000 can copy onto regular plain paper. That said, the cheapest color copier — which is made by Canon — costs around $4,500, so if you are prepared to put up with limitations, these machines may not be totally out of reach for those on moderate budgets.

If you want a color copier that makes as few compromises as possible, the optimum budget range is $23,000–$50,000 in list price terms. Actually, these prices aren't quite as horrendous as they may seem, because you can often take 30 percent off, and sometimes 35 percent, to get a street price. In other words, buyers with $15,000 should be able to get something quite good.

Most color copiers whose basic list prices start at over $20,000 are capable of being upgraded to double up as color printers connected to a PC or a network. As I'll be showing in this chapter, there is a widespread belief in the industry that the rosiest future for color copiers is as multifunctional devices that connect with computers. The market for expensive stand-alone devices is pretty limited outside the most obvious sectors, such as copy shops. Be warned, however, that the cost of interfacing a color copier to a computer is still very high. More on this later.

If I haven't totally put you off with this reality check, read on. In this chapter, I'll explore what's cooking in the color copier market and introduce you to the vendors. Even if you end up deciding that now is not the right time to buy one of these machines, this chapter should, at the very least, help you make a rational decision to "just say no" (or, maybe, "not yet").

# Permanently Poised for Take-Off?

The color copier market seems to be in a state that I will call "perma-poise" — defined as "permanently poised as though about to take off." Industry analysts are forever speculating whether the moment is about to come, but somehow it never does.

These machines are not new. Japanese manufacturers have been parading them for several years at US trade shows. They tend to be displayed behind roped-off sections, nervously guarded by technicians flown over from Osaka (the color copier market is more advanced in Japan and virtually all the equipment comes from there).

An aura of prototype surrounds them, even when they are supposedly ready for the market. Adding to the atmosphere of unreality is the tendency of vendors to heavily promote features, such as copy editing, that don't get used much in practice even by organizations that do buy these machines.

Though the machines are marveled at by copier reps sent to Las Vegas conventions as rewards for beating their sales targets, few make their way into end users' offices. Several reasons account for this. One is that most color copiers are very expensive, as I pointed out above. Running costs have also been steep — color copies generally cost in the region of 25 cents a copy in consumables and service.

What's more, color copiers have usually not been suitable for doubling up as the copier that handles your everyday black-and-white copying. Some make no pretenses of trying to do that job, but even those that do tend to offer productivity that compares unfavorably with regular copiers costing far less.

### The dearth of originals
Perhaps a more fundamental reason why color copiers have remained in perma-poise is that, when it comes down to it, not a lot of people really feel they need one. Most businesses can think of occasions when it would be neat to make some full-color cop-

ies, but it's another matter to conjure up the volume to justify handing over thirty or forty thousand greenbacks. (Especially when an outing to your local copy shop gets you the use of someone else's machine.)

The plain truth is that there is a shortage of originals — there are simply not enough color documents and pictures floating around corporate America that need to be copied. Ah, you may say, but surely with all these color monitors and color software programs, this is going to change — is it not a fact that Microsoft Windows is introducing color into just about every area of daily office work?

Up to a point, it is. But the only way that you can get a color image out of your color computer is to get a color printer. And if you have a color printer, you may well decide that you don't need a color copier. Just ask the printer for 10 prints instead of one, and you've produced the original plus nine color copies — all without leaving your desk. Whereas printer running costs are much higher than those of copiers in the black-and-white world, the same does not necessarily apply in the color market. It may well be that a color printer is all you need.

As you may already have gleaned from browsing through the previous chapter, color printers are a lot less expensive than color copiers. You can get a pretty decent one for just $1,500–$2,500. And a laser model can now be bought for under $8,000.

True, the color laser printer will be somewhat slower than a color copier (though not all that much slower: an $8,000 laser printer can produce color prints at about three a minute, while a moderately priced laser copier typically churns out prints at about five or six per minute). And, of course, the color printer is restricted to printing images created on, or scanned into, a computer. But if you only need to make several hundred color prints a month, and if most of them are of computer-generated documents, a color printer is probably the way to go.

### The way forward

All these points are not lost on color copier vendors. As a result, the shrewdest among them have long ago seen the need to do one of two things. Either start making color copiers that are not so expensive that they give everyone sticker-shock (this means exploring new copying technologies). Or make color copiers that are expensive, but that are able to communicate with computers so that they can act as what are, by color standards, high-speed PC output devices — faster and generally more versatile than the cheaper dedicated color printers that they indirectly compete against.

While it may be true that the brightest future for color copiers is as multifunctional devices able to link into computer networks, this vision also confines most of these machines as viable options only for very large companies with mighty sophisticated requirements — and budgets to match. And that, in my opinion, is why full-color copiers seem likely to remain in permapoise for a while longer.

# The Four Types of Color Copier Technology

Though most color copier vendors boast certain proprietary technology refinements, all their machines fall into one of the four following categories:

### (1) Ink jet digital color copiers

At the bottom of the market are ink jet machines. These are the only color copiers that come close to being "affordable" — they start at "just" $4,500 (list price). The drawback is that models currently available can't really copy onto regular plain paper (unless you're willing to put up with pretty disappointing results).

They are also slow: each copy takes around 90 seconds to emerge. And copy quality, even with the special smooth paper, is not as good as you get from other, admittedly much more expensive, types of color copiers.

Still, I don't want to sound too negative about ink jet copiers: the fact is that they are the only budget option and for that we should be grateful. At the time of this writing, only one vendor — Canon — sold them (do not confuse these with Canon's much more expensive color laser copiers).

The technology involves first scanning an original into digital format, and then printing it out using a method very similar to that found in color ink jet printers (discussed in the previous chapter). Between the scanning and the printing, you can — if you like — edit the image to leave bits out, manipulate parts, and so forth.

### (2) Thermal transfer color copiers

This isn't a very important category, as only one vendor — Toshiba — uses it. What's more, the machine in question is neither very new, nor very interesting. My guess is that thermal transfer color copiers will no longer exist as a category in a year or two.

The basic reproduction technology is similar to that used

with thermal transfer color printers (though Toshiba's implementation isn't as good) — a thermal process causes an image to be transferred from heat-sensitive color ribbons onto a special type of paper (plain paper is not an option). The best thing that can be said about it in the color copier market is that it's one of the least expensive options. The Toshiba model concerned lists at just under $11,000.

But copy quality is not the best, and running costs are high. If you're looking to narrow your options, leaving this one out should be a fairly easy decision.

### (3) Analog xerographic color copiers

The third of the four color copying technologies is the one closest to that used by regular copiers. Images are copied using a process involving light, lenses, drums, and toner. This technology delivers good results, and you can copy onto regular plain paper (though you may get better quality if you use paper recommended by the machine manufacturer). There is usually an image editing feature, albeit of a comparatively limited nature. However, you can't interface an analog copier to a computer so that it doubles up as a printer.

Analog color copiers of this type are not at the cutting edge. If you accept the view that full-color copiers have a limited future as stand-alone devices (i.e., as copiers that can't be connected to computers), the logical conclusion is that analog machines are gradually on the way out.

### (4) Digital laser color copiers

This is the premium color copier technology: it offers the best copy quality, the most extensive connectivity with computers, the fastest speeds, and the widest number of features. Not surprisingly, you also have to pay the highest prices: the lowest list prices are usually over $20,000 and the highest are over $50,000.

Here, for those of you who are interested, is a very brief (and simplified) description of how they work. Like ink jet copiers, laser models scan images electronically and encode them into a series of digital signals — the stream of 1s and 0s that form the binary code that computers use to communicate.

The image is then reconstructed on a drum with a laser beam, rather than by an optical reflection of the image (as with analog copiers). The electronic signals that make up the scanned image have the effect of switching the laser on and off, so that the drum is charged positively or negatively. The positive areas attract particles of electrostatically-charged toner to create an image, which is offset from the drum onto the page and fused to the paper using a heat process. The imaging process occurs separately for each of the four process colors, out of which all shades of color are made (there are four separate toner supplies in the machine and, depending on the model, there may be either one drum or four separate ones).

As with ink jet copiers, the fact that the image is captured in digital format allows it to be edited in all sorts of ways before it is printed. The range of editing options with laser copiers tends to be very fancy (more on this shortly when I talk about features). As with analog color copiers, you can copy on regular plain paper, but you may be advised to use a special type of plain paper — probably one with a very smooth finish — in order to achieve the best results.

At the time of this writing, the companies that manufactured digital laser copiers were Canon, Xerox, Ricoh, Minolta, and Konica. Kodak also sells them, but its models are, in fact, relabeled Canons.

# Features & Performance

By now you should have a general idea of what to expect in this market. Now let's look a little more closely at features and issues to do with quality and performance.

### Copy quality

This means different things to different people. To some, very faithful reproduction of original colors is paramount. For the most precise results, look for machines that boast "Pantone" color matching: Pantone numbers are the industry-standard method of identifying specific shades of color for commercial printing and graphics arts purposes. This level of sophistication is available only from some laser models.

Other people look for vivid, forceful colors and aren't too bothered if the reproduction is a shade or two off the original. Some people are concerned about very fine detail not getting lost in the copies. Others look for black text that is as sharp as on a regular copier. Most people look for a combination of all of the above.

At the risk of stating the obvious, it is essential that you take a good look at a machine's copy quality for yourself. Try it with the sort of originals that you will be copying — don't just settle for the salesperson's demonstration originals which are carefully chosen to show the machine in its best light. Always be present when the copies are made — if you tell the rep to take the originals away and then bring back the copies, you'll never know how easy it was to achieve the quality.

Most of the vendors will attempt to blind you with science about the exact ways in which their machines are designed to achieve optimum copy quality. They generally look for a detail in their machine's design that's different from the competition, package the technology into an acronym, and then throw this at you hoping that you'll be suitably impressed, even though you don't really understand it (but don't want to appear dense by admitting this).

For example, Canon has its unique "Digital Image Processing System" (DIPS), Minolta offers its unique "Laser Intensity Modulation System" (LIMOS II), while Ricoh boasts its unique "Ricoh Synchro-Drive System" (RSDS). All these terms describe technology that works well and that deserves praise, but the buyer is on the wrong track fretting with "DIPS or LIMOS II?" anxiety. Just look at the machines, judge them for what they do, and don't feel guilty if — within reason — you slightly switch off when the sales person dwells on jargon (which he or she probably doesn't understand much more than you do).

### Image resolution

With the exception of analog xerographic copiers, all color copiers scan images by turning them into tiny dots, each of which produces a signal that drives the printing device. One factor determining image quality is the scan resolution — in other words, the quantity of dots that make up the image (the more, the better). The resolution is measured by the numbers of rows and columns of dots per square inch (dpi).

Although the dpi figure is important, it isn't a factor that will swing a purchasing decision — at least, not right now — since all color copiers turn out to have the same 400 x 400 dpi resolution (often abbreviated to "400dpi").

### Color copying speed

Color copiers are not speedy. The fastest full-color speed you can currently get out of a digital copier is 15 copies per minute (cpm), while most labor at less than 10cpm. Actually, this isn't as big a deal as it sounds, since most of these machines are worked for fairly low volumes. While a brisk pace is nice, it is — within reason — usually less of a consideration than quality or price. Remember that ink jet copiers are particularly slow — expect each copy to take around a minute and a half to emerge.

Usually, the first copy takes longer to produce than subsequent ones — for example, a machine capable of making seven copies per minute on a multiple run might take over 20 seconds to make just one. Since a lot of people do only make one color copy at a time, the first-copy time can, therefore, be as important as the more-often-quoted copies-per-minute number. The fastest time is 15.5 seconds, a record held by a new Ricoh model.

### Copy volumes

As you may have noticed from earlier chapters in this book, I am generally skeptical about copier manufacturers' recommended volumes. For the record, though, the recommended volumes for color copiers are set pretty low — partly because actual usage is pretty low, and the vendors don't want to scare people away by quoting numbers that customers can't relate to.

Typically, a laser model costing something in the region of $30,000 would be rated for up to 5,000 color copies a month. The most expensive models might be rated for up to 10,000 a month — maybe more — but generally get used for under 5,000 a month in practice. In other words, 5,000 copies a month is considered quite high volume in the color market.

### Suitability for black-and-white copying

Some color copiers are more adept than others at handling your black-and-white needs. The most versatile can, in theory, be the only copier serving an office or department, though keep in mind that the black-only copy quality on a digital color copier isn't always quite as good as on the best regular machines.

Features to look for include black-and-white copying speeds and the range of paper and document handling features and options. Some machines that are pretty sophisticated when it comes to the color market nonetheless turn out to be pretty cumbersome if you ask them to do a simple black-and-white job. For example, the Canon CLC 550 is widely regarded as one of the finest color machines (it costs over $50,000), yet its black-and-white copying speed is only five copies per minute — half the speed of a Canon Personal Copier costing less than $1,000!

However, a number of color copiers are able to make black-and-white copies at speeds of around 25–35cpm — on a level with mid-volume "ordinary" copiers. These are not necessarily the ones that are best purely on color jobs, but they are the ones that stand the best chance of also handling routine office copying requirements.

If you do want one machine to perform both functions, look for reasonably large on-line paper supplies and options such as document feeders and sorters. Many color copiers do not have these, even though they're essential in mid-volume, black-and-white copying environments.

And be advised that the document handling options that do exist tend to trail behind those found on regular mid-volume copiers. For example, the sorters tend to be quite small: typically, they can only handle up to 10 sets at a time, and the sets can't be longer than 20 pages. They are also very expensive — the sorter option on Xerox's Majestik color copier lists for no less than $3,600 (more than twice what you'd normally expect to pay for a sorter of its type). Moreover, not a single color copier offers a sorter with automatic stapling. Likewise, no color copier can do double-sided copying automatically, and most aren't even suitable for doing it manually.

The problem is that most organizations with the needs and budget to justify a full-color copier tend to be the sort that have high-volume black-and-white copying requirements — and no color copier has the speed and features suitable for that. Interestingly, the color copiers that are best suited for black-and-white work tend to be those in the middle of the color price scale. The reason is that the most expensive color copiers tend to be designed for specialized color applications.

A further problem about using the same copier for your color and black-and-white copying concerns the question of access. A black-and-white copier is usually available on a walk-up basis, and not many offices consider it worth restricting usage to too great an extent (except, perhaps, when copies are billed to clients). But with color copying, the much higher running costs mean that you probably don't want anyone in the office to use the machine on a casual basis (especially as unskilled operators often make several copies before managing to optimize the reproduction quality).

A final reason why the idea of making black-and-white copies on a color copier may not appeal is that they generally cost more in consumables than those made on a regular copier, because of the different toner used.

### Reduction/enlargement

One feature of color copiers that might surprise you if you've previously only been exposed to black-and-white machines is the extent of the zoom reduction/enlargement feature. Color copiers usually have zoom magnification ranging all the way from 50–400 percent — a much higher range than you get on normal copiers. A few go all the way from 25–400 percent.

### Paper sizes

Almost all color copiers can handle paper sizes up to 11" x 17". One Canon copier can handle sizes up to 22" x 33" — useful for a number of specialized applications — but the list price for this fine piece of equipment is no less than $120,000 (a little beyond most budgets, I suspect).

### Copying 35mm slides

Quite a few color copiers come with optional adapters that allow you to make enlarged copies of 35mm slides — a handy feature if you have the right application. Expect to pay around $1,250 on top of the regular price of the copier. Canon also offers a neat option on its laser color copiers that allows you to copy still clips directly from a VCR or TV set.

### Image editing

Image editing refers to the ability to alter an image before making the copy. This feature often dominates the presentations that color copier vendors give when selling their equipment, though there's evidence to suggest that it only gets used to a limited extent in practice.

At its most basic level, editing can involve moving or omitting parts of the image. Often, however, it can involve rather more fancy tricks, such as:

✔ Reversing out text or graphics (i.e., turning white-out-of-solid into solid-on-white, or vice versa).

✔ Introducing colors into selected parts of black-and-white originals.

✔ Changing the colors of a colored original.

✔ Making copies that omit parts of an original that are a certain color.

✔ Reducing or enlarging only selected parts of originals.

✔ Reducing or enlarging images by a different percentage on one axis from the other (this feature, sometimes known as "anamorphic zoom," enables you to produce altered copies that fit a specific set of vertical and lateral dimensions).

✔ Slanting, compressing, and extending text and graphics.

✔ Mirror imaging (changing an image from left to right, or top to bottom).

✔ Image repeat (producing multiple images from a single original to fill an entire page with same-size or altered-size repeat copies of the same original).

✔ Combinations and variations of all of the above.

There are three ways of making a color copier perform these party tricks. One is by entering instructions from the machine's built-in keypad and control panel — this is the least user-friendly method, however, and it may not give you access to all the editing features.

The next involves using something called an "edit board," which is an external device connected to the copier. This is offered as an option on some machines; occasionally, it's standard. You place your original on the board, mark out the areas you want to highlight for special treatment using an "electronic pen," and then select the editing features required.

Edit boards are generally a little easier to use than built-in copy editing features, and may offer a broader range of functions. Expect to pay $750–$1,500 extra to get one. When an edit board is offered, you should still be able to use some, or possibly all, of the editing features without one, but it won't be as easy.

The third method involves marking your black-and-white originals with a colored pen to designate the areas of the original that you want to single out for editing (you use the editing features in a way that ensures that the marks themselves won't show up on the edited copies). However, this method is usually associated with a narrower range of functions than an edit board.

Image editing is a common feature of color copiers, especially digital laser models which have the fanciest range of functions. A more straightforward version has also been available on some black-and-white machines for some time. In the black-and-white market, the feature has flunked big-time — very few people have chosen it as an option and few who have it really make much use of it.

It is unclear what makes vendors think that the feature is more promising in the full-color arena. Some of the explanation about why they continue to push it is that it is, apparently, more popular in the Japanese domestic market. One of the reasons why few people in this country take to image editing on copiers is that most documents that are edited are originally created on computers, and it generally makes much more sense to do the manipulation at that stage of the document creation process. Editing on computers is both easier and more economical.

### PC connectivity

If image editing seems a somewhat gimmicky feature, PC connectivity is the opposite. Connectivity means interfacing the color copier to a computer, so that it can double up as a printer and — in some cases — also function as a scanner for inputting color graphic images.

Color copiers acting as printers can outperform dedicated color printers in terms of speed and, arguably, quality. However, the premium is steep — the least expensive laser copier equipped with the optional hardware to perform as a printer is likely to cost over $25,000 at list price and most will be a great deal more — you can easily drop over $60,000 on a connected color copier. (You can, however, purchase an ink jet color copier equipped with a PC option for a little over $8,000.) Keep in mind when assessing these figures that, as I pointed out earlier, list prices for dedicated color laser printers now start at below $8,500.

The most expensive and ambitious color copier-PC connectivity options involve using third-party devices made by a company called EFI — short for Electronics for Imaging — whose Fiery Controller products provide link-ups designed to appeal to large network users. The Fiery Controller is used by Xerox, Kodak, Ricoh, and Minolta — and generally costs in the region of $20,000–$30,000 depending on the version selected and the vendor (that's in addition to the cost of the copier).

Despite the high expense involved in connecting color copiers to computers, a high proportion of people who buy connectable machines do indeed go for the link-up (if not immediately, then later). While connectivity costs a lot of money, it also gives the color copier an additional role in the office — without which the machine can be hard to justify in the first place.

# Buying a Color Copier

One of the reasons why the color copier market has been slow to develop concerns the problem of how to sell and support them. Most of the Japanese manufacturers sell only through dealers — except, occasionally, in some major cities — but most dealers lack the experience (and, arguably, the interest) in handling them.

Moreover, when it comes to connectivity, a large number of copier dealers are totally clueless about the technical issues involved. The copier dealer industry has remained remarkably unmoved by the computer revolution of the past decade, and the typical dealership would be out of its depth dealing with computer professionals inside the companies that are the most promising buyers for PC-connected color copiers. (This is an issue I discuss in the chapter of this book dealing with multifunctional equipment in general.)

Of course, there are exceptions: Canon, in particular, has some dealers who clearly do have the know-how to sell these machines; Ricoh has also made a big investment in educating its dealers. But the computer-savvy copier dealer is still an uncommon breed. Part of the solution to this problem may involve the color copier manufacturers beginning to distribute through computer industry channels, not just through traditional office equipment channels. In the meantime, the vendors that sell direct — notably Xerox and Kodak — sometimes have an advantage.

### Buyer's tips

The points I have just made are important, because it is absolutely essential to get excellent service in your local area. Color copiers are maintenance-intensive, even more so than regular black-and-white ones. The choice of who to buy from can be more important than the decision about what to buy.

You should be wary about being a guinea-pig — if you are the first customer a dealer has had for a color copier, you are taking a bigger risk than if you buy from a dealer that already services places like the local copy shops which are relatively high-volume users of color copiers. It's a good idea to ask for the names of existing color copier customers in your area who you can call for references.

When shopping for a color copier, get a clear indication of what the running costs will be. As with regular copiers, running costs are made up of the consumables, regular preventative maintenance (essential), and the cost in parts and labor of fixing the machine when it breaks down. Get the vendors to give you the running costs in writing, and be sure that these are based on a copy volume close to what you're likely to make. A bottom line is likely to average something in the region of 20–25 cents per copy.

However, running costs will vary depending on what you're copying: for example, originals densely packed with color will cost more to copy than ones with lighter coverage (on account of the toner consumption), and black-and-white copies should be a lot less expensive than full-color ones. For this reason, it can be hard to budget exactly.

Beware of items that are excluded from a vendor's running costs estimate. For example, if the machine requires special paper, is that included in the quoted cost or not?

This is a market where many people prefer to rent or lease. Vendors are keen to get more of their color copiers into the market, and can be quite flexible in structuring deals to suit the needs of different buyers. But read the small print to make sure that any deal you strike is as flexible as you want it to be. However you structure a deal, do not be afraid to negotiate!

Keep in mind that discounts of around 30 percent off list prices are far from uncommon in this market — even 35 percent may not be out of reach in some instances. If you are leasing the copier, make sure that the finance is based on a capital sum that reflects this.

Look for additional guarantees that go beyond the very limited standard warranties that are normally offered with these machines. By far the best guarantee in the business is offered by Xerox, which promises to replace your machine if you aren't happy with it during the first three years or longer.

Remember that when manufacturers sell through dealers, they generally offer little in the way of help if you aren't satisfied with either the equipment or the service. They usually take the view that customers with grievances should battle it out with the local firm that sold the machine and is servicing it.

# Vendor Profiles

Next, brief comments on the vendors active in the color copier market — for more background on these companies, and how they go about their business, refer to the vendor profiles in Chapter 5 covering mid/high-volume black-and-white copiers.

## *Canon*

*Canon USA, Inc.*
*One Canon Plaza*
*Lake Success, NY 11042*
*Tel: 516 488 6700*

Canon is, arguably, the class leader in color copiers. It has by far the widest selection of equipment, ranging from an ink jet costing under $5,000 to a laser copier costing over $50,000. During the past few years, Canon has established itself as something of a benchmark for quality in the color laser arena, and the company's equipment is widely used in the quick-print industry. However, the company faces tougher competition now than in the past.

Canon is the only manufacturer to sell ink jet color copiers. It has three ink jet models. Prices for these start at around $4,500, which is very low by color copier standards. Remember, though, that ink jet copiers require special paper in order to produce good results. Copy quality is not as sharp as on a much more expensive laser copier, and per page running costs are higher.

Canon's flagship color copiers are its two laser models. Both the current models — the CLC 350 and CLC 500 — were introduced in spring 1993 as updates of earlier ones, rather than totally new machines. The CLC 350 is the one that is more suitable for doubling up for regular black-and-white copying duty: its black-and-white speed is 20cpm — four times that of the 550 — and it also has a wider variety of paper handling options (a document feeder and additional on-line paper supplies, but no sorter). With street prices for this machine around $14,000–$15,000, the CLC 350 is one of the least expensive laser models and is a good choice for entry-level applications. The CLC 550 is the finer machine when it comes to the detail of color reproduction.

Both the Canon laser models have connectivity options enabling them to act as PC printers and scanners via Canon's Intelligent Processing Unit (IPU) or PostScript Intelligent Processing Unit (PS-IPU) options. At around $4,500 and $13,000 (list), these are significantly less expensive than the EFI Fiery Controller add-ons sold by other vendors with connectivity options, though they do not offer the same sophistication.

Canon's two laser copiers are also sold relabeled by Kodak; the Kodak versions are identical, except that they come with different connectivity options (which are much more expensive, but may appeal to very large network users).

Canon has a very strong position in the print shop market. The significance of this to people who aren't in the print-for-pay industry is that some Canon dealers are a lot more experienced than dealers for other brands at servicing and supporting color copiers.

# Kodak

*Eastman Kodak Company*
*343 State Street*
*Rochester, NY 14650*
*Tel: 800 344 0006*

Kodak's presence in the black-and-white copier market is focused on the top end: the company sells direct to high-volume users and major accounts and it does not have any dealers. It has a first-class reputation for service and support. With this distribution platform, Kodak is better positioned than most to operate in the color market.

Kodak currently sells three color copiers. Two are relabeled Canon lasers, and the other is a Kodak-manufactured analog machine. There are no significant differences between the Canon and Kodak brand lasers, except for different PC connectivity options: Kodak offers its versions with EFI's Fiery Controller in place of Canon's much less expensive IPU interfaces.


# Konica

*Konica Business Machines USA Inc.*
*500 Day Hill Road*
*Windsor, CT 06095*
*Tel: 203 683 2222*

Konica has achieved a pretty good reputation in the black-and-white copier market, but is not a particularly major player in the color arena. At press-time, it was about to launch its first model with a connectivity option — its previous model, though digital, was only standalone.


# Minolta

*Minolta Corporation*
*Business Equipment Division*
*101 Williams Drive*
*Ramsey, NJ 07446*
*Tel: 201 825 4000*

Minolta is a relatively new arrival in the color copier arena. It launched the CF80, an upscale digital laser model, in spring 1993. This machine is an upgrade of an earlier version called the CF70 which was introduced in Japan and Europe about a year earlier, but never made it to the US.

Minolta has chosen to go in right at the top of the market, challenging the most upscale offerings from Canon and Xerox in the over-$40,000 sector. This machine is pitched directly at the specialized color market, not at the general office market — the CF80 has neither the speed nor the paper and document handling features to make it suitable for regular black-and-white work as well as color. An EFI Fiery Controller option was introduced in 1994. User feedback during this machine's first year on the market, though limited, has been pretty positive.

# Ricoh

*Ricoh Corporation*
*5 Dedrick Place*
*West Caldwell, NJ 07006*
*Tel: 201 882 2000*

Ricoh is emerging as a strong contender in the color copier market. At press-time, it was still selling one analog color copier — list-priced in the mid-teens — though it was unclear how long this was going to remain in the range. This machine's real strength is that it's one of the color copiers most suitable for handling an office's black-and-white copying needs as well as its color requirements.

Ricoh's other color copiers are all lasers; the two most recently announced models have EFI connectivity options, though neither these had begun shipping at press-time. Ricoh is making a big play to establish itself as a leader in the emerging multifunctional market, and connected color copiers form part of that larger strategy.

# Toshiba

*Toshiba America Information Systems Inc.*
*Electronic Imaging Division*
*9740 Irvine Boulevard*
*PO Box 19724*
*Irvine, CA 92713–9724*
*Tel: 714 583 3000*

Toshiba is not a big player in the color copier market. It has one machine, the ChromaTouch 1000, which was introduced early in 1991 and remains the only thermal transfer machine on the market. With a price tag of just under $11,000, it is also the cheapest color copier apart from Canon's ink jets.

As I indicated earlier, thermal transfer is not the technology of choice in the context of color copiers: speeds are slow, running costs are high, suitability for regular black-and-white copying is nil, special paper is required, and copy quality is not the best.

# *Xerox*

*Xerox Corporation*
*PO Box 1600*
*Stamford, CT 06904–1600*
*Tel: 800 832 6979*

Xerox's color copier range received a huge boost in 1993 with the introduction of the Majestik, a connectable laser model priced in the middle of this market. This is an excellent machine which has superb color fidelity. It is also one of the best models from the point of view of handling black-and-white as well as full-color copying. The Majestik is made in Japan by Fuji Xerox.

Although this is now Xerox's main color copier, the company continues to sell its older and in some ways more upscale 5775 SSE — though the Majestik appears to be taking quite a lot of business away from that model. ✍

# Chapter 9

# Multifunctional Equipment

# Multifunctional Equipment

The big buzzword in office equipment these days is "multifunctionality." This is the ability for one machine to perform tasks that were previously handled by two or more separate ones. This chapter reviews what's cooking in this emerging market and discusses the pros and cons of the new "all-in-one" machines.

In this chapter, I will assume reasonable familiarity with computers and with all the individual functions that these new machines bring together — refer to the relevant "single function" chapters in this book if you need clarification on any of them.

## Introducing Multifunctionality

The notion of multifunctionality in office equipment is actually not new. Since the early 1980s, the personal computer — along with software and assorted peripherals — has been "the mother of all multifunctionality," steadily taking over some or all of the functions previously carried out by separate equipment in areas as diverse as word processing, addressing, accounting, voice mail, typesetting, faxing, and entertainment — among others. Soon, the personal computer will even begin encroaching on the hitherto protected turf of the postage meter.

### Defining the new genre

Nonetheless, certain functions have, until now, remained largely the preserve of dedicated, single-function equipment — the office copier is a prime example. So, to a lesser extent, are the fax machine and computer printer. What is quite new, therefore, is an emerging genre of multifunctional machine that can handle at least two (and sometimes all) of the following four imaging functions: copying, printing, faxing, and scanning.

When the word "multifunctional" is used in an office equipment context these days, it is — in the absence of an indication

---

**Inside This Chapter ...**

---

to the contrary — a reference to a machine that falls in this new genre. Keep in mind, though, that multifunctionality is occurring in other areas of office technology too, such as the merging of computers and phone systems.

Multifunctional imaging machines can, in all cases, be connected to a PC and often directly to a network (of course, two of the functions — printing and scanning — require this by their very nature). The words "connectivity" and "multifunctionality'" are, therefore, often heard together.

A growing number of office equipment vendors are beginning to introduce, or at least talk about, multifunctional machines — but most are approaching this new market from different directions. A multifunctional machine can be anything from a sub-$1,000 ink jet product offering only fax and printing, to a $25,000 laser product offering the full set of all four functions. In this chapter, I identify six separate categories of black-and-white multifunctional machines that address some or all of the copying/printing/faxing/scanning functions. It would be easy to break this out into a few more categories, if one wanted to, as not all models fall perfectly into any of them.

### How the equipment differs

Multifunctional products differ from each other in a number of respects:

    ❑ The number and type of functions they bring together.
    ❑ Whether they are upgrades of machines that are already available as standalone, single-function units, or whether they are totally new products designed for the multifunctional market.

❑ What their "lead function" is — most machines, though they may be able to handle more than one function, are likely to be used most heavily for one of them in particular.
❑ The level of the market that they address (larger office, smaller workgroup, very small office, etc.).

### What's holding it back?

Although multifunctional machines are generally spoken of as a "new" development, the idea has been around for quite some time: prototypes have been displayed at trade shows for a number of years and one low-end product — the Oki DOC.IT — was launched commercially in 1992. What is new is the fact that a stream of models, aimed at different levels of user, is at last beginning to make its way to the market — though few industry insiders believe they will be an overnight sensation.

Although the multifunctional concept sounds very attractive and forward-looking, there are a number of reasons why it is taking off slower than than you might imagine:

❑ The cost of a multifunctional machine does not always compare all that favorably with the cost of buying separate, single-function machines.
❑ Likewise, the performance of the individual functions is not always as good as that of dedicated, single-function equipment.
❑ With a number of machines, there is a marked unevenness in the caliber of different functions addressed by a single model — for example, some machines meet high-end printing applications, but only act as low-end copiers.
❑ There can be potential user-conflict and bottleneck issues.
❑ Traditional office equipment dealers that are meant to be handling this type of equipment can get out of their depth in connectivity waters.

### What's in this chapter?

In this chapter, I describe the six categories of multifunctional equipment. You will see that I illustrate them with more "model-specific" detail than you find elsewhere in this book, because this is really the only way to describe what is happening in this emerging market where different companies are mostly going about things in a slightly different way — there are not enough established norms for generic descriptions to suffice.

After that, I introduce you to a new software standard — Microsoft At Work — that is intended to introduce a new set of common standards in multifunctional and connectable office equipment. Finally, there is comment on the way in which multifunctional equipment is sold.

This chapter does not talk about the super-high end of the multifunctional market, which is currently only addressed by Xerox and Kodak (prices at this level begin at $75,000 and rise well into six figures). The largest and most expensive machines that I am talking about here are ones costing up to $30,000 and capable of producing images at up to 40 per minute (though at press-time, the fastest models actually available or announced had speeds of 30 images per minute). Also missing from this chapter is any discussion of color multifunctional machines — but these were discussed separately in Chapter 8.

Keep in mind that there is not a Vendor Profiles section at the end of this chapter, as I am talking about vendor specifics as I go along, and there is general background on all of the companies elsewhere in this book. For addresses and phone numbers, look at the Vendor Profiles sections in the chapters dealing with copiers and printers — all the companies mentioned in this chapter feature in one or more of those as well.

# (1) Mid/Upmarket Copier-Printer Combos

The companies that are making most efforts and noise in promoting the multifunctional concept in medium- and larger-size offices are those with backgrounds in copiers. Most of the companies concerned are also in the printer business, but it is their copier divisions that are handling multifunctional product development.

This is ironic since, as I will suggest, these machines are likely in practice to be used much more heavily as printers than as copiers. In other words, although the lead function in terms of design and product origin is copying, the lead function in terms of actual usage is printing.

The machines concerned are based on copiers that use digital technology, rather than the conventional analog "light-lens" method of traditional xerographic equipment. What "digital technology" means in this context is that originals are scanned electronically and the stored images — consisting of millions of computer instructions — are then processed in much the same way as data sent to a PC printer. Once you produce copiers that employ this type of technology, the same machine can then be connected to a PC and a phone line and made to perform other functions.

### The typical product

The typical product in this category will have something like a 30 images per minute print engine — in other words, it will be able to function as a 30 copies per minute (cpm) copier or as a 30 pages per minute (ppm) printer. It will also be capable of acting as a fax device and, perhaps, as a scanner for inputting graphical images into a PC. It will probably cost around $12,000 for a stripped-down copier-only version, but a fully-configured system for copying, printing, and faxing is more likely to set you back over $20,000.

### Early examples

Although there are quite a few prototypes that make appearances at industry trade shows, few products had been formally announced at the time of this writing. Early ones include the Canon GP55, which was already being sold at press-time, and the Ricoh DS5330, which was announced but not yet shipping (other than on a very restricted basis).

Not all machines in this category will support all the functions: for example, the Ricoh DS5330 does not handle fax (though, as I will show later, Ricoh does have other multifunctional products which do approach the market from a mainly fax-led direction).

### Copier function pros and cons

Although this category of multifunctional device enters the arena from the door marked "copier vendors," these machines are likely, in practice, to be used more heavily for printing than for copying.

The reason is that the copier functions are not, in reality, all that better than what you get from traditional analog machines. First, it is by no means clear that digital copiers do necessarily deliver better image quality than analog ones. Moreover, the copier functions of these machines are distinctly midmarket — viewed as copiers, they are unlikely to offer better productivity than any regular 30cpm device.

True, the digital copier may be able to perform some party tricks that an analog model can't — super-fancy copy editing and ultra-wide zoom magnification, for example — but these things tend to be peripheral to most people's needs. My view, therefore (and one widely shared in the copier industry) is that digital technology is not really that exciting from a purely copier perspective.

Moreover, the speed of these machines — typically 30cpm — is pretty unremarkable. Most of the offices that have the needs and budgets to buy fancy multifunctional equipment are probably already used to analog copiers that work somewhat faster. If first-generation multifunctional machines are going to replace existing copiers, it may actually mean asking people to trade down in terms of speed. (And if they are viewed as additional machines, rather than replacements, this undermines the whole all-in-one ideology.)

### Printer function pros and cons

Nonetheless, the same multifunctional machines viewed as printers seem pretty upmarket. Whereas a 30cpm copier is regarded as fairly slow, a 30ppm printer is exactly the opposite. Print speeds on most office laser printers are typically below 20ppm. For example, the fastest Hewlett-Packard LaserJet available at press-time cruised at 17ppm (though a somewhat faster model was rumored to be in the works). Moreover, many people currently work contentedly with 8ppm laser printers — despite the fact that they'd go crazy if asked to put up with an 8cpm copier.

The bottom line, therefore, is that most people have totally different ideas of what the word "fast" means when they are printing compared with when they are copying. Actually, this isn't quite as irrational as I may be making it sound — print runs are usually shorter than copy runs (partly because with separate machines, there is a running cost incentive to make only one print of a computer-generated document and then use the analog copier to make additional sets). Moreover, you can print without getting up from your desk and you can usually be doing other things on your computer at the same time. So speed may not be quite as critical as it is with a copier, where you often end up literally standing by the machine waiting for quite long jobs to finish.

Another big advantage of these machines viewed as printers is that they will also offer sorter and sorter-stapler functions — these are hardly ever available in the dedicated printer market. It is not totally obvious why you can't get these functions on dedicated printers: the usual explanation is that printer companies like Hewlett-Packard don't have the background in more mechanical paper handling peripherals to make this work reliably (not an explanation I find terribly convincing).

A further benefit is that multifunctional machines will be able to print onto 11" x 17" paper — this is something that only a relatively small number of dedicated printers can handle.

On the other hand, the first generation of multifunctional machines will trail the best dedicated printers when it comes to image quality. This is because they will only offer 400dpi resolution, not the 600dpi variety that is rapidly becoming the main standard in the printer industry. Likewise, their performance as scanners will trail that of dedicated machines, which these days can almost always scan in color and which also work at much higher resolutions.

Summing up so far, this category of machine typically offers mediocre copying capabilities, fast and productive printing, but unexciting image resolution. The fax and scanner functions on these machines are secondary: few people will buy them for those functions, though they may opt for them if they are buying the machine anyway.

### The user conflict issue

Multifunctional machines of this type are designed so that more than one function can be accessed at a time. For example, if you are copying something, someone else can be sending a print job from their PC. At the same time, the machine could be receiving a fax into memory for printing out at a later time — or transmitting one from memory.

However, a potential bottleneck occurs in the imaging function itself — if the machine is physically printing something out, you obviously can't make a copy of something at the same time or vice versa (though you might be able to interrupt the other function, and you could still scan an original into the machine so that a copy is made as soon as the machine is done printing). You can generally set up a hierarchy, so that different types of work can be prioritized — for example, whether you want incoming faxes to automatically jump ahead of a print queue of documents sent from PCs on the network.

Clearly, there is some scope for user conflict in the imaging function — by making your printing, copying, and faxing functions share the same print engine, you run the risk that people will find their output waiting in a queue when they are used to having it handled immediately on a dedicated, single-function machine.

Against this is the argument that your computer and fax printing are likely to work faster than on a dedicated machine when they do get to the front of the queue. And if you find that your current standalone copiers, printers, and faxes are not actually in use for most of the time, it may follow that the output queues won't be very noticeable anyway.

### Is integration an intrinsic benefit?

Still, these points underline the fact that integrating different functions in one machine may not, in itself, be a benefit — and may be a step backwards from a productivity perspective. Despite this, some vendors tend to tout integration as though it were an intrinsic advance — in other words, as though a three-in-one machine were necessarily more efficient than three separate ones.

The only intrinsic argument in favor of integration that I can see is that it results in space savings — having one machine handle the job of three or four separate ones can save some square feet. This is more of a plus for some offices than for others — the space-savings argument tends to have most force in Japan, where floorspace is at a premium and where the multifunctional concept is much more advanced.

A further reason why integration may of itself not be smart is that if a machine goes down, it probably takes out all the functions with it. Having separate machines spreads the downtime risk.

Another negative is that buyers don't necessarily need to buy, or replace, all the functions at the same time: it can get expensive if, say, upgrading your copier means simultaneously replacing existing fax and printer equipment that already meets your needs.

### Cost comparisons

If integration is not, of itself, a benefit, and if the process can lead to bottlenecks in document output, is there at least a cost savings in going for one of these multifunctional machines? The answer, unfortunately, is no — on the contrary, you may end up spending more to be an early user of this technology. That said, the premium isn't necessarily all that big.

The list price of a 30cpm analog copier with a good range of options is around $12,000 (sometimes less); the list price of a reasonably upmarket laser fax is around $3,000; the list price of two 17cpm Hewlett-Packard laser printers (delivering 34ppm combined output) is about $7,500 total; and a competent black-and-white scanner lists for $750. Total list price for all these items: around $23,250 (discounts will bring that price down by at least 25 percent). If you only included one laser printer in the total, the list price would be just about $19,500.

These totals are less than what you could expect to pay for a multifunctional machine with an equivalent level of features and paper handling capabilities. How much less is hard to say, as only one vendor — Canon — had announced pricing at presstime. However, a fully-equipped Canon GP55 would probably cost over $25,000 at list price — depending on the options selected.

Remember, though, that one advantage of going with the Canon would be that your printer could use the sorter-stapler — this is something that you don't get with dedicated printer products. Also keep in mind that the price of multifunctional equipment is likely to fall as this market begins to take off (perhaps it would be more accurate to say that it will have to fall if the market is to take off!).

Another point to consider is that this type of multifunctional machine could have lower running costs than dedicated printers. At the time of this writing, the market was too young and scattered to draw firm conclusions, but it appears that buyers might enjoy running costs that are closer to those of traditional mid-volume copiers (1¢–2¢ per page) than to those of traditional printers (1.5¢–2.5¢ per page).

### Human factors

On a related note, owners of these machines will not have to worry about whether to print or copy originals that are created on a computer. With separate analog copiers and dedicated printers, there is usually a cost-incentive to make only one print of a computer-generated document and then use the copier for additional sets. However, this two-step process can be tedious — the notion of being able to control the entire document creation process from your PC without paying a premium for supplies, and while enjoying copier-style document finishing (sorting-stapling, etc.), is one that many people will find very attractive. The savings in human time is definitely something that has to be considered in an overall cost analysis.

On the other hand, some users could find that multifunctional machines will put more demands on their time — this is because having these pricey machines take over from slower dedicated printers will inevitably mean more people having to share the same centralized printers — and this means having to spend more time getting to the printer, checking that it is available for use, and so forth.

### Are they worth it?

If someone bought one of these pretty expensive multifunctional machines and then ended up using it mainly as a copier, it would probably not be money well spent — as I pointed out earlier, the copier function is nothing special. Likewise, the fax and scanner functions are really icing on the cake — they are not the lead functions.

The real added productivity (compared with the office equipment you already use) occurs when you employ the printer function. And some vendors privately estimate that over 80 percent of the images created on these machines could be pages printed from a PC.

But this then raises the following question: if these machines are really best used as printers, and if the copier function is nothing special, and if the integration aspect is not intrinsically a big plus (and may create user conflict), why not just build a new class of dedicated 30cpm printer with sorter-staplers?

The big threat to these multifunctional machines would come if companies such as Hewlett-Packard did indeed start selling 30ppm printers with sorter-staplers. There seems no reason why this should be beyond their skills.

# (2) High-End "Fax-Led" Multifunctional Machines

The products I was talking about above were essentially copier-led, in terms of the equipment platform, and printer-led in terms of the likely usage. Faxing and scanning, though available, were secondary functions.

The next class of product is fax-led both in terms of the equipment platform and usage — as a consequence, the fax features are very high-end. Secondary functions in this case are printing, copying, and scanning.

The class of machines that I am talking about here are ones that are designed from the ground up as multifunctional units: at press-time, Ricoh was the only vendor with announced products that fall into this category. However, as I will be showing afterwards, there is another category of fax-led multifunctional machine that consists of upgrades of laser/LED faxes that are mainly sold as standalone, single-function units.

### Introducing the Ricoh MV715 & IFS66
The Ricoh MV715 is a combined fax/copier/printer (it does not have a scanner function). Its fax capabilities are more advanced than its printer and copier functions and it is, therefore, likely to be used more for faxing than for anything else. The fax functions include 14,400bps transmission, 11" x 17" send-and-receive (very unusual in the fax market), a 1.5-second fast-scan, and a 500-sheet paper supply. All of these features place it right at the top of the plain paper fax market. Like other PC-connected faxes, it allows you to send transmissions directly from your PC (as though it were a fax modem).

However, the MV715's copier capabilities compare with those of low-volume dedicated machines — the copy speed is just 15cpm and there is only a tiny three-bin sorter option; there is a duplex option, however (which you wouldn't typically find on a 15cpm dedicated copier). As a printer, the MV715 operates at 10ppm with 300dpi resolution — this means that it is slower, and has lower resolution, than the Hewlett-Packard LaserJet 4 Plus, which defines the standard of dedicated, mid-market printers.

The MV715 is, therefore, another case of a multifunctional machine which seems uneven in the caliber of its component functions: it offers one function that is very upscale, and two others that are somewhat basic. The problem is whether the people who need the upscale function will be satisfied with the basic nature of the other two — and, conversely, whether people who are satisfied with the two basic functions will want to pay for the upscale nature of the lead function. The list price of this machine is $5,995 for the unit with fax/copier functions plus another $695 for the printer option.

Ricoh also has another product which falls in this category, but was still waiting in the wings at press-time. The IFS66 has 14,400bps fax as a lead function, and also offers scanning and 10ppm/300dpi printing as secondary functions. This model is not being marketed with a copier function. Pricing for this model had not been announced at press-time, but it can be expected to cost less than the MV715. What is special about the IFS66 is that it will be one of the first products to use the new Microsoft At Work architecture discussed later in this chapter.

# (3) Multifunctional Upgrades of Standalone Laser/LED Faxes

The products discussed above were fax-led, but were designed from the ground up as multifunctional devices. The next category of machines are also fax-led, but are upgrades of laser/LED products that are also sold as standalone, single-function plain paper faxes.

With these machines, the lead function continues to be fax, and up to three other roles are added as secondary functions: (1) printing; (2) PC fax modem capability (i.e., allowing you to fax from your PC); (3) scanning. This category of machine does not offer a credible copier function.

### The printer function

The printer function is usually very unexciting. The fastest plain paper fax prints at just 10 pages per minute, which is 2ppm slower than Hewlett-Packard's mid-market LaserJet 4 Plus (an excellent printer with a street price of around $1,500). In fact, many laser faxes only print at 4ppm. Moreover, no fax currently in production can print in 600dpi, which has become the main standard in the dedicated printer market (and is available on 4ppm dedicated lasers costing under $1,000).

In addition, laser/LED faxes tend not to offer performance-enhancing RISC processors which are now the norm among dedicated mid-market printers. Also, they tend not to offer PostScript, and they usually don't work with Apple Macs.

In other words, a laser/LED fax that performs as a printer is a very unexciting printer to say the least — it is about as good as laser printers were three years ago, but it is not as good as what people are buying today in the dedicated printer market.

### More pros & cons of fax-based printers

If these machines were aimed at budget buyers, all of these negatives might be overlooked. But the fax platforms on which they are built generally have upscale features and quite hefty price tags. The problem is that the sort of people who need, and are willing to pay for, this level of fax machine won't be impressed with the printer function — and the type of people who will be happy with the printer function won't typically want to pay so much for their fax. Therein lies the problem.

That said, if one wanted to construct a case in favor of printer options on laser faxes it would be this: although the printer function may not be as good as that of a dedicated model, the price can be less. For example, the list price of the printer upgrade on Ricoh's laser faxes is $695. For this you get 10ppm output at 300dpi. You may or may not be able to get a discount off this figure. By contrast, a typical 8ppm/300dpi dedicated printer — if you can find one (they are a vanishing species) — would probably cost about $800–$900. In other words, it would be a bit slower and a bit more expensive. As I pointed out above, a state-of-the-art mid-market (12ppm/600dpi) printer would probably cost you around $1,500 (that's without PostScript).

So the best that can be said for the printer interface on the fax is that it can be an inexpensive way of getting a so-so printer. Fair enough — but not exactly consistent with the "technological breakthrough" message that the vendors in this market like to spread!

### The PC fax modem/scanning functions

The other benefit that often comes from this type of multifunctional fax is that you can send fax transmissions directly from the PC without first preparing a hard-copy print-out. In this sense, the fax machine effectively acts just like a regular PC modem. This is a useful capability, but it is really nothing special — there are dozens of fax modems, costing as little as $100, that allow any PC to do exactly the same thing. Despite this, the capability is often presented to buyers as though it were amazingly advanced.

Some fax-based multifunctional machines can also act as scanners for inputting graphical images into a PC — but, again, the function is not particularly impressive when compared with that of dedicated equipment (in terms of resolution and lack of support for color).

### What these products can't do ...

One thing that multifunctional machines that are upgrades of regular faxes can't do in a credible manner is act as copiers. True, you can make copies on any fax machine, but all you get are images that look like faxes in terms of the quality and resolution. Despite this, fax vendors often have a habit of touting a "convenience copier" function as a benefit of their equipment. Treat such claims with caution!

# (4) $2,000–$3,000 All-Purpose Machines for Small Workgroups

The three categories of multifunctional equipment discussed so far have been mainly targeted at larger companies. The next category consists of all-in-one machines that are aimed at smaller offices (including workgroups in larger offices with four or less people). However, unlike the sub-$1,000 ink jet category that I'll be talking about shortly, this one requires budgets of a few thousand dollars — so it's quite pricey for the so-called "SOHO" (small office/home office) market.

In this category, no single function is generally identifiable from the design of the equipment as the lead function, although the machines are likely, in practice, to be used most heavily as printers.

### Introducing the Oki DOC.IT

The most prominent machine in this category is the Oki DOC.IT

— introduced in 1992, this machine was the first truly multi-functional product to hit the market. Though the machine uses the same LED engine that Oki employs in its printers and fax machines, it is not really a "conversion" of an existing single-function product — instead, it was designed from the start to serve the multifunctional market. The functions it contains are: an 8ppm, 300dpi or 400dpi printer; a so-so low-volume 8cpm copier; a 400dpi grayscale scanner; and a decent mid-market fax (including PC fax modem capability).

The case against the DOC.IT is that the performance/features of the individual functions are not that great compared to those of dedicated, single-function equipment. However, the plus point is that the DOC.IT now costs a little less than you'd pay for four individual machines serving the same functions (this wasn't always the case, but price cuts have made the DOC.IT's economics look more attractive).

At press-time, the DOC.IT's list price was $2,499/$2,999 depending on the version selected; these prices had recently been cut, and it was unclear how large any additional discounts would be. To get all four functions on dedicated equipment, you'd probably pay a little less than $3,500 after discounts. Of course, not everyone wants all four functions — the scanner, in particular, is surplus to some people's requirements. If you only wanted a copier, fax, and printer, you could get away with below $3,000. Also, people who are willing to buy ink jet printers and faxes could get all four functions on separate machines for under $2,200 — the $3,500 figure assumes you're buying laser/LED equipment.

The weakest link in the DOC.IT chain is the copier function: image quality is generally not as good as that of dedicated low-end copiers costing under $1,000. The plus point, however, is that you can use the unit's document feeder for making copies of multi-page originals — the cost comparisons above with dedicated equipment assumed a less-than-10cpm copier without a document feeder (because feeders are not available on that size of copier).

### DOC.IT competitors

At the time of this writing, the DOC.IT had few direct multifunctional competitors. However, more machines like it can be expected during the shelf-life of this book — these will come from both the printer and copier ends of the market.

For example, Konica was expected to introduce a model called the 7310, which is a 10ppm copier/fax/printer expected to sell at a street price of $2,500 or less. I believe that this product is being made by Sanyo, though I have not been able to obtain confirmation of this.

A DOC.IT competitor that was already announced at presstime comes from QMS, a vendor known best for upmarket laser printers and color printers. The QMS 2001 Knowledge System is a laser-based product, which offers low-end printer/copier/scanner/fax functions. In this case, the printer is a 6ppm/400dpi unit. As with other products of this type, the copier function is the one that is least likely to impress. The price for this model is $2,999 (QMS list prices approximate to actual selling prices); QMS also sells a version bundled with a 486-based PC. QMS doesn't have much of a presence in the market to which this model is targeted, and I doubt it will get very far.

# (5) Laser Printers With Fax Add-Ons

This category of multifunctional machine consists of a laser printer with a fax modem capability added to enable it to receive and print faxes, and allow the host PC to send them and display incoming ones on-screen. The lead function, however, is definitely printing. The fax function is secondary — and there are no scanning or copying functions. Keep in mind, moreover, that this set-up does not allow you to fax hard-copy originals (unless you have a separate scanner for inputting documents into the PC prior to faxing — a slow and awkward approach).

The concept is being promoted by Adobe, the company behind PostScript software, as a means of widening the appeal of PostScript printers. Adobe has developed a PostScript fax card that goes inside printers and it is trying to encourage printer vendors to design machines that accept this as an option. Apple was the first to do so. NEC also offers a similar, non-Adobe feature on some of its printers, as did Compaq before withdrawing from the printer market.

My impression is that not many users are choosing this approach in practice — the lack of a fax scanning function for transmitting paper originals severely restricts the appeal.

# (6) Sub-$1,000 Ink Jet Multifunctional Equipment

The final category of multifunctional machine is the type that is aimed at very small offices and home users. These units are typically based on ink jet print engines (though thermal transfer technology may have a walk-on role in this sector as well). Early examples include machines from Canon and Ricoh.

Most machines in this category are ink jet plain paper faxes that are upgraded with add-on PC printer interfaces. Soon after this book was published, however, Xerox was expected to introduce a sub-$1,000 fax/printer/scanner ink jet product that is not an upgrade of an existing single-function machine.

With this class of product, the performance of individual functions may not be very different from that of single-function equipment. And the price may be less than buying separate ink jet faxes and printers — typically, the list price for a fax/printer combo ink jet machine is about $150 over the price of the same machine in a fax-only version. By contrast, a single-function, black-and-white ink jet printer typically sells for around $275 — so you may be saving about $125 by going for the combo approach.

It seems to me that the multifunctional concept is more viable in the short term at the low end of the market than it is higher up. In small offices and home offices, space can be a premium consideration. In addition, the equipment tends not to get used so much that user conflict becomes a problem. And savings in the region of $100 are significant at this level.

There should be a steady stream of multifunctional ink jet products during the shelf-life of this book. I imagine that Hewlett-Packard has something up its sleeve: not only is HP a strong player in ink jet fax, it is also the leader in the ink jet printer market. This market would seem to be a natural opportunity for HP.

# Introducing Microsoft At Work

At the same time as copier and printer vendors are working to bring out multifunctional hardware, Microsoft is introducing a new software architecture that promises to promote the multifunctional concept in a different manner.

This new architecture — called Microsoft At Work — is a standard that will drive and connect different types and brands of digital office equipment, enabling them to share the same user interface and giving them significant communality in terms of features; it will also enable them to share information with each other and with the computers they work with; and it will enable users to control more office equipment from their PC screens.

Microsoft At Work impacts each of the four imaging technologies covered by the multifunctional hardware discussed in this chapter — copying, printing, faxing, and scanning. But it will also cover other types of equipment — most notably business phone systems which have, to a large extent, remained remarkably "unconnected" in terms of PC integration.

### Making equipment easier to use on its own

Microsoft At Work will work at two levels: (1) making individual machines more easy to use on their own; (2) linking different equipment together, to make information easier to share.

The goal of making individual products more easy to use by themselves will typically be achieved by using touch-screen displays that will give intuitive, Windows-style access to individual features. This in itself isn't all that dramatic a step forward — several vendors offer this sort of thing already on copiers, using a graphical "folder-style" metaphor — but the new architecture will introduce a common user interface on different types and brands of equipment. Once you have mastered the operation of one, you will be well on your way to understanding others.

The whole concept will seem more novel on some types of equipment than on others — the benefits might be most noticeable on phones, which could end up with graphical point-and-touch screens to replace complex button-and-code combinations needed today for common tasks such as transferring calls or checking for voice mail messages.

### Making information easier to share

The second, and perhaps more significant, benefit is that Microsoft At Work will enable users to control different, connected equipment from their Windows-equipped PCs — with standardized point-and-click, on-screen dialog boxes as simple as the touch-screen displays on the equipment itself.

If the standard takes off — as seems likely from the support it is getting from hardware manufacturers — most future multifunctional products will eventually be Microsoft At Work-compatible. But PC-connectable single-function equipment will also be controllable in this way — and by connecting several different single-function devices on a network, using the same software and user interface, Microsoft will be providing users with many of the benefits of multifunctionality while allowing them to retain the advantages of having separate machines.

### Nuts-and-bolts give way to bits-and-bytes

Among people with roots in traditional copier/fax markets, the name "Microsoft" tends to evoke images of awe mixed with deference, of enthusiasm tempered by resignation.

Perhaps the most important long-term implication of Microsoft At Work is that it is, for the first time, making software, rather than hardware, the driving force in traditional office equipment markets. If the moving force in office imaging becomes software, the makers of imaging equipment will increasingly find themselves building compatible boxes to meet industry standards, rather than designing total, proprietary solutions which are sold through distribution channels that have little to do with computers. I pointed out at the start of this chapter that the PC is the "mother of all multifunctionality" — Microsoft At Work confirms and extends this description and will have a major effect on how the multifunctional hardware market develops.

That said, it is important to remember that office imaging machines are, by their nature, in the business of handling paper — this is what copying, scanning, faxing, and printing is all about. And handling paper automatically, reliably, and at very high speeds is an intrinsically electro-mechanical skill that is not going to become obsolete. So long as there is paper in the office, there will be machinery to move it — and so long as there is machinery, software will have its limits.

### What next for Microsoft At Work?

Microsoft At Work was announced on June 9, 1993 — at its formal unveiling, Microsoft was joined by more than 60 major companies representing the office equipment, telecommunications, and computer industries which came together to endorse it. These included some very heavyweight names — for example, Compaq, Hewlett-Packard, NEC, Northern Telecom, Ricoh, Xerox, Dialogic, Intel, Minolta, Octel, Sharp, Mita, Muratec, and Oki. The first compatible hardware products were not shipping at the time this book was published, but Ricoh had shown a prototype at trade shows and Xerox was close to announcing one.

It would be wrong to assume that Microsoft At Work will be an instant hit, rendering all non-compatible office equipment obsolete overnight. On the contrary, it will in the short term add a further cost burden to an already slow-moving transition from standalone to connected office equipment. In addition, not all hardware vendors that count have endorsed it with enthusiasm — Canon, for example, has been guarded in its reaction. But it will also produce common standards that should, in time, galvanize this emerging market. While the possibility of a false dawn should not be discounted, I would be inclined to regard Microsoft At Work as something that will feature prominently in the years ahead.

# Multifunctional Distribution Issues

One of the things holding up the development of multifunctional equipment is the problem of who is going to sell it. Most of the multifunctional equipment aimed at medium-size and larger offices is manufactured by companies with backgrounds in standalone copiers and fax machines — and with distribution channels developed to handle those products.

The problem is that dealers selling copiers and fax machines have, for the most part, remained remarkably unaffected by the computer revolution of the 1980s and 1990s — and many observers doubt that they have what it takes to sell sophisticated multifunctional equipment which is, by its very nature, computer-connected.

These traditional office equipment dealers have a culture that is characterized by detailed knowledge of the mechanical workings of their machines mixed with a tradition of hard face-to-face selling. But the people who sell copiers and fax machines do not, in the main, deal with the "techie" managers in larger organizations who run networks — the "traditional" office equipment purchasing function tends to be separate from the so-called "MIS" (management of information systems) function.

At the same time, it is not easy for the makers of multifunctional machines to switch channels and start selling their new wares through computer industry channels — the reason is that they would risk alienating their copier/fax dealers on whom they still rely to sell the traditional equipment that will remain the larger part of the office equipment market for a number of years. For that matter, computer resellers themselves can leave a lot to be desired — in particular, they would lack expertise in servicing this type of equipment which will continue to have significant electro-mechanical aspects. What is really needed, therefore, is the emergence of a new class of reseller.

There is no quick and easy answer to these problems. The companies that are making the biggest commitment to this market — notably Ricoh and Canon — are making a big investment in retraining their dealers to handle the new challenges.

The fittest and largest dealers will probably rise to the challenge: the long-term outlook for those that don't is not particularly bright. Those companies that sell equipment direct will have to undertake a similar internal re-engineering of their sales forces.

The problems of selling low-end multifunctional equipment are much less daunting. These models — especially the sub-$1,000 ink jet variety — have the necessary characteristics to become commodity items, sold in boxes by mass market retailers, and requiring little expertise on the part of either the buyer or the seller.

# Conclusion

The office equipment market seems at a turning point. The golden era that began in the mid-1970s, with the multiplication of vendors in the copier industry, and the subsequent emergence of new types of standalone electronic office equipment, may now gradually be drawing to a close — to be replaced by another, centered around the network, in which the driving forces are different. This has big implications to all those who make, sell, use, and, indeed, write about office machines.

But the changes are evolutionary, not revolutionary. For example, most copier manufacturers will continue to introduce standalone, analog machines for at least the remainder of this decade. What is perhaps most remarkable about some of the developments reviewed in this chapter is not that they are happening, but that they took so long to come about — much of this type of thing has been the talk of office equipment pundits for years. And don't be surprised if the factors, discussed in this chapter, that delayed the start of this new era may continue to retard its progress in the years ahead. ✍

# Chapter 10

# Phone Systems

# Phone Systems

A new phone system is one of the most complex purchases you can make for your office. Which type of system should you get — KSU-less, key system, hybrid, or PBX? Which of the many vendors should you consider? What are their backgrounds, what do they sell, and how do they sell it? Should you buy direct, from a dealer, or from your local phone company? Does it matter whether the dealer gets its products from a wholesaler or from the manufacturer? How can you increase your chances of getting a quality installation? Which of the many features really matter? What are the arguments in favor of a digital system over an analog one? What should you expect to pay for your phone system? What is Centrex and should you consider it?

These are some of the subjects covered by this chapter. I have written it mainly to help people buying anything from a very small phone system up to one for offices with about 100 people. The chapter should also provide some useful information for people needing a larger system, but that isn't its main focus.

### *Need advice on voice mail and related functions?*
This chapter is devoted to helping you choose a completely new phone system for your office (it also discusses the used equipment option). However, you may also want to consider adding a third-party voice mail system to the one you are buying or already have — that subject is dealt with separately in the next chapter entitled "Voice Processing."

Keep in mind that many of the complete phone systems being discussed in this chapter do themselves include voice mail and related voice processing functions, so there is no necessity to turn to third parties. I will, therefore, be touching on that subject in this chapter, but I still recommend that you also read the next chapter for a fuller discussion of voice processing features and technology.

# My Most Important Piece of Advice ...

If I could only give you one piece of advice in this chapter, it would be this: it is vital that you deal with first class people when you get a new phone system. It is better to buy an average phone system from a superb group of people, than to buy the finest system from a bunch of idiots or from people who lack experience or who just don't care. A poor installation will sabotage the best phone system. Bad or thoughtless wiring will leave you with a headache that will bug you for years. Careless programming will mean that you'll never get the most out of all those fancy features. And inadequate training will mean that no one will have a clue how to use them anyway.

This advice matters less if you are buying a very small system — perhaps one for less than 10 extensions — where the range of installation and programming options will be limited compared with a medium or larger system. But even smaller system buyers have to look at the people as well as at the equipment. The only buyers who don't have to worry about this are those needing only a handful of extensions — less than five — who can buy the sort of system you install and set up yourself.

I'll be talking more about this later, but I just wanted to put that piece of advice on the record right at the beginning. You should have it in mind when reading everything else!

# Introducing the Different Types of Phone Systems

Phone systems can be divided into five categories:

### Two-line phones for very small offices

The very smallest users don't really need a "system" at all. If you only need a couple of outside lines and two, or perhaps three, phones, you can get by with a regular two-line phone that you plug into the phone jacks in the wall just like an ordinary single-line phone. Pressing a key allows you to select line-one or line-two when making or answering a call. Calls placed on hold on one phone can be picked up by someone else on another phone — but don't expect an intercom allowing you to tell someone in the room next door that there's a call holding. This type of arrangement therefore works best if everyone is in the same room; it's also an ideal arrangement for a home office.

The best place to buy them is at consumer electronics or office supply warehouse stores. Expect to pay around $70–$130 for a two-line speakerphone with a reasonable number of features. Pick out the one you like the look of most and that seems the best deal in the place you're shopping. I won't be talking more about two-line phones, as there really isn't a great deal to say about them.

### KSU-less systems — budget buys, mainly for up to five people

If you are a small office, but need something a bit bigger than a two-line phone, consider a KSU-less system. A "KSU" (or "key service unit") is the central apparatus that usually goes on the wall to control a larger phone system. A KSU-less system is one that doesn't have any central apparatus — all the gadgetry to run the system is inside the phones themselves and all you have to do is wire them together.

KSU-less systems do offer intercoms as well as the things you'd find on a regular phone — such as speakerphones, speed dialing, etc. They don't offer much else in the way of system features, but they are inexpensive to buy and you can set them up yourself. They are typically good for two or three phone lines, and four to six extensions. They won't give you much room to expand, however. Expect to pay around $150–$175 per phone in the system.

### Key systems — good for 5–50 people, sometimes more

Key systems are the most common type of phone system for smaller and medium-size offices. If you have between five and 50 people in your office, chances are you'll get one (some are suitable for up to 100 people). You'll probably end up paying a total of anywhere from $250 to $600 per phone installed (this includes the price of all the central apparatus and wiring), though there are numerous variables that affect phone system pricing as I'll show later.

Key systems allow any extension user to answer incoming phone calls. The person who answers a call can then place it on hold, call another extension user, and have him or her pick up by pressing a key dedicated to the phone line that the call came in on. There's no need to have a full-time attendant (i.e., operator) to take all the calls before directing them to the desired extensions. When you want to make an outside call, you press a key for a line, get a tone, and then dial the number without first pressing "9."

Key systems are ideal for smaller offices, where you can't count on any one person always being at his or her desk to handle all calls. They're also suitable for offices where it doesn't really matter who answers the phone: sales offices where several people take enquiries, for example. However, many key system users do have one or two people who are designated as being mainly responsible for answering incoming calls. And if the notion of a key system sounds a little too informal for the way your office is organized, don't immediately write them off — there are also some variations known as "hybrids" which work a bit more like conventional phone systems. I'll be talking about these shortly, after making a few other introductions.

### PBXs — good from 50–100 people, up to hundreds or even thousands

A PBX is the traditional type of phone system generally requiring an attendant to answer outside calls before transferring them to the right extension, and requiring extension users to dial "9" for an outside line.

The letters "PBX" stand for "private branch exchange." Sometimes, you'll hear the term "PABX" and this refers to the same thing — the "A" stands for "automatic," a useful distinction in the days when some PBXs were "manual" (i.e., when outgoing and transferred calls all had to go through an operator who furiously fought with wires and plugs to keep everyone happy). These days, thankfully, that distinction is no longer necessary.

PBXs are most common in larger offices with over 50 extensions. This is because the amount of phone traffic in a larger office makes a full-time attendant more or less a necessity. It would be chaotic if no one had specific responsibility for ensuring that calls were answered. (In fact, very large offices require more than one full-time attendant.)

All PBXs now being sold are capable of serving over 100 extensions; there are no versions designed specifically for smaller offices. However, a PBX with a maximum capacity of over 100 extensions may be economical if configured with only about half that amount or less. Expect the cost of a PBX to work out to around $500–$600 per person in the office, including all the phones, central apparatus, and installation.

### The phones on your desk

The other difference between a PBX and a key system relates to the type of station instruments found on users' desks. A "station instrument" is the jargon term for what most of us simply call "telephones." PBXs can use regular single-line instruments — in other words, they use phones like the ones we use at home. Key systems, by contrast, provide each extension with a special phone designed for that particular system. According to the FCC (Federal Communications Commission), it is the ability to use regular single-line phones that distinguishes a PBX from a key system.

That said, most PBX vendors do offer optional proprietary "feature phones" as well. These are designed to give one-touch access to important system features. The station instruments used for key systems include special buttons — or "keys" — for accessing each outside phone line. They are sometimes called "keyphones." Like the proprietary phones for PBXs, they also often offer additional keys dedicated to controlling important system features. There is usually a choice of instruments for each key system offering a variety of different facilities; therefore some extensions can have more fully-equipped versions than others.

### Hybrids — the compromise solution for medium-size offices

Sometimes, it's hard to determine whether something is a key system or a PBX. That's because some large key systems and smaller PBXs have hybrid features — in other words, they are a bit of one and a bit of the other. "Hybrids" — as these are known — are usually based on key systems. But unlike regular key systems, they allow you to use ordinary single-line phones on some of your extensions; users who have these phones dial "9" for an outside line, as on a PBX. This saves money compared with giving everyone fancy keyphones.

Hybrid users generally have one person in charge of answering most incoming calls — a sort of part-time attendant. Often, there is also an attendant console — not unlike the one used on a PBX. But any extension user with a keyphone on his or her desk can still use a hybrid as though it were a key system. One other advantage of hybrids over conventional key systems: it's generally easier to integrate facsimile and modem phone lines within the system.

Some quite small key systems are hybrid. In general, though, it's offices with between around 30 and 80 people which have the most to gain from a hybrid. This is the size of business that may be a little small for a conventional PBX, but big enough for a conventional key system to have its drawbacks.

There is a growing amount of fusion between the top end of the key systems market and the bottom end of the PBX market. For example, there was a time when PBXs could be counted on to be much more feature-rich than key systems. That is no longer always the case, and sometimes it is hard to be too precise about whether a system is a key system, a hybrid, or a PBX. Don't fret too much about these distinctions. Choose the sort of system that fits your office best. What people choose to call it is ultimately a matter of semantics and not very important.

### Using key systems with PBXs

A key system clearly isn't an option for a large organization with hundreds of extensions. But sometimes an individual department within a large organization would operate most efficiently if it had its own key system. This can be achieved through "piggybacking" (also known as "behind-PBX operation").

Piggybacking allows you to install a key system in one department; outside callers can access it either by calling it directly, or via the PBX attendant after dialing the organization's main phone number. Likewise, calls can be transferred from the key system to the PBX and vice versa, and internal calls can be made between the two systems. These days most key systems are PBX-compatible.

### Making a match

The phone system you buy should match the way your office is organized — you shouldn't have to reorganize your office to accommodate the design of the phone system. Before contacting vendors, it makes sense to analyze your own needs.

Consider how well your current system operates. What could be done to improve it? If you don't have a system already, what are you really looking for? Talk to the people in your office who make most use of the phone — not forgetting your switchboard attendants. Find out what features of your existing system actually get used. Often, many users don't even know what features exist, let alone how to use them. What features of the existing system do users find most irritating? What saves time? And what wastes it?

There are also issues wider in scope. How much do you expect your workforce to expand — or retract — in the next few years? The system you buy now should be able to keep pace with your business. Ideally, you should be able to add extra lines and extensions without any major hardware upgrade. At the very least, you should be able to upgrade your system by replacing only the central apparatus and retaining all your station instruments.

Ultimately, it's necessary to strike balances. You want to be able to expand the system as your business grows, but you don't want to waste money on a system that's far larger than you need. You want to maximize efficiency, but you don't want to waste money on snazzy features that sound good but don't get used in practice. But remember, don't make compromises on the most important decisions — in particular the need to deal with a reliable supplier.

# Phone System Costs

It is very hard to know exactly what a phone system is going to cost until a supplier submits a detailed quotation for a particular contract. There is really no such thing as a price list in the phone systems market. The price you end up paying for a given installation is determined by a wide range of factors.

A major variable is the installation itself, which can form a very significant part of the total system cost. Installation is usually performed by the dealer, and priced locally — rates for this are not set by the manufacturer. In addition, many systems are heavily discounted so that the price you pay even for the pure hardware element may vary widely from dealer to dealer. Another variable is the mix of equipment selected — usually there's a wide range of station instruments to choose between. Optional program modules can be another cost factor.

### Key system price guidelines
Having said all of that, I can give you some information on pricing to give you an idea of what to expect. It is common in the phone systems market to express system cost on a "per station" (i.e., extension) basis by taking the total cost of the central apparatus, station instruments, and installation, and then dividing this by the number of extensions. For example, if the total cost of an installed system is $25,000, and you have 50 extensions, the cost is expressed as "$500 per station."

Phone system prices have been falling in recent years (as,

incidentally, has the volume of sales). Key system prices generally vary from lows of around $250 per station to highs of about $600 — something around $450 is average. Larger systems sometimes work out to be more expensive than smaller ones on a per station basis — this is because the tendency of larger offices to get more sophisticated equipment outweighs the economies of scale enjoyed by running more stations off the same KSU. Also, installation tends to be more complex in larger offices.

### PBX price guidelines

I can also give you some idea of what to expect price-wise if you're shopping for a PBX (with all the same caveats). In this case, the lowest per station figures tend to be around $450 and the highest are generally a bit short of $600. The "typical" range (if there is such a thing) seems to be around $500–$550. Again, there is no consistent pattern that shows that larger offices always pay less per station than smaller ones — though this can be the case in many instances.

### Getting quotes

Before a supplier can quote a price that includes installation, they'll want details on how your office is laid out, and what type of wiring you have in place. The cost of installation will depend heavily on your premises. In addition, labor rates around the country for telephone installation vary considerably.

When obtaining suppliers' quotes, always be sure that you know what the price includes. Aside from installation, ask about training (very important when the system has lots of features), warranties, and after-sales service. And be prepared to negotiate: there is no such thing as a fixed price in the phone systems market.

It's a good idea to prepare a written specification for the job and to give this to all the companies that are bidding. Always get proposals back in writing. Make sure that the different proposals are prepared on a like-for-like basis. Try to get the prices broken down as much as possible — so if the bottom line seems high, it's easier to see where there might be scope to cut back. If, in the process of reviewing one of the bids, you decide to alter the original specifications of the job, it makes sense to get all the other suppliers to rebid.

### Buying versus leasing

There is no easy way for users to make a definitive choice between leasing and purchasing without using discounted cash flow methods and taking into account both taxes and residual values. Small companies often prefer leasing, simply because it is easier to obtain than bank loans and it avoids tying up working capital.

But beware of what are, in effect, high interest payments hidden in leasing contracts. Often, lease packages are quoted without a clear indication of the capital sum on which they are based. This makes it hard to assess whether the deal is a good value. It could be that the capital value is being overstated — in other words you're being overcharged for the equipment. Or it could be that the finance element is uncompetitive.

Unless you know what the purchase price would be, there's no way of telling. So I advise negotiating the deal on the basis of outright purchase price and then, when that has been settled, working out the lease arrangements if they are required. Leases can be arranged through the phone system supplier, via a third-party leasing company, or through a bank.

# Who Makes and Sells Phone Systems?

The key systems market is characterized by a large number of vendors, most with a fairly small slice of the pie. They tend not to be names that you encounter in the mainstream office equipment or computer markets (though there are exceptions, such as Toshiba and Panasonic). The PBX market has a much smaller number of vendors, most of which are larger companies.

The methods by which phone systems are sold can be as confusing as the equipment itself. Here's a guide to the maze which leads from the phone systems factory to the end user's desk.

### Made where?

The term "manufacturer" is often used in a rather loose sense in the phones market. I often come across companies that claim to "manufacture" the systems they sell, when the truth is that they have manufacturing agreements with producers in the Far East. The equipment may be made to the US company's specifications, but it is still imported. Other products are marketed as imports without any pretense of being American.

The number of key systems that can truthfully be said to be "Made in the USA" are few. There are American manufacturers, such as Comdial and, indeed, AT&T, but they are a diminishing breed. In 1991, TIE — a prominent American manufacturer and number-two to AT&T in the key systems market — filed for Chapter 11. Although TIE is now back on its feet (details later in the Vendor Profiles section), it shed its manufacturing operation as part of its reorganization.

American manufacturers have a better grip on the PBX market, though they face stiff pressure from imports there as well. For example, Northern Telecom — a strong number two to AT&T — is Canadian.

### Who sells?

Until 1968, choosing a phone system was easy — by law, you could only get it from your local phone company (also, you could only rent it). Today, by contrast, phone systems are sold through a wide variety of channels.

Some manufacturers and importers sell direct to their customers. This is especially common in the PBX market, but it is also becoming more common in key systems. A lot of people prefer to buy direct, because it intuitively seems a safer bet from the point of view of getting better support later on. There is something in this. And it is becoming easier to buy direct — several leading key systems vendors have been on a spree in recent years buying up dealers and turning them into direct sales outlets.

Nonetheless, most systems are still sold through independent local dealers, often called "interconnects." The term "interconnect" goes back to the days when it was still novel for a non-Bell company to dare to connect customer equipment to the sacred Bell system; these days, the terms "dealer" and "interconnect" are interchangeable.

Dealers range from small family-run businesses to regional or nationwide operations. They usually also act as installers and provide maintenance. A good dealer can be just as service oriented as a direct sales operation, perhaps even more so. But there is a lot of variation in dealer quality — you have to be careful (more on this shortly).

Although AT&T manufactures the phone equipment it sells, anti-trust rules dating back to the Bell break-up prevent local phone companies — the Regional Bell Operating Companies (RBOCs) — from doing the same. Instead, they can only act as distributors for other companies. The RBOCs sell directly to end users, but they also have their own dealers. They usually sell equipment under the manufacturers' own brand names. None of the RBOCs have been spectacularly successful in selling end user equipment, though some manage better than others. Most of the RBOCs only sell equipment in their own regions, though there are exceptions.

The other main operators in this market are wholesalers

known as "supply houses." The largest is North Supply. These companies sell mainly to dealers and retailers, but occasionally direct to end users on larger orders. Supply houses generally carry several competing brands.

Remember that a dealer that gets its equipment from a supply house is two steps away from the manufacturer — perhaps even three steps away if the supply house buys from an importer, rather than from the manufacturer. Whether this is likely to have an affect on the quality of support is debatable, but it's a point to keep in mind. It's never a bad idea to ask a dealer where it gets its equipment from. A dealer that buys from supply houses may have less commitment to one particular brand and, hence, less experience in the intricacies of the system it wants to sell you. On the other hand, it may be able to offer you a wider choice and a more independent recommendation.

Very small phone systems — especially KSU-less ones — can also be bought at office supply warehouse stores and in some retail stores. For example, AT&T sells its small Partner key system this way — you can still arrange to have AT&T come around and install it for you, though the Partner is so straightforward you could think about doing this yourself.

Mail order small system sales exist, but are not very common. If you are looking for a small system and you like to shop by mail, check out a catalog called *Hello Direct* (tel: 800 HI HELLO).

That completes my round-up of distribution channels, but keep in mind that often the same system is sold through more than one of them. In other cases, vendors have parallel product ranges or brand names for different channels. The Vendor Profiles section later indicates how the different phone system suppliers sell their goods and, in most cases, where the systems are made.

# Vendor Quality Matters

My advice is that it is better to buy an average phone system from a good dealer, than the best system from a bad one. If the system is not installed and programmed efficiently, you'll never get the most out of it. If training is inadequate, you might as well have done without all those expensive features. And if repairs are not carried out promptly, the result could be a nightmare.

### What makes good support

Good support starts before the system is even installed. It is vital that the supplier should have a complete understanding of the system, in order to advise you of the programming options. That might sound like the least you should expect but, sadly, it's not something you can take for granted. There are endless programming permutations, and you shouldn't just settle for the default ones. Consider the choices carefully, or you'll waste an opportunity to ensure that your phone system really does what you want it to do. A system can be reprogrammed later on, but this costs money and, without good support, you probably wouldn't even know what could be done to improve it.

Effective training is equally important. Many businesses don't make the most of their telephone system, because people in the office simply do not know how to use it. Training should cover all users, not just the boss's secretary and people with time on their hands. Some vendors offer formal training as part of their basic contract and you should raise this issue at an early stage of negotiations.

Remember that even a diligent supplier won't be able to provide the highest quality initial support unless you're prepared to make some effort as well. If you don't make time to consider the programming options carefully, you can't blame the supplier if you don't get what you want. If staff treat phone training as a waste of time, it's pretty obvious that they won't use most of the features you're paying for.

A thoughtful installation process can save you a lot of headaches down the road. When you install a new phone system, think expansion. It's a lot easier — and ultimately less expensive — to put in the extra wiring and jacks to cope with future growth now, than to have the system supplier come back a year later and start tearing up the carpet and drilling through walls.

This is a good example of where a supplier will respond better if you are prepared to get involved — don't just sign the contract and leave the supplier to figure everything out on its own. And do take an interest in the wiring (boring though this may sound) — there may be options and complexities which you won't know about unless you make a point of asking. Also, let it be known that you will not be satisfied with unsightly wiring!

### Checking out a supplier

So much for initial support and installation. But the worst nightmare for a business is if a system goes down after it has been installed. That can cost you a lot more than you paid for the equipment itself. You could suffer lost orders. And lost goodwill. Usually, faults don't knock out the whole system, but this can happen. So it's absolutely vital that your supplier is able to guarantee fast emergency service.

Although it is difficult to be 100 percent sure of future service, it is possible to get a pretty good idea by making certain inquiries. How long has the supplier been in business? Even if the equipment is made by an established manufacturer, an individual dealer's pedigree might not be as strong. How many customers does the supplier have in your area? How many service technicians are employed and where are they located? Is there always some techie available who you can call up if you have a question and need immediate assistance over the phone?

If possible, get the names of a few existing customers in your area. Call them to check whether they are satisfied both with the equipment and with the service. In addition, I strongly advise you to visit a supplier during negotiations, rather than have the salesperson always come to you. Just walking around a supplier's premises should give you some feeling for the culture of the operation.

As I indicated earlier, some buyers prefer to avoid phone system dealers, and instead choose manufacturers and importers that sell direct. However, this narrows your choice of equipment considerably, and the option is usually only available in large cities. On the other hand, there are very strong grounds not to buy a phone system from a dealer that refers you to a third party for subsequent service. That's a classic recipe for buck-passing later on.

Another service tip: look for a feature on some medium and larger phone systems called "remote diagnostics." This allows your supplier to check out faults by accessing the system over the phone with a modem. Sometimes, bugs can be removed "remotely." Programming changes can also be carried out this way.

### The obscure brand risk

Sometimes, the least-known phone systems offer an attractive combination of features and price. But there may be a big risk if you choose a fairly obscure brand. What will you do if the dealer you buy from turns out to offer poor support?

If you buy from a leading supplier, there will generally be alternative dealers in your area to whom you can turn for support or to expand your system. But with a lesser known brand, this is unlikely. Even if the support is of acceptable quality, what will you do if the dealer decides to stop carrying the brand you bought? Or if the importer simply stops bringing the equipment into the country? In that case, the dealer would probably continue to service your existing equipment, but might not be able to sell you additional compatible equipment as your business grows and spare parts could take longer to obtain.

When it comes to phone systems, there is a strong case to stick with leading, mainstream suppliers which have extensive distribution. You should find the comments in the Vendor Profiles section of this chapter helpful in deciding who to shortlist.

### Warranties and service contracts

Don't forget to check out the warranties offered with your new system. Often, the price you pay for the equipment includes full parts and labor service for a year. The case for taking out a service contract after the warranty expires is that you can expect priority when it comes to service calls. Merely having a service contract is no guarantee that the service will be satisfactory; but you're on firmer ground if the supplier has contractual obligations to support you. The case against service contracts is that paying for maintenance on an *à la carte* basis often works out cheaper, though you are not insured against large expenditures if you happen to be stuck with a lemon.

Annual service contracts typically work out to around 10 percent of the system cost. Note that in some cases, leasing companies require you to take out a service contract. If you decide on one, don't forget to peruse the small print for price escalation clauses, and to check whether you have a right to renew. Try to avoid paying for service contracts annually in advance: it's better to insist on quarterly payments, in case you discover that you don't receive the type of support you're entitled to.

One final tip on service: sometimes a single telephone instrument can go on the blink, so you might want to keep a spare one around just in case this happens.

# The Secondary Market

The secondary market deals in surplus, used, and refurbished equipment. It's quite a healthy market — during the boom years of the eighties, a lot of vendors overproduced and were forced to sell off surplus stock through secondary channels. And in the tougher times of the nineties, companies that have been driven out of business or forced to downscale have been obliged to get rid of equipment that is still quite serviceable. In general, the focus of the secondary market right now is more on used and refurbished equipment than on surplus stock. Also, a lot of the activity is in supplying parts and additional equipment to existing users, rather than selling entire systems on a turnkey basis.

Until not so long ago, what you got when you bought a used system was something fairly antiquated. But these days, you may find that yesterday's phone systems have more than enough features to meet your needs. Even if you don't plan to buy used or surplus equipment, you may want to consider the secondary market as a means of getting rid of your old system. This may result in a better deal than a trade-in with the new system vendor.

### How to find a secondary market supplier

There are hundreds of secondary market dealers. The low costs of entry into this market have attracted some pretty fly-by-night operators that have at times given it a bad name, but there are many others that are established and stable. One of the best ways of studying your options is to get hold of one of the all-advertising publications in which secondary market suppliers take space. The largest of these is *Telecom Gear*, which in a typical issue has over 150 pages of secondary market advertising. Call 800 866 3241 (or send them a fax on a company letterhead saying why you want a copy, and they'll send you a sample free; their fax number is 214 233 8269). Another publication which is mainly given over to secondary market phone system advertising is *The Mart*; you can call them at 214 238 1133.

# The Centrex Alternative

There is an alternative to buying your own phone system — you could also consider using someone else's. The "someone else" is your local telephone company. The equipment that it uses in its telephone exchange relies on the same technology as a phone system you'd buy for your own office. And it's possible for most of the features of a PBX to be supplied directly to you from the local phone company ("telco" for short) without the need to install your own equipment.

This service is called Centrex. It has been around for years, but it went into decline in the 1980s when the PBX market was booming. Recently, however, it has begun to stage a bit of a revival. It seems quite fashionable in telecommunications circles to argue that Centrex deserves another look.

### Centrex explained

If you sign up for Centrex, the local phone company allocates you a bunch of lines and provides you with PBX-type services from its central switch. It's a bit like a much enlarged and enhanced version of the various special phone services that the telcos offer to residential users — but you get things like four-digit intercom (so you can call another extension) as well as various PBX-type advanced features.

One thing that Centrex does not provide is an attendant at the phone exchange to answer your incoming calls and transfer them to the right extensions. In its purest form, it operates on the assumption of "direct inward dialing" — i.e., callers dial straight through to the individual person they want to speak to (an option also available with many PBXs).

That's fine if you're confident that callers will know the extension number to dial, but what happens if they don't? One solution is to buy a special Centrex-compatible attendant console. This sits in your office, just like a regular PBX console, but you don't require the central switching apparatus that you'd need if you were a PBX user. Another option is to have an automated attendant that allows callers with touch-tone phones to spell out the name of the person they want to talk to, or to choose from a menu of options.

Alternatively, you can buy a whole key system for use in conjunction with Centrex. A Centrex-compatible key system is able to function on its own, sometimes in a basic sort of way, but derives extra features from being linked to Centrex. Many phone systems are Centrex-compatible, and some are marketed mainly with Centrex in mind — the latter are usually small KSU-less systems. The best provide easy one-button access to important Centrex features. Some companies use Centrex to serve the overall needs of a large office building, but nonetheless give certain individual departments a Centrex-compatible key system of their own.

### Centrex pros and cons

Don't go away with the idea that Centrex is a cheap option. Over a five year period, it tends to be more expensive than buying your own PBX — and even when it doesn't, it probably won't produce significant long term savings. Centrex tariffs vary across the country. Whereas they have traditionally been subject to state regulation, the tendency these days is to allow the "telcos" (short for local phone companies) much more latitude in how they charge for the service. In some parts of the country, Centrex requires more of an upfront set-up charge and commitment period than in others. Your telco will be able to advise you what's available locally.

In general, though, the advantage of Centrex is that it does require less commitment than if you were putting in a new PBX of your own. It is therefore particularly useful for companies that are very uncertain about their future needs, or about their future location (you don't want to install a PBX in a building you think you may be moving out of). Centrex also frees you from the worries associated with PBX ownership — maintenance, housing the central apparatus in a suitable room, and so forth. In addition, Centrex can be the best solution for larger organizations whose premises are scattered all over a town, rather than centralized in one building.

The last point may help account for the fact that over 60 percent of all Centrex users are in government or education. But another reason why the public sector tends to favor Centrex is that it can enable the telephone system to be budgeted as an administrative running cost, rather than a capital item — something which can be useful when funding for new equipment is short. Most private sector Centrex users are companies with 50 or more extensions. Usage among smaller businesses is not common, though that doesn't mean that it can never make sense — especially in parts of the country where the tariff structures encourage smaller users.

Centrex service is sold by the telcos direct, by independent agents operating on commission, and by some equipment suppliers who offer Centrex-compatible equipment.

# Digital or Analog?

You'll be bombarded with sales claims that you're being short-sighted if you don't buy a digital phone system. And you'll hear rival claims that it's no big deal. You don't need a master's degree in telecommunications to form an intelligent opinion on the digital versus analog debate, but it helps to have a basic grasp of the technology. So, with as little jargon as possible, I'll talk you through the subject.

### A very brief introduction to digital technology
At the risk of stating the obvious, I'll begin by reminding you that when you hear someone talking on the phone, you aren't actually hearing his or her voice. You are hearing a reconstruction of the voice from signals created from the original. The digital/analog issue centers around how these signals are created, transmitted, and reconstructed.

Analog is the traditional method. This way, your voice is transmitted through the system in the form of a continually varying electrical current. The term "analog" is used because the changing patterns in your voice are directly analogous to changing patterns in the current. If analog phones had the voice equivalent of a tachometer, you'd see the needle rising when your voice reached a shrill pitch, and falling when you groaned.

The alternative is digital transmission. This relies on the "binary" method of transmission. In this case, the sound of your voice is encoded into computer data. Each tone in your voice is represented by an eight-digit series of "1s" and "0s" known as a "byte." If you consider the huge number of permutations of "1s" and "0s" that can form an eight-digit sequence, you'll realize that every possible tone can be catered for. The sound of your voice is encoded — or "digitized" — at tiny fractions of a second, a process known as "sampling." The signals are transmitted down the wire in exactly the same way as computer data. A pulse of electricity down the line represents a "1," and a gap — no pulse — a "0." At the other end, the signals are reconstructed into the original sound.

In an ideal world, digital is better than analog. The signals are clearer, which means that voice reconstruction is more accurate (in plain English, you'll get fewer crackles and distortions). In addition, you can send computer data over digital phone lines faster and more accurately. Dialing may also be quicker over digital lines.

But the world — as most of us don't need reminding — is not ideal. Although there are plenty of digital phone systems on the market, most lines provided by the local telephone companies to connect offices and homes to the rest of the world are still analog. A phone conversation is only as good as its weakest link. You can have the swankiest digital phone system at either end of a conversation, but if the lines connecting two locations are even partly analog, all the voice signals will at some stage have to be converted from digital to analog in order to get from A to B.

### Is it worth it?

That doesn't mean there isn't any point in buying a digital phone system. For a start, if you're buying a PBX you'll find that everything is now digital anyway (though only some digital systems guarantee you the ability to enjoy future digital phone services, as I'll explain shortly).

Secondly, some users may derive benefits from a digital system right away — the digital premium doesn't only have to be an investment for the future. For example, you may be able to use a digital phone to transmit data between computers within your building. It's a way of networking computers, though performance generally falls short of what you can expect from a dedicated PC network. Large phone users will also enjoy the full benefits of a digital phone system if they have private leased digital lines connecting two locations (T1 lines, for example).

In addition, key systems with the largest number of features tend to be digital anyway. So you may end up getting a digital phone system simply because that's the only way to get all the features you want, rather than because you were drawn to the digital aspect specifically. The only new analog key systems being introduced tend to be fairly small and straightforward ones.

### Introducing ISDN

Eventually, almost all calls within and between large cities will travel along something called "ISDN," which stands for "Integrated Services Digital Network." This is a new international standard for high speed voice, data and video transfer; once fully implemented, it will add all sorts of new gizmos to the way we use the phone.

Analog phone equipment will be able to work on a network which is mainly digital, but it will never enjoy the benefits. Right now, however, ISDN is still a system for the elite. It is only a practical and economical option if you're a very heavy sender of computer data. But the idea is that within 10 or 15 years, most businesses will be on ISDN; many households will as well, so its proponents assure us.

ISDN doesn't require laying new phone lines across the country or into your building. Instead, a new type of telephone exchange sends a different type of signal over existing lines. But even if you are in a city served by ISDN, you won't benefit from it unless you have a phone system in your office that is ISDN-compatible; and even if you have that system, you'll only enjoy ISDN benefits on phone calls to people who are also in an ISDN area and who also have ISDN-compatible equipment in their office.

For all practical purposes, it will not be possible to upgrade an analog system to become ISDN-compatible. But that doesn't mean that any digital system you buy now will necessarily be able to work with ISDN. Being digital is a requirement for ISDN compatibility, but it is not sufficient. You will need an ISDN interface as well. Only a small number of phone systems on the market now offer these. Eventually, all vendors of digital systems will offer ISDN adapters for their new equipment, but you can't count on upgrades being offered on existing systems.

### Summing up digital versus analog

Let's sum up the digital versus analog debate. The buyer who really wants to be certain that a phone system bought now will still be up-to-date in the year 2000 should not merely choose a digital system, but an ISDN digital system in particular. But making that decision restricts your choice considerably; it will almost certainly force you to spend more than you otherwise would; and it is usually not even an option unless you are quite a large user.

My advice, therefore, is not to worry about ISDN unless you have a major requirement to send a huge amount of data over the phone lines. If ISDN isn't a factor in your purchasing decision, it follows that it may not matter a great deal whether your phone system is digital or analog. However, since the most up-to-date phone systems tend to be digital anyway, most medium businesses — and all larger ones — will end up with something digital even if they don't specifically intend to. Smaller offices, and some medium-size ones, may still end up with an analog system, and — frankly — they'll probably never notice the difference.

# Phone System Features Glossary

Look at the literature that phone systems vendors put out, and you'll see endless confusing lists of features. Many vendors seek to impress potential buyers by claiming the highest number of features — some literally try to put a number on them, with sales lines such as "The XYZ system has 175 features, etc."

But some of these features are pretty arcane. And it is often hard to compare features, since different vendors use different terms, or define the same terms in a different manner. Also, many features have a host of "sub-features," so to speak. For example, two systems may both have automatic call distribution (defined shortly), but one may be infinitely more sophisticated than the other.

So if you, as a buyer, find the literature and sales pitches confusing, don't assume that this reflects badly on you — the fact is that the whole subject is confusing! But it is important to understand the main features, and to help you do this I have prepared the following glossary. This doesn't attempt to be exhaustive, but it should fill you in on most of the things that really matter. Features are listed alphabetically.

***Automatic attendants:*** Automated attendants greet callers with a digitally recorded message and then allow the callers to route themselves through the phone system to the correct extensions. Typically, the greeting informs callers which company they've reached and asks for an extension number to be keyed in. This action connects them through to the person they want, or, perhaps, to a called party's voice mailbox. In some cases, the automated attendant offers callers the option of entering the name of the party they're calling — the system then matches this to an extension number.

Automated attendants do not generally replace human operators, they work with them. This means that if a caller doesn't have an extension number, or needs help for any other reason, a human voice will come on the line as soon as one is available. Keep this in mind when assessing the overall cost-effectiveness of the equipment — you may be able to reduce your staffing costs at the switchboard, but not eliminate them.

Sometimes when you call up a company, you don't have a specific individual to contact, but you need anybody in a particular division or department. Automated attendants can deal with this situation by offering callers the option of pressing a number to route to a particular department — the often-heard "Press 1 for accounts payable, press 2 for sales, press 3 for service," and so on.

Many PBXs and key systems — even relatively small ones — come with automated attendants, often as options. If a system doesn't come with one — or if you would like to add the feature to a phone system you already have — there are numerous third-party add-on products that work with most phone systems. More on this in the next chapter.

***Automatic call distribution (ACD):*** This is a feature for users, such as travel agencies and telemarketing operations, which have a large amount of incoming traffic handled by a group of agents/attendants. It places calls in a line until the next person is available. Some can also balance the traffic load among individual agents, and provide management information about the pattern of incoming calls (how long people had to wait, how many people hung up before being put through, who dealt with how many calls, etc.).

Most PBXs and larger key systems and hybrids offer ACD as a built-in feature. It only used to be something of interest to pretty large companies, but its widespread availability now makes it a feature that can benefit any business with an uneven, and sometimes hard to predict, quantity of incoming sales calls. ACDs vary a great deal in terms of their sophistication — don't expect too much if you see it on a smaller phone system. People with very advanced requirements sometimes turn to third party add-on products.

**Automatic route selection:** See "least-cost routing."

**Busy lamp field (BLF) indicators:** See "direct station selection" (DSS).

**Call accounting:** Many phone systems have a feature known as "station message detail recording" (or SMDR), which provides a straight chronological print-out detailing every call made from each extension. Call accounting goes a step or two further by providing management reports that analyze phone traffic. Like most features of this type, the degree of sophistication varies significantly between vendors. Sometimes, you can have forced account entry, which means that people can't make a call without first entering a code costing it to a particular client or project.

**Call forwarding:** This allows you to program the system so that if calls are not answered by an extension after a given number of rings or because a line is busy, they are automatically rerouted to another extension. Call forwarding is not the same as "user call divert," which is offered on the actual station instruments and allows calls to be diverted on an ad-hoc basis by the extension user.

**Call waiting:** If you're on the phone and someone else is trying to call you internally or transfer an outside call to you, this feature gives an audible or visual signal. If you like, you can place the first call on hold while answering the second. It's just like the call waiting feature you can get at home.

**Camp on busy:** If you're calling another extension within the system and it's busy, this feature allows you to hang up and get rung back automatically as soon as the person gets off the phone. A few systems allow you to camp onto an outside line if they're all busy when you first try.

**Capacity:** The maximum capacity of a phone system is usually expressed by the number of trunk lines (i.e., outside phone lines) and extensions/station instruments that the system can handle. The short way of referring to system size is to talk about, say, a "4 by 10 system," as a way of indicating that it can go up to 4 lines and 10 extensions. Some systems' capacity is measured by the number of "ports." This generally means that it can be configured with almost any combination of lines and extensions up to the maximum number of ports. However, on some systems there are restrictions on how the balance is achieved in terms of the ratio of lines to extensions.

When choosing a phone system, be sure to get one that will accommodate your reasonable growth projections without major and expensive upgrade costs. Only a business with no hope of growing wants to install a phone system that is virtually maxed out on day one.

It's pretty easy to figure out how many extensions you need when first installing a phone system. Rather harder to determine is how many outside lines are required. Buyers often look for some magic ratio, but, sadly, there is none. It all depends on your pattern of calling. Some small offices with heavy phone usage need one line for every extension, or perhaps more lines than extensions. At the other extreme, a hotel which has phones in every room, but not a great deal of outside calling, may only need one outside line for every 20 extensions. A ratio of one line to every three extensions is quite common in offices, but this doesn't mean that it applies to you.

It's hard to win on this one. Nothing will cause more user complaints about the phone system than difficulties getting an outside line. Likewise, callers will be irritated by constant busy signals. On the other hand, you aren't going to feel too good about paying the phone company every month for line rentals that, in practice, are surplus to requirements. Strike a balance — and don't forget to periodically review your line rentals, in case you do have more than you need. Many businesses waste money on lines that never get used without even realizing it.

**Central office (CO) line:** This is a slightly antiquated — but nonetheless commonly used — term for the phone lines that carry your calls out of your building to the local telephone exchange. "Central office" is another term for the exchange. The term "central office line" is synonymous with "trunk line" and "exchange line."

**Conferencing:** This feature allows you to set up a call between three or more people, of whom usually no more than one can be calling from an outside location. Keep in mind two alternatives when you want a conference call. One is simply to have more than one person at your end sharing a speakerphone.

Another is to use your local or long-distance telephone company's own conference calling service; the latter is especially suited to conference calls involving people in more than two locations.

**Direct inward dialing (DID):** This PBX feature allows a caller to by-pass the attendant and go straight through to an extension. All that's required is to know the number to dial; usually, this will be the normal area code and exchange for the company, followed by four digits that correspond to the internal extension number. Although an extension with DID has what amounts to its own exclusive phone number, it does not generally have its own exclusive trunk line.

DID is a handy feature, because it saves time for the caller and reduces pressure on the attendant. In fact, it can save large organizations money, allowing them to employ, say, only one attendant when otherwise they'd need two. DID is a major feature of Centrex, though many PBXs and hybrids have it too.

**Direct inward system access (DISA):** This allows outside callers to dial directly into the system and gain access to its facilities as though they were in the building. For example, if you're calling your office and talking to a colleague, you could place that call on hold and dial another extension in the building without making a second phone call. A common use of this feature is to call into the office when you are working from home and then make a long-distance call to another location using the office's cheaper phone rates or leased lines.

Beware that this feature sometimes leads to so-called toll fraud, when unauthorized people dial into your system and make long-distance calls at your expense. It's a phone system equivalent of computer hacking. The phone industry is working hard at ways of battling this crime, which is estimated to cost businesses in excess of $1 billion a year.

**Direct station selection (DSS) keys and busy lamp field (BLF) indicators:** Many key systems have station instruments that include dedicated keys for one-touch dialing of individual extensions. These are known as "direct station selection" (DSS) keys. Often, there are also lights next to them that show whether an extension is busy. These are known as "busy lamp field" (BLF) indicators — also referred to as "extension status indicators." DSS keys and BLF indicators tend to go together, but it is possible to have one without the other.

On a large key system, it is very unlikely that there will be enough DSS keys and BLF indicators on a station instrument to cover all the extensions in the building — there simply isn't room. In fact, you don't often get more than around 16. In this case, you can program the phone to select which extensions you want covered. Sometimes, there are also programmable keys that can be used for DSS, but that can alternatively be programmed to control other features on the system.

If you want your DSS/BLF to cover all the extensions on a large key system, you'll have to opt for a separate DSS/BLF console. This is a unit that sits next to a station instrument. It is bit like an attendant console on a small or medium PBX. These are commonly used in hybrids, where there's a need to have some sort of attendant at the hub of the system.

With PBX systems, extension users don't get extension status information, since they generally use conventional telephone instruments. However, a display on the attendant's console provides detailed information on the status of all extensions on the system.

**Distinctive ringing:** Most systems produce different ringing sounds to indicate whether a call is coming from another extension or from outside.

**Exclusive hold:** With key systems, calls placed on hold can usually be picked up by any extension user and not only by the person who put it there. Exclusive hold is a feature you activate to prevent this from happening.

**Flexible line assignment:** This key system feature allows you to program the system so that certain departments or individuals have groups of outside lines assigned to them specially. It's a way of ensuring that people in your office who need the phone most don't find that all lines out of the building are busy.

For example, if you have 20 lines and 60 extensions, you may want to reserve 10 of the lines for the 20 extensions in the sales department. That way they would have a better ratio of lines to extensions than the rest of the office. Outside callers aren't affected: they still dial the main number, no matter who they want to speak to.

This feature is standard on just about every system, but buyers sometimes aren't made aware of it. A good vendor will suggest that you consider your options at the time the system is installed and programmed; lazy vendors don't tell you about it and the result is that the feature never gets used.

**Flexible ringing assignment:** This allows you to program

your key system so that only selected extensions ring with incoming outside calls. This is useful if some people don't want to be disturbed by constant ringing. The feature is available on just about every system. Some systems also feature "time of day services," which means that ringing assignments vary according to the time of day and the day of the week.

**Hold call reminder:** An audible signal reminds you when you have someone waiting on hold. This can be irritating, especially if you don't often forget about calls on hold. However, you can generally program the system to include this only on designated extensions or to lengthen the period before or between signals.

**ISDN:** See the discussion earlier in this chapter in the "Digital or Analog?" section.

**Key service unit (KSU):** As explained earlier, this is the wall-mounted box which is the central apparatus of a key system. Some very small key systems don't have a KSU, and all the necessary circuitry is contained within the station instruments themselves; these are sometimes known as "KSU-less systems."

**LCD displays:** Many key systems have station instruments with LCD displays. These usually show which features you have activated, the number you have just dialed, and other information to help you track calls. There's often also a clock feature that allows you to time a call. In addition, the displays sometimes show messages left by other extensions (see "messaging").

It's arguable how useful displays are in practice, and they are often found only on the premium station instruments, not on the ones generally given to most people in an office. If you're a PBX user, you can attach any single-line phone as an extension, and there are plenty available that include displays of some sort or other.

**Least-cost routing:** The more you study long-distance tariffs, the more you discover that the carrier that is cheapest on one phone call isn't necessarily going to be cheapest on another. The solution is to use more than one carrier, but the problem then is how to figure out who to use for each call. "Least-cost routing" — or "automatic route selection" — directs each call automatically onto the least expensive facility available. The feature is transparent to the user and it makes no noticeable difference to the speed with which a call is connected. Businesses that do a lot of long-distance calling will find this one of the most desirable features they can get on a phone system.

Least-cost routing only used to be available on pretty large and upmarket systems, but recently it has begun to be more common on medium and even smaller systems. It doesn't work without a certain amount of human input, however — it requires careful set-up at the beginning, and regular reprogramming to reflect phone tariff changes. It's a good example of a feature that's a lot more effective if you've got a first-class supplier to help you get the most out of it.

**Line status indicators:** These are buttons on key system station instruments that light up to show the status of each outside line. Depending on whether a button is lit, flashing, or unlit, you can tell whether a line is busy, on hold, or free. On most key systems, every station has a button for every outside line. By pressing the button, you gain access to the line. Line status indicators are the very essence of what traditional key systems are all about.

**Messaging:** This feature enables an extension user to leave simple messages which show up on the display of someone else's station instrument. The feature can work the other way too: when you go away from your desk, you can leave a message (e.g., "Back at 3:30 p.m.") which shows up on the display of other extension users who call while you're gone. Some PBXs allow extension users to send a similar message to the attendant.

This type of visual messaging is arguably a little redundant if you have voice mail (discussed later), which is altogether more flexible. However, it does have some functions that distinguish it from voice mail. For example, a receptionist may be able to send you a message while you are on the phone telling you the name of someone who is holding for you. The exact detail varies from system to system — the term "messaging" really covers quite a lot of different things.

**Music-on-hold:** This generally means that callers on hold hear a tape or radio station connected to the system. Less satisfactory are the built-in synthesized tunes found on some low-end systems; these repeat every 15 seconds or so and cannot be turned off. Some people find music-on-hold irritating, but at least it assures callers that they haven't been cut off.

An increasing number of companies use sales messages instead of music to keep people entertained while on hold. There are companies that specialize in recording these with appropriately breezy voices. If you wish to play this sort of recording, you may want to look for a system that starts each caller at the beginning of the message instead of making them join in the middle. There are various third-party add-on devices that can enhance the music/message-on-hold features that come standard.

***Night service:*** This PBX feature provides the ability to route incoming calls to specific extensions when the attendant has gone home for the night. See also "flexible ringing assignments" for the key system equivalent.

***Non-blocking architecture & path restrictions:*** The number of outside calls that can take place simultaneously is governed principally by the number of outside lines. However, some mostly older or smaller systems impose a limit on the number of "speech paths" — i.e., the number of people who can be talking on the phone at the same time. This means that if a lot of people are making internal calls simultaneously, the system could block — even to the extent of denying access to outside lines that aren't being used. This doesn't occur often in practice, but it's a factor worth keeping in mind. Digital systems are non-blocking.

***Off-hook voice announce:*** This enables someone in your office to tell you something over your speakerphone, even though you are on the phone. Typically, it's a way for a receptionist to alert you to another call that's waiting. Sometimes, there's a hands-free reply feature — you can bark your answer back into the speakerphone microphone without putting the first call on hold.

***On-hook dialing:*** See "speakerphones."

***Off-premise extensions (OPX):*** This can mean one of two things. The traditional definition is that you can have an extension in a different office or building to your main one, but connected by a dedicated line. The OPX can effectively operate just like any other extension.

The other meaning is what I term "external call transfer." If someone calls your office, and you're some place else, this feature allows either the attendant or an extension user to transfer the call to where you are over the regular public phone system — whether it's across town or across the world. The caller is unaware that this is taking place — as far as he or she is concerned, it's just like a transferred call within the building. The caller only pays the regular tariff for calling your office, but your business picks up the tab for the onward connection. This is great for when you're working at home but want to take calls that come in for you at the office. The feature is sometimes known as "patching."

**Paging:** Paging allows announcements to be broadcast through all the speakerphones connected to a key system. Usually any extension user can make an announcement which then sounds on every extension loudspeaker where the user isn't already on the phone; it is also possible to program the system so that you can page certain groups of extensions.

In some cases, systems are designed with "dual speech paths"; this allows you to make an announcement which sounds on a user's speakerphone even if he or she is in conversation. PBXs don't generally offer built-in paging, but they can be connected to separate paging systems.

**Patching:** See "off-premise extensions."

**Ports:** See "capacity."

**Priority override:** This feature allows designated extensions on both PBXs and key systems to break in on other phone conversations. It is sometimes called "executive override," a polite way of saying that it's a feature for impatient bosses and not for humble workers.

**Speakerphones:** Two-way speakerphones allow you to talk into the speaker as well as listen. Be warned that vendors sometimes say that there is a speakerphone feature, when all you get is on-hook dialing — the ability when making a call to listen to the dial tone/ringing over the speaker, and pick up only when the other party answers.

Sound quality on two-way speakerphones varies widely, but you generally get that "hollow" sound that often annoys the people you're talking to. Performance is affected by the operating environment: speakerphones work best in a quiet carpeted office. Keep in mind that all speakerphones only allow one person to talk at a time — the result is that words can get cut out when one person tries to break in while someone else is talking.

**Speed dialing:** This is a standard feature on almost all

key systems and PBXs. It enables you to store frequently dialed numbers as short codes; you can then dial them by pressing just one or two keys. Speed dialing is available in two flavors: system-wide and by extension.

With system-wide speed dialing, the system stores a large directory of numbers that are accessible from any extension. This is particularly useful for dialing frequently called corporate contacts or branch offices. Extension speed dialing allows individual users to store their own most frequently dialed numbers in their own station instruments. Most systems provide both forms of speed dialing.

***Station message detail recording (SMDR):*** This feature — common on both key systems and PBXs — enables you to keep a log of outgoing phone calls. It involves attaching a regular computer printer to a port on the system's central apparatus. In most cases, the print-out shows the number dialed, the call duration, the extension that made the call, the date and time, and, in some cases, the cost of the call. Larger phone systems generally give you more information on an SMDR print-out than smaller ones.

SMDR print-outs list call details chronologically but don't, as a rule, include any analysis. See "call accounting" if that is what you need.

***T1 lines:*** These are high-speed, privately leased digital lines used by phone users to connect two locations with heavy voice/data traffic. If you use them, you'll need a digital phone system with a "T1 interface."

***Toll restriction:*** This enables you to place restrictions on the types of calls that particular extensions can make. For example, you can bar international calls, long-distance calls, and 900 calls. Few systems don't offer toll restriction of any kind. However, some are more flexible than others. For example, some allow long-distance calls to certain area codes, but not to others.

***Trunk line:*** See "central office line."

***Uniform call distribution:*** See "automatic call distribution."

***Voice mail:*** Many phone systems — including some quite small ones — now have this feature, which allows callers to record messages for people who are away from their desk or on the phone. If a phone system doesn't have this as an integrated feature — or if you want to add it to the phone system that you already have — there are numerous third-party voice mail add-on devices. I cover the third-party option, and voice mail in general, in the next chapter.

Voice mail is now such a common part of everyday business life that it seems unnecessary to describe how it works. But keep in mind that there are some more advanced voice mail features that you don't get on all systems. One example is "message broadcasting" — this allows you to send the same message simultaneously to multiple mailboxes. It can be useful, for example, when someone needs to notify a group of people about the time and venue of a meeting. Another is the ability to set up temporary "guest mailboxes" for people visiting your office who don't have their own extension on the phone system.

You should also consider the different methods that alert extension users to the fact that there's a message waiting in their voice mailbox. Key system users, and PBX users with special feature phones, may have a special light on their station instruments; otherwise, you usually have to settle for a special "stutter tone" that you hear in place of the continuous dial tone when you pick up the phone. More on voice mail — and related voice processing functions — in the next chapter.

***Wireless systems:*** A very new development in the key systems market is the wireless phone system, where all the station instruments are portable units that operate like cordless phones over an area of a few thousand square feet. At the time of this writing, only one vendor — Premier — was selling an all-wireless key system. AT&T offers you the option of using some cordless phones on what is mainly a conventional key system, but no other vendors do so.

# Key System & PBX Vendor Profiles

Following next are short profiles of over 30 vendors of key systems (including KSU-less systems) and PBXs. My intention here is to give you a general idea of the types of systems that each vendor has to offer, of where the systems come from, and how they are sold.

Vendors' addresses and phone numbers are included in each entry — call the numbers shown for details of sales offices and/or dealers in your area (though keep in mind that some companies will refer you to supply houses which, in turn, will give you the names of dealers they sell to). Vendors are listed alphabetically in order of brand name.

## *ATC*

*American Telecommunications Corporation*
*1180 Seminole Trail*
*Charlottesville, VA 22901*
*Tel: 800 473 5282*
ATC is a subsidiary of Comdial, a prominent vendor listed separately in this section. Whereas Comdial specializes in American-made systems for smaller and medium businesses, ATC sells imported products aimed only at very small users. Most of ATC's products are regular single-line phones, but it also sells one KSU-less system that can be used either in a small business environment or with Centrex. Sales are through dealers and supply houses.

## *AT&T*

AT&T Global Business Communications Systems
211 Mount Airy Road
Basking Ridge, NJ 07920
Tel: 800 247 7000
AT&T is still the market leader in the business phone systems market. The company sells its phone systems direct and through dealers. All are made in the US — AT&T has manufacturing facilities in Shreveport, LA and Denver, CO.

AT&T has become a more interesting vendor since it began to revamp its smaller and mid-size phone systems range in 1991. It is no longer fair to accuse the company of charging high prices for under-featured equipment. Though AT&T is still not a bargain supplier, and though it still doesn't always match its fanciest competitors feature-for-feature, it can be a tempting choice for buyers who want to play it safe. Even if you end up not buying an AT&T system, I recommend at least considering one — at the very least, it'll give you a measure against which to compare offerings from other vendors.

AT&T's smallest key systems make up the Partner series. Introduced in 1990, the Partners come in three shapes and sizes, ranging from 4 lines/12 extensions to 24 lines/48 extensions; the larger systems have significantly more features. An interesting, and unusual, feature of all the Partners is that AT&T supplies an optional multi-line cordless phone that can work as an extension on the system. At the time of this writing, no other key system vendor offered this (though Premier had just introduced a system which only uses wireless handsets).

Moving up from the Partners, you get to AT&T's Merlin systems. The one to check out is the Merlin Legend which was introduced in 1991. This is an ISDN-compatible digital key system/PBX hybrid that can handle up to 104 lines/200 extensions, with a maximum of 230 ports. However, AT&T is also pushing it for businesses with as few as 10 extensions. You can use old Merlin telephones with the Legend, if you already have a pile of them left over from your old system, but the new ones are much nicer if you can start afresh. There is an impressive list of features available on this system, and there is also the unique AT&T cordless extension option I referred to above.

AT&T's smallest dedicated PBX is the Definity G3vs, which is a downsized version of its super-large, all-bells-and-whistles Definity systems.

## Comdial

*Comdial Corporation*
*1180 Seminole Trail*
*PO Box 7266*
*Charlottesville, VA 22906*
*Tel: 800 347 1432*

Comdial is a prominent supplier of small/mid-size business phone systems, with a history that leads quite a long way back. What sets it apart from most of its competitors is that it manufactures its products in the US. Comdial has built a solid, if not dazzling, reputation in the market. Comdial sells a variety of digital and analog key systems and hybrids ranging from a 4 line/8 extension key system to a 120 line/192 extension hybrid. Comdial is one of the few major phone systems vendors that is still introducing new analog products.

All Comdial sales are through dealers and supply houses. Comdial also owns a company called American Telecommunications Corporation (ATC) which sells single line phones and KSU-less systems that are made overseas.

## *Cortelco*

*Cortelco, Inc.*
*4119 Willow Lake Boulevard*
*Memphis, TN 38118*
*Tel: 800 866 8880*
Cortelco sells key systems and large PBXs. It is part manufacturer, part importer — in general, its smaller systems come from overseas. Like many companies in the telecommunications industry, it has a long and somewhat complicated history.

The business was started by ITT in 1957 as the Kellog Switchboard & Supply Company. It went through several name changes under ITT ownership until 1987 when ITT merged its telecommunications business with Alcatel, the French conglomerate. It then became part of Alcatel's US operation and was renamed Corinth Telecommunications Corporation (it was based in Corinth, MS), which subsequently became abbreviated to Cortelco. In 1990, Alcatel decided to sell the company as part of a larger restructuring of its operations, and Cortelco was acquired by private investors.

Corporate headquarters were moved to Memphis, but the plant at Corinth remains open producing a PBX system and some older key systems and hybrids. The company's newer key systems, however, are imported from the Far East. Cortelco still has a license to use the ITT brand name when selling phone systems, even though ITT no longer has any involvement in the company. Sales are direct, through dealers, and through supply houses.

## *DBA*

*DBA Communication Systems Inc.*
*Q101–19428 66th Avenue South*
*Kent, WA 98032*
*Tel: 206 251 0526*
DBA is a Canadian company — founded in 1979 and headquartered in Vancouver — that specializes in small KSU-less systems that can be used on their own or behind Centrex. Sales in the US are through dealers, supply houses, and some telephone companies.

The company has a good reputation and sells some excellent products for people needing no more than 3 lines/8 extensions. I would definitely check them out if I were looking for a system of this type and size.


# DEKA

*DEKA Corporation*
*1800 New Highway*
*Farmingdale, NY 11735*
*Tel: 800 248 0084*
DEKA is another small KSU-less specialist — and is also worth considering if you're in the market for a very small and pretty inexpensive system.


# Eagle 1

*AVG Corporation*
*132 Wilbur Place*
*Bohemia, NY 11716*
*Tel: 516 244 9600*
Eagle is quite an old name in the phone business, though it has lately entered an unsettled phase. The Eagle brand name belonged to a company called Eagle Telephonics, which sub-contracted the manufacturing to AVG, a Fortune 500 company that's big in electronics and automation control.

Around 1992, Eagle Telephonics ran into financial difficulties and settled its debts to AVG by giving the latter its inventory and the right to sell and continue manufacturing the equipment. The Eagle products are now being sold by a new division of AVG known as Eagle 1/AVG. The Eagle 1/AVG product range, which is made in the US, consists of some fairly straightforward analog key systems and hybrids, serving smaller to medium buyers — don't expect the latest in phone systems technology. Sales and support are through dealers.


# Executone

*Executone Information Systems, Inc.*
*Six Thorndal Circle*
*Darien, CT 06820*
*Tel: 800 458 4802*
Executone is well established in the phone systems market. It also owns the Vodavi brand, which is discussed separately in

these Vendor Profiles (the Vodavi operation tends to focus on sales to smaller/medium-size users, while the Executone brand is targeted chiefly at medium/larger-size companies with more advanced needs).

Executone markets a digital hybrid called the Integrated Digital System (IDS), which is available in several sizes accommodating fairly small to quite large organizations (the largest system goes all the way to 432 ports). The IDS can be quite a sophisticated system, especially in its larger configurations. It is manufactured under contract by suppliers in Hong Kong and elsewhere in the Far East, though some work is also carried out in Executone's own facility in the US. The IDS was first introduced in 1987.

Executone sells direct and through dealers. The company has a very wide sales and support network — one of the best in the business. I regard Executone as one of the more conservative choices for buyers seeking an advanced system from a solid vendor.

## Fujitsu

*Fujitsu Business Communications Systems*
*7776 S. Pointe Parkway West*
*Phoenix, AZ 85044*
*Tel: 602 921 5900*
Fujitsu Business Communications was created in 1988 by the merger of units from Fujitsu America, Inc. and GTE Communications Systems Corporation. The company makes PBXs and concentrates on the top end of the market. Its smallest system is its Series 3, a hybrid system ranging from 30 to more than 400 stations. The company also sells a range of other very large PBXs going all the way to 9,600 ports. Fujitsu has a strong pedigree in telecommunications. It targets buyers with sophisticated needs — and budgets to go with them.

## Hitachi

*Hitachi America, Ltd.*
*Telecommunications Division*
*3617 Parkway Lane*
*Norcross, GA 30092*
*Tel: 404 446 8820*
Hitachi concentrates on the top end of the business phone systems market. The HCX 5000 series is a digital PBX range that was introduced in 1989 and comes in several sizes ranging from

500 to as many as 6,000 ports. These are very upscale systems that offer just about all the features you could hope for. They are also ISDN compatible. Large corporations looking for a state-of-the-art phone system will want to consider Hitachi. Specialized software packages are available for a number of vertical markets, including — bizarrely — prisons.

# Inter-Tel

*Inter-Tel, Inc.*
*7300 W. Boston Street*
*Chandler, AZ 85226*
*Tel: 602 961 9000*

Inter-Tel is a well-established name in the phone industry. It sells a variety of key systems and hybrids aimed mainly at smaller- and medium-size users, though the company's largest system goes up to 832 ports.

Sales are through dealers, supply houses, and 17 direct sales offices in major markets. The products are manufactured for Inter-Tel by a number of mainly offshore contractors, including Samsung in South Korea and a company called Maxon in the Philippines.

# Iwatsu

*Iwatsu America, Inc.*
*430 Commerce Boulevard*
*Carlstadt, NJ 07072*
*Tel: 201 935 8580*

Iwatsu is a Japanese manufacturer with a respectable share of the world market for smaller- and medium-size phone systems. It sells through dealers and supply houses.

# MacroTel

*MacroTel International Corporation*
*6001 Park of Commerce Boulevard*
*Boca Raton, FL 33487*
*Tel: 800 826 1627*

MacroTel sells a variety of Korean-manufactured systems for smaller and medium businesses. The company was founded in 1980 and began life by focusing on Latin America (it claims to have 23 percent of the Mexican key systems market, for example). It has been selling systems in the US for a number of years, and it seems to be getting a higher profile.

MacroTel's product line ranges from small analog KSU-less and key systems to digital hybrids for medium-size companies. Sales are through dealers and supply houses.

# Mitel

*Mitel, Inc.*
*11921 Freedom Drive*
*Suite 500*
*Reston, VA 22090*
*Tel: 800 648 3579*

Mitel is a major manufacturer of PBX systems; it no longer sells key systems. Until a couple of years ago, Mitel's controlling shareholder was British Telecom (BT) — the UK's equivalent of AT&T — but, in June 1992, BT sold its holding to venture capital investors. All of Mitel's manufacturing now takes place in Canada.

Mitel has a fine reputation for offering systems that are good values, easy to use, and productive — there are a large number of very satisfied users. Many of Mitel's customers are very large organizations but, unlike some other PBX vendors, it does not overlook the needs of smaller offices wanting a traditional operator-controlled phone system.

# NEC

*NEC America, Inc.*
*8 Old Sod Farm*
*Melville, NY 11747*
*Tel: 800 626 4952*

NEC, the Japanese telecommunications and computer giant, is a significant force in the US phone systems market, with a product line ranging from quite small to very large systems. Sales are direct and through dealers.

NEC's offering for smaller/medium-size users is the Electra Professional, which is a digital hybrid. Large users are offered the NEAX series of PBXs.

# Nitsuko

*Nitsuko America, Inc.*
*4 Forest Parkway*
*Shelton, CT 06484*
*Tel: 800 999 8630*

Nitsuko is a long-established and respected Japanese manufacturer of phone systems, which for a long time only operated in the US through OEM agreements with companies relabeling its products. Lately, however, Nitsuko has begun to operate under its own name. This came about partly as a result of the 1991 collapse and subsequent reorganization of TIE, previously number-two to AT&T in the key systems market. As part of the reorganization, Nitsuko acquired TIE's manufacturing rights and some of its inventory.

Nitsuko now manufactures the key systems that are sold under the TIE name, but also markets similar systems under the Nitsuko brand name through dealers and supply houses. I understand that most of Nitsuko's key system manufacturing currently takes place in Thailand (no pun intended); some, however, takes place in North America and the company stresses its ability to make any of its systems in any of its locations (handy when bidding for government contracts).

The main product in the Nitsuko range — and the one it makes for TIE — is called Onyx, which was originally developed by TIE itself. This is a digital system that comes in several flavors, ranging from small key systems to hybrids and PBXs that go up to 72 lines and 180 extensions. The company also sells smaller analog key systems — in fact, it is one of the few major phone systems manufacturers that is still introducing new analog products.

# Northern Telecom

**Key systems:**
*Northern Telecom Inc./Norstar Division*
*565 Marriott Drive/Suite 300*
*Nashville, TN 37210*
*Tel: 800 667 8437*

**PBX systems:**
*Northern Telecom Inc.*
*2305 Mission College Boulevard*
*Santa Clara, CA 95054–1591*
*Tel: 800 667 8437*

Northern Telecom — a Canadian company — is one of the biggest names in the phone systems business. Traditionally a supplier of large PBXs, it has lately also made considerable progress in the mid-size key systems market with its Norstar system.

The Norstar, which was first introduced in 1988, is a digital hybrid which is supplied in configurations ranging from 3 lines/8 extensions to 128 ports. In its off-the-shelf version, the Norstar lacks some advanced system features offered by its strongest rivals, but one of its most distinctive attributes is its so-called "open architecture," which allows developers and value-added resellers to enhance it in customized versions. Sales are through dealers and regional telephone companies; there are also some direct sales for very large accounts.

Northern Telecom is best known as a PBX vendor. It is number-two in that market to AT&T. Its Meridian 1 PBX is available in different sizes going all the way up to 10,000 ports. The version most likely to interest readers of this book is the Meridian 1 Option 11, which is designed for businesses wanting between 30–200 total lines and extensions. Much emphasis has been placed on making the Option 11 easy and quick to install. There is a very wide range of available system features, as you might expect. Sales are mainly through dealers.

## *Panasonic*

*Panasonic Communications & Systems*
*2 Panasonic Way*
*Secaucus, NJ 07094*
*Tel: 800 435 4327*

Panasonic — the trading arm of Matsushita, the Japanese office equipment and consumer electronics giant — sells a variety of small and medium phone systems. The range stretches from small analog and digital key systems, to a 144-line/288-extension hybrid.

Panasonic won't win prizes for offering the widest number of features or the most ambitious implementation of telephone technology — some of its systems are distinctly low on frills. But it could be a good choice for people who want a straightforward, big-name system — providing, of course, that the price you're offered reflects what you're getting.

# Premier

*Premier Telecom Products Inc.*
*600 Industrial Parkway*
*Industrial Airport, KS 66031*
*Tel: 800 326 8775*

Premier is owned by North Supply, the largest of the business phone systems supply houses (remember that supply houses are distributors that buy products from manufacturers and then sell them to dealers and, occasionally, direct to very large end users). Premier, which was launched in 1983, is effectively North Supply's own brand for products that are made for it under contract by a number of mostly Far Eastern manufacturers. North Supply, in turn, is owned by Sprint — yes, the same Sprint that is number-three in the long-distance phone service market.

Premier is becoming more ambitious in the type of phone systems it sells and has also begun using the Sprint connection in its marketing. The company sells digital key systems and a PBX called the Premier Answer.

Premier also has a very unusual product called the Premier Microcel. This a digital wireless key telephone system, in which portable handsets replace conventional deskbound station instruments. Premier stresses the innovative nature of the wireless technology, which is different from cellular or conventional cordless phone technology. The Microcel system can handle up to 4 lines and 24 stations.

# Redcom

*Redcom Laboratories, Inc.*
*One Redcom Center*
*Victor, NY 14564–0995*
*Tel: 716 924 7550*

Redcom is a PBX manufacturer, concentrating on larger installations. Sales and support are all direct. The SBX — or "Small Business Exchange" — is Redcom's smallest system, and this can range from 4 to 384 ports. It was first introduced in 1981. Larger versions can go up to 1,200 ports. Redcom makes sophisticated equipment. A distinctive Redcom feature is its Radio Line Interface, which enables you to connect two-way radios into your business phone system.

# Rolm

*Rolm Inc.*
*4900 Old Ironsides Drive*
*Santa Clara, CA 95054*
*Tel: 408 492 2000*

Rolm is a famous force in the telecommunications industry. It made a name for itself in the 1970s by being one of the first to challenge AT&T's dominance of the PBX market. In the mid-1980s, Rolm was acquired by IBM when the latter was trying to buy its way into telecommunications. The IBM and Rolm corporate cultures proved an awkward match. Over the next few years, IBM became uncomfortable in the phone systems market and, in 1989, it sold half the business to Siemens, the German telecommunications giant, which assumed responsibility for running the operation. Subsequently, Siemens bought IBM's remaining stake.

Rolm is active in the top portion of the PBX market. Its main product is the 9751 CBX series, which comes in several sizes ranging from 50 to 20,000 lines. Rolm has a great reputation in the telecommunications industry for quality and service. Sales are direct.

# Samsung/Prostar

*Samsung Telecommunications America, Inc.*
*1350 E. Newport Center Drive*
*Deerfield Beach, FL 33442*
*Tel: 305 426 4100*

Prostar used to be the name of a telephone distributor which was once owned by STC — a British telecommunications company — but was later acquired by Samsung, the South Korean conglomerate. Recently, the company has been renamed to operate under the Samsung identity. As you might expect, the phone systems it sells are all made by Samsung.

The company focuses on analog key systems and hybrids for small- and medium-size businesses. The systems tend not to be at the cutting edge when it comes to features and technology, but they can appeal to buyers in search of fairly straightforward solutions to mainstream requirements.

# Solitaire

*Solitaire Telecommunications Corp.*
*2100 Roswell Road NE*
*Suite 200-C*
*Marietta, GA 30062*
*Tel: 404 971 4811*

Solitaire, which was formed in 1987, sells a KSU-less system called the Plus Five Basic. Each station can be configured to access up to five lines — which is more than most KSU-less systems — and the company says that you can set up a system with a "virtually unlimited" number of extensions. It can be a good bet for Centrex applications or for smaller standalone environments. Sales are direct and through dealers.

# Southwestern Bell

*Southwestern Bell*
*7442 Shadeland Station Way*
*Indianapolis, IN 46256*
*Tel: 800 255 8480*

Southwestern Bell is a regional Bell company that distributes phone equipment nationwide, not just in its own area. Its Freedom Phone branded equipment is aimed at small business users and is sold through dealers and supply houses. Most of it is imported.

# SRX

*SRX Inc.*
*3480 Lotus Drive*
*Plano, TX 75075*
*Tel: 214 985 2600*

Founded in 1983, SRX is a medium-size manufacturer focusing on mid-market and larger systems, which are made in America. Sales and support are entirely through dealers. SRX is a reputable vendor for companies wanting a reasonably upscale phone system. It is not an obvious choice for smaller users.

# Tadiran

*Tadiran Electronic Industries Inc.*
*5733 Myerlake Circle*
*Clearwater, FL 34620*
*Tel: 813 536 3222*

Tadiran is an Israeli electronics firm, with a background in the defense industry, which also sells telecommunications products for the commercial market. The company has been in the telecommunications industry for over 20 years; before selling products in the US under its own name, it sold them through OEM agreements with GTE.

Tadiran sells a variety of analog and digital key systems and hybrids. The flagship of its product range is the Coral line. Introduced in 1987–1989, this comes in several sizes, the largest of which can go all the way to 3,840 ports (though few Tadiran customers are as large as that). The Coral systems are innovative in design and rich in system features — there are few mainstream requirements which can't be handled.

Tadiran is one of the more high tech vendors serving medium-size businesses. Buyers with advanced needs — and, presumably, budgets to match — should consider calling them. Sales are through dealers.

# Tandy/Radio Shack

*Tandy Corporation*
*1800 One Tandy Center*
*Fort Worth, TX 76102*
*Tel: 817 390 3011*

Tandy sells a variety of imported small KSU-less systems through its Radio Shack stores under the DUo-FONE brand name. The equipment is nothing remarkable, but buying a small phone system at a Radio Shack store is easy and convenient if there's one close by. Some buyers may consider this a better option than trying to locate a dealer for another KSU-less brand they've never heard of before.

# Telrad

*Telrad Telecommunications, Inc.*
*135 Crossways Park Drive*
*Woodbury, NY 11797*
*Tel: 800 628 3038*

Telrad is an Israeli company, which was founded over 40 years ago and has worldwide sales of over $165 million. Telrad has a fairly strong presence in the US market, and an excellent reputation. All sales are through its own dealers.

At press-time, Telrad was still selling some older small/medium analog systems. However, these are being played down in its marketing, and the emphasis is now on its digital hybrid and PBX products. The Digital KeyBx systems, which were introduced in 1991 and are marketed as hybrids, stretch from 8 lines/18 extensions up to 128 ports. The new Digital 400 is a PBX which goes up to 384 ports.

Telrad is a strong supplier with first-class products. It is a good choice for smaller/medium-size businesses looking for a system from an established vendor.


# *TIE*

*TIE/Communications, Inc.*
*4 Progress Avenue*
*Seymour, CT 06483*
*Tel: 203 888 8000*

TIE is a leading supplier of business phone systems. It has traditionally been number-two to AT&T in the mid-size phone systems market, though it has recently been through an unsettled phase. Previously a manufacturer, TIE ran into financial difficulties and was forced to file for Chapter 11 in 1991. After only 84 days, a successful reorganization was completed which resulted in 100 cents on the dollar being paid to creditors and ownership of the company passing to the Marmon Group, a $3.8-billion, privately-held conglomerate.

As part of the reorganization, TIE sold its manufacturing rights and inventory to Nitsuko, a leading Japanese manufacturer of smaller and mid-size phone systems. The key systems that TIE now sells are bought from Nitsuko and relabeled, though the latter also sells them through other dealers and distributors. TIE also acts as a distributor for Mitel, selling the latter's PBXs under the Mitel brand name.

The TIE product range is narrower than it used to be before the reorganization, when there were several parallel ranges for different distribution channels. TIE sells and supports its equipment through 60 direct sales offices and through dealers. Though TIE is not the company it once was, it retains excellent distribution and offers a solid product range. It is still worth considering if you are looking for a mid-range business phone system, though it isn't what it used to be.

# *Toshiba*

*Toshiba America Information Systems, Inc.*
*Telecommunications Systems Division*
*9740 Irvine Boulevard*
*Irvine, CA 92718*
*Tel: 800 222 5805*

Toshiba is one of the few office equipment "generalists" — i.e., companies that sell a wide range of equipment types — to be involved in the phone systems market. In fact, it is the only company with a foothold in several traditional office equipment markets (copiers, fax, notebook PCs, printers, etc.) to have a full range of phone systems for businesses of all sizes (Panasonic's phone systems range is a lot narrower). That of itself doesn't amount to a case to rush out and buy a Toshiba system, but it's an interesting point to note. All sales and support are through dealers and telephone companies, though there is also direct sales support for its largest PBXs.

Toshiba's Strata series consists of digital key systems and hybrids aimed at everyone from very small offices to ones with almost 100 people (the older analog versions have recently been discontinued). Toshiba's top-of-the-line systems form its Perception series, which ranges from a 32 line/180 extension hybrid to a PBX which can handle as many as 1,920 ports.

Toshiba sells a remarkably wide range of phone systems, addressing everyone from very small offices to pretty large organizations. It can be a good mainstream choice for businesses of all sizes — with such a wide product range, it should be able to work its way onto many shortlists.

# *Vodavi*

*Vodavi Communications Systems Inc.*
*8300 East Raintree Drive*
*Scottsdale, AZ 85260*
*Tel: 602 998 2200*

Vodavi is a major — and respected — player in this market, concentrating on smaller- to medium-size companies. It is part of the same group as Executone (discussed earlier in these Vendor Profiles); there is some overlap between the two brands, though Executone tends to focus on slightly larger systems.

Vodavi's products are manufactured for it by Far Eastern suppliers. There are two product ranges under the overall Vodavi brand umbrella. The best known is the Starplus line, which is made by Goldstar (a leading South Korean manufacturer); this is sold exclusively through supply houses. Vodavi's other product line — Infinite — goes through dealers (which is where Vodavi competes against the Executone brand products). Both lines contain small/medium key systems and hybrids. Starplus contains both analog and digital products, while Infinite is all analog.

Vodavi covers the small/medium-size phone systems market with a comprehensive product range and strong distribution. Its equipment is good, and the company is well established. It is definitely worth considering.


# *WIN*

*WIN Communications Corporation*
*1770 Corporate Drive*
*Suite 535*
*Norcross, GA 30093*
*Tel: 404 925 0087*

WIN, formerly known as Walker Communications, was acquired by Nissho Iwai — a Japanese company — a few years ago, but became independent again in August 1992. It sells a range of analog key systems and digital key systems/hybrids, which are mostly made in Malaysia. WIN focuses on the middle of the phone systems market. It isn't an obvious choice if you are very small or very large, but it may be worth thinking about if you're somewhere in the middle. ✍

# Chapter 11

# Voice Processing

# Voice Processing

This chapter is about third-party voice processing systems that you add to a phone system you already have, or to one that you are buying at the same time. I'll be defining "voice processing" shortly, but the term covers voice mail, automatic attendant, and a lot more besides.

I am not discussing voice processing modules that come as same-brand options on complete phone systems. That is why you won't find coverage of vendors such as AT&T, Northern Telecom, Vodavi, Comdial, etc. However, complete phone systems were dealt with separately in the previous chapter.

It's worth keeping in mind, incidentally, that some of the phone system vendors' own voice processing modules are actually developed for them by third-party companies that are discussed in this chapter. Later in this chapter, I'll be reviewing the pros and cons of getting a voice processing system bearing the same brand name as the rest of your phone system, instead of taking the third-party route.

## What is Voice Processing?

Most people, when they think of this sort of system, call it "voice mail," because that's the function they're most familiar with. Today, however, most voice mail systems are capable of doing a lot more than just taking messages, and more applications are being added all the time. For this reason, the term "voice mail" is experiencing shades of obsolescence as a means of describing entire systems, despite the fact that there isn't yet a truly viable, or standardized, alternative.

The best all-encompassing term that exists at present is "voice processing" (which I'll sometimes be referring to as "VP"). This originally applied specifically to applications that involved systems "speaking" information — for example, the ones used by banks that allow customers to call up their account balances using a touch-tone phone. Today, however, it is emerging as the best available phrase to describe systems that handle all or some of the following range of functions:

❑ **Voice mail:** The system of personalized voice mailboxes that is at the heart of most systems.

**Inside This Chapter ...**

❑ **Automatic attendant:** The module that routes callers through the system without them having to talk to a human attendant (this usually goes hand-in-hand with voice mail, but it's possible to have one without the other).

❑ **Audiotex:** An automated system allowing people to call in and hear recorded information on subjects of their choice.

❑ **Interactive voice response (IVR):** A much more sophisticated system for giving information to callers, which allows them to access a computerized database with a telephone and retrieve information that is electronically converted to speech via a voice synthesizer. At present, people wanting to go up the IVR path are almost invariably going to require custom work.

❑ **LAN connectivity:** A means of allowing users to view and share information relating to their use of the voice processing system on their regular networked PCs (for example, you could view a summary of traffic into your mailbox on your PC screen).

❑ **Fax capabilities:** This can mean various things, including allowing users to receive faxes into the same mailboxes as their voice messages before printing them out on laser printers and/or distributing them to other users on the system.

❑ **Fax-on-demand:** A system allowing people to call into the system and request specified documents to be faxed to them automatically without any human intervention at the sending end.

I'll be talking more about all of these functions later in the chapter, as well as describing other features associated with them. Clearly, the term "voice processing" is not an ideal one to describe what is being discussed, as some of the functions go beyond voice. Still, it seems the best of the bunch for the time being — eventually, some other term, such as "message processing," may take its place.

### What the systems consist of

Most systems today are based on industry-standard personal computers containing "voice boards" and running special software programs. This is the route that most buyers take — it involves buying the voice processing system from your third-party supplier and then connecting it to the rest of your office phone system.

It's not a matter of each extension user having a specially-configured PC — instead, you just have one central PC platform serving the whole office. Normally, the PC in question doesn't also get used for other functions; however, very small offices might get away with using a computer that has other jobs as well.

Often, VP vendors supply turnkey systems that include the PC itself, with the boards in place and all the necessary software installed. All your local dealer has to do is make the connection with your phone system (something that some technically-proficient end-users might consider doing themselves, though this isn't generally recommended).

Sometimes, though, you have the choice of buying the voice boards and software separately, which can be handy if you have old PCs needing a new reason for carrying on — in general, voice processing has surprisingly modest hardware requirements and does not require the latest level of PC power. More on this later.

Not all voice processing systems are based on industry-standard PCs, however. Some third-party vendors don't use regular PCs, but instead base their systems on "dedicated" hardware platforms. These are non-standard computers using proprietary ingredients. Dedicated systems are usually associated with the high end of the market. While most of the companies that sell them have impeccable pedigrees for both product and support, the logic of using dedicated platforms is diminishing. As in other fields of computer-related technology, industry-standard platforms are catching up in performance terms, while offering significant advantages in cost. I'll return to this later.

### Gray areas

Most voice processing systems can be configured in a wide variety of ways. It can, therefore, be quite difficult to define the exact features and parameters of a system, or to compare two different ones, since most don't come out of boxes and can be customized. Comparisons are also made tricky by the fact that there are frequently gray areas, and a lack of standard terminology, when it comes to describing detailed features (as opposed to broad functions).

Two systems might claim to have the same feature, for example, but may go about it in two totally different ways — one quite elegant, perhaps, and the other somewhat makeshift. Likewise, a feature as implemented on one system might be a great deal more sophisticated than the same one on another. In addition, some features may vary depending on which phone system a VP product works with.

On a related note, it is difficult to get a firm handle on pricing in this market, without getting custom quotes for your particular situation. This is because there are so many variables with every system depending on the size, software, configuration, installation, and the margin a dealer chooses to work with.

### The service bureau option

You don't have to buy your own equipment to take advantage of voice mail. As an alternative, you can use the services of a bureau. This means that your unanswered calls are forwarded to voice mailboxes on the bureau's central equipment (which also services lots of other businesses). You can access the messages from any phone, just as if you had your own system.

Basic voice mail bureau services are provided by local telephone companies ("telcos"), and their Centrex services generally offer slightly more advanced versions. There are non-telco bureaus as well, some offering fairly straightforward services on a local level and others — such as Tigon — providing a more sophisticated service to businesses nationwide.

In general, bureaus are most cost-effective for smaller offices — those with fewer than 20 people, say — or for people very unsure of their future needs who don't want to commit to something long-term. I'll be discussing the case for and against the bureau approach later in this chapter.

### Voice processing controversy

Back in the late 1970s, AT&T came up with some interesting statistics. Ma Bell (as it then was) discovered that three-fourths of all calls were not completed on the first attempt. Either the party being called was not at his or her desk (so the phone just kept on ringing), or the line was busy.

AT&T also determined that half the calls made were to convey information in one direction: put another way, 50 percent of calls were placed to tell someone something to which no response was really necessary. AT&T also found out that a full two-thirds of calls were considered less important than the work they interrupted.

Since then, voice processing has stepped in to remedy these inefficiencies. Many companies have met the goal of eliminating the busy signal, the endless ringing of the unanswered phone, and the "please holds" spat out by harried receptionists. At the same time, attitudes have changed: the recorded announcement inviting messages no longer bears the stigma it once did, when it was a tell-tale sign of a very small business with a single-line telephone answering machine. In fact, voice mail has been a leveler, enabling small businesses to deal with outside callers using an interface not much different from that of much larger organizations.

The increasingly widespread use of voice processing in corporate America is not without its critics, however. Some people find these systems frustrating to deal with, and most have their own anecdotes about being given the run-around. In general, the complaint boils down to the fact that callers often spend more time maneuvering their way through a system before they complete their business than they do with a human-attended system.

In other words, the supposed benefits are all on the side of the organization that owns the equipment and are at the expense of the outside callers who have to use it. What's more, the breezy manner in which voice menus are delivered can do little to soften the irritation of having to listen to them. Sometimes, moreover, voice mail provides a cover to people who just don't like to answer their phone.

There's some validity to these complaints, but it's also true to say that companies that are infuriating to deal with via their voice processing systems are generally the ones that are dreadful to deal with anyway. Voice processing is neither a panacea for old communications problems, nor the root cause of new ones. It is the people behind a system that make it work or fail.

### Budgeting for voice processing

Traditionally, voice processing has been a tool for medium and larger size companies, but today it can be of interest to businesses of all sizes. Most smaller and medium size organizations should budget a minimum of a few thousand dollars; this excludes the cost of the PC itself (which these days can easily cost no more than about $1,000). Very small offices wanting pretty straightforward voice mail might get away with under $1,000 (again, plus the cost of the PC). Larger organizations will be in for a five figure bill, with the largest and most complex installations running well into six figures.

### Who are the vendors?

This is a highly fragmented market: there are a large number of fairly small vendors, and even the market leaders are companies you probably haven't heard of unless you happen to follow this industry for a living, or you've encountered them as a buyer or user.

Most of the vendors are first-and-foremost software developers. They buy in voice boards from a small number of companies that produce them, write the software, and put everything together in turnkey systems. Most develop systems based on voice boards supplied by one of two companies, Dialogic and Rhetorex. Although end-users don't deal directly with board manufacturers, those two names are as pivotal to a discussion of voice mail as Intel and Microsoft are to a discussion of personal computing. There will be frequent references to them throughout this chapter.

Some of the companies that develop Dialogic- and Rhetorex-based systems have become quite large businesses with strong distribution. Most, however, are fairly small. Many employ fewer than 10 people and/or have been around for less than five years (voice processing itself is not much more than a decade old anyway). Their typical profile can be described as: small, brainy, entrepreneurial, driven by technology, and yet to make the big time. The people who have gone into this business see it as a new frontier: as with previous frontier businesses, some pioneers may live out the American dream, while others will fall by the wayside.

In practice, the smaller vendors tend to sell the smaller systems. However, most are at pains to stress their ability to configure systems for virtually any size of buyer and few are prepared formally to cede major account territory to the big vendors, even though the reality is that they have so far had very little impact at that end of the market.

Many of the smaller vendors are keen on striking alliances with PBX/key system manufacturers, so that they supply the voice processing modules sold under the umbrella of the phone systems vendors. Those that succeed in forging these relationships are probably the ones that have the best chances of doing well. The others that stand a better-than-average chance are those that develop reputations in particular industries and vertical markets for customizing specialized systems.

A new twist is that some of the very big names in this market, which previously concentrated on Fortune 1000-type businesses, are now becoming more interested in addressing a much wider market, partly in response to a flattening out in their major account business. For example, Octel — the largest company in the business — has acquired Compass, a manufacturer of mid-market Dialogic-based systems, while VMX — one of Octel's main competitors — has acquired Rhetorex as its means of addressing the mass market. It remains to be seen what effect this will have, but the downward migration of the upscale vendors will do nothing to make life easier for the very small companies.

### Who you will buy from

Most voice processing systems are not bought from the manufacturers or developers direct, but from dealers. Even small developers can have a national presence of a sort by developing their dealer network. Some dealers merely act as resellers and installers, perhaps providing support services as well. Some — known as "value added resellers" (VARs) — do something to enhance systems, perhaps by customizing the software. And others act as systems integrators, creating turnkey systems by mixing software and boards they buy from developers with PC hardware they obtain from elsewhere.

# Voice Mail Features

There's clearly more to voice processing than leaving messages, but this is nonetheless its most prominent feature and it's the main reason why people get into it. Here's a little more on what it involves.

### Mailbox basics

The telephone answering function of a voice processing system answers users' lines when they are on the phone, away from their desk, or when they have told the system that they are unavailable. Messages are then recorded and stored on a computer disk, where the traditional analog method of storing sound is replaced by the digital method of encoding it into computer data — it's like the difference between a tape and a CD.

Each user has his or her own voice mailbox on the computer, which is effectively a data file. This mailbox can be checked regularly for messages, and — as I show below — most systems automatically alert users when one is waiting. One of the nice things about voice mail is that a caller can generally leave a message even if someone else is already doing so. Providing there is enough capacity in the system (something I'll be discussing later), the dreaded busy signal should not be encountered.

Every mailbox has its own voice greeting for callers. These days, the greeting is usually recorded in the user's own voice and many people change them on a daily basis to leave specific details of their comings and goings. You can do this easily from any phone. Less satisfactory are the systems that require the mailbox user to record his or her name in the middle of what is otherwise a generic greeting.

Some systems route callers directly into a mailbox when a phone is busy or unanswered, but others play them a short message asking whether they want to leave a message, or whether they'd like to select another option. Some people prefer the flexibility, but others find the repetitive announcements of options tedious. Users who know their way around a system are generally able to press a key to go directly into their desired option without waiting for the system to offer it. Up to a point, variations of this type represent not so much intrinsic differences between one voice mail product and another, as differences in how they are set up at the time of installation.

You can access your mailbox from any touch-tone phone, usually by entering a password. The keypad on your phone is also your vehicle for getting around the mailbox — pressing different numbers allows you to play, store, delete, scan, retransmit, and so on. Some super-friendly systems allow users to un-delete messages that have inadvertently been erased.

### User-programmable options

Many systems allow individual users to program other options from their phone, like choosing how many times a particular extension rings before the voice mail picks up. Another user-programmable feature is "call screening," which prompts callers to speak their names in order to give the mailbox owner the choice of either picking-up or having the voice mail take a message (an irritating feature, in my opinion, but some people seem to like it). Likewise, "do not disturb" routes all calls directly to the mailbox without ringing in the office, so users can remain uninterrupted when they need to concentrate.

Also in the user-programmable category is "call cascading," which allows users to program a series of numbers for the system to call to attempt delivery of messages it has recorded. The number of retries and intervals can also be selected. So, for instance, you could program the numbers for your cellular phone, home phone, and a friend's house, and the system would try one after the other every, say 15 minutes, until it is able to deliver the message. And, of course, all of the above can be programmed from any phone, anywhere, so travelers can stay in touch.

Some voice mail systems and services also provide the capability of controlling what kind of messages are forwarded using the cascade feature. For example, with systems where it is possible for callers to add an "urgent" tag to their messages, it may also be possible to have only the urgent ones forwarded to another number.

Another delivery option is a "time-of-day" feature that forwards messages only at certain times of the day. For example, medical and emergency personnel may arrange for voice mail messages to be sent to their home numbers at night.

### Features available to callers

Some voice mail systems allow callers to review messages they've left before hanging up — if a caller is unhappy with a message, he or she can scrap it and record another. That's quite useful if you're leaving complex messages (not to mention if you've just said something you'll later regret).

Callers may also have delivery options such as "urgent," "private," or even "future." "Urgent" messages are placed at the head of the line, so that they're delivered first when the called party checks his or her mailbox. The trouble with this feature is that some people routinely prioritize all the messages they leave, urgent or not, so the effect is nullified. "Private" usually means the message cannot be transferred by the recipient to someone else. "Future" allows callers to select when they want a message to be delivered.

Another function is message broadcasting — sending the same message simultaneously to multiple mailboxes. This can be useful, for example, when someone needs to leave the time and venue of a meeting for all potential attendees.

### Dealing with non-mailbox users

If you need to regularly send messages to someone outside your organization who doesn't have a voice mailbox, you may be able to provide them with a "guest" mailbox. This could be a full-fledged mailbox or it may be restricted, allowing the guest access to just a few system features.

Many voice processing systems have a feature called "message delivery," a variation of the message broadcasting feature referred to above. This allows the user to program the system so that it calls a series of outside numbers and delivers a recorded message — it will go on trying a number until it gets an answer. Many readers will be familiar with this technology in the form of annoying telesales devices that call prospective customers to deliver recorded sales pitches. However, it can also be used in more productive ways when you need to disseminate information quickly to a group of people outside your voice mail system.

### Message receiving features

So far, I've been talking mainly about features that are available when you're sending voice messages, but there are also several related to receiving them. One handy feature allows you to forward a received message to someone else's mailbox — you might want to do this if, for example, you felt it would be more appropriately dealt with by one of your colleagues or if you simply wanted to share the information.

Likewise, when you pick up a message that someone has left, you may be given the option of responding to it and having the reply forwarded automatically to the message leaver's own mailbox. A very useful and commonly-found feature is a "date/time stamp," which automatically records the time and day each message was left — I'd place that on a "must-have" features list!

### Message waiting

How do you know if you have a message waiting? That depends on your equipment. In some cases, there's no way of knowing, short of dialing into your mailbox to check. That's pretty low-tech, and it's clearly better to be alerted automatically when you've received a message.

This can be done with a light that flashes on your telephone when there's something in your mailbox (like the message-waiting light on a hotel phone). With sophisticated phones, a more detailed message-waiting notice may appear on an LCD display (it might show how many messages are waiting, for example). As I'll discuss later, message-waiting indicators of this kind require a fairly high degree of integration between the VP equipment and the phone system installed at your office.

Another kind of message-waiting indicator is a special dial tone, called a "stutter tone," which replaces the normal continuous one with a series of very short tones. The only problem with stutter tones is that you don't know you've got a message until you pick up the phone and put the receiver to your ear.

Other systems have a call-back feature: if a message came in while you were on the phone, the mailbox will call you as soon as you hang up.

Some systems can work with pagers, so that you automatically get beeped every time someone leaves a message in your mailbox. This is a very useful way of keeping in touch with your messages when you're on the road, as it saves calling in speculatively.

### Voice "forms"

Voice forms — also known as "audioforms" — are a specialized VP feature, whose job is to collect information from callers in an interactive manner. They ask you to respond to a series of questions, store the responses on disk, and then provide you with options for retrieving or processing the data. Voice forms are effectively the voice equivalents of a questionnaire.

# Automated Attendants

With voice mail, callers hear recorded messages when they reach the extension they're trying to get through to. Often, though, callers also find that a company's main phone number is answered by a machine rather than a human operator — this is the automated attendant.

Automated attendants greet callers with a digitally recorded message and allow people to route themselves through the phone system to the correct extensions. The technology is closely related to voice mail, and these days almost all voice processing systems cater to both applications. Some users who put in voice mail choose not to install an automated attendant as well — on the basis that the initial reception should be more personal — but it is rarely not an option.

### How they operate

Automated attendants are usually activated on the first or second ring. Typically, the greeting informs callers which company they've reached and asks for an extension number to be keyed in. Many systems set up name directories for callers who are unsure of the extension number: by having the caller spell out the person's last name on their keypad, the system attempts to make the connection automatically.

Automated attendants do not generally replace human operators, they work with them. This means that if a caller doesn't have an extension number, or needs help for any other reason, they can request an operator, either by pressing zero or doing nothing, and wait for a human voice to come on the line.

Keep this in mind when you're assessing the overall cost-effectiveness of the equipment — you should be able to reduce staffing levels at the switchboard, but not do away with them entirely. Technically, it is possible to run an auto attendant system without an operator, but this arrangement is likely to lead to a lot of unhappy callers (especially those with rotary phones). Many users with automated attendants regard them as devices to handle overflow during peak calling hours — they prefer the initial reception to be personal, workload permitting.

Sometimes callers aren't trying to speak to a particular person, but rather to a particular division or group. Automated attendants can be set up to deal with this situation: instead of, or in addition to, asking for an extension number or name, the greeting message can offer the option of selecting a particular department — the often-heard "Press 1 for Sales, Press 2 for Service," and so on.

Many auto attendants come with time-of-day and, often, day-of-year features, which allow users to customize morning, afternoon, after-hours, and holiday greetings that are played automatically at the appropriate times. This feature often accommodates daylight savings time.

Keep in mind that with direct inward dialing — the phone system feature that allows outside callers to come straight through to individual extensions — a lot of inward traffic can bypass both automatic and human attendants.

# Audiotex & IVR

Audiotex (sometimes spelled "audiotext," though purists argue that this is wrong) is a fancy name for a recorded information service. While early audiotex services were tape-based, they are now fully integrated into digital voice processing technology. Audiotex is one of those features that comes in levels of sophistication that vary enormously. At its most basic, it amounts to little more than an "announce-only" voice mailbox that gives out information, but doesn't allow the caller an opportunity to leave a message.

More advanced audiotex can be set-up to progress to many "levels," so that callers have numerous options and sub-options about what they want to hear. In all cases, though, the information was originally recorded from someone reading it out. That is the fundamental difference between it and a somewhat more sophisticated voice processing function called "interactive voice response" (IVR).

IVR is also a method of allowing callers to listen to information, but in this case what they hear is computer data that has been converted to speech sound using a digital voice synthesizer. In other words, you aren't actually hearing a human voice, but a computer rendering of one. The information is drawn from a computer database that is integrated with the VP system.

IVR can be used for disseminating any type of information that is suitable for storing in database format — including real-time information (i.e., data that is constantly updated). It is often found in very upscale installations (e.g., banking systems and airline arrival/departure information lines).

However, IVR can also be used in more straightforward applications as an alternative to audiotex. In fact, callers may find it hard to tell whether information they are listening to is upmarket audiotex or entry-level IVR. While many voice processing vendors claim to have IVR capability, buyers should keep in mind that this almost always involves custom work — having IVR capability is not the same as having considerable experience in implementing it.

# Integrating With Fax, E-Mail, & LANs

A further option to consider is integrating voice messaging with your fax and/or electronic mail communications. This is the latest trend, and the market is still young.

Fax link-ups with voice processing systems can involve a number of things. One is having faxes arrive in a fax mailbox that's part of, or connected with, your voice mailbox. This is bit like using a fax modem to receive faxes into a PC, but the difference is that the fax management hardware and software is part of the voice processing system.

Faxes received in a mailbox can be stored, copied to other mailboxes, forwarded to regular fax machines at other locations, and output on a laser printer. Mailbox users can be notified of received faxes, in much the same way as they are told about voice messages. A voice processing/fax link-up may involve fax mailboxes having their own direct dial numbers, or it might require senders to route through an automatic attendant and specify a fax extension number — something which can confuse people who aren't used to sending faxes this way. Some vendors offer features that allow mailboxes and/or automated attendants to distinguish automatically between incoming voice and fax calls, so that you only need to publish one number.

This technology is clearly interesting, but it is also young. Anyone who has ever lived with the often unpredictable quirks of PC fax modems and voice/fax line-sharing might be wary about forgoing the reliability and convenience of dedicated fax machines with their own lines until the integration of fax with voice processing has become more mature. Besides, fax mailboxes alone are unlikely to dispense with dedicated fax machines, as they are essentially to do with receiving and forwarding faxes — you still have to make other arrangements to send your own fax originals.

### Fax-on-demand

Of wider interest, perhaps, than fax mailboxes is an increasingly common function known as "fax-on-demand" — a.k.a. "auto fax-back." This allows people to call into a voice processing system and select information to be faxed to them automatically with no human involvement at the sending end. They make their requests after hearing an audiotex menu of available documents. The documents themselves are scanned into your VP system by faxing them in from a normal machine.

Fax-on-demand can work in a couple of ways: "one-call" and "two-call." One-call systems require the caller to initiate the request from the phone built into their fax machine and then stay on the line: the information is then faxed over during the same call. The benefit of this approach is that the information provider doesn't have to pick up the tab for the phone call.

With two-call systems, callers are able to initiate the request from any touch-tone phone — in this case, the sending system calls their fax machine back a minute or two later to transmit the information (the caller would have entered in his or her fax number as part of the initiation process). Some fax-on-demand systems can be set to work either way.

Many voice processing systems now offer fax-on-demand, usually as an option. The amount of faxed material you can have available to callers is limited only by disk space in your VP hardware. Often, callers are encouraged to request a faxed description of all the documents you have available the first time they use the system, as this makes it much easier to choose further documents compared with wading through endless voice menus.

Some systems offer built-in credit card processing, for when you want callers to pay for information they access. Others are able to work with subscriber PIN codes that are only usable for a preset number of requests — this provides another method of charging for information.

Prices for basic fax-on-demand options generally start at between $1,000–$2,000 and can be more depending on size and complexity. Adding the function to a PC-based VP system involves inserting an extra board into one of a computer's vacant expansion slots and loading additional software. There are a handful of manufacturers that supply the fax boards to the VP companies, among them Intel.

There are also standalone fax-on-demand products (i.e., ones that are not part of a wider voice processing system), some PC-based and others built around proprietary platforms. The latter are sometimes sold under the brand name of fax machine companies, but are more expensive than the PC-based variety with prices usually starting at around several thousand dollars. One company that's quite prominent in proprietary systems is Brooktrout Technology.

### LAN & E-Mail Link-Ups

Some voice processing systems can also be linked into a PC local area network (LAN), although I should stress that this is taking us into the very high end of the market — a level that isn't a realistic option for most buyers. LAN link-ups enable users to view summaries of what's in their voice mailboxes on screen, as well as viewing fax documents they have received.

Integrating voice messaging with a LAN also allows you to combine it with electronic mail (which is effectively the text-based equivalent of voice mail). The combination opens up a number of possibilities, many of them with a distinctly futuristic flavor. These can include text-to-voice and — more difficult and rarely implemented — voice-to-text functions that allow messages delivered as electronic mail to be retrieved as voice messages or vice versa. Another application is adding voice annotations to electronic mail or faxes.

Fax, voice, and electronic mail are moving closer together, in a quest to establish a new kind of multi-media messaging platform. Right now, no more than a dozen vendors claim to offer PC network connectivity in some form, and it is still viewed as being at the exotic end of the market. In addition, not all vendors that say they have it have really had much experience in implementing it.

Nonetheless, the ultimate goal is to provide users with single "mailboxes," containing their voice, text and fax messages, viewed from PCs that also serve as telephones. It is with this destination in mind that most steps in this industry are being taken.

# The Three Approaches to VP Hardware

Voice processing hardware sold to end-users (as opposed to bureaus and telephone companies) falls into three very broad categories:

❑ *The PBX/key system vendor option:* First, there are the voice processing options designed for, and sold alongside, specific PBX or key systems. These are supplied by the PBX/key system vendors under their own brand names — you can buy them from the same dealer or direct sales office that supplied (or is supplying) the rest of your phone system. Keep in mind, however, that smaller and older phone systems may not always have them available.

❑ *The proprietary option:* The other two options involve buying from third parties which supply equipment that links into a number of different phone systems, and isn't tied to one brand in particular. The first involves "proprietary platforms" — in other words, the hardware and operating system are not industry-standard PC stuff. These are also known as "dedicated" systems, and some people call them "dedicated standalones" (the word "standalone" in this context seems to be a reference to the fact that it's an add-on to the phone system, not an intrinsic part of it).

❑ *The PC-based option:* The other third-party option involves buying a voice processing system based on a regular industry-standard PC running DOS, Windows, OS/2, or some other familiar operating system. As I pointed out earlier, these work with voice cards made by a small number of board manufacturers (principally Dialogic and Rhetorex) and with software written by a large number of developers. The voice cards go into vacant expansion slots in PCs.

### Own-brand versus third-party

This chapter is chiefly concerned with the last two options — in other words, the ones that involve third parties. My lack of attention to the "own-brand" voice processing options offered by PBX and key system vendors should not be taken as an implied criticism of this approach — on the contrary, your first step should be to check out what, if anything, your phone system vendor has to offer. But in these cases, the question of what to buy is effectively predetermined by your choice of phone system. Remember that complete phone systems were the subject of the previous chapter.

Buying a system from your PBX/key system vendor may be the easiest guarantee of a smooth integration into your existing telephone environment. The mere fact that you are dealing with just one vendor can keep things simpler (I'll be discussing what's meant by integration later). But third-party systems can often offer better value, are still usually reasonably easy to integrate, and may be more easily expandable. In addition, third-party systems can offer a greater range and depth of functions than the other variety, which are more likely to concentrate on core voice mail.

Note that proprietary add-ons offered by PBX/key system vendors use the same technology as third-party solutions (some use proprietary platforms, while others are PC-based) and frequently are developed by third-party vendors working under contract. The distinctions are more to do with marketing channels than differences in the core product.

### PC-based versus proprietary

Between the two types of third-party product, the big plus of industry-standard PC-based systems is that they're generally less expensive. For this reason, PC-based products dominate the market for smaller and medium-size installations. However, they are also making inroads further up the market: although all voice messaging boards have some sort of capacity restriction (I'll be talking more about that later), you can expand almost indefinitely by adding additional boards in the same PC and then by networking additional PCs.

There can come a point when PC systems catering to thousands of extensions become unduly complicated. However, the ceiling generally has less to do with the hardware itself, and is more a function of how much experience most PC-based vendors have in selling to, and supporting, the largest customers.

That wasn't always the case. A few years ago, dedicated systems enjoyed the advantage of using more powerful hardware than what were then state-of-the-art 286- and 386-based PCs. This made them intrinsically better suited to catering to the most complex installations — especially those involving multiple voice processing functions (voice mail, auto attendant, audiotex, IVR, etc.).

Today, however, that argument is harder to sustain, due to the emergence of reasonably affordable and very powerful 486- and Pentium-based PCs. Not that you need a particularly powerful PC to handle most mainstream voice processing tasks —

for example, a mid-market system catering to 20–30 people should be able to work with a 386 PC, or even an old 286, with a 40MB drive and a pretty standard amount of memory.

Despite the advances in PC-based voice processing, dedicated hardware is still going strong at the top of the market, even if its supremacy is less assured. The companies that specialize in installing very large and complex systems mostly use dedicated platforms, simply because that's what was available when they first designed their systems in the 1980s. They made a big investment in developing these systems, and they have stuck with them. If you are a large user, you may choose to go with one of these vendors for a whole host of reasons, but it probably won't be because of the dedicated hardware as such.

Lower down the market, dedicated systems have mostly been squeezed quite hard, though there are a few exceptions which manage to offer reasonable value. One other reason why dedicated systems are sometimes unattractive to smaller and medium-size offices is that the scope for building onto your system might be less if you've boxed yourself into a proprietary design.

### Looks deceive

Keep in mind that there can sometimes appear to be a gray area between industry-standard, PC-based systems, and dedicated, proprietary ones. That's when a vendor develops a system that uses Intel chips, and runs on a standard operating system, such as DOS or Windows, but configures it in a "box" that doesn't resemble a normal PC (it might not have a monitor or keyboard, for example). Likewise, some systems that are proprietary actually look like PCs — they come with screens and keyboards — whereas others look like "boxes."

What you have to keep in mind is that all voice processing systems are based on computers in one form or another. What the system actually looks like is less important than the components it uses — the real clue that a system is industry-standard, even if it doesn't look like a PC, is if it uses Dialogic or Rhetorex boards and/or runs on PC operating software. The only advantage of having a monitor and keyboard as part of the system is that it can make set-up easier — the alternative is doing all the initial set-up, and any revisions, with touch-tone instructions over a phone.

### What PC platform?

Finally, if you're looking to buy an industry-standard system, but want something quite upmarket, look for one that's based on an upscale PC platform. As I indicated earlier, an old 286 system running DOS is fine for humdrum applications, and should be able to handle a few fancy ones such as fax-on-demand — but there's a limit to what you can get out of it.

Right now, some of the snazziest PC-based systems require 486 systems running the OS/2 operating system rather than DOS. Surprisingly little VP software has so far been written for Windows, and there is virtually nothing for the Apple Mac.

# The Bureau Option

As an alternative to buying voice processing equipment of your own, you could use the services of a bureau. The technology of voice mail bureaus isn't any different from the technology that you employ when you put in your own equipment. Indeed, the equipment that is used by a voice messaging service bureau is often the high-end product from a vendor that also supplies end-users. All you're doing when you sign up for a voice mail service is hooking up to the bureau's voice messaging equipment and sharing that with other users.

### Bureau pros
The main advantage of using a bureau is that there are few up-front costs — you simply pay a monthly charge for each mailbox on the system, though there may also be a per-mailbox set-up fee at the outset.

Bureau-based solutions are also much easier to set up. All you need is a fixed call forwarding arrangement, which routes calls to the voice mail system when your phone is busy or when it rings more than a specified number of times. Likewise, bureaus are much easier to walk away from than equipment you purchase or lease. Bottom line: you keep your options open.

### And bureau cons
But there's also a downside to using a service bureau. If you have your own equipment, you have more control. You can customize the system to meet your specific needs. A bureau arrangement may be simpler at the outset, but when you want to add new features you'll be totally at the mercy of the service providers. Bureaus may or may not keep up with the latest technology.

Moreover, you get a pretty low level of integration with your phone system. For example, don't expect visual message-waiting indicators on your phones — the most you normally get are stutter tones and, in some cases, you may have to call into your mailbox to check for messages not knowing whether any have been received.

Also, while bureaus cater to voice mail applications, and often offer audiotex as well, that's about all they do. They don't provide automatic attendant features, they don't do IVR, and they don't allow for fax or e-mail integration.

### Bureau economics

Another factor working against the service bureau option is cost. If you've got more than about 15–20 people in your office and are able to plan ahead several years, it's generally cheaper to get your own system. With fewer people, a bureau could prove cost-effective, at least over a three-year period.

Bureaus can also make sense as a means of linking numerous small branch offices into a national network (more on this below). In addition, they can suit larger companies unsure of their future requirements.

### Finding a bureau

Your local telephone company may be a good place to start in your search for voice mail service. All the Bell companies now offer it, as do their Centrex divisions (Centrex is the telco service that provides PBX-like features over-the-phone to offices without their own equipment).

There are also independent bureaus, mostly local and a few national. Check your *Yellow Pages* for local listings. A national bureau, with its own privately-leased long-distance lines, can make most sense if you have offices all over the country: signing up with one can provide a very economical means of sending internal voice messages between far-flung locations. The largest national bureau is Tigon, which is now owned by Octel (best known as the largest vendor of upscale voice processing equipment).

# Picking the Right Size of System

If you do decide to go with a bureau system, the process of setting it up is fairly straightforward — you simply tell the service provider to open a mailbox for everyone who needs one. If, on the other hand, you decide to put in your own system, the process of sizing it at the outset is a little bit more complicated.

### Ports explained

There are two dimensions to sizing a voice processing system —

the number of ports and the message capacity. A port is an entry point into the system. When someone goes into a mailbox, either to leave a message or to collect messages, he or she is connected to a port. The number of ports determines the number of people who can access mailboxes at any one time.

People sometimes get confused on this point, because they assume wrongly that the number of ports equates to the number of people who can have mailboxes on the system. They imagine, for example, that a 24-port system is suitable only for a fairly small business (i.e., one with up to 24 people), which it definitely is not. A 24-port system would be more likely to serve hundreds of people.

The point here is that not all voice mailboxes are used simultaneously. In fact, a typical voice mailbox is actually in use for only a fraction of the time. Consequently, the number of ports required is a fraction of the number of users that need to have mailboxes.

Unfortunately, determining the exact number of ports required is quite a complex process. Special tables are available from voice mail vendors to help you, and most vendors will be happy to advise, but it doesn't hurt to check the calculations yourself — you don't want to be sold a bigger system than you need, or one that's too small. However, remember that it always makes sense to buy a system with enough excess capacity to accommodate likely growth without hardware upgrades.

### How many ports?

To determine the optimum number of ports, you must first decide on an acceptable "blocking factor." This is the proportion of calls into a voice processing system that end up getting a busy signal or, in more technical parlance, end up getting "blocked." The blocking factor varies depending on usage, but many vendors recommend something called a "P.02" factor, which means simply that the probability (P) that a call will get blocked is two in a 100 (i.e., 0.02).

At this point, you need to figure out how many calls you're going to get during your busiest hours and what their average length will be. It pays to carry out as good a survey as you can of your phone traffic to establish this (your phone system itself may be capable of generating the required reports). You can then turn to the P.02 blocking table — which your vendor will hopefully use — and read off the number of ports you require. For example, if the average call is 30 seconds in length, and the system gets up to 60 calls per hour, it turns out you need three ports.

These calculations only cover voice mail, but you also need to take into consideration the other functions of your system. More ports must be installed for automated attendants and for audiotex. And while the calculation of the number of ports will proceed along the same lines (and using the same tables) as for voice mail, the call patterns may be completely different. For example, the average voice mailbox in your system may be in use five times an hour, for one minute. But the automated attendant may be in use 40 times for 30 seconds.

Note that the calculations referred to above are based on aggregate calls into the system and the average length of the calls, not on the number of mailboxes or users. It's difficult to give a general indication of the number of ports required for a VP system based simply on the number of mailboxes. In some offices, voice mailboxes are frequently used, so more ports are needed, while in others, voice mail isn't an important form of communication, so fewer are needed.

That said, vendors frequently do quote rules of thumb that are related to the number of mailbox users. For example, one leading vendor offers this advice: "Assume that 30 people use each port for automated attendant, 20 people use each port for voice mail, and 10 people use each port for voice mail and automated attendant." These rules-of-thumb can be helpful, but the trouble is that you hear quite different figures from different vendors. Unfortunately, there is no definitive answer to the "How-many-ports-do-I-need?" question — you've just got to make the best judgment you can based on a combination of formulas, rules-of-thumb, and gut feeling.

### Disk capacity

As mentioned above, ports aren't the only capacity measure that you need to take into consideration when buying a voice processing system. The other dimension is its message capacity — that is the number of messages that can be stored at one time. This comes down to a function of disk capacity.

Once again, an initial survey should help you make some determinations. As part of your survey, you should find out not just how many messages users expect to receive and their average length, but also the typical time they'll be kept in the system. Using this data, it's possible to calculate how many hours of storage you'll require.

A commonly quoted rule-of-thumb is that you should allow three minutes worth of capacity for every mailbox on the system. For example, an office with 50 people will need to have 150 minutes worth of storage. That doesn't sound very much, but you needn't fret too much about what to allow: the chances are that you'll end up with plenty more message capacity than you need, due to the large hard drives that come standard on today's PCs.

Most vendors rate the storage capacity of their system in hours, so you can compare your calculations with vendor product literature. However, a few vendors only give their specifications in terms of the megabyte (MB) capacity of the hard disk.

The number of hours of storage that can be squeezed onto a hard disk varies from system to system, though about 10MB-20MB per hour is fairly typical. It all depends on the technique used to digitize voice and whether compression methods are utilized. This means that an 80MB drive (which is pretty small by today's standards) can typically hold 8–16 hours of messages — enough for 160–320 people if you use the three-minutes-per-person formula (minus a few megabytes for the software).

Talking of disk drives, it's essential to have some system in place for back-ups to prevent the loss of all your messages should the hard drive ever crash — this could be a second hard drive, for example. Ideally, look for a system that backs up automatically at preset intervals. And talking of back-ups, it can also be a good idea to think about an uninterruptible power supply — especially if you're in a part of the country were outages are not uncommon.

### Other capacity restrictions

Keep in mind that some systems restrict the message capacity of each individual mailbox, although the limit imposed is rarely going to cause a problem. Outgoing greeting messages are also often restricted in length, but, again, the restrictions are generally more theoretical than real. For example, one Octel system places a 30-minute restriction on outgoing greeting messages.

Similarly, some systems place restrictions on the total number of voice mailboxes that can be accommodated, but these are, once again, of little practical importance for most users — you'll almost certainly run into one of the other capacity constraints (ports, hard drive size, etc.) before you reach this ceiling.

### Expanding your system

If you do find yourself outgrowing your system, it should be possible to expand it. Putting in a larger hard drive is the simplest method of all — this allows you to store more messages on the system, though it doesn't allow more people to use it at the same time. If people get busy signals more often than you find acceptable, you have to add more ports.

Industry-standard PC-based systems are generally very easy to expand in this way: it's simply a matter of adding an extra voice board or, possibly, taking one out and replacing it with another. Typically, smaller and medium-size systems are configured using four-port boards, so expanding means adding extra ports in multiples of four. (Larger systems are based on eight-port boards, and there are also some two-port ones.)

If you run out of vacant slots in your PC, you may have a choice of scrapping the four-port boards you already have and replacing them with eight-port ones, adding a second PC to accommodate extra four-port ones, or replacing the old PC with another that has more expansion slots. You'll have to draw on the advice of your vendor to figure out which approach makes the most sense in a particular set of circumstances.

Many of the proprietary system vendors have been responding to the flexibility of PC-based systems by making their boards and chassis more interchangeable and versatile — but remember that if you only have one source for a board, there won't be much price competition. Whereas PC-based systems tend to have more or less infinite expandability, proprietary ones often have fixed ceilings on the number of ports for any given model. If you outgrow one model, you have to move up to the next one. You may be able to take some of your hardware and software with you, but you can't count on it. Generally, the less swapping and the more adding you can do, the less expensive your expansion will be — that goes for both PC-based and proprietary systems.

Remember that change can mean more than just vertical growth. As you get more sophisticated in your use and understanding of voice processing, you may find yourself wanting to add additional functions to what began as a fairly straightforward system. So look at the horizontal as well as the vertical growth options before you buy a system — even if you don't need certain options right away, it's nice to know they are there.

# Integrating VP With Phone Systems

As I've explained earlier, the voice processing systems covered in this chapter are supplied separately from the phone systems they work with, although most PBX/key system vendors supply some sort of option of their own. Nevertheless, phone systems and voice mail systems do not operate independently, even when they are acquired separately.

Just about any VP system can be connected to any phone system, simply in order that calls can be transferred from one to the other. There is, however, a big difference between integrating a VP system with a phone system and merely connecting it. The point of integration is to make sure that the phone system and VP system work together in a manner that's user-friendly and makes for effective communications. True integration requires that the two systems should be able to talk to each other over a data communications link. This link allows them to work in harmony, passing voice messages and information back and forth.

Functions such as return to operator, and moving on from one mailbox to another extension, are clear benefits of integration. Integration is also vital in providing message-waiting information.

The link can provide a VP system with information from a PBX about the status of an extension — for example, you can arrange for all callers to be automatically routed to an attendant or to another extension when the called party is on the phone, and to a mailbox when the line isn't busy but is unanswered.

It isn't difficult for callers to tell when a VP system is poorly integrated. One tell-tale sign is when a call that isn't answered by an extension routes back to the attendant, who then has to transfer the caller into a mailbox as a separate step. Long transfer times, accompanied by annoying clicks on the line, are another indication.

### Integration limitations

Most third-party voice processing vendors now claim to be able to provide integration with most PBXs and modern key systems, though some specialize in integrating with certain leading brands, such as Mitel and Northern Telecom. The one very big exception is that AT&T Merlin systems — the most widely-used business phone systems in the US — are notoriously difficult for third-party systems to work with. If you are a Merlin user looking for a third-party solution, my advice would be to check out a company called Voysys (listed in the Vendor Profiles).

In general, integration with key systems is harder to achieve than with PBXs. Something can usually be worked out, but you may have to settle for a lower level of integration. The older the key system, the more likely there will be difficulties. "Hybrids"— the key systems that have more PBX-like qualities — should present less of problem. (The differences between PBXs, key systems, and hybrids were explained in the previous chapter.)

Keep in mind that the term "integration" means different things to different vendors — it isn't an either/or affair. Different pairings between particular voice processing systems and phone systems allow for different integrated features to be provided.

Sometimes, the degree of integration depends on how open the PBX/key system vendor is in its dealings with third parties. In some cases, the phone system vendor publishes detailed specifications of its equipment allowing third-party VP vendors to provide tight integration. In other cases, the third parties have to feel their way around in the dark, resulting in fewer integrated features.

Although most third-party systems are technically capable of working with most phone systems, this does not mean that the dealer installing the system will have had any experience in making the specific match that's needed in your office. Larger vendors tend to have the most experience in dealing with a wide range of phone systems and may, therefore, be able to provide better technical support to their dealers.

Some voice processing system developers also produce software and documentation that makes the dealer's job of installing a system easier, while other products are fundamentally harder to install. Likewise, some phone systems are intrinsically easier for the third parties to work with than others — Panasonic phone systems are among the favorites of VP developers.

### The change-your-phone-system option

While you are talking to VP dealers, you may be encouraged to change your entire phone system if they find working with it to be difficult. They may or may not have a point — but before you take that very expensive path, you should definitely talk to other vendors as well. Sometimes, dealers tell you that you ought to replace your whole phone system when all they really mean is that they can't work with it — even though others might be able to!

# VP Networks & AMIS

Most readers of this chapter will probably be thinking of installing a voice processing system at a single location. However, larger multi-location companies can obtain advantages by installing voice processing networks spread across different places. With one of these in place, an employee in San Francisco can leave a message for a colleague in New York with the same ease, and using the same procedures, as leaving a message for a co-worker across the hall. Often, multilocation networks use privately leased lines, resulting in big savings compared with dial-up long-distance service.

### Introducing AMIS

Constructing a voice processing network is a complex matter, not to be attempted by the technically faint-hearted. Voice processing networks are particularly tricky to implement if you happen to have VP equipment from one vendor at one location, and from a different one at another location. This frequently happens if Location A has implemented voice processing independently of Location B, and corporate management now wants to install a VP network that includes both locations.

However, multi-vendor networks of this kind are becoming easier to set up as the result of a new industry standard called AMIS ("Audio Processing Interchange Specification"), which was devised by a group of leading lights in the industry. AMIS comes in two flavors: analog and digital. AMIS-Analog supports sending, receiving, and replying to messages using tone dialing over regular analog phone lines. AMIS-Digital, which is intended for very high-volume users, uses digital transmission and also allows for the integration of voice mail and e-mail.

AMIS is being adopted by upscale VP users in the Fortune 500 category and by the largest service bureaus. Most of the major voice processing equipment companies, and some of the smaller ones, are now making equipment that conforms with AMIS, and most others claim to be working on it.

If you are not interested in networking, AMIS will not be of much importance to you. And if you are, you should treat AMIS with a little caution, since some insiders are reporting that, while AMIS helps a lot, it still does not provide fully transparent interconnection for equipment from different vendors. In other words, AMIS networks are still not as straightforward as networks with hardware from a single vendor.

# Buying a VP System

Most voice processing systems — especially those aimed at smaller and medium-size offices — are sold through dealers. Unless you are in the market for a very large system, it is unlikely that you will be dealing with the manufacturer/developer direct.

However, as I pointed out earlier in this chapter, some dealers enhance or integrate the systems they sell — so it can be a bit of a gray area as to whether the firm you are buying from is merely a dealer or a bit of a developer as well. Either way, who you buy from can be as important as what you buy. The quality of the initial installation and integration is paramount. I cannot stress this enough!

### Who are the dealers?

Dealers that sell VP equipment are often ones that also peddle complete phone systems. Such dealers are often called "interconnects." That term goes back to the days when it was still novel for a non-Bell company to dare to connect customer equipment to the sacred Bell system; these days, the terms "dealer" and "interconnect" are interchangeable.

Dealers range from small family-run businesses to regional or nationwide operations. They usually also act as installers and provide maintenance. A good dealer can be just as service-oriented as a direct sales operation, perhaps even more so. But there is a lot of variation in dealer quality — you have to be careful.

### Look for experience

Ideally, you should look for a dealership that has experience in matching the particular VP system it sells with your particular phone system. At the very least, you should look for a dealer who has had quite a lot of experience with the VP system it represents — while everyone has to start somewhere, you don't want that "somewhere" to be your phone system!

I strongly encourage you to request names of recent customers who you can call for a reference. This is a slightly tedious thing to do, but it's worth it. I also encourage you to visit the dealer's premises rather than having all discussions take place in your office — this can give you a feeling for the culture of the operation.

In practice, your choice of what to buy will be restricted by availability: if you take the view that a good local dealer is essential, you'll have to choose out of what is available in your area. Only the largest vendors have comprehensive national coverage.

### Sizing up the systems

One of the hardest things about choosing a VP system is quite simply getting a sense of how good it really is. One way is to rigorously test the dealer's or manufacturer's own system, simply by calling in and navigating your way around.

It's advisable to do this on a number of occasions — try

calling at different times of the day including peak times, during holidays, even in the evening — how a system handles out-of-hours callers can be as important as how it operates nine-to-five when there's a human attendant to help it. Also try transferring in and out of voice mailboxes and audiotex announcements, using directories, and, if applicable, sending faxes and requesting documents via fax-on-demand. If a vendor has a poorly implemented system at its own offices, it hardly inspires confidence.

### Be prepared

The more information you have available for your local supplier, the better. If you read the earlier discussion of sizing VP systems, you'll recall that you should come up with as much data about your calling patterns as possible.

The key to success in choosing between voice processing options is beginning with applications — before you do anything else, think hard about what you want from your VP system or service. This will put you well on the way to determining just what kind of system or service you require, how big a system you need, or whether you need voice processing at all.

Depending on your size of organization, it can be a good idea to conduct a survey among employees to discover exactly what they'd like from a system. Their needs can vary quite widely. Individuals, such as sales people, who are frequently out of the office may have a much greater need for voice mail — possibly with cascading or beeper notification. Departments that provide regularly updated, but relatively standardized, information may need audiotex or even IVR, and may also want to consider fax-on-demand.

At this stage, you should be on the look-out for both problems and opportunities. Problems to look for include places where customers complain they have difficulties getting through to people or obtaining information. Opportunities include situations where voice processing can open up new channels of communications or even create new products.

As a result of your initial survey, it can be a good idea to prepare some sort of document which will be the basis for inviting bids. I'd encourage you to talk to several vendors before deciding what to buy. The more specific your initial document, the better your ability to attract like-for-like bids. However, it's possible that as a result of your initial discussions with potential vendors, you may fine-tune your requirements and only then put out a definitive document as the basis for bids. You'll have to feel your way along a little, but don't feel you're being unreasonable if you get everyone to bid a second time as a result of you changing your mind about various things — this sort of thing is perfectly normal!

### Technical support

Be sure to get a clear statement in writing about support arrangements. At the very least, you should expect technical support to be provided free for as long as it takes to get the system fully up-and-running and debugged. In general, people who buy from dealers are expected to turn to their dealers for all ongoing support. Some manufacturers/developers do provide technical support over the phone to end-users, but usually a little reluctantly — they say it's there in case an end-user isn't getting satisfaction out of a dealer, but that it isn't meant to be the normal first point of contact. In general, manufacturers prefer to direct all their tech support toward dealers.

Training is very important. At the risk of stating the obvious, there's not much point in having this wonderful new system if people only have the vaguest notion of how to use it. You should probably think in terms of getting one or two key people in your organization trained on every last detail, and then conducting further training of other users internally.

The key operators should also be trained in housekeeping functions, such as setting up new mailboxes — you don't want to rely on your dealer for what are routine administrative tasks. But to avoid too much subsequent housekeeping, you should work with your dealer at the time of installation to make sure that the system is set up the way you want it. There are numerous options and parameters that can be set at installation — unless you spend some time going through them with the dealer, you'll end up with the defaults which may not make the most sense. They can be changed later, but it's better to get everything set up the way it should be from day one.

Incidentally, you should take a look at the manuals and other support documentation that go with all the systems you're thinking of buying. Ask to see what, if any, easy-to-use summary guides are available for individual mailbox owners (as opposed to the ones for the system administrator) — and check whether you get one copy for each person who will be using the system.

### Warranty anomalies

Warranties can be anomolous in this market. Often, the system developers offer, say, one-year warranties even if some of the important components in the system were supplied to them with longer ones. For example, all Rhetorex voice boards now come with three-year warranties (not that most end-users would probably know this), yet most Rhetorex-based turnkey systems are sold by the developers with only one-year warranties. So if your system goes down in year two, you could be charged for a replacement board, even though the developer gets it for free! With voice boards often costing four-figure amounts, this is no trivial matter.

Likewise, some vendors only offer paltry 90-day warranties on their systems, even though they probably get a one-year warranty on the PC platform from their own supplier. A further complication is that sometimes the system developer passes a warranty on to the dealer, but the dealer sets its own warranty terms when selling to the end-user.

It is confusing, and there are anomalies, which is why you should make sure that everything is set out very clearly in writing. If you end up with a no-exceptions parts-and-labor warranty running for a full year, you're getting a fair deal — except when you know for a fact that certain important ingredients of the system have a longer manufacturer's warranty, in which case you should press for that to be passed on. At the time of this writing, there was talk that Dialogic might up its one-year warranties to match the better ones offered by Rhetorex — but nothing had been decided.

### Ongoing support

Once you are out of the warranty period, it may not make sense to take out a service contract on the hardware. There's quite a strong case for saying that you'll probably be better off self-insuring and paying for fixes only when you need them. The counter-argument, though, is that you are on stronger ground in the event of serious problems if someone is under a contractual obligation to support you.

The other reason why you may want to consider a service contract is if this covers software upgrades. Minor software fixes to iron out bugs should be supplied free during the warranty period (this is something you should check), but they probably won't continue at no charge after the warranty — and major upgrades almost certainly won't be supplied free.

An extended warranty is similar to a service contract after the initial warranty has expired — up to a point. The difference is that an extended warranty is usually sold and paid for at the time the system is delivered — like when Circuit City tries to sell you one on your new TV.

Similar pros and cons apply as per service contracts —

except that I'd be inclined to view extended warranties with more caution: why pre-pay for years' worth of service before you know whether it is any good, and especially if you're dealing with a smaller vendor whose future may be hard to predict?

### Remote diagnostics

These days, most systems allow your dealer, or the VP manufacturer/developer, to get into your system and perform minor software fixes over a modem — without anyone turning up in your office. This can be a useful way of keeping your support costs down, though keep in mind that this capability also provides a back door into your phone system that could be used by "toll fraudsters" — these are the crooks who hack their way into companies' phone systems and then dial out of them on international calls. Toll fraud is a multi-million dollar racket, with some very organized and highly-skilled gangs making a fortune out of selling "cheap" overseas calls to people in poor city neighborhoods. There are ways of protecting yourself, and your supplier may be able to advise.

### Negotiate!

Finally, don't be afraid to negotiate! This is a market where end-user list prices in the normal sense do not generally exist. Systems tend to be priced individually — installation paying quite a major part in determining the bottom-line figure.

If you like a system, but it seems overpriced, tell the dealer what you'd be happy to pay. If you like a system, but you think that you're getting a lousy warranty, say so — the chances are you can get a better one! You should respect the dealer as a source of wise and useful advice on a subject that gets pretty technical, but not stand in such awe that you lose your confidence to strike a good deal!

# What to Buy?

Following next is a summary of recommendations that were made in the most recent *What to Buy for Business* guide to third-party VP systems. These recommendations do not refer to specific systems, but to vendors that are good choices for readers with various requirements. The recommended names were picked from an analysis of over 50 third-party vendors. After this summary, I'll be providing brief descriptions of the companies listed.

❑ *If you are looking for a PC-based system — probably one with quite a wide range of features and functions — and would prefer to deal with one of the largest vendors:*
**Active Voice**
**AVT**
**Compass**
**Microlog**

❑ *If you are looking for a PC-based system, but are interested in talking to a smaller vendor with a good reputation (some of these may be nimbler than the bigger vendors when it comes to custom work):*
**ABS TALKX**
**Digital Speech**
**ITI**

❑ *If you are an AT&T Merlin/Merlin Plus user:*
**Voysys**

❑ *If you are a very large user looking for an upscale, multilocation system (probably, but not necessarily, using a proprietary platform):*
**Centigram**
**Digital Sound**
**Octel**
**VMX**

❑ *If you're looking for vendors focusing on small/low-cost/basic systems:*
**DuVoice**
**Telekol**
**VSR**

❑ *If you're looking for vendors offering advanced fax, E-mail and/or LAN integration:*
**AVT**
**Digital Sound**
**Malibu**
**VMX**
**Wygant**

❑ *If you're looking for a noteworthy IVR specialist not mentioned under other categories:*
**Voicetek**

# Vendor Profiles

Below, in alphabetical order of brand name, are short profiles of the vendors that appeared above in my recommendations summary. Keep in mind that these are by no means the only players in this market — the *What to Buy for Business* guide on this subject contains much fuller profiles of over 50 vendors.

The information shown was current as of the start of 1994. The figures for the number of installations/employees/dealers, etc., should provide some idea of the size of the different companies. Keep in mind that I have not been able to independently verify those details, which were provided by the vendors themselves (sometimes reluctantly).

## *ABS*

*ABS TALKX, Inc.*
*2500 Shames Drive*
*Westbury, NY 11590*
*Tel: 800 825 5944*
*Fax: 516 333 7953*
*Year established:* 1988
*Approximate number of installations:* 3,000
*Number of direct sales offices:* 1
*Number of US dealers and/or distributors:* 70
*Number of employees:* 12
*Manufacturer warranty:* 1-year/30-day money-back
*Vendor overview:* ABS started out with a product that used its own voice boards. Late in 1992, ABS decided to join the crowd and redeveloped its software to run with Dialogic and Rhetorex boards. The current product is called TALKX-Ultra and is supplied to dealers only as turnkey systems; ABS also sells direct.

ABS is one of the first voice messaging companies to introduce customer service policies that resemble those offered by mainstream PC software companies. These include a 30-day money back guarantee, a 24 hours/seven days technical support line, and free software upgrades for one year.

# Active Voice

*Active Voice Corporation*
*2901 Third Avenue*
*Seattle, WA 98121*
*Tel: 206 441 4700*
*Fax: 206 441 4784*
*Year established: 1983*
*Approximate number of installations: 15,000*
*Number of direct sales offices: None*
*Number of US dealers and/or distributors: 450*
*Number of employees: 140*
*Manufacturer warranty: 1 year*
*Vendor overview:* Active Voice, one of the pioneers of the PC-based voice mail business, has its roots in technology developed at MIT. One of its founders was, and still is, the principal research scientist at MIT's Media Laboratory for Speech and Artificial Intelligence.

From this beginning, Active Voice has become a voice processing manufacturer to emulate. Rated the 17th fastest-growing, privately-held business by *Inc.* magazine in 1992, it offers a line of products which, though seldom the cheapest, have a reputation for being high in quality and easy to install and use. It has an extensive, well-trained dealer network which is backed up with what are exemplary instruction manuals and documentation.

Active Voice sells several turnkey, Dialogic-based systems under its own name ranging from 2–60 ports. In addition, it makes equipment that is relabeled by several other vendors. The company also has a separate standalone IVR system.

# Applied Voice/AVT

*Applied Voice Technology, Inc.*
*11410 N.E. 122nd Way*
*PO Box 97025*
*Kirkland, WA 98083*
*Tel: 206 820 6000*
*Fax: 206 820 4040*
*Year established: 1982*
*Approximate number of installations: 10,000*
*Number of direct sales offices: 6*
*Number of US dealers and/or distributors: 160*
*Number of employees: 80*
*Manufacturer warranty: 1 year*
*Vendor overview:* Applied Voice Technology (AVT) was founded

in the early 1980s and has since gone on to become one of the top three vendors of voice processing systems. Over 20,000 of the company's Dialogic-based systems have been installed worldwide under a variety of names. AVT's product range services offices with between 20 and 2,000 users. Its systems are state-of-the-art, fully upgradable, and offer the latest voice processing options including fax mail, IVR, and Windows interfacing.

Sales are through a well-picked selection of dealers, though Applied Voice sells direct to its very large accounts. Almost all of its dealers sell turnkey systems that are configured by AVT itself; however, the company is making a move to focus more on software, rather than hardware, so some larger dealers can buy the components and build their own systems to resell. In either case, all technical support and service is provided by the dealers unless you purchased from the company direct.

# Centigram

*Centigram Communications Corporation*
*91 East Tasman Drive*
*San Jose, CA 95134*
*Tel: 408 944 0250*
*Fax: 408 942 3732*
*Year established: 1977*
*Approximate number of installations: 6,000*
*Number of direct sales offices: 10*
*Number of US dealers and/or distributors: 26*
*Number of employees: 250*
*Manufacturer warranty: 1 year hardware/2 years software*
*Vendor overview:* Founded in 1977, Centigram is one of the oldest voice processing companies. Like most other vendors of its size and vintage, it sells proprietary, rather than PC-based, systems. It was incorporated in 1980 and then acquired Speech Plus in 1990 to add IVR and text-to-speech capabilities to its voice processing repertoire.

Centigram is a publicly traded company. It targets businesses of all sizes, universities, government offices, service bureaus, and telephone companies. It is also responsible for the voice processing systems used on Fujitsu PBXs. Centigram does not really have many regular dealers — its systems are mostly sold by large distributors and resellers such as BellSouth Communications, Mitel, NEC, PacTel Meridian Systems, Voice Plus, and WilTel Business Systems.

# Compass

*Compass Technology Inc.*
*Live Oak Office Center*
*Suite 116*
*Sarasota, FL 34232*
*Tel: 813 371 8000*
*Fax: 813 377 5600*
*Year established: 1989*
*Approximate number of installations: 4,000*
*Number of direct sales offices: None*
*Number of US dealers and/or distributors: 500*
*Number of employees: 90*
*Manufacturer warranty: 1 year*
*Vendor overview:* Compass's roots were originally in custom applications and fax processing software. The company then moved into developing turnkey voice mail/auto attendant/audiotex products, and it became one of the leading suppliers of PC-based systems. In 1992, it was purchased by Octel Communications (see separate entry), a major vendor that specializes in dedicated proprietary products that dominate the high-end of this market. The two companies are currently being run separately, though Octel will probably start selling Compass products through its direct sales force at some point.

Compass sells systems using Dialogic and Rhetorex voice boards. Most systems are sold as software and voice board "kits" to dealers who package them into turnkey systems (this is somewhat unusual for such a prominent vendor). Because of this, the warranty on the computer will vary from deal to deal, but should generally be about one year. Compass claims to provide its authorized dealers with unrivaled technical support and training.

# Digital Sound

*Digital Sound Corporation*
*6307 Carpinteria Avenue*
*Carpinteria, CA 93013*
*Tel: 800 366 0700*
*Fax: 805 684 2848*
*Year established: 1977*
*Approximate number of installations: 1,300*
*Number of direct sales offices: 20*
*Number of US dealers and/or distributors: None*
*Number of employees: 130*
*Manufacturer warranty: 1 year*

*Vendor overview:* This company's roots are in the professional audio industry. In 1985, it introduced the first of its VoiceServer models: these proprietary systems were designed from the ground up to integrate voice mail, fax, and e-mail on a single platform together with IVR.

Digital Sound systems are used by service bureaus, phone companies, Fortune 500 companies, and large government agencies. Distribution is direct for major accounts, and also through GTE, Pacific Bell, and various distributors and VARs. Digital Sound is not for small companies, or those looking for budget prices, but it is worth considering if you're a medium or larger size user looking for an advanced system to handle a variety of messaging and IVR applications.

## Digital Speech

*Digital Speech Systems, Inc.*
*1840 N. Greenville*
*Suite 156*
*Richardson, TX 75081*
*Tel: 214 235 2999*
*Fax: 214 235 3036*
*Year established: 1983*
*Approximate number of installations: 3,000*
*Number of direct sales offices: 1*
*Number of US dealers and/or distributors: 200*
*Number of employees: 10*
*Manufacturer warranty: 1 year*
*Vendor overview:* Founded in 1983, privately-held Digital Speech Systems is a mid-size and growing vendor that supplies PC-based systems using Rhetorex and Dialogic boards. The company's products are sold through a network of dealers, and also through major telecommunications firms including Telrad Telecommunications.

## DuVoice

*DuVoice Corporation*
*PO Box 938*
*Kirkland, WA 98083–0938*
*Tel: 206 821 9228*
*Fax: 206 821 9646*
*Year established: 1990*
*Approximate number of installations: 250*
*Number of direct sales offices: None*

*Number of US dealers and/or distributors: 24*
*Number of employees: 12*
*Manufacturer warranty: 1 year*
Vendor overview: This is a small company with modest distribution that sells a system using Dialogic or Rhetorex boards, but packaged in a neat box without a keyboard or monitor — effectively, it looks like a proprietary system even though the insides are PC-based. This approach provides some of the simplicity of the former, with the economies of the latter. The system, which is targeted at smaller offices, first appeared in late 1992. Sales are through dealers.

## Innovative Technology/ITI

*Innovative Technology, Inc.*
*1770 Corporate Drive*
*Suite 540*
*Norcross, GA 30093*
*Tel: 404 806 8140*
*Fax: 404 806 8804*
*Year established: 1982*
*Approximate number of installations: Vendor declined to answer*
*Number of direct sales offices: 5*
*Number of US dealers and/or distributors: 300*
*Number of employees: 15*
*Manufacturer warranty: 90 days*
Vendor overview: Innovative Technology (ITI) was founded in 1982 and became a supplier of voice boards and development kits used by other vendors, VARS, and resellers — effectively a somewhat smaller version of Dialogic and Rhetorex. In 1993, it was acquired by Teleco, a Toshiba phones relabeler which was already using ITI voice boards in its own system. ITI also has a successful "TDD" product for the hearing-impaired.

## Malibu

*Malibu Software Group, Inc.*
*23715 West Malibu Road*
*Suite 356*
*Malibu, CA 90265*
*Tel: 310 456 8940*
*Fax: 310 456 6225*
*Year established: 1985*
*Approximate number of installations: 210*
*Number of direct sales offices: None*

*Number of US dealers and/or distributors: 12*
*Number of employees: 10*
*Manufacturer warranty: 1 year*
*Vendor overview:* This business goes back to 1978 and has been in its current incarnation since 1985, although the name was changed in 1990. Malibu's VORAMS (Voice Reception And Mail System) is a PC-based system, using NMS voice boards, that offers some options that are usually only found on much larger systems from bigger vendors. These include PC networking capabilities and e-mail functionality which enables users to view a voice message count on-screen with their faxes and e-mail.

What is most unusual is that VORAMS can convert fax and e-mail to voice. The company says the speech synthesis technology used to do this is accurate, though interested buyers might want to have this demonstrated to their complete satisfaction. Malibu claims that accuracy on a "good, clear fax" will be 90 percent and that on e-mail it's 100 percent. The company adds that this function is probably most useful for getting the gist of messages when you're traveling and that it isn't a substitute for viewing them in a normal way when they are readily available.

VORAMS was introduced in 1990 and is sold through a dealer network. Although Malibu's official policy is that it does not sell direct, it says it will send out a turnkey demo system to buyers who want to attempt to set it up themselves — only those with some PC background need apply. The company has, however, recently introduced a more user-friendly graphical user interface.

## *Microlog*

*Microlog Corporation*
*20270 Goldenrod Lane*
*Germantown, MD 20876*
*Tel: 301 428 3227*
*Fax: 301 972 6208*
*Year established: 1977*
*Approximate number of installations: 10,000*
*Number of direct sales offices: 7*
*Number of US dealers and/or distributors: Uncertain*
*Number of employees: 130*
*Manufacturer warranty: 1 year (on-site)*
*Vendor overview:* This publicly-held company has been around since 1969 and is one of the largest companies in the voice processing market. In 1991, it acquired Genesis Electronics, another major player in this field.

In the same year, Microlog announced the Dialogic-based CallStar product line, which is designed principally for smaller and medium-sized organizations. This is a combination of the Genesis CINDI systems, which are no longer being sold, and its larger VCS 3500. In addition to the CallStar range, the company still markets the VCS 3500, a large high-end system with a focus on IVR and audiotex applications.

The CallStars are so-called "plug-and-play" products distributed through wholesalers, distributors, and major resellers, including GTE and North Supply. The VCS 3500 is sold direct through offices in California, Florida, Maryland, Minnesota, Missouri, and Utah. The company has some good support policies, such as 24-hour technical support and third-party on-site service.

## *Octel*

*Octel Communications Corporation*
*890 Tasman Drive*
*Milpitas, CA 95035*
*Tel: 408 321 2000*
*Fax: 408 321 9801*
*Year established: 1982*
*Approximate number of installations: 14,000*
*Number of direct sales offices: 36*
*Number of US dealers and/or distributors: 26*
*Number of employees: 1,280*
*Manufacturer warranty: 1 year*
*Vendor overview:* Octel Communications is one of voice processing's biggest success stories. Started in 1982 by two mathematician entrepreneurs, it pioneered third-party voice mail at a time when this technology was aimed only at large companies.

Today, Octel is publicly owned and is the largest supplier in the business. Its systems still all use proprietary hardware. It has very strong sales to Fortune 1000 corporations, and also has a over a third of the market selling large-scale voice mail equipment to local phone companies, cellular carriers, and service bureaus. In addition, it has been very successful in the export market. By combining a wide range of compatible system sizes with a direct sales force, Octel is well positioned to serve major accounts with multiple locations across the country (apparently, Octel's top 25 customers average 88 systems each).

Recently, however, Octel has been trying to diversify from its traditional core business of selling premium systems to buyers at the top end of the market. In 1992, it acquired Compass Technology, a leading PC-based voice processing vendor (see separate entry), and Tigon, the largest service bureau in the US.

Headquartered in the heart of Silicon Valley, Octel sells and supports its equipment through its own direct sales force and a network of distributors and major resellers which includes names like US West, NEC, and RCA Business Telephone Systems. The average price of a system shipped by Octel is reportedly over $80,000. Octel's direct sales force appeared likely to start selling Compass systems soon after this book was published, though the company was reluctant to confirm this.

# *Telekol*

*Telekol Corporation*
*560 Harrison Avenue*
*Boston, MA 02118*
*Tel: 800 688 6423*
*Fax: 617 451 6226*
*Year established: 1989*
*Approximate number of installations: 800*
*Number of direct sales offices: None*
*Number of US dealers and/or distributors: 95*
*Number of employees: 15*
*Manufacturer warranty: 1 year*
Vendor overview: Telekol has two products aimed mainly at smaller users — a proprietary voice mail/auto attendant system called TeleMail, and a separate fax-on-demand product called FaxExpress. Both systems are sold turnkey through dealers. TeleMail is also relabeled by two phone systems manufacturers.

# *VMX*

*VMX, Inc.*
*2115 O'Nel Drive*
*San Jose, CA 95131–2032*
*Tel: 408 441 1166*
*Fax: 408 441 7026*
*Year established: 1978*
*Approximate number of installations: 12,000*
*Number of direct sales offices: 10*
*Number of US dealers and/or distributors: 37*
*Number of employees: 500*
*Manufacturer warranty: 1 year*

*Vendor overview:* VMX is one of the old names in voice processing which has grown steadily — partly through acquisitions — to become a major force in the industry. It sells a proprietary line of fully-featured systems aimed principally at very large buyers. Some of the largest service bureaus, like Tigon (which ironically is now owned by Octel, a major VMX competitor), use its equipment (easily recognized by a distinctive four-tone opening greeting that sounds a bit like the first notes of Beethoven's "Ode to Joy").

VMX now also owns Rhetorex, the board manufacturer whose products are used by many of the PC-based vendors in this industry. VMX sells about half of its systems direct, and the rest through a well-trained dealer network. It offers excellent support policies, as you would expect of a vendor at this level of the market.

## *Voicetek*

*Voicetek Corporation*
*19 Alpha Road*
*Chelmsford, MA 01824*
*Tel: 508 250 9393*
*Fax: 508 250 9378*
*Year established: 1981*
*Approximate number of installations: 550*
*Number of direct sales offices: None*
*Number of US dealers and/or distributors: 4*
*Number of employees: 50*
*Manufacturer warranty: 1 year hardware/90 days software*
*Vendor overview:* One of the older names in voice processing, Voicetek specializes in IVR systems. Its software is used by four large vendors selling equipment under their own names: Northern Telecom, Digital Sound, NYNEX, and Bell Atlantic.

Voicetek also sells several different-sized systems under its own name, all of which use Voicetek's highly-successful Generations software. Unlike most products being discussed in this chapter, these are IVR systems first, and voice mail/audiotex can then be added as custom options — usually, it's the other way around.

# Voysys

*Voysys Corporation*
*2450 Junction Avenue*
*San Jose, CA 95134*
*Tel: 408 954 9500*
*Fax: 408 954 9501*
*Year established: 1986*
*Approximate number of installations: 15,000*
*Number of direct sales offices: None*
*Number of US dealers and/or distributors: 60*
*Number of employees: 75*
*Manufacturer's warranty: 1 year*
*Vendor overview:* Voysys is a medium-size vendor that sells voice processing hardware and software that's relabeled by some pretty big phone system suppliers including Northern Telecom, Mitel, Premier, and Tadiran. The Voysystem is the first product it has introduced to be sold under its own name. Voysystem is made specifically to integrate with the AT&T Merlin and Merlin Plus phone systems — which are usually very difficult for third-party products to work with. In addition to being sold by phone systems dealers, this product is offered in the traditional office equipment dealer channel (which is somewhat unusual)

# VSR

*Voice Systems Research, Inc.*
*4095 Delmar Avenue*
*Suite 10*
*Rocklin, CA 95677*
*Tel: 916 632 9400*
*Fax: 916 632 9555*
*Year established: 1989*
*Approximate number of installations: 1,000*
*Number of direct sales offices: None*
*Number of US dealers and/or distributors: 300*
*Number of employees: 17*
*Manufacturer's warranty: 1 year*
*Vendor overview:* VSR was founded in 1989 and is 51 percent owned by a $200 million-a-year telecommunications company call Pana-Pacific. VSR focuses specifically on low-end, small systems for voice mail, auto attendant, and audiotex — although IVR and other more complicated applications can be customized. The company's products are PC-based, using Rhetorex boards.

VSR sells only turnkey products through authorized dealers and Alltel, a wholesale telephone distributor. Support is left largely to the dealers.

# *Wygant*

*Wygant Scientific, Inc.*
*813 S.W. Alder Street*
*Portland, OR 97205*
*Tel: 800 688 6423*
*Fax: 503 227 8501*
*Year established: 1983*
*Approximate number of installations: 150*
*Number of direct sales offices: None*
*Number of US dealers and/or distributors: 49*
*Number of employees: 15*
*Manufacturer warranty: 1 year*
*Vendor overview:* Wygant Scientific was founded in 1983 by a physicist who specialized in solving specific voice processing applications in the days when the available choices were few. Sales were direct and most of the company's business was in the Pacific Northwest. In 1987, the company introduced a more mainstream product called the Micro-ITC system; in 1992, it established a national dealer network and, for the most part, ceased selling direct.

Wygant was able to develop a dealer base fairly quickly, largely due to a strategic alliance it developed with Tadiran (a manufacturer of business phone systems). Wygant's focus is to offer voice processing systems that include IVR capability.

All systems are turnkey; applications generators are available to customize features, but the company does not sell developers' kits. ✍

# Chapter 12

# Typewriters

# Typewriters

When I first started a publishing business in 1980, just about the first thing I did was buy a typewriter. That was before the age of the PC, and it was back when word processors were dedicated machines costing over $10,000. I chose a good old electromechanical, IBM Selectric "golfball" typewriter — one of the all-time office equipment greats. In those days, a directly-employed IBM salesman — dark blue suit, white shirt, and all — would turn up in your office to negotiate the sale of just one unit.

I haven't personally used a typewriter for about six or seven years (even though I do all my own typing), and no one in my company does either. We are not atypical — during the past five years, large and small businesses alike have discarded typewriters in droves and replaced them with laser printers connected to personal computers running word processing software. IBM, the former typewriter supremo, has divested itself of its typewriter business. Xerox has also gotten out. And most of the European manufacturers have pulled out of the US market.

I debated whether to feature the subject at all in an office equipment guide being published in 1994, but eventually decided to do so. Apparently, several hundred thousand of these machines are still being sold in America every year — it seems that the typewriter has found a niche catering to those on very tight budgets and to people who find them convenient for certain odds-and-ends tasks. Also, the typewriter industry has spawned a related product known as the "personal word processor" (a concept that I will be defining shortly). So although the typewriter has become marginalized, it is still hanging in there.

## Why Would You Possibly Want a Typewriter?

It's easy for me to sit here smugly at my fairly expensive Apple Mac and wonder why anyone would possibly want a typewriter, but — to be fair — they do have some points in their favor. In fact, a typewriter can do a few tricks that even my Mac can't manage. So here are some nice things to say about them:

✔ A typewriter is still the cheapest way of producing a letter, apart from handwriting it. In fact, it is the only method that allows you to write and print a letter for a total investment of under $500.

✔ Using a typewriter can be the fastest way of putting something short down on paper. (Apart from using a pen — personally, I've never understood why more business correspondence can't be handwritten.)

✔ Print quality is usually very good.

✔ A typewriter is very easy to learn.

✔ Sometimes, it's a whole lot easier to type an envelope than to figure out how to do envelopes on your PC word processing software and laser printer.

✔ A typewriter can still be handy if for some reason you need to work with multi-part (i.e., NCR/carbon) forms — that's something that no laser printer can manage (though dot matrix printers are able to do this).

### What sort of typewriter?

All these typewriter plus points lean in favor of fairly lightweight models. The main reasons for getting a typewriter seem to be either that you have very low needs and/or budgets, or that you want one to help you with those small, fiddly jobs. Either way, you won't want to spend much, and you certainly don't require the ultimate in heavy-duty construction. There are quite a few machines selling for up to $250 that are designed for this type of user. Prominent vendors of low-cost typewriters include Brother, Canon, and Smith Corona (SCM).

But it is increasingly hard to understand why anyone would want to pay $500–$1,000 or more for a very heavy-duty office typewriter — the type that is designed to take a pounding all day, every day. These heavy-duty machines are still being made, though by a diminishing number of vendors. The two companies that seem to be soldiering on with most determination are

Lexmark — the company that was formed to take over IBM's typewriter business — and Swintec (a company that has put most of its eggs into the typewriter basket).

# Introducing "Personal Word Processors"

A lot of typewriters have limited text memory and display functions enabling their owners to perform basic editing on fairly short documents. But some typewriter vendors sell products that they market not as typewriters, but as word processors. The difference between a typewriter and this type of word processor can amount to little more than semantics, but some historical perspective may help clarify the matter.

### A little bit of history
In the olden days — which, in this context, refers back to the early eighties — the term "dedicated word processor" referred to very expensive computers that were designed solely for word processing and that usually couldn't do anything else. These machines were proprietary — they could only use the software developed for the particular model by the hardware manufacturer. Their keyboards were tailored to the software, often with keys labeled with the functions they controlled. They worked with "daisywheel" printers — the type that used a printwheel similar to that found on typewriters. Upmarket dedicated word processors prospered for a while before the IBM Personal Computer was introduced in 1981, and they survived for a few years after that because early PC word processing software was a lot less elegant.

Some of the companies that were big in that market have long since folded or gone on to find new niches. These include Exxon Office Systems (a spectacularly unsuccessful subsidiary of the oil company), NBI, CPT, and others. Hardly any — apart from IBM — made the transition into becoming successful vendors of PC hardware or word processing software. Those who soldiered on, after most had pulled out, ended up getting hurt — none more so than Wang which entered a period of terminal decline culminating in its Chapter 11 filing in 1992.

### The budget dedicated WP
Today, however, there is a new breed of dedicated word processor. Like their early eighties counterparts, these machines incorporate proprietary word processing software built into non-industry standard hardware. Unlike the early eighties vintage

dedicated WPs, they are aimed at the rock-bottom budget end of the market. The dedicated word processor has turned from being a machine targeted at people who wanted something better than a PC-based word processor, into something for people who can't afford a PC-based word processor.

These personal word processors — let's call them "PWPs" — are usually based on typewriter technology and it can be a bit of a gray area as to whether a particular machine is best defined as a memory typewriter or a PWP. However, the hallmarks of a PWP are: (a) it has a screen showing at least a dozen lines of type and ideally about half a page; (b) it has some type of disk storage; and (c) it can perform a full range of text editing functions on longer documents, as well as very short ones. Many of these machines incorporate a typewriter printwheel mechanism, and others are connected to a daisywheel printer device which amounts to the same thing. Canon makes some models that incorporate built-in ink jet printing.

### PWP pros and cons

Some PWPs physically resemble typewriters — the screen is literally an add-on to a typewriter chassis — while others are more distinctive (and sometimes rather ungainly in appearance). What most have in common is that they are not very good — they work as advertised, but they tend to be pretty rudimentary and unrefined. Anyone used to state-of-the-art word processing software on a personal computer would be an unhappy camper if forced to move over to a PWP. On the other hand, someone who knows nothing better, and who has a limited budget to match limited requirements, might be perfectly satisfied.

Above all, PWPs are cheap. A PWP typically costs around $300–$400. That compares with about $1,000 for the absolute lowest-priced PC-based word processing system including software and a letter-quality printer. The PC-based product may be a better and more flexible solution in all sorts of ways, but there's no getting away from the fact that it's two to three times the price. That's why college students, home users, and some very small businesses continue to buy PWPs.

But few businesses can't justify the cost of a computer these days when you think of all the things you can do on them besides word processing. If you are considering buying a PWP, I would strongly urge you to think again whether a PC wouldn't be a better investment. If, nonetheless, you do decide to go ahead and buy a PWP, Brother and Smith Corona (SCM) are the two obvious brands to consider.

# Typewriter Features Guide

Next, a guide to typewriter features. I'll be talking here mainly about features relating to typewriters, though many of the points are also relevant to the PWP buyer.

### Correction memory

"Correction memory" is a feature found — to a greater or lesser extent — on every electronic typewriter; do not confuse it with "text memory" which allows you to store documents for subsequent revision and automatic retyping.

A correction memory is a buffer which stores the characters you have just typed. This means that in order to make a lift-off correction to something that's just been typed on the paper, you need only press a single key — when you do this, the printwheel backspaces and automatically lifts off the mistaken character(s).

Although all machines have this feature, correction capabilities vary widely. Some machines are only able to correct the last half dozen characters automatically; others can correct anything on the current line; and top-end models can correct up to several hundred, or even a few thousand, characters spread over several lines or even a whole page. Many machines also allow you to lift off an entire word — sometimes even a whole line — at a single keystroke. This feature is often known as "word-out correction."

On some machines, it's awkward to make a lift-off correction outside the correction memory. At worst, you have to go through a complicated series of coded keystrokes and retype the mistake back into the correction memory so that you can then backspace and lift it off.

Keep in mind that the speed at which different typewriters make lift-off corrections varies significantly and some are painfully slow. The quality of lift-off correction also varies — some machines leave noticeable traces of the corrected characters, while others leave virtually none. Just about all machines have a relocate feature, which means that you're automatically returned to the typing position you were at before going back to make the correction.

### Text memory

As mentioned above, the other type of memory is internal text memory. This enables you to store text for subsequent editing and automatic re-typing. Memory capacity is measured in thousands of characters — an "8K" memory, for example, is one that can hold up to eight thousand characters. As a rule of thumb, a full page of text usually takes up around 4K of memory. Memory size varies from around 8K to highs of about 80K — though, in general, anything over 24K is considered quite a lot by typewriter standards (even though it's negligible by PC standards).

Many memory machines have disk drive options (disk drives come standard on a few top-end models). This allows you to store text on a disk in the same way you would if using a personal computer — this is where you get into the gray area between typewriters and personal word processors. Without a disk drive, you have to delete the contents of the memory when it becomes full before you can add anything else.

A few machines have text memory that isn't really suited to editing, but only to storing commonly used sentences or short paragraphs for automatic insertion into a document as you're typing it. These usually only have 1–2K of memory and are sometimes known as "phrase memory" typewriters. Typewriters without any form of text memory are often referred to as "correction-only" machines.

### Displays

Almost all memory machines have some sort of display, and the most common are LED "line displays." These serve two main purposes. First, you can see each line before actually printing it out and make changes on the display before committing anything to paper. Second, the line display acts as a window on what's stored in the memory; you can scroll through the memory, viewing the stored text and making any changes as you go along.

Usually, a line display actually shows rather less than a full line of type at a time — 15–30 characters is typical. However, a handful show around 80 characters at a time and some show two lines; often, however, the second line is devoted to status information (e.g., it shows you what features you have selected, what line in a page you are on, etc.).

Full-size displays are similar to line displays, except that they allow you to view a lot more text at a time — up to 20 or 25 lines in some cases. In addition, some use CRT technology, which results in much clearer lettering than LEDs — this takes you into personal word processor (PWP) territory. Whereas line displays are located just above the top row of keys on the keyboard, full-size displays are often connected to the typewriter with a swivel arm.

### Editing features

If you're planning on getting a text memory machine, you'll have to decide whether to opt for one with fairly basic editing features, or whether to pay for something a little more sophisticated.

The basic variety merely allows you to make changes and corrections one character at a time. If you want to delete a whole sentence, for example, you'll have to delete each character individually. If you want to move a particular sentence, you'll have to delete it and then retype it at its new location. This is known as single character editing.

By contrast, many machines offer more advanced editing facilities. Some allow you to define blocks of text and then move, copy, or delete them as necessary. Some will automatically search for a specified word in a document and replace it with another one. All this is pretty mundane stuff to anyone used to PC-based word processing — but these are things you can't take for granted in a typewriter context.

A few advanced memory machines — especially PWPs — also offer a mail merge feature, enabling you to keep lists of names and addresses and merge these with standard text to automatically produce a series of personalized letters. Keep in mind that mail merge is much less effective if you don't have a sheet feeder to insert each page automatically one after the other — but sheet feeders are expensive options on typewriters and are not often available anyway.

"Stop codes" are useful when printing out phrases, paragraphs, or standard letters from memory that contain variables — names or a date, for example — in the middle. The way they work is that when you are entering the standard text into memory, you insert a stopcode where the variable occurs. When print-out takes place, the typewriter automatically stops printing when it reaches a stop code; you then type in the variable, before telling the typewriter to resume printing automatically from memory. Almost all machines with text memory have this feature, but a handful don't.

### Other typewriter features to look for

A typewriter's **pitch** is the number of characters that you can type in an inch. All electronic typewriters offer at least two pitches — 10 and 12 — and many offer 15 pitch and proportional spacing as well.

**Proportional spacing (PS)** varies the number of characters per inch in proportion to their individual width and provides a neater and often more compact effect. Proportional spacing can, however, be a problem when it comes to making lift-off corrections beyond the machine's correction memory (and sometimes even within it). This is because the characters are not spaced evenly, so the lift-off correction may be imprecisely aligned when you have to backspace.

Check out the **maximum paper width** if you anticipate needing to type onto wide paper. All typewriters can accept letter-size paper sideways (i.e., they can accept paper that's 11" wide). Relatively few typewriters can accept 17" paper should your needs require this — a limit of 15.5" or 16.5" is common even on most medium- and heavy-duty machines. Keep in mind that the maximum typing line is always shorter than the maximum paper width.

**Bold print** can help improve presentation by highlighting headings and key phrases. Keep in mind, though, that the quality of bold print varies, since it requires the printwheel to hit the same character twice, so exact alignment of the printing mechanism is very important.

**Justification** creates a straight right-hand margin. Combined with proportional spacing, bold print, and auto centering, justification can produce an impressive-looking end result. Justification is usually only found on memory machines.

**Automatic paper insertion** means that a typewriter can automatically feed paper into a predetermined position ready for typing — you only need to press a button or pull a lever. Some machines go a step further, allowing you to program how far down the page the paper stops when it's automatically inserted.

**Expanded print** increases the spacing between characters for presentational purposes — it's a useful way of making a heading stand out, for example. It's not very common, however.

**Format memory** allows you to store the layout of forms or invoices by combining a number of tab settings, both vertical and horizontal, so that by pressing a single key you can skip from one tab position to the next, downward as well as across.

**Paragraph indent** enables you to automatically indent a paragraph or block within a document by setting a temporary left-hand margin. It's very common, but not all machines have it.

A much smaller number of machines offer **column layout**, which automatically works out tab positions when you need to type in columns. All you have to do is tell the machine how many columns there are and type in the longest word or figure that will appear in each of them. The machine then automatically works out and sets the optimum tabs.

**Line framing**, available on relatively few machines, allows for easy line and box drawing, so that you can produce neatly laid-out forms and tables.

**Spell checks** warn you — usually with a beep — whenever you type a word they don't recognize from their built-in "dictionaries." These dictionaries usually consist of around 50,000 words, which users can supplement with a few hundred words of their own choosing. The main problem with typewriter spell checks is that the dictionaries aren't sufficiently large. This means that the machine frequently sounds an alarm when you're typing words that aren't misspelt, but that simply aren't in its dictionary. By and large, typewriter spell checks aren't nearly as good as their equivalents on PC word processing software programs.

Some spell checks not only warn you of mistyped words, but also suggest correct spellings. One manufacturer goes further still — not only does its spell check suggest alternatives but, once you give the go-ahead, the machine automatically corrects the mistyped word and retypes the alternative for you. Again, this type of thing is routine on PC word processing software — but it's advanced stuff on a typewriter. Spell checks are sometimes options, costing $100–$200 depending on the sophistication offered. But in my opinion, typewriter spell checks are more bother than they're worth. It's a case of typewriters getting too big for their britches.

**Typing speeds** are measured in characters per second (cps). The speed is of most interest on memory machines, as it's an indication of how fast the machine can print out from memory. That said, typing speed is still important on non-memory models, since it's possible for a very fast typist to outpace a machine with a slow typing speed (13cps is considered slow; 20cps, moderate).

The other reason why the print speed might be of interest is if you're considering a computer interface option, which allows the typewriter to double up as a rudimentary PC printer. Many models offer these and the cost is usually around $150. But beware that print speeds are almost unbearably slow compared with dedicated computer printers. In addition, you may well find compatibility problems with your software — and this type of printing is not suitable if you use Windows software (or an Apple Mac). My advice is to think at least twice before taking this path.

### Features you can normally take for granted

These days, there are a number of features you can really take for granted, even on inexpensive lightweight machines. Here are the most important ones. **Automatic carriage return** ensures that when you come to the end of a line, you move to the next one automatically — there's no risk of accidentally typing too far over to the right or going off the paper. (You don't have to stop typing while the printhead is moving down to the next line — a small buffer memory holds the letters you type while this takes place.)

**Automatic underscore** means that words can be underlined as you type them — you don't have to go back and do this afterwards. **Automatic centering** means that you don't have to rely on your eye or judgment to center headings — the machine will do it for you.

**Decimal tabulation** automatically lines up a column of figures around the decimal point. **Caps lock** means that you don't have to keep your finger on "shift" in order to type in capital letters. **Express backspace** whizzes you back along the line on which you're typing. **Flush right** automatically aligns text to the right-hand margin, useful for setting things like dates and addresses.

# Buying a Typewriter

Low-cost typewriters and personal word processors are sold mainly through consumer electronics outlets, office supply catalogs, and office supply warehouse stores. Heavy-duty typewriters are sold by traditional office equipment dealers. Family-owned dealerships specializing in typewriters used to be pretty common, but they are now increasingly few in number — there simply isn't the volume to support them. Many traditional typewriter dealerships have been driven out of business; few made a successful transition into selling computers and other more high-growth types of office equipment.

Typewriter list prices are, on the whole, set at a level that virtually assumes you're going to get a discount of 25–40 percent. Shop carefully before you buy: the same machine often sells at significantly different prices depending on where you buy it.

Getting a typewriter fixed is a problem if you don't know an old-fashioned dealership with its own technicians; even if you do know one, you may find that it doesn't service your particular model (especially if it hadn't sold it to you). A $175 budget typewriter is viewed by many as almost a disposable item — if you get three years' use out of one, you may consider it not worth getting fixed.

# Typewriter Supplies

Typewriter supplies could be the subject of a chapter of their own. Some buyers who get a good deal on their machines end up getting robbed on their ribbons. Some machines use intrinsically more expensive ribbons than others, but in most cases there are compatible ribbons from third-party supply companies so you needn't be stuck with the manufacturer's "own brand" variety.

If shopping around, remember that ribbons are the ultimate discount product — so much so that the concept of a "list price" hardly exists. But for every dealer who sells ribbons at half price, there's another who sells them at double or even triple the price — unscrupulous dealers take advantage of the fact that most buyers have only the vaguest notion of what they ought to be paying. The safest places to buy ribbons are the big office supply stores such as Office Depot, Staples, or OfficeMax — this way you can be more or less sure you're not a getting bad deal.

When comparing costs, it isn't sufficient to look only at the unit price — you also have to take account of the ribbon yield (measured in thousands of characters). Unfortunately, this isn't always easy, as many ribbon vendors don't publish this information. As a rough guide, if you're paying $3–$5 per 100,000 characters for top quality ribbons you're not getting a bad deal.

But not all ribbons are the same — there are two main varieties to choose between. "Carbon correctable" ribbons give the crispest image, but are also the most expensive. "Multistrike" ribbons last longer, because each time you print a character the ribbon only advances by less than a full character space. This means that costs work out cheaper, but print quality isn't quite as good since parts of the ribbon get hit more than once.

Ribbon costs tend to be highest at the lightweight end of the typewriter market (where you can pay up to $10 per 100,000 characters) — though the whole issue is less important there, because if you've got a light workload you won't get through many ribbons anyway.

# Who's Who in Typewriters and PWPs?

Most of the action in the typewriter market is at the low end, and the two vendors which put most energy into marketing themselves are Brother and Smith Corona (SCM).

### The mother of all typewriter wars

The word "rivals" would misstate the relationship between Brother and SCM — they are, in fact, bitter sworn enemies. Rarely in the office equipment market has there been a case of two companies hating each other's guts as much as these two. The reason has to do with a long-running dispute over which company is dumping imports and which is making typewriters in America.

It all began when SCM — historically an American company — accused Brother — a Japanese one — of dumping imported machines at artificially low prices to stifle competition. Brother responded to Federal anti-dumping measures by moving assembly into the US. SCM countered that Brother was only running a screwdriver operation and that the "Made in America" machines were, in essence, foreign.

SCM, meanwhile, was itself forced for reasons of costs to source an increasing amount of its parts and completed products from the Far East. Then, in 1992, SCM closed its upstate New York factory and shifted production to Mexico.

This led Brother to accuse SCM of dumping. Brother also claimed to be the only American manufacturer of budget typewriters, and accused SCM of also being a "foreign" company since it has for several years been approximately half-owned, by a British conglomerate called Hanson Industries. To rub the point in, Brother started sponsoring the US Olympic team. All of this drove SCM management crazy. Fighting Brother in the courts and in the lobbies of Washington became their top concern — some saw it as an obsession.

Buyers, meanwhile, were happy. To them, dumping simply meant lower prices. And with the typewriter industry struggling to justify its existence, there seemed little threat that prices would surge upwards if one vendor was driven out by predatory pricing from another — the fact is that even if typewriter manufacturing were a monopoly, there would be plenty of downward price pressure caused by events in the PC and laser printer markets.

Early in 1994, the two companies halted legal hostilities, realizing that the battle had become pointless and damaging to both sides — but relations remain chill.

### Other players in the typewriter market

Other vendors that are still in the typewriter and PWP markets are: Olympia (an old German vendor, whose low-end machines are now made in the Far East by Nakajima and whose other manufacturing has been shifted to Mexico); Canon; Sharp;

Panasonic; Royal (an old, but substantially diminished name in the office equipment business, now owned by troubled office equipment giant, Olivetti; its typewriters are actually made in South Korea by Samsung); Swintec (a major distributor, which has manufacturing arrangements with Nakajima and also performs some assembly in the US); and Lexmark (the typewriter company that was spun off from IBM and focuses only on the top end of the typewriter market). ✍

# Vendor Addresses & Phone Numbers

Below are the addresses and phone numbers of the vendors still active in the typewriter market. Remember that none of them sell direct, except occasionally to very large accounts.

Brother International Corporation
200 Cottontail Lane
Somerset, NJ 08875–6714
Tel: 908 356 8880

Panasonic Office Automation
Two Panasonic Way
Secaucus, NJ 07094
Tel: 800 843 0080

Canon USA Inc.
One Canon Plaza
Lake Success, NY 11042
Tel: 516 488 6700

Royal Consumer Business Products
765 US Highway 202
Bridgewater, NJ 08807
Tel: 908 218 5518

Lexmark International Inc.
740 New Circle Road
Lexington, KY 40511
Tel: 800 426 2468

Sharp Electronics Corporation
Sharp Plaza
Mahwah, NJ 07430–2135
Tel: 201 529 9200

Olympia USA, Inc.
1330 River Bend Drive
Dallas, TX 75247
Tel: 800 832 4727

Swintec Corporation
320 W. Commercial Avenue
Moonachie, NJ 07074
Tel: 800 225 0867

# Chapter 13

# Postage Meters

# Postage Meters

If you think the only name in the mailing equipment game is Pitney Bowes, you're wrong. While it's true that this $3.4-billion dollar Connecticut firm dominates the market for postage meter systems with about an 87 percent share of installed equipment, it is not the only player. Although Pitney Bowes makes some very fine equipment, the sheer extent of its dominant position is due more to history, the clever use of patents, savvy marketing, and — some would argue — an historically close relationship with the Postal Service, than to the innate superiority of what it sells.

Lately, Pitney's grip has been slipping. Though no one doubts that it will continue to lead the market, it has lost some ground to three very real competitors which have products that are usually just as well made, sometimes better, and often less expensive. More fundamental threats are on the horizon, due to a combination of technological and regulatory pressures which will likely be opening up this market during the next few years.

The three challengers to Pitney Bowes in today's postage meter market are Ascom Hasler, Friden Neopost, and Francotyp-Postalia. All three rely on equipment imported from across the Atlantic; Pitney's marketing makes much of the fact that it is the only all-American vendor in the business. Of the three challengers, Ascom Hasler and Friden Neopost are serious forces. Francotyp-Postalia is far smaller in this country, and these days its US operation sells mainly relabeled Neopost equipment.

### An important explanation

A postage meter system comprises two connected parts: the first is the "base," and the second is the "meter" itself. The base is the part that physically handles the envelopes — feeding them in, sealing them, and so forth; and the meter is the part that prints the postage. Under postal regulations, you are allowed to own your base, but you can only rent the meter. There will be further discussion on these points in this chapter, but it is important to keep these basic definitions in mind.

The terminology can be confusing, because the popular way to refer to the base/meter combination is to call it a "postage meter." To reduce confusion, I sometimes use the term "postage meter system" to refer to the combined unit.

# The Culture of Today's Postage Meter Market

Despite growing use of electronic technology, mailing as it exists today is one of the few remaining areas of office equipment that is intrinsically mechanical in nature. This fact has kept it apart from the rest of the office equipment industry. None of the Japanese or Koreans have shown any interest in getting involved. The imports come from Germany, France, and Britain — nations that have been virtually obliterated from the rest of the office equipment market — and from Switzerland (which was never there in the first place).

In recent years, the postage meter world has been an oasis of calm, where a handful of Western manufacturers have been producing traditional machinery, competing only with each other just as they did in the olden days when the Orient was known more for its rice than for its microchips. No new manufacturer has entered this cozy market in a generation. It's not just that the technology has been pretty static, it's also that the industry is protected in all countries by government regulation. In order to supply postage meter equipment in this country, you have to be licensed by the United States Postal Service (USPS).

### The ban on meter ownership

Users of the equipment are not even allowed to buy much of it outright. As I indicated above, the part of a postage meter system that keeps a tally of how much money you've paid and how much you've spent — the actual "meter" itself — can only be rented.

The ban on end-user meter ownership has helped depress competition by acting as one of a number of barriers to new entrants in this market. It has also provided an excuse for manufacturers to send out a literally never-ending stream of rental invoices to businesses needing to use what are pretty straightforward pieces of equipment.

Hundreds of thousands of these meters have been paid for by users many times over, yet prices continue to rise. On prices current at the time of this writing, the cost of renting Pitney Bowes' most heavily-promoted meter over a five-year period amounts to $2,145–$4,665 (depending on how much postage you put through it: the lower figure applies if your quarterly amount totals less than $1,000). That, of course, is in addition to the "base" that is required for the meter to operate (which typically costs anywhere from around $2,000 to over $8,000 for an outright purchase).

The situation is reminiscent of the days when it was illegal to own your own telephone, and you were forced to rent one from Ma Bell. Indeed, the arguments that are used to defend the status quo in postage meters are comparable in tone to those that were deployed to justify the ban on phone ownership.

The equipment vendors are beneficiaries of the current system. When pressed whether they think it is fair, they stonewall by pointing out that they have nothing to do with setting the rules. The Postal Service, which does set them, has rationalized the ban by arguing that postage is a currency equivalent and that equipment capable of printing it cannot, therefore, be owned by ordinary citizens.

This has always struck me as an unconvincing argument: dishonest people who are intent on defrauding meters are not likely to refrain from doing so because legal title to the meter is vested with their equipment vendor. If they want to tamper with their meter, they will do so regardless of who owns it. (A more philosophical objection is that postage meter imprints are not a currency equivalent: they are simply vouchers used by a delivery organization that happens to be owned by the government.)

Proponents of the ownership ban argue their case by quoting the large amounts that the Postal Service loses through fraud. USPS estimates have lately put the amount as high as $100 million annually, though some in the industry consider that to be an exaggeration.

Be that as it may, the very fact that tampering takes place on this large a scale is evidence that the ownership ban does nothing to prevent fraud! Moreover, end-user ownership is allowed in other countries, notably Britain, in which the same meters are used.

In my opinion, meter fraud has nothing to do with meter ownership, and everything to do with meter design. The overwhelming evidence suggests that postage is only stolen via old-fashioned mechanical meters. In fact, the Postal Service has recently decertified some very old Pitney Bowes mechanical models that it saw as particularly vulnerable (these were the R-Line meters, of which about 10,000 were still in use). As far as I am aware, there has never been a case of someone stealing postage using an electronic meter designed to be refilled over the phone (postage credits by phone are now offered by all three major vendors in this market: more on this later).

Despite the fact that existing electronic meters have a very good security track record, the USPS view is that they can be made even more fraud-proof. The Postal Service would like to see everyone switching to a new type of tamper-proof meter that will begin to appear in 1995. When that happens, well-placed sources indicate that the Postal Service could drop its objections to meter ownership — this is not something that would be welcomed by the bulk of the meter suppliers, but it is something that customers should look forward to. More on this shortly when I talk about impending changes in this market.

### Ethical standards

The postage meter market is pretty mature. The vast majority of sales are replacement units, not first-time placements. The rapid growth of fax, e-mail, computer modems, and overnight letter services has blunted the role of traditional mail. While the mail will continue to be the main method of transmitting business papers for the foreseeable future, it is not at the cutting edge. In addition, there has recently been limited technological development in postage meters (especially in the low- and medium-volume sectors of the market) and the equipment tends to be very reliable and durable: thus people who have postage meters are usually content to keep them for a long time.

As a result of all of this, the life of a postage meter sales rep can be a tough one. The pressure to maintain sales quotas is significantly higher than the natural demand for the products. This leads to a culture of hard sell and, at times, to questionable sales methods.

I have come across cases in which businesses were told by postage systems reps that a lease had expired when, in fact, it still had time to run. There have also been cases of businesses being told that equipment is being used too heavily or is beyond repair, when that is patently not the case. In one incident I came across not long ago, a sales rep got a junior secretary to sign a piece of paper that turned out to be a new lease; the secretary, who thought she was just renewing a service contract, was in no way authorized to enter into a lease.

In Britain, Pitney Bowes has been the target of government action for anti-competitive and dishonest sales practices. Cases of dishonesty in the US postage meter market have always been more sporadic. Moreover, Pitney Bowes — while not explicitly admitting that they have occurred — has lately started to take steps to stamp them out by imposing a new, customer-oriented culture on its sales force.

### Pitney's new procedures

The company's new "Procedures Guide" for its sales force includes the following instructions: "Always honestly state who you are, whom you represent ... Never endorse, sign or initial any agreement or document on behalf of the customer ... If you obtain a signature or endorsement from an individual whom (sic) you know is not authorized to commit the customer, you are violating Company policy."

Employees are made aware that they can be fired for breaking these rules. Likewise, the "Procedures Guide" instructs its sales reps never to announce themselves by saying things like: "The post office sent me to check your meter."

Pitney Bowes is to be commended for setting out, and enforcing, standards of acceptable behavior. But the very fact that it has to tell its sales force, in such specific terms, not to be sleazy is, perhaps, indicative of problems that have occurred. In the past, I used to say that while PB did not condone unethical sales practices, its middle management tended to look the other way. Now I am inclined to accept the company's assurances that this type of thing is no longer tolerated and that the culture of the company is changing.

### What to remember about postage meter reps

But Pitney Bowes is naturally as keen as ever to increase its sales revenues — like any public company, it is under shareholder pressure to grow. Customers should keep three things in mind when dealing with its sales force: (a) all Pitney sales reps earn their living mainly by getting existing customers to upgrade and/or commit to ever-longer lease agreements; (b) Pitney Bowes is the only direct sales business equipment company of its size which still pays most of its sales force solely on commission; and (c) postage meter reps (not only Pitney's) routinely advise buyers to get somewhat larger equipment than is really required.

The rep who turns up in your office without an appointment offering to replace your old machine with a new one may produce figures showing that your monthly payments will not be much higher. Maybe they don't appear higher at all (though watch the small print for what will happen in year two). But the intention is to commit you to making those monthly payments for much longer than you were committed before. Anything to stop you from being a target for predatory vendors. Pitney's strength as a business rests on the fact that it has over one million customers locked into long-term, cash-producing contracts.

One of the reasons why vendors encourage you to lease their bases, rather than purchase them outright, is to create a trap where, once you have signed up, it will always seem cheaper for you to stay with your existing supplier rather than switch. They try to get you to extend your commitment by switching equipment before it is necessary, so that you never escape.

The same Pitney Bowes "Procedures Guide" that tells the reps not to be sleazy also decrees the number of times that they must call on existing customers in their territory — it is mandatory that every Pitney customer be visited at least twice a year, and some larger accounts must receive sales calls quarterly or even monthly. My advice: be wary of postage meter reps who say they have come to help you.

There can be a very thin line between a commission-only sales rep being motivated, and becoming a pest: some cross that line. Over-selling occurs in many other industries besides postage meters, but it takes on a special significance with Pitney Bowes, because of the company's near monopoly position in a market to which access is controlled by an arm of the government.

That said, I certainly do not want to cast doubt on the professionalism of all who earn their living by selling postage meter systems: there are many out there who get the balance right and service their customers without alienating them.

### Customer alienation & the billing problem

Besides sales tactics, the main source of discontent among users concerns billing. Though the vendors have improved their systems, postage meter users have for years had to put up with confusing bills, chronic errors, and poor handling of complaints and inquiries. And the problem has been particularly serious with Pitney Bowes.

The most common errors have been rental billing for equipment that the customer no longer has, and billing for meter rentals based on a higher volume of postage than the customer puts through the equipment (both Pitney Bowes and Friden charge meter rentals which are banded according to use). Combined with the confusing presentation of bills, this has led to money being paid that was not owed.

Pitney Bowes, while conceding that problems were widespread in the past, claims that they have now largely been addressed. PB concedes, however, that billing clarity still has to be improved. Friden tells us much the same thing, and also speaks of new steps it has taken to make it easier for customers to deal with the company.

In my opinion, the lack of competition in this industry has been a factor behind billing problems. It is hard to imagine that the problems would have become so widespread, and lasted for so long, had there been more effective competition or, failing that, proper regulation.

### The What to Buy for Business user poll

In a 1994 guide to postage meter systems, *What to Buy for Business* published the results of a poll of over 500 users. Worth mentioning here is the high degree of alienation that many users feel towards their vendors. Pitney Bowes takes the brunt of this — partly by virtue of being the largest — but the others by no means escape it. In summing up the results of the poll, *What to Buy for Business* wrote:

> "If the vendors of postage meter machines choose to portray their customer base as, for the large part, very satisfied, that is their right. All we can do is report the evidence that we come across. And our conclusions are as follows:
>
> "First, postage meter equipment is, in general, reliable (notwithstanding the iffy performance of certain features, such as sealers). In fact, its very reliability is what causes many of the problems in this industry — i.e., commission-hungry reps trying to persuade people that they need new equipment when the existing machines are doing just fine.
>
> "According to our poll, Ascom Hasler's stuff is more reliable than the rest. It may be — but we don't argue that the poll proves this conclusively by any means, as users who have had bad experiences with Pitney over things like billing may be less generous towards rating their machines' performance than Ascom Hasler users who are not so frustrated about the total experience of dealing with their supplier. That said, although the poll does not provide conclusive evidence that Ascom Hasler's equipment is better than that sold by Pitney Bowes, there is absolutely no reason to believe it is any less good.
>
> "Second, a significant minority of Pitney Bowes cus-

*tomers dislike the culture of the company they deal with. PB is viewed by those people as something of a bully.*

*"In private briefings with very senior people at PB during the past year, What to Buy has been told about things that Pitney Bowes is doing to change the company's culture and make it far more customer-oriented. However, there is a time lag between senior management in a near-monopoly giant instigating a cultural revolution, and customers forgetting what they have experienced hitherto. In our opinion, the jury is still out on the question of how different the PB of today is from the PB of the past."*

In the interests of fairness, I should add that Pitney Bowes responded to the above by saying that its own surveys of its customers — based on a larger number of responses — yielded much more positive results. The full results of the poll are published in *The Postage Meter Systems Guide,* which also contains full product information and ratings on the equipment from all four vendors in this market (the guide costs $24 including shipping; call 800 247 2185 to order by credit card).

# How the Postage Meter Market is Set to Change

Though the postage meter market has lately seemed sleepy, people in it are bracing themselves for stirring times ahead: more will happen to change this industry during the next five years than has occurred in the previous quarter of a century.

This will come about as a result of technological innovation, legal maneuvering, and regulatory pressures. The changes will be more fundamental than you might imagine — the whole concept of postage equipment will soon be redefined, as will some of the assumptions that surround its use.

### The birth of PC-based postage

For example, by the end of 1995 it could be possible to get PC software that prints postage directly onto an envelope, together with the address, using a normal laser printer — in other words, the need for dedicated postage equipment could soon become a thing of the past at certain levels of the market.

The three main suppliers of traditional postage equipment are all working on PC-based postage software. However, the first company to offer it may be a complete newcomer to this industry. "Outsiders" are at an advanced stage in getting PC-based postage software ready for the market, and they are working with the full knowledge and cooperation of the United States Postal Service which fully expects these products to be available before long. So, during the next few hundred days, you may find that you can choose not only new postage technology, but also new sources of supply.

It is likely that PC-based postage will — at least initially — have the most impact among smaller businesses, including those that do not already have meter equipment, and that the intrinsically mechanical aspects of heavier mail handling will assure the traditional meter of a continuing market. Nonetheless, larger mailers could also find themselves with a computer-driven alternative to traditional postage meters.

So-called "mail manifesting systems" will enable users to deliver items to the mail carrying unique numbers, which would be read by Postal Service equipment that would track them and debit customers' prepaid accounts. In a large office, users on a network could all produce mail-ready envelopes at the point of printing, rather than having to send mail to a special room to be processed. Every time an envelope was produced, the information about it would be sent to a file in the network containing a mail manifest for the day. At the end of the day, the mail would be collected from users and handed to the USPS with a manifest printout. Systems like this are already being shown at mailing industry trade shows.

The more one thinks about it, the more it becomes obvious that technology exists already that threatens to make the traditional postage meter obsolete — sooner or later.

### New generation meters

Nonetheless, the traditional postage meter will not disappear — at least not in the foreseeable future. But it will itself undergo major changes in the next few years. As part of its efforts to outlaw meter fraud, the Postal Service is insisting on new designs that are tamper-proof.

If the Postal Service gets its way, the entire installed meter base could be withdrawn during the next five years and replaced by a new generation of electronic meters which the three main vendors will begin introducing in 1995. Whether the Postal Service succeeds in forcing all users to trade in their rental meters — even relatively new electronic ones — remains to be seen. Such a widespread change would prove expensive to people who currently rent the oldest, and hence the least expensive, meters. Moreover, Pitney Bowes — with so much market share to lose and little to gain — might not welcome a change which could prompt users to review their vendor loyalties.

However, any mass switch-over towards a new generation of meters could have far-reaching and positive consequences in this industry. This is because the tamper-proof design of the new meters will remove the theoretical justification behind the ban on end-user ownership. Privately, senior sources in the Postal Service agree that the ban on ownership will become untenable.

The only question is who would precipitate a change in the rules. The Postal Service maintains that the request would have to come from the vendors. Yet the vendors are those who have a vested interest against change: interviewed by us, they all say that it is up to the Postal Service to set the rules and that, as mere suppliers, their job is only to follow orders. Nonetheless, someone is likely to break ranks at some point and, once meter ownership is legalized, entry into the market would become easier, a strong second-hand market would develop, and downward pressure would be exerted on prices.

### Patent wars

The ban on meter ownership isn't the only reason why competition in this market has been restricted. Another is that Pitney Bowes has cornered a whole load of key patents.

Critics charge that this is the result of an historically cozy relationship with the Postal Service: PB's clout, they argue, meant that it was able to develop its patents in tandem with influencing the Postal Service's technical standards for meters, such that smaller vendors subsequently found it hard to bring out competitive equipment that passed USPS requirements without violating those patents. This, the critics argue, has stifled competition, led to higher prices, kept two European manufacturers from selling their equipment in the US market, and deterred other possible entrants from getting started.

In 1959, a Justice Department antitrust suit accused the company of illegally monopolizing the postage meter market. Part of the settlement that followed obliged Pitney to license its patents, royalty free, to qualified manufacturers (in agreeing to this, Pitney never admitted guilt). But this, and various other constraints, were lifted in the late 1960s.

Friden, which also has a number of its own patents under its belt, later accepted a Pitney offer to use certain of the latter's patents in return for a royalty payment. Friden's attitude towards opening up patents seems to be that it has paid its dues to be part of this closed market, and that it doesn't want to make things easier for anyone else. Postalia also agreed to pay royalties.

Ascom Hasler, however, has refused. At first, it argued over the size of the payments but then balked over the principle. In plain English, Ascom Hasler's case is that PB patented stuff which resided in the public domain. In spring 1993, Pitney Bowes filed a lawsuit against Ascom Hasler, citing patent infringement. Ascom Hasler counter-sued, alleging unfair trade practices.

As this book was published, legal maneuverings were underway. Ascom Hasler had come up with legal precedents which, they said, showed that PB's patent lawsuit should be against the government, not against Ascom Hasler; this was because the government had put itself in the front line by certifying (not to mention using) Ascom Hasler equipment. In other words, according to Ascom Hasler, the law says that if the government is a party to an alleged infringement, then the government has to be the first target of a lawsuit.

As a result, it appeared at press-time that the US Postal Service would be forced to take a position on an issue crucial to the future competitive structure of the postage meter industry. The result of this lawsuit may not make much difference to a purchase you make during the shelf-life of this book — but it could change the industry during the remainder of this decade and beyond.

# Introducing Today's Equipment

Having briefed you on the culture, politics, and future of the postage meter market, let's get down to talking about the equipment as it is available today.

As I explained at the start of this chapter, a postage meter system comprises two elements: the first is the "base" and the second is the "meter" itself. Closely related are postage scales, which are sold by all of the meter manufacturers but also by quite a few others. Although they are distinct products, bases, meters, and scales all work together. Without a good handle on how they relate, it can get a bit confusing — here's what you need to know.

### Bases

The base of a postage meter system doesn't actually print or keep track of postage. Its job is to sit underneath the postage meter, guide the envelope under the meter for stamping, and then eject it out the other end. Bases vary in their capabilities in terms of how fast they process envelopes, how automated the envelope loading feature is, and whether they can perform special functions like sealing the envelopes and dispensing postage tapes for parcels. Each base is configured to be compatible with one or more specific types of meter. However, you can never mix one brand of base with another brand of meter.

Postal regulations allow you to purchase bases (meters, as I have explained, can only be rented), though many users prefer to rent or lease them. Renting may seem like a more flexible arrangement but, in practice, the only flexibility you get is the ability to trade up — short term rentals of bases are usually not available and vendors are much more keen on locking you in than on giving you outs!

Renting and leasing generally works out to be more expensive in the end, though you may be able to claim a fuller tax deduction — ask your accountant for advice. If you are buying outright, prices start at under $700 and rise to around $20,000 for something very fancy. A typical mid-market base with some automation, but not a huge number of advanced features, costs in the region of $3,000–$4,000.

### Meters

The meter is a mechanical or electronic device attached to the base that stamps the "indicia" (the indicia — pronounced "in-dish-a" — is the red-ink image printed on the envelope that saddens stamp collectors worldwide). You set the correct amount on the meter, usually by sliding levers (older models) or pushing buttons (newer electronic ones). Ascending and descending registers keep a running account of how much postage you've "spent" and how much is left in the meter. When you get low, you need to "fill" the meter again. You can do this by taking it to the post office and writing a check, or by utilizing one of the over-the-phone postage replenishment systems described later.

As explained previously, postal regulations prohibit the purchase of meters — you can only rent them. What you pay is partly a function of the features, but it's often also related to the amount of work you put through the unit. Monthly rates vary from around $15 to over $75. The most common range is around $30–$60.

Keep in mind that most of the rental plans have significantly lower monthly payments in the first year than they do thereafter. For example, new customers may be offered the low-volume usage rate for the first year, even though their workload will place them in the top band thereafter. Make sure you know what you're committing yourself to — and beware that the mailing industry likes its small print!

Also, be vigilant to ensure that you are not being charged a higher band then you should be — the vendors are often more adept at putting your rent up when you increase postage expenditure, than on reducing it if your postage decreases.

### Standalone meters

At the low end of the market, a few meters can be used on their own without any form of base. So for the cost of an average meter rental, you can be all set up without having to pay for anything else. This arrangement is well worth considering if you're a small office and if you don't need features like automatic postage label dispensers (discussed later) and sealers.

Pitney Bowes, Friden, and Francotyp-Postalia all have standalone meters; Ascom Hasler does not. Standalones aren't necessarily downmarket machines — for example, Pitney has a very nice-looking electronic model which can be used with its over-the-phone telephone refills service and which costs from around $77 a quarter to rent.

Standalone meters will be most vulnerable to the new type of PC-based postage software described earlier, which will allow you to print postage directly onto envelopes using a regular laser printer. The chances are that standalone meters as a genre will be obsolete within a few years.

### Scales

This chapter isn't discussing scales in detail, but I will be referring to them in passing because people often buy them at the same time as postage meter systems. Electronic scales weigh your mail and automatically calculate the postage. They typically cost from a few hundred dollars to around a couple of thousand. They work out postal rates based on both the weight and your chosen method of mailing (e.g., 1st class, 3rd class, air mail, etc.).

Keep in mind that you can also get low-cost mechanical scales that only weigh your mail and leave you to figure out the postage either by referring to a chart or reading off a card placed on the dial — these are less accurate, but may be all that a small office needs.

Although electronic scales normally operate independently of postage meter systems, some are designed to interface automatically — this means that they set the correct amount of postage on the meter. In some cases, they can cause a mailing label to print without the operator pressing anything on the base.

Pitney Bowes and Ascom Hasler electronic meters can all interface with compatible same-brand scales at no extra charge as far as the meters are concerned; however, you'll generally have to pay for an interface option on the scale itself and this can be expensive — you're talking about a minimum of a few hundred dollars and sometimes a lot more. With Friden, the interface option adds to the cost of the base (and not all of its bases can be interfaced). Pitney Bowes's top-end Paragon base comes with a built-in weighing device — more on this later when I look at advanced weighing features that work with bases.

If you don't need an interface feature, there are several manufacturers of electronic scales in addition to the postage meter vendors being discussed in this chapter; prominent ones include Detecto, Micro General, and Pelouze.

### So what do you need?
Once you understand what the different types of equipment are, and how they all relate, the next logical questions are: do you really need them and, if so, how sophisticated do they need to be?

If you're sending less than, say, 20 envelopes or packages per day, you can arguably get by with stamps. In fact, you can probably use stamps if you send out more items than that if they all weigh the same amount. Stamps only become a pain if used in large quantities or if you need to keep lots of different denominations to cater to all possible postal rate levels.

Sometimes, stamps offer an advantage: they help get your mail read, because they look more personal. Direct mail wizards maintain that sales letters sent with stamps are received more sympathetically than ones that are metered. This is a counter-argument to the slightly patronizing sales line that even very small businesses should have their mail metered because it makes it look "more professional."

In pure productivity terms, there's no doubt that postage meter systems can offer several advantages when you send out several dozen items a day. Using one should prove quicker and more convenient than sticking on stamps. Most models offer additional time-saving features, like automatic sealing. Your mail may be processed faster at the post office, since metered mail by-passes postal cancellation equipment and goes straight into the sorting unit. In addition, meters make it easier to keep financial records and to control how much you're spending on postage.

But don't over-order: buyers are often subjected to intense pressure to upgrade their equipment or to order a very fancy system in the first place. If in doubt, under-order. You'll always be able to trade up later, but you'll never be able to trade down without incurring a hefty penalty!

### The detail factor

Let's look next at the features in a little more detail. You should be warned that the vendors in this market tend to sell against each other by stressing points of fine detail. Each vendor looks to see what is different about the way in which its machines are designed and then builds a case around them. The points they dwell on tend to be somewhat arcane, of interest more to post-age meter aficionados than to regular buyers. I make no apologies for glossing over some of them, since they tend to cancel each other out and, if I repeated them all here, I doubt that anyone would finish reading this chapter!

Privately, some people who work in the industry at a senior level concede that sales pitches based around "levers and switches" don't really amount to a whole lot, and that issues to do with customer service are of much more importance to buyers.

# More About Bases

Having made that last point, here are the main things that you do need to know about bases.

### Envelope feed methods

The least expensive bases have manual feed. Although these machines are motorized, you have to feed each envelope in and help it go through. That's fine for small offices, but it becomes a bit tedious with larger quantities of mail. Keep in mind that a base that is entirely manual in operation is, arguably, not a lot more productive than a standalone meter (i.e., a meter that is able to operate on its own without a base).

Semi-automatic envelope feeders work a bit faster: with one of these, you can "stream feed" envelopes by inserting them in rapid succession into the machine, which grabs them from you and does the rest. For the highest productivity, consider a fully-automatic feeder: here you place a pile of envelopes in the feeder, and the base automatically processes them one by one with no need for operator involvement (jams and misfeeds allowing!).

Envelope feeders are not inexpensive. For example, Ascom Hasler charges $1,350 for a fully-automatic feeder and $350 for a semi-automatic one (those prices include a sealer as well). Often it's hard to specify exactly what you're paying for a feeder, as the option comes along with various other enhancements to the non-feeder version of the same basic machine (faster speed, etc.).

### Machine speeds

All vendors quote speeds in terms of envelopes per minute. Speeds vary from around 30–40 on low-end machines to 240 at the top of the market. On a manual feed machine, the quoted envelopes per minute figure is pretty theoretical — it offers some comparative indication of how fast a machine's motor is relative to that of other models, but manual dexterity, rather than motor speed, is what will really determine how long it takes you to meter your mail. The same applies to a lesser extent to semi-automatic models.

The quoted speed figure is more realistic on machines with a fully-automatic envelope feeder, but even here only mailing athletes manage to maintain the theoretical speed for long periods. The inevitable misfeeds, plus the need to keep the feeder replenished with fresh supplies of envelopes, invariably slow things down. Machines with fully-automatic feeders usually have quoted speeds of around 150 envelopes per minute or more.

### How fast a machine do you need?

One of the questions I am asked most frequently about postage meter systems is how fast a system people should get for given volumes of mail. Unfortunately, it's quite hard to answer this: for example, an office that sends out 300 pieces of mail daily, but handles them evenly during the whole day, should be able to make do with a slower machine than one that needs to meter 300 pieces every day in a rush just before the mail is collected.

Nonetheless, as I have already pointed out in this chapter, you should be careful not to buy a faster machine than you really need. Even if you assume that the actual throughput of a machine will be just 20 percent of its official envelopes per minute speed, this still means that a 150-envelopes-per-minute base will be able to process 30 envelopes a minute, or 1,800 envelopes an hour. There is no way that you are over-using a base if you run it for an hour every day, so it follows that a base like this is sufficient for fairly high volumes of mail.

Despite this, most postage meter reps routinely recommend much faster bases to people who send 1,000 letters a day or more, and, likewise, offer 150 envelopes-per-minute bases to people who might only be sending a couple of hundred letters a day. Of course, it follows from this discussion that if you count your mail by the dozen, rather than by the hundred, you should go for one of the slowest bases.

### Tape dispensers

Next question: what do you do when you need to mail a package or parcel? Obviously, these can't be run through a meter because of their size. The solution is a tape dispenser. This produces a strip of gummed tape that's run through the meter and stamped with the correct postage. All you need to do is stick it on the package.

The tape comes in two forms depending on the machine: (a) self-adhesive, peel-off strips that are pre-cut to a certain size; or (b) gummed rolls which are cut and, if you wish, moistened by the machine as they're dispensed. The roll tape method has a slight speed advantage if you're a very high-volume user.

Most bases do have tape dispensers (the exceptions are some entry-level models). If you buy a machine without one, you can still run pre-cut tapes through the meter manually, but this can be tricky to do correctly. If the tape isn't properly aligned, the postage mark will miss the tape. Do this often enough and it becomes expensive — because the meter is still debited every time it happens.

### Envelope thickness

Most bases can handle envelopes up to 3/8" thick and 1/2" is the maximum on any model. Some machines allow you to adjust the feeder manually for envelope thickness; a few do so automatically.

If you're metering thick items, it can be helpful to adjust the position of the imprint, to stop it from getting too close to the edge. Some machines allow you to do this manually; a few do it automatically.

### Sealers

This potentially handy option seals your envelopes as they pass through the meter by moistening the gummed flaps and pressing them shut. These days, almost all bases have a sealer as a standard feature. Keep in mind, though, that sealers can be one of the most problematic features on a meter system — they do not always work in practice as well as users would like.

Normally, all that's required for a sealer to operate is that the envelopes be stacked and fed into the machine. However, certain models require them to be "nested" — this means that the gummed flap of each envelope has to be revealed so that the glue is exposed. A "seal-only mode" is useful if you want to seal envelopes that aren't destined for the mail — payroll envelopes, for example.

### Piece counters

Need to keep a count of how many pieces you're mailing at a

time? Then look for a machine with a resettable counter. This feature is often found on bases; if it isn't, you may find that your meter can perform the same task.

### Stackers
On high-performance systems, metered envelopes are churned out at a rapid rate, so it can be helpful to have some mechanism to handle them as they emerge sporting their newly-printed indicias. A power stacker — also known as a "conveyor" — does this by guiding the processed envelopes away from the meter via rollers and fanning them out for easier collection. Power stackers are expensive, generally costing around $1,000–$1,600.

### Ink cartridges versus reservoirs
Putting red ink on envelopes is what postage meter systems are ultimately all about. There are two ways to store the ink that's run over the meter's "die" to create the image: you can either have a dry ink cartridge, or a reservoir of liquid ink that's slowly released.

These days, most bases have cartridges; with this method, you just replace the whole cartridge when the ink is depleted. The reservoir method obliges you to replenish supplies from a bottle; this has the potential to be a lot messier, though some ink aficionados see advantages relating to flow control.

### Advertising messages
Keep in mind that you can have a special advertising message or logo printed out alongside the postage indicia — your equipment vendor can arrange this for a modest charge.

# Advanced Weighing Features

Nothing slows down mail handling quite like having to process a wide range of mixed size and weight items. The solution is usually to weigh each item individually on an interfaced electronic scale, have the amount set automatically on the meter, and then run the item through the envelope feeder or produce a metered tape. The drawback is that this is very much a two stage operation — weigh first, then meter. Here are your options if you'd like to streamline the process. ...

### WOW from Pitney Bowes
Pitney Bowes's top-end postage meter system — Paragon — incorporates a unique built-in weighing platform that resides be-

tween the envelope feeder and the meter. In other words, the item is weighed after it has been fed into the machine using a normal automatic envelope feeder, but before the postage is printed.

PB calls this feature "Weigh On The Way" — or "WOW" for short. It's an impressive feature which works as advertised. The drawback, however, is that it slows down the machine's overall speed — without WOW, the Paragon cruises at 240 envelopes per minute, but with WOW deployed, this drops to just 90 per minute.

### Ascom Hasler's Champ

No one else has a feature quite like WOW, but Ascom Hasler has come up with an alternative approach to the mixed-weight weighing challenge, which is found in a system it calls The Champ. This involves putting a pile of mail onto a special mailing scale that is connected to both a special PC and a postage meter system. Each time an item is removed from the pile, The Champ calculates the differential weight and sets the postage amount on the meter accordingly.

The Champ is a less automated weighing system than WOW, as you still have to manually transfer the items from the scale and feed them into the postage meter system; in addition, it does not automatically recognize the size of an item, only the weight. However, The Champ costs less and allows you to place items haphazardly in a pile without checking to make sure that they're all facing the same way.

### Pitney Bowes's "One Step"

Pitney Bowes also offers an option on some of its mid-market systems that it calls "One Step." This connects a mailing scale to a postage meter system with a sort of conveyor — you place envelopes on the weighing platform one at a time, and they are weighed and transported into the meter system which is automatically set with the correct postage.

"One Step" only allows you to weigh one item at a time, and it can't automatically recognize mixed sizes. While it clearly automates the metering and weighing process, it's arguable how much it really speeds it up.

# More About Meters

Next, a more detailed look at the meter part of your postage meter system. Remember that meters — unlike bases — can, by strict order of the United States Postal Service, only be rented, not purchased outright (see the earlier part of this chapter for a discussion of this regulation, which may be rescinded in years to come).

Remember too that many meters are compatible with a variety of bases supplied by the same vendor — providing you don't mix brands, you may be able to mix and match your meters and bases to come up with your dream combination.

### Maximum meter setting

A key difference among meters is the maximum amount of postage you can set the machine to print on a single letter or label. Generally, you choose between 99¢, $9.99, or $99.99. What's best for you is obviously determined by the frequency with which you mail heavier items.

Sometimes you'll see that a meter can be set for amounts such as $9.999; this isn't a misprint on the brochure — the extra digit is there for bulk mailing purposes (when you're sending out large quantities of mail by third class, the rate may be expressed in tenths of a cent). These are known as "decimal" meters.

### Maximum capacity

This refers to the amount of postage a meter can hold at any one time. Usually the choice is a maximum of between $9,999 and $99,999. You've got to be a pretty heavy mail user to want to make advance payments to the Postal Service of over $10,000, so the smaller capacity is usually plenty.

### Electronic versus mechanical

You'll need to decide whether to get a mechanical or an electronic meter. You may find it surprising that, in the 1990s, not all meters are electronic and that the mechanical ones are still cheaper. But the mailing world is nothing if not slow-moving — and the meter market moves even slower than the rest, because the all-rental system means that old machines are constantly refurbished and recycled (chances are the meter you get won't be brand new, even if you're buying a brand new base).

With a mechanical meter, you set the amount of postage by sliding levers until the correct amount is shown on a rotating dial; additional dials keep track of how much you've spent, and how much is left in the machine. An electronic model, by contrast, has a pushbutton keypad for setting the postage amount, which is displayed on an LED or LCD window. The same display shows how much credit you've got left.

Electronic meters are probably a bit easier to use, but the difference really isn't all that great. An electronic meter typically costs about $10 a month more than a mechanical equivalent. Mechanical meters are in their twilight era and it's only a matter of time before they are phased out entirely — the Postal Service would like to see the back of them as soon as possible, because they are less tamper-proof than the electronic variety. Friden Neopost has already stopped supplying mechanical meters, though Pitney Bowes and Ascom Hasler still have them available for those who want them.

The main practical advantage of going for an electronic meter is that you can link up with an electronic scale. They are also better suited to working with telephone refills (more on this shortly) — though both Ascom Hasler and Pitney Bowes offer phone refills with some of their mechanical meters too.

### Cost-center accounting

Some meters allow you to set up multiple customer/user accounts, and then allocate all postage expenditure to one of them. In some cases, cost-center accounting is a feature of the base rather than the meter. One Ascom Hasler base with this feature also includes a built-in printer that's able to produce information reports on narrow paper rolls.

### Auto high-value cut-off

This is a safety device to prevent the operator from accidentally setting the meter too high. With this feature, the machine refuses to print out anything over a specified amount — usually 99¢ — unless the operator presses a special button. This prevents you from accidentally paying the Postal Service $57 when you only needed 57¢.

There are several variations on this theme. For example, some meters automatically reset themselves to, say, the cost of a regular first-class letter every time they have been used to print a higher value. This covers someone who walks up to the machine and meters an ordinary letter, without checking whether the previous user had set the meter for a much higher amount.

# Refilling Postage Meters

One of the least popular chores in many offices is taking the meter to the post office to get a refill. However, more and more offices are saying good-bye to standing in line at the post office and are opting for meter refills by phone.

This service was pioneered by Pitney Bowes, which calls it "Postage By Phone," but Ascom Hasler now offers its own "Telephone Meter Service" (usually called "TMS") and Friden Neopost offers "Postage-On-Call." Francotyp-Postalia is the only vendor in the US market not to offer telephone refills.

### How telephone refills work

The concept is the same between the three vendors, though the methodology differs. In all cases, you need to have sent a check to the service provider, and that check will need to have cleared, before you can get a refill.

There are ways of obtaining credit in an emergency, but penalties usually apply (for example, Pitney charges $30 for an emergency credit equivalent to your average reset amount). The bottom line, therefore, is that the system works on the basis that you pay before you pump. For this reason, it can actually be harder to obtain postage if your machine runs out unexpectedly than if you use the traditional method of taking the meter to the post office — you have to think ahead. (A meter capable of being refilled over the phone cannot also be credited at the post office — you have to opt for one method or the other.)

Despite this, the equipment suppliers market telephone refills as though they are a protection against running out of postage when you need it in a hurry. That argument only works if you keep deposits of cash permanently lodged with the meter companies — which the latter would dearly love you to do. But unless you particularly like making interest-free loans to the likes of Pitney Bowes, you'll probably only send the money in shortly before you need the postage and then you'll withdraw the full amount.

Once you have paid your money, getting the meter credited is fairly straightforward. With Pitney, you call a special number using any regular phone, and enter various numbers on the touch-tone keypad; the system at the other end gives you a numeric code which you then enter on your meter keypad and, hey presto, your meter's ready to roll. You don't talk to a person, and you don't need a modem.

With Friden, the system is similar, except that you do talk to a person at the other end. With Ascom Hasler, the TMS meter comes with a special modem and the credit is sent over the phone line directly from Hasler's TMS apparatus into your meter. There is no need to have a dedicated phone line, however. Ascom claims that its system involves fewer steps than Pitney's. Friden places emphasis on the value of human contact.

In practice, all three systems work perfectly well and the

different methods do not amount to major reasons to go with one vendor over another. Remember, though, that Postalia does not offer any over-the-phone refill service at all.

### What it costs

The service is not free. All vendors levy a resetting charge — Pitney's is $8.50, Friden Neopost's is $8, and Ascom Hasler's is $7.50. In addition, you may end up paying more for your meter rental in order to get one that can handle telephone refills, though this is less the case now than before because the equipment suppliers want to encourage everyone to sign up for the service.

There are sometimes package deals that include unlimited meter resets in a single charge. These are not necessarily huge bargains, however. For example, Pitney offers a package that offers unlimited resets, and emergency resets, for $18 a month over the normal rental charge of its most popular meter, the A900.

# Buyer's Tips

Next, some advice on how to go about getting your postage meter system:

✔ Pitney Bowes only sells direct. Friden sells direct and through dealers in different parts of the country (the split is about 50/50). Ascom Hasler sells through dealers, as does Francotyp-Postalia.

✔ Prices can be negotiable, especially if you don't mind playing one supplier against another. A salesperson may not have the authority to discount unless there is clear evidence that it is necessary to win business against a competitive bid or to displace a competitive incumbent. Nonetheless, this is not a deep discount market — you are probably doing well to get 10 percent off the list price. Even the government, which commands the lowest prices, generally pays about 20 percent below full list (in other words, the government is itself a victim of the near-monopoly it has helped to create!).

✔ Be sure to watch the small print! And a reminder of a point made earlier: don't just focus on the size of rental and lease payments during the first year, but ascertain what they will amount to thereafter.

✔ Maintenance agreements covering bases for repairs typically cost 7–12 percent of the equipment cost (that includes parts and labor). Don't automatically sign up for one without pausing to consider whether it's really worth it. The salesman will strongly encourage you to get one, because these agreements are very profitable to the vendors. For precisely this reason, you should consider paying for service only as and when you need it, since bases are in general very reliable. Meter rental prices always include service. Consider also third-party service — this is often offered by independent dealers who sell used mailing equipment.

✔ Used postage meter systems make more sense than most other types of secondhand office equipment — more on this shortly.

### Meaningless guarantees?

Pitney Bowes offers buyers something it terms its "Customer Satisfaction Guarantee." This states that for a period of five years, Pitney will replace any product that does not perform to specifications, providing you purchase a full service agreement; it goes on to say that if the replacement does not perform to specification, they'll give you a full refund.

That sounds good — but it is, in fact, pretty vague when you think it through. This is because Pitney is far from clear about what the specifications are that a machine is meant to perform to. There are no published figures on what constitutes an acceptable level of misfeeds, for example, nor for mean-time between failures. All that the guarantee really amounts to is a promise that if they sell you a total lemon (which is very unlikely), you can get some sort of justice. PB's guarantee also promises prompt responses to phone calls and letters and easily understood and accurate bills — not things for which PB is historically noted.

Not to be outdone, Friden offers its own set of guarantees. These are similar to Pitney's, but they go a step further by promising a loaner if your machine can't be fixed within eight business hours. Friden also offers its lease customers the "guaranteed right" to upgrade their equipment (without saying anything about the terms). This, again, seems a fairly unspectacular sort of guarantee (to put it mildly), since no meter supplier has ever been known to say "no" to a customer wanting to upgrade — in fact, as I pointed out earlier, their sales reps spend most of their working days trying to persuade people to do just that.

# Buying Used (Oops, Pre-Leased) Equipment

Mailing equipment doesn't change a great deal from one year to the next, and machines can generally go on performing just fine for very long periods — a sizable number of users get more than a decade of use out of their equipment.

For these reasons, good secondhand equipment can be a good buy — much more so than in most areas of office equipment, where technical obsolescence and/or five-year natural lifespans often make the used option not very attractive.

Dealers that sell Ascom Hasler and Friden equipment sometimes have something used in their inventory — it's always worth checking. Pitney Bowes also sells some used equipment, though it destroys much of what it takes back as trade-ins — Pitney, like the other manufacturers in this market, is none too keen on allowing a strong secondhand market to develop.

### Introducing Evcor

There are also a number of companies that specialize in selling used mailing equipment. Following a number of court cases, the equipment manufacturers have been forced to supply them with spare parts and supplies. Most are small local dealers, but one company has emerged as something of a force nationally....

Evcor Systems, Inc. is the largest independent supplier of used mailing equipment, with 34 offices nationwide. Most of these are independently owned and operated. Evcor specializes in handling Pitney Bowes equipment.

Evcor discourages words like "used" or "secondhand," and instead talks about "pre-leased" (a euphemism borrowed from the used car market) and "remanufactured." The use of the word "remanufactured" is always a tricky one in office equipment and is sometimes misused. However, Evcor does give the equipment it sells a pretty good going-over, cleaning it thoroughly, painting it, and replacing certain wearing parts. The equipment then goes out under the Evcor brand name and with an Evcor model number, not under PB colors.

Whether you choose to call this "refurbishing" or "remanufacturing" is, up to a point, a matter of semantics. However, I do believe that Evcor's used/pre-leased — call it what you will — equipment is sold in excellent working order.

Prices are definitely tempting — while some Evcor units correspond to Pitney models that are no longer sold brand new, Evcor claims that prices are in general 40 percent below PB list prices. Evcor also offers a plan where if you lease one of its machines, you get a replacement unit every 12 months.

If you buy an Evcor base, you still have to rent a meter from Pitney — anyone can sell meter bases, but only the manufacturers are allowed to supply the meters themselves. However, Evcor offers a service where its customers can send them their PB meter invoices which Evcor then pays on their behalf — thus eliminating the need for the user to grapple with PB's not always very user-friendly customer interface.

Evcor also offers enhancements to some PB products. For example, it offers something called the Evcor Pentagon, which is an enhanced version of the Paragon. In addition, it has developed a number of PC-based mailing, shipping, and receiving products.

Evcor seems to be doing well. The company has been named to *Inc.* magazine's list of the 500 fastest-growing private companies and claims to have over 15,000 customers — that would give it a larger customer base than Francotyp-Postalia. I have had some good feedback from a few people who use Evcor, and I definitely think that the company is worth checking out. If you are interested, you can call them at 800 873 8267.

# Vendor Profiles

Next, a closer look at the four companies that supply new postage meter systems.

## *Ascom Hasler*

*Ascom Hasler Mailing Systems, Inc.*
*19 Forest Parkway*
*Shelton, CT 06484–6140*
*Tel: 800 243 6275*

Ascom Hasler is a Swiss company that has been making postage meter systems for almost as long as Pitney Bowes, though it has only been in the US for around 10 years. Postage equipment is only one part of the company's business. The Ascom group is a $2.4-billion conglomerate involved in a diverse range of businesses, including telecommunications, fiber optics, and money-changing equipment. For a long time, Ascom Hasler reps used to boast that the company made most of the famed Swiss railways' signaling equipment, though I haven't heard that said lately.

Ascom Hasler is pretty big in the European postage meter market (where postage meters are called "frankers"), and over the past few years it has begun making significant strides in the

US. At the end of the third quarter of 1993, Ascom had 87,208 meters installed in this country, compared with a little over 72,000 at the end of 1991. This gives it about a 6.3 percent share of the installed market, up from 5.4 percent at the end of 1991.

Ascom Hasler is now comfortably in second place and has become the main thorn in Pitney Bowes's side — as I report elsewhere in this chapter, Ascom has rocked the mailing industry boat by challenging PB over the issue of patents and bringing an anti-trust lawsuit. Ascom Hasler's senior management in the US is largely ex-Pitney Bowes and appears to relish the battle with the zealousness often associated with converts.

Ascom Hasler used to sell through an independent US distributor called International Mailing Systems (IMS), which also traded as Better Packages. But the Swiss manufacturer purchased IMS in 1989, and the US operation is now a wholly-owned subsidiary.

Ascom Hasler sells mainly through dealers. Recently, the company made itself unpopular in some circles by attempting to put pressure on smaller dealers that were not performing and at the same time trying to gain stronger representation from larger, multi-product office equipment dealerships. The company now has 207 dealers, of which the largest have been marked as "Star" dealers; at press-time, there were a total of 18 Star dealers and this number was expected to rise to 22 soon afterwards. The company sees the Star dealerships as a spearhead for breaking into the major account market more effectively as well as increasing its overall share in large urban markets. A small number of the existing non-Star dealers have been dropped as part of the refocusing.

All of Ascom Hasler's machines are made in Switzerland. The product range has a fine reputation for quality. The *What to Buy for Business* user poll, referred to earlier in this chapter, suggests that Ascom Hasler users are, in general, more satisfied both with the equipment, and with their total experience as a customer, than users of the other two main brands.

## *Francotyp-Postalia*

*Postalia, Inc.*
*1980 University Lane*
*Lisle, IL 60532–2152*
*Tel: 800 341 6052*

Postalia, Inc. is the "fourth" player in the US postage meter market, with a market share that is a long way behind the others. The company now does business as Francotyp-Postalia, which is the name of its German parent.

Although Francotyp-Postalia manufactures its own postage meter systems in Germany — where it is the market leader — the products that are marketed in the US are relabeled ones manufactured in Britain by Roneo Neopost, a sibling company of Friden Neopost.

The Francotyp-Postalia products therefore correspond somewhat to certain models sold by Friden in the US. The match is not exact, however. Previously, Francotyp-Postalia — as it was then known — also sold some pretty uninspiring German-made systems in the US, but these are no longer available new.

Francotyp-Postalia's US operation is all-dealer. It is the only one of the four vendors not to have a meter refills by phone service. At the end of the second quarter of 1993, Postalia had 18,150 meters installed in the US, representing an approximately 1.3 percent share — that's about the same as the figure a couple of years earlier.

Why should anyone consider a Postalia system? The one advantage that Postalia offers is that its meter rental prices are quite low. There's nothing particularly special about the equipment, which is of the plain-vanilla variety.

## *Friden Neopost*

*Friden Neopost*
*30955 Huntwood Avenue*
*Hayward, CA 94544*
*Tel: 510 489 6800*

Friden is a long-established American postage machine company: originally the creation of a Swedish immigrant who started making mechanical calculating machines in San Francisco in 1933, the company later moved into mailing machines and became the only American manufacturer of postage equipment aside from Pitney Bowes.

In recent years, Friden has had a somewhat unsettled ownership history. About 12 years ago, it was acquired by Alcatel, the giant French telecommunications, electronics, and defense conglomerate which already owned a small French manufacturer of postage equipment. At around the same time, Alcatel acquired Roneo Neopost, a British postage meter systems manufacturer that had been in the business since the 1930s.

Friden then became known as Friden Alcatel, and it formed a close operating relationship with its French parent and with Roneo Alcatel, as the British company came to be known. The product range offered in all countries was a mixture of French, British, and US-made equipment.

In 1990, Alcatel shut down Friden's US manufacturing. As a result, all the bases are now imported from Europe, with the exception of one not very prominent model which is made in America by an outside supplier working under contract. Meters are refurbished in Mexico.

In 1991, Alcatel decided to get out of the postage meter market, and it divested itself of the entire business. Early in 1992, the French, British, and American mailing operations were spun off in a single company which was acquired by primarily French institutional investors. This company adopted the name Neopost. With annual sales of $400 million worldwide, Neopost claims to be the number-one producer of mailroom equipment in Europe and the second largest in the world.

In America, Friden Alcatel was renamed Friden Neopost, and the strategy is now to play up the "Neopost" name. In fact, the word "Friden" will not appear on new equipment, which will be decorated only with a "Neopost" logo. Sources in the company don't discount the possibility that the Friden name will eventually be dropped altogether.

After spending a lot of effort and money during the 1980s trying to educate American mailers to recognize one European name (Alcatel) that was then discarded, it seems odd that the company is now trying to do the same to promote another (Neopost), which — although strong in Europe — has little recognition on Main Street America. I was surprised that the company didn't just decide to focus on the Friden brand. However, the view is that the benefits of being identified as part of a global brand outweigh the drawbacks of having to ingrain the Neopost identity in the American consciousness.

Although there is some evidence that older Friden models proved disappointing in terms of reliability, the *What to Buy for Business* user poll suggests that machines sold during the past three years are proving as reliable as equipment sold by Pitney Bowes. Friden's main claim to fame in terms of mailing technology history is that in 1979 — two years ahead of PB — it introduced the first electronic meter (it was only somewhat electronic, as far as I can recall — though that was a long time ago!). Today, about 85 percent of Friden Neopost's installed meters are electronic, well ahead of the figure for all of its competitors.

Friden seems to us to have a somewhat different culture from Pitney Bowes (determined to do what it takes to hold onto its near-monopoly) and Ascom Hasler (managed largely by ex-Pitney people who pursue their former employers with relish).

The Friden culture is a bit more relaxed: unlike Ascom, Friden does not appear to be over-keen on rocking the mailroom boat and it went along with paying Pitney royalties on patents rather than getting drawn into an anti-trust dispute. Friden's attitude seems to be that the company has paid its dues to be a member of a closed circle of postage meter suppliers, and that it has little interest in making it easier for others to break in. Instead, it would rather operate as part of the mailing establishment, chiseling away at Pitney's market share rather than trying to turn the industry upside down.

At the end of the third quarter of 1993, Friden Neopost had 75,702 installed meters in the US, up from 71,076 at the end of 1991. This translates to about 5.4 percent of the installed population — compared with Ascom Hasler's 6.3 percent. For most of the 1980s, by contrast, Friden was in second place.

The momentum in the battle for second place seems to be favoring Ascom. Whereas Ascom's installed base grew by over 14,000 meters between the end of 1991 and the end of the third quarter of 1993, Friden's grew by under 5,000 (Pitney's grew by over 42,000, though its share of the market decreased). However, Friden maintains that it is still well ahead of Ascom in terms of its US revenues from the postage meter business (figures are not available, as both companies are privately held).

Friden is the only vendor in this market to have a dual-track distribution strategy, selling both through its own branch network and dealers. The split is apparently about 50/50. Friden has 22 direct sales branches in major markets, and about 120 dealers elsewhere. Unlike most Pitney Bowes reps, salespeople employed directly by Friden are paid a basic salary as well as commission; in addition, they get a commission if a customer renews a lease on existing equipment, as well as ordering new stuff. According to Friden, this reduces pressure on customers to upgrade when there is no real benefit in doing so.

Although the company has not had as bad an image problem as Pitney Bowes, it has by no means escaped the negative feelings that postage meter users in general often have towards their suppliers. The company is doing a number of things to improve its "customer interface" — for example, making it easier for customers to resolve problems in a single phone call.

Friden is a decent company and it has some fine equipment and good dealers. It lacks the market clout of Pitney, or the aggressiveness of Ascom. In recent years, it has tended to try to sell by stressing points of technical detail. Today, however, the company's senior management is banking on overall customer satisfaction with the company being of more importance in determining loyalties than the design of levers and switches. It remains to be seen whether this change in focus will help it to regain some of the momentum it seemed to lose during the later stages of the Alcatel era.

## Pitney Bowes

*Pitney Bowes Inc.*
*World Headquarters*
*Stamford, CT 06926–0700*
*Tel: 800 672 6937*

Pitney Bowes, a $3.4-billion company, pioneered postage meters in the 1920s and has been the clear world market leader ever since. At the end of the third quarter of 1993, PB had 1,209,783 postage meters installed in the US — down from 1,328,265 at the end of 1991. This represented an installed market share of fractionally under 87 percent, compared with almost 88 percent at the end of 1991.

As you can tell from these figures, Pitney's grip is weakening — but only very slowly. With most of its customers locked into long-term rental and lease contracts, Pitney's continued dominance seems assured.

Part of PB's strength in this market stems from the fact that it also sells a wide range of mailing equipment besides postage meters — folders/inserters and addressing systems, for example. And since the launch of its Paragon system, its postage meter range has extended further up the market than those of its competitors. What this means is that large users who are looking for one-stop shopping are more likely to find all their needs met by PB than by anyone else. Although mailing equipment is its core business, Pitney Bowes is also a relabeler of copiers and fax machines. In addition, it owns Dictaphone.

Pitney manufactures most of its postage meter systems in the US. Some of its meters are made in Britain, however. And quite a lot of its ancillary equipment — postage scales, for example — is imported (in some cases, it is made for Pitney by other companies). Pitney is an all direct-sales company. It is the only one of the four vendors in this market not to have any dealers at all.

As I indicate elsewhere in this chapter, Pitney Bowes attracts negative comments from some users about the attitude of its sales force, the efficiency and clarity of its billing system, and the quality of its support. Put simply, there are quite a few of its customers who do not particularly like the company they deal with. Negative feelings towards Pitney Bowes are largely directed against the company, rather than against the equipment which is widely perceived as being durable and generally reliable.

During the past 18 months, PB's senior management has begun a concerted effort to make the culture of the company more customer-driven. How successful this will be remains to be seen: there is an inherent conflict between the best interests of postage meter users — who would benefit from more competition leading to lower prices — and those of Pitney Bowes stockholders who would suffer. Nonetheless, PB is correct in realizing that treating its customers better — and not getting up their backs — could help stem the gradual erosion of its market share.

The problem that PB faces in the US postage meter market is that it has, arguably, got nowhere to go but down: it has an overwhelming share of a market which is pretty mature. PB hopes that there is room for growth from the huge number of American businesses that do not currently own postage equipment. However, it is by no means clear that current technology will draw those users — who for years have resisted it — nor that PB will dominate any new market for the type of PC-based postage software that I discussed earlier.

PB's near-monopoly position in this industry attracts criticism from a number of quarters and there are those — I count myself among them — who would like to see the market opened up. However, it would be unfair to "blame" the management of PB for the monopoly or expect them to take steps to end it. The proper job of PB's management is to grow their company and increase shareholder value, not to make life easier for competitors.

Blame should instead be directed against the Postal Service, which has historically controlled the market for its own purposes without properly regulating it in the public interest. It should also be directed at others in Washington, DC who have allowed anti-competitive practices to continue in this ultimately "boring" market — practices that would never have been tolerated in a more politically-sensitive industry! ✍

# Chapter 14

# Shredders

# Shredders

Shredders were invented by the Germans in the 1930s and brought to the US in the fifties. The machines remain fundamentally unchanged to this day. Though electronics now have a walk-on role, the shredding industry has been largely undisturbed by the office equipment revolution of the past 15 years.

To the outsider, this is a dull market. It lacks the glamour of computers, the trendiness of fax, and the rivalries between global titans that characterize the copier market. But the shredder market is more complex than you might imagine — not because the machines are all that difficult to get to grips with, but because of the sheer number of machines and the complex relationships between the different brand names.

## The Shredder Market in a Nutshell

Shredder companies tend to be ones that few people have heard of. Those who work for them have a habit of importing glamour by association, with references and innuendo concerning the more notorious uses of their products. Model names borrow from recent political history. Insiders confide in a "I-really-shouldn't-be-telling-you-this" tone about who uses their machines in Washington, DC.

Every now and then, shredders become fashionable as a result of some scandal. No other industry seems so prone to short and furious bursts of publicity, only to slide back into the obscurity from which it emerged. Underneath it all, the shredder industry has been steadily plugging away for years. Occasionally, vendors come and go, but not much really changes.

German companies remain by far the dominant force, though some have opened US factories or bought into American distributors. Of the almost 200 machines available in the US, approximately two thirds are made by German companies.

The number of companies that manufacture shredders is much less than the number that sell them under their own names. There is a whole lot of relabeling going on in this industry, with multiple brands relying on a few factories to churn out the goods. One manufacturer — Schleicher — is so prolific that it is responsible for over a quarter of all the models available.

Machines from the same manufacturer that are sold under more than one brand name are often very similar, but they tend not to be identical. A company such as Schleicher manages to vary the features on almost all of its machines ever so slightly, thereby ensuring that all of its relabelers have exclusives — but also confusing the poor buyer trying to make comparisons.

Be warned that specifications quoted by shredder manufacturers are not always reliable. I have often come across cases where I know that two machines selling under different brand names are the same, but where the numbers quoted by different vendors are quite different. Inconsistent data is not necessarily the result of vendors being disingenuous or sloppy, since some of the criteria by which shredders are rated are far from precise in their very nature (as I'll explain later when I discuss things like speed).

The shredder buyer seems to have a lot more choice than he or she really needs. But not all of the plethora of machines are readily available in every town or city. Quite often you will find that your final decision will be a matter of negotiating the best deal you can find between the brands whose turf you happen to be sitting on.

# Pros and Cons of Shredding

Shredder salesmen spend a good part of their time not just trying to convince buyers of the merits of the brand they represent, but trying to sell people on the idea of shredding in general. Some people need no convincing, as they have confidential material that simply has to be shredded, period. But here, very briefly, are the two most commonly heard sales pitches used to convert people who don't have such an obvious need.

### Security

By far the more convincing argument concerns security. This means hiding things from prying eyes, as well as protecting your business against inadvertent leakages of information that could conceivably result in a lawsuit for violating the Privacy Act. That legislation, which was put into effect in the early 1970s, puts the responsibility for the misuse of any information contained in records squarely on the shoulders of whoever was responsible for producing them. So, if someone gets a hold of some damaging piece of information at the dump, and then uses it to blackmail somebody, the victim's basic right to privacy has been violated, and he or she has a legal right to sue the party that has carelessy discarded it. Of course this is an extreme example, but you get the idea.

The upshot is that banks, hospitals, large corporations, and government agencies were quick to act to protect themselves. Today, in an ever more security-conscious world, this example seems to be trickling down to smaller businesses. Everything from personnel records to accounting documents are prime candidates for shredding.

Clearly, businesses have to pay heed to this sort of thing. But don't be paranoid — shredder reps have a habit of painting the world out there as a more dangerous place than it really is!

### The environment: beware of phony arguments

The shredder industry has also taken to using "green" arguments to try to persuade people to buy its machines, but most are pretty phony. There is nothing about shredded paper that makes it more suitable for recycling than unshredded paper. The process of shredding paper merely creates the illusion that you are somehow "reprocessing" the material. In fact, what you are doing can be positively unhelpful from an environmental point of view: this is because recycling organizations really prefer unshredded paper, as they need the larger fibers.

If the paper is not being recycled, then you'll find conventional strip-cut shredding just increases the bulk going to the landfill. The only truly green option is to use the bulking factor to your advantage by converting paper and newspaper destined for the trash into packing material to replace environmentally unfriendly styrofoam "peanuts." But, this isn't a practical option for most businesses, added to which I suspect that unbiodegradable styrofoam peanuts are probably on their way out anyway.

So that's that — the bottom line is that shredder reps who go on about the environment are generally talking rubbish.

# Shredder Sizes

Once you've decided to buy a shredder, the next item on the agenda is what type of shredder to consider.

### *Personal shredders*

This is a fast growing (by shredder standards) section of the market. Personal shredders are defined in this book as machines that list for less than $500; but they can generally be bought for under $200. These machines are mostly about the size of a deskside waste basket; some actually sit right on top of your wastepaper baskets, or can be clamped to the side of a desk. They are entry-level, lightweight, and fairly slow. Some can optimistically shred up to 10 pages at a time, most manage less.

Personal shredders are popular items for small offices. But they are also catching on in medium and larger organizations: the idea is that each individual in an organization who handles sensitive material should have their own. The benefits of this approach are that if the machine is close by, it's more likely to get used and the sensitive material is less likely to get seen by other people. When people are obliged to take a walk to get to the shredder, you have a higher likelihood that documents won't get shredded at all — or that they will be seen by prying eyes while they pile up waiting to be shredded later.

The good news is that there are some very low-priced and competent personal shredders that have been introduced lately — particularly by Fellowes. In today's market, you can think about buying 10 of these for the cost of some department shredders. The other plus point is that they are very easily found at office supply superstores and retailers.

As I'll be explaining shortly, there are two broad types of shredding — strip-cut and cross-cut (the latter makes a better job of ensuring that spies won't be able to reassemble the shredded pieces). Almost all personal shredders are strip-cuts, but most have surprisingly narrow shred widths — so these machines shouldn't be regarded as Mickey Mouse shredders. They are also very reliable.

But if service is required, it's handled much like any other small appliance — you ship it back, or you may be able to take it into some sort of local service center if there's one in your area. If you are unfortunate enough to have a problem soon after you get it, the retailer you purchased it from should be able to arrange a replacement rather than a repair.

### Department shredders

There are a host of reasons why lightweight personal shredders might not do the trick for you. You might find that you generally have to shred thicker documents, you may create too much volume for personal shredders, you might have too many people who generate sensitive material, or you may need a smaller shred. Then it's time to think about a department shredder.

This is a fairly broad category that encompasses a large percentage of the shredders on the market. These machines generally have an appearance consistent with an office environment (i.e., no unsightly specimens); they are operated by different people in a so-called "walk-up" environment, much like a fax or a copier; they are generally placed for easy access close to where people work; and they are usually about three feet high.

Department shredders are normally purchased from office supply retailers or traditional office equipment dealers. Some can be found in catalogs like Quill and Reliable. Others are sold direct by manufacturers or relabelers. Department shredders run the full gamut when it comes to price, but if you buy a $2,000 list price machine you'll probably be reasonably close to the national average.

In general, on-site service is available for department shredders — at least it should be. Most of these machines exceed UPS shipping dimensions, and you won't want to have to deal with freighting one back if it develops a problem. Keep in mind that a well purchased shredder should last for much longer than most types of office equipment — your shredder should outlive generations of copiers and computers.

### Centralized shredders

The line between department shredders and centralized shredders can be a bit blurred. In general, though, centralized shredders tend to be more heavy duty, a bit less pretty, and, most likely, louder. Some are over five feet tall. In short, they will be less friendly office companions. While they are geared to higher workloads, their actual shredding capabilities are not necessarily any different from those of lower volume machines.

Centralized shredders are often kept in a mail room or as an adjunct to a centralized copying department. Some very large users might even have a shredding plant down in their basement, with dedicated employees operating the equipment; this takes you into the light industrial shredding category, which is outside the scope of this chapter.

What all centralized shredders have in common is that the process is one step removed from the source; often there will be one employee, or a small group of employees, who are most likely to be operating the machine. People drop off their material, or it's picked up from workstations. This concept is obviously not ideal for maximum security, but really comes into its own for large quantities of fairly unsensitive material.

These machines are most commonly purchased through traditional office equipment dealers or direct from the manufacturer. Some require special electrical installation. The price range for centralized shredders again varies a great deal, depending on your requirements, but expect to pay anything from around $3,000 on the low side to over $8,000 on the high side.

# Shredder Speeds

Now that you've had a chance to think about what type of shredder you will need, the next step is to consider how fast a machine to get. Speed is actually measured in two different ways: how fast paper goes through the machine, and how much paper can go in at once.

### Feet per minute speed

Throughput is generally measured in feet per minute (fpm). With some slower machines, you might come across references to sheets per second speeds.

The most important thing to keep in mind when looking at quoted figures is that there's no scientific method for calculating throughput speeds. A variety of factors, including paper weight and even fluctuating voltages, can produce different results. In fact, even vendors that relabel identical machines can't agree on the speeds. The quoted figures therefore put you in a ballpark — don't attach undue significance to differences of five or ten feet per minute.

Feet per minute speeds for office shredders range from a low of about 6fpm to a high of about 140fpm. The average mid-market, strip-cut shredder would run around 35–40fpm — but, as I'll show, the cross-cut shredding method slows things down considerably. Clearly, you'd get a workout trying to manually feed over 100 sheets of paper into a shredder each minute to take advantage of its speed potential. However, very high fpm ratings can be useful when you have machines with automatic feeding for piles of continuous computer paper.

### Paper capacity

If, however, you have large stacks of paper which are not printed on continuous stationery (e.g., multi-page 8.5" x 11" documents), then you become particularly interested in the second way of measuring speed — capacity, which refers to how many sheets can go through at once.

Capacities for shredders are measured in "sheets per pass." Think of this as referring to the thickest document you can toss into the machine whole. Again, measurement is not a precise business — the figures quoted for the same, or near identical, machines can vary.

If possible, choose a shredder with a somewhat higher capacity than your average document so you don't find yourself frequently overloading the machine. But you'll find that high capacities, even more than fpm speeds, rapidly add to the price — it takes a more rugged machine to handle thickness than it takes to create speed. Capacities for office shredders range from one to about 70 sheets per pass. The typical $2,000-ish shredder would generally take less than 20 sheets per pass.

### Assessing your needs
Undoubtedly the most important factor in choosing a shredder is accurately assessing the quantity and nature of the material you need to shred. You don't want to pay a premium for speed and capacity you won't use, but neither do you want to buy a shredder that won't stand up to the job. Speed and capacity are at the heart of shredding productivity — everything else, except possibly shred type and size, is secondary.

# Types of Shreds

There are two basic categories of shred: strip-cut and cross-cut. Cross-cuts are then further divided into two sub-categories: particle-cut and high security. Here's what you need to know.

### Strip-cuts
Like the name implies, strip-cut shredders tear paper lengthwise into ribbons that resemble uncooked fettucine. These machines are the infantry of the shredding market — they are what most people choose for mainstream work. The shreds vary in width from about 1/12" to 5/16". Generally, the machines require little or no maintenance.

Like many other specs in the shredder industry, quoted shred widths can be slightly suspect. This is partly because many of the vendors are converting European manufacturers' millimeters to fractions of inches. It is also because shredded paper is not really cut, but torn, so there are inconsistencies in the shreds themselves. And with some of the very small high-security shreds, you are hard pressed to pick out a particle, let alone accurately measure it. Some of the fractions used in quoted shred widths require a bit of effort to visualize — 3/128", for example. Likewise, you may have to pause for a moment or two to figure out whether 1/12" is larger or smaller than 3/32". The upshot is that when it comes to comparing quoted shred sizes, you're going to wish you hadn't fallen asleep that long ago day when they were teaching fractions; or you might wish that conversion to metric had happened after all.

Luckily, if you're on a budget, you'll find that, as a group, the newer lower end shredders actually have narrower shreds. One reason is that narrow shreds slow down speed, which is crucial to high-end machines. Another is that the lower end of the market tends to have the newer machines, and although there have been fairly few changes in shredders over the years, shred sizes are ever so slowly getting narrower.

On the whole, it's nice to have anything less than a 1/4" shred width. Shreds wider than 1/4" are, in my opinion, best used for packing material, or high volumes of fairly unsensitive data. Also, since recyclers actually prefer unshredded paper, because they need the bigger fibers, you might consider wider shreds for them. I really can't see the point of anything over 1/2".

### Cross-cuts (1): particle-cuts

If you have very sensitive material, you may be uncomfortable about even the narrowest width strip-cut. In that case, you should consider a cross-cut machine, which cuts the paper both lengthwise and crosswise. The less expensive cross-cut shredders are the particle-cut variety, which are generally defined as machines that fall short of the high-security Department of Defense (DOD) specifications of 1/32" x 1/2". For the most part, the widths are similar to the strip shreds, and the lengths vary from just barely missing DOD standards of 1/2", to over 2". As well as providing better security, particle-cuts significantly reduce the volume of your shreds, which means emptying the bin less often.

So, should you go for a long, narrow shred, or a shorter but wider particle, or one that's both narrow and short — and what about the longer, wider ones? It's easy to wonder if we really need all this choice for such a seemingly simple task. The bottom line, obviously, is that "smaller" is "better," but unless you face an extremely determined snoop, all these shreds do an adequate job of providing security for most mainstream business applications. So, providing the shred size seems pretty small, and assuming you aren't up against professional espionage, going for overall speed and capacity are probably more important than going round in circles fretting about the more arcane aspects of shred size.

Keep in mind that cross-cutting can reduce speed and capacity by as much as half next to comparable strip-cut machines. So if you have larger quantities of sensitive material to shred, you might choose a larger particle, so you can have better performance (or drop the idea of cross-cuts altogether). If you buy that kind of machine, you'll probably end up with a particle a bit smaller than 1/4" wide and 1" long. Cross-cut shredders are generally more finicky than their strip-cut siblings, incidentally, and require more maintenance.

### Cross-cuts (2): high-security shreds

If you are still having doubts about the security of your shreds, or you are obliged to conform to DOD standards, then you may be in the market for a high-security shredder. These are generally defined as machines that produce shreds that conform to DOD specifications for "Top Secret," which is 1/32" x 1/2", plus or minus 1/64" on either axis.

About 25 out of the approximately 200 machines on the market conform to DOD specs, and these are the ones that tend to give this dullish industry its only hint of pizzazz. You can bet all the people most famous for shredding were using one of them. Shred sizes in this sector vary from those that just barely meet the minimums, which puts them very close to some of the machines classified as particle-cut, to ones that manage an amazing 1/42" x 3/8".

### Specialty high-security shredders

There are also specialty high-security shredders that handle things like typewriter ribbon cassettes, microfiche, camera film, ID cards, and other objects of this sort. All machines in this category are cross-cuts of some sort; not all are also suitable for shredding your paper.

At the risk of stating the obvious, it's important to remember not to put these types of items in machines that are not specially made for this purpose. You could end up with melted plastic all over your cutting assembly, or worse. Just about any shredder takes staples, incidentally, though paperclips can cause problems on some models.

# Throat Widths

Throat width refers to the size of the opening that you put your paper in. These range from a low of just over 3", to a high of 18", with just about every increment you can think of in between. For maximum efficiency and speed, it's best to choose a width that will comfortably accommodate the paper you use most without crumpling.

Anything less than 8 1/2" is simply not ideal for much besides credit card receipts, invoices, and similar non-standard items. Once you get above 8 1/2", there's little additional benefit to be gained until you reach 9 1/2": this is the size that will begin to fit unburst letter-sized continuous computer paper (the pins for computer paper add 1/2" on each side to all sizes).

The next big jump for usefulness is 12", because this is the size of a standard file folder. Of course, you can always toss files in the short way, but even then they are almost 10" wide. A 12" throat also allows you to feed letter-size paper the long way, which could help it to go through the machine faster — but don't do that on a strip-cut machine, because it could result in entire lines of type emerging from the shredder intact.

A 12" throat will be wide enough for mid-size computer paper. Beyond 12", the most common throat sizes accommodate large-sized computer paper, which measures 15 7/8" wide with its pin holes intact. You could put it in the short way, which measures 11", but you wouldn't be able to feed it in automatically (and you might find yourself unhappy with the number of consecutive characters that stay intact). One thing to keep in mind about the very wide throats is that they add a hefty premium to the price of a machine.

# Cabinets

One of the biggest changes in shredders over the last 10 years has been the increased use of enclosed cabinets, which keep the unsightly bag for the shredded paper hidden behind closed doors. This has encouraged the spread of shredders into the mainstream office environment.

Old-style external bag shredders still have a role for people who don't want to be restricted by the size of the bin in the cabinet: they can be useful if you're shredding very high volumes, perhaps to create packing material. But, for the most part, people prefer cabinets these days because they help contain the dust and the noise and they look tidier.

Cabinets come in all shapes and sizes. Sometimes they are an optional item costing about the same amount — $200–$300 — as the stands for non-cabinet versions. Most are fully enclosed, with a door to get inside. Some don't have a door, but leave a side exposed.

### Bin/bag access

One thing to think about when choosing a cabinet model is how you access the bin or the bag which catches the shred. Many of the smallest personal shredders have what I classify as a "lift to empty" type of access: this means the motor and the shredding mechanism form a unit that has to be lifted to allow you to get at the built-in waste basket when you need to empty it. This isn't too big a deal — most aren't very heavy — but it is slightly cumbersome.

Rear access is also far from ideal, and is often a clue that a machine is old: it means the machine has to be pulled away from the wall to empty the shreds — or, even worse, it makes people position the shredder in the middle of a room.

The best solution is front access. This is definitely the most convenient design, and it also means you can put the shredder up against a wall to save space.

### Feeding continuous paper

If you are shredding continuous computer paper, one thing to watch for is the position of the racks that hold the stacks waiting to be fed in. If they attach to the rear of the machine, you've effectively made your shredder larger. If they hang on the front, they can interfere with your front access.

Most brands address this by putting the racks on top of the shredder, or by making ones for the front that fold or can be removed. There are many different configurations out there, all of which have their pros and cons.

# Electronic Features

Depending on your viewpoint, you'll either find shredders refreshingly void of electronic features — or depressingly old fashioned. Either way, there's virtually no learning curve, and you shouldn't have that nagging feeling that you've wasted money on a pile of features that nobody's going to bother to use. Here are the ones you can get and expect to use:

### Auto start/stop

This is a handy feature: the machine can be left on standby mode, so that it automatically comes to life when you insert some paper — you don't have to switch it on and off every time. This usually works by means of an electronic "eye" like the ones you get on alarm systems: when the beam is broken by the inserted paper, the machine starts shredding; and soon after the paper is gone, it shuts down again.

### Auto reverse

Unfortunately, jams are a fact of life in the shredding world. There are a number of design solutions to prevent them from happening, but the most common way of dealing with the problem is to put the machine in reverse when they do occur.

All shredders have a manual reverse function, but some also have auto reverse. This can be particularly handy if the machine jams after you have tossed something in and walked away leaving it to shred unsupervised. But auto reverse is a fairly upmarket feature that you can't count on getting.

### Bin-full indications

In the bad old days when most shredders sported external catch sacks, there wasn't any need for bin-full indicators. The shreds exited to the rear into a bag and, if this overflowed, so be it — the only person who might be bothered was whoever had to push the broom.

But in this day of sleek cabinet models, with shreds that exit straight down into an enclosed bin, an overflowing bag can cause shreds to back up into the cutter and jam the machine. Hence the need for bin-full indication.

The best is the type that also shuts the machine off, so unattended shredders stay out of harm's way. (Often this sort of shut-off also kicks in if the shredder is overloaded.) If you can't have that, then an audible beep of some sort is nice. Least satisfactory are visual-only indicators, because they are easiest to miss. Most systems offer a partial combination of the three methods, some do it all.

### Other electronic features

Some different companies have very brand-specific electronic features that you might come across — like audible beeps that alert you if the cabinet door is open, or LED lights that tell you what capacity the machine is running at. These types of features can be nice to have, but they are unlikely to be a major factor swinging your decision. As I indicated earlier, when it comes to specifications, speed and shred type/size are really all that seriously matter.

# Where to Buy

The are three main options when it comes to where to buy your shredder: office supply outlets of all kinds (including superstores, retailers, and catalogs), traditional office equipment dealers, and direct from the manufacturer or relabeler.

### Office supply superstores/retailers/catalogs

These can be excellent places to buy small personal shredders. They can also be good sources for discounts on smaller and medium department shredders.

Since the shredder market has a huge number of relabeled machines, and a relatively small number of manufacturers, you'll actually find similar shredders in these channels as you would at traditional office equipment dealers — but they'll usually be sold under different brand names. Machines sold through these channels are generally heavily discounted.

On-site service is usually available through third party providers, or sometimes through the manufacturers' own service centers. Some low-end machines have to be sent away for repair, however. Big names to watch for in these channels are Fellowes and GBC.

### Traditional office equipment dealers

These dealers tend to sell more of the mid- and high-end shredders, but they offer complete ranges so you can get smaller models from them as well. Discounts vary widely among the dealers, partly reflecting the prices they pay which are related to how much volume they handle. Often, though, traditional office equipment dealers charge higher prices than the office supply retailers referred to above in the sector of the market where they overlap. In general, a discount of 25 percent is reasonable. Keep in mind that you'll generally find more room for negotiation in the traditional dealer market than in the office supply channels.

Most dealers of this type are able to provide on-site service. Warranty terms are not always very generous — partly because the dealers like to make money out of the service. Prominent brands sold through this channel include Destroyit, EBA, Intimus, and Shredex — though some vendors span more than one of the channels.

### Direct from the manufacturer

There are a few manufacturers and relabelers that sell direct. Discounts tend to be lower, but then so are the list prices — so it all usually evens out in the end. Service is available on-site (in some areas, the manufacturers arrange this to be carried out by third parties). Vendors that sell direct include Allegheny, Ameri-Shred, Cummins, and Oztec.

# Shredder Vendor Profiles

Here are brief notes introducing the shredder vendors that are vying for your business. Also shown are their addresses and phone numbers: contact them for details of dealers and/or direct sales offices in your area. Entries are listed alphabetically according to brand name.

## Achiever

*World Office Products, Inc.*
*6073 NW 167th Street, Building C5*
*Miami, FL 33105*
*Tel: 305 825 4500*

World Office Products is a Miami importer that distributes one Chinese-made personal shredder that is sold under the Achiever brand name through some office supply warehouse stores. Warranty arrangements involve shipping the machine back for repair. The company does not seem to like talking to office equipment scribes such as myself, so I am unable to tell you more about it.

## Allegheny

*Allegheny Paper Shredders Corporation*
*Old William Penn Highway East*
*Delmont, PA 15626*
*Tel: 800 245 2497*

Allegheny is a more than twenty-year-old manufacturer of large industrial shredders and balers. It also offers three high-end, strip-cut office shredders. Sales and service are direct.

# Ameri-Shred

*Ameri-Shred Corporation*
*PO Box 46130*
*Monroeville, PA 15146*
*Tel: 800 634 8981*

Ameri-Shred is a manufacturer and relabeler whose sole business is shredding. At the time of this writing, its range consisted of 13 models, four of which it makes itself — the other nine are made in Germany by Ideal (whose machines are also sold as Destroyits and Heyers). Ameri-Shred offers better warranties on these machines than you get elsewhere. Sales and service are direct and through dealers.

# Boston

*Hunt Manufacturing Company*
*230 South Broad Street*
*Philadelphia, PA 19102–4167*
*Tel: 215 732 7700*

Boston is the almost 100-year-old office products brand usually associated with things like pencil sharpeners and staplers. Hunt Manufacturing, which owns the Boston brand, has one personal shredder that it has been selling for years. This is widely available through office supply channels. You have to ship the machine back for repair should it ever need fixing.

# Cummins

*Cummins Allison Corporation*
*892 Feehanville Drive*
*Mount Prospect, IL 60056*
*Tel: 800 621 5528*

Cummins is an old American company with deep roots in the document security and paper handling industry — it started making perforators in 1887. It started in shredders in around 1955, about 10 years after the Cummins family sold the business.

Cummins manufactures most of its office shredders, as well as a range of very industrial baler-type machines; it also relabels two German models it imports from EBA (these differ from the EBA shredders sold by SEM). Sales and service are direct.

# Dahle

*Dahle USA Inc.*
*7 Old Dock Road*
*Yaphank, NY 11980*
*Tel: 516 924 2600*

Dahle A.G. is a German shredder manufacturer that is also the world's largest producer of pencil sharpeners. Actually, the German Dahle company puts out all sorts of blade-oriented products containing blades for the office, home, and art markets — including shears and scissors.

Dahle USA is a separate company, with different ownership, that has been in the shredder market for about nine years. Most of the Dahle shredders found in this country are assembled in America by Dahle USA, using cutter heads imported from the German Dahle. However, one low-end model is imported from Germany complete.

Dahle USA's shredder line concentrates on the lower to middle sections of the market, though it also contains what the company terms "industrial workhorses." Sales are through office supply retailers and, to a small extent, traditional office equipment dealers. Service is through dealers or third parties.

# Datatech

*Datatech Shredders*
*10 Clipper Road*
*W. Conshohocken, PA 19428–2721*
*Tel: 800 523 0320*

Datatech started in the shredder business in 1971 and went on to become the largest distributor of Schleicher machines in the US in the days before Schleicher had a directly-owned North American distribution operation (Schleicher, a German company, is the world's most prolific manufacturer of shredders).

Today, Datatech still sells relabeled Schleicher equipment, but the company has been overshadowed to some extent by Intimus, the Schleicher-owned US distributor that was established several years ago. Datatech has also recently begun to distribute three conveyor shredders and balers made by HSM Pressen, but these fall outside the office shredder market being discussed by this chapter (HSM Pressen also makes office shredders — but these are distributed in North America by SEM — see separate entry). Datatech tends to sell the more dated table-top Schleicher models, while Intimus offers a sleeker line of mostly cabinet models.

Datatech also owns a shredder company called Novatech, which used to have its own separate relabeled product line, though this has since been discontinued. Today, the Novatech name has largely been phased out. Datatech also sells labeling and other types of mailroom equipment. Sales and service are through dealers. Datatech is a major player in the government market.

## Destroyit

*Michael Business Machines*
*3134 Industry Drive*
*North Charleston, SC 29423–0249*
*Tel: 800 223 2508*

Michael Business Machines (MBM) was one of the first companies to start distributing imported shredders in the US when it linked up with a German company called Ideal in 1956. About three years ago, Ideal bought 50 percent of MBM.

Ideal itself is one the oldest and largest forces in this market. Ideal machines are also relabeled by Ameri-Shred. The Destroyit line is strongest in the middle and higher levels of the market. Sales and service are through dealers.

## EBA

*Ecco Business Systems, Inc.*
*45 West 45th Street*
*New York, NY 10036*
*Tel: 800 682 3226*

A grand old name in shredding, EBA is a German company that claims to have invented shredders in the 1930s. EBA's machines first appeared in the US in the 1970s under the Swedish Lindaco name. In the 1980s, they were relabeled by Standard Duplicating. In 1989, EBA began selling in the US under its own name for the first time, through a New York-based distributor called Ecco Business Systems (which has about 100 dealers nationwide).

EBA also exports from Germany directly to two relabelers: SEM and Cummins. EBA's line is particularly strong in the higher levels of the market.

# Fellowes

*Fellowes Manufacturing Company*
*1789 Norwood Avenue*
*Itasca, IL 60143*
*Tel: 800 955 0959*

This family-owned company started in 1917 with Liberty Boxes (which are now known as Banker's Boxes) and is today an industry leader in records storage products. Fellowes also manufactures and distributes computer accessories, copyholders, and various office/desk accessories.

Fellowes began selling shredders in the early 1980s, with a range of relabeled Schleicher-made models that span the low to middle sections of the market. In the early 1990s, it introduced its own line of personal shredders. The latter, which are excellent values, are made by Fellowes in the USA. These products have been very successful — Fellowes is now the largest manufacturer of personal shredders in the world.

Sales of both lines are through dealers and retailers. Service of the Schleicher-made models is through dealers; the personal shredders are shipped back to Fellowes for repair.

# GBC Shredmaster

*GBC Office Products Group*
*500 Bond Street*
*Lincolnshire, IL 60069*
*Tel: 800 477 9900*

GBC — standing for General Binding Corporation — is a large, publicly held, American company that's big in all sorts of mechanical paper handling equipment like punchers, binders, and laminators. Although it has been in shredders for over 20 years, it became a major force in the low and middle sectors of the market when it purchased a Florida company called Shredmaster 13 years ago.

GBC makes most of its 15 machines, but fills a few gaps in its line — mostly in cross-cuts — with brandings from EBA and Dahle. Headquartered in Illinois since 1947, it has 35 direct sales branches throughout the US and Canada, as well as a wide dealer network. GBC also markets heavily through office supply catalogs and retailers. Service is direct or through dealers and third parties. GBC's smallest unit must be shipped back for repair.

# Heyer

*Heyer Inc.*
*1850 South Kostner Avenue*
*Chicago, IL 60623*
*Tel: 800 621 3884*

An old-time, family-run, American company that specializes in old-fashioned duplicators. Its shredder line consists of nine German-made Ideal machines that it gets from Michael Business Machines (which sells an Ideal line called Destroyit).

One thing to keep in mind is that Heyer tends to keep the same model numbers when models are updated. This means that there could be times when an old version of a machine is sold under the same model number as the new one until stocks are sold out. Sales and service are through dealers.

# Intimus

*Schleicher & Co. of America, Inc.*
*5715 Clyde Rhyne Drive*
*Sanford, NC 27330*
*Tel: 800 334 5162*

Intimus is the brand name now used by Schleicher, the most prolific producer in today's shredder market. Schleicher, a German company, began making shredders in 1965; shortly thereafter it began distributing them in North America through a company called Datatech (see separate entry in these Vendor Profiles). In 1978, it established a manufacturing and assembly facility in North Carolina. Today, most of its machines sold here (and the components — except for motors) are made in the USA, and Intimus has overtaken Datatech as the main distributor. Olympia, Fellowes, and GBC also sell brandings of Schleicher machines.

Schleicher actually accounts for over a quarter of the shredder models that the buyer has to choose from — even though the name "Schleicher" doesn't appear on any of them. But, even though key components are the same, and the machines come out of the same factories, Schleicher has cleverly created around 50 "different" models for all the different brands by mixing every possible combination of speed, capacity, shred size, and features. Sales and service of the Intimus models are through dealers.

# Kutter

*C.R. Resources Inc.*
*49 Natcon Drive*
*Shirley, NY 11967*
*Tel: 516 620 9674*

New to the US market, and not very prominent, these Italian machines are distributed by an offshoot of Shredex called C.R. Resources. The range stretches from a personal shredder to a fairly upmarket cross-cut machine. Sales and service are through dealers, except for the personal model which has to be shipped back for repair.

# Martin Yale Premier

*Martin Yale Industries, Inc.*
*251 Wedcor Avenue*
*Wabash, IN 46992*
*Tel: 219 563 0641*

Martin Yale is a more than 50-year-old US firm that specializes in paper handling equipment like electric paper folders. Shredders came into its picture when it acquired Swingline of stapler fame. But it is currently getting out of the shredder business, with the exception of one new, low-end machine. Sales are through office supply retailers. Machines have to be shipped back for service.

# Monroe

*Monroe Systems for Business*
*1000 The American Road*
*Morris Plains, NJ 07950*
*Tel: 201 993 2480*

An old distributor that was big in the bang-on-every-door style of sales that characterized the pre-electronic office machine era. Today, Monroe has adjusted to modern times by pulling in the infantry and concentrating largely on distributing relabeled copiers and fax machines to major national accounts.

Monroe's shredder line consists of some relabeled German-made Geha machines that it gets from Shredex. Sales and service are direct.

# Olympia

*Olympia USA, Inc.*
*1330 River Bend Drive*
*Dallas, TX 75247*
*Tel: 800 832 4727*

Olympia is an old German office equipment company with roots in the typewriter market. Today, Olympia sells a variety of office equipment in the US, including relabeled copiers.

In the shredder market, Olympia used to sell relabeled Ideal models, but in 1992 it introduced a line of products mostly made by Schleicher. Most of these correspond roughly to the Schleicher machines sold by Datatech, Fellowes, GBC, and Intimus (Schleicher's own brand). Sales and service are through dealers.

# Oztec

*Oswald Business Machines*
*65 Channel Drive*
*Port Washington, NY 11050*
*Tel: 516 944 5007*

A division of a 20-year old Long Island manufacturing company that got its start in shredders by manufacturing components for other vendors. For the last five years, it has also been selling its own shredders under the Oztec name.

There are three fairly heavy-duty machines in the range which are sold and serviced through dealers. The factory provides back-up service if required. Oswald also has two other divisions specializing in industrial equipment like concrete vibrators and grinders.

# Panasonic

Panasonic Company
Special Products Division
Secaucus, NJ 07094
Tel: 201 348 7490

Not a strong force in the shredder market, Panasonic has three machines — all made in Japan by its parent company Matsushita. Two are personal shredders that have been around for some time, and one is a newer low-end cabinet model.

Sales and service are mostly through office supply retailers. The personal shredders have to be shipped back for repairs, though on-site service is available for the cabinet model.

# Sanyo

*Sanyo Business Systems Corp.*
*51 Joseph Street*
*Moonachie, NJ 07074*
*Tel: 201 440 9300*
Sanyo dabbles in office equipment of all kinds, but is not a major force in any sector (with the possible exception of the declining dictation equipment market where it is quite strong). It has one low-end personal shredder, which is available in places like office supply superstores. It has to be shipped back if it ever needs repairing.

# SEM

*Security Engineered Machinery Co., Inc.*
5 Walkup Drive
PO Box 1045
*Westboro, MA 01581*
*Tel: 800 225 9293*
In business since 1967, this privately-held company is a distributor of relabeled shredders, as well as fierce-sounding machines called "disintegrators" and various other types of equipment for destroying "off-spec" and returned products in the pharmaceutical, medical device, and food industries.

Its office shredder range includes a mix of the oldest and most respected German shredder names — EBA, Schleicher, and, since 1987, HSM Pressen (for which it's the only US distributor). Most of the models it sells are cross-cut shredders.

SEM is apparently the largest supplier to the federal government, and it also specializes in multiple sales to larger companies. It sells direct through field offices in Texas, Maryland, California, Florida, and Georgia. Service is direct or third party.

# Shredex

*Shredex, Inc.*
*49 Natcon Drive*
*Shirley, NY 11967*
*Tel: 516 345 0300*
Shredex is a New York distributor that's been around since 1982. It has managed, for a relative latecomer to shredders, to make excellent inroads. Shredex relabels a range of machines manufactured by an old German company called Geha that's particularly known for cross-cuts. In addition, Shredex sells Geha ma-

chines to Monroe, which in turn sells them under its own colors.

Most sales are through dealers, but some Shredexes are also available through Office Depot at pretty low prices. Service is through the dealers or third parties; the personal shredder models have to be shipped back for repair. Shredex shares offices and staff with C.R. Resources, which distributes a new Italian arrival called Kutter (see separate entry in these Vendor Profiles).

# Suncom

*Suncom Technologies*
*6400 W. Gross Point Road*
*Niles, IL 60648*
*Tel: 708 647 4040*

Suncom is a privately-held, US company that's been in business since 1982 primarily selling joysticks for computers, but also niche office accessories. It has one unusual battery-powered shredder that can be bought through a number of mail order catalogs, some office supply stores, and also direct from Suncom. It has to be shipped back if it ever needs repairing.

# Wilson Jones

*Acco USA, Inc.*
*77 South Acco Plaza*
*Wheeling, IL 60090–6070*
*Tel: 708 541 9500*

Wilson Jones is a 40-year-old vendor that was acquired a while ago by Acco, a company that specializes in office supply. It was subsequently merged completely into its adopted parent. Wilson Jones's machines once dominated the low end of the market, where shredders and office supply share common distribution channels, but over the last few years the company has lost its edge.

The shredders are made in Britain by Acco/Rexel. Sales are through dealers and office supply retailers; service is through dealers or direct from Wilson Jones's eight nationwide service centers. ✍

# Appendix

**What to Buy for Business**

# What to Buy for Business

If you're interested in obtaining more "model-specific" information and product evaluations, here is some information about *What to Buy for Business*, the consumer guide to office equipment published and edited by the author of this book.

### "What is What to Buy for Business?"

*What to Buy for Business* is the leading consumer guide to office equipment. It refuses to accept advertising, so you can count on it for unbiased advice. Published 10 times a year, it is an indispensable resource for buyers seeking value, reliability, and good service. It has a loyal following: people who use it swear by it.

There are *What to Buy* reports on all the major types of office equipment — copiers, fax, computers, printers, phone systems, mailing equipment, shredders, and more. You can either subscribe to all the guides, or buy individual ones.

More end-users choose *What to Buy* than any other no-advertising office equipment guide. They value its thorough and intelligent approach to a market full of flattery and hype. With *What to Buy*, you can say good-bye to "buying office equipment anxiety." You'll no longer have that nagging feeling of "Did I make the right decision?" or "Was there something better and less expensive?" Every purchase will be based on full knowledge of all the facts.

You don't have to buy a large amount of equipment to justify using the guides. Individual ones cost only $23, and a subscription is $121 — less than $13 per guide. There are also some great special offers — read on for details!

### "What do the reports contain?"

Most *What to Buy* reports include detailed charts — usually in double-page, grid-style format — summarizing the specifications and pricing of available machines. The charts also include the Editor's "verdicts" — short, punchy comments on the pros and cons of each machine (in some reports, the verdicts are separate from the charts for reasons of space). Some charts show not only the list prices, but also the lowest discount prices.

All reports include clear recommendations on the best buys — when appropriate accompanied by negative comments on the bad ones. There are also articles explaining the features and technology in plain English, and vendor profiles that examine the companies behind the products and compare policies on service and support.

Many subscribers turn first to the letters' section, in which readers share experiences and opinions on subjects covered by *What to Buy*. This also serves as a forum in which scam artists who prey on businesses are exposed — crooked office supply telemarketers, for example.

### *"How often do the reports come out?"*

*What to Buy* is published 10 times a year. Most issues are devoted mainly to one topic — so every issue is effectively a standalone publication, as well as part of a series. Most subjects are covered about once a year, though some slower moving markets may be visited less frequently in order to make room for new topics.

In spring 1994, *What to Buy* introduced a new update service. Readers can call a special number and, using a touch-tone phone, request update information to be faxed to them automatically. Regularly updated bulletins summarizing important developments are being made available in conjunction with most reports. There is no separate charge for this service.

### *"How long are the guides?"*

They vary, but they're generally around 40–90 pages (remember, that's with no advertising). Page size is 8.5 by 11 inches. *What to Buy* is printed on high quality, recycled paper. Most reports include product photos.

### *"What to Buy doesn't take advertising, so where does its money come from?"*

Only from people like you who buy subscriptions and single issues. Unlike other publications, *What to Buy* refuses to sell partial reprints to equipment manufacturers who want to use its findings in their promotional activities. Nothing compromises its independence.

### *"How long has What to Buy been publishing?"*

*What to Buy for Business* was started in 1986. (Its sibling publication in Britain goes back to 1980.)

### "How does What to Buy do its research?"

Behind every report are many years of cumulative research and analysis. There is no single formula behind the reports. *What to Buy* examines equipment hands-on, carries out benchmark testing (copiers, for example), conducts user polls (postage meters, for example), and also receives constant informal feedback from users about equipment and suppliers. The Editors talk off-the-record to dealers and manufacturers, visit trade shows and manufacturing facilities worldwide, and are able to inspect many new machines before they are offered to the public.

The best proof of the quality of the research is the renewal rate: almost nine out of every 10 businesses that use *What to Buy* renew their subscriptions or buy additional single issues.

### "Are there money-back guarantees?"

Definitely. In fact, there are three.... *One:* If you buy single issues and you aren't pleased, send them back within 30 days for a full no-questions-asked refund. *Two:* If you subscribe, you can cancel within the first 30 days and receive a full refund (no need to send anything back). *Three:* You can cancel your subscription at any time after that and receive a refund on the unused portion.

### "How much does it cost?"

A year's subscription (10 guides) costs $121. Single issues are $23 each (plus $3 per order for shipping). There are also two special offers:

> ✔ You can request any three recent issues free with your prepaid subscription — take your pick out of any listed in this catalog.
> ✔ As an alternative, you can buy three single issues for the price of two ($49 including shipping). A great value!

*Note:* The above prices may increase in 1995, but *What to Buy* will hold them for people who identify themselves as readers of this book when ordering and/or who use the order form at the end of this book.

### "How can I order What to Buy?"

*What to Buy for Business* is available from the publisher direct — you can't buy it on newsstands or in bookstores. For fastest service, you are encouraged to order by credit card over the phone — call 800 247 2185 (Visa, MasterCard, American Express). Orders received before 3:00 p.m. Pacific time are generally shipped same day and take 2–3 days to arrive. (Overnight shipping is available if you provide your Federal Express account number.) Alternatively, mail a check to:

What to Buy for Business, Inc.
PO Box 22857
Santa Barbara, CA 93121–2857

**California residents:** Please add sales tax for single issue orders, but not for subscriptions.

### "What guides are available?"
Below is a list of the reports that should be available during the second half of 1994 and throughout 1995. You may want to request an updated list before ordering — this will include the approximate dates of publication of current and scheduled reports. To obtain this updated list by fax, please call the *What to Buy* automated information system at (805) 963-5749: when calling, please have your fax number ready, follow the recorded instructions, and ask for Document Number 21. The information — which includes an order form — will be sent to your fax within minutes. You can call from any touch-tone phone: you do not have to make the call from your fax machine. (If you do not have access to a fax machine, you can, of course, still call the regular number — 800 247 2185.)

❑ ***"The Low-Volume Copier Guide"***
Copiers that work at below 25 copies per minute — mostly suitable for below 10,000 copies per month.

❑ ***"The Mid-Volume Copier Guide"***
Copiers that work at 25–49 copies per minute — mostly suitable for 10,000–35,000 copies per month.

❑ ***"The High-Volume Copier Guide"***
Copiers that work at 50cpm–135 copies per minute — mostly suitable for over 35,000 copies per month.

❑ ***"The Plain Paper Fax Guide"***
Laser, LED, ink jet, and thermal transfer plain paper fax machines — from around $600 to over $3,000.

❑ ***"The Laser, LED, & Ink Jet Printer Guide"***
Black-and-white printers — from under $300 to around $5,000.

❏ ***"The Multifunctional & Color Guide"***
Three-in-one guide: (1) multifunctional machines that combine copier/printer/fax/scanner functions in a single unit; (2) full-color copiers; (3) full-color printers.

❏ ***"The Business Computer Guide"***
Desktop PCs, notebook PCs, and networks. (Note: This guide does not contain as much model-specific information as most of the other guides.)

❏ ***"The CD-ROM & Scanner Guide"***
Two-in-one guide: CD-ROM drives and scanners that work with PCs and Apple Macs.

❏ ***"The Phone Systems & Voice Processing Guide"***
Covers PBXs, key systems, hybrids — plus third-party systems for voice mail, automatic attendant, etc.

❏ ***"The Postage Meter Systems Guide"***
Detailed coverage of products from all four vendors — includes the results of a 500-company user poll.

❏ ***"The Shredder Guide"***
Full coverage of office shredders from all the vendors.

# Index

*Bold* page numbers refer to *"Vendor Profile"* entries included in most chapters

# C

*(Computers continued)*

# N

# O

# Y

# Z